ENCYCLOPAEDIA OF EDUCATIONAL TERMS

(In 5 Vol.)

ENCYCLOPAEDIA OF EDUCATIONAL TERMS

(In 5 Vol.)

Edited & Compiled by:

Ekta Thani, Rohit Sharma, Anoop Jain, Mohit Sharma, Kanika K., C.H. Judd, & L.B. Earhart

Vol. III

SPORTS PUBLICATION

4264/3, Ansari Road, Darya Ganj, Delhi-2
Ph.: 23290142, 27241050, 27562163 (R)

Published by:

Lokesh Thani

SPORTS PUBLICATIONS

H.O. 4264/3, Ansari Road, Darya Ganj, New Delhi-110002
B.O. WP-474, Ist Floor, Shiv Market, Ashok Vihar, Delhi-52
Phones: 23290142, 27241050,
(R) 27562163, (M) 9868028838
E-mail: sportspublication1@rediffmail.com
Website: *www.sportsbookshouse.com*

I.S.B.N. – 81-87818-68-9

PRINTED IN INDIA 2004

Laser Typeset by:

JAIN MEDIA GRAPHICS

B-4/40-A, Lawrence Road, (Keshav Puram),
New Delhi-110035 Ph.: 27183573, (M) 9811430646

Printed by:

BANDEMATRAM PRESS

Maujpur, Delhi

Price: Rs. 4,200/- (In 5 Vol.)

VOL. III

PART 3

COMMERCE

The present book exhibits many important terms and its meaning along with instances where necessary.

The present book has been compiled as a clear immediately accessible reference book. Every aspect of its conception and layout has been planned to help the reader to find information he/she needs with minimum difficulty.

The purpose of this study is to clarify definitions and obscure meanings of technical terms and phrases that form the vast vocabulary. Many of the words defined are common words, which have been given unusual meanings in different countries by different researchers.

Some of the words find their roots in the slang in different languages, and have been very well accepted in common usage. Most the terms came from a wide range of disciplines, particularly Commerce.

Commerce is the life-line of modern civilization. Its essential knowledge is a must to oil the wheel of any business—a shop, a departmental store, a manufacturing unit, an export-import house, a sales organisation (retail or wholesale), a private firm or a limited company.

The present study will be of immense value to the university commerce students and to those appearing for competitive examination, research, scholars, teachers and authors but also to administrators, planners, insurance agents etc. It will give an unimaginable pick-up to his studies of the subject in the classroom and a better success in the examination hall.

The salient features of this book are:

- A to Z terms that covers many subjects which comes under Commerce.
- Vast definitions are explained with instances where necessary.
- Alphabetically arranged terms from A to Z.

The reason why this work is created is that most of the students enter college and university departments of Commerce without having any background in the subject. Just as it is impossible to solve the riddles of mathematics without knowing the importance of numerals, it is impossible to do commercial study without knowing the meaning of those key concepts that one comes across in commerce literature.

The prima facie duty of every student of commerce is to get acquainted with the commercial terms. The only way to get acquainted with such terminology is to approach the present book which provides the student with a brief elucidation of a term or a concept.

An overview of commerce is also important to everyone running any business or participating in a business activity of nay kind a proprietor, director, sales executive, production supervisor, financial expert, company secretary or any other functionary will find this book of immense help as a reference guide, aid to decision making, understanding and solving day-to-day problems of commercial law and otherwise ease the performance of his everyday duties.

Although the dictionary mainly provides brief elaboration of commercial, managerial banking (industrial, financial and allied terms, it does provide guiding lights in planning, controlling, executing and expanding business programmes to the businessman.

All comments from users on omissions or shortcomings will be most welcome.

PART 4

GEOLOGY

This book covers terms which have been carefully selected from the various branches of geology such as geomorphology, geophysics, geochemistry, mineralogy, hydrology, petrology, etc. All these terms have been explained with their specific geological meanings.

The aim in making the present study is to provide the nonspecialist with accurate definitions of the working vocabulary of earth sciences. While compiling the dictionary, the author has concentrated on terms which seem to him to be in the widest use; special and local terms have been excluded.

A number of obsolete and popular terms have been included since the former may be encountered in older works frequently still in use, and the latter in some of the books and articles which purport to explain geological terms, stratigraphical divisions are restricted to stage names.

The present work contains vast entries which cover definitions of terms relevant to Geology. Because of the overlap which exists between the many branches of the Earth Sciences, for instance between Geomorphology and Sedimentology or between Palaeontology and Biology, some of the entries might be considered to be at the borders of Geology, but they are included because of their significance to the subject.

It is endeavoured to write the entries in a clear and in a lucid style to provide both straight forward definitions and invaluable background information. The network of cross-references has been kept throughout the dictionary.

All comments and suggestions regarding shortcomings and omissions will be appreciated.

PART 3
COMMERCE

aala
abbreviation of Associate of the Association of International Accountants.

aar
refers to the initials for against all risks, with special reference to freight insurance. Also, refers to the initials for Association of American railroad.

ab
abbreviation of aktiebolag which literally means share company. A limited company organized according to the laws of Sweden.

abacust
an elementary form of calculating machine not often used in the West today, though it may be seen in the British Museum or in the nursery. It normally takes the form of beads strung upon wire. The operator moves the beads along the wire in the process of counting.

abandonment
a martin insurance term for abandoning a ship as dangerous or unseaworthy. This would normally be a total loss and the insurer would have a right to claim the subject matter. Notice of abandonment should be given to the insurer immediately.

abatement
the cancellation of all or part of a past or prospective expenditure. A reduction or cancellation of an assessed tax. Also, any items of incidental income accounted for as a reduction of general cost.

ability to pay
a wage theory that holds that the wage level should be based on a company's ability to pay. Under this theory wage levels should this theory rarely increase as profits increase. Those who support recommend the converse, lowering wages as profits decline. Also, a theory of taxation holding that taxes should be based on the taxpayer's ability to pay, the rich paying proportionately more than the poor.

able-bodied seaman
strictly, one who has served three years before the mast, at least one of them in a trading vessel.

above par
as used in the securities market, a premium price, which is either paid or quoted, that is higher than the face value of the item.

above the line
those items on a balance sheet or other financial statement that are given in support of the sum of the details.

absenteeism
failure of workers to report for work on scheduling-owing to unwillingness rather than incapacity.

absentee ownership
the ownership of capital, like land or factories, by one or more persons living away from their property and employing others to manage and work it

for them.

absorption

1. in transportation, the assumption by one carrier of the shipping charges of another, without any increase in charges to the shipper. This might include, for example, charges normally applied to switching from one conveyance to another.

abstinence theory of interest

the concept that interest gained by saving money in an interest savings account is a reward for not spending the money on goods and services.

accelerated depreciation

depreciation of an asset at repaid, nonlinear rate, generally during the early years of its useful life.

acceleration clause

a provision in an agreement for the repayment of a loan by instalments that if a specified number of instalments are not paid then all the outstanding payments are due immediately.

accelerator

relatively small change in demand for consumer goods resulting in a comparatively substantial change in demand for capital plant supplying these goods.

accelerator-co-efficient

it tells by how much investment will increase given a particular rate of change in consumption or in national income. More simply it is known as accelerator. In terms of formula, it may be put as follows:

$$\text{Accelerator co-efficient} = \frac{\text{increment in investment}}{\text{increment in income}}$$

acceptance

the signature on a bill of exchange indicating that the person on whom it is drawn accepts the conditions of the bill. Acceptance is usually written : Accepted, payable at. A bill of exchange that has been so accepted. Agreement to accept the terms of art offer.

acceptance supra protest

if a bill of exchange is protested and then accepted by another party to save the name of the drawer, this is known as acceptance protest, or acceptance for honour.

accepting house

a financial enterprise whose principal function is facilitation of negotiation of Bills of Exchange either by accepting them or guaranteeing them. The main offices of these houses are situated near the central bank and other institutions concerned with the smooth running of the country's financial system. The signature of an established acceptance house on a bill of exchange is a sign of the reliability of that bill and enables the holder to discount the holder to discount it at favourable rates.

accepting houses committee

some of the bigger merchant banks and acceptance houses

are affiliated to this committee. This indicates that they are of high and that bills of exchange drawn of them are likely to be discountable at fine rates.

acceptor

the person drawing a Bill of Exchange is the drawer and the person on whom the bill is drawn is the drawee. When the drawee has accepted the bill, i.e. has accepted liability, he is known as the acceptor. The normal from of acceptance is by signature on the face of the bill. He cannot deny the existence and capacity of the drawer or payee or the signature of the drawer-he can however question an endorsement (he would not be obliged to pay on a forged endorsement). Delivery is necessary for complete acceptance: this means the acceptance: this means the acceptor willingly parts with possession or gives notice of acceptance. If the bill in the hands of a holder in due course, delivery is presumed. It is possible for a bill to be negotiated before acceptance. It is then up to the holder of the bill to present if for acceptance before, or at the time of payment. Presentation for acceptance is not obligatory except where the bill so stipulates or where it is payable after sight, or payable elsewhere that at the residence or place of business of the drawer.

acceptance for honour

the drawer of a bill and any enforcer may insert in the bill the name of a person to whom a holder may resort in case of need that is in case the bill is dishonoured by non-acceptance or nonpayment.

acceptor

the drawee-the person on whom a bill of exchange is drawn-becomes an acceptor on signification of his asset to the document in writing. In short, a person who accepts the bills of exchange by witting his name across it.

acceptor for honour

the person, not already liable on the bill, who with the holder's consent accepts it after protest for the honour of any party liable thereon, or for the honour of the person for whose account the bill is drawn.

accident insurnce

this is a loosely used term to include personal accident insurance or other forms of insurance in which accident may be a factor, e.g. accidents at sea, accidents on the highway and accidents involving building.

accommodation bill

a bill which is drawn, accepted or endorsed for the sole purpose of discounting it, no goods being given or received for it, thus offering short-term a accommodation.

accommodation endorser

a person or a bank that endorses a loan to another party; for example, a parent company may endorse a bank loan to a subsidiary. The endorser becomes a guarantor and is secondarily liable in case of default. Banks may endorse other banks acceptance notes, which can then be traded on the secondary market.

account

a statement of indebtedness from one person to another; an invoice. A provider or professional services or of goods may render an account to a client or customer, a solicitor selling a house on a person's behalf will render an account of the sale, which may show that the solicitor owes the seller the proceeds of the sale, less expenses. A named segment of a ledger recording transactions relevant to the person or the matter named. Accounts consist of two sides; increases are recorded on one side and decreases on the other, accounts may be kept in a written from in a ledger, they may be on loose cards, or they may be on a magnetic medium in a computer. A record maintained by a bank or a building society of the amount of money a customer has deposited or been lent. A period during which dealings on the Stock Exchange are made without iomediate cash settlement. There are 24 accounts in the year most of two weeks duration but a few last for three weeks to accommodate public holidays. Up to the end of each account transactions are recorded but no money changes hands, which enables speculators to operate with the minimum capital outlay. Settlement of all transactions made within an account is made ten days after the account ends. Most other world stock markets use rolling accounts in which deals are settled a fixed number of days after the transaction is agreed.

accountable

liable to be needed by a specified person (or group of people) to report on and justify actions in relation to specified matters.

accountant

a person trained in accounting who may either be employed by a firm or work independently.

accoutant's return

alternative term for return on capital or book rate of return.

account day

the day on which all transactions made during the previous account on the Stock Exchange must be settled. It falls on a Monday, ten days after the account ends.

account, income and expenditure

the shows the income and expenditure for a stated period and the surplus or deficit resulting. These accounts are usually used by clubs and other non-profit-making organizations.

accounting

the recording and summarizing of business transactions, and the interpretation of their effects on a business enterprise or other economic unit. Accounting embraces bookkeeping, which involves primarily the recording of transactions, as well as auditing, the design and installation of a accounting system, tax services, Cost accounting, and budgeting (the advance planning of business transactions).

accounting basis

the conventions used when dealing with items of a particular kind of accounts.

accounting concepts

the basic theoretical ideas devised to support the activity of accounting. As accounting developed largely from a practical base, it has been argued that it lacks a theoretical framework. Accountants have therefore tried to develop such a framework; although various concepts have been suggested, few have found universal agreement. However, four are deemed to be important; the first, the on-going concern concept assumes that the business is a going concern until there is evidence to the contrary, so that assets are not stated at their break-up; the second, the accruals involves recording income and expenses as they accrue, as distinct from when they are received or paid; the third, the consistency concept, demands that accounts be prepared on a consistent basis from one period to another; and the fourth, the prudence concept., calls for accounts to be prepared on a conservative basis, not taking credit for profits or income before they are realized but making provision for losses when they are foreseen. Depreciation and deferred taxation are concepts relating to accounting, but are not often considered when reference is made to accounting concepts.

accounting department manual

a manual which outlines the system of accounting, the entries or number of typical transactions in the books and giving sample entries. It also outlines the duties of the cashier.

accounting equation

it implies that any increase or decrease in total assets of business house must simultaneously result in a corresponding increase or decrease in the total equities. But since the later comprise external, (outsiders, or creditors) equity and internal (owners), equity, either of these or both change by a variation of total resources. In order to introduce clarity, liabilities and 'equity' are narrowly used to represent respectively the creditors, claims and proprietors' interest. .Accordingly the equation becomes as follows:

$$A = L+P$$

where L denotes outside liabilities and P for proprietors' equity (or' proprietorship' or capital'). As creditors have a definite and prior claim against the assets, proprietorship is also termed as 'residual equity' which is expressed as

$$P = A-L$$

accounting for inflation
in times of inflation accounts do not give an accurate picture of real profits or the real present value of capital employed. In order to give both the public and the investor a proper appreciation of business results it is thought desirable to eliminate, as far as possible, variations that result from, and changes in the value of money, e.g., if the price level has doubled over five years, or, which is to state the same point, the value of money has halved over that period.

accounting period
businessmen devise timely measurement by artificially business into annual intervals, called accounting periods. The last or closing day of an accounting period is termed accounting date. On this date, the management prepares income and position statements to show the result of business operations and the changes in resources occurred since the construction of the last statements.

accounting policies
the accounting bases selected and constituently followed by a business enterprise.

accounting principles
have been defined as the body of doctrines commonly associated with the theory and procedure of accounting, serving as an explanation of current practices and as a guide for the selection of conventions or procedures where alternatives exist. Rules governing the formation of accounting axiom and the principles derived from them have arisen from common experience, historical precedents, statements by individuals and professional bodies and regulation of government agencies. In other words, these are guidelines to establish standard for sound accounting practices and procedures in reporting the financial status and periodic performance of a business.

accounting rate of return
the net profit to be expected from an investment, calculated as a percentage of the book value of the assets invested.

accounting ratio
1. in assessing the viability or performance of a business, certain ratios often regarded ratios calculated from the figures appearing in the accounts of the business are

termed as accounting ratios.
2. It is also known as a financial ratio.

accounting records
the records which have to be maintained according to the needs of the business concern. Sometimes they are also maintained according to the legal requirements relating to that business. Accounting records of sole proprietors, partnership firms and joint stock companies differ from one another to a great extent. The causes of this difference have been two-fold.
(a) Individual needs of the business.
(b) legal requirements of the business.

accounting reference date
the date which is the end of the accounting reference period of a company. The day may be chosen by company (though it must normally be the same each year) but if no choice is made then it is 31 March.

accounting reference period
a period of time ending on an accounting reference date and starting on the day after the preceding accounting reference date.

account payee
the words added to a crossed cheque ensuring that the funds will only be paid to the individual to whom the cheque was made payable.

account payee cheque
this type of crossing a cheque indicates a direction to the collecting bankers that the proceeds of the cheque have been intended to reach the hands of the payee. He should therefore collect the cheque only by credit into the account of the payee. It is also a term used in double-entry look-keeping to indicate the records of the amounts charged to others for goods and services, sold, and amounts received.

account receivable
1. the amount owned to a business by its customers, who are customarily granted any-where from 10 to 90 days to pay for merchandise already shipped.
2. In simple words, account receivable refers to advancing funds against the book debts of the customer.

account receivable financing
the use of money owned to a firm (see accounts receivable) to funds for current operating expenses or other purposes.

account records
these are records maintained according to the needs of the business concern. Sometimes they are also maintained in accordance with the legal requirements relating to that business. Accounting records of sole proprietors, partnership firms and joint stock companies differ from one another to a great extent. The cause of this difference are two fold. (a) individual needs of the business.

(b) legal requirements of the business.

Whatever may be the shape and form of accounting records, the basic minimum is the same because all business are to answer certain quarries regularly. Accounting records are mainly concerned with the basic records of any form of business.

account rendered

a statement sent by a seller to his customer of the amount that the customer owes, details of which may have been previously sent.

accounts

the profit and loss account and the balance sheet of company.

accounts, final

final accounts is the summary of accounting records. The fundamental objects of business is the service to the society with a motive to earn profits for the living of the businessmen. All business transactions directly result either in profit and loss or the creation of assets and liabilities. To known the position of profit and loss, we prepare the Profit and Loss Account and to known the position of assets and liabilities, we prepare the Balance Sheet. Preparation of the Balance Sheet is the final object of keeping accounting records. Balance sheet cannot be prepared until and unless the Profit and Loss Account is prepared. The preparation of profit and loss account and the balance sheet is thus known as the final accounts.

Profit and loss basically arises from trading transaction the relating to sale and purchase of the merchandise trading transactions are recorded in the shape of goods account. The difference between the two sides of the goods account gives either profit or loss. If the total of the side is more than the debit side total, the difference is profit and if and debit side total is more than the total of the credit side, it is loss.

The profit or loss arrived at from the goods account is known as either gross profit or gross loss. It is known as gross profit or loss because to earn it, the businessman has to incur certain expenditure as salaries, rent, electricity and water charges, repairs, stationery, carriage etc. The businessman incurs all these expenses to facilitate the work of trading and with a hope of earn profit from trading transactions.

accounts payable

the amounts due to suppliers of goods and services to an organization.

accounts receivable

the amounts owed to an organization for goods and services that it has supplied.

accounts sale

an account which is sent by one agent to the consignor

'showing the total quantity and the amount to be realised after deducting freight, commission, etc.

accounts, consolidated

some companies posses subsidiary companies. The holding company must; in addition to the normal requirements of the Companies act, file group accounts.

account stated

the simple acknowledge of a debt.

accretion

in finance, an addition of principal or income to a fund as a result of plan of accumulation.

accrual

an amount incurred as a charge in a given accounting period but not paid by the end of that period.

accrual basis in accounting

n accounting, a system of charging income and expenses to the period in which they are earned or incurred rather than to the period in which they are actually received or paid.

accrual concept

a fundamental accounting concept that revenues and costs should dealt within the accounts for the period in which they are earner or incurred so far as this is consistent with the concept of prudence in accounting.

accrual costing

in accounting, the expensing of goods and services as they are consumed.

accrued depreciation

in accounting, the difference between the cost of replacement of equipment of equipment or real property as of the date of the appraisal at the time of acquisition and the appraised value at the present time.

accumulated depreciation

the total amount written off the value of an assets. It is the sum of the yearly instalments of depreciation since the asset was acquired.

accumulated distribution

in accounting, income that has been received and accumulated by a trust for future distribution.

accumulated dividend

a dividend which has not been paid when due and which has become a liability of the corporation to be paid, presumably, as some future time.

accumulated income

net income retained and not paid out in dividends or dissipated by subsequent losses. Also reference to as accumulated earnings and accumulated profit.

accumulated profits

the amount showing in the appropriation of profits account that can be carried forward to the next year's accounts, i.e. after paying dividends, taxes, and putting some to reserve.

accumulation plan

an arrangement under which

the purchaser of shares in a mutual fund agrees to acquire more shares over a given period of time.

accumulation units
in a unit trust where net units income instead of being distributed to the unit-holders, is automatically reflected in the increased value of the units.

accruals concept
one of the four principal accounting concepts. Merely to record cash received or paid would not give a fair view of an organization's profit or loss since it would not take account of goods sold but riot yet paid for nor of expenses incurred but not yet paid. Accordingly it is considered good accounting practice to prepare accounts taking note of such accruals.

accured benefits
the benefits that have accured to a person in respect of pension, for the service given up to a specified date, whether or not that person continues in office.

accured charges
the expense incurred by a creditor. For example the fees chargeable for an audit may appear under this heading when the accounts printed before the auditor has submitted his account.

accured interest
interest that has accumulated but which has not been paid or collected. In the case of bond purchase, it is customary for the buyer to pay the seller accrued interest up to but not including the date of delivery, in addition to purchase price.

acquisition accountings
the accounting procedures adopted when one company is taken over by another. This often involves controversial issues as to the way in which goodwill is to be treated.

aquisition cost
the funds required to acquire goods or services.

acquittance
a written acknowledgement that a debt or other financial obligation has been discharged, or paid in full.

active circulation
the notes which are in circulation, that is, notes which have been issued from a bank of issue and are in the hands of the public, as distinguished, for example, from those held by the Banking Department of the Reserve Bank as part of the reserve.

active money
money in circulation in contract to money held in the form of idle cash balances.

active partner
a partner in a firm who takes an active or working part in the business of the firm.

act of bankruptcy
an action committed by a debtor that a court will recognize as a ground for making a receiving order (the first stage of making the debtor bankrupt).

act of god
an act of nature that is not reasonably foreseeable. In insurance, a natural event, such as flood, lightning, earthquake, or hurricane, that leads to a property loss and could not have been prevented by reasonable care or foresight.

actuals
goods or commodities that are physically available and which are bought and sold immediately(for example, at spot markets), as distinct from market futures where trading in contracts for future delivery.

actual cost
cost data based on transactions that have been complete as contrasted with costs that have been estimated.

actual output
it means what a nation does produce.

actuary
an actuary is defined in the oxford English dictionary as an expert in statistics, especially one who calculates insurance and premiums.

ad damnum clause
a clause in a legal declaration or complaint of a plaintiff that makes a demand for damages and sets out the amount.

addressing machines
addressing machines are used to print address on envelope, wrappers or labels, to be sent frequently to regular customers. They are also used for putting the names and addresses of customers on the monthly statements of accounts. They may be adapted to compile wage lists, dividend lists, and to put addresses of shareholders on notices of meeting, dividend warrants, annual returns, etc. They are particularly useful in Insurance Companies and Electricity Undertakings which have to send regular communications to a large number of customers. For example, Premium Notice are to be sent at regular intervals to the policy-holders; electricity bills are also to be sent to the users of electric energy, every month. Addressing such communications by hand would be a tedious task, and would take a long time. Here, addressing machines are used for placing the addresses which save time and labour.

adelaide stock exchange
one of six member stock exchanges of the Australian associated Stock Exchanges.

ademption
the gift by will of a specific legacy is 'adeemed' and can therefore no longer take effect if the item in question no longer exist in the testator's ownership at the date of the death.

ad hoc
latin, "for this". Refers to a limited particular situation. An ad hoc committee is one limited to a specific purpose

and may be dismissed on completion of its task.

adjusted basis
in income taxes, the basis used to compute decreiation or gain or loss on sales or fixed or noninventory assets.

adjusted cost basis
for accounting purposes, the value of property equal to the original cost plus improvements less depreciation.

adjusted gross income
taxable income that is earned income.

adjusted gross income
for income taxes, the gross income of an individual less business expenses where applicable, deductions allowable for income producing property, certain losses from sales or exchanges of property, self-employment expenses, and moving expenses.

adjuster
in the insurance industry, an employee of an insurance company authorized to study, and make recommendations to his employer relative to the use of an event that has resulted in a claim, the amount of the loss, and the extent of the insurance company's liability. Adjusters may be salaried employees of the company or they may work independently, adjusting losses for whatever firm hires them.

adjusting entry
in accounting, an entry made to correct or offset an error, accrual, write off, determent, etc.

administered price
a price that is purposely influenced by the government. For example, the interest rate for the use of money is determined by the demand, for and the supply of, loanable capital; it is not generally considered to be determined by a free market.

administrative accounting
that part of the accounting process generally associated with management.

administrative expense
expense incurred in the general direction and management of an enterprise; contrasted with expenses incurred by specific functions such as selling or manufacturing.

ad referendum
when applied to a contract, this means that although the contract has been signed, certain matters have been left over for consideration.

ad valorem
a property tax or import or other duty computed as a percentage rate of the value of the property.

ad valorem subsidy
a fixed-percentage subsidy granted to producers of commodities as a form of financial aid or relief from hardships resulting from economic conditions beyond the control of the producers. The subsidy is calculated on the basis of

the current or prevailing market value of the commodity.

advance against securities

a Central Bank's assistance to the banking system in a country is made available, in the main, through the alternative facilities of advance from the Central Bank. The advances which are authorised under law are repayable on demand or on the expiry of fixed periods not exceeding 90 days (in 180 days in case of export bills).

advance bill

an invoice submitted before the goods or services intemized therein have actually been delivered or performed. It is usually requested by buyers for tax purposes or some similar reason.

advanceiment

a payment made by a trustee out of the capital of trust funds to a beneficiary for the purpose of establishing him in life.

advantage

the ability of one nation, region, or supplier to produce a goods or services at a lower cost (with less labour, or less land, or less machinery) than others.

adverse balance

a balance on account of a revenue loss or a liability. It is particularly applicable to accounts of a nation where the amounts payable to foreign countries exceed those receivable from aboard.

adverse selection

the insuring of a group of risks that represents an above-average expectation of loss.

advertising

the art of making known to the public, in one way or another, goods and services, offered for sale, and various methods of persuasion to induce public to buy those goods and services. Today we are surrounded on all sides by many types of advertising. No matter whether we walk on the streets, drive an automobile on the highways, ride a bus, watch television or read a newspaper or magazine, or open out mail, we are brought face to face with advertising. This creates a difficult situation for the manager, for he must determine what advertising on his part will justify its cost amid the bewildering array of advertisements by other companies.

Any of a number of advertising techniques are used to induce the customer to purchase specific products. Some have a rational basis while others are largely psychological or emotional. Thus, when you buy aspirin, you are to insist on a given brand because it is pure, it dissolves, and it acts more quickly. At other times reliance is placed primarily upon repetition of the brand name so that the consumer will automatically select that particular product.

advertising agency

an organization concerned with

Marketing. It considers the goods and services that clients wish to offer to the public and advises on the best method of a advertising them in order to maximize profit or goodwill. The agency is therefore interested in the product itself, in alternative methods of promotion, in presentation, and in effective copywriting. It may wish to study the product, and the persons to whom it is hoped to sell it, and will wish to know the pattern and areas of distribution. It will need to be conversant with all methods of advertising, with appropriate magazines, journals, newspapers, etc.

advertising agencies are 'necessarily independent but in order to preserve standards and prevent abuse, an Institute was formed as long ago as 1917, becoming known in 1954 as the Institute of Incorporated Practitioners in Advertising. There is a British code of advertising practice attempts to establish legal, honest and truthful advertising. The practice and interpretation of this code is supervised by a Code of Advertising Practice Committee. The institute helped to from the code of practice and is also represented on the Committee. It also took part in forming the Advertising Standard Authority.

advertising copy

advertising copy is the name given to the published advertisements issued by a company. The advertising copy should give the message in the briefest, most interesting and forceful manner. The copy must be addressed to the type of people who are exposed to the advertising medium.

advertising informative

advertising intended to inform the public of the existence or quality of goods, and most often found in technical journals. For instance, a new invention might be advertised as useful to a manufacturing industry.

advertising manger

an employee of a firm who supervises the production of the firm's advertisements and decides which media will carry them.

advertising standards authority

an independent organization composed of five persons connected with advertising, five with no connection and an independent chairman. The objects are 'to promote and enforce throughout the United Kingdom the highest standards of advertising in all media and to ensure in cooperation with all concerned that no advertising contravenes or offends against these standards.'

advice

when a banker issues a draft, he sends an advice, called a letter of advice, to the banker

upon whom the draft has been drawn, giving him particular of the amount, number, date and payee, so that, when the instrument is presented for payment, the drawee banker may be able to satisfy himself that the draft is in order. In the absence of an advice, a banker would hesitate to pay a draft; at least, this would be so when the practice has been followed previously,.

advice note
a document sent by a seller to a buyer stating the description and quality of goods that have been despatched, to him.

affreightment
a contract for transporting goods by sea. Also known as character party-or ocean bill of lading.

a forfait
a from of export finance which has traditionally been more common among banks in continental Europe but which some British and US banks have actively developed in recent years.

after date
a term used with reference to Bill of Exchange, indicating that they are payable at a certain time after the date of the bill.

after date, after sight
terms specifying the due date of a note, bill of exchange, or other credit instrument. After date refer to a given period following the date appearing on the instrument; thus, "payable 30 days after date" on a note drawn on February 10 means that payment is due on March 12. After sight rears to a given period following presentation of the note for acceptance, and the date for acceptance must similarly be specified.

after sight
a bill of exchange drawn after sight, payable when it has been accepted and the acceptor has indicated a date of acceptance.

agency bills
bills of exchange drawn on and accepted by the branches of foreign banks.

agency, fiduciary nature of
a contract of agency is a contract that creates a special relationship between the parties. The agent must act in good faith, and even though their is no express agreement he must not make any private or secret profit out of the agency. He must always act in his principal's interest, and if he professes any skill he must use this to the best of his ability.

agency of necessity
this occurs where one person acts on behalf of another without that other's express permission, in order to safeguard the interest of the other party. The other party will be bound by the agency. Agency of necessity cannot arise, and there would be no legal agency unless: (1) it is impossible to communicate with the

principal, (2) a contract of agency already exists, and (3) immediate action is necessary.

agenda

details of business to be transacted at a meeting , made out by the person calling the meeting or the secretary appointed to do so. The agenda is sent out to those invited to attend. It is generally accompanied by an invitation to appoint a proxy if a member cannot attend personally.

agent

when a banker employs a correspondent or agent in carrying out a transaction for a customer, the banker is responsible to his customer for any loss arising from the conduct of the agent.

agent de change correspondent

stock broker who may deal on the Brussels Stock Exchange, but only through an Agent de Change.

agent, general

an agent with authority to act for his principal in all matters concerning a particular trade or profession, or in some specified field. A travelling representative is one example.

agent misrepresentation

misrepresentation by an agent is equal to misrepresentation by his principal, whether fraudulent or innocent. However, if an agent makes an innocent misrepresentation it does not become fraudulent by reason of the principal's knowledge of the true facts. **e.g.** A contract with B through agent C.B. Is aware of faults in goods being sold to A. C is not. A relies on C's representation. A cannot then claim damages for fraudulent misrepresentation.

age of debt

management accountancy term meaning extent of customer credit.

agglomeration

concentration of labour, retailing.

aggreate income

an amount which is lying being between the value of the gross product and net national product. It is another name for national income.

aggregate demand

the flow of money and expenditures for goods and services during a given time period. The expectations of aggregate demand influence the aggregate supply.

aggregative inder number

an index constructed from totals rather than from individual categories.

aging

an analysis of individual accounts receivable according to the time elapsed after the due or billing dates.

agio theory of interest

the theory states that "interest arises out of a process of lending present income against the promise of future income; some individuals in the community are apparently willing to pay a premium or agio on present income for the privilege of disposing of it as they see fit for a period of time".

agrarian revolution

also, Agricultural Revolution. The transformation of farming from the growing of substance crops to a profitable business.

agraian syndicalism

a movement which is intended to protect and promote agricultural interests.

agreed procedure

negotiated between management and trade union (s) as the procedure to be followed in attempting to solve any grievances before resorting to strike action.

agribusiness

the sector of the economy involved with the process and procedures of agriculture, including farming and supplies.

agricultural bank

a bank specially established to assist agricultural development by granting loans or longer duration.

agricultural labour

the term includes all persons who are hired for carrying on agricultural operations on a permanent or temporary basis, such persons may or may not own any plot of land which they cyultivate on their own account.

aided-receall method

technique for assessing the effectiveness of advertising in which an interviewer show someone on advertisement (or quotes from it) and asks whether he remembers having seen or heard it.

air freight

the first type of air freight was mail, which took up relatively little space. As time progressed producers of goods saw the competitive advantages of being able to fulfil orders, particularly those for light-weight goods in a far shorter times by using air transport. The transactions is still greater where the weight-related transport. The transactions is still greater where the weight-related charges offer a particular advantage. Now, far from seeing cargo as an 'extra,' airlines are becoming increasingly conscious of its economic benefits. Sometimes aircraft design planes for 'cargo only'.

airway bill

1. a term used to describe the document made out on behalf of the consignor of goods by air as evidence of the contract of carriage. It, or a copy thereof, accompanies the goods throughout their journey.
2. a way bill which is covering carriage by air.
3. it may also be known as air consignment note. It is issued as a contract of carriage by air.

all commodity rate

a freight that generally allies to any and all commodities.

all-in

everything included (usually to describe rates of pay, deductions or trade union subscriptions).

all-in rate
wage rate that incorporates various extras, such as bonus payments in addition to the basic time-related payment scheme.

allocate
to spread a cost systematically over two or more time periods, objects, activities, processes, operations, or products. In government accounting, to transfer an appropriation, or a part thereof, from one agency to another.

allocated cost
in accounting, the assignment of expenditures to various accounts. For example, fire-insurance premium costs might be spread among fire's departments in proportion of the value of insurable assets located in each department.

allocation
any planning needs, for allocation of the available resources to provide the best possible result, but before the resources have been allocated the meaning of 'best possible result' must be established and it will be essential of devise some criterion for judging the economic effect to each complete set of such allocations.

allocation problem
a problem concerning the distribution of limited resources among competing alternatives in such a way as to minimize total cost or maximize total income. Also called a 'programming problem'.

allonge
a slip attached to a bill of exchange to allow for extra endorsements. It does not need a stamp.

all-or-none-order
a market or limited-price order given to a stockbroker to be executed in its entirety or not at all.

allot
to assign newly issued shares to their first owners.

allotment
the acquisition, by one or more persons, of newly issued securities; commonly as a result of an administrative decision by which the securities are allocated among applicants.

allotment of shares
when a company receives an application for shares issued by means or a prospectus, it allots the shares on a predetermined basis (which is set out in the prospectus).

allowance, age
some of those over sixty-five may claim total exemption from tax. There are; single people whose incomes do not exceed Rs.504, and married people (they must cohabit, and one party must be over sixty-five) with an income not exceeding Rs.786. Marginal relief is given where incomes slightly exceed

these amounts.

all-risks insurance

this may take the form of a separate policy of insurance or it may be part of the insurnce policy covering the content of a house. In either case, it covers loss or in some case damage to personal belongings in circumstances where cover would not normally be available under a household contents policy. An all-ricks policy would, for example, cover the loss of personal possessions in the home in circumstances other than normal perils of theft or fire covered by the contents policy. It would also cover personal possessions being carried or own on the person.

all-risk protection

a contract that covers all causes of loss except those specifically, and that presumes that the cause of any loss is not he deliberate action of the insured. A high percentage of inland marine insurance policies are written on all risk basis.

along-side date

date on which ship is expected to ready and in position to take on a particular cargo.

alternate

a person who is appointed to act as a substitute for another person in performing specified duties whenever the other person is unavailable.

alternate director

a person appointed to act as an alternate for a director of a limited company.

alternate directors

if the articles of association of a company permit, a director can nominate an alternate or substitute director, who can act when his principal is absent, and his acts done within the scope of his authority are binding on the company. The appointment of an alternative direotor should be in writing and notice given. Unless provided by the article, and alternate director cannot look to the company for his fees which are the responsibility of his principal. Particulars of alternat directors must be included in the annual return to Companies Houses.

alternative cost

that will be incurred if management takes one of the particular alternative courses of action before it. The different alternative costs have to be taken into account in assessing opportunity cost.

alternative payee

a bill of exchange may be made payable in the alternative to one of two, or one or some of several payees.

amalgamation

a merger by agreement of two or more concerns with or into a major organization.

amortization

it is the wiring off of assets— the lives of which are determined not by a deterioration or obsolescence but by the expire of the tenure of ownership, The principle instance would be a leasehold property.

amortize
to write off all or a portion of the cost of an asset; to depreciate or deplete.

amortized cost
in accounting, the cost of an asset minus the portions written off or depreciated.

analytical forecasting
forecasting gross national product by estimating the components for demand and then combining them into an overall estimate.

anchorage
charges paid for anchoring in certain ports or harbours.

anchor lease
a lease, usually favourable, given to a large or well-known retail business in order to attract the public to an area such as a shopping centre.

and reduced
words appended to the name of a Company where, after reorganization, the Capital is reduced, with court approval. The court may order these words to be added to the name.

annual audit
a audit by a professional accountant that cover transactions for a period of one year.

annual closiong
accounting, the posting of closing entries that takes place at the end of a fiscal year.

annual report
a formal financial statement issued once a year by a corporation to all its shareholders, listing assets, liabilities, revenues, and earnings, and indicating the company's standing and profits at the end of the business year.

annual return
a return that a business hosue is obliged to make annually. Specifically, the details of membership and financial structure that each registered company must sent to the registrar of companies who makes it available for public inspection.

annual usage value
in stock control, the total cost of the quantity of a particular stock-keeping unit used during a year.

anticipated profit
a profit that is recorded before being realized; paper profit.

anticipation stock
raw materials, parts or finished goods purchased or manufactured in advance of expected demand or in anticipation of rising costs and prices.

antitrust law
law relating to, legislation or action (especially in the USA) to turn monopolies and restrictive trade practices.

application form
1. a form completed by someone who applies for a job with an employer and on which he sets out basic facts about

himself and his suitability for employment.

2. A form completed by a person who wishes to buy securities in a public offer on which he states the number of securities he would like to buy.

application for shares

a form of application for shares usually accompanies a prospectus offering to the public for subscription or purchase shares in a company.

appreciation

1. a rise in value, especially of one currency in terms of another.

2. Appreciation means increase in the value of an asset. Appreciation may be caused by rise in the price of the asset as a result of inflation, increased shortage or increase in its demand in general.

apprenticeship

training period, usually for young person who apprenticed to a craftsman and helped and copied him.

appropriated retained earnings

retained income that is earmarked of specific or general purposes, taking the form a separate account to which retained earnings are transferred. The financial record, and the statement earning of a corporation that has established such an account in the existence of such a fund or account.

apropriation

the earmarking of funds for some specific or general purpose; a distribution of net income to various accounts: the amount of future expenditures that has been approved.

appropriation account

an account term referring to that part of the annual accounts of a business where the net profit is allocated to various claimants as the directors so determine. It disclose the amounts to be declared as dividends and amounts transferred to named reserves.

appropriation period

in government accounting, the period of time, usually one year, for the expenditure or obligation of an appropriation.

approval, sale on

a transaction that does not become final until the buyer approves or accepts the goods in question.

approval bill

a bill of exchange to which no reasonable objection can be raised.

arbitrage

buying and selling currency, bills of exchange, etc. in different markets, taking advantage of different rates to make a profit. Persons engaged in arbitrage can be providing a useful service in making money or bills available where they are wanted.

arbitrator

a person chosen by the parties

to a dispute to suggest a way of settling the dispute.

arrived ship
a vessel that has arrived at the agreed of discharge or loading, proper notice having been that is ready to start discharging or loading.

articles of association
it contains the regulations concerning the constitution and management of joint-stock companies registered under the Companies Acts. It includes the by-laws governing the internal working of a joint-stock company, such as elections, functional, power , salary etc.

articles of association, alternation of
the articles may be altered by a Special Resolution at a general meeting. The alternation must be within the powers given by the Memorandum of Association. It must concern legal acts and must not be a fraud on a minority of shareholders: that is, it must for the good of the Company and must not be an attempt by the majority to take advantage of their position. Where alternation of the rights of any class of shareholders is concerned, the articles often provide that special class meetings must be held and that the consent of the class must be obtained. Where the rights are fixed by the memorandum, then if the method of alternation is not specified it may be necessary to appeal to the court.

artifical person
an enterprise, business firm, or organization that has power, either granted by law or by custom, that resemble those of a natural person.

artisan's lien
a legal claim against another's property as security by a person who has invested labour upon, or added value to, such property and who has not been reimbursed for the value of the labour and materials.

'A' shares
ordinary shares of joint-stock company, carrying no votes, or simply non -voting shares.

asian dollars
the term applies to United States dollars dealt in, whether by deposit or loans, in Asian countries, notably Japan, Hongkong and the Pacific Basin.

As in goods
condition of sale that a buyer will accept delivery or goods ordered 'as they come' and without warranty.

ask
1. in business, the price offered by a seller; in effect, the same as bid.
2. also, offer. In the securities and commodities trade, the lowest price a seller is willing to accept.

asking price
the price at which a goods or a security is offered for sale.

assented stock or bond

a stock, or bond, the owner of which has agreed to some voluntary organizational change in the company issuing the stock or bond and has deposited it pending the issue of a definitive stock certificate or bond.

assessment

1. the process of valuing property for establishing taxation. Any recurrent tax levied by a government authority, such as for property or real-estate taxes. A special tax levied for improvement or repairs to community property under the direct control of a municipal authority; also known as a special assessment tax or improvement tax. A levy on stockholders, members of an organization, or owners of special beneficial interests for the purpose of raising additional capital.

2. in insurance, the practice of certain mutual companies or reciprocal exchanges of requiring the insured to pay additional charges to meet loses greater than anticipated. A policy that limits the insured's liability to the amount of premium paid is called nonassessable.

assessor

a person appointed to give specialist advice to a Court of Inquiry or an arbitor; also a person appointed by the Manpower Services Commission to an industrial training board to monitor its work.

asset

a physical object or a right that has economic value to its owner. For balance-sheet purposes, assets broadly grouped as current, fixed or intangible, and within these grouping are descriptive titles, such as receivables, inventories, investments, plant and equipment, goodwill, and patent.

assets

in accounting, any physical property or right that is owned and has money value. Accountants view an asset as source of wealth, usually expressed in terms of its cost, capable of giving its owner future benefits.

assets and liability statement

usually a Balance Sheet, the term is sometimes used by accountants to indicate a statement of what is owned and what is owed, prepared for single-entry books or sources other than double-entry books.

asset stripping

a situation which arises where a company rich in asset is taken over and the assets are sold off at a profit.

asset value

the value of a company calculated by reference to the current value of the underlying assets, for which is then deducted the amount of the company's liabilities. The asset value per share in the amount of the net asset so calculated divided by the number of ordinary shares in issue.

assignee

a person or party or parties to whom an assignment is made. An assignee may also be one to whom a title, interest, or right of some kind has been transferred. The person from whom the transfer is received is the assignor.

associated company

a corporation, wherein 50 per cent of the voting capital stock is owned by another. In British usage, a corporation in which another company holds a trade investment.

associated director

title sometimes given to senior managers, e.g., heads of major functions or divisions, which, implies status and recognition. Such directors are neither members of the board not have the duties and responsibilities of directors under the Companies Act.

association

a group of individual united voluntary for achieving a dterminate purpose/s and hold together by mutually determined code of procedure and rules.

association of international accountants

a professional institute for accountants in all parts of the world which aims to promote international accountancy standards.

assortment

the selection of goods offered sale by an intermediary or by a retailer.

assurance

tends to be used interchangeably with insurance in practice, but, technically, an assurance policy what is bond to happen but at an unknown time, while an insurnce policy is taken out against what might happen.

assured

a beneficiary of an insurance policy; a person who would be indemnified by another against a risk of loss.

atomistic society

an economy, in which there is a distinct preponderance of small independent producing units, as compared with large aggregates of capital in industry and trade.

at par

the term is generally used in relation to share value. It refers to an equality in value; the legally established value of the monetary unit of one country in terms of that of another using the same metal as a standard of value; the state of the shares of any business, undertaking, loan etc., when they may be purchased at the original price or at their face value.

at sight

a term used for bills of exchange payable on presentation, as opposed to on a particular date.

attendance bonus

an addition to normal wages which an employer promises to give to the his employees who achieve a certain standard or timekeeping lack of absence from work.

at-the-close order

a stock market order to buy or sell that is to be executed at or near to the close of the trading day as is practicable; any such order or portion thereof not so executed is treated as cancelled.

at-the-opening order

a stock market order to buy or sell that is to be executed at the opening of the stock or not at all; any such order or portion thereof not so executed is treated as cancelled.

attorney

in England, a person practising at the bar. It may also mean someone who holds a power of attorney.

attorney's opinion of title

in real estate, a legal document written and signed by an attorney, stating his opinion as to whether a seller may transfer a good title.

attornment

an attornment clause in a mortgage deed is one in which the mortgagor attorns tenant i.e., acknowledges himself to be the tenant of the mortgaged property, normally at a rent equal to the periodic instalments under the mortgage. The original idea was to confer on the mortgaged the right of distraint for rent in the event of non-payment of the mortgage instalments. This is no longer possible and attornment clauses have largely fallen into disuse among banks and buildings societies.

audit

critical examination and analysis or accounts performed by an independent person in order to asses their accuracy and, often, to detect fraud.

audit adjustment

an adjusting entry to a journal resulting from an examination by a public accountant.

audit certificate

the certification of a financial statement by a certified public accountant; and auditor's report.

audited net sale

average net sale of a publication excluding vouchers and other free copies, but accepting requested copies of controlled circulation journals.

audited voucher

a voucher that has been examined and approved for payment.

auditing

a deducting a defined as the examination of the books of account and of documents of a business by an independent person, qualified for the job and not in any way connected with the preparation of the accounting records, in order to verify the accuracy and correctness of the financial position as disclosed in the profit and loss account and the balance sheet for a particular period. It is an intelligent and critical scrutiny of the books of account of a business along with the documents and vouchers from which they have been written up.

auditing—process of

the process of auditing involve five different stages: (i) recognition of the proposition to be proved; (ii) evaluation of the proposition; (iii) collection and evaluation of evidence and (iv) formation of judgement.

audit internal

regular and independent appraisal, by a staff of internal auditors of the accounting, financial and other operations of an enterprise. Although more often limited to the auditing of accounts, in its most useful aspect internal auditing involves the appraisal of operations generally, weighing actual results in the light of planned results. Internal audit is an effective tool or management control.

auditor

a person engaged to examine the financial record of a firm and to report his observations and findings. He may be an employee of the firm whose records are being audited or an outside individual or member or a professional auditing group.

auditor, appointment of

the auditor of any company, registered under the Companies Act, 1956, is appointed by the members of that company at the annual general meeting and holds office till the next meeting when he may be reappointed by a resolution of members. The directors may appoint the first auditor (a) and fill in any casual vacancy. But such appointment must be confirmed at the next annual general meeting. The remuneration of auditor is fixed by the company at the annual general meeting.

auditor—duties of

an auditor must satisfy himself to his best about the accuracy of accounts and correct maintenance of records. He must see that the Balance Sheet discloses the true financial position of the business. Auditor is not only to ascertain that final accounts have been prepared in accordance with the books, but he must also satisfy himself that they are correct record of the transactions of the business. He must report to the shareholders if he finds that the balance sheet does not represent the true state of affairs of the company or the accounts have not been properly kept, otherwise he will be liable for breach of duty. If he wilfully certifies accounts knowing them to be false, he will be held criminally liable.

He must report all the facts with which he is not satisfied, not only to the directors but to the shareholders. An auditor must give all information in clear and unambiguous terms to the shareholders so as not merely to arouse any enquiry but to inform them of all the facts about the business as it stands. Auditor should not give any advice unless specially consulted for it. Auditor will be held liable for negligence if he reports overvaluation of assets through inadequate provision for losses to directors alone and not to the shareholders.

auditor, removal of

an auditor can be removed at any time. If he is auditor of a company there are certain formalities, to be observed; he must be removed by a resolution of a general meeting; notice of the resolution must be given to the company twentyeight days prior to the meeting; the company must then give members twenty-one days' notice and must also notify the auditor. The auditor may then speak at the meeting, or may make a written statement, and request that this be notified to members and/or be read at the meeting. (This need not be none if the statement is judged in court to be in any way defamatory.)

audit trail

a notation accompanying a transaction entry or posting that refers to its source records or documents.

audit year

the year covered in an annual or balance-sheet audit; usually the fiscal year.

audit voucher

a voucher that has been examined and approved for payment.

autarky

self-sufficiency, especially of a country with no international trade.

authorized capital

the total nominal value or stated value of all the shares that a company is authorized by its constitution to issue.

authorized capital stock

the number of shares and the par or state value of capital that may be issued by a corporation under its articles of incorporation.

authorized issue

the sum of shares of capital stock corporation may sell under its charter, or the sum of bonds that may be sold under a given mortgage. A corporation wishing to issue more stock must have its charter amended, with the approval of the shareholders.

automatic dividend reinvestment plan

an agreement between a shareholder and a mutual, fund, whereby dividends are automatically used to purchase additional shares of stock in the fund.

automation

application of such mechanise in business industry which automatically operate or perform acts of interrelated operations with virtually no human labour.

automated funds transfer

also, AFT account, technically speaking, two bank accounts, one checking and the other savings, where money can be transferred from one to the other automatically by a computer. This practice was instituted in 1978 and has come to be widely used.

autonomous investment

investment that is made independent of current or anticipated economic conditions (such as anticipated increases in national income).

available assets

assets that are free for general use, free of encumbrance or lien, not saving as collateral for an obligation.

average adjuster

a loss adjuster is employed by an insurer to determine the extent of his liability to reimburse an assurer to determine the extent of his liability to reimburse an assured who has to meet a claim for general average contribution or his liability to reimburse an assured sum when there is a particular average loss.

average bond

a bond given by a person receiving cargo, stating that he will contribute to any General Average Claim.

average demurrage agreement

in transportation, an agreement to offset debits with credits.

average due date

the average date on which a number of payments due at different times, may be paid.

average fixed cost (AFC)

1. the fixed cost of producing a quantity of a goods divided by the quantity produced.
2. total fixed cost divided by output.

average total cost (ATC)

the total cost of production a quantity of good divided by the quantity produced.

averaging (stock exchange)

a 'bull' speculator on the Stock Exchange buys more of a certain stock he holds, when the price has fallen, so as to make the average price of the whole purchase less than the price paid for the original purchase; and a 'bear' speculator, when the price rises against him, sells more of the stock as to average the price.

aviation insurance

a category of insurance covering, as the name implies, risks arising from aviation.

avoidable costs

those that are incurred as a result of specific action or management decision rather than being an inherent and unavoidable part of the very existence of a business or organization (unavoidable costs of the latter kind might include factory buildings and basic equipment and labour costs).

backdoor financing
a method is used by various government agencies to by pass the conventional way of obtaining funds divided by instead borrowing money directly from the treasury.

back-door selling
the practice of attempting to sell a product directly to its ultimate industrial users instead of dealing with the company's authorised purchasing personnel.

back duty
tax which should have been paid in the past by an individual who failed to provide adequate information at the time for a correct assessment to be made of tax payable.

back note
an authority, endorsed by broker, the master of ship arranging the loading of goods for shipment.

back order
the portion of a customer's order that has not been shipped against as accepted order that is in backlog.

back pay
wage/salary for work already done but for which proper payment has not been received.

back-to-back loan
a loan from one company to another in a different country, often in a different currency, using a bank or other financial institutions as a middle man to provide the loan but not the funding, which comes from a third party.

bad debts
accounts going out of business and still owing money to suppliers. Also an item in financial accounts referring to actual amounts of monies so lost, or written off.

bail
the security that is pledged to enable an arrested or imprisoned person to be temporarily released until his appearance is required at specified place and time.

bailment
a transfer of possession of goods without the passing of title, as on consignment for safekeeping, repair, or sale.

balance
in accounting, the balance of an account is the difference between the total of the credit entries and the total of the debit entries. It is ascertained at certain intervals, monthly or weekly for debtors or creditors, and perhaps annually for the annual accounts.

balance certificate
the certificate received by a shareholder for the remainder of his holding when he has sold part of his holdings.

balanced budget
a budget in which the expenditures forecast for given period of operations are equal to, the expected revenues for

the same period.

balanced economy
when imports equal exports in dollar value, the national economy is said to be in balance.

balance of payments
refers to record of all transactions between the residents of one country and the rest of, the world, with payments expressed in terms of the country's currency.

balance of trade
the difference between the money value of a country's merchandise imports and the money value of its merchandise exports. A country is said to have a balance-of-trade surplus if it exports more than it imports and a deficit if it imports more than it exports.

balance on current account
the net value of a nation's exports goods and services plus or minus all unilateral money transfer abroad, such as remittances social security payments, and grants in aid.

balance sheet
balance sheet is the statement of account which is prepared at the end of every financial year. It gives the total picture of the business at the point of time. Balance sheet is the sum of the liabilities and assets of the business house at a particular time or the point of time. Balance sheet provides immediate answer to all questions which may be asked by the businessman at the end of the financial year. It is essential that the total liabilities of the business must be equal to the total assets of the business and that is why the two sides of the balance sheet always remain equal.

balance sheet total
refers to the total value of assets shown in a balance sheet.

balancing charge
an amount that is added to the taxable trading profits of a person or company when an asset is sold and the writing-down allowances taken up to the date of sale exceed the difference between the cost of the asset and the proceeds of the sale.

balloon
also, balloon payment. A large final payments made at the end of a term or other long-term obligations, following a series of a smaller payments.

bank
a commercial institution licensed as a taker of deposits. Bank are concerned mainly with making and receiving payments or behalf of their customers, accepting deposits, and making short term loans to private individuals, companies and other organizations.

bank acceptance
a bill accepted by a bank. A merchant in one country, purchasing goods overseas may arrange for his bankers to accept a bill drawn on them by the shippers, the various

shipping documents being attached to the bill. The shipper may then sell the bill and thus receive immediate payment for the goods. Banks show the total of these acceptances in their balance-sheet as a liability with contra-entry on the asset side of the customers' liability to the bank.

bank account, deposit
an account kept buy a customer at a bank. It differs from a current account inasmuch as the money is intended to remain for a longer period. Withdrawals are made subject to notice (often waived); payments out cannot be made by cheque (though this again is a rule not always enforced provided the cheques are infrequent). Depositors have a pass book recording the balance—interest is at deposit rate (normally 2 per cent below bank rate).

bank advance
bank's loan to its customer against approved securities. Such advances include secured as well as insecured advance.

bank bill
a bill which has been drawn or accepted by a bank.

bank certificate
a certificate, signed by a bank manger, stating the balance held to a company's credit on a specified date.

bank discount
refers to the difference between the volume of a bank loan and the amounts credited to the borrower. Interest on a loan is deducted in advance from the face value of the same.

bank draft
bank drafts are basically cheques drawn on a particular bank and obtained from that bank by a debtor for the paying a debt where the creditor will not accept the debtor's personal cheque or the debtor does not have a bank account.

banker's acceptance
an instrument which is used in financing foreign trade. It makes possible the payment of cash to an exporter for all part of the amount of a shipment made by him.

banker's clearing houses
an agency through which the interbank indebtedness is cleared. Usually the central bank acts as a clearing house for member banks.

banker's deposits
bank's cash reserves with the central bank of the country.

bank failure
refers to the inability of a bank to honour the withdrawals of its depositors. Bank failure may set off sudden large withdrawals.

banking
method used by 'payment by results' workers to 'store' work done, by delaying its booking and recording; also implying the falsification of records. Business of accepting deposits and lending money.

bank loans and overdrafts, disclosure of
bank loans and overdrafts must be disclosed in the balance sheets of limited companies. Only one figure need be given.

bank note
a financial document by which a bank promises to pay the bearer of the document, on demand, a specified sum of money. In England and Wales the bank of England may issue bank notes. In India only the Reserve Bank does so.

bank of issue
a bank authorized to issue its own bank notes to circulate as currency. Now usually the central bank of a country is the bank issue.

bank overdrafts
basically an amount due to a bank by a customer on his account. The bank will give overdraft facilities in place of a bank loan to a person or organization, with or without security. A charge is made by the bank and is calculated on the amount overdrawn on a day to day basis. A limit is usually placed on the amount a customer may draw in this way, i.e. in excess of the amount which he has deposited. An overdraft should be distinguished from a bank loan; the overdraft varies from day to day, the loan is a stated amount, and interest is paid on the total, or in the balance outstanding at certain times. Banks overdrafts, like bank advances, are sometimes indirectly State controlled.

bank rate
the rate at which the central bank is prepared to lend to the others banks in the banking system.

bank reserve
the stock of money a bank must set aside (and not lend) to meet the demands of depositors.

banks
banks provide means by which capital is transferred from those who cannot profitably use it to those who can use it most productively for the benefit of the society as a whole. Banks provide rate of interest. They advance loans to businessmen on credit, provide facilities for making remittances at home and a-broad and settle credit payments. The system of banking and finance not only brings the distribution of goods among the consumers but also enables modern productive processes to go on. Where the manufacturing process is very long it becomes necessary that throughout its course the producer should not fall short of money.

banker's draft
a bill of exchange drawn by banker on himself. It is often used in international trade. A foreign exporter receiving a banker's draft may cash it at the local branch of that bank.

Bankers, Institute of

this was founded in 1879 to afford opportunities to acquire knowledge of banking theory, and to facilitate consideration and discussion of matters of interest to bankers. It is also intended 'to help our members to educate themselves not only for banking but also for responsible citizenship' (Sir E. A. Carpenter). The institute has a series of examinations leading to a banking diploma. Holders of a diploma may use the letters. A.I.B. (Associate of the Institute of Bankers). The may also be elected fellow (F.I.B.). Syllabuses may be obtained from the institute without charge. Exemption from certain papers is given to persons with other recognized professional qualifications.

bankruptcy : arrest of debtor

where a debtor shows signs of absconding, or appears to be making efforts to prolong or delay the bankruptcy proceedings, or hides his books and papers, the court has power to issue a warrant for his arrest. This also is so where after the receiving orders, or presentation of the petition, he removes goods of more than Rs.250 in value without the leave of the official receiver or trustee.

bankruptcy offences

when a bankruptcy does certain things after an adjusdication he may be guilty of a misdemeanour. The offences are generally speaking deeds by the bankrupt which hinder the realization of his property and payment of his creditors.

bankrupcy : proof of debts

a creditor wishing to share in the proceeds of a bankrupt estate must prove his debt. He does this by submitting to the official receiver or trustee an affidavit giving a statement of account. This statement must be detailed and give means of verification. If the creditor has any security he must say so; if he does not he may be deemed to have surrendered it. Trade discounts are deducted and also agreed cash discounts but not exceeding 5 per cent. (Special rules apply to moneylenders). The cost of the proof must be borne by the creditor. Double proof is not allowed, i.e. two creditors cannot prove for the same debt (both guarantor and creditor cannot prove, for instance). However, one credit could prove in two bankruptcies. Proofs must be stamped and be dealt within a specified period. Proofs may be admitted, rejected or held over for consideration. It is not necessary for each employee to prove separately for wages.

banks: shipping

banks frequently deal with problems involved in shipping goods, and financial problems attached to owning ships; for example they will see to registering vessels, placing insurance and handling claims. They will also receive freight, and make remittances to captains.

bargain

a agreement between two persons on the terms of a contract between them.

barrister

one how acts for a client in court, pleading or defending a case. He does not deal directly with the client but through the clients's solicitor. By custom a barrister cannot sue for debts incurred in his profession. One becomes a barrister by being called to the bar, which involves sitting various examinations, serving an apprenticeship, and eating a number of meals at what are known as Inns of Court.

barter

refers to the exchange of goods and services without the use of money is called barter. In this system a particular quantity of one goods may be exchanged for some quantity of another goods, persons or organisations basing the exchange on manually matching requirements.

barter terms of trade

bareter terms of trade to the quantity of real imports that a nation can buy which each unit of its real exports. A nation's barter terms of trade very with the ratio:

$$\frac{\textit{The price of exports}}{\textit{The priceof imports}}$$

base rate

the variable part of the interest rate charged by a bank on loans to its customers. A customer is charged a fixed rate in addition to the base rate.

base year

a reference year established for purpose of comparison and the indication of trends or changes.

basic producer

a manufacturer who uses natural resources to produce materials for other manufacturers.

basic rate

the minimum wage rate for a job excluding any allowances such as overtime premium of bonus. Used as a nominal rate from which other rates (e.g., overtime rates) are calculated. Also called 'base rate' or 'basic wage rate'. It is also the minimum wage rate for a job agreed in a national agreement but subejct to local increases.

basic standard cost

in accounting, it refers to a standard cost that serves as a point of reference from which to measure changes in current standard cost as well as actual cost. Also, a standard cost that is developed from engineering studies, using specific assumptions.

basket loan

a loan by an institution that is higher than the usual maximum allowed by law. In many states insurance companies and mutual savings banks may invest a higher percentage of their assets in mortgages under particular conditions.

batch costing

refers to a process or activity of allocation costs to a batch of identical items of production, treated as a single unit.

batch processing

operation of a computer in such a way that individual jobs or programs are dealt with one at a time : one jobs is not started until the previous job has been completed.

bear

someone who thinks that the stock market prices or activity will decline.

bear account

when the speculative sales exceed the speculative purchase, the position is a bear account or oversold position.

bearer bond

a bond that does not have the owner's name registered on the book of the issuing company and that is payable to the bearer.

bearer cheque

a bearer cheque is open in the sense that it does not have two parallel lines drawn across its face and the banker is required to pay the specified sum to the one who (bears) presents it.

bearer debenture

a debenture which is payable to bearer with or without power for the borrower to have placed it on a register or to have it at any time withdrawn from it. It is transferable by delivery.

bearer security

a security which can be transferred from one owner to another simply by handing over a certificate of ownership.

bearer share

a share, ownership of which is evidenced by a bearer security. Also the bearer security, usually called a share warrant, that evidence ownership of such a share.

bear market

market is which speculators are operating on assumption in any name.

bear raid

when the tone of the market is bearish and the bears want to press down the prices still lower by spreading this pessimism, it is called a bearraid.

benefical interest

an interest in a property held in trust or in the benefit of an insurance policy or other contract. In its plural form, beneficial interests are the proprietorship represented by the outstanding shares of stock of a corporation.

benefits-received principle

the idea that tax assessments should be based on the extent to which taxpayers benefit from the goods and services paid for by taxes.

betterment

also, improvement. In cost accounting, the replacement of an asset of part of an asset with a superior unit or part, resulting in a higher valuation of the asset (any presumably also greater productivity or better quality and/or durability.

bicolumnar

a term used to describe a two column balance sheet or income statements, or double-entry bookkeeping, wherein one column is used to display credits, and the second column, debits.

bid

an offer to buy. A bid proposal may be presented by a vendor to a potential buyer, in effect stating that the vendor would accept a bid from the potential customers in conformity with terms of the bid proposal.

bid price

the price at which stocks and shares, commodities and indeed any item of property may be sold, it is the price 'bid' by the prospective buyer.

bilateral flow

the expression refers to a flow of funds from the Government to the private sector of the economy in exchange for commodities and services.

bilateralism

exclusive dealings between two countries, as opposed to dealings among a larger group of nations (multilateralism).

bilateral monopoly

a market structure in which a moniponist buyers faces a monopolist seller.

bilater oligopoly

a market situation in which a small number of buyers confront a small number of sellers.

bill

as used in commerce and finance, a generic term identifying a variety of documents having to do with currency, the shipment of goods and the collection debts. The term is used as an abbreviation of a bill of exchange or as synonymous with a draft often in association with one of a number of qualifying or descriptive objectives.

bill broker

the person or firm that buys bills of exchange and promissory notes at a discount and either rediscounts them or holds them in order to receive payment from drawees.

bill discount book

a bank book in which the details of all bills discounted are entered.

bill for collection

bills left for collection or 'short bills,' as they are sometimes called.

bill in a set

in some countries, foreign bills are usually drawn in several parts, and, for safety, the parts may be transmitted by separate mails. Where a bill is drawn in that way it is said to be drawn in a set, and the various parts constitute the bill.

billing

in business and trade, the

submission of invoices for goods or services.

bill of credit

fiat currency issued by American colonies.

bill of entry

a document which is prepared by the importer for the purpose of paying the customs duties.

bill of exchange

this is defined officially as 'an unconditional order in writing, addressed by one person to another, the person to whom it is addressed to pay on demand, or at a fixed or determinable future time, a certain sum of money, to, or to the order of, a specified person, or to the bearer. Bills of exchange involve the payment of the money only. The time of payment must be definite.

bill of exchange : stamping

bills of exchange are not stamped on an Ad Valorem basis. All bills negotiated in U.K. pay a stamp duty of 2d. The stamp may be an adhesive stamp or the bill itself may be stamped. The stamp is cancelled by the person stamping the bill. If foreign bills are drawn and payable abroad, stamp duty is not payable : the liability arises when the bill is negotiated in U.K.

bill of lading

refers to a shipping documents on which the ship owner or his agent certifies the consignment to a specified party to have been received by them; a document providing a description of goods received for shipment, term on which these are to be carried and, regarded as the title for goods received for shipment.

bill of material repetitions

the number of times a part number referenced in a bill of material. This information can be useful in determining order quantities for specific part numbers, as developing kits of materials for production.

bill of sale (absolute)

document indicating transfer of title and possession, and witnessed by a solicitor.

bill payable

a bill of exchange, payable at some time in the future, considered as a liability of its acceptor.

bill receivable

a bill of exchange, payable at some date in the future, considered as an asset of the person entitled to payment of it.

bin card

a card kept in a storehouse recording the actual quantity of material in a bin or other receptacle. The card is marked each time items are purchased or requisitioned.

binder

in insurance, a document that is used extensively as a means for providing immediate insurance protection to an applicant for policy. The binder-oral or, preferably, written-is evidence that consideration has been given to purchasing a formal policy. In effect the binder is itself a temporary insurance policy that is enforceable as though it were the final, formal policy.

In real estate, a temporary document, usually requiring a monetary deposit, executed by a buyer and a seller in contemplation of a more formal contract for the purchase of real property.

black capitalism

an effort begun in the late 1960s to increase the ownership and control of business by black people. Its objective is to improve the job market, the ghetto economy, and the condition and status of black community.

black economy

economic activity that is concealed from government agencies (and so not recorded in official statistics) in order, usually, to evade taxation.

blacking

action of employees who during industrial action refuse to handle or work on goods or components that they consider are being processed or supplied by employees in a way which evades the industrial action.

black market

a market consisting of illicit buying and selling of goods in violation of legal price control, rationing, etc.

blank cheque

a cheque where no sum of money is stated. The holder can fill in the amount himself. Blank cheques are often used in latter transactions where the price of the goods to be purchased is not known. The buyer may send a blank cheque but write 'not to exceeds Rs.....on it. The blank will need this instruction.

blank credit

credit granted by a banker on the personal security of his client.

blanket order

an order placed with a vendor, usually for large quantities of materials, such as for an annual supply, against which individuals releases are made.

blanket policy

an insurance term for a policy which covers many different types of risk. For instance property may be insured against fire, theft, etc.

blank indorsement

where an indorsement on a bill of exchange specifies no indorsee, it is an indorsement in blank.

blank transfer

a blank transfer of stock or shares is a transfer which a material particular is lacking; the date is not, in this sense, a material particular.

blind entry

in accounting a journal entry that states only the name of an account and the amounts debited or credited, without explaining the transactions or providing the information essential to an ad equate record; a posting in a ledger that is not supported by a journal vouchers or other evidence.

blocked accounts

non-resident funds which cannot be transferred freely.

blocked currency

a currency of a country is said to be blocked when the government of that country creates categories of its currency that can be used only for purchase within the country.

blood stock insurnce of

in some countries, a number of insurance companies will provide cover for death or injury to animals which are valuable for racing or breeding.

blue chip

a listed company which, because of its large size, long history of profitable trading and good management, commands a high level of confidence among stock-market investors. Also an ordinary share of such a company. (Highvalue chips for gambling-e.g., in poker—are coloured blue.)

blue chip company

company whose shares price is high and whose shares are sought after, especially by investment institutions.

blue chip investment

a colourful term for that type of investment which, though not gilt-edged, is considered to be safe, so that there is little likelihood of losing capital or income. They are usually the shares of particularly well known and sound companies.

board of directors

the person elected by the shareholders of a corporation to set company policy.

board room

a room for customers in a broker's office where opening high, low, and closing prices of leading stocks are posted on a quote board.

board wages

a term for payment made to hotel staff etc. for buying their own meals.

bona vacantia

this refers to property where there is no apparent owner and no claimant. This could be property remaining in the hands of a liquidator when a company has been dissolved. Such property passes automatically to the Crown or the Royal Duchies of Lancaster or Cornwall. They could also disclaim it, and then its ultimate destination would depend on the nature of the property: shares would be surrendered to the company; land would probably be compulsorily acquired by a local authority. A liquidator may need to apply to a court for direction.

bond

a certificate on indebtedness of an international organization, a national, or local government, public body or a company, bearing on its details of interest rate, dates and conditions of .naturity.

bond and prefei red stock fund

a mutual fund whose policy is to invest in bonds and preferred stocks.

bonded block loading

an effective and secure method for loading freight; the items are stacked in the manner of overlapping "bricks".

bonded lighterman

a person responsible, with bonded carmen, for moving goods from one bonded warehouse to another.

bonded warehouse

a warehouse in which goods may be stored without customs duty or excise duty being pad until they are withdrawn from the warehouse.

bond note

a term used in shipping with reference to export of goods. Dutiable goods must be put in bond. A bond note is issued indicating that the necessary formalities have been observed. The note acts as authority for recovering the goods from the warehouse and exporting them.

bond price

it is a price which includes all the expenses till the goods are transferred to the bonded warehouse at the port of destination. The importer can take delivery of the goods from the bonded house on payment of necessary custom duties.

bonus

any payment in addition to regular or base wages. It may be in the form of an annual allotment, or it may consist in high rates paid for night-work, overtime, hazardous work etc.

bonus account

a savings account that pays higher than normal rate of interest.

bonus formula

the formal provision in an incentive bonus plan that determine the total funds available for bonus purposes in a given year individual bonus awards are made from this total pool.

bonous issue (shares)

it is the free issue of shares to existing share holders with the intention of bringing a company's capital structure into line with the true value of its assets. Bonus shares are issued to those who are already shareholders by using undistributed profits and reserves.

bonus pool

the total amount of bonus funds generated by an incentive plan in a given year and available for awards. In most companies the pool approximates the total bonuses that would be paid if all participants received "normal" awards.

bonus stock

common stock offered as a bonus, either to the underwriter of the issue as additional incentive, or to buyers of bonds or preferred stock in the same company.

boodle
money obtained by corrupt dealing in public affairs, and also counterfeit money.

book
as recorded in the books of account of a firm.

book debts
the total amount of due from the customers of the concern for sales made to them on credit.

bookkeeping
keeping the financial records (books) of business or other economic unit, recording all the transactions in which it' engages. Book-keeping is the branch of accounting.

book-keeping and accounting machines
these machines are used for ledger posting, cash book writing, payroll preparation, posting and analysis of costing records, etc.

book of account
the records of a firm's financial records.

book of final entry
in accounting, a record book to which the money amounts of transactions are transferred, or posted, from other books; a ledger.

book of original entry
in accounting, a record book in which transactions are recorded and that serves as the sources of postings to ledgers; a journal.

book of secondary entry
book of final entry.

book-rate of return
alternative term for return on capital or accountant's return.

book value
as applied to stocks, the proportionate amount of money that would accrue to each share of outstanding capital stock of a corporation if all the corporation's assets were converted into cash at the values appearing on the books, and all of its creditors and other prior claimants, if any, were paid in full.

book value per share
an indicator of the financial status of an enterprise, BV/share represents the sum of the common stock, paid-in surplus, and retained-income accounts of the balance sheet, divided by the number of common shares outstanding.

boot
as applied to trading, something given in addition to the thing exchanged to equalise the exchange.

borderean
in insurance accounting, a tabular register or report that contains abstracts of insurance that has been written.

bottom line
on a balance sheet or other financial statement, the sum or total of the details listed above the line.

bottomary bond
a master of a ship may need money quickly during a voyage. He may then borrow it on the security of the ship and cargo

by means of a bottomary bond. He only does so when money is necessary to complete the voyage when communication with the owner is impossible. If money can be obtained on the shipowner's credit, this must be done. A Lottomry bond holder loses all his money if the ship is lost. If there are serveral bond holders, the last is paid first. The ship cannot be disposed of until the bond is paid.

bought ledger

the ledger consists of individual creditors accounts. This ledger is posted from the books of original entry when goods are purchased, payments are made, goods are returned and bills are accepted, etc.

bourse

a word of French origin applied to any stock exchange or commodity market in continental Europe.

bracket creep

the slow but sure progression of individuals and families to an ever higher income tax bracket during a period of high employment and high inflation.

brand

a name, term, symbol, or design (or a combination of these) that serves to identify goods or services of one seller or group of sellers and to distinguish them, from those of competitors.

brandburys

a slang term for Rs.50 and 10s. notes, issued by the treasury in place of gold coin in 1914. The name derives from the then Secretary of the treasury, John Bradbury. In 1928 the Bank of England took over the issue of notes from the Treasury.

brand leader

a branded product which has the largest market share for all products of its type.

break-even analysis

computing costs and revenues for different volumes of production in order to determine the break-even point i.e., the point at which an enterprise starts yielding a margin of profit.

break-even chart

management aid for identifying the relationship between costs, of output and profit.

break-even point

that level of production at which total cost equals gross income; in other words, the rate of plant utilization when neither a loss is incurred nor profit is made.

breaking bulk

function of wholesaler who buys in bulk and then distributes in smaller qualities to local retailers.

break-up value

a term for asset value, common in the field of company accounts. Shares have various values, each corrected according to the viewpoint of the value they have a nominal value; selling price (listed price when quoted on a Stock Exchange); buying price—

which will differ from the selling price marginally, also depending on the commission paid to intermediaries.

bribe

a bribe is a payment by which the payer obtain some right, benefit, or preference to which he has no legal entitlement and which he would not have obtained but for the payment of the money. It is a criminal offence to accept a bribe. Any bribe taken by an agent must be handed over to the principal. It is an offence, punishable by two years imprisonment and/or a fine of Rs.10000 for an agent to accept a bribe, or for a person to offer a bribe to an agent.

British Export Houses Association

the association formed by British Exports Houses to give free advice to exporters on finding an export house and/ or confirming House suitable to their needs.

British Overseas Engineering Services Bureau

this was set up with government help in order to promote overseas work by British consulting engineers, architects, management consultants, etc. It helps by collecting and passing on information, sends mission overseas, and may help meet the cost of feasibility studies. It also helps to form organized consortia. Part of the cost is met by the government and part by members' subscriptions.

British road services

this was once an independent organization controlled by the transport holding company, and is now part of the national freight corporation. It is concerned with general haulage, and operates about 7,000 vechiles of all types; most types of loads can be carried. Some 200 branches are linked by teleprinter; there are regular overnight services between main industrial centres, as well as nationwide warehousing and distribution services. Thee are direct services to the continent, northern Ireland and Eire. Vehicles include bolster vehicles, bulk carriers, cable carriers, coiled steel carriers, insulated containers, livestock containers, low loaders, pole carriers, etc. There is also a specialized car-carrying service, and British Road Services Parcels Ltd. specializes in collecting, conveying and delivering pacels and small consignments.

broker

a merchantile agent, who in the nature of his business, makes contracts to shares, goods or property. He need not carry the goods or documents of ownership. There are also specialized brokers, in stock exchange, commodity markets, and even insurance or in services. A broker is not bound by any personal liability unless customs dictates. He has implied authority to sell on normal credit, receive payment, and do other things consonant with his trade.

brokerage

a commission that accrues to a broker for having brought about an arrangement or transaction between a buyer and a seller.

broker's loan

money borrowed by brokers from banks to buy or carry securities, finance the underwriting of new issues, or carry their clients margin' accounts

bubble company

a company that has never has any real business or intended to trade honestly, or a company formed with the intention of defrauding the public. It probably takes its name from the South Sea Bubble.

bucket shop

a place where bets are made on the prices of securities or commodities bought and sold on the stock and commodity exchanges. An enterprise which sells securities or futures contracts for commodities but which is not a member of an organized market and is not regulated by government or other agencies.

budget

the term is derived from the old English word Bougette.

The term budget refers to anticipated revenue and proposed expenditure by a government in the year (next financial year).

The budget may be surplus or deficit or balanced. However, deficit budget are more common.

In India, the budget is divided into (1) revenue budget and (2) capital budget. The former includes revenue receipts and revenue disbursements while the latter contains capital receipts and capital disbursements.

The central budget is presented by the Union Finance Minister to the parliament a few days before the commencement of never had new fiscal year.

budget account

system of retail trading in which a customer makes fixed payments to a trade and is allowed credit up to a certain amount.

budgetary control

a system of controlling expenditure and income used by the management of a business. Each department in the business forecasts its probable expenditure or income for the coming financial period. There forecasts or budgets are scrutinized and approved at top management level, so that a provisional profit and loss account for the coming year can be drawn up and, if necessary, expenses checked and sales policies revised. The system varies from firm to firm. Generally speaking budgets must be adhered to and any deviations during the relevant period are reported so that action can be taken if necessary.

budget, cash

it is a forecast of cash receipt and disbursements against which actual cash experience is measured. This is perhaps the most important single control of a business. Cash budgeting indicates availability of excess cash, thereby making possible planning for profit making investment of this "cash.

budget, flexible

budget which is elastic in nature. It indicates a number of possible outputs and different cost structures in contract to Fixed Budget which shows one volume os output and related costs in a manufacturing industry. Since it is very unlikely that the volume depicted in the forecast and budget will be the one obtained in practice, the flexible budget is the only one which enable costs to be controlled effectively.

budget, functional

budget prepared to indicate performance and cost for each function in a department.

Functional budget is prepared in addition to departmental budget with a view to controlling more effectively a function as administration, production, purchase, sales, research and development. The budget for, say, the Machine is clearly a departmental budget yet, because this budget relates to production, the figure may be summarised in the functional budget for production.

budget, master

the principal or supreme budget and the budget of all budgets of an enterprise. It puts together all others into one overall integrated budget. Its purpose is to harmonise and collate the different sectional budgets of the enterprise for top management control.

budget summary

budget summary takes into account master budget, balance sheet budget and income statement to present a complete budgetary programming quantitative and terms. Budget summary thus aims at assisting overall management control in an enterprise.

budget surplus

an excess of total revenues over total expenditures. The effect of surplus in the national budget is to reduce the level of economic activity.

builder's risk

fire insurance written to cover the constantly increasing value of a building under construction.

building society interest

where interest is paid to building societies approved by the Inland Revenue, be deducted from taxable income.

Tax is not deducted at source.

bulk cargo

a shipping term meaning cargo which can fill the whole space by one commodity.

bulk freight

material that is shipped loose rather than in packages or containers, as coal in a hopper car or sulphur in the hold of a ship.

bull

one who believes that the stock market prices or activity will rise.

bull account

when the speculative purchases made by the bull operators exceeds the speculative sales, it is called a bull account or overbought position.

bullion

gold and silver of a recognized degree of purity. It may be in various forms, normally gold or silver bars.

bullish market

when the market shows signs of rising and a feeling of optimism prevails, the tone of the market is called bullish.

bull liquidation

when the bull begins to unload his holdings to reduce his loss because of the fact the prices show signs of going lower than expected, it is called bull liquidation.

burglary insurance

basic protection against loss due to crimes committed by outsiders rather than by employees of an organization or authorized visitors.

business agent

in labour relations, the highest official in a union or labour organization operating on a local basis. The business agent is usually salaried and is either elected or appointed to perform the principal work of the local union, such as negotiating contracts, settling grievances, and building membership rolls.

business club

it is an association formed by members not necessarily for gain but for some common advantages like social service, games, recreation, entertainment, etc. But a partnership is primarily formed with a view to earn profits from a business. A member of a club is not liable for the debts of the club unless he had participated in its transactions.

business deposits

the bank deposits held by a businessman, a manufacturer or a speculator for business purposes.

business enterprise

an enterprise engaged in business activities.

business entity

the concept of business entity is the universal acceptance of the business world. Such business has a separate entity of its own besides that of the businessman. The registered partnership firms and joint stock companies have separate legal entities of their own but sole proprietorship business has none. However to provide that business the same status, this concept of business entity has been recognised.

business interruption insurance

a type of insurance that covers the insured for loss of earnings sustained as a result of fire.

business life insurance

insurance on the life of a member of a partnership or on the officer or stockholder in a corporation payable so as to finance purchase by surviving owners of the insured's interest at his or her death.

business management

the term 'business management' has acquired an unenviable position in the modern society these days.

business profits

revenue minus business expenses can be called business profits because this is the profit concept of the accountant and of the businessman. Business profits are always larger than net profits because business expenses are always less than full costs.

(Full cost = Fixed costs + Variable costs)

(Net profit = revenue-Full costs)

business ratio

a ratio used in analysing activities of a firm. (Also known as a 'management ratio').

business risk

the risk that a firm's profits will decrease because of the nature of the activities - e.g., because there is a decline in the demand for its product or an increase in the cost of its materials.

business savings

net income earned by firms that has not been paid to Stockholder or other owners of the business. It represents saving by the firm on behalf of tis owners.

buyer

in a retail business, an executive who undertakes the purchasing and stocking of various items for the store.

buyer credit

a method of financing exports in which a bank in the exporter's country loans money to foreign buyers for purchases from the exporter. Such a deal is usually set up on the exporter's initiative and the money is in practice paid direct to the exporter.

buyer's panic

a market in which buyers suddenly greatly outnumbers sellers at a particular price level.

buying behaviour

way in which a buyer behaves when deciding whether or not to buy a product or service and the factors that determine the behaviour.

buying-in

the process of enforcement of delivery of securities by buyers, when the seller has failed to deliver the shares within the stipulated time.

buying office

a centralized purchasing office that serves a number of retail stores.

buying power

in the securities trade, the total amount a stock broker will allow a customer to buy on margin without putting up more cash or securities.

calculating machine

a machine used for mathematical calculations, particularly calculations other than straightforward addition and substraction, e.g. percentages.

callable bond

a bond that is issued, subject to a condition that the issuer may at any time, demand that the bond be presented for redemption. (Also known as 'redeemable bond.)

callable issue

a bond issue, all or part of which may be redeemed by the issuing cooperation under defined conditions before maturity. The term also applies to preferred shares redeemable by the issuing corporation.

called up capital

when the full price of a share is only partly paid for an issue the remaining capital not called may be payable on allotment of the shares or in the future. In the event of winding up or liquidation the shareholder is liable for the outstanding capital.

call in pay

a guaranteed minimum payment for being specially called in to work. (Also known as call-back pay).

call loan

a loan that may be terminated at will by either party; primarily a loan made by a bank to a stockbroker. A loan that has been terminated in this way is known as a called loan.

call money

1. loan on which pre-payment can be demanded any day the bank desires.
2. money lent at a day's or week's notice to the money market (also to the stock exchange for the "account".)

call-off system

an arrangement for buying manufactured parts for use in assemblies by which the purchaser places a firm order for a specific quantity of the parts to be manufactured over, say, the next year on the basis that required quantities will be delivered as an when the manufacturer needs them.

call over

the term used for the practice (practise) in some smaller exchanges of securities being offered for sale, and in effect auctioned, at specific times.

callover price

the price agreed for a transaction at a callover; it may be used subsequently by the general market dealers.

Callover prices, though verbal at the outset, may later be formally printed.

call price
the price at which a callable bond is redeemable.

call rate
1. the rate at which the market can borrow short-term money from the banks.
2. the rate at which money is advanced for very short periods to bill-brokers etc.

cameralism
a form of mercantilism extensively implemented by German government during the eighteenth century with the chief objective of increasing the revenue of the sate.

cancellation price
the lowest price at which the manager of a unit trust may offer to redeem units on a particular day. The cancellation price is calculated on the basis of a formula laid down by the Securities and Investment Board.

cancellation right
the assumption that both the insured and the company have the right to cancel the contract, unless otherwise defined in the terms of the contract.

cancelled cheque
a cheque that has been perforated or ink-stamped on its face to indicate that it has been paid by the bank on which was drawn and so cannot be used again. Banks normally return cancelled cheques to depositors, who treat them as receipts from payees.

cancel order
a market or limited-price order given to a securities broker, to be executed in whole or in part as soon as it is represented in the trading arena. The portion not so executed is to be treated as cancelled.

capacity of firms
the amount of land, building, plant and machinery and other fixed capital of a firm.

capital
the tangible resources of a person or organization, including cash, machinery, land, building, raw-materials etc.

capital account
business account stating the owner's or shareholder's interest in the assets.

capital allowance
the proportion of annual profit (gross) allowed by tax authorities as a deduction to cover changes such as special depreciation and other incentive allowance prior to computation of taxable income.

capital appreciation
increase in the market value of equity capital; or increase in the money value of capital assets.

capital asset
an asset in continuous use or possession, including land, buildings, equipment, leaseholds mineral deposits, goodwill, patents, trademark, and copyrights.

capital authorized
the amount of capital a new development bank or an enterprise indicates to, and is authorized by, the company law authorities as its ultimate equity level.

capital budget
in finance, the portion of a budget, or a separate budget, dedicated to proposed future additions to capital assets and their financing.

capital callable
when the shares of a development bank or a limited company are not fully paid at the time of issue, the development bank or the company may call for payment of the amount outstanding or a portion of it when it requires additional capital.

capital charge
provision in the profit and loss account for payment of interest on borrowed capital, repayment of annual principal borrowed and depreciation charges on fixed assets.

capital coefficient
1. Ratio of capital stock to output;
2. Capital output ratio;
3. Also known as capital-output ratio, it is the ratio between the book-value of capital (machinery and equipment) in a plant and the gross value of its output. It is the amount of capital necessary to produce an additional unit of output. It varies from one industry to another.

capital commitments
capital expenditure contracted for by companies or other organization of which nothing has been paid by balance sheet date. These commitments should be shown in the accounts of limited companies, as a note or otherwise, and that a distinction should be made between items contracted for, and those agreed by the directors but not yet contracted for.

capital consumption allowance
in national income accounting, the equivalent of what is called depreciation in private business accounting.

capial debt
the part of a company's capital represented by long-term loans and debentures.

capital employed
the total shareholder 'or proprietors' stake in the business. This normally means the total paid up share capital plus reserves (as capital invested).

capital expenditure
it is that outlay which benefits several accounting period. It is a long term asset (called fixed assets) and its useful life is estimated by experts for spreading the cost over this life-period. The amount allocated and expired in an accounting year is an expense : termed 'depreciation.' The rest is the cost-residue (or unexpired

cost) and carried forward as an asset for future expansion.

capital for blook
finance for fixed and permanent assets like machines; tools, appliances, structures, land etc., (which are required by industries).

capital gains
personal income earned through the sale of such capital assets as securities and real estate.

capital gains tax
this is a tax on profits or gains made on capital transactions on the buying and selling of assets other than those in the normal course of a business.

capital gain tax, short-term
a tax levied on gains from assets held and imposed of within twelve months. These gains are taxes as income. Loses may be set against profits and carried forward. The tax applies to all tangible movable property and to land, but not to motor cars. Where the consideration is less than Rs.50000 no tax is payable. If the consideration is greater than Rs.50000, the tax is limited to half the difference.

capital inflow
process of inducting foreign capital through various means such as unilateral, multilateral and private investment capital by providing various incentive such as repatriation facilities, controlling interest of enterprises, infrastructure facilities, helpful fiscal and monetary policies.

capital investment
the total funds invested in an enterprise.

capitalism
the economic system in which a person who contributes capital to an enterprise is allowed freedom to be financially rewarded.

capitalist
denotes a class of persons who, under a system of private property, own the stock of goods, i.e., capital. The capitalist gets an income by way of a remuneration for allowing the use of his property for production.

capital levy
in finance, a nonrecurring tax on capital. Capital levy is also known as capital debt.

capital lors
the opposite of capital profit but calculated in the same manner. For tax purposes capital losses can be set off against gains.

capital market
the market for buying and selling long-term loanable funds, in the form of bonds, mortgages, and the like.

capital paid-up
the part of the issued capital which is actually called up and paid-in by subscribers. Also known as subscribed capital or paid-in capital.

capital profit
profits made by the sale of assets not bought for resale.

At one time these sales were not taxable but now they are subject to capital gains tax.

capital rationing
in corporate finance, capial rationing occurs any time there is a budget ceiling, or constraint, or the amount of funds that can be invested during a specific period of time, such as a year.

capital redemption reserve
account representing the nominal value of shares that have been redeemed in so far as the redemption was not paid for by the proceeds of new issue of shares and is not a payment out of capital.

capital surplus
that part of the paid-in capital of an enterprise that is not assigned to capital stock.

capitalisation
the process of computing capital value from the income which they yield.

capital industry
an industry in which the material instruments of production are owned or hired by private persons and are operated at their orders with a view to selling at a profit, the goods or services that they help to produce.

car hire
there are three kinds of car hire business: (1) the taxi business, (2) the business which hire cars for specified periods at an agreed rate, normally based on time and mileage, (3) a variation of (2), the organizations which put cars at the disposal of customers at particular places and for specified purposes. These customers may then leave the cars at agreed places at the end of their journey, for example : a business arrives at London airport, takes a self-drive car for the remainder of his journey to Glasgow, as planes are grounded. The car is then collected at Glasgow by the owners. Car hiring in this third sense should be distinguished from car rental where a person, rather than purchase a car, rents one on a permanent basis. He does not own the car but enjoys all the privileges of ownership. The charges and responsibilities will depend on individual contracts. The car is usually replaced at specified intervals.

carrying charges
interest charged on the balance owed when paying by instalments.

carrying costs
cost of holding items stock including interest of funds invested in stock warehouse, space depreciation, obsolescence, insurance, etc.

carry-over day
a stock exchange term. Accounts are made up at stated intervals, normally of two weeks. The first day of each new account is known as the carry-over day, because those who have not the money, when the time comes for settlement,

to take the shares they have asked a stockbroker to buy, often wish to carry over payment into the following accounting period.

cartel

a term implying together of business houses producing similar type of goods with a view associate to secure a monopoly of the market. A cartel is a voluntary agreement of capitalistic enterprises of the same branch for a regulation of the sales market with a view to improving the profitability of its members's business by agreeing to limit competition among themselves.

cash and carry

a retail business that provides no credit or delivery services, requiring customers to pay cash and pick up their purchases (or pay extra for delivery).

cash-and-carry wholesaler

a merchant who requires that his customers come to his warehousing, elect the products from the warehouse shelves, pay cash for what they select, and carry away the products they have thus purchased. This type of wholesaler operates much like a supermarket, dispensing with delivery and credit services in an effort to introduce operational methods that are expected to reduce costs.

cash asset

cash and any asset that can be immediately converted into cash without disrupting day-to-day operations. Also known as cash resource.

cash book

basic book of account for recording all receipts (debits) and payments (credits). Often each side has two columns (or more) indicating whether transactions were for cash or via the bank.

cash budgets

a state of the estimated totals of cash that will be received and payed by a firm during each of a number of future periods. If a significant surplus is forecast for month then plan can be made to invest it ; if a deficit is forecast then arrangements must be made to borrow the necessary cash.

cash credit

cash credit is similar to overdraft except that it is comparatively for a longer period. In fact some prefer not to make any difference between these two terms. The account holder is allowed to draw on the account up to the limit sanctioned. The facility may be secured by any tangible security or may be granted against the personal security of the borrower. Frequency of transactions is expected and interest charged is higher than that charged on loans. If the turnover in the account is good the facility may be renewed periodically, usually once in a year.

cash deposits

cash deposits are the sum of income deposits and business deposits.

cash discount

a deduction that a firm will allow from the total value of an invoice sent out if payment is made within a short time. (Also called a 'settlement discount').

cash dividend

a dividend paid in cash rather than in property stocks, bonds, or any other substitute for cash.

cash dividend's refunds

from of sales in which customers collect tokens or stamps supplied with goods, which can be exchanged for cash.

cash-flow statement

a statement of a firm's actual or projected cash inflows and cash outflows measured at suitable intervals over a period.

cashier

generally this term is applied to a person who has the responsibility of accounting for cash transactions and keeping a record thereof. In a narrower sense it denotes a particular job at a bank—normally that of handling cash transactions with the public at the bank counter.

cash sale

the delivery of goods or services in the immediate receipt of cash in payment. In stock market terms, a transaction on the floor of the stock exchange calling for delivery of the securities the same day.

casting vote

the chairman of a meeting's vote, used if the votes cast for and against a particular resolution are the same. The casting vote is not a legal right—the chairman must be given it by, for example, the particles or association.

caveat venditor

Latin, "let the seller beware." In commerce, the principle that unless a seller by express language disclaims responsibility he shall be liable to the buyer if the goods he, delivers are different in kind, quality, use, or purpose from those described in the contract of sale.

ceiling price

the highest price obtainable or permissible in the sale of particular goods or services. It is the price to charge above which is an offence.

central area shopping

buying in shopping areas or centres with large thresholds of customers.

central bank

a bank which specializes in the transaction of government business and which advises on and implements the government policy.

central banker

the man who exercises his discretion, not the machine that works according to the value.

central processing unit

the principal data-processing device within a computer ; consisting of an arithmetic unit, a control unit and a store. The store in the CPU is normally an immediate-access store.

centre for 'nter-firm comparison

this was established by the British Institute of Management and the British Productivity Council in 1959. Membership is voluntary, and information supplied confidential. The object is to advise business whether or not they are above the average and suggest reasons for any apparent inefficiencies.

certificate

in stock market terminology, the actual piece of paper that is evidence of ownership of stock in a corporation.

certification of a transfer

statement made on an instrument of transfer of a company's shares that a company official or Stock Exchange official has seen documents that establish prima facie that the transfer owns the shares he is transferring.

certified cheque

a cheque drawn by an individual on his account on the face of which the bank has certified that the cheque is valid and will be paid on presentation.

certified financial statement

a statement of the financial position of a company attested to by an independent auditor who is certified public accountant.

certified invoice

export invoice certified by approved body such as a Chamber of Commerce.

certified public accountant

an accountant who has been registered or licensed to practice public accounting and is permitted to call himself a certified public accountant and use the initials CPA after his name.

certified transfer

when a shareholder wants to sell only part of his holding, he sends the share certificate with the transfer form to the secretary of the company. The transfer form is then certified, i.e. endorsed by the secretary showing that the certificate has been deposited.

chain discount

a series of trade discounts, usually related to quantity purchases and indicated as a progression of percentages.

chain of title

in real estate, history of the conveyances and encumbrances affecting a title from the original grant or patent, or as far back a records are available.

chain store

a shop, or store, which is one of many, each in a different location. Examples in India are Bata—manufacturing and selling shoes, Kwality—producing and selling variety of icecreams, etc. Structually, these shops are organised on a branch basis.

chamber of commerce

an association of business and professional men and women and of trade and professional organization, formed to promote the interest of the business community.

In India the private sector has chambers of commerce on stated levels, and an apex institution on the national level called FICCI—The Federation of Indian Chambers of Commerce and Industry.

champerty

this occurs when a person pays for a court action in which he is not sufficiently personally involved, in return for a share of any damaged received. It is illegal, and any contract concerning champerty is also illegal.

chance of loss

in insurance, the relative probability of specific property being destroyed. If the property is certain to be destroyed, the chance of loss is 100 percent. If the property cannot be destroyed, the chance of loss is zero. The greater the chance of loss, the more likely a person or a company will be to seek insurance.

change date

in accounting, the date the standard cost of material and labour for produced goods was also revised by the company official responsible for establishing standard costs.

charge

an agreement between a debtor and a creditor that if the debt is not paid when due then the creditor may appropriate certain property of the debtor (called charged property') and use it (by selling it) to obtain payment of the debt. A creditor who has a charge on property is called a 'charge' of the property.

charge account

another name for a credit account offered by a retailer with a view to attracting more trade by giving customers extended credit items.

charging order

a court order attaching to a debtor's goods for the benefit of a creditor. If the dent is not paid within a specified time the creditor may have the right to sell the goods for this own benefit.

charted accountant

member of the Institute of Charted Accountants. Members are recognized by the government to audit public company accounts.

charted secretaries (Institute of)

this was founded in 1891, and given a royal charter in 1902. Its present membership is approximately 30,000. Members are not only company secretaries. The institute's objectives are: (1) to provide examinations to test the capacity of potential administrators in the fields of commerce, industry and the public service, (2) to hold conferences and meetings and publish papers, documents and lists of members, (3) to represent members' interests in dealings with government departments and the public, (4) to provide professional supervision over membership through a disciplinary committee. Members may be Associates (A.C.I.S.) or Fellows (F.C.I.S.). An Associate must be twenty-one or over, have passed the necessary examinations and have had appropriate experience (which might be as much as six years).

chartering, marine

a vessel is chartered when it is, as it were, hired in part of whole for a particular time or a particular purpose. The contract is known as a charter party. Where the contract does no otherwise specify it is covered by the carriage of goods by Sea Act. There are various forms of charter.

chart of accounts

a systematic listing of accounts by name and number serving as an index for recordkeeping and as rapid account identification for posting and others uses in book-keeping.

chattel mortgage

a mortgage on tangible personal property of a movable nature, such as automobiles or large appliances.

cheap money

a term signifying that the value of a particular currency is low compared with the value of goods and services.

cheap money policy

1. the government's imposition on the Central Bank of the policy of keeping the rate of interest stable at the lowest point.

2. a deliberate monetary policy of keeping the rates of interest low to stimulate the borrowing of money and achieve economic recovery.

The Reserve Bank of India, in the wake of unending inflation, is following dear money policy.

checkoff

a procedure by which an employer, with written permission of workers, withholds union dues and other assessment from paychecks and transfer the collected fund to the union.

cheques, alternation of

bankers are wary of altered cheques. Alterations should be initialled by the drawer or customer. When a crossed cheque is opened, the full signature of the drawer should appear. Bankers will even then refuse to pay over the counter unless they known the customer.

chircular velocity of money

the so-called income or circular velocity of money indicates the number of times a unit of money is spent on the real constituents of the national income.

choses-in-action

strictly speaking a chose-in-action is a right to, but not possession of, property or a sum of money; taking possession may be contingent on some event. The right can be enforced in a court of law. Examples of choses-in-action are debts, negotiable instrument, mortgages, insurance policies warrants. A particular quality of a chose-in-action is that it can be assigned to another person, though this may be conditional upon permission obtained from some other party.

christmas tree

in manufacturing, a bill of material in graphic form that displays the structure of a product and how its assemblies are related.

circular flow of income

the passing of income between household and firms, which arise from the purchase by households of the goods and services supplied by firms.

circulating capital goods

a capital good that is destroyed in the course of use by a sign use. Coal expendable fuels are examples.

classified advertisement

an advertisement in a section of a newspaper or magazine that contains many advertisements, all set in the same simple style, grouped according to a classification scheme say, matiomoninl, situations vacant etc., devised by the publisher of the newspapers.

classified stock

a stock issue that is divided into two or more classes, carrying different rights and privileges.

class rates

insurance rates established for large general class of risks, according to the construction, occupation, and location of the insured property. Also known as minimum rates and tariff rates.

clearance sale

a retail sale of merchandise at reduced prices, to clear out seasonal stock, over-stock, or slow-moving items.

clearing

the process by which a cheque is collected from the bank on which it is drawn when deposited in some other bank.

clearing house

a central agency for the collection, classification, and distribution of information. In finance, an establishment maintained by banks for settling mutual claims and accounts among the members of the establishment.

clearing house, bankers'

each day a great number of cheques are drawn a various banks and their branches. The clearing house exists to set off the amounts owing between banks so that only one sum need be paid by one bank to another. That is, rather than that Lloyds should have to a hand over to Barclays the amount due on each cheque drawn by its customers and banked at Barclays bank, and vice versa, cheques are effectively set one against the other at the clearing house, and the total balance owing to or by each bank is calculated.

clearing union

a kind of International Clearing House composed of the central bank of members countries, whereby international payments are settled by means of each nation's trading surplus or deficit.

clock cards

cards used in a factory to record the time worked by employees paid on a time basis. Times are stamped automatically by a clock in an office or entrance to the works.

close company

company controlled by fewer shareholders and in which the public holds less than 35 per cent of the equity.

closed account

an account the sum of whose debits and credits are equal.

closed-end company

a company that maintains an investment service for a limited group of stockholders, often specializing in a particular type of security, without redemption priviledges. Its shares may be listed on stock exchange.

closed mortgage

a mortgage that cannot be paid off before maturity.

closed-end investment company

an investment company that has a fixed number of shares of stock outstanding. These share are traded like other shares of common stock and are not redeemed by the investment company.

closed stock

merchandise sold only in sets, such as silverware or china, with no guarantee that replacements for lost, broken, or damaged pieces, will be available. Open stock, in contrast, can be purchased piece by piece and, at least for a time, replacements will be available.

closing price

the price at which a listed security not changed hands at the end of a trading day. Stock prices listed in the financial pages of leading newspapers normally are the closing prices.

coalition bargaining

a method of bargaining by which a federation of unions tries to coordinate and establish common termination dates for contracts with firms that deal with a number of unions at their plants throughout the country. Its purpose is to enable the federation to strengthen bargaining positions by threatening to close down all plants simultaneously.

coin

a piece of metal of prescribed size, shape, and weight usually stamped with a number denoting its face value as well as other special marking, that is used as money. Today just about all coins are token money and are issued only by governments.

collateral

term for security put up by a borrower in addition to his own promise to repay—it may take the form of a guarantee from a third party or deposit of documents of title.

collateral agreement

an agreement or contract running alongside an existing agreement or contract. If the initial contract is void the collateral agreement is not necessarily void: much depends on whether the second contract restates the void agreement. However, if the initial contract is illegal, the collateral agreement will also be illegal.

collateral loan

a loan secured by some kind of property, which is either held by the lender until repayment is made or is merely pledged.

collateral security

for a debt given by someone other than the debtor. An extra security for a debt given by a debtor in addition to a major security that in some circumstances might be considered sufficient. A security for a debt that consists of right over property, as opposed to personal guarantees.

collecting officer

in government accounting, an employee who is bonded and authorized to receive, deposit, and report moneys owed to the government.

comaker

a person who, together with one or more others, signs a engotaible instrument and hence is liable for its payments.

combination

in business the joining of two or more companies in order to pool resources, cut costs, and or limit competition.

command economy

an economic system in which an authorities government exercise primary control over decision concerning what and how to produce; the government may also decide for whom to produce.

commmerce-definition of

commerce refer to and includes all those activities which are necessary to bring goods and services from the place of their origin to the place of their consumption. It signifies the exchange of all reciprocal goods and services and includes the whole of the labour engaged in rendering services to help this exchange. Thus, it includes, trade, i.e., the buying and selling of goods and services as well as transport, banking, insurance and warehousing. In

the words of Evelyn Thomas "commercial occupations deal with the buying and selling of goods, the exchange of commodities and the distribution of finished products".
Production of goods has no meaning in a market-economy unless these goods are exchanged for money or money's worth. The exchange of goods is not a simple process. The wheels of commerce have to keep on moving to ensure as smooth an exchange of goods as possible. As stephenson writes, commerce "constitutes the sum total of those processes which are engaged in the removal of hindrances of persons, place and time in the exchange of commodities.

commerce-scope of

for a proper understanding of all the activities covered by commerce, different aspects of the various branches of commerce must be studied. To understand trade, one has to know both home trade and foreign trade ; the types of traders, such as wholesalers and retailers, the mercantile agents engaged in the home trade and steps involved in import and export business. The place of warehousing and transport, banking and insurance and the process of the removal of hindrances of time, person and place have also to be studied. The sell the goods effectively, help of salesmen and publicity is called for and commercial office established. Hence the study of salesmanship and publicity also gets a place in any scheme of study of commerce. Many time-saving appliances are used for the efficient and economical working of a commercial office, hence office-appliance have to be known. Documents like bill of exchange, promissory notes, cheques, hundis, etc., have become indispensable for the smooth flow of exchange of goods. These are included in the study of commerce. And lastly, various commercial activities are to be organised in a suitable form. The choice of the suitable form has to be made like the sole trader, partnership, joint Hindu family firm, joint-stock company and cooperative undertakings. Certain activities are organised in the form of organisation with special characteristics, such as public utilities and state-enterprises. Also, in the process of marketing of goods, assembling and buying, grading, packing, etc., have to be done. All these are included in the study of commerce.

commercial bank

a financial institution chartered by federal or state government, primarily engaged in making short-term industrial and commercial loans by creating demand deposits or checking deposits, and in retiring loans by cancelling demand deposit, it may also perform other financial functions such as holding time or savings deposits and making long-term loans.

commercial bill

trade bill which is a device for raising money on goods during their transit from one place to another.

commercial floater contract

an insurance policy issued to cover business property that is in the hands of the owner.

commercial law

the branch of law that relates to business enterprise and commercial transactions, including contracts, negotiable instrument, estates and trusts, sales debtors, creditors, corporation, real estate, and securities.

commercial revenue

the revenue received by the government in the form of prices paid for government produced commodities and services.

commission

payment to someone in return for obtaining work, orders or sales for others; especially a payment that is a fixed percentage of the value of the business transacted. For example payment to a salesman of a percentage of the value of the sales he makes, payment to an agent of a percentage of the value of work he procures for others. An action or a document confers authority to perform duties specified in such a way. A task entrusted to someone who is to act as an agent in performing it. A body of people given authority to perform a specific task. Especially a government agency with investigative or administrative duties. A task given to an artist or designer to create something according to outline instructions in return for a fee fixed in advance.

commission for oaths

a person given a commission by having porter to take affidavits and similar sworn statements.

commission merchant

an agent or factor through whom goods, wares, merchandise are sold or to whom they may be consigned for resale, for a compensation referred to as a commission.

committee of incompetent

a coutappointed guardian or guardians of the persons or estate of one adjudged incompetent or insane.

commodity exchanges

markets where dealings in commodities are made on national and international scale. London is a very important centre for these exchanges. Many organizations specialize in one particular commodity.

commodity money

a medium of exchange consisting of a given commodity or group of commodities, as opposed to some kind of paper currency.

commodity pool
also commodity fund. A kind of mutual fund for speculators in the commodity market, which includes not only commodities but futures on stock price and other financial instruments and options. Such pools combine the money of many investors and are managed by professional commodities traders.

commodity rates
a system of freight charges that takes into account the special characteristics of a particular commodity moving between specified points, as related to volume and distance. For example an economical rate may be established for automobile parts moving from o Detroit to Cleveland because of heavy volumes between these two places.

commodity standard
a monetary system in which the purchasing power of the money unit—the standard of value—is kept equal to the value of a designated equality of a particular commodity or of a group of a commodities.

commodity terms of trade
also called barter terms of trade, it is a type of terms of trade. It refers to the rate at which a country's exports exchange for imports. Also "barter terms of trade."

commodity theory of money
a theory that attempts to explain the fluctuating value of money in terms of changing demand for and supply of the commodity by which money is backed, chiefly gold and silver.

commodity warehouse
a warehouse specializing in storing and handling commodities such as wool, cotton, potatoes, or tobacco.

common market
where two or more countries agree to from a customs union between themselves and a common external tariff against goods and commodities imported from other countries.

common money
money which is universally acceptable within a given political area.

common stock fund
an investment company whose investment policy is to seek profits by investing in common stocks.

communication
the word 'communication' is derived from the Latin word 'communist' which means 'common' that stands for sharing of ideas in common. The term 'communication' has varied meanings.

communications world
monthly journal published by International Association of Business Communicators to provide information about the profession of organizational communication and news of

IABC an Francisco.

Companies (Amendment) Act 1960.

this amending act was enacted on the recommendations of Shastri committee which was appointed by the government on 15th may, 1957, to review the Act and point out the defects and to give suggestions. Under this Act some restrictions were imposed on management of companies, managerial remuneration and private companies. By adding Section 43A a new class of companies, 'Deemed to be Public companies' was introduced.

Companies (Amendment) Act, 1969

this Act prohibited companies from contributing any amount to any political party or for any political purpose, and abolished the institution of Managing Agents and Secretaries and Treasurers with effect from 3rd April, 1970.

Companies (Amendment) Act 1974

this amendment Act plugged the loopholes in the law and made it an effective instrument for implementation of the socio-economic policy of the government. Thus, the Act was designed not only to streamline the administration of the Companies Act but also to promote greater efficiency and social justice in the working of the corporate sector. The Amendment Act came into force on 1st February 1975.

companies, register of

the register which is maintained by the Registrar of Companies. Name, address, business, and other details of every company are recorded in this Register. Name of the companies are struck off from the Register if the Registrar has reasonable cause for believing that they are not in business.

company

a body corporate, whose regulation is governed by one of the various Companies Acts, reduced effectively to the Companies Acts 1948 and 1967. In popular usage it is a company with a share capital. Companies may be created by royal charter, by a specific act of parliament, or may be registered with the Registrar of Companies under one of the various Companies Acts, particularly act of 1948.

company bargaining

collective bargaining in quest of a company agreement.

company : change of name

this may take place inter alia: (1) by Special Resolution with Board of Trade consent, (2) at the board of Trade's direction, (3) where the name is considered undesirable. The change does not affect proceedings pending in the old name.

company, chartered

a company established by the

Royal Charter of England. These were once more common than they are today-they were used for developing international trade. One well-known company still in existence is the Hudson's Bay Company.

company director

the member of the board of directors appointed to run a company by its shareholders. A director may or may not be a shareholder himself. Broadly equivalent to vice-president in USA.

company formation

anyone wishing to form a new company must file certain specified documents with the Register of Companies: (1) the Memorandum of Association, (2) the Articles of Association, (3) a list of the persons who have consented to become Directors, (4) written consent of the directors to act, (5) a statutory declaration that the requirements of the Companies Act have been complied with, (6) notice of the situation of the registered office, (7) particulars of directors and secretary. [(3) and (4) not required for private companies.] Certain fees and duties must be paid before the Registrar will issue a certificate. If the company is a public company certain other conditions must be fulfilled before it can commence business.

company, investment

a company engaged in using its funds to acquire shares or securities instead of carrying business on its own account. They are not trusts in true sense.

company legislation in India

the origin of India's Company Law can be traced back to 1850, when the first Indian Companies Act providing for the registration of joint stock companies was passed on the lines of English Companies Act of 1884.

company law after independence

amendments made after independence include the adaptation of laws order, 1950, which came into force on the 26th January, 1950 the date on which the constitutional status of India was changed into a Sovereign Democratic Republic. The government felt the need for a further revision of the company law in view of the far-reaching change in the English Companies Act of 1929 brought about by the English Companies Act of 1948, and also because of the developments in the trade and industry of this country during the war and port-war years.

company life cycle

as suggested by Wroe Alderson, the theory follows a process of establishment (continued product development, service to buyers), expansion (increased advertising expenditure, competitive pricing) and consolidation (struggle to maintain market position). This forms and upward S curve but unlike the product life cycle, shows no decline.

company, objects of

the memorandum of a company must contain the object or objects. The general practice is to make the object clause as comprehensive so to include every conceivable lawful act since subsequent alternation of this clause is difficult. Any activity which is outside the expressed provisions of the object clause is considered ultra viers.

company, private

about 97 per cent of the limited companies registered in Great Britain are private companies. A private company is one which restricts the right to transfer its shares, limits its members to fifty (but has a minimum of two), and cannot invite the public to subscribe for shares. It has certain legal privileges, but these are not of great consequence and the tendency today is towards removing them.

company, public (limited)

a company registered under the Company Law of a country unless it satisfies the conditions necessary to constitute it is a private company.

company seal

every limited company must have a common seal, which must be affixed to certain documents. The company must keep a seal book recording details of all these documents.

company secretary

person in a company responsible for ensuring that the legal obligations of the company are met, in particular the requirements of the Companies Acts.

company, statutory

these were companies needing specified powers (for instance to purchase land). They were intended to develop communications such as railways, roads, or canals, or to provide services such as gas, water, or electricity. They were set up and governed by special act of parliament. Shares were normally only transferable by deed. Most of these companies have now been nationalized.

company, unlimited

it is nothing but large partnership registered under the Company Law of a country and the members, like partners of recognised as a separate legal entity, and (ii) that the liability of members is limited to the nominal value of the shares they have taken up.

company : winding-up

a company may be wound up but cannot be made bankrupt. Winding-up may be (1) voluntary, (2) by the court, (3) voluntary but under supervision of the court.

company's liquidation account
when a company is dissolved and monies are left with the liquidator (because dividends have been unclaimed, etc., or more than six months) these monies must be paid into the company's liquidation account at the Bank of England.

comparative advantage, law of
in economics, the principle that if one nation can produce each of two products more efficiently than another nation, and can produce on of these commodities more efficiently than the other, it should specialize in the product in which it is most efficient and leave production of the alternative product to the other country. The two nations will then have more of both goods by engaging in trade. This principle is applicable to individuals and regions as well as to countries.

comparative cost
opportunity costs, comparison of costs between producing one product rather than another in terms of raw materials, labour, overheads, warehousing distribution and perhaps servicing.

compensation of employees
the term applies to supplementary payments for maintenance pension funds, social insurance, and the like received by the labourers in addition to their wages.

compensatory transactions
transactions among nations that are a direct response to balance-of payments conditions.

competition
rivalry among buyers and sellers of goods, services, or resources. Competition tends to be related to the freedom with which buyers and sellers may enter or leave a marketplace.

competitive film
firm working under perfect competition. The perfectly competitive will be in the long run-equilibrium earning only normal profits.

competitive marker
a competitive market is easily defined only for perfect market or perfectly competitive market; it is then a market in which the individual buyer or seller does not influence the price by his purchase or sales.

competitive price
the price that is established in a market through the independent actions of a number of buyers and sellers.

complentary goods
two or more commodities that are related because a change in the quantity demanded of one causes a direct change in the quantity demanded of one causes a direct change in the quantity demanded of the other, within a consumer's given budget.

complete refund offer
offer by manufacturer to refund

entire cost of purchase after a complaint by a customer. Frequently includes reimbursement of postal expenses in addition.

completion bond
an obligation under notary seal posted as a guarantee by a contractor of completion of a project according to conditions described in the contract.

composition
a partial payment, or promise of partial payment, of debts made by a debtor and accepted by his creditors as a complete discharge of his liability of them.

composition of creditors
an arrangement whereby a debtor who cannot make payment to all his creditors in full pays each of them the same fixed percentage of the amount owed, in exchange for their freeing him from the balance of the indebtedness.

compound
to add interest to principal at periodic intervals, thereby establishing a new basis for subsequent interest calculations.

compound duty
a customs duty consisting of a specific duty to which an ad valorem tax is added.

compound interest
the charges made by a lender or a creditor for the loan of money: calculated by the periodic addition of simple interest to principal. The new base thus established becomes the principal amount for computing the interest for the next accounting period. Individuals or organizations placing funds on deposit with a bank or other financial institution that offers savings accounts in effect become lenders to or creditors for the financial institutions.The money placed or creditors for the financial institutions. The money placed on deposit thus earn interest on principal, generally calculated at a compound interest rate.

comprehensive crime insurance
covers burglary, robbery, and other types of theft-loss, destruction, or disappearance of property. Coverage may be offered on an all risk basis, including losses from forgery and counterfeiting.

comptroller
the head of the General Accounting Office, an arm of the legislative branch of the federal government. The GAO reports directly to the congress on the financial position and accounting systems of government agencies, at the request of Congress, provides critiques related to agency organization and management.

compulsory winding up
a winding up of a company ordered by a court. (Also called 'compulsory liquidation'.

concealment of the receipts
cash sales may not be fully accounted for and amounts

may be transferred to bad debts account, while they have actually been recovered. Unauthorised discounts and allowances may be adjusted against customer's accounts. The sale of scarp and other sundry receipts like rent, etc. may not be recorded. In addition to these, there are many other ways to under-account the cash receipts. These can be checked by a thorough scrutiny of all the books of account, particularly cash book, cash memo books, sales vouchers and wage sheets etc.

concentration banking
a means of accelerating the flow of funds of a firm by establishing strategic collection centres. The purpose is to shorten the period between the time a customer mails in his payments and the time when the company has the use of the funds.

concessionaire
one who operates a business or trade within premise supplied by another.

conditional sale contract
a legally enforceable agreement for the purchase of property on an instalment payment basis. The buyer does not receive clear title to the property until all payments have been completed.

confirmed credit
a credit which the advising bank undertakes to honour or not it receives funds from the issuing bank.

confirming house
an enterprise in one country that will confirm orders for gods made by buyers in others countries to exporters in the confirming house's country.

conflict of interest
in business finance, and government, any situation where a decision made by an individual in an official capacity is likely to bring personal benefit.

conflict of law
in contract, difficulties sometimes arises as to which particular law applies, where more than one country is concerned. As a general rule, the law of the country where the contract is to be performed will apply, though the intentions of the parties as expressed in the contract are relevant. There are various supplementary provisions. For instance, one country may not enforce a contract valid according to its own law but illegal in the place where it is to be carried out.

conglomerate merger
a merger of firms with unrelated activities to corn a conglomerate.

consequential-losses insurance
a type of insurance providing coverage for indirect losses.

consignment account
special accounts must be kept by both a seller (or principal) and his agent to record the true

ownership remaining vested in the seller, the transaction is said to be 'on consignment'.

consignment note

a shipping term for a note accompanying a consignment of goods. This is sometimes an alternative to a bill of lading.

consignment selling

goods sent to distributors who take possession but title remains with manufacturer until consignment is paid for.

consolidated accounts

accounts of a parent or holding company which incorporate those of any subsidiaries.

consolidated balance sheet

in accounting, a balance sheet in which the assets and liabilities of a controlling company are combined with the corresponding financial data of economic units of the total organization in such a way as to present a combined fiscal report, as though all units of the organization were acting as a single unit.

consolidated financial statement

the statement of the financial condition of two or more economic units of an enterprise, presented in a combined formats as though they were one unit, this specific data for one unit not identified separatelty from those of any other in the same enterprise.

consolidation

the preparation of a balance sheet or other financial statement into a single format that combines that data or related enterprises, which may be affiliates, division, or subsidiaries of a parent or holding company.

consols

government consolidated stock. This stock is irredeemable. It is used at various times at various rate of interest prevailing at the time. In fact , the price of consols is a good indication of current gilt-edge interest rates because there is no question of capital repayment to be taken into account. Consols are quoted per Rs.100. That is, if $2\frac{1}{2}$ per cent consols are quoted at fifty, this means that to obtain Rs.5000 worth at 2½ per cent it is necessary to pay Rs.2500, and the gilt-eged interest rate is therefore 5 per cent, i.e. 2½ over 50.

consortium

large contracts are often tendered for by a consortium of companies or firms none of which is competent to fulfil the contract alone. It is generally a rare combination for the purpose of bringing together a number of quite different operative skills of areas of specialized knowledge under one organisation.

consortium bank

a bank is owned by two or more other banks and has been set up to provide specialized banking services.

constant capital
the cost that is not only uniform but also remains the same whether the total output be larger or smaller.

constant-dollar value
subsidiary company belongs to a parent or group of companies.

consular invoice
when goods are exported the importing country may insist that they are accompanied by an invoice certified by their own consul in the exporting country. This enables import duties to be correctly charged. The consul will charge a fee known as consulage.

consumer
strictly, the ultimate consumer of a product, the ultimate user of a product of service, the person who derives the satisfaction or the benefit offered.

consumer cooperative
a retail business (and sometimes also a wholesale business) that is owned and may be operated by some or all of its customers in order to reduce the costs of marketing.

consumer credit
facilities which enable consumer to obtain consumer goods by delaying all or most of the price for them for some time after acquiring possession of them. The term includes credit facilities given by retailers, loans by finance companies for the purpose of specific goods and hire-purchase agreements.

consumer expenditure
total expenditure in a national economy on goods and service for immediate consumption.

consumer good
a product used directly to satisfy needs or desires, such as food or clothing, as opposed to a capital goods, used to product some their product or service.

consumer goods market
market where entrepreneur sell goods and services to consumers in exchange for money; examples are foodstuffs, permanent wares, and symphony concerts etc.

consumer surplus
difference between the actual price of a product and its maximum worth to the consumer.

contango facilities
provisions by which, at the end of a stock exchange account period, a speculator does not settle his account but instead arranges to pay interest on the value of his share purchases until he sells them or until the end of the next account period.

container port
specially constructed seaport for container ships which are unloaded and loaded by giant computerized cranes.

contigency table
a table designed for the purpose of analyzing, or discovering association between, qualitative

characteristics. It is distinguished from a correlation table, which is restricted to the study of quantitative characteristics.

continuing appropriation
in government accounting, an appropriation whose remainder, if any, at the end of fiscal year is carried cover to the next fiscal year and may be expended under the conditions of the original appropriation.

continous billing
preparation of invoicing procedure throughout a business period rather than at a single time each month.

continuous budget
a moving projection of financial operations for a series of accounting periods immediately ahead.

contra account
one or more accounts that partially or totally offset other accounts. On financial statement they may be merged or may appear together.

contract
in law, a transaction involving two or more individuals whereby each becomes obligated to the other, with reciprocal rights to demand performance of what is promised.

contract, ambiguity
where a contract is in writing, or needs to be evidenced in writing, and there is ambiguity, the court may allow oral evidence to determine the intentions of the parties. So far as oral contracts are concerned, ambiguity is more likely to arise from mistake or mispresentation.

contract, anticipatory breach of
this happens one party to a contract announces in advance that he does not intend to perform his part. This other party may then sue immediately for anticipatory breach or he may refrain from taking action and wait until the contract date. If he does this he may fail to recover anything if, by that time, the contract has become impossible through the fault of neither party, i.e. has been frustrated.

contract for differences
stock exchange transactions are controlled by the normal rules of contract. Contracts for differences on the Stock Exchange come into slightly different category. There is no deliberate intention to take or sell stocks and shares—the investor buys and sells on the same account, receiving or paying the difference. These are known as dealings in differences and are, strictly speaking, wagers, so are governed by the rules relating to wagering contract.

contract, infant's
generally speaking an infant, that is, a person under 18 cannot make contracts enforceable against him, except contract for necessaries

(goods suitable to the infant's condition in life and his actual requirement at the time of sale or delivery',), or beneficial contracts of services (e.g. contracts for apprenticeship). Indian Majority Act 1875 also provides that all contracts made by an infant (1) for repayment of money lent or to be lent, (2) for goods, other than necessaries supplied or to be supplied, (3) for accounts stated, are absolutely void. Although an infant cannot be sued on contracts generally, he will find it difficult to bring an action himself where he has obtained some benefit. Generally speaking an infant cannot ratify on coming of age a contract made in infancy; there must be a new contract. There may be an exception where the contract is a continuing business contract (e.g. a partnership) which the infant does not repudiate within a reasonable time of coming of age. If he continues to act as a party to the contract he may be held liable on it, but only for the period since his coming of age.

A person legally comes of age on the day before his eighteenth birthday.

contract note
a document sent by a broker to his client immediately after the broker has carried out a transaction for him. It gives details of what the client will have to pay or what he can expect to receive for the deal.

contract of insurance
a contract between an insurer and an 'assured' under which the insurer promises that if a specified peril causes a loss to the assured or if a specified event occurs then the insurer will pay the assured a specified sum of money.

contract : of married women
a married woman may now contract quite freely, as though she were single. At one time in common law the husband and wife were one person, the husband being that person. The wife was not allowed to contract on her own account.

contract of record
this is not a contract in the normal sense of the work, but takes the form of, e.g. a court order where one person is obliged to perform some act such as payment of maintenance. The obligation is entered in the records of a superior court and is binding for this reason—it does not depend on the consent of the parties.

contract out
to give notice that one does not wish to incur a minor obligation under a contracting-out arrangement.

contract, trade union
the position is somewhat anomalous. Where the union is registered, it is governed by certain rules applicable to corporate bodies. It can sue and be sued in its own name.

However, it has not yet been decided whether a union is a legal person distinct from its members or an association of individuals who can appear in a collective name. It may be sued for breach of contract both by persons outside the union and by its own members.

contract void

a contract which in fact never existed, for example where there is a fundamental mistake on both sides as to the subject matter or the identity of the parties. No action can be taken on a void contract.

contra entry

an item of an account that partially or totally offsets one or more item on the opposite side of the same account.

contributed capital

payments in cash or property made by stockholders to a corporation in return for capital stock, or in response to an assessment on the capital stock, or as a gift to the corporation.

contrabution margin

in accounting, the excess of sales revenue over variable expenses. The contribution margin ratio is necessary for cost-volume-profit analysis were the information is expressed in terms of dollars instead of units.

contribution theory

the doctrine that sales of commodities and services provide a source of funds from which production overhead and other costs are paid.

control accounts

an accounts term for accounts showing total trade debtors and total trade creditors. When invoices or cash receipts are posted to individual accounts, the total for the day is entered in the control account. The balance on the control account should therefore always equal the total of the individual balance on the personal accounts.

controllable cost

in accounting, a cost that varies with changes in production. Also, any cost that they be directly controlled and regulated by the management of the unit of an enterprise to which the cost is allocated.

controller

an accountant whose technical skills and activities are dedicated to a single organization or unit of an organization and who is generally the manger of the bookkeeping and financial recording and reporting functions.

controller's deed

an instrument transferring the little to real estate; issued by the state, usually when property is sold due to tax deliquency.

controller-general of accounts

the organisation of the Controller-General of Accounts (CGA) was set up as part of the

Ministry of Finance, Department of Expenditure in October 1976 to administer matter pertaining to the departmentalisation of accounts of the Union government. These include prescribing the form of accounts relating to Union and state Government; laying down of accounting procedures, framing and revising rules and manuals relating thereto; overseeing the maintenance of adequate standards of accounting by Central (Civil) Accounts Offices; consolidation of the monthly and annual accounts of the Governments of India (including preparation of Summary Civil Appropriation Accounts); and the administration of rules under Article 283 of the Constitution relating to the custody, etc. of the Consolidated Fund of India, the Continency Fund of India and the Money credited to public accounts.

convenience goods

products bought for personal consumption, usually, through retail outlets located near the consumer's residence. Such goods are generally staple items of low unit value, purchased frequently and in low volume.

conventional financing

a loan made without government participation.

conversion

an act of a exchanging for and equivalent especially exchanging a convertable security.

convertible loan stock

fixed interest stock whose holders have an option to convert the stock into ordinary shares at a later date.

convertibility

the degree to which something is convertible especially the extent to which the holder of a specified currency is permitted to convert it into other currencies.

convertible debt

debt capital obtained by selling securities which may be exchanged by their holders at a future date for equity shares.

convertible loan stock

occasionally companies issue loan stock, with a right to convert this stock into ordinary shares or preference shares to some stated time in the future. This is known as convertible loan stock. The term is also applied to stock issued by the government, which the holder has right to convert into new stock instead of obtaining repayment.

convertible securities

those preference shares and debentures which can be redeemed by converting them into new class of shares or debentures.

co-operative selling agencies

association of producers of a certain commodity for the better standardisation and marketing of their product.

cooperative soceity

a cooperative soceity is an economic enterprise set up by economically weak individuals to eliminate middle men, competition, waste and to bring the producer and consumer together. It is a voluntary association with unrestricted membership and collectively owned funds. It implies association of individuals on equal terms to fulfil their economic needs to promote thrift and self-help among themselves.

cooperative society-dividends of

a co-operative society does not distribute all its surplus in form of dividend on shares held by its members. Rather it gives them bonus which need not be in proportion to the capital contributed by the members. In case of consumer co-operatives, the bonus is generally paid to the members in proportion to the purchases made by them during the year, while in case of producers' co-operative stores, the goods delivered for sale may form the basis of distributing bonus. In fact, the whole of the surplus is not distributed among the members but a portion of this is usually utilized in extending amentities and facilities to the members. Law, however, requires that each society must transfer at least one-fourth of its profit to a general reserve and provides that it may utilise a portion of the profit, not exceeding 10 per cent, for the welfare of the locality in which the society is functioning.

cooperative societies-privileges of

cooperative societies generally enjoy special privileges in regard to taxation, finance etc. The are exempt from income-tax and also from stamp duty and registration fees for the purpose of registration. They are also provided cheap finance and other facilities by the government. No such privileges are enjoyed by a company organisation.

coordination

coordination is a very important function of management inasmuch as it harmonizes, synchronises and unifies individual specialised efforts for better action and for the achievement of business objectives. Coordination implies synchronisation of the efforts of subordiantes towards common objectives.

Just as division of work is necessary for a good organisational structure, similarly coordination and integration of the various division, functions or activities is essential for the harmonised functioning of any business.

copartnership scheme

form of profit of sharing scheme in which employees normally acquire shares in the employer's company in proportion to the net profits of the company and their own earnings.

copyright

this refers to an amalgam of legislation and common law which attempts to protect the work of one writer from being freely copied or in any way reproduced by another. Apart from certain limited exceptions, e.g., short 'quotes' as part of another work, the law does not allow and author work to be used or reproduced without express permission and will punish all parties to such an offence, including the printer and the publisher.

cornering the market

a person corners a market when he obtains a virtual monopoly over particular goods or services. He is then able to name his own price. In the past this sometimes happened to the market in raw materials. Markets may be cornered for a short term; a person may make a fortune by controlling the supply of a particular raw materials for a particular period. The possibilities are now somewhat restricted by state intervention.

corporate capitalism

industrial society directed by a consensus of three constellations of power, business corporations, trade unions and central government.

comparate image

image or impression of a company, based on knowledge of its activities, experience of is behaviour.

corporation

an artificial being created under law; an association of shareholders, or even a single shareholder. Corporations are legal entities entirely different and distinct from the shareholders, with the capacity of continuous existence or succession.

corporation de facto

created when a group of persons has attempted in good faith to organize a corporation under a valid statute and has failed in some minor particular, but has thereafter exercised corporate power A minor particular might be the oversight or failure to have the incorporations' signatures notarized on applications for charter.

corporation income tax

also corporate income tax. A tax imposed on the annual net earnings of a corporation.

corporation tax

a straight percentage levy on profits of all companies in place of income and profits tax. It applies to all bodies corporate or unincorporated associations, but not to partnerships. Income tax remains payable on dividends distributed. Assessments for accounting periods, e.g. the accounting year ending 31 December, are taxes at one rate till 5 April and at another from 5 April to 31 December. Losses may be carried forward, including previous income tax losses. The tax was introduced in 1965; its present rate is 40 per cent.

corpus

the principle or capital of an estate, fund, or trust, as distinguished from the income received.

correspondent banking

system by which banks, usually large ones, perform certain services for other banks in return for holding their balances.

cost accountant

he is an account or to accounts officer whose job concerns the fixing of monies due for work done in manufacturing a product (i.e., reckoning the cost of material and labour consumed) but who is increasingly called upon to estimate the probably unit cost of a manufacturing process so that the price to the buyer can be determined by the company for the purpose of making a tender.

cost absorption

accounting procedure for allotting indirect costs to a particular product

cost accounting

the branch of accounting that deals with the classification, recording, allocation, and summarization of cost factors in the planning or operation of an organization.

cost analysis

study and interpretation of all cost figures; of particular use in considering future likely costs in the launch or development of a product or service.

cost and freight

a kind of foreign grade contract, which is similar to a cost, insurance, and freight contract, except that the importer looks after the insurance. The seller must give the buyer sufficient notice to enable him to do this.

cost and revenue theory

reasons that profit earned during a period is different between revenue accrued and cost incurred (Leonard Hardy).

cost benefit analysis

a systematic comparison between the cost of carrying out any service or activity and the value or the benefit of that service or the activity, quatifying as far as possible, all costs and benefits, whether direct, indirect, financial or social.

cost center

a department, division, unit, or other clearly identifiable segment of a business that has no capacity for income.

costing

the technique of determining the cost of activities, processes, products, or services.

cost insurance and freight

the price quoted for materials delivered to and unloaded at a named location. The seller assumes responsibility for securing all insurance coverage.

costing system

set up to monitor and control a company or organization's costs, keeping them as close as possible to budgeted costs and giving management a check on company operations and performance.

cost insurance and freight basis

method of computing a nation's balance of payments taking into account the value of invisible exports and imports such as finance insurance and shipping services. The term is used particularly in the USA.

cost ledger

a subsidiary ledger for the accumulation of accounts used in computing of summarizing the cost of goods manufactured or services produced.

cost of capital

the minimum rate of return which the firm must give to the supplies of its capital. The capital of company is supplied from three main sources; the purchasers of shares, retained earning and the suppliers of debt capital. It is usual to take a weighted arithmetic mean of the cost of the three types of capital.

cost of living

index number representing the trend of a series of prices paid by consumers for a representative sample items, so revealing the changes in the cost to house holds of typical purchase needs.

cost of production

in a manufacturing business, total cost of materials, labour and overhead charged to producing a particular item. It is the single most important factor in determining that item's ultimate price.

cost of market

a method of inventory valuation in which stock is valued at either the price for which it was bought (cost or the price at which it could currently be replaced (market) depending on which is lower.

cost of reproduction on yield

the estimated cost, under present production of finished goods that have been sold. It excludes overhead, marketing, and the selling expense. In retail operations, cost of sales includes the total cost of goods sold during a given accounting period and is based on the invoices and other costs related to the cost of goods purchased.

cost plus contract

a purchase contract whereby the seller is paid whatever it cost him to supply a given item, plus some extra fee as profit.

cost push

it is the theory which states the inflation in caused or intesified by trade unions insisting on higher wages regardless of output.

According to it, the trade unions with their strong bargaining power succeed in raising wages and thus push-up costs.

counterclaim

the claim by a defendant against a plaintiff where he hopes to reduce or wipe out the damages he may have to pay, the claim being one which could give right to a cause of action as opposed to set-off.

counter purchasing

in international trading, the placement of an order by a purchaser with a supplier in another country on condition that goods to an equal or specified value are sold in the opposite direction between the two countries.

country of origin

that from which goods or commodities are being exported in a particular transaction.

cover

an abbreviation of the phrase 'times overed' with particular reference to company dividends. The cover for a dividend is determined by the total net profit available for distribution; it is expressed as a multiple of the amount paid out, e.g., a dividend which is three times covered means that only one third of profits available for distribution were paid out by way of dividend.

coverage

in insurance, the face amount of an insurance policy or the amount of compensation provided by the insurer in the event of specified losses on the part of the insured; all the risks and perils covered by and insurance policy.

covered bear

a person who is believing that prices would fall, sells securities with a view to repurchasing them alter at a lower price. He does not, however, deliver the securities sold hoping to save expense on repurchases; if however, prices rise, he is in a position to deliver stock without paying inflated price.

covering warrant

in government finance, a document issued by the Secretary of the Treasury and countersigned by the Comptroller General that accompaneis a deposit of cash receipts within the federal government.

cover note

a contract of insurance which gives insurance temporarily while negotiations about a permanent contract continue or while administrative work connected with preparation of the final contract is in progress.

credit

the ability to buy or borrow in consideration of a promise to pay within a specified time period following delivery. In accounting, a book-keeping entry that records the reduction or elimination of an asset or an expense, or the creation of or addition to a liability or item or net worth of revenue. Credit entries are made on the right-hand side of an account.

credit account

(1) purchase made on credit and account settled, monthly or otherwise by agreement.

(2) regular monthly payments made by a banker's in order to retail establishment against, which person may make purchases up to an agreed multiple of the monthly insalment.

credit bank

in continental countries commercial banks are called credit banks.

credit card

a card issued to an individual called the card holder'), which identifies him and permits him to obtain goods or services on credit. Credit cards are either two-party or three -party.

credit control

the activity of (1) deciding whether a firm should grant credit to a customer and how much credit should be granted (2) ensuring that customers who have been granted credit are paying on time.

credit inflation

a concept of inflation. It means creation of money through a process of credit expansion in the banking system.

credit insurance

intended to cover losses arising out of credit customers' inability to pay their debts, but only to the extent that losses for the year due to this cause exceed normal losses for the year. Generally written for a 12-month period.

credit line

an agreement by a creditor, lender, or bank to extend credit or to make a loan up to a maximum specified amount, when needed by a customer; usually informal and for an indefinite time period.

credit outstanding

or line of credit. Amount of money a company is prepared to allow a particular customer to owe at a particular point in time.

credit sale

sale made on credit over a short-term, where the ownership of the goods passes with possession.

credit sale agreement

defined by law as 'an agreement for the sale of goods under which the purchase price is payable by five or more instalments not being a conditional sale agreement'. Such agreements are covered by the hire-purchase and consumer credit laws.

credit slip

a form completed by a customer of a.bank when depositing money into his account which gives details of the deposit.

credit theory of business cycle

this theory explains the trade cycle in terms of changes in the volume of bank credit. It is said that there is a tendency for bank periodically to over-expand credit due to inter-bank competition. Each bank vies with the other to give advances to the customers. Each bank vies with the other to give advance to the customers. After time, it is pointed out, the banks become alarmed and so apply the reverse gear and start contracting credit. This undue expansion and contraction of credit leads to ups and downs in business activity.

credit transfer

a method of setting a debt. It is used by persons or businesses with a great debts to settle at any one time. A list of the creditors is given to the bank, together with the amounts due, and the name and address of each creditor's bank. The bank then transfers the amounts due. The debtor then notifies each creditor that the transfer has been made. The obvious advantage of this method is that it saves writing out and signing a greater number of cheques.

credit union

a cooperative whose purpose is to promote thrift and to make small loans to members.

creditworthiness

degree to which it is prudent to grant credit to someone or to a firm.

crop loan

1. the loan that is granted to the farmer not against the security of land but on the basis of an estimate of the future buying capacity of the borrower.

2. an innovation suggested by the All-India Rural Credit Survey committee. According to this, the agricultural loan must be granted not on the basis of the value of the land but on the basis of the value of the anticipated crop on the land.

cropper

a farm labourer who receives a specified share of the crop.

crossed cheque

a cheque may be either an open cheque or a crossed cheque. Crossing is an indication appearing on the face of the cheque that it should be paid only through a banker ; it is usually done by drawing two parallel lines on the face of the cheque. Crossing has been evolved to avoid wrongful person from obtaining payment on it. An open cheque is payable to any person who presents it and it would be very difficult to locate him later if it is desired.

crossing

two parallel lines drawn or printed across (from top to bottom) a cheque or similar order to pay money, as an instruction to the drawee that the money must be paid only to a bank. If the name of bank is stated between the parallel lines then the crossing is called a 'special crossing', if not it is called a 'general crossing.

crossing, general

two parallel transverse lines drawn across the cheque. These prevent payment over the counter at the bank; the holder would have to pay the cheque into an account. It is common to include the words 'and Co..' between the liens but this is quite unnecessary.

crossing : special

a cheque with a special crossing has the name of a banker stated between the lines, or the name of an account and a bank, such as Boggy's Charities Account, Diamond bank. The instructions must be followed by the holder and the banker.

cross order

in the securities trade, an order to a broker to buy and sell the same security.

cross-referencing

cross-referencing means that a card or sheet describing a particular paper is placed in other position in the files when someone might look for that paper. Usually cross-reference sheets are of some colour that will make them distinctive from other field materials. All commercial filling systems provide a cross-referencing form.

cross-subsidizing

where the profit from one activity or enterprise is used to offset on another activity. They may be quite different activities linked only by being in joint ownership.

cumulative dividend

a dividend on cumulative preferred stock that is payable, under the terms of the issue, at stated intervals and before any distribution is made to the holders or common stock.

cumulative preferred stock

stock having a provision that if one or more dividends are omitted, the omitted divideds must be paid before dividends may be paid on the company's common stock.

cumulative preference share

a preference share that carries the right that, if in one year the company cannot pay a divided it must be paid in the next year in which sufficient profits are made together with the dividend for that year.

cumulative voting

a method of voting for corporate directors that enables a shareholder to multiply the number of his shares by the number or directorships being voted on and cast the total for one director or for a selected group of directors.

curb exchange

former name of the American Stock Exchange, second largest exchange in the United States. The name comes from the market's origin on a street in downtown New York City.

currency depreciation

autonomy of currency appreciation. It implies automatic decline in the external value of a currency as brought with by the forces of demand for and supply of the currency.

currency note

a price of paper that is used as currency in a particular country (usually a banknote).

currency of a bill

period of time between the drawing of a bill of exchange and the final date when it becomes payable.

currency school

a 19th-century English school of thought concerning the role of the central bank in the economy. Its adherents believed that only currency (bank notes and coins) was actual money, and that the central bank should regulate the money supply to keep in a fixed proportion to the amount of gold backing it.

currency speculator

person or organization calculated exchanging one currency for another in the expectation or making a profit from alternations in exchange rates.

current asset

something owned by a firm which is either a liquid asset available for use in current operations or owned by the firm with the intention of selling it for cash within a short period.

current cost accounting

also current-dollar-accounting. A method of accounting in which figures are adjusted for changing price level, specially higher prices (inflation). It is one or two methods required of large public corporations in publishing their annual reports.

current demand

present willingness in the market to pay the ruling price for goods.

current deposits

they are deposits engaged in some form of business where usually frequency of operation in the account is expected. There are no restrictions placed on the number of withdrawals of deposits in the account. The deposits are withdrawable without any prior notice and the banker has always to be ready to meet huge withdrawals on such accounts.

current dollars

a value expressed in dollars and reflecting actual of the current year. Economic data are often quoted in current dollars.

current liabilibities

an accounting term for those monies owed in the near future, usually within the next accounting period. These will include trade creditors, current taxation, and dividends declared and due. They should be distinguished from long-term liabilities and share capital or loan capital.

current maturity

the portion of a long-term obligation that is to be retired during the next twelve months; usually classified as a current liability.

current money
the aggregate of state money and bank money.

current outlay
it represents expenditure other than investment, and includes expenditure on revenue account on plan schemes.

current ratio
one of many ratios used to measure the performance of an enterprise and its management; determined by dividing current assets by current liabilities.

current revenue
revenue of the government from tax measures.

current yield
the yield of a security determined by dividing its annual interest or dividend payment by the current market price and converting this figure into percentage terms.

customer flow
measure of flow of customers throughout shop, reporting sections visited and intensity of flow.

customer records
tabulation of inquiries and orders received, deliveries, and any other pertinent information concerning a customer and his satisfaction.

customs : airports
regulations at airports are similar to those at seaports, particularly in the case of stores. Commanders of aircraft arriving from or leaving for abroad must use, except in emergency, customs airports, and declare cargo carried inwards and outwards. There are facilities for clearing goods from the airports before the entry of the goods is passed and the duty paid. A 'provisional' entry is made and the importer leaves a sizeable cash deposit with the Customs Authorities. Airports often have a duty-free shop for the convenience of departing passengers. Goods are sold here free of duty and are controlled by Customs officials.

customs duty
a tax that is levied on goods transported from one political juridication to another, especially a tax on goods imported from a foreign country. Such a duty is distinguished from a customs tariff, which is a comprehensive schedule of such duties.

customs invoice
an invoice for goods shipped from one country to another, prepared in a form that provides the information and date required by the country to which the goods are shipped, and sworn to before a consular officer stationed in the country from which the goods are shipped. Also known as consular invoice.

customs: lading cargo
the landing of cargo is supervised. A customs officer ensures that all cargo landed is declared and that nothing

declared has not been landed. Cargo is also examined: this is done on a selective basis. The importer or agent opens the cargo on the direction of the customs officer. Customs officer do not open, unpack or repack any goods.

custom permit

the forwarding agent produces a custom permit so that he may not face any difficulty in exporting the goods. He applies to the custom office for granting him a custom permit in regard to the goods he wants to export to any foreign country. In his application he will give full details of the commodities and also their place of destination.

customs service

an office of the Department of the Treasury. Customer examines all persons and merchandise entering the United States from foreign countries to ensure compliance with documentary and tariff regulations.

cut-throat competition

price in the market reduced to the point where no supplier is likely to make a profit.

damages

a sum of money claimed or award as compensation for loss or harm suffered by a person or by his property or reputation.

damaged, liquidated

damges stated in a contract to be payable on breach. They must be a fair estimate of the damage likely to be suffered. Round sums which do not appear to be related in any way to possible damage are known as penalties and are not enforceable. Where damages are difficult to assess, what might appear to be a penalty may be adjudged to be liquidated damages, if the court considers that the sum was an attempt to evaluate the possible loss.

dandy note

a document used for obtaining goods from a ware-house officer which are required for exportation, etc. It is issued on the authority of the customs house.

data base

a large, comprehensive central or otherwise significant collection of data; especially when carefully organized and recorded so that information may be derived from it by using electronic data processing.

dated security

bill of exchange or bond or other security with a stated date or a range of dates for cash repayment of the face value of the security. Short-dated security is one for which the repayment date is near while long-date security is that for which it is a long time ahead.

day book

in accounting, a diary of business activities; a chronological record of the transactions conducted by an enterprise. Entries in the day book are subsequently entered in a journal and posted to a ledger. Day books have become virtually obsolete.

day order

in the stock market, an order to buy or sell that expires if not executed by the end of the trading day on which it was entered. DBA Short for Doing Business As. The legal name under which a person or firm is doing business.

dcp

trade terms under which the seller is responsible for the carriage of goods by a usual route and in a customary manner to an agreed point, but the buyer is responsible for insuring the goods for the journery.

ddp

trade terms under which the seller must deliver the goods to a named place and must bear all the cost and risks involved in getting them there.

dead freight

payable where the character is unable entirely to fill a ship with cargo and is therefore charged against empty space.

dead heading

as used in the transportation industry, the movement of empty cars, buses or trucks to a given destination or the practice of furnishing free transportation to employees of a transportation company is called dead heading.

dead rent

a minimum amount payable, for example, on a lease of mine (where rent is usually charged as a royalty on the quantity mined.)

dead time

time lost through no fault of the employee and for which he is usually paid at the full rate. Time lost because of machine breakdown or delays in delivery of material are examples.

deal

1. a transaction: especially a large-scale transaction in securities.

2. a form of promotion in which a price reduction is given for a limited period.

dealer

1. middleman in distribution chain, buying goods in order to sell them, usually but not always to the general public: generally synonymous with 'retailer' but often applied to the larger distributor.

2. in the securities trade, a trader, who buys and sells for his or her own account rather than as an agent for customers.

dealer leaders

promotional device providing incentives to retailers to stock a product, or range or products, at predetermined quantities.

dealership

right to deal in a product as appointed dealer. Usually occurs with product which require after-sales services, or when distribution is restricted to network of selected agents as with cars, sewing, machines, typewriters and consumer durable.

debasement

a reduction in intrinsic value, especially referring to reducing the amount of precious metal contained in a coin.

debenture

a promissory note issued by a company and backed by the general credit of the company; usually not secured by a mortgage, lien, or any specific property. A debenture ranks ahead of preferred stock in the event of liquidation of corporate assets.

debenture bond

(US) a bond for which the issuer gives no security e.g., in the form of a floating charge or a mortgage. (Equivalent to unsecured loan stock in the UK).

debentures at a discount

debentures may be issued at a discount without any restrictions. The amount of the discount must be shown separately in the balance sheet.

debeture trust deed

a deed by which a company that has borrowed money by means of a marketable loan appoints a trustee to look after the interest of the stock holder or debenture holders and usually, gives security for payment of interest and repayment of principal. (Equivalent to an 'indenture' in the U.S.A).

debit note

a term used in accounting. A debit note is sent to a customer when it is intended to debit his account, normally in an unusual situation—say when a person has been insufficiently charged for goods.

debt

a debt is money owed by one person or firm to another. It may carry interest covering the period which it is due but not paid, although common business usage allows an agreed period of interest-free credit before payment is demanded. Creditors often offer inducements by way of attractive discounts for quick settlements of debts. The usually term of credit in the business world for goods applied is one month. Debts which are not intended to be paid for a longer time may sometimes be covered by a bill of exchange or some other negotiable paper. Longterm debts, carrying interest, take the form of mortgages, etc. Debentures are a common form of long-term debt in the company world.

debt capital

money that has been loaned to a company for more that a short time (conventionally, more than one year).

debt collection

the activity or process of getting debtors to pay their debts.

debt conversion

the issue by the government of new securities to replace

existing or maturing debt. Conversion is a part of debt management technique.

debt discount
the difference between the face value of a loan and the net amount received by the borrower. When the discount relates to a loan, such as a bank loan, that represents a current liability, it is treated as a prepaid expense.

debt-equity ratio
to market analysts, a company's long-term debt dividend by the stockholders equity or net worth in general, the total amount owed to outsiders divided by the stockholders equity.

debt limit
in public finance, the maximum indebtedness permitted to a government by law.

debt management
the process of managing the national debt, i.e., arranging for the payment of interest and the refinancing of maturing bonds.

debt ratio
refers to the ratio of a company's debt capital to the sum of its debt capital and its contributed capital.

debt service ratio
a country's repayment obligations of principal and interest for a particular year on its external debt as a percentage of its exports of goods and services (i.e. its current receipts') in that year.

debt-to-equity ratio
refers to a ratio that measure a company's financial Leverage. It is calculated dividing all debt (both short and long-term) by all equity capital, including preferred and common stocks, earned and unearned surplus, and surplus reserves.

decentralization of industry
the opposite of localistation of industry which is also called territorial division of labour. The term refers to dispersal of industries throughout the length and breadth of the country.

decision accounting
this is not separate accounting system, but the accounting in for nation which helps arrive at a decision. For example, decision on capital expenditure, whether to make or buy, what price to charge, whether to subcontract, and other important matters, may all be assisted by the employment of accounting information.

decision-making
the process or activity of selecting, from among possible alternatives, a future course of acting.

decision tree
a diagram of a sequence of decision, each of which involves choosing between a known number of alternatives and depends on the results of previous decisions.

deck cargo
cargo stowed on deck rather

than in the ship's hold. Deck cargo may often be of a hazardous nature and must, therefore, be easier to jettison in a situation of jeopardy.

declared dividend
a dividend which has been authorized by the board of directors to be paid to the stockholders of record on a specified date.

declining balance
a method of calculating depreciation of a fixed asset in which the amount of depreciation is a fixed percentage of the previous year's depreciated value. (Also known as 'diminishing balance'.)

decreasing costs
you have increasing cost if a producer sets a price at which he is willing to sell a given quantity or less, and decreasing costs if he be willing to sell at that price a given quantity or more.

dedicated manger
a manager who tends to dominate others. He gives many verbal directions to subordinates.

deductible clauses
insurance clauses that eliminate coverage for minor losses there by reducing the relatively high costs of processing and investigating the small claims and restraining the growth in premium. There are two forms of deductible clauses found most frequently in property and liability insurance deductible and the franchise deductible.

deductible coverage
an insurance clause providing that the insured will assume any losses below a given amount.

deed lieu of foreclosure
the transfer of a little from a borrower to a lender to avoid foreclosure.

deed of arrangement
a deed by which a person who is insolvent, transfer his property to trustee who uses it to pay the person's creditors as best he can.

deed of assignment
a term used in bankruptcy, when rather than become bankrupt a debtor assigns all his property for the benefit of his creditors generally. As it is an alternative to bankruptcy, agreement with his creditors would be necessary for it to be legally enforceable.

deed of trust
a deed to real property held by a trustee to secure the performance by the grantor or another of an obligation owed to the beneficiary of the trust.

deed, warranty
a deed containing a convenant of guara-ntee, in which the grantor assures that the title is free from defect, that the property is free of encumbrances other than those listed, and that the grantor agrees to protect the grantee agaisnt any loss by reason of the existence of any

other title or interest in the property at the time the deed is executed.

defensive investment

any investment, domestic or foreign, undertaken principally to insure against loss rather than to make a profit.

defence bonds

government securities introduced in November 1939, and on sale.Bonds were issued in units of Rs.290 and there was a maximum holding. At maturity certain issues had a tax free bonus, free of capital gains tax. Holders could always convert into anew issue. These were similar to National Development Bonds.

deferred annuity

an annuity which begins only after a specified period of time has elasped following its purchase or other arrangements for its payment. Deferred annuities often provided for in life insurance policies. An annuity is a sum of money due today but payable after stated time in the future.

deferred demand

demand that must be postponed owing to a shortage of the desired good or service.

deffred income

also, deferred credit, deferred revenue. Income that has been received but not yet earned (and hence is sometime called "unearned" income).

deferred rebate

rebate or discount goods accumulated for an agreed period; used as an incentive to customers to remain loyal to supplier or to buy all needs from one supplier.

deffered shares

these are shares which rank for dividend and return of capital after all other classes of shares have received a fixed rate of dividend or have been paid out in the case of winding-up of the company.

A deferred share in a company carries rights which are in some way inferior to those of the ordinary shares in the company. Typically a dividend on deffered shares in payable only if their is any money left after a specified dividend has been paid to ordinary shareholders.

deficiency account

a statement of the changes in assets and liabilities of a bankrupt over the twelve months proceeding the date on which a receiving order was made against him. It forms part of the bankrupt's statement of affairs.

deficit spending

another name for deficit financing. It is distinct from deficit budgeting. The newly generated high voltage money is termed as deficit spending.

deflation

a decline in the general price level of all goods and services, equivalent to a rise in the purchasing power of money, as contrasted with inflation.

Also, a statistical adjustment

of date which an economic time series expressed in current dollars is converted into a series expressed in constant dollars of a previous period. The purpose of the adjustment is to compensate for the distorting effect of inflation.

deflationary motive
one of the reasons for holding money. It is the reverse of inflationary motive for avoiding holding money.

defunct company
a company that has been struck off the official register of companies because it has ceased to function. This may arise after a winding up or where, after proper formalities have been completed, the Registrar of Companies concludes that the company is no longer in existence. When the name of the company is removed from the Register of companies it is entered in another book known as the Register of defunct companies, referred to colloquially as the 'dead book'.

degressive tax
the tax is called degressive when the higher incomists do not make a due sacrifice, or when the burden imposed on them is relatively less.

del credere
a del credere commission is an extra commission paid by a principal to an agent when the agent guarantees the solvency of customer to whom he has sold goods on credit.

del credere agency
from the Italian, "or belief" or "trust". An agent, factor, or broker is operating under a del credere agency of commission when he undertakes to guarantee to his principle the payment of a debt due from a buyer of goods.

del creadere agent
he is an agent employed by a principal to buy or sell goods on credit. He ensures the recovery of payments. In the case of the default of the purchaser in paying the price, he shall indemnify the seller of the goods for any loss arising on account of bad debts. He gets extra commission for bearing this extra risk. Such commission is called commission.

delinquent tax
a tax not paid when due. Usually penalties are invoked, which for a property tax may involve a Tax Lien.

delivery note
a note similar to an advice note accompanying goods sent by a vendor, often in duplicate, the recipient returning one copy and signing the other. The signed copy is then taken by the person delivering the goods to the vendor is evidence of proper delivery.

demand
its usual reference in marketing is to the aggregate of effective purchasing intentions in a community regarding a particular product

or service.

demand deposit
a sum of money deposited by someone in a bank on condition that he can withdraw it on demand.

demand effective
the total effective volume of sales anticipated for a product at a given price, that is, the want backed by purchasing power to the extent required for making purchases upto the quantity desired.

demand, inelastic
a positive relationship between changes in price and total revenue.

demand price
the highest price a buyer is willling to pay for a given quantity of a commodity.

demand schedule
a list of the demand for something when it is offered for sale at various prices.

demurrer
a procedural method used in a suit by which the defendant admits all the facts alleged in the plaintiff's complaint, but denies that such facts state cause for action. It raises a question of law on the facts, which must be decided by the court.

departmental management
a departmentally managed undertaking is the oldest and the most traditional type of public enterprise in all the countries of the world. It has been mainly used for railways, communications, power, ports, etc. Under Departmental Management, the enterprise is managed by the officials of the government in one of its departments, under the charge of the Secretary of the Ministry concerned. They are managed by civil servants who are government employees and who work under the control of a Minister.

departmental stores
a departmental store may be described as a large retail establishment having in the same building a number of departments each of which confines its activities to one particular kind of trade and forms complete unit in itself and is centrally controlled. A departmental store implies the opening of a number of shops under one roof and control, each dealing in a certain line of goods. The idea of departmental stores is to provide a large variety of merchandise from a pin to a motor car at one place. It aims at providing convenience in shopping and acts as a universal provider. The customers can get all their requirements at one place and need not go from place to place making purchases.

depletion
lessening in value of a natural resources at rate greater than its replacement rate.

deposit
an amount of money paid to a vendor as part of the purchase

money and to secure the sale. The depositor is entitled then to buy the property if he pays the balance within a stated period. Normally, if the balance is not paid, he will lose the deposit, assuming good faith on both sides.

deposit account

an account with a bank from which deposits are repayable only to the depositor, who is required to give notice in a advance if he requires repayment.

deposit money

bank deposit against which cheques can be drawn. It can also be cheque book money.

depreciation accounting

a branch of accounting that deals with systematically distributing or allocating the cost or other basic value of a fixed asset over its estimated useful economic life by means of periodic charges to expense or against revenue.

depreciation base

the recorded cost of a fixed assets or, fixed-asset group that is to be recovered through depreciation, not including the estimated amount that may be recovered from sale or salvage of the asset.

depreciation expense

the portion of the cost of a fixed asset or fixed-asset group that is charged against operations for an accounting period. Also, any provision for depreciation.

depreciation insurance

insurance that is added to a fire insurance policy by endorsement and that covers the difference between the actual cash value and the replacement cost of the insured property.

depression

period during which a nation's productive resource are persistently undereployed; often manifests itself through a long period of high unemployment among a community's labour force.

derived demand

the demand for a good or service that arises from the demand for some other good or service.

destroyed bank note

where notes have been partly or wholly destroyed, their value can be recovered from the bank which issued them, provided that full particulars, including the numbers, are supplied, and the bank is otherwise satisfied. The bank will require a sufficient indemnity to be given before paying notes which are stated to have been destroyed.

deustscher industrie-und handelstag

association of Federal German Chambers of Industry and Commerce linked with chambers of commerce in most principal towns and with seven regional organizations.

devaluation

an official act that makes a domestic currency cheaper in terms of gold or foreign currencies, generally to increases a nation's exports while reducing its imports.

development expenditure
the cost of development in a business that does not necessarily result in visible assets but is aimed at promoting sales by advertising and various other devices. This expenditure is sometimes capitalized, i.e. it is shown as an intangible asset in a balance sheet, or sometimes as a fixed asset, and then written off over a period. The period will depend upon the estimate of the time sales are expected to benefit.

diagonal combination
this type of combination takes place where ancillary services as repair works, distribution services such as transport or packing are run along with the main activity of production. Dependence on others for such services is done away with to ensure speed and continuity of production.

differential tax incidence
it refers to the distributional changes that result when one tax is substituted for another assuming that the money yield of the two taxes is the same. Here the public expenditure should be held constant.

diminishing-provision method
a method of depreciation, more popularly known as Declining-Balance method.

deminishing returns
the principle that as more of a variable factor is applied to a fixed factor, the output increases less than proportionately. An input whose quantity a business can very at will is the variable factor of production; an input cannot be increased is the fixed factor. For example, if it is known that a two-operator machine can produce a certain number of widgets per hour, adding a third operator may not cause a proportionate increase; in fact, the third operator may cause interference, resulting in a negative change in output.

direct cost
a measurement, for the purpose of cost accounting of the value of whatever a firm has parted with or is liable to part with in making an expenditure on goods, services or labour which can reasonably be said to have been directly used by, or to have directly benefitted, only a specified activity, product or cost centre of the firm. Also the total direct costs incurred in manufacturing an item.

direct costing
method or producing a statement of costs which are directly attributable to a particular product, brand, or function.

direct expenses
expenses which can be directly associated with the cost of producing a particular article or service, as opposed to

overhead expenses.

director

a person selected by shareholder, to establish company policies. The directors appoint the president, vice presidents, and all other operating officers. They also decide, among other matters, if and when dividend shall be paid.

director's emoluments

sums of money and benefits in kind received by directors. These may include fees, salaries for acting as director (or some other capacity) for the company, the use of company property, and certain expense allowance. The Companies Acts require that the accounts of a company shall distinguish between amounts received in respect of services as director of the company or any of its subsidiaries, and remuneration received for management of the company's affairs or the affairs of any subsidiary. They also require that director's emoluments should be distinguished from directors' pensions or compensation for loss of office. The Law details be given of the number of directors receiving salaries within certain range, for instance Rs.0-Rs.100, 500,-Rs.250, 000, etc. This also applies to highly paid persons who are not directors. The Law does not apply to independent companies where the total emoluments are less than Rs.37500.

directors : over age

generally speaking a person who is over seventy cannot be appointed director of a public company or of a private company that is a subsidiary of a public company. This is does not apply where the appointment is made by the company in a general meeting, after special notice has been given of intention to do so.

directors' service contracts

companies must keep (in an appropriate place) details of service contracts with directors. If the contract was in writing, a copy of it must be kept. If not, a memorandum will suffice. The appropriate place is the registered office, the place where the register of members is kept, or the principal place of bushiness. The place where it is kept must be notified to the Registrar of Companies, it must be open to inspection on every bushiness day for at least two hours, free of charges to all members of the company. There are certain limited exceptions in the cases of directors working wholly outside the united kingdom , and of contracts for very short periods.

direct placing

a placing of shares in a company direct to investors, without recourse to underwriters to back the deal or to public subscription.

direct taxation

taxes on individuals or organizations levied directly by income or wealth.

director

he is an officer of a company. Strictly speaking, directors are person concerned with managing a company on behalf of the shareholders. They are they representatives of the company. Any person according to whose instructions directors are accustomed to act is to all intents and purposes a director when it comes to directors shareholders, closure of companies, etc.

dibursement list

a printed list containing the identity and quantity of part and assemblies to be withdrawn from stock and dispatched to the starting point of manufacturer or assembly on a given day.

disbursing officer

in government accounting, a bonded employee who is authorized to pay cash or to issue cheques in settlement of vouchers that have been approved by a certifying officer.

discharge of contract

this means the fulfilment of the obligations imposed by a contract, or else an agreement to negate the contract or put in its place. It can also mean a situation where a party may be released from his obligations by impossibility of performance or by operation of law. For example, alternation of a written instrument without the consent of the other party will preclude the party altering the instrument from taking action on it and release and other party from all obligations.

discount

a deduction from a standard or nominal price or value of something that is made to arrive at the price of the thing in a specified transaction.

discount agent

commission agent who sells for cash at well below recommended price, usually holding no stock and giving no demonstrations, working from a catalogue, goods being supplied direct from manufacturer.

discount broker

a broker who neither buys nor sells bills or exchange but acts as intermediary between those who wish to sell and those who wish to buy. If a broker deals on his own account he becomes a discount house. The question to be asked is, 'Do they run own book?'

discounted cash flow

any profitable investment, whether it be the purchase or an income-earning asset, must generate a cash flow. The investment will provide the investor with a cash return over a period, the return being monies earned by the asset after deduction of the costs of making the asset productive.

discounted net benefit cost ratio

the same as the undiscounted net benefit-cost ratio except that the present value of annual cash inflows minus depreciation is compared to the present value of annual cash outflows.

discovery period
the period of time allowed by the insured after the expiration date of an insurance contract or bond to discover and report losses that may have occurred while the contract or bond was in force and that would have been covered by the term of the insurance.

discretionary income
amount of income left over after fixed regular outgoings have been paid. It constitutes the amount of money not yet committed and therefore its expenditure is subject to persuasion techniques.

discriminating monopoly
a market situation in which the monopolist divides his sales among a different number of 'markets' and charges different price in each market.

disequilibrium
the state of imbalance in any economic organism or system (such as household, a firm a market, or a national economy) wherein the quantities supplied and demanded of a commodity at a given price are unequal, resulting in a tendency for market prices and or quantities to change.

disgorging
the removal of sediment from wine. The bottles are stood on end, the sediment settles in the neck of the bottle, the cork is removed and the sediment disposed of.

display bonus
special trade terms to retailer to encourage use of POS material or to display actual product.

disposable income
this term is used to describe the amount of a person's wage or salary after all compulsory deductions, such as direct taxation, pension contributions, compulsory savings deposit and national insurance contributions, have been made.

dissaving
paying for current consumption by drawing on past savings, by borrowing, or by receiving aid from other sources. Spending at a rate that exceeds one's disposable income.

dissolution of company
a company is dissolved when winding up proceedings have come to an end (winding UP), or when the Registrar of Companies has struck the company's name off the Register as defunct.

distribution expense
in accounting, an expense associated with selling and distributing any product or service, including warehousing, advertising, sales commissions, and delivery charges.

distributive trades

collective term for wholesalers and retail firms, especially those directly involved in selling to the public. Often abbreviated colloquially to 'The Trade.'

diversion

a change in routing while a shipment in under way. Some railroad permit shipping of a carload of goods in a given direction without a specific destination-for example.

divestment

action or process, undertaken by a firm, a transferring ownership and control of part of its activities to another firm.

divided account

in the sale of securities through underwriting syndicates, a divided account is one in which the liability of the members of the syndicates is limited to their percentage participation.

dividend

a share of profits taken by a shareholder of a company. Dividends may be preference or ordinary. Preference dividends have precendence as to payment. A company need not pay dividends. Payment depends on monies available and the policy of the company. A dividend is not payable until declared (normally at an Annual General Meeting) and the amount is agreed by the Directors. The normal practice is to pay one dividend per year shared as a percentage of nominal capital. Part of this dividend may be paid durng the year as an interim dividend. Dividends are paid by dividend warrants and after deduction of tax.

dividend cover

the number of times a company's dividends to ordianry shareholders could be paid out its net profits after tax in the same period. For example, a net dividend of E400,000 paid by a company showing a net profit of EIM is said to be covered 21/, times Dividend cover is a measure of the probability that dividend payments will be sustained (low cover might make it difficult ot pay the same level of dividends in a bad year's trading) and of a company's commitment to investment and growth (high cover implies that the company retains its earnings for investment in the bushiness). Negative dividend cover is unusual, and is taken as a sign that a company is in difficulties. In the USA, the dividend cover is expressed as the pay-out ratio, the total dividends paid as a percentage of the net profit. Dividend Equalization Reserve a Reserve formerly created to smooth out fluctuations in the incidence of taxation so that dividends could be maintained. Such reserve are now normally referred to as deferred-tax accounts.

dividend mandate

documentary by which a

shareholder authorizes a registered company to pay the dividends due to him into his bank account by credit transfer.

dividend tax

a tax introduced in 1965 at the same time as the Corporation Tax. It is in the form of an income tax payable on dividends paid by limited companies. The tax is paid in addition to corporate tax and is deducted from the dividend before payment and accounted for by the company to the Inland Revenue. There are certain complicated provisions with reference to dividends received by a company and then paid over to its members. The aim of these is to prevent double taxation.

dividend waiver

a decision by a major shareholder in a company riot to take dividends, usually because the company cannot afford to pay it.

dividend warrant

the cheque issued by a company to its shareholders when paying, dividends. It states the tax deducted and the net amount paid. This document must be sent by non-taxpayers to the Inland revenue when claiming back the tax.

dock warrant

a document issued by a dock company stating that the gods as described therein are entered in its books and are deliverable to the person mentioned or his assigns by endorsement.

doctrine of international distribution of gold

its essential points are the following two ideas:

1. that gold is a commodity whose circulation from one country to another is determined by the same circumstances as other commodities.
2. that just as commodities are exported from a country where they are cheap to one where they are dearer, so is gold exported when it is cheaper in one country than in others and this export of gold tends after a short time to equalize the price levels in the different countries.

documentary bill

a bill of exchange to which the payee (who is also the drawer) has attached documents to show that he has sent goods, to the value of the bill, to the drawee who will then be willing at least to accept the bill (if not actually pay it) before receiving his goods. The documents involved are usually a copy of an invoice and a bill of lading.

documents against acceptance

a term used with reference to foreign trade, where documents of title to goods expoted are handed over by the master of the ship or some other person when the importer signs a Bills of exchange. (The bill would be a period bill.)

dollar area
the group of countries, where the United States Dollar was freely convertible after the second world war.

dollar diplomacy
a term of denigration suggesting that the monetary strength of the United States has been used for advancing her political influence.

dollar shortage
also, dollar gap, the situation in which the demand for U.S. Dollars greatly exceeds their supply. As a result, the dollar is undervalued in relation to other currencies.

domestic bill of exchange
inland bill of exchange as distinguished from foreign bill of exchange. In India it is called hundi.

domestic corporation
a corporation that is created under the laws of a given state of country in which the corporation is officially located.

domestic gold standard
the modern gold standard serves two function. In the first place it is a method of controlling the volume of the currency. The second function of the gold standard is it to preserve the stability of exchange rates.

door-to-door
practice of selling by calls upon householders, may also be used to distribute promotional material.

double entry
normal method of book-keeping or accounting in which transactions are entered both as a debit to one account and as a credit to another so that the totals of debits and credits are equal.

double-entry book-keeping
a form of a book-keeping devised centuries ago, whereby each transaction is entered twice, a transaction being by its nature two-sided. The purchase of an asset necessitates the recording of the asset and also, separately, of the debt incurred or the money paid. The book in which all the accounts are kept is known as the ledger, though the cash account in normally kept in a separate book, known as the cash book. At any time the total debit balance in the ledger should equal the total credit balances. If this is so, it is an indication that (in the absence of compensating errors) double entries have been properly made. This is because, of the two entries made, one is always a debit and one a credit entry.

double indemnity
a provision in an insurance policy that the insurer will pay twice the face amount of the policy if the insured dies as a result of an accident.

double indemnity
a provision in an insurance policy that the insurer will pay twice the face amount of the

policy if the insured dies as a result of an accident.

double taxation agreement

a treaty between two countries designed to avoid double taxation occurring if someone lives in one country but earns money in the other.

down theory

a theory of stock market analysis based on the performance of the Dow-Jones industrial and transportation stock price averages.

down tick

in the stock market, a transaction at the same price as the preceding sale but lower than the preceding different price. Indicated at each trading post on the floor or the NYSE by a minus sign next to the last price of the stock traded. Also called minus tick.

downtime

period when a machine could be working but does not work because of a fault or because of a break in planned maintenance operations.

dow payment

a partial payment of the total purchase price rendered by a buyer to a seller at the time of purchase, with the understanding that the rest will be paid later, according to the terms of their agreement.

dow payment

a partial payment of the total purchase price rendered by a buyer to a seller at the time of purchase, with the understanding that the rest will be paid later, according to the terms of their agreement.

draft

a written order drawn by one party, the drawer that orders a second party, the drawee to pay a specified amount of money to a third party, the payee.

drawback

a rebate which may be obtained for duty paid on imported materials used in the manufacture of exported goods. Drawback is avoided if goods are kept in a bonded warehouse for ex-export. Goods for repair may be imported free of duty.

drawee

the person, or firm that is instructed by the drawer of a bill of exchange, a cheque or a draft, to make a payment.

drive-in

a business enterprise whose customers drive their cars to the establishment and conduct their business without leaving the automobile.

dry goods

older name for cloth by the yard rather than being made up into a garment or other item.

dual unionism

where two or more trade unions represent similar types of workers in the same bargaining unit.

due bill

a statement of charges for services rendered, containing details of the services and terms and dates when the amounts due are considered payable. In transportation, a due bill covers additional charges when an original bill for freight charges was to low or in error.

due date

in purchasing the expected date or receipt for a part; in manufacturing, the expected completion date of a part.

due from banks

the sum that a bank may have on deposit with other banks (perhaps to take advantage of the clearing house facilities of another banks that have been received by the bank unquestioning and are in the process of collection).

dumpbin

a container for displaying goods in a retail establishment which consists of an open-topped box or bin in which goods are piled in an unarranged jumble.

dumping

a term used in international trade for the unloading of large quantities of a particular product in another country at a low price. This may be done where the first country is over-producing and wishes to sell at a low profit rather than at none at all (or even to sell at a loss, so that it may get a foothold in the other market). Again, it can be a rather ruthless way of maximizing the profit of a particular industry; where there is a monopoly at home output is restricted and a high price charged. The bulk of the output is pushed into another country and sold at prices which producers in that country cannot afford. Dumping is therefore frowned upon by governments, and steps are often taken to prevent it happening. These may be direct, e.g. by duties, or indirect, e.g. by retaliatory action.

duopsony

the condition that exists when two buyers control the demand for goods and services offered by many producers.

durable goods

goods purchased for use over a period, such as washing machines or refrigerators. The consumer's equivalent of a fixed asset.

dutch auction

a sale in which the price of an article is set rather high and then gradually reduced (often on a daily basis) until the article is sold.

duty free shop

retail establishment in which selling prices do not include Customs and Excise duties and may, therefore, be fixed at a lower level than those prevailing generally within a particular country. Most often located at air or seaports where operators can, as a result, take a higher margin of profit than other retailers.

dynamic programming

mathematical or logical techniques for dealing with multistage decision problems that involve deciding an optium sequence of decisions where each decision in the sequence depends on the ones before it.

earned for ordinary
the amount of he earnings of a company for a period that could be distributed to its ordinary shareholders; in other words, net profits after deducting corporate income tax, payments of interest on debt capital and payments of preference dividends.

earned income
it is the of a person's income which is obtained as a result of the application of labour either as an employee or as a self-employed person.

earnings drifts
extent to which wages or earnings rise above national rates through the influence of such factors as local rates, overtime, work place bargaining, payment by-results schemes bargaining, creep,etc. Also known as wage drift.

earning power
the ability of an individual or an organization to make money from its goods or services. Used in the valuation of an enterprise as a whole or in the valuation of a class of securities.

earning report
a statement issued by a company showing is earnings or losses over a given period, usually one fiscal year. It lists the income earned, expenses, and net results.

earnings yield
the relationship between profits and capital. It is used frequently with reference to stock exchange investments and generally means the ratio of annual profit (after tax and fixed interest or fixed dividend payments) to total equity capital (at the current market value, the value per the official lists). It should be distinguished from the 'dividend yield', this being dividend over stock exchange price. 'Dividend yield' would apply of course to fixed-dividend shares as well as to equity shares. This dividend yield as a percentage will differ from the rate of dividend stated by the company, insofar as the latter is based upon nominal value and the former on market value.

easement
a right, which is automatically acquired by whoever owns a specified piece of land, to use a second piece of land in a specific manner apart from a right to take something from that land. The most important easements are rights of traffic, a right to sun-light and a right to avail of public utilities at reasonable costs.

econometrician
economist, with mathematical expertise, who constructs models of interaction of economic variables.

econometrics
the integration of economic theory, mathematics, and

statistic. It involves expressing economic relationships in the form mathematical equations and verifying the resulting models by statistical methods.

economic activity
the production and distribution of goods and services.

economic dynamics
analysis of economic system, through time, and particularly in relation to behaviour of markets, firm and national economy in general.

economic growth
rate usually measured annually, at which a nation or other community's real income or national income, or flow of goods and services, increases.

economic income
money income plus imputed income (rental value of owned homes).

economic sanction
where the government of one nation, or of many acting in concert wish to make a token objection to the policies of another, then a common tactic is adopted to disrupt the economy of the offending nation by the imposition of boycotts and embargoes on trade with that country. For example, many Asian and African nations have imposed economic sanctions and declared an economic boycot against South Africa for its apartheid policies.

economic union
a trade association of two or more countries that permits the free flow of capital, goods, labour, services, and traffic from one member nation to or another.

economist
someone who known the price of every thing and the value of nothing.

economy
ordinarily means thriftiness. It also indicates, the advantage or benefit available to or produced by.

eighty-twenty rule
in marketing, an empirical rule reflecting the common experience that relatively small proportion, of items in a company's catalogue generate a large proportion of the company's total activity in sales. The rule also states that approximately 20- per cent of the customers are responsible for 80 percent of the sales volume. Some managers claim the same is relatively true of the sales effort, total 20 per cent of the sales force produces 80 per cent of the orders.

ejusdem generis rule
a rule of law (the words mean 'of the same kind'). The rule might be applied in, say, insurance: the court might decide that although a policy may cover losses not expressly mentioned in the policy, they must be of the same kind as those which are mentioned, and not of a compeltely different kind.

elastic demand

effect which a price change has on the demand for goods or services. Those which are very sensitive to price change are said to be elastic. The opposite is inelastic demand.

elasticity of demand

demand is considered elastic when a decrease in price results in an increase in total revenue.

electronic funds transfer system

a technique using computers to transfer funds between banks.

embargo

when it is forbidden to export goods to certain countries, then goods are said to be subject to embargo.The embargo may be imposed by either side, and prevents the unloading or loading of certain goods, or else prevents ships entering or leaving certain ports. Goods subject to embargo are listed in the Board of Trade Journal.

emerson efficiency plan

under this system a minimum wage is guaranteed to the workers. Conditions of work are standardised and a standard task is fixed after careful study. The standard task is considered to be a full and fair task for a hundred per cent efficient work. For the attainment of the desired standard a bonus is offered. Smaller bonuses may. be provided for those who are short of the standard.

emolument

the return from personal labour received or accrued in the form of compensation, such as salary, wage, fee, commission, price concession, or other personal benefit.

employee

person who enters into a contact with another (the employer) to perform work-under the control of the employee or another of that employer's employees and as part of the organization run by the employer-in return for wages or salary or some other valuable consideration.

employee contribution

they money individual employees pay to participate in company benefit plans, especially common in the areas of insurance, pension, and savings plans. The usual pracgice is to deduct employee contri-butions directly from their paychecks.

employee's share scheme

a scheme for encouraging or making it esiser for the employees of a company to own its shares.

employment

indicates regular occupation, opportunities of regular occupation depend on a country's overall economic development achieved. In any country, employment opportunities are created broadly by industrial sector, agricultural sector and service sector. With the expansion of those sectors employment opportunity increases, in the sense that new jobs are created for people.

employment exchange

an office at which work people seeking employment and employers requiring work people may notify their respective needs. It is market place for labour, intended to replace the unguided individual research for work or for employees.

endorsee

the person designated in an endorsement as the one to whom the endorser is transferring the right to receive money.

endorsement

a term used with particular reference to bills of exchange. When a bill is negotiated the person negotiating will write his name on the reverse of the bill. This transfers the property in the bill. A valid endorsement must be written on the bill itself or on an allonge. It must be of the entire bill and must be by all parties to whom the bill is made out unless one has authority to act for the others. If the bill is payable to order and the payee's names wrongly spelt, the endorser may sign it in the incorrect way and add his correct name if he wishes. Where there are a number of endorsements on a bill, they are presumed to have been made in the order in which they appear. Unless the country is stated, a bill is presumed to have been negotiated before it is overdue. Any person endorsing a bill becomes liable on the bill to all subsequent endorsees or holders. He cannot deny the drawer's signature or the signatures of persons endorsing the bill if asked to pay by a holder in due course. Endorsements may be of various types: (1) a bill may be endorsed in blank, no endorsee being named; the bill then becomes payable to bearer, (2) there may be a special endorsement when the name of the endorsee is specified; the bill then becomes a bill payable to order, (3) there may be a restrictive endorsement, where the bill is endorsed 'pay A only'; the bill then ceases to be a negotiable instrument, (4) the endorsement may be limited, e.g. without recourse. If an endorsement is forged, the position is more difficult. Generally speaking title cannot pass through a forgery and a holder of the bill can only claim from persons signing the bill subsequent to the forgery. Sometimes bills are endorsed conditionally, e.g. 'To a provided he cashes the bill in X days'. The payer can please subsequent or not he observes the condition.

endowment

it is a term used with reference to assurance

policies. An endorwment assurance is one where the holder of the policy, by paying a certain annual premium, is entitled to a fixed sum at the end of a stated period.

endowment assurance

a policy of assurance which is payable on the assured surviving to a certain age, or payable at death if it occurs before that age.

engineering

an inclusive term embracing the discovery through research of laws and formulation of principles and methods of utilizing them through the design, construction, maintenance, and operation of mechanical and other devices.

entrerprise

a business undertaking. Unless otherwise qualified, the entirely of an organization rather than a unit or subdivision. Also, that quality of business management identified with energy, inditiative resourcefunless, and adaptability.

entrepeneur

a person who is skilled at identifying new products (or sometimes new methods of production), setting up operations to provide new products, marketing the products and arranging the financing of the operations.

environmental sensor department

department in a company which tests the markets or provides intelligence helpful to marketing. e.g., market research, economic, consumer relations, public relations, legal departments.

equilibrium of the firm

when a firm is producing the output at which marginal costs equal marginal revenue, it is in a position of equilibrium. That means there is no incentive to expand or contract the output.

equilibrium rate of exchange

the rate at which the demand for each currency, would be equal to the supply of it, ignoring speculative and abnormal capital movements.

equity

in finance, right or claim to an asset. A holder of an equity may be creditor, part owner, proprietor, or stockholder. Also, an interest in the property or in a business that is subject to claims of creditors. Generally used as a statement of the amount or percentage of ownership interest.

In matters of law, early English courts did not always give an adequate remedy to an aggrieved person; redress was sometimes sought from the king. The appeal having been made to the sovereign's conscience, he therefore referred the case to his spiritual adviser, the chancellor, who was expected to decide the case according to rules of fairness, honesty, right and natural justice. The rules in equity were developed from this practice. The laws of trusts, divorce, rescission of contracts for fraud injunction, and specific performance are enforced in courts of equity.

equity capital

it is that part of the capital of a company that belongs as of right to the true owners, i.e. those who take the greatest risk that are entitled to all profits and reserves after the contributors of fixed interest capital have been paid their due.

Money, or other assets, put into a business enterprise by investors in return for an unlimited share in the profits of the business that are left after paying its creditors and alter paying persons who supplied capital in return for a limited share of profits.

equity dilution

dilution of the influence or control of the original shareholders as a result of the issue of new shares.

equity of redemption

it implies the rights of a mortgagor to redeem his property on the repayment of money borrowed. The law does not approve of clogs on the equity of redemption by way of difficult conditions imposed on the mortgagor, or of conditions aimed at making it difficult for him to redeem his property.

equity security

a transferable certificate of ownership; sometimes used in connection with capital stock, stock warrants, or indebtedness convertible into stock. Also a controlling company's interest and holding of stocks, bonds, notes and other formal evidences of ownership of indebtedness of a subsidiary.

errors and omission excepted (E. & O. E.)

these initials are commonly included at the end of an invoice. The idea is to absolve person issuing the invoice from clerical doubtful error.

escape clause

a clause in a contract which enables enables one party to escape an obligation he would normally have under contracts with similar subject-matter.

escheat

an old legal term for the right of the lord or the grantor of land or interest in land, to take the land when the tenant died leaving no heir.

estate agent

an agent or brokers is a person who is concerned with the sale, letting, management and valuation of real and leasehold property. The work is often combined with that of an auctioneer. The agent works on an ad valorem commission. He is a general agent. He is not legally bound to belong to any organization or to have any special educational qualifications in order that he may call himself an estate agent. There is, however, a senior professional body known as the Chartered Auctioneers and Estate Agents Institute, and movements are afoot to provide for the registration of estate agents for the better protection of the public.

estate duty

a former tax on the state of a deceased person at the time of death. This tax applied in the UK from 1894 to 1974, when it was converted to capital-transfer tax. The latter tax became inheritance tax in 1986, when it reverted to a form of taxation similar to the former estate duty. The tax is levied on the assets less the liabilities of the deceased, taking into account (to forestall avoidance) certain gifts made in a defined period before the death.

estate duty

taxes payable to the government imposed on property passing after the death of the owner.

estoppel

a rule of law, whereby a person is prevented (or estopped) from denying a statement he has made either orally or in witting (or possibly by conduct). It applies particularly to statements made in a contract by deed. It also prevents a principal from denying the authority of his agent, or a person denying the existence of a partnership, where the conduct of the parties has implied that this exists.

eurocheque

a cheque drawn on a European bank, available in 39 countries which can be cashed at any bank or bureau de change in the world that displays the EC sign (of which there are some 200000) It can also be used to pay for goods and services in shops, hotels, restaurants, garages etc., that display the EC sign. The cheques are blank and are made out for any amount as required, usually in the local currency. They have to be used with a Eurocheque Card which guarantees cheques for up to about. In most cases, a commission of 1.25% is added to the foreign currency value of the cheque before it is converted to sterling and there is a cheque charge.

eurodeposit

a deposit using the currency of another country, i.e. a transaction in the eurocurrency market.

eurofrancs

the monetary franc dealt in and traded outside France but within the member states of the Common Market.

euromark

the monetary mark dealt in and traded outside the Federal Republic of Germany but within member states of the Common Market.

euronote

a form of euro-commerical

paper consisting of short term negotiable bearer notes. They may be in any currency but are usually in dollars or ECUs. The euronote facility is a form of note issuance facility set up by a syndicate of banks, which underwrites the notes .

European Free Trade Association

formed in 1959 as an alternative to the European Economic Community. It was intended as a much diluted form of common market. The object were to reduce progressively tariff barriers and other trade restrictions between the member countries, and thus to foster trade between them. It was looked on as an aid to economic development. There was to be no common tariff barrier against the rest of the world. Members are : Austria, Denmark, Norway, Portugal, Sweden, Switzerland, and the United Kingdom. Finland became an associate member in 1964.

exceptional items

an accounting term used for items of expenditure or income which do not normally arise in the type of business being considered. If material, the amount should be shown perhaps separately in the accounts.

excess

an amount that insurer and assured agree will be deducted from any claim made by the assured under his contract of insurance. (Also known as a deductible).

excess issue

in manufacturing, the quantity of parts issued to a shop order in excess of the quantity required by the bill of material.

excess profits tax

a tax levied (in England) upon excess profits arising from the Second World War.

excess reserves

any stock of cash and deposits a commercial bank holds over and above what it is required to hold.

exchange broker

an agent operating on a commission basis on behalf of others on the foreign exchange market.

exchange cheque

a cheque given in exchange for cash or for another cheque.

exchange control

action taken by government of a country to regulate or restrict international settlements by residents of the country.

exchange distribution

in securities trading, a method of disposing of large blocks of stock on the floor of an exchange.

exchange rate parity

the fixed rate of exchange between one currency and another. In foreign exchagne, the value of one currency in terms of another is determined by their respective gold backing. When there is difference between the values of two currencies, one is referred to as being parity or below parity.

exchange-speculation
buying and selling by speculators; claims against money just as buying and selling securities and commodities, with the hope of gaining or at least avoiding losses, from price changes through time (Exchange) speculation occurs in two types of markets; forward exchange markets and spot markets.

exculpatory clause
a section in a lease that relieves the landlord of liability for personal injury to occupants and for property damage.

executive
in organizational behaviour, descriptive of a manager who uses a high task orientation and a high relationships orientation in a situation where such behaviour is appropriate and who is therefore more effective. Such a manager sets high standards, treats everyone somewhat differently prefers team management, and is therefore often perceived as a good motivating force.

executive director
the director of a company who is also a fulltime employee of the company.

exemplary damages
in a tort action, the sum assessed as punishment by the jury, above the compensatory damage, in order to make an example of the wrongdoer as a deterrent to others who might consider similar conduct. Injuries caused by willful, malicious, wanton, and reckless conduct will subject the offender to exemplary damages.

exemption clause
it is a clause entered into a contract, particularly a contract for the sale of goods, excluding the vendor from liability for breach of condition, or warranty, or both.

ex-new
a stock exchange term. Shares are quoted ex-new when their price does not include the right to take new shares being offered.

expenditure
a relinquishment by a firm of money or some other asset or an incurrence of a liability in exchange for a benefit received or to be received.

expense account
a statement of special expenses incurred while conducting business outside the office, for such items as business-related travel and entertainment, normally such expenses must be authorized before reimbursement.

expired cost
a measurement for the purposes of accounting, of the cash value of whatever a firm has parted with (or is liable to part with) when making an expenditure on goods or

services that are no longer available for use within the firm (e.g., because they have been used in manufacturing something that the firm has sold).

export bank

the banking organization particularly concerning themselves with export trade for which usually they proved special assistance. In India, in 1982 on such bank with an authorized capital of Rs. 1,000 million was established in the public sector.

export finance house

financial institutional specializing in arranging non-recourse finance for exporters.

export house

an experienced organization specializing in selling other people's goods abroad. These set themselves up as market experts regarding language and local conditions abroad. They deal with packing, shipping, insurance, import regulations, tariffs, quotas, licences, exchange, and payment terms. Export houses sell on commission or on behalf of foreign importers. They also help to finance exporters, e.g. by buying direct and guaranteeing payment. When acting for the overseas buyer they will do so as confirming houses and receive a commission from the buyer.

export import merchant

a merchant who specializes in international trade, selling domestically produced goods in markets overseas, or purchasing goods made overseas and reselling them to customers in the domestic market.

export incentives

these are inducement subsidies given by the state to promote exports. They may be in the form of grants or cash subsidies to exporting industreis, additional credit facilities, tax exemptions, duty drawbacks, import licences, etc.

export license

a permit to export specific goods to a particular country

export quota

1. a limit on the amount of a particular item that may be exported during a given period of time, usually set in order to protect a domestic industry.

2. "voluntary" export quota. A device use either to prevent imports from gaining too large a share of the domestic market or to ensure an adequate supply of raw material for a domestic industry.

exright

in securities transactions, synonym for "without the rights" Corporation raising additional capital may do so by offering their stockholders the right to subscribe to new or additional stock, usually at a discount from the prevailing market price. The buyer of a stock selling exrights is not entitled to the rights.

extented coverage (EC) endorsement
extends a fire insurance policy to cover additional perils.

external currency market
the market for lending to firms outside of a particular country, through deposits of the currency that of country.

externalities
the benefits or costs accruing to some individual or group not involved directly as a buyer or seller in a market transaction.

externmal debt
it refers to the obligations of a country to foreign Governments or nationals or international financial institutions.

extractive industry
any industry that removes irreplaceable natural resources, such as petroleum, iron, ore, and other minerals.

extraordinary general meeting
a general meeting that is not an annual general meeting. The word 'extraordinary's is used because an annual general meeting used to be called an 'ordinary general meeting'.

ex-warehouse
a term indicating that the buyer is responsible for all charges to the destination of the shipment and has to arrange insurance to cover the goods from the time they leave the warehouse at the place of shipment until their arrival at the final destination.

fabin socialism
a form of socialism advocated by a group of socialist. It emerged as an outgrowth of utopian socialism and advocated gradual, evolutionary reform within a democratic framework. It is the philosophical basis of the British Labour Party.

face amount
the maximum loss payment an insurance company will make under the terms of a specific policy.

facilitating agency
such as transportation, banking insurance, advertising agencies communications services, which contribute to marketing without acquiring or selling goods.

facility
the aggregate amount of credit that a bank or other lender will grant to a particular borrower.

factor
a general mercantile agent dealing with a specified category or categories of goods. He is distinguished by the fact that, provided he has possession of the goods coming into these categories with the consent of the owner, he can sell and give a good title to an innocent purchaser for value, whether or not the true owner has given his permission to sell. An art dealer, for instance, could sell pictures lent to him for display, provided the buyer was not aware of this fact.

factor endowments
the amounts of factors of production the country possesses.

factory
any premises in which person are employed in manual labour in manufacturing or related process by way of trade or for purposes of gain.

factory ledger
a subsidiary ledger that contains the operating costs of a manufacturing establishment, such as materials, labour and factory overhead.

fad
trade terms under which the seller is responsible for delivering the goods to an air carrier at named airport of departure and for arranging (but not paying for) carriage by air to a named destination.

fair trade
also, resale price maintenance. An agreement between a manufacturing and distributor, and a dealer, stipulating that the latter will not resell an item below a specified minimum price.

family allowance plan
a plan that provides every family, regardless of income, with a certain amount of money based exclusively on the number and age of its children. Families above certain designated income levels return all or a portion of the money with their income taxes, but those below specified income level keep it. More than 60 countries have family allowance plans.

family budget
the term adverts to a detailed statements of the income and expenditure of a family for a period of time, say, a month.

farming co-operate societies
these are voluntary associations of small farmers who join hands with the object of achieving the economies of large scale farming and maximising agricultural output.

fat work
work on which it is relatively easy to earn high bonus under a payment-by-results scheme. May also be known as gravy jobs. Work on which it is difficult to earn bonus may be known as lean work or stinkers.

federal reserve system
the central monetary authority of the Unites States.

feedback
part of the output of a system that is used to evaluate the performance of the system.

fellow subsidiaries
subsidiary companies of the same holding company are known as fellow subsidiaries. Amounts due to and from fellow subsidiaries are normally shown as a separate item in the annual accounts.

fiat standard
a principal class of monetary standard. It is a monetary system in which the value or purchasing power of the

monetary unit is not kept equal to the value of a specific quantity of a particular commodity or of a group of commodities.

fiduciary

a person in a position of trust and confidence, as a broker with respect to a principal. The broker as a fiduciary owes a loyalty that cannot be breached under the rules of agency.

fiduciary issue

that part of the note issue of the Bank of England that is backed not by government and other securities. The total is controlled by Parliament. Any profits on sale of these securities go to the government, being paid into the Exchange Equalisation Fund.

fiduciary issues of notes

one of the different systems of note issue. In this system, the central bank can issue notes without gold backing (unpacked by gold) up to a limit and the limit is known as fiduciary limit.

field warehouse

a section of the premises of a firm on which it stores its products which is cordoned off and put under the control of a warehouse company. In effect the warehouse is brought to the goods rather than the goods to the warehouse.

film loop

an 8 mm movie film, not more than 50 feet long, of which the ends are joined. Film loops are shown continuously on specialized projecting equipment, showing the same piece of action again and again, for example, in training or as part of an exhibition.

final dividend

refers to the final payment of dividend paid by a company in respect of its profits for a financial year.

finance

the management of public revenues; the conduct or transaction of matters generally and particularly those affecting the public as in the field of banking and investment. Finances refer to the pecuniary resources as a government, company, company organization or of the individual; to supply with capital or obtain or furnish credit for; the provision of money at the time it is wanted.

financial circulation

deposits used for the purposes of finance.

financial document

an instrument used for obtaining payment of money. For example, a bill of exchange, a cheque, or a promissory note.

financial report

fortnightly confidential newsletter containing comment and analysis on world-wide financial matters.

financial risk

in the securities market, the uncertainty of future returns from a security because of changes in the financial capacity of the organization that issued the security. Some times called business risk.

financier

a fairly meaningless term for those earning their living by financing other people's business. They take the place of what were know as usurers.

finder

a person, acting as an individual or as an enterprise, who brings together a buyer and a seller and earns a fee for the service.

fineshed goods

the goods that a manufacturer has in stock for ready sale. Also the value of a stock of such goods.

fire legal liability

an insurnce policy written to cover possible legal liability to others as a result of a fire that develops through the negligence of insured.

firm

strictly the name given to a partnership business though often used more generally. In Scotland a 'partnership firm' is a separate legal person, though it does not have all the attributes of a corporate body. In England a partnership firm cannot contract in its own name.

firm, theory of the

the theory relating to the ways in which prices are determined and resources allocated among different uses in respect of the products of an individual firm.

first-class mail insurance

this type of coverage is for stock certificates, bonds, coupons, stamps, money orders, and other securities of institutions such as banks, trust companies, insurance companies, stock clearing corporations, and general corporations.

first in system served

a rule used in decision-making for production scheduling that is based on the due dates for orders waiting in line. The order that has the earliest planned date will be assigned first.

fiscal

the world, fiscal, adjective of fisc, is generally used to refer to all matters pertaining to the public treasury, is revenues, and its expenditure.

fiscal monopoly

a government monopoly created to gene-rate revenue. Commodities such as salt and tobacco, for example are sometimes reserved for sale by the government, and their profits are used for public purposes.

fiscal year

from 1st April to 31st March of any year such as 1987-88; it is different from agricultural year as well as from calendar year.

fixed asset

an asset of an firm that is not a current asset and is intended to be used by the firm for some time (usually, longer than a year or longer than one operating cycle). Fixed assets are often described as 'property, plant and equipment' as these are the main types of fixed asset.

fixed budget

budget which is based on a forecast of ideal or normal capacity. It does not take account of possible variations in the level of activity as would a flexible budget.

fixed charge

a term used to describe a mortgage of distinct assets against which a loan is made. The charge applies to assets specifically identified and is distinguished from a floating charge. These terms usually arise in connection with an issue by a company of debentures, which may be described as fixed or floating debentures. Occasionally the term fixed charges in also used as a synonym for the fixed cost.

A recurring liability that a firm has (e.g., to pay rent or loan interest) the size of which does not depend on the scale of operations of the firm. Also known as a 'fixed expense'. A charge on a specific and identifiable item of property.

fixed cost

an operating expense that does not vary with the volume or activity of business or of production. Also known as fixed expense, or constant cost.

fixed expenses

those that remain constant regardless of the level of business activity. Expenses that vary with output or activity are variable expenses.

fixtures, fitting etc.

an accounting term for immovable assets affixed to a building in some way though not strictly part of that building itself.

flat tax

a single uniform tax rate applicable to all income, replacing graduated tax rates.

flat yield

the true rate of interest on a fixed interest security, found by relating actual income to present purchase price, without taking into account any benefit or otherwise that might arise from the proxsimity of redemption date.

float

in finance, money usually in the form of cheques, en route to the payee but not yet credited to the payee's account. The payer of the cheque may have, in the process of effecting payment, deposited the cheque with a corresponding bank.

floater policy

a type of insurance policy or contract covering property that floats" or moves about from place to place, or goods or a class in which the particular items change or shift in quantity over relatively short time periods.

floating address

in data processing, an address

written in such a way that it can be easily converted to a machine address by indexing, assembly, or some other means.

floating currency
a currency is said to float when it is allowed to find its own level in relation to other world currencies.

floating debt
a debt consisting of short-term obligation. The term is used in contradistinction to long term or funded debts.

flood insurance
such insurance is generally difficult to obtain in areas subject to flooding because of the frequency or catastrophic losses. A federal flood insurance program has been authorized to make such protection available at reasonable rates.

floor
popular term for the trading area, about two-thirds the size of a football, where stock and bonds are bought and sold on the New York Stock Exchange. Also used in reference to the trading area of any exchange.

flotsam
goods or parts of a shipwrecked vessel found floating on the surface of the sea. If not claimed within a year and a day they belong to the Crown.

flow diagram
a diagram or model, to scale, showing the location of specific activities carried out in a work-place and either the routes followed by workers or the routes along which materials or requirement are moved.

flyback timing
a method of timing of job using a stopwatch in time study in which the hands of the stopwatch are returned to zero at the end of each element of the job.

for
trade terms under which the seller is responsible for delivering the goods to a railway.

forbearance
the act of giving up the right to enforce a valid debt, right, or obligation. The act of forbearance is treated; as sufficient consideration to make a new promise given by the debtor legally binding.

forced-sale value
the amount derived from a sale of assets or goods on an urgent basis usually where the seller is under legal or economic compulsion to sell.

foreign corporation
in state corporation laws, a corporation that has been created under the laws of a state or country other than the one in which the corporation is officially located. In federal law, a corporation established under the laws of another country.

foreign exchange market
a market in which foreign exchange can be bought and sold. Such a market consists of foreign exchange dealers

and brokers who are in touch with each other and with other similar markets elsewhere in the world.

foreign investment

the acquisition by the government or the inhabitants of a country of assets abroad.

foreign judgments

where a judgment is made in a foreign court and the judgment creditor wants to enforce it in this country, he must appeal to the High Court within six years to have the judgment registered. If registered, it is equal to a judgment in this country. If it is to be registered, it must be final and conclusive and must not involve payment of taxes, fines, penalties, etc.

foreman

a foreman in an industrial house is a supervisor who undertakes to supervise the work of the skilled and unskilled labour. Foremen supervise the procurement of needed materials and tools for their workmen,plan and assign work to each man, train the new workers, check the quality of products produced by the workers, see that the machines and equipment are kept in smooth functioning, maintain discipline, look into the grievances of the workers and represent the management to the workers and vice-versa. A foreman may also be a fist-line supervisor responsible for planning and supervising the work (usual manual work) of others but may not usually perform work himself.

forex

this is an abbreviation for the International Foreign Exchange Market. This is the largest market of any kind in the world and is believed to have a daily volume estimated of around $2000,000 million. The market does not have a physical location as such is made up of the banks and foreign exchange brokers dealing in currencies throughout the 24 hours of each day.

forfeitures

funds relinquished by a terminating employee in qualified profitsharing or thrift plan. These funds are sometimes used by the company to reduce future company contribution to the plan, or they may be allocated to current' participants to increase their shares.

formal authority in a company

the formal authority is the delegation of authority upwards from any managerial position, from various subordinate managers upto the president of the company, who in turn derives his authority from the shareholders of the company. According to the authority theory the ultimate source of authority lies in the institution of property.

The theory views the concept of authority as being power-transmitted from basic social institutions, the individual managers. It may also be considered as hierarchical, originating from the top in the institution of property and being delegated through owners to their representatives called the managers and through them to their subordinates.

forward buying

buying at a current price for future delivery, based on the anticipation that prices will rise.

forward dating

the practice of dating commerical documents in advance. Invoices may be dated forward, perhaps to give the customer additional time to pay, or where devilry has been delayed. Cheques may be forward dated where the drawer has no present funds but expects to be able to meet the cheque at the date specified. The bank will not cash the cheques before that date.

forward exchange

foreign currency bought or sold for future delivery is known as forward exchange and its price, called the forward rate, is expressed as being at a premium (or discount) to the spot rate.

forward integration

where the manufacturer or main supplier of a product or service acquires or takes over certain customer or retail outlets in an endeavour to secure a further part of the market for the product or service. The opposite process, usually intended to give control over materials, supplies is backward integration.

forward price

the price at which someone is willing to buy or sell something for delivery at some specified future time or date.

forward rate

an exchange rate at which someone promises to buy or sell foreign currency at some date in the future.

founders' stock

stock in a new venture issued to the founders and, in some cases, to key executive. Typically, the stock of this category is priced below the amounts paid by other investors.

franchise

a clause in a marine insurance policy which disallows claims of less than a cetrtain amount unless the insured ship is standed or sunk. If the damage is over the minimum, all is recoverable, if less, then none is recoverable unless the ship is stranded or sunk. The purpose of this clause is to prevent petty claims, and also to restrict liability on perhaps risky cargo.

franchise deductible

a clause found most frequently in ocean marine insurance policies for property and liability coverage. It provides that if losses are less than a specified amount as a percentage of the value of "the property, nothing will be paid. If the loss exceeds the percentage, the insurance company pays the full amount of the loss.

franchise tax

a tax on the right of a corporation to do business under its corporate name.

fraud and foregery

fraud under the Indian Companies Act means acts committed by a party to a contract or with his connivance, or by his agent, with intent to deceive another party thereto or his agent, or to induce him to enter into the contract.

fraudulent conveyance

an act of bankruptcy. The debtor deliberately signs away part of his property with an intent to defeat creditors.

fraudulent preference

a payment made, by a person who is incapable of paying his debts as they fall due, to one of this creditors with the intention of preferring that creditor to others.

free banking

the principle that any group could establish a bank under a general incorporation law by meeting prescribed requirements.

free from particulars average

a marine insurance term meaning that the insurers are not responsible for anything other than total loss and general average loss. The clause may be qualified in various ways, i.e., the insurer may take responsibility for certain specified items of cargo.

freehold

a poverty, without any encumbrances except to the state. There may, however, be such encumbrances as Easements, etc. The term 'Freehold land and buildings' is more commonly used in accounts to denote freehold land owned by the business, and buildings on it. If anyone has the freehold to land he has the best title of becoming its absolute owner. This term is related with property e.g., land, building, etc.

freehold estate

an interest in real estate that continues forever, or for the lives of more than one individual. An estate-less-than-freehold is one that lasts for a certain or uncertain number of years; for example, a commerical lease is an estate that continues for a fixed term, which a tenancy at will is an estate that continues at the will of either the landlord or the tenant.

freehold property

it is a property which is free of any lien or any other condition or cess for its holding by the owner.

free negotiable credit

a negotiation credit under

which the beneficiary may get any banks of his choice to negotiate his bills.

free on board (f. o. b.)

when an exporter delivers goods 'free on board,' he pays all charges involved in getting them actually onto the ship. His responsibilities include putting the goods in a condition for shipping taking them to the ship and loading them (free on board and trimmed). The buyer must provide the ship, and the seller's responsibility ends when the goods are on board. The seller must notify the buyer to enable him to insure the goods; otherwise he may himself be liable for damage at sea. Property in the goods normally passes with risk, though the buyer may reserve the right to reject goods if he has had no previous opportunity to examine them and they are not up to specification or quality when he receives them.

freeboard

the distance between the main deck and the waterline of a ship.

free port

a restricted area at a seaport for the handling of duty-exempted import goods. Also known as foreign trade zone.

free trade area

an area consisting of several independent countries in which no costumes duties are imposed on goods going from one of those countries to another.

freezing

in the commerical world, freezing denotes creation of blockade in order to prevent a person or an enterprise to use the owner's fund, assets. etc. This term is also used in connection with accounts, wages, salary, dearness allowance, etc.

freight consolidator

an independent contractor who receives many small shipments for the account of one industrial company and combines them into one carlord or trucload.

freight liner

a door-to-door container service offered by British Rail. The emphasis is on speed and efficiency. Loaded containers are taken by road to a freight liner terminal then transported speedily to anther terminal. Space can be reserved in advance. The containers are delivered by road from the terminal. The containers (of a fixed size) are owned by the railway but packed by the user at his own premises. They conform with international standards. There are freight liner lines between most major industrial centres. The containers are loaded onto British Railways vehicles free, but there is a charge for any delay over a stated limit, e.g. fifteen minutes per capacity ton. Containers must be returned within a specified time after use.

freight-out

freight charges paid or allowed by the seller on goods or materials shipped out.

freight prepaid

this expression means the seller will pay transportation charges to the carrier and the buyer will remit the full amount of the invoice without deduction for freight charges.

frozen assets

assets tied up to that transactions in them are restricted or impossible. Where a company has floating debentures and they become repayable, the assets of the company are frozen from the point of view of the debenture holders.

full-bodied money

full valued or natural money. When the value printed on them (coins) (or their face value) is equal to the value of the metal contained in them (or their intrinsic value), they are called full-bodied coins.

functional authority

functional authority permits a number of specialists to exercise authority within their area or competence. It is the right and power given to a specialist or a department to issue orders to instructions to other departments. It is binding on the line authority. But it does not carry the right to discipline for noncompliance. Functional authority is pursued for the sake of convenience and efficiency.

functional finance

the doctrine in commerce that the government should pursue whatever fiscal measures are necessary to achieve noinflationary full employment and economic growth without regard to budget balancing.

functional income distribution

the allocation of the national income to the owners of the economic resources-land, labour, and capital-that contributed to its production. Also known as factorial income distribution.

functional organisation

in order to avoid the difficulties faced in the case of line organisation, Talyor, the pioneer of scientific management, suggested a new organisational structure known as Functional Organisation at the shop level. He aimed at providing specialisation in management since the he was not able to find all the qualities of a good manager in any one person. He suggested for the division of responsibility among different people who were specially qualified for their special duties. Thus, instead of the employment of several general purpose foremen, he recommended the employment of specialists to perform various functions. Taylor put all supervision in the hands of the functional specialists.

fundamental accounting concepts

broad basic assumptions underlying the financial accounts of business enterprises, notably the accruals concept, the consistency concept, the going concern concept and the concept of prudence in accounting.

fundamental terms

under the law of contract, these are terms in a contract which are so fundamental that breach of them would be considered to be complete non-performance, as opposed to breach of conditions of warranties. The distinction is important, for exemption causes that apply to conditions or warranties do not apply to fundamental terms.

funded debt

that part of the national debt which the government is not obliged to repay at any particular time, e.g., consols. A debt that does have to be repaid, especially one represented by an irredeemable security.

funded reserve

any of several types of reserves for pensions, bonuses, the retirement of preferred stock, or any other prospective liability against which certain: assets have been accumulated, set aside, or earmarked.

funding bond

bonds that are issued for the purpose of retiring current, or long-term indetedness or to finance current expenditures.

funding company

the name gives to a type of a financial company that offers investors a package of mutual fund shares and life insurance.

fund surplus

the excess of the amount accumulated in a specific fund over its obligations.

fur auctions

these take place at beaver house, which is also the head office of the Hudson Bay Company. Sales of individual furs are held throughout the year, and more general sales about four times a year. Buyers inspect the furs at the borkers"s warehouse (anyone may attend the sales). By tradition the wares of the Hudson Bay Company are sold first. Setting day, or prompt day, is usually thirty days after the first day of the sale. Brokers may refuse bids from undersirable buyers.

futures

the items for contracts to buy and sell commodities, usually traded on a commodities exchange.

futures, dealing in

buying and selling by middlemen of options to purchase shares, stocks, goods, to sell them. This helps to put forward buyers in touch with forward sellers (the dealer, of course, takes a commission).

futures market
an organized market for buying and selling futures contracts.

future tax
a term used in accounts with reference to tax calculated on the profits of the accounting year but not payable until some distant date and then only if the business was still in existence.

gain-sharing
operation of a premium bonus scheme in which the incentive payment per unit of time saved decreases as the time save increases.

gambling
indicates playing game for money or a prize. Specifically, this is an agreement whereby one party pays a sum if an event occurs on consideration of the other party paying a fixed sum if it does not. The subject matter of the agreement is nothing but a sum of money. And neither party has any personal interest in the event or stand to lose anything other than the money.

gaming contract
a contract involving the playing of a game of chance by any number of people for money. A wagering contract involves only two people. In general, both gaming contracts and wagering contracts are by statute null and void and no action can be brought to recover money paid or won under them.

garnishee
a person upon whom a garnishment is served. He is the debtor or a defendant and has money or property that the plaintiff is trying to reach in order to satisfy a debt from the defendant.

garshee order
a legal order made on a person owing money to a judgement debtor intructing him not to pay the debt until the debtor has made goods the claims agaisnt him. It effectively (though not legally) gives the judgement creditor a lien on debts owed to the judgement debtor.

garnishment
a legal proceeding by which a plaintiff seeks to reach the money or property of the defendant that is in the hands of a third party.

geared investment trust
in investment trust that borrows money, usually to increase investment in equities. The shares of a genered investment trust tend to rise faster in rising markets and fall faster in falling markets than ungeared trusts.

gearing effect
the way in which the capital gearing of a company affects its shareholders' dividends.

gearing of capital
after the ascertainment of the total needs of the industry, planning of capital structure involves the selection of the different modes of raising the total amount. Determination of

some proper ratio between any two or more methods of raising the total amount. Determination of some proper ratio between any two or more methods of raising capital is called gearing of capital. Capital may be high or low geared according to the small or higher proportions respectively of equity capital in the total capital of the company. Gearing of capital plays a very importance role in determining the structure of capital.

gearing ratios

there is no hard and fast rule for the desirable level on gearing for commerical and industrial companies. It will vary from industry to industry, from company to company and from time to time.

general accountant

an accountant who is competent by education or experience, or both, to deal with any type of accounting situation in the organization.

general average loss

a term used in marine insurance. When there is a partial loss of ship or cargo incurred for the benefit of others than the owner of the ship or that particular cargo, the loss is approtioned over all persons involved. For instance, if there is a fire in a ship and in putting out the fire, cargo other that which caught fire is damaged, then the loss is apportioned between owners of all the cargo, the freight and the ship. In order that a loss may be a general average loss there must be an extraordinary sacrifice or expenditure, voluntarily made at a time of necessity for the purpose of preserving all the propriety involved in the venture. The danger must be common to all those called on to contribute; contributions will be assessed at the port of discharge; the shipwoners must collect contributions from the shippers, and it is then up to them to claim their insurance company.

general average sacrifice

a sacrifice made by the master of the ship for the benefit of the shipowner, characterer, and cargo-owners. The term is related with marine insurance.

general deposits

as opposed to special deposits, interest bearing general deposits consists of money of deposit currency in which the bank becomes the owner of the deposit. Should the bank fail, the general depositor becomes a general creditor.

general meeting

a meeting which may be attended by all the members of an association and which gives them some opportunity to control the association's affairs.

generic term

in marketing, applied to brand name which have come to be adopted as the general descriptive term for a product, often as the result of extensive promotion, Hoover, Biro, Linoleum.

general merchanside warehouse

this operation stores and ships a great variety of merchandise rather than specializing in one tupe, provided that controlled environmental conditions are not required.

general partner

an active member of a partnership who has unlimited liability for the actions of the partners. An enterprise formed as a partnership with or more partners is required by law to have at least one general partner for liability purposes.

general store

a type of retailing institutions that usually sells in limited selection of a wide range of goods. The general store is distinguished from the, department store in that its limited selections of goods in each line are not departmentalized.

In real estate, a covenant in a deed whereby the grantor agrees to protect the grantee against any claimant.

genetic industry

an industry engaged directly in increasing the supply of some form of plant of animal. Life. Farming and cattle raising are examples.

giffen effect

the income effect can be negative. But again, the substitution effect is positive and outweights a negative effect, so that in price sill causes the customer to buy more.

gift

a voluntary transfer of property by one person to another, no consideration being given. Promises to given freely in this way are only enforceable if they are made by deed. When a gift is of some property other than money, it is subject to capital gains tax (payable by the donor) which is levied as if the property had been sold at the date of a transfer for its proper market value.

gift cheques

decorative cheques made available by certain banks for rise on festive occasion. The main beneficiary of such a cheque is the issuing bank which normally charges high to the account of the donor.

gilt bond

loose terminology for a single-premium life assurance policy invested in government stocks.

gilt-edged bond

a high-grade bond issued by a company that has demonstrated its ability to earn profits over a period of years and pay its bondholders their interest without interruption.

give-up

the splitting a stockbrokers commission with participating brokers following a large trade; now forbidden by the stock exchanges.

glut

to choke up; to flood the market with a certain article or commodity so that the supply greatly exceeds the demand; the supply of commodity being greatly in excess of the previous demand, there is in consequence a considerable fall in price.

goal

a desired result of activity by an individual or an organization. The end result of a plan. A state which an individual, consciously or unconscious by, strives to achieve.

going value

an owner's equity in a business enterprise, is established by accounting records and reports; equivalent to net worth.

gold certificate

in the Unites States form of paper money in circulation from 1885 to 1933. The certificate represented gold bullion that fully secured the certificate. From 1933 to 1955 gold certificates were issued, in a revised form, only to Federal Reserve Banks for reserve purposes. Since 1955. the reserves have been indicated only by bookeeping entries in a record known as the interdistrict Settlement Fund.

gold coins

the law insisted that all gold coins or bullion should be submitted to an authorized dealer. They may be sold through a jeweller. Collectors may retain coins which were minted before 1816, or have a greater numismatic value than their gold content.

gold flow

also, gold movements. The movement of gold into and out of a country, which directly affects its gold reserve and therefore its money supply.

gold points

limits of fluctuations of currencies under the gold standard and gold bullion standard, determined by the cost of gold imports and exports.

gold standard

a country on the gold standard agrees, by definition, to convert its currency freely into gold through its central bank. It implies a system of controlling the foreign-exchange market by specifying an amount of gold for which a country's central bank will always exchange a unit of its currency if requred. The amount of gold is called the 'gold content' of the currency.

gold sterilization

a monetary policy that prevents the accumulation of a Country's Gold Reserves from expanding the amount of money in circulation within the country.

good

a single element of wealth; a commodity an item of

merchandise, raw material, or finished goods.

good delivery

on the stock exchange a security is not 'god delivery if it is affected with some irregularity such as absence of coupous, or necessary stamps; or in the case of a bearer, security, if holder has written his name on it. A certificate is accepted as a 'good delivery'.

goodwill

the likelihood that customers will return to the same supplier. Also an estimate of the value of goodwill of the supplier. The standing of an enterprise as successful business house.

goods

the definition of 'good' is important because of the obligations imposed and the protection offered by, the Law. Goods are generally personal chattels, emblements, industrial growing crops, and ships, but not choses-in-action or money. Contracts for the sale of goods should be distinguished from contracts for work and materials, which are not governed by the Sale of Goods Act. (The test is, whether the payment was made for the work done rather than for the materials supplied. A contract for work done where the materials are incidental, e.g. the painting of pictures, will be a contract for work and materials.)

goods on consignment

an arrangement whereby an agent takes possession of goods but no title to them. The agent will normally be working for a commission on their sale and the goods are returnable in the absence of a buyer being found for them.

go-public

to become listed company on a stock exchange for the first time—usually by making a public offer securities.

go-slow tactics

also called "working to rule". It is an alternative to the strike, in which the labourers work more slowly than usual.

government bond

a financial obligation of a government. In the United States, U.S. government bonds are regarded as the highest-grade issues in existence.

government borrowing

it often stands for an excess of Government spending over tax-collection combined with borrowing from the public equal to this difference.

government securities

fixed interest securities issued by the government. They may be in the nature of bonds or other types of security and may or may not be redeemable. They may be issued to banks and other institutions in the money market or to the general public through banks or the post officer. The treasury bill is a specific type of government security which is issued only within money market, and particular to discount houses which tender for these bills each week. The rate of discount at which they are allotted is a pointer to the general health of the economy and can influence the current minimum lending rate.

graduated lease

a lease of property that provides for a variable rental rate, often based on future determination such as a periodic appraisal. A feature primarily of long-term leases.

grant

a bestowal of a right by authority as in the 'grant of a patent'. Also the right that is bestowed. An allocation of money from a fund. Also the amount that is allocated. Conveyance of property by means of a deed.

grant, bargain, and sell

in real estate, a phrase sometimes used in a deed to pass title, meaning the grantor promises that he or she has good title to transfer, from encumbrances, and warrants it to be such.

gratuitous coinage

in a system of free coinage if no fee is charged by the government for the working of mintage, the coinage is called gratutious.

graving dock

a dry dock where ships are taken for repairs and maintenance, particular by to the exterior of the ship below the waterline.

green money

special exchange rates used under EEC's common agricultural policy (CAP) to convert common farm prices into national currencies so that movement in currencies are not reflected in national farm prices.

green revolution

a term descriptive of the development of high-yielding varieties of seed grains, which has had a dramatic impact on the agricultural output of developing nations.

gross annual value

the rent that could be obtained for a year for a piece of land if it were let, on the open market, with the conditions that the landlord would pay for all repairs and the tenant would pay all rates.

gross cash flow

the sum of net profit (after tax has been paid) and the amount of expense determined as depreciation of a firm over a period. (Sometimes also known as cash flow').

gross income

the amount of revenue received by a firm over a period.

gross loss

the excess of the cost of goods or services sold over the amount of sales; opposite of Gross Profit. Also known as loss.

gross national disproduct

the sum of the social costs or reductions in benefits to society that result from producing the gross national product.

gross operating spread
in retail accounting, gross mercha-ndise margin minus the cost of merchandise procurement.

gross profit
a vague term. Where the buying or selling of goods is concerned, it is used for the proceeds of sales, less the cost of putting the goods into a condition for sale. Where the goods are also manufactured, this cost will include part of the overhead expenses. Otherwise, overheads concerned with distributing or selling the goods and administering the business generally are charged after gross profit (also known as 'gross profit on trading') to produce net profit on trading. This will then be adjusted for exceptional items or items not connected with the major objects of the business, to produce the actual net profit.

gross requirement
in production procedures, the total requirements for a part assembly; quantity on hand is not considered.

gross working capital
the total value of the currency assets of a firm.

ground rents
rent paid for land as opposed to rent paid for the buildings on the land. Rights to receive ground rents can be bought and sold. At one time prior to 1964, tax was deducted by the payer, and the payment was treated as an annual charge. Payment is now made gross, i.e. not tax-deducted.

group account
a British accounting term for a consolidated statement. Group dynamics. The study of the behaviour of group and of the interacting behaviour of individuals as members of the group.

group dynamics
area of study concerned with the nature of people, their patterns of development and their relationships with individuals and other groups.

guaranteed annuity option
or annuity option rate. A provision in an endowment assurance scheme guarateeing a minimum rate at which the endowment sum assured may be covered into an annuity on retirement.

guaranted bond
a bond issued by one company to another company (e.g., the parent company) guaranteeing that interest will be paid on the capital borrowed from the parent company.

guaranteed security
a bond (or stock) whose interest or principal (or dividend) is backed by some company other than the issuing one.

guarantor
a person who promises that if a second person fails to fulfil some obligation then he will

fulfil it instead or pay money (up to a specified limit) to compensate for any loss caused by the second person's failure.

guaranty

the undertaking of responsibility by one person for another's debt or obligation to perform some act or duty, or generally to assure that a thing will be done as promised.

guinea

originally a U.K. gold coin from gold mined in Guinea in Africa, but nowadays simply the sum of 21s. Professional fees are often quoted in guineas, but will probably cease to be after the introduction of the decimal system.

gunsmith

a maker or repairer of firearms, particularly the small ones.

haggling

colloquial expression for the prices of bargaining or negotiating the price of a sale or purchase.

half commission man

a Stock Exchange term denoting a person who is neither a stockbroker nor a stock-jobber. In return for a share in the commission, he introduces clients to a broker.

hall mark

a mark made on precious metals after an assay test. At present there are two qualities of silver and four of gold. The British hall-mark is accepted internationally as a guarantee of standard. There are four marks: the maker's mark, the hall or assay-office mark, the quality mark, and the date letter. The hall or assay-office mark may be made at London (leopard), Chester (the arms of the city), Birmingham (anchor), sheffield (crown), Edinburgh (caste), Glasgow (fish, tree, bell and bird) and Dubin (Irish harp with crown).

Gold must also have the carat mark on it to indicate its quality—there are four recognized carat marks at present, 22 carat (i.e. 22 parts gold,. 2 parts alloy), 18 carat, 14 carat and 9 carat. In Dublin there is an additional 12 carat. The date is indicated by a letter, each year having a separate letter, the letters being changed on different dates at different centres. Quality marks for silver are a lion passant for England and a thistle or a lion rampant for Scotland. All objects made of gold or silver must be stamped, but there are exceptions, which are briefly; (1) chains, e.g. watch chains, alberts, dress chains, key chains, but not chain bracelets, etc. (articles attached to the chains are not necessarily excepted), (2) lockets, (3) the actual settings of precious stones, (4) imported articles over one hundred years old, (5- gold only) jointed sleeper ear-rings, rings other than wedding, rings, thimbles, percial cases, or items richly engraved or set with stones that might be damaged by marketing, and items too small to be marked (weighing less than 10 dwts), (6-silver only) items too small to be marked, stamped medals, and certain items weighing a very small amount.

hallmarks
the impressed stamps on gold, silver and platinum under the authority of the Goldmiths Company and the various assay offices.

hammering
public announcement at the Stock Exchange that a member cannot pay his debts. In the past attention was drawn to the announcements by an attendant striking a rostrum three times with a mallet.

hard-core unemplopyed
people who are unemployed because they lack the education or skills required by a complex economy. Discrimination may be a contributing factor. The ranks of the hard-core unemployed consist mainly of members of certain minority groups such as blacks and Mexicans, person who are too young" or " too old", highschool droupts, and those who are permanently displaced because of technological change.

hardware
physical apparatus used for some purpose (especially computers) as opposed to 'software' i.e., the instructions for using the apparatus.

harvest theory
another name for climatic or agricultural or sunspot theory of business cycles.

haulage
the charge made for carrying goods, though not usually for loading or unloading them.

hazard
the various factors or the primary factor contributing to uncertainty in a given insurance situation. The risk of loss to any particular person or company may be calculated as the total of all hazards presents. A hazard may be anything that may conceivably bring about a loss, whereas the word peril is used to denote the factor that actually caused the loss.

head-end business
the transportation of property such as mail, baggage, and express in the cars immediately behind the locomotive of a passenger train.

heavy market
also, active market, broad market. In the securities and commodities trade, a market in which there is very active trading, with many shares changing hands.

hedge
to protect against financial loss; especially to make a transaction in a futures market for a commodity or for foreign currency which reduces the risk of loss from a commitment one already made in connecection with that

commodity.

hedging

a method by which wholesale dealers in basic raw materials and food-stuffs or manufacturers of certain products can transfer risks of adverse price fluctuations to professional speculators in the commodity exchange.

hidden reserve

the amount of the understanding of net worth that may result from a variety of accounting practices, for example, classifying additions to fixed and other assets as expense. Disclosure of hidden reserves is required for any substantial amounts that may be so classified. Also known as secret reserve.

hidden tax

an indirect tax is termed as hidden tax since it is merged in the price of the commodity, without being shown explicitly.

hierarchy

an arrangement of the positions in an organisation into ranks so that the holder of a position in one rank is responsible to the holder of a position in the next higher rank for the performance of his job.

high-profile strategy

the launching of a new product with high price high promotion expenditure, thus assuming that high price will repay high promotion cost because market, whether aware of product or not, is willing to pay high price.

higher purchase finance

this is a particular aspects of instalment credit. It is the provision of finance to be repaid by instalment over a period in accordance with a contractual arrangement.

high purchase

the equivalent of instalment buying. The buyer pays an initial deposit, takes possession of the goods or receives the benefits of the services, and then makes regular payments that cover the remainder of the purchase price plus interest or carrying charges. The buyer does not take title to be goods until the last periodic payment or instalment is paid in full.

hire purchase finance

retailers selling goods on hire purchase or on credit, may need cash more quickly than they receive it. They may therefore employ a hire purchase company, which will make agreements directly with the retailer's customers, who will make their payments, including interest, direct to the hire purchase company. The interest is usually about 10 per cent per annum and the period of repayment depends on government policy. The hire purchase company may require the retailer to guarantee the debt or repurchase the goods if the customer defaults. The hire purchase company will pay the retailer a proportion of the

hire purchase price when cash contract is signed.
Alternatively, the retailer may sign hire purchase agreements with his customers and sell these agreements to a hire purchase company, which will immediately pay, say, 75 per cent of the hire purchase price, which the retailer will repay over the period of hire. The retailer collects the instalments on behalf of the hire purchase company. The charges for this type of block discounting vary according to the risk, and may be between 5 and 7 per cent.

historical cost
the original cost of an asset as opposed to its saleable value, replacement value, or value in present or alternative use.

historical cost accounting
a method of accounting (supported by most professional organizations) whereby assets are maintained at their original cost in the books of the company or other organization and depreciation charged accordingly. The could mean that insufficient profit is set aside for replacement of the assets in a time of rising prices.

holder in due course
this concerns bills of exchange, including cheques. A holder in due course is a person who has taken a bill, complete and regular on the face of it, not overdue and without notice of any previous dishonour. He must have taken it in good faith for value and without notice of any defect in the title of the person from whom he took it.
The holder of a bill is presumed to be a holder in due course, unless the opposite is proved. If, however, fraud is proved at any stage he must (to be recognized as holder in due course) prove that value was given after that time. The advantage of being a holder in due course is that one has the best possible title, and can claim from all parties who have signed the bill.

holding company
a form of business organization which is created for the purpose of combining industrial units by owing a controlling amount of their share capital.

holding out
pretending that a partner who has in fact left a partnership is still a members of it and obtaining credit on the strength of his name. An ex-partner who is "held out" in this way is liable for debts thus incurred : hence the practice of widely advertising the departure of a partner.

hold order
in manufacturing, a written order directing that certain operations or work activities be interrupted or cancelled, pending a change in design or material.

home loan plans

in many countries this is the title normally applied to schemes which enable orler people to mortgage their house, with the benefit of tax relief, and purchase an annuity. In this way, capital would otherwise be locked up is turned into income during the lifetime of the owner.

home produced real income

total net national real income minus property income from overseas.

horizontal merger

a merger involving firms that produce closely related products and sell them in the same market. The usual objective is to round out a product line that is sold through the same distribution channels, thereby offering joint economies in sales and distribution.

horticulture improvement scheme

grants of up to one-third of some costs are available to horticural growing, landlords, and co-operatives. These are costs involved in growing, storage, preparation for market, and transport, of horticultural produce. Grants of less than Rs.10000 are not made.

hot holder in due course

a holder who has taken a bill complete and regular on the face of it before it was due, and without notice of dishonoured and in good faith and for value and without notice when the bill was negotiated to him of any defect in the title of the person who negotiated it.

hour-for-hour plan

payment-by results system in which pay is directly to the achievement of standards performance.

house bill

a bill drawn by a company or firm upon itself, as between different branches.

housekeeper allowance

in many countries this is an income tax allowance which a widower or window may claim in respect of any person, whether a relative or an employer, who lives in the home and acts as housekeeper. If, however, the housekeeper is a relative and is married, the allowance will not be available if the husband of the housekeeper is claiming the married man personal allowance.

housekeeping

in data processing, the setting up of constants and variables to be used in preparing a computer program.

human resource development

a term connected with one of the operative functions of personnel management. Human Resource Development is essentially a part of corporate manpower planning, aims at educating, training and retraining the employees of the enterprise.

hundi

indigenous bills of exchange are known as "hundi" which are mostly of 60 days duration.

hundred percent location
a retail business location considered optimum for attracting business.

hyper-inflation
the conditions when all the equilibrating effect of inflation is lost and the value of the monetary units sinks almost to zero.

hypermarket
an increasingly popular term for those very large supermarkets which offer a wide range of goods including consumer durables such as T.V.'s, Videos, furniture, refrigerators, etc. 'occasionally these large indoor market-places concentrate on a limited range of durables,. In this way they can offer customers an immense choice and, due to savings on rent, rates, bulkbuying, etc., afford to sell at concessional prices.

hypothecation
the pledging or property as collateral for a loan, the lender is not given title to the property but is given the right to sell it is case of default. Hyporthecation is widely used in buying securities on margin.

hypothecation, letter of
shippers may borrow from a bank, using the goods they are shipping as security. Until repayed, the banker has a lien on the goods , as they are listed in the bill of lading. The lien, which of course of course is not a possessory lien, is conveyed by a 'letter of hypothecation'.

icc
International Chamber of Commerce and Interstate Commerce Commission.

ICICI
the Industrial Credit and Investment Corporation of India Ltd.

idle capacity
in manufacturing, unused productive potential, in reference to machinery, operating, or a factory's facilities that are not in use or are used only partially. Idle capacity may be expressed in units of output capability that could be realized through full usage, or in hours available for use.

immediate holding company
a legal and accounting term for the company which actually holds the controlling interest in another company, even though the first company itself be controlled by yet another company.

impact day
the day on which the terms of a public offer of securities are first made generally known.

imperfect competitor
anyone who buys or sells a good in large enough quantities to be able to affect the price of that good.

implied contract
a contract that is inferred from actions of the parties who fulfil

promises without the existence of an expressed contract.

implied terms

terms which are not included in a contract, but which the law considers would have been included had the parties remembered or though it necessary to do so, which any reasonable man would have taken for granted. For instance, if a man builds a house for another, although the contract says nothing about it, it is taken for granted the house will be fit to live in. Terms may also be implied by custom or by statute. These terms may be excluded by an express clause to that effect in the contract.

import duty

a tax imposed on the imporation of goods into a country.

import licence

items of which restrictions are imposed against their importation could be had only when the government permitted party to do so. The permission for importing these items is granted under a licence. The import licensing serves many purposes besides conserving foreign exchange, it is also used to protect certain industries like the small scale units, and it could even accord priority treatment to different categories of importers such as established importers against New Units or Exports Units against domestic suppliers.

import licence is one of the five different types of direct import quotas, the other four being: (i) tarrif or customs quotas, (ii) unilateral import quotas, (iii) bilateral quotas, and (iv) mixing quotas.

import liencesing was introduced to overcome the difficulities in the administration of the global quota. It prevents the rush to import. It introduces equality of treatment for different importers.

import prohibitation

prohibiting by Law or allowing only under defined conditions the importation of certain commodities.

imposta complementare progressive seel reddito complessivo

complementary tax or progressive surtax charged on an individual's total income from all sources in Italy.

impound

in government accounting, to reduce authority to incur obligations by withholding all or any portion of a congressional appropriation. Also, any action by the Office of Management and Budget that has the effect of modifying the character of an agency's operations is an impounding action.

impulse goods

consumer goods that are normally bought by consumers without any previous planning.

inactive post
a trading post on the floor of the New Stock Exchange where in active securities are traded in units of ten shares instead of the usual 100-share lots. Known among professionals as post 30.

inactive stock
an issue traded in relatively low volumes on an exchange or in the over-the-counter. (OTC) market. Volumes may be no more than a few hundred shares a week and are sometimes even less. On the New York Stock Exchange many inactive stock share traded in 10-share units rather than the customary 100.

inchmaree clause
may be made part of hull insurance to protect the shipowner damage to the machinery of the vessel caused by breakdowns or accidents in loading, discharging, to handling cargo, bunkering, and entering dry docks.

inchote instrument
a term used with reference to bills of exchange. Where a blank signed piece of paper is given to another party to be made a bill of exchange, that other party may fill in all necessary details, but he must do so, within a reasonable time. Similarly, when a bill is in any way incomplete, the holder may make goods the omissions, and provided is done within a reasonable time the will be enforceable agaisnt prior signatories.

incident process
a method of training in which: the trainer gives trainees an account of a business situation (the 'incident') which describes a problem and calls for a decision although not enough information is given for a decision to be made.

income bond
generally, an income bond promises to repay principal as stipulated but to pay interest when earned.

income deposits
a man must hold a stock of money or a ready command over it in the form of a bank deposit, both to bridge the intervals of time between receipts and expenditure and to provide against contingencies. Deposits of this kind replenished by individuals out of their personal income and employed by them to meet their personal expenditure and their personal savings we shall call them income deposits.

income fund
a type of investment company whose main investment goal is to obtain liberal current income for shareholders of the fund.

income policy
a policy aimed at reducing inflation by limiting increases in wages and prices, and therefore the income of workers and producers.

income tax
direct taxation levied on

persons receiving an income above a minimum amount. The amount varies from country to country and is determined by the current level of personal relief. This rate is usually on a sliding scale with higher taxes on higher incomes. Income rather than earned income may also be subject to further taxation by way of an investment income surcharge or, when assets are sold, by way of capital gains tax.

income tax allowance: national insurance contributions

no allowance is now given for these contributions though it was prior to 6 April 1965. Employees can of course deduct from profits sums paid on account of employees.

income tax repayment of

if a person has over-paid tax he can claim repayment at any time within the following six years. Claim forms are available from the Inland Revenue. Persons who do not pay tax at the standard rate, may need to claim repayment when they receive dividends or interest from which tax has already been deducted at the standard rate (tax is deducted from nearly all interest and dividend payments).

income terms of trade

barter terms of trade multiplied by the quantity of exports. Income terms of trade is one of the different concepts of terms of trade, the other being: (i) gross barter terms of trade, (ii) net barter or commodity terms of trade, (iii) single factorial terms of trade, (iv) double factorial terms of trade; and (v) utility terms of trade.

to calculate the income terms of trade (P_x/P_m) we multiply the commodity terms of the trade with the index of the volume of exports (Q_x). The formula for income terms of trade is:

$$\frac{O_X P_X}{P_m} \times 100$$

inconvertible paper money

when a country's currency is not redeemable in either gold or silver, it is said to have an inconvertible paper money system, or a nominal currency.

inconvertible paper standard

a monetary system by which a nation's unit of currency cannot be converted into any metal or other precious substance in terms of which it may or may not be defined. Historically, this standard has existed on a domestic basis in all countries since the worldwide abandonment of the gold standard in the 1930s.

Increased net worth theory

profit accruing to business over given period of time is difference between net worth of business at beginning and close of period.

incremental payment system

giving pay increments arising

from increased merit, age or service in accordance with a predetermined scale.

indemnity

the legal protection or security whereby a person or an organization is obligated to make good a loss or damage another has suffered. The compensation for that loss or damage. Also, legal, exemption incurred by one's actions.

indenture

a form of deed, but different from a deed poll in having serrated rather than straight edges. These were originally two copies of an indenture. They were both written on the same parchment, which was afterwards torn in half. The impossibility of matching the tear was a guard against foregery.

index numbers

an index number may be a ratio or other number derived from a series of observations and used as an indicator or measure of a condition or a phenomenon. Index numbers are a composite made up of many part.

Indian Council of Trade Fairs and Exhibitions

government body responsible for organising trade fairs and exhibitions or promotes trading of industrial products of India. Address; Jhansi Castle. Cooperage road, Bombay-400 039.

Indian Journal of Industrial Relation's

quarterly publication of the Shri Ram Centre of Industrial Relations and Human Resources. Address: 4 Vaswani Marg, New Delhi-110035

Indian National Trade Union Congress

founded in May, 1947 it is one of the four central all-India trade union organisations. It "aims at establishing an order of society which is free from hindrances to an all-round development of its individual members; which fosters the growth of human personality in all its aspects".

It further aims at progressively eliminating social, political and economic exploitation of labourers and inequality and anti-social concentration of power in any form. It covers over 200 trade unions with approximately 2,250,000 members.

Indian Standards Institution

Central Government enterprise established in 1947 to determine and improve the qualitative standards of agricultural and industrial products, raw materials, machinery, spare parts, etc. This institution gives certificate to products which satisfy the qualitative standard fixed for the same. The institution also allows the producers to use ISI stamp on products approved and certificated. ISI-stamped product ensures quality and thus facilitates domestic and foreign trade.

indian stock exchanges
major fice stock exchange in India are (a) Ahmadabad Share and Stock Brokers' Association (b) Bombay Stock exchange; (c) Calcutta Stock exchange Association Ltd.; (d) Delhi Stock Exchange Association Ltd.; Madras Stock Exchange.

indirect cost
a cost of an expenditure on goods, services or labour used by, or benefitting, a number of activities, products or cost centres where the extent of the use for each individual purpose cannot easily be measured. Also a portion of such a cost that is associated with a particular activity, process or cost centre by means of overhead absorption. Also the total amount of such apportioned costs associated with a particular activity, product or cost centre.

indirect labour
workforce not engaged (like direct labour directly) in the manufacturing of a product or the provision of a service but doing work without which the product could not be produced or the service provided effectively.

indirect material cost
an indirect cost that relates to an expenditure by a firm on materials or supplies.

indirect taxes
taxes imposed on items which enter into consumption pattern of the individual; such taxes are paid if the assess makes use of those items. Examples of indirect taxes are commodity taxes, sales taxes, etc.

individual demand
an individual demand for any good is a schedule of the respective quantities of that good which is as ready to buy at all possible prices.

indorse
when a payee writes his name upon the back of a bill or cheque, he is called an 'indorser', and when the instrument is negotiated to other persons, each person may indorse it in turn and become an indorser. Each indorser of a bill (or cheque) is liable thereon.

Any indorser, however, may add after his signature such words as 'without recourse to me' or 'sans recours'.

induced investment
investment made in response to actual or anticipated increase in demand, either for a specific good or service or throughout the entire economy (owing to increased national income, large population, etc.). Induced investment usually consists of purchases of capital equipment to increase productive capacity. According to some economists, specific increase in income or output will generate specific increases in investment. Most economists, however, feel that

although a relationship undoubtedly exists it is not numerically fixed.

inducement to break a contract
generally speaking if a person induces another to break a contract, he is committing an actionable wrong. This does not appear to apply to trade unions. Nor is there anything to stop one person persuading another to end a contract in a lawful manner.

induction
a term frequently used in Personnel Management with particular reference to Recruitment and Hiring of personnel.

Industrial Artists and Designers, Society of
the was formed in 1930, and is the only professional association of designers in Great Britain. Its objects are to preserve standards of performance and professional conduct and integrity, and also to provide educational facilities and information regarding the profession. There is a code of professional conduct. Members may be Fellow (F.S.I.A.), Members (M.S.I.A.), Asscoaites (A.S.I.A.) or Licentiates (L.S.I.A.(, depending on merit and experience , but not on examinations. The society produces a monthly, the Designer and also the S.I.A.D. Year Book.

industrial broker
a natural or legal person who acts for another in a transaction and who specializes in industrial real estate.

industrial credit
the debts of manufacturers and other primary producers.

industrial goods
goods that are normally bought for incorporation in, or to aid the production of, other goods or services.

Industrial Development Bank of India
the industrial development bank of India is a specialised financial institution to provide long-term finance to industry. It is functioning with the object of providing direct loans, subscribing to shares and debentures to industrial ventures, underwriting of shares and bonds and guaranteeing of loans and deferred payments.

industrial estate
a planned industrial area, with factories organised to provide varied employment. Such an estate provides necessary zoning, land, shopping facilities, waste disposal outlets and other infrastructure facilities.

industrial insurance
insurance where premiums are collected on a house-to house basis. Payments are made, say, weekly and premiums tend to be higher to cover the cost of collection.

industrial relations

rules and regulations governing the relations between a labour union and management. They often deal with such matters as contract negotiation, the type of recognition accorded the union, the financial arrangement for collecting membership dues from employees, the methods of controlling the quantity and kind of union membership through apprenticeship requirements, licensing provision, initiation fees, seniority rules, and the handling of grievances.

industrial union
a labour union that admits to memberships people who work within an industry, irrespective of their occupation or craft.

industry
the activities of processing or manufacturing goods on a large scale using extensive plant and equipment. A class of firms that are sufficiently similar in their main activities or products to be grouped together for purpose of description, analysis or classification.

inflation
although this is a term in Economics, in modem trade and commerce the term is frequently used. Popularly, inflation refers to a rise in price level or, which is the same thing, fall in the value of money.

inflation accounting
financial accounting procedures that take cognizance of the likely effect of inflation on costs, revenues and profits, normally within an accounting period.

inherent vice
in insurance, this refers to a characteristic of an article that makes it tend to destroy itself. An improperly constructed machine or a precious stone with imperfections that could cause it to break apart under normal handing is said to have an inherent vice; it would therefore not be covered by insurance.

inhertance tax
tax imposed on the right of heirs to receive descendant's property; tax levied on what is received by the individual heirs to an estate.

injunction
a court may order someone to perform or not perform some action. This order is called an 'injunction' in England, and an 'indirect' in Scotland. Injunctions are often issued to prevent someone from continuing to act in a certain capacity, or in a manner harmful to someone else.

in kind, payment
strictly speaking, an exchange of equivalent good such as buying merchandise in exchange for other, comparable items.

inland bill
a bill of exchange drawn and made payable within a country

or drawn upon a resident within the territory.

inland waterways,

a system of canals, river and lochs used both for commerce and pleasure. Inland waterway transport is governed by the British Waterways Board Mulbury House, Mulberry Terrace, London NWI. The Board provides .(1) storage accommodation and up-to-date handling equipment, (2) road transport from depots and trans-shipment points, (3) a container service, and (4) three independent docks equipped as trans-shipment points between oceangoing vessels and inland transport. There are : Weston Point Docks (on the south bank of the Mersey; cargo capacity 1,600 tons), Sharpness Docks (on the east bank of the Severn; 5,000 tons) and Glucester Docks (750 tons).

Inland waterway traffic consists largely of raw materials in specialized vessels (e.g. bulk liquid in tankers, or coal in compartment craft). Trains of barges may be towed by one motorized vessel. Canal transport may be slow, but the routes are usually more direct. For instance, on the Caledonian Canal, the speed limit is 6 m.p.h. on the canals (about twenty miles) though there is no limit on the lochs which make up the remaining forty miles; by using the canal, ships are saved the long and perhaps difficult voyage round the north coast of Scotland. Locks are the canals' main drawback.

innovation

introduction, of new thoughts, policies, products, market distribution, mechandising or other deliberate change.

in-service training

training that is relating to the trainee's current employment and takes place where the trainee is employed.

insider dealings

transactions in shares and securities by people who posses special knowledge affecting the value of those shares. Such people are generally the company directors and auditors who may have prior knowledge of events likely to influence the market value of shares in their companies.

installments, delivery and payment

if according to a contract, delivery or payment is to be by instalments, problems crop up from a failure to comply with the instalment system. Failure of one instalment discharges the other party. The court will generally ascertain the intention of the defaulting party in case of delivery.

instalment selling

involves taking an initial deposit against goods purchased and collecting the balance of the selling price over an agreed period of time in fixed instalments.

institutional advertising
advertising that is intended to create a favourable estimation of the advertiser rather than of any particular product of the advertiser. It is also called goodwill publicity.

institution for collective investment
synonym for collective investment institution.

institutional finance
the term as opposed to individual finance refers to credit made available by financial institutions such as banks, insurance companies and corporations.

institution
stock exchange term for certain large organizations that have large shareholders in various public companies and whose buying and selling of shares has a major influence on the stock market and, sometimes, the control of particular companies.

insurable interest
an interest of such a nature that the insured party would be financially injured by the occurrence of the event insured against. An insurable interest is required in all lines insurance before a contract is legally valid.

insurance
a legal contract in which an insurer promises to pay specified amount o to another party, the insured, if a particular event, happens and the insured suffers a financial loss as a result. The insured's part of the contract is to promise to pay an amount of money, known as the premium either once or at regular intervals. In order for an insurance contract to be valid, the insured must have an insurable interest. It is usual to use the word insurance to cover events that may or may not happen, whereas assurance refers to an event that must occur at sometimes.

insurance company
company that enters into contracts with individuals or with companies, organization, etc., to pay compensation in specific circumstances in return for the regular payment of insurance premiums. Sometimes an insurance company does business with an insured person or organization through an insurance broker.

insurance, double
a risk insured twice is called Double Insurance. But the insured cannot get compensation from two insurer, nor can obtain reimbursement more than the actual loss suffered. And if a risk is insured with two companies, both of them, in the event of paying compensation, will share the loss either equally, or proportionately to the value of risk insured.

insurance export finance company
an organization set up to help finance exports. Members are insurance companies affiliated to the British Insurance Association, and funds amount to about Rs. 75,00,000,000. The Company purchases long-term promissory notes on behalf of its members. It tends to deal with long-term finance (e.g. five years and over). Its rates of interest are approximately $6\frac{1}{2}$ per cent.

insurance industry in india
insurance industry in India has taken remarkable strides towards its objectives. The growth of this industry was particularly marked after the First World War. When, in 1947, Indian attained independence, there were at that time well over 200 Indian and non-Indian insurance and provident societies in the field. independence heralded the beginning of a new era of growth of insurance business in India but the main watersheds were the nationalisation of life insurance business on 1 September, 1956, and the nationalisation of general insurance business on January 1973. The major objective of nationalisation was achievement of wider spread of business more particularly in the rural areas, so that the benefits of insurance should become available to an increasing number of persons and to all sectors of the economy. For this purpose, great emphasis has been laid on strengthening the field force to cater to the needs of different sections of the community. A progressive policy for establishment of more and more branch offices in the rural and mofussil areas has also been adopted.

insurance policy
a document setting out the terms of a contract of insurance.

insurance premium
what the insured agrees to pay to the insurer annually. It is payable on a stated date though a number of days of grace are normally allowed.

intangible assets
an accounting term for those unseen assets which have a value to the business and perhaps also a saleable value e.g., goodwill, patents, trademarks, copyrights, etc. These are called intangible assets.
It is something that is owned by a specified person or firm, is useful and for some time, can be assigned a value on the basis of its usefulness, but has no physical form, e.g., patent rights, known-how, goodwill.

intangible cost
also, intangible expense. A cost incurred in order to

acquire an intangible assets, such as good will or a patent.

integrated manager

a term describing the manager who likes to become part of the people things, and processes he or she managers. Such manages are joiners and take pains to get involved with individuals and grc ɹp about their work. They like to communicate in group settings and therefore use frequent meetings.

intensive cultivation

methods whereby a farmer seeks to obtain the grates possible yield from a given, acreage, using large amounts of fertilizer, irrigation, and special seeds, as well as a great deal of a labour and equipment.

inter-bank loan

a loan from one bank to another for a fixed period from overnight to 12 months.

interest

the amount paid by a borrower to a lender in payment for a loan. Interest may be simple or compound. Simple interest is a fixed rate on a stated sum. The same amount is paid or accumulated each year irrespective of the amount borrowed, for instance Rs. 5000 lent at 5 per cent simple interest would earn Rs.250 a year. If the interest were not paid when due, it would not itself earn interest. But if a sum is invested at compound interest and the interest is allowed to accumulate, the interest is calculated each year on capital and interest already accumulated.

interest, compound

interest calculated not as a fixed amount per annum based on the capital to which it applies, but on an accumulating balance consisting of both capital invested and the interest already earned.

interest and discount

the charge made by a lender for advancing funds. When the charge is paid at maturity, it is interest; when it is deducted in advance, it is discount.

interest certificate

a certificate issued by a bank, building society or other lender of money, showing the interest charged on a particular loan in a given period, usually the income tax year from April to April.

interest cover

similar to dividend cover, it relates to the number of times that the total fixed payable can be met out of the current income of a company or an organization.

interest in subsidiaries not consolidated

accounting terms for the value of holdings in subsidiary companies where the accounts of the subsidiaries and not consolidated when group accounts are presented.

interest out of capital

the Companies Act 1956 does

not permit distributions of dividends paid out of capital, except in one instance: when the capital is for the construction of works, no profits being earned, and the payment is authorized by the Articles or Association and sanctioned by the Board of Trade. The rate must be fixed by the Treasury. Where interest has been paid out of capital, the accounts must show both the capital involved and the rate of interest.

interests in subsidiaries not consolidated
an accounting term for the value of holdings in subsidiary companies, whether the accounts of the subsidiaries are not consolidated when group accounts are presented. Subsidiaries need not be consolidated, where, for example, the amounts involved are immaterial, or when the business of the subsidiary is quite different from that of the holding company.

interest warrant
an order or warrant for payment of interest on stocks, debenture and loan stocks and other fixed-interest securities.

inter-locking directorship
it means the existence of common directors on the Board of Director of several companies, that is to say, interlinking of two or more firms by common directors and thereby concerned companies tend to blend into one another in respect of policies of common interest. There may be three types of interlocking directorships : (a) Inter-locking between competing units ; (b) inter-locking between different groups and (c) inter-looking between manufacturing and financial companies. In India, inter-locking between competing firms in the same industry is found in tea, jute, coal and textile industries.

intermediate products
producers' goods which are not original means of production but which come between the original means of production and consumers' goods.

internal check
in-built system of accounting control, part of the general system of internal control.

internal control questionnaire
accounting/audit designed to probe the effectiveness of procedures and the way in which they are being implemented. Analysis of the questionnaire leads to an internal control report.

internal trade
called interregional trade by Berti Ohlin, internal trade or home trade or domestic trade (as constrasted with foreign or international or world trade) is trade within the geographic boundaries of a country.

internatinal air transport association
the aim of this association is to ensure that all international

airline traffic moves the maximum speed possible, consistent with convenience, safety and efficiency. It provides a means of expending cooperation between various independent or national airlines by crossing language barriers and seeking to synchronize, as far as possible, the legal requirements of the various countries represented by overcoming procedural difference. The latter has been approached by attempting to standardize documentation and handling procedures, particularly where hazardous cargo is involved. One innovation is the standard. I.A..T.A. air waybill.

international air transport association

association of airline service companies. The object of this association is to ensure that all international airline traffic moves with maximum possible speed, without causing inconvenience and inefficiency.

international bank

the banks which have most, if not all, of their branches overseas and whose principal business is centred in their overseas and particularly between their overseas branches and London. While their most profitable assets are their loan and advances to overseas customers, they hold their main reserves of cash and other liquids assets in London.

International Bank for Reconstruction and Development

often known as the World Bank, this was set up together with the international monetary fund by the Bretton Woods Agreements of 1944. Its purpose was to help finance post-war reconstruction by making loans to governments or guaranteeing outside loans. The loans are for fifteen to twenty-five year periods. The bank is a specialized agency of the United Nations. About one-third of the funds come from Europe. Members must also be members of the International Monetary Fund. Two off-shoots of the Bank are the International Finance Corporations (1960) and the International Development Association (1961). Both of these place particular emphasis on aid to less-developed member countries, which have become more demanding in recent years.

international depositary receipt

Also IDR. A substitude stock certificate that makes it easier for a citizen of one country to own stock in a firm located in another country.

international division of labour

international specialisation. Each country will produce those goods for the production of which it is specially suited on account of its climate, of the qualities of its soils, of its other natural resources, of the innate and acquired capacities of its people.

International Federation of Stock Exchange
or Federation International des Bourses de Valeryrs. Set up in 1961 to promite understanding among its members stock exchanges and to represent them internationally.

International Fiscal Association
set up in 1938 to promote the international study of public finance, fiscal law and taxation. It has members in more than 60 countries. Based in the Netherlands.

international investment
also, foreign investment. Ownership by a private individual, business, institution or government of assets in the form of securities; titles to land, buildings, or equipment; bank deposits; etc.; in a foreign country.

International Monetary Fund
one of the fruits of Bretton Woods. Agreements in 1944. The fund was formed in 1946 and began to operate in 1947. Its object is to maintain and stabilize rates of exchange and facilitate multilateral clearing system, and also to eliminate unnessary restrictions on foreign trade. It has the power to advance money to countries in balance of payment difficulties : it will supply a country with the currency it needs in return for that country's own currency. There is a repayment period of about five years. It also gives countries credit guarantees, that is, without actually, lending, it agrees to lend, if asked. These facilities are obviously only available to member countries. Members finance the fund by making contributions according to an estimate of their means. The higher the contribution the higher the voting rights. The amount paid in is partly in gold and partly in the currency of the country.

International Savings Bank Institute
set up in 1925, the Institutes is an advice and intelligence center (center) serving savings banks in more than 40 countries. Based in Switzerland.

International Trade Centre
the Internatinal Trade Centre (ITC) was established at the request of the developing countries to help them promote their exports. Set up in 1964, it has been jointly operated by GATT and UNCTAD since 1968.

International Trade Secretariat
organization of national trade unions with membership from particular industries or occupations. Such secretariats

are linked with the international confederation of free trade unions.

internship training
the method of training refers to a joint programme of training in which the technical institutions and business houses cooperate. The object of such cooperation is to provide such training as will bring about a balance between theory and practice. For this purpose, students may be sent to factories for practical training from their schools/ colleges during vacations.

intervention
foreign exchange operations by the monetary authorities with the object of preventing or causing movements of exchange rates in accordance with the aims of the policy or tactics they pursue.

intrinsic value
the value contained in the substance from which an article is produced. In trade and commerce the term is most often used in relation to metallic currency.

invention
from business point of view the term means finding out something new or a new method of producing a thing, or a new product.

inventory
a quantity of something that is kept or stored for use as the need arises ; especially quantities of raw materials, goods-in-process, finished goods and supplies. A detailed list of goods or articles in a particular place or of the assets of an organization.

inventory control
also, inventory management, material requirements planning. The mangement in inventories so that there is always enough stock on hand for production yet no investment of capital that could more profitably be used otherwise. Inventory control involves determining how much stock must be kept on hand, the rate at which stock will be consumed, the most economic order quantity for purchasing or manufacturing, and the lead time required to obtain the needed materials.

inventory valuation adjustment
a technical device to remove artificial changes in corporate profits introduced by price movements. Its effects is to reduce profits when they are inflated by rising price of inventories and to arise profits unduly depressed by falling of inventories.

invested capital
the equity of all security-holders in a business, that is, both stockholders and holders of long-term liabilities (such as bonds). This can also be described as net, worth plus long-term debt, and is sometimes called capital structure.

investment bank

an organization that assist business corporation and governmental bodies to rise money through the sale of stocks and bonds for usually long-term purposes.

investment company
a generic term that describes a company handling mutual funds or closed-end funds, or any of several other types of companies engaged in the business of investing the money of their shareholders in securities and in other organizations.

investment consellor
an individual or firm whose principal business consists of guiding the investment of its clients, generally making for them all decision to buy and sell securities and/or commodities and seeing that these decision are executed.

investment curve
the cover indicating the relationship between the rate of interest and the volume of investment. Lower the rate of interest, the more investment.

investment grants
government grants a available to industry for specified purpose, e.g. the purchase of machinery used for certain qualifying industrial process. They applied to the manufacturing industries but were also available for the purchase of computers, ships and hovercraft. The grants were of 20 per cent, but of 40 per cent in development areas. These rate were increased to 25 per cent and 45 per cent for expenditure between 1 January 1967 and 31 December 1968. Grants have been discontinued as from 27 October 1970.

investment policy
attempted rate of expansion and profits expected will determine investment policy. Market may oblige businessmen to chose investment policies for which expected rate of returns is at least as great as the discount.

investment trust
a collective investment institution organised as a limited company. Only a few of the earliest investment trusts were organized as trusts but the name survived because it symbolised a prudence and solidity and attracted small investors.

investment trust (or company)
company that exists to invest its capital in other companies, usually in quoted securities but sometimes more riskily. An investment trust is said to have the advantage of giving small investors and opportunity to spread their investment widely and therefore safely.

invisible imports
payments by a country for the kinds of services noted under invisible exports.

inviation to treat
retailers putting goods on show in shop windows or display

cabinets are inviting people to make an offer the retailer is not, as popularly believed, making any offer.

invoice

a document that shows the quantity, price terms, character nature of delivery, and other details for goods sold or services rendered.

invoice discounting

the practice of obtaining money on the security of books debts (i.e. money to be received). A company which finds that it has too much working capital tied up to book debts may sell these debts to a finance company. This is known as invoice discounting. In a typical case, finance company would agree to advance, say, 75 per cent of outstanding debts of a certain category The security might be either goods, where the debtors are hire purchase debtors, or bills of exchange accepted by the borrower. The borrower would act as agent in collecting the debts, and monies would be payable to the finance company, the additional 25 per cent being paid perhaps, when the first 75 per cent is satisfied, i.e. when the bill of exchange is met. The borrower is normally responsible for all bad debts and the finance company would charge a commission, depending on the financial state of the borrower.

inward correspondence

the starting point of the correspondence work is the incoming letters. Incoming letters may pertain to orders, remittances, complaints from customers or may relate to offers, quotatios, invoices, etc., from the suppliers. The prompt handling of such letters is essential from the standpoint of business goodwill. In the words of Thomas Evelyn, "The organization of inward correspondence is very important, for on this depend the prompt despatch of orders the safe handling of remittance, adequate attention to complaints, and in general, smooth running of the business as a whole."

irreddeemale debt

also known as perspective debt, refers to a debt which may not be redeemed at all but the government promises to pay the interest regularly.

irrevocable documentary acceptance credit

used in export trading. An overseas buyer opens a credit with a bank in the country of the exporter, the bank then issuing to the exporter a letter of credit in which it undertakes to accept a bill of exchange drawn on the bank against delivery of the relevant shipping document.

iso-cost map

a diagram in which the variations of the cost of supply with distances from any centre of supply can be shown by means of isorithms, that is by lines down on a map through all points having the same numerical value.

issue
a block of securities that are issued at the same time and all carry the same rights.

issue by tender
where tenders are invited for shares in a company and the shares are sold to the highest bidder(s).

issue price
the price at which a new issue of shares is sold to the public. Once the issue has been made and securities will have a market price, which may be above (at a premium on) or below (at a discount on) the issue price. In an introduction, offer for sale, or public issue, the issue price is fixed by the company on the advice of its stockbrokers and bankers; in an issue by tender the issue price is by the highest bidder; in a placing the issue price is negotiated by the issuing house or broker involved.

issuing house
a financial institution which acts as intermediary between seeking capital (usually industries) and those able to provide it. These houses handle issues on behalf of companies, either by full prospectus or by an introduction or placing. They also often work as underwriters of share issues or as merchant banks.
A firm that specializes in obtaining capital for its clients and advises them on the timing and pricing of new issues of their shares.

issuing houses association
formed in 1945, the association has fifty-six members, not only in the city but also in other parts of London and in the province. It aims to represent the issuing houses' interests in dealing with other financial institutions and with government departments.

itayose
the Japanese concept for stock-exchange dealing in which all orders that arrive at a broker's or dealer's office before the exchange has time, i.e. the opened are treated as having arrived at the same time the exchange opened.

jaw bone control
a name applied by Paul A. Samuelson to normal suasion a method of credit control.

jerry building
quick building by speculators aiming at profit rather than durability, and therefore using inferior materials, This kind of building was common in the boom years of the industrial revolution.

jobber
in the distribution of goods, an individual or a firm, that intervenes between a wholesaler-distributor and the retailer. Jobbers may act exclusively as brokers or sales agents, carrying no inventory of the goods purveyed, or they

may so organize and finance their activities as to provide warehousing facilities for the goods.

jobber

a merchant middleman who buys from an importer or manufacturer or some large wholesaler and sells to retailers.

A wholesaler is a person or firm that buys and sells securities especially on the Stock Exchange taking ownership and possession of them as opposed to a stock broker who arranges purchases and sales as an agent for others and never takes ownership. Also called a 'stockjobber'.

jobber's turn

a stockjobber always quotes two prices for shares or securities: a buying price and a selling price. The selling price is higher than buy price and the difference is known as the jobber's turn.

jobbing backwards

looking back on a transaction or event and thinking about how one might have acted differently, and one known then what one knows now.

job clinic

technique use particular in sales training where specific problems encountered by an individual are discussed with two or three colleagues and solution suggested.

job enrichment

changing features of a job other than compensation, physical working conditions and the essential tasks of the job in order to increase the job satisfaction of the person performing it.

job grading

non-analytical job evaluation technique in which jobs with similar responsibilities, job content, etc. are grouped into grades usually having similar rates of pay.

job number

in manufacturing processes, a number assigned to each job or kit for purpose of identification, the number travelling with the job or kit throughout the plant.

job price

the price or paid for completing a specified task without regard to time required for completion.

job rotation

transferring an employee from one job to another of a similar level in an organization in order to give him experience before promotion.

joint account

1. a bank account of a building-society account held in the names of two or more people often husband and wife. On the death of one party the balance in the account goes to the survivor(s), except in the case of partnerships, executors's accounts, or trustee's account. It is usual for any of the holder of a joint account to operate it alone. 2. In the USA a

syndicate of investment banks acting together in an underwriting venture.

joint and several liability

a liability that is entered into by a group, on the understanding that if any of the group fail in their undertaking the liability must be shared by the remainder. Thus, if two people enter into a joint and several guarantee for a bank loan, if one becomes bankrupt the other is liable for repayment of the whole loan.

joint annuity

an annuity payable during the lives of two or more persons and during the life or lives of the survivor or survivors.

joint product

two or more products that inevitably result from processing single raw material and that are of equal importance, so that none can be designated as the major or primary product.

joint sector

joint sector has been adopted as a part of government policy to promote economic development of the country on the lines indicated in various economic policy statements issued from time to time to reduce concentration of economic power in the private and to promote new and medium entrepreneurs to build up viable units.

The concept of joint sector implies the participation of both the government and the private sector in industry. In other words, joint sector means the establishment and running of an industrial enterprise on a joint basis by the government and a private entrepreneur. The idea of joint sector as a form of private entrepreneur. The idea of joint of sector as a form of business organisation is basically an extension of the concept of mixed economy wherein the growing public sector and regulated private sector are enjoined upon to herald the socialistic pattern of society.

joint stock banks

the ordinary banking organizations which carry the banking operations, capital of which have been raised by issuing shares and debentures. These banks are operated on the principle of joint companies.

joint stock company-general meeting

meetings of the members or the shareholders of the company are called General Meetings. They are different from the meetings of the Board of Directors or Committees of Directors. Generally, Directors have the authority to convene a General Meeting-whether an Annual General Meeting or an Extraordinary General Meeting. The Secretary sends out notices to the members on the instructions of the directors. It is the duty of the secretary to ensure that the Board meeting is properly convened and that it has properly resolved to call a General Meeting. Every limited company is required under the companies Act, 1956 to call a General Meeting once annually.

joint stock company-prospectus

it is essential for a public company to issue a prospectus if it intends to appeal to the public for the capital to carry out the objects for which it has been constituted. Prospectus is a document inviting general public to subscribe to the share capital of a company. It can be issued by a company at any stage of its commencement. A private limited company need not issue a prospectus or file a statement in lieu of prospectus since it cannot invite public to subscribe for its shares.

joint tenancy

in law, a single estate is property, whether real or personal, owed by two or more persons under one instrument or act of the parties, with an equal right of all to share in the enjoyment of the property during their lives. On the death of a joint tenant, the property descends to the survivor and at length to last survivor.

joint tenants

person who hold property jointly in such a way that should one tenant die other takes the property. This is unlike a tenancy in common, where the representatives of the deceased tenant take his share.

joint venture

a business relationship similar to a Partnership but formed for the purpose of carrying out a single project rather than as an on going business.

Joplin Thomas

the inventor of the currency doctrine as opposed to the doctrine of banking with reference to the method of note issue.

journeyman

a skilled worker who has completed an apprenticeship and is an employee, not an employer and not self-employed.

judgment creditor

one who has proved a debt in a court of law, or won an action for the recovery of debt.

juniopr mortgage

a mortgage second in line to a previous mortgage; a subordinate mortgage. Also known as junior financing.

jurisdictional strike

a strike caused by a dispute among craft unions over which shall have jurisdiction over a specific job.

kaffirs

a Stock Exchange term for South African gold mining shares.

kangaroos

a stock exchange term for

shares or securities in Australian land mining and tobacco companies.

kapitalertragstauer
capital yield tax on dividends and other distributions of company profits in Austria, Federal German and Luxembourg.

kennedy round
an extensive renegotiation of multilateral tariff agreements, within the limits set by the General Agreement on Tariffs and Trade. The kennedy Round Pact is the world's biggest ever tariff cutting deal and was supposed to give a new boost to trade among developed and developing countries.

kerbside conferences
post-interview discussion between a salesman and his sales supervisor, involving analysis of selling method, performance and achievement.

key lot
a marketable parcel of land one of whose sides adjoins the rear of others lots. Usually one of the least desirable lots in a subdivision because it does not offer optimum access or privacy.

key-man insurance
provides temporary protection to ensure financial solvency in the event of loss through death of a key executive. The business firm pays the premium and is the beneficiary. Premium cost are not tax-deductible; however, proceeds from the policy are not subject to federal income taxation.

keyword
the work in the little of a book or article or other piece of information which is selected as best characterizing the contents of the item and is therefore used to index it in certain kinds of information retrieval system. Thus a book called making the most of your talent would be under 'Talent' in a key word index.

kirkeskat
church tax, a form of income tax in Denmark in addition to national income tax, local tax and net wealth tax.

kite
an accommodation bill. A cheque drawn by someone who known there is no money in the bank account he is drawing on.

knock-for knock agreement
agreement between insurers that whenever a vehicle insured by one of them is involved in an accident with a vehicle insured by the other then each insurer will pay for the damage to the vehicle he has insured. This procedure is adopted-instead of the normal one in which an insurer (exercising his right of subrogation) pursues a claim for damages against the person alleged to have caused the accident—in order to simplify settlement of claims.

know-how
a term used to describe saleable knowledge of

technique or special skill which have been developed within an industry for use on certain projects. This may be the result of many years of intensive research and development in the manufacture of a valuable product.

Knowledge of the techniques or practical details that enable a process or operation to be carried out efficiently.

known-how agreement

an agreement by which the possessor of known-how promises to disclose it to someone else. When the disclosure is made to enable the other person to perform his own research or to evaluate the usefulness of the know-how, the agreement is called a 'secrecy agreement'. When the disclosure is made so that the other can use it in commerical production, the agreement is called a 'know-how licence'.

kondatrieff cycle

in economic analysis, a 40-to-60 year wavelike movement in economic activity that is approximately divided between good and bad times.:

labour

the element of production represented by those hired workers whose efforts or activities are directed toward making the product; also, all personal services including the activities of wageworkers, professional people, and independent businessmen.

labour force

the labour force or working force denotes that part of population which is economically active or "gainfully employed".

labour market

the market for labour in a particular area : the available workers, the firms that wish to employ them and the kinds of contracts they enter into including rates of pay.

labour relations

relations between trade unions and employers, or between an employer and the unions representing his employees.

labour-standard rolled-up cost

the total labour cost required to build an assembly. The figure includes the labour cost of both the assembly and its subssemblies.

laesio enormis

the doctrine in certain continental legal systems that consideration, when a matter of prices, must be fair and serious, otherwise the other party could rescind the contract. The doctrine is of Roman origin, and the cash offered had to bear some relation to he value of the object.

laisses-faire

the doctrine that government should let thing alone and allow economic activity to go forward in response to individual and private objectives.

laity
persons in a profession who are not skilled with respect to that profession. In accounting, for example, the laity includes those who are not skilled in accounting but who might need auditors reports in the completion of their own tasks.

lame duck
although this term was once reserved for members of the stock exchange who, not being able to meet their debts, were due to be hammered, it has recently been accorded a much wide use in the industrial sphere. The term 'lame duck company' is now applied to companies which can be kept from complete ruin with the help of public funds. Lame duck companies may also be called sick-units.

landed price
the quoted or invoiced price of a commodity, including costs of loading, shipping and unloading at its destination.

land factor
ratio of the cost of the equipment in a plant used in process industry to the total cost of erecting the plant. The ratio is observed to be constant for a large number of plants in broadly defined categories (e.g., all plant processing fluids).

landing book
a book kept by dock companies for noting details of all goods received off incoming ships. Lading accounts are made up from this book and sent to the relevant cargo owners. It gives them an indication of the state of the goods, and of when the rent due for e.g. use of warehouse, becomes payable.

language sheet
a term used by central government agencies, in their accounting practice, to denote the narrative portion of an appropriation bill that accompanies an agency's submission of its budget to Congress.

last cycle count date
in manufacturing, the date on which a particular part was counted in an inventory. This date is used to determine when the next physical inventory should be taken.

last transaction date
the last date on which a transfer of a particular material was transacted.

laundering money
processing money acquired illegally so that it appears to have come from a legitimate source. This is often achieved by paying the illegal cash into a foreign bank and transferring its equivalent to a bank with a good name is a hard-currency area.

layaway plan
a form a retail selling in which merchandise is held by the retailer while the customer make periodic partial payments on its.

lay days
the days allowed by customs for loading or unloading a

vessel. Failure to complete the job within these days may make the guilty party liable to pay demurrage. Lay days may be counted in working days, running days, or weather working days. Where the number of lay days is not specified in the contract, the work must be done in a reasonable time (this might allow for delays due to strikes, etc.).

lead time
the length of time between ordering ·the supply of something and receiving it. Also an estimate of such a length of time.

lease
a contractual agreement that transfers possession and use of property for a limited period under specified terms and conditions. A lease is an encumbrance against the title, since the rights it grants to the lessee are likewise binding on the successor successors to the title.

lease assignment
a written legal document that generally conveys all rights of the assignor for the remaining term of the lease.

lease back
a long term lease of real estate of equipment that has been sold to an independent agent and is then taken back under the lease agreement by the original seller.

lease purchase agreement
an instrument whereby it is agreed that a portion of the note payment will be applied to the purchase price. The title is transferred on completion of the agreement.

leasehold
in interest in land under the term of a lease; normally classified as a tangible, fixed asset.

lease purchase agreement
an instrument whereby it is agreed that a portion of the note payments will be applied to the purchase price. The title is transferred on completion of the agreement.

ledger
a book where an organization's individual accounts are kept. For practical reasons it is usually divided into several books: cash books, personal ledger, private ledger, and general ledger. In the pat, ledgers were great tomes where information was recorded in copperplate hadnwriting by little men with long quills. Now they are usually trays of cards handwriting, with information printed by accounting machines.

ledger journal
a book with multicolumned pages, used as a record of transactions, functioning as both a journal and a ledger. Usually the record contains debit or credit columns or both, and is used only when the number of accounts is few and transactions are relatively few

and simple.

ledger—posting to

the process of copying entry from the journal to ledger is called 'posting'. In the posting procedure, journal debits are copied and become ledger-account debits; conversely, journal credits are copied and become ledger-account credits. From a general journal, each item is posted individually, and the number of postings is (a) two in a simple journal entry, and (b) three or more in a compound journal entry, according to three or more accounts involved. Whereas a transaction is journalised as and when it occurs, the posting is usually periodically, say weekly or bi-weekly as per the business needs. In a banking concern, accounts are, however, posted daily, if not instantaneously.

legal capital

the part of a corporation's paid-in capital that becomes the par or stated value of the capital stock, as determined by law, agreement, or resolution of the board of directors. Also, the portion of net assets that is restricted from withdrawal, under corporation law.

legal entity

any individual, partnership, corporation, or organization empowered by law or custom to own property or engage in business transactions.

legal list

a list of investments selected by various state governments in which certain institutions and fiduciarises such as insurance companies and banks may invest. Legal list are often restricted to high quality securities that meet defined specifications.

legal mortagage

a form of charge in which a debtor transfers property to his creditor on condition that the property will be transferred back again when the debt is paid. Also called 'mortgage'.

legal tender

money, which being offered in payment of a debt at an appropriate time and place, must be accepted by the other party in satisfaction of the debt. It the creditor refuses, the debt remains, but if the debtor is sued, the creditor will probably have to pay the costs. An offer of money in this way stops interest running, and usually extinguishes the creditor's right of lien. Legal tender of money must be an unconditional offer in legal currency of the exact amount owed, to the creditor or his agent, the money being produced. It consists of banks of England notes to any amount-silver not exceeding Rs.100, bronze not exceeding, 1s., twelve-sided threepenny pieces not exceeding 2s.

The debtor cannot demand change, though if the creditor accepts a larger amount he will be obliged to give change. It might be noted before refusing to takes as change on a bus what is strictly no legal tenders, e.g. 1s. 11d. in pennies on the offer of 2s. for a ld. bus ride, that once one is on a bus one has no alternative but get off or give the larger amount together with one's name and address and ask that the change be forwarded. A bus conductor is not obliged to give change.

legatee
the person to whom 'person' property is left, or bequeathed, in a will. The person who takes all the personal property remaining after legatees have received their shares is called the residuary legatee.

less developed countries
a less developed country is simply one with per capital income that is low relative to the present day per capita incomes of such nations as Canada, the United States, Great Britain and Western Europe generally. Optimistically, a less developed country is one regarded as being capable of substantial improvement in its income level.

lessee
on who is given possession of someone else's property by means of a lease.

lessor
one who gives possession of his property to someone else by means of a lease.

letter of credit
a document issued by a bank or similar institution allowing a borrower to draw a bill or exchange on it for specified purposes. In the case of internatinal trade, an overases buyer may arrange for a bank in the country of the supplier to issue a letter of credit to the supplier accepting a bill of exchange drawn on it upon delivery of the relevant export shipping documents. Normally, the overseas buyer opens an irrevocable letter of credit with the vendor's bank in the vendor's country.

letter of credit—anticipatory
also known as packing credit, the latter of credit contains a clause printed in red authorising the negotiating banker to advance to the beneficiary for purchase of goods. The amount of the advance is recoverable from the bill drawn under the credit on shipment.

letter of credit—transferable
when it is expressly provided so in the credit, the letter of credit can be transferred by the beneficiary to some third party and the letter of credit is called a transferable letter of credit. This is usually done where the beneficiary under the bill is only an intermediary who procures goods from the supplier and arranges it to be sent to the importer.

letter of hypothecation
document held by a bank as

evidence of its lien on goods which are the security or collateral against which it has granted a loan or credit.

letter of lien
in foreign trade, a document signed by a buyer stating that the seller retains a lien, or possession of the goods, until they have been paid for.

letter of renunciation
where shares have been allotted to a person and he does not wish to keep them, he may renounce them in favour of another person. The document by which this is effected is called the letter of renunciation.

letters patent
a document by which the government grants authority to someone. To stress the fact that authority should be available for everyone to read, the document is not folded i.e., it is 'patent' or 'open'.

letter stock
stock issued to founders, early executives, and investors that is not registered with the Securities and Exchange Commission, and thus is not subject to restrictions on sale and dispostion. It is called letter stock because a letter of intent to invest, not to trade, must be field with the appropriate regulatory body.

levy
a tax assessment. In management, a request made on members of an organization for contributions of capital. In law, a writ of levy refers to the seizure of a defendant's property by the sheriff to satisfy the plaintiff's judgment.

levey
a tax assessment. In management, a request made on members of an organization for contributions of capital.

liability
an obligation, especially an obligation to pay money. The amounts of money that a firm owes to others, usually classified as current liabilities and long-term liabilities.

liability of a bank
the sources of its funds which are employed by a bank in the ordianry course of business.

liability risk
sometimes called third-party risk or legal-liability risk, this involves the possibility that the insured party may become legally obligated to pay money to a third party.

licence
a document permitting its holder to do something otherwise forbidden, and usually obtainable by paying a fixed sum. Licence are a means of raising revenue and of controlling the use or abuse of certain rights. They are needed inter alia for driving or conducting a bus, carrying goods or passengers for money, selling wines, spritis, beer or tobacco, using premises for dancing or singing, or for unting , shooting or fishing. Anyone in doubt as to whether

or not he needs a licence should consult his local authority or the police. Conditions vary between parts of the country. Some licences are obtainable from post offices, e.g. broadcast receiving, dog, drivers, export, game, hounds, local taxation and excise, and vehicle licences; others from magistrates, e.g. for the sale of alcohol; others from various authorities. Members of the public can oppose the issue of particular licences by magistrates, if they attend the court.

licensed institution

an organization that is licensed by the Bank of England to operate a deposit-taking business in the UK but may not suggest to the public that it is a bank.

licensee

a person who is entitled to do something (that is otherwise unlawful) under the terms of a licence. A person who is entitled to use some one else's property under the terms of a licence.

licensor

a person who grants a right to use his property to someone else by means of licence.

lien

a right one person has to keep possession or control of the property of another in satisfaction of a debt. Among the many kinds of liens are the artisan's lien, the attoney's lien, innkeeper's lien, the mechanic's lien, and the vendor's lien.

lien, equitable

this is not a possessory lien, although it could be. It is conferred by equity and is a right to have property disposed of in a certain way, e.g. the lien of a partner on the property of a partnership, or the lien of the vendor of land for the purchase money.

lien, maritime

in certain circumstances, certain persons have a lien attaching to a ship and/or its cargo which enables them to recover money owed to them. These are : bottomry bond holders; the master, for wages and dispersement; sailors, for work done; seamen, for wages; and the owner of another ship damaged in a collision. Possession is not necessary.

lien, particular

a possessory lien enabling the holder of goods to retain the goods until money due on those goods is paid. Common law affords such liens to unpaid carriers and unpaid sellers. The lien arises when goods are held for improvement rather than maintenance. The work must be completed. The fact that the goods do not belong to the person who deposited them does not always defeat the lien.

lieu bonus

a payment made to worker who, for special reasons, is not able to participate in an incentive payment system or who is unable, because of abnormal circumstances, to do the work required to entitle him to an incentive payment.

life insurance corporation
the life insurance corporation of India (LIC) was established on 1 September 1956 to spread the message of life insurance in the country and to mobilise people's savings for nation building activities.

life annuity
an annuity whose payments temrminate on the death of the beneficiary. In the business world, it may be an annuity derived from the purchase of an insurance policy of a special type, or the result of a special perquisite provided as part of an employment contract.

lifo
a method of inventory and cost-of-sales valuation in which the individual items constituting the inventory are valued according to the cost of the earliest acquisitions, and the cost or articles sold or used are valued at the cost of the most recent acquisition.

limited and reduced
being a limited company of which the nominal share capital has been reduced (written as the last three words of the company's name, usually by order of the court that sanctioned the reduction.

limited company
a company whose members are required to contribute capital to the company but only up to a known limited amount agreed between members and company. No further contribution can be required even if the company is unable to pay its debts.

limited liability
this applies to a company limited by shares or a company limited by guarantee. No member can be asked to pay more than the nominal value of his shares or the amount of his guarantee. Holders of fully-paid shares have not liability whatever. The memorandum of associaiton must contain a clause stating that the member's liability must contain a clause stating that the members' liability is limited. The word 'limited' or the abbreviation 'Ltd.' must always appear as part of the name of the company.

limited partner
a member of a partnership whose liability to creditors of the partnership is limited to the amount of his or her investment. A limited partner may not participate in management.

limited price order
in securities trading, an order to buy or sell a stated amount of a security at a specified price, or better price, if obtainable after the order is presented on the floor.

limping standard

a monetary standard which has two legs one of gold and one of silver bui that of silver is cripped and deformed.

line and staff conclict

line and staff conflict arises because of sharp differences in the training, experience and outlook of the two groups. Staff, because of their specialised knowledge acquired by training or experience, tries to assume the role of an expert. Line manger because of his broad responsibilities and general competence takes pride in what he calls a common sense view of things. Thus, staffmen faced with opposition to their ideas, tend to see the line manger as basically stubborn, resistant to change and improvement and not appreciative of their special qualification and capabilities. Line managers, on the other hand, often regard staff proposals as impractical, too academic or building castles in the air. They see personal staff as interested only in their techniques and procedures, talking a professional jargon which no one else can understand.

line authority

authority that is, or is like, the authority exercised by a line manager.

link financing

an arrangement whereby a firm borrows the amount of a compensating balance from someone else.

liquide assets

those assets of the business which comprise cash or items which can easily and quickly be converted into cash, money at call.

An asset that is either cash or can be turned into a known amount of cash very quickly.

liquidation

this term is applied to the winding-up of the affairs of a company when it ceases business. In most publicized instances it indicates bankruptcy, but it is equally applicable to the winding-up of a company by its shareholders when the purpose for which it was initially founded has been completed.

The action or process of liquidating. The state of being liquidated is called liquidation.

liquidation value

the price that can be obtained from the sale of assets of liquidation proceeding. In the event of the liquidation of a corporation, liquidation, value is the agreed upon amount per share to be paid to preferred shareholders.

liquidator

an individual appointed to manage the winding up of a company.

liquid funds

balance on current account, sight deposits, short time deposits, long-time deposits with escape clauses, money at call or at short notice, bill which have a good market.

liquidity
a term for the ease with which funds can be raised by the sale of assets. In any business, cash is needed at various times for various purposes, but on the other hand idle cash earns no money. Cash may therefore be used to purchase assets, e.g. bills of exchange, securities, market investments, or may be deposited for short periods, so that interest is earned but the asset is quickly realizable. These funds are said to be near-liquid.

liquidity of the bank
a bank is liquid only to the extent that it turns its assets into cash to meet the demands of its depositors and other creditors as rapidly as they are presented.

liquidity ratio
the commerical banks under banking regulations are required to maintain in liquid assets certain specified proportion of their total deposits if various categories. Cash or near cash substitutes are thus kept so that the demand for cash can be readily met. The proportion of these two, that is, the total liability and the cash and substitutes is known as the liquidity ratio, which the bank are expected to maintain always.

listed company
a company that has issued securities the are listed on a stock exchange. (Also known as a 'public company' or a 'quoted company').

listed security
also on-board security. A security listed on an organized exchange, meeting that it has met the requirements set by the exchange.

list price
a published price, intended to be the price paid by the ultimate consumer. Any trade of other discounts are calculated from the list price.

Live Load The orders or the load of manufacturing orders that are actually available to be worked on by a manufacturing facility.

livery
style of design adopted by an organization for the uniform symbol of the commerical vehicles that it owns.

livestock insurance
intended to provide coverage for groups of animals, or for individual animals such as a valuable racing horse. Insurance is available to those who professionally raise or breed game or fur-bearing animals for profit.

lloyds register of shipping
a soceity formed to survey and classify ships for the benefit of insurers and other interested parties. If a ship is constructed under the supervision of Lloyds surveyors it is marked with Maltese cross. Ships are generally given periodic surveys. The society is responsible for an

annual publication known as Lloyds Register of British and Foreign Shipping. This contains details of all vessels alfoat of 100 ones or more.

loan

something lent for the borrower's termporary use, especially money lent with conditions about repayment and the payment of interest.

loanable funds

the supply of lonable funds is compounded of saving (in the Robertsonian sense) plus net additions to loanable funds new money and the discarding of idle balances.

loans and discounts

they represent as asset of the bank because they are right or claims of the bank against its borrowers to the collected at some specific date in the future, the date depending upon the length of the loan.

loan shark

person or organization making loans at extortionately high interest rates.

loans to directors

a company may not make loans to its directors unless: (1) it is an exempt private company (these companies were obsolished by the Companies Act 1956), (2) the director is a holding company, (3) the money is necessary to enable the director to perform his duties to the company and the loan is approved by the company in general meeting, or (4) the loan is made in the ordinary course of business by a company whose ordinary business includes lending money. Particulars of loans must be shown in the accounts.

loan value

in insurance, an amount of money available to the owner of the policy and which the owner may borrow from the insurer. The insurance policy serves as collateral for the loan repayment.

lock-box system

a means of accelerating the flow of funds from the time of customer payment to the time of deposit in the company's bank account. A lock-box arrangement usually is on a regional basis, with the company choosing regional banks according to its billing patterns. The company choosing rents a local post office box and authorizes if patterns. The company rents a local post office box and authorizes if; bank in each of the cities in which a box is rented to pick up the remittances in the box. The bank picks up the mail several times a day and deposit the checks in the company's account.

lock out

the closing of a business or wholesale dismissal of employees by the employer because of a disagreement over terms of settlements; the refusal of an employer to admit his employees to their place of work.

London Association for the Protection of Trade

a organization giving status reports regarding the credit-worthiness of potential customers, principally within the London area. There are branches in certain other towns and also affiliated organizations.

London Gazette

a weekly bulletin enjoying the unique distinction of being 'published by authority.' Any information published in the London Gazette (or in Scotland, the Edinburgh Gazette) is notice to the world,, or rather to the nation, and no one can deny knowledge of it, even though he has neither heard of, nor seen, the publication. Matters include in the Gazette apart from certain traditional items, are notification of public appopitments, etc., details of winding-up orders, bankruptcies, meetings of creditors, change of names of companies, partnerships, and individuals, changes in the constitution of partnerships, and all other matters which they requires to be gazetted.

long

in securities trading terms, this signifies ownership of securities." I am long 100 U.S. Steel" means speaker owns 100 shares of that company's stock.

long period

in this period as defined by Marshal, there is time for firm's fixed equipment to be altered so that output is capable of adapting itself more fully to changes in demand conditions than it is in the short period. There is time to build new machines, factories and old ones can be closed down or allowed to fall to pieces.

longs

government stocks that are to be redeemed more than 15 years hence.

long term

a general expression for a period of time that extends through one or more fiscal years.

long-term contract

any contract for goods or services that extends beyond one-year.

long-term debt

an obligation or liability that is due after one year, as contrasted with short term debts or liabilities that are current and due within the next 12 months.

loop

in a graph, an edge that has the same vertex at each end. A sequence of instructions in a program that are to be obeyed repetitively by the computer.

loro accounts

current accounts of banks with foreign banks in terms of a foreign currency held on behalf of their clients.

loss

an amount by which the revenues of a firm are less than all expenses and lost costs over a period. An amount by which the proceeds of selling something are less than the expenses associated with the sale.

loss leader
something which a retailer sells at a loss in order to attract customers to his shop where they will buy (other goods on which he hopes to make a large profit).

lost cost
an amount of expenditure by a firm for which it has not received any benefit.

lost-size inventories
the quantity of supplies or materials required to support production for a specific time period, usually expressed in weeks. Also known as cycle inventories.

lottery
in business transaction, any scheme for the distribution of goods that involves the three elements of payment of consideration; (1) return promise, (2) an act performed, and (3) a forbearance. This involves a prize to some but not all of those who give consideration and also involves chance.

low-level language
a programming language which has few or no macro-instructions but has a code for instructions that is more easy to remember and use than computer instruction code.

machine-hour
a unit for measuring the usage of machines which is equivalent to the use of one machine for one hour. Thus a use of 3 machines for 1 hour each or 6 machines for $\frac{1}{2}$ hour each, etc. are measured as 3 machine-hour.

machinery and equipment
the category of industrial goods that includes all machines of all sizes used in production and office work, not intended for resale.

madras stock exchange
one of seven major Indian stock exchange.

mail order
system of retailing in which customers send orders to the seller by post and goods are delivered to the customer's home.

mail order firm
a firm selling a very wide selection of goods, but by post rather than through retail premises. It employs agents who take orders, which are dealt with by a central organization. The agent has an elaborate catalogue and is paid a commission on his sales. The goods are sold at competitive prices, the economies in marketing enabling the firm to allow the customer to pay in instalments without necessarily charging him a higher price.

mail order firm or house
business organization concerned with direct mail selling.

mail-order wholesaler
serving as a middleman in the distribution of goods, this merchant substitutes mail-order catalogues and order forms for a personal sales force. Such a wholesaler meets the needs of retailers who are located at great distances from regular merchant wholesalers.

mail transfer
an applied to banks, Mail Transfer is an advice sent by one branch of the bank by mail to another branch to credit the account or pay amount to the beneficiary of the transfer.

mailtenance
work undertaken on plant, equipment or machinery in order to keep it at, or restore it to, an acceptable standard.

make or buy
determining the differential costs arising from making a product or component or buying it from an outside supplier. Involves the use of marginal costs.

managed money
money having no fixed value in items of an objective standard.

management accountancy
it is defined as business accounting practice concerned with provision of information to management for policy-making purposes as opposed to that required for the preparation of a balance sheet. This branch of management helps managements in arriving at correct business decisions and targets of plants set by governments.

management accounting
branch of accounting geared to making the decision making of management better informed by providing detailed information, present and project, on the costs of individual products departments and activities.

Management, British institute of
an independent, non-political, nonprofit-making company, limited by guarantee and not having a share capital. It was established in 1947 on the recommendation of the Bailieu Committee, set up by the Board of Trade, and is the national clearing house for information on management policies, practices, and techniques, and management development including education and training. Its members include industrial and commercial companies, nationalized industries, government departments, banks, finance houses trade and employers' associations trade unions, management consultants, professional bodies, educational institutions and individuals. It has a library and a consulting services information bureau. Its publications include the monthly, Management Today,

the bi-monthly, British Institute of Management Notes for Collective Subscribers, the quarterly, Management Abstracts, and also various books. The institute holds courses, conferences and seminars. Individual members may be fellows (F.B.I.M.), Members (M.B.I.M.) Or Associate Members (A.M.B.I.M.). Qualification for Fellowship is eminent achievement in the practice of management, for Membership, general management experience at board or general management level and for Associate Membership, a Diploma in Management Studies or equivalent qualification in management subjects, and one years's acceptable experience. Persons with long experience in management may be admitted to an Associate Membership with a Diploma. Individual subscriptions: Fellows and members Rs.420 others Rs.315.

management by exception
a management method under which subordinates handle normal details or their assignments and are sensitive to exceptional events that they bring to the attention of their supervisors.

management company
a company which decides what securities should be bought and sold by a unit trust and arranges the sale of units in returns for a fee that is deducted from the fund's income.

management consultant
someone whose principal business activity is management counselling.

manager
in the most fundamental interpretation of the word 'a person who occupies a formal position in a formal organization, is responsible for the work of at least one other person, and this formal authority over that person. It is policy among some companies to set the minimum number of persons or subordinates in a group as the determining factor, or one of the determining factors in the application of the title manger.

managing director
the chief executive of a company. The title is generally preferred in areas outside the North American continent. Broadly equivalent to president of a company, the title preferred in the United States.

manament information system
a system for providing mangers with information relating to their management tasks.

management—nature of
the nature of management is very complex. It is a hard fact that no two persons agree upon a common definition of management. An economist considers it purely a theoretical subject but a

mathematician thinks management as a logical process capable of being expressed in terms of symbols. A behaviour scientist looks at management as a complex of inter-personal relationships. He considers it as a part of psychology or sociology. A functionalist looks at management as a process concerned with getting things done through the efforts of people working in organised groups.

manager

a person who has been appointed to carry out a job of management. Also a person who undertakes such job as a profession.

managing director

the director of a company who generally ranks first in seniority under the chairperson or president and is essentially the chief executive. He is, as such, the key figure in the running of the business with responsibility for all actions that are taken in the area of management.

Managing Director is a director who, by virtue of an agreement with the company or of a resolution passed by the company in a general meeting or by its Board of Directos or by its Memorandum or Articles of Association, is entrusted with substantial powers of management which would not otherwise be exercisable by him and includes a director occupying the position of a Managing Director, by whatever name called.

mandate

instructions given by an organization to its delegate or representative on how he should vote an particular issue at a meeting or conference.

man-honour

a unit of measuring employment equivalent to the employment of one person for one hour. Thus employment of 3 men for 1 hour each, or 6 men $\frac{1}{2}$ hour each, etc. are measured as 3 men-honours.

manpower planning

estimating how many employees and what types of employees an organization or a nation will require at some time in the future and making plans to meet those requirements.

manufacturing

general term for the process of producing or assembling goods, by hand or machine, for sale to other.

manufacturing expense

the cost of manufacturing, other than the cost of raw materials consumed and direct labour. Also known as factory expense, indirectly expense, and factory overhead.

margin

a margin is strictly the difference between the cost of an asset or investment and the amount that a lender of money of willing to advance for its purchase; or (and this is much the same thing) the amount of money a speculator puts down in forward dealings. Where a person wishes to buy or speculate in a property he may not intend to take it up, but the margin or deposit is an earnest of his intentions. The term is particularly used with reference to forward dealings in commodities or even currencies. Dealing in margins occur when a speculator, having secured a certain quantity at a fixed price in the future, sells the margin by selling the options at a profit or loss.

marginal costing
pricing of additional sales on the basis of merely the direct costs, leaving overheads to be recovered from existing sales.

marginal cost pricing
a method of setting prices in which price is made equal to marginal cost. Since price must be set in such a way that all output is sold, and since marginal cost varies with output, marginal cost pricing implies that the price should be set at the point at which the demand curve cuts the marginal cost curve. Marginal cost pricing in considered an appropriate policy for nationalized industries on the grounds that it—maximizes economic welfare.

marginal relief
if a personal relief is given only when income is below a particular amount then a proportion of the relief is usually given to people with incomes that are slightly above the limit. This proportion is called marginal relief.

marginal revenue
the increase (or loss) in total revenue resulting from selling an additonal unit of output. It is measured by the equation: Marginal revenue = change in total revenue change in quantity marginal revenue product the gain (or loss) in total resulting from adding an extra unit of a variable factor of production, such as labour cost.

marginal unit
any unit of a commodity which a consumer is momentarily considering whether to buy-whether he in fact buys it or not.

margin call
a demand on a customer to put up money or securities with his or her broker. The call is made at the time of a purchase, or if a purchase, or if customer's equity in a margin account declines below the minimum standard set by the exchange or by the firm.

marine insurance
a marine insurance contract is concerned with a marine policy of insuring ships, cargo, passengers, etc. The risks insured against include damage by fire, storm and tempest; detention by foreign

princes, seizure under legal process and dangers occasioned by fire, enemies, pirates, rovers, thieves, jettisons etc.

markdown
in retail merchandise, the amount by —which an original selling price is reduced.

marketable securities
a balance-sheet classification for negotiable stocks, bonds, and treasury securities carried as a current asset in the form of investment.

market economy
economy in which the most important influence on the prices and quantities of products to be supplied is consumers' decision on whether or not to purchase a particular product at a particular price.

market equilibrium
the economic state in which the supply of goods is limited to the quantity already produced and placed on the market.

marketing
the activities, of a firm, that are concerned with acquiring and maintaining markets for the firm's products and for ensuring that the firm's output reaches those markets in time and with needed supplies.

marketing accounting
process of collection and analysis data, and providing the necessary information for. decision making in relation with marketing.

marmeting research
marketing research is distinguished from market research in that while the latter deals with the pattern of a market, the former deals with problems involved in marketing a particular product.
Marketing research begins with market research and then studies practical difficulties in selling and such matter as what lines might be adopted in particular areas and what special problems might be met many particular regions. It is concerned with the problems attached to selling a particular product for a particular manufacturer.

market-out clause
a clause in some securities underwriting contracts whereby the underwriter may withdraw from the agreement if the market should become unfavourable for selling the securities.

market price
it is the price at which specified goods can be sold in the market.

Market Research Society
a professional association for persons using survey techniques in market, social and economic research. Founded in 1947, it seeks to promote and protect the interests of its members and those employing their services. It also attempts to publicize the profession. Members are bound to observe a standard

code of practice in conducting scientific sample surveys and reporting results. Various conferences are held to exchange information, and liaison with government departments, universities , scientific institutions, etc., is preserved. Members may be Full Members (M.M.R.S.) Or Associates (A.M.M.R.S.), the former having obtained full professional standing. They now must also have been Associates for more than two years. Full Members pay Rs.367.50, associated Rs.210 per annum.

Various organizations offer market research in particular areas on behalf of exporters. Plans are sometimes offered without obligation. The Market Research Society has a register of members and will provide the address of the the nearest assoriation.

market risk

in the securities market, the condition of uncertainty about future prices because of changes in investor attitudes.

market share

the ratio of a firms sales of product, either the number of units sold of the value of sales during a period in a specified market to the total sales of that type of product during the same period in that market.

mark-up

the selling price of an article is different from the cost of its production. The traders add a particular percentage on their cost of the product to determine the selling price. This proportion is known as mark-up.

marriage brokage contracts

some persons offer for reward to provide a partner in marriage. These contracts are illegal. The locus poentientiate rule does not apply and money may be recovered even after part performance or marriage itself.

master tariff

a tariff field with the Interstate Commerce Commission applying to a large number of applicable tariffs,

matched and lost

in securities trading, when two bids to buy the same stock are made on the trading floor simultaneously and each bid is equal in price or larger than the quantity of stock offered, both bids are considered to be on an equal basis. The two bidders flip a coin to decide who buys the stock.

material current cost

each time a purchase order is issued, the cost date for the relevant material are updated. The latest purchase cost becomes the current cost for the material.

materials

the goods that a manufacturer buys for conversion into manufactured products. Also the value of a manufacturer's stock of unconverted materials.

maturing liability

generally refers to bonds; an obligation that is about to reach maturity. Maturity-the date on which loan, bond, or debenture falls due and is to be paid off,

maturity
the time when a debt becomes repayable. The period for which money is loaned.

maturity basis
the method of calculating the values of bonds and their rates of return, based on the assumption that bonds will be held until maturity.

maturity date
the date on which a debt is repayable—especially when a security is to be redeemed.

mean (arithmetic)
a statistical term for the average of a series of numbers, obtained by totalling the series and dividing this total by the number of items in the series.

mechanic's lien
a lien that has been created by statute to assist labourers in collecting their wages. Its purpose is to subject the land of an owner to a lien for materials and labour expended in the construction of buildings. Having been placed on the land, the buildings become a part of the land by the law of accession.

medium-term liabilities
those which must be met within about three years but are not so imminent as to be classed as current.

meeting, extraordinary
this is a meeting other than the annual general meeting. It may be called by the directors at any time, either of their own volition or after being requisitioned by the holders of not less than one-tenth of the paid-up capital (voting). (The articles of associations of the company may increase this percentage.) The requisition must be signed by the requisitionists. If the directors do not act within twenty-one days the requisitionists (or more than half of them) may call the meeting themselves. A printed notice of the resolution passed must be sent to the registrar within fifteen days.

meeting, statutory
a meeting that must be held within a period of not less than one month, and not more than three months, from the date on which a comapny commences business. At this meeting members may inspect a list showing names, descriptions and addresses of members, together with the number of shares held by each. The meeting discusses matters relating to the formation of the company or to the Statutory report.

member corporation
a securities brokerages firm organised as a corporation and having at least one member of the New York Stock Exchange as a director and a holder of voting stock in the corporation.

member firm
a securities brokerage firm organized as a partnership and having at least one general partner who is a member of the New York Stock Exchange.

members of companies
a person becomes a member of a company when his name is entered in its register of members. SubscriLers to the memorandum of association become members automatically. Other person are entitled to registration when allotted shares on application, or when alloted shares on application, or when shares on application, or when shares are transferred to them. Strictly speaking, anyone whose name does not appear on the register is not entitled to the rights of membership. A court may order rectification of the register if a person's name is wrongly omitted. On the other hand, entries in the register are not conclusive and a person may have his name removed if it has been wrongly entered, though application to the court may be necessary first.

memorandum of association
one of the documents of a company to be formed. It contains the title of the company, the nature of the business to be undertaken, the amount of the authorized capital, the address of the registered office, particulars of the shares and a statement that liability of the shareholder is limited.

memorandum of satisfaction
a document stating that a mortgage or charge on property has been discharged by repayment of the money lent. It should be signed by all parties concerned. A copy should be sent to the Registrar of Companies if the mortgage has been made by a company and registered.

memorandum of satisfaction
document stating that a Mortgage or charge on property has been discharged by repayment of the money lent. It should be signed by all parties concerned.

mercantile agent
agent dealing with a specified category or categories of goods. As an agent he is distinguished by the fact that, provided he has possession of the goods coming into the category or categories with the consent of the owner, he, can sell and give a good Title to an innocent purchaser for value, whether or not the true owner has given his permission to sell.

mercantile credit
or commercial credit. Term used to indicate the allowable limits of a transaction. Strictly speaking, it covers business between manufacturer or wholesaler and other levels of the trade before it reaches the

consumer.

merchandise

to buy and sell goods, either as wholesaler or a retailer, without altering the physical form of the goods. To take action intended to help retailers to sell products one has manufactured. For example, by supplying point-of-sale advertising or designing packaging. Also to inform retailers on one's plan to advertise a product and persuade them to stock up their shops to meet the demand created by advertising.

merchant

type of wholesaler, and sometimes retailer, who is not committed to handling goods from a particular supplier or selling to particular outlets.

merchant banks

these, unlike the clearing or joint stock banks, evolved from the need to finance foreign trade. They tended, historically to trade on their specialized knowledge of overseas financial organizations and institutions and their contacts with them. Their major concern has always been with the facilitation of international trade; also with the problems of exporters seeking assurance of payment for goods delivered abroad and importers looking for convenient methods of settling indebtedness to overseas suppliers. They are the principal brokers for international trade though much of their business in this sphere is connected with the acceptance or negotiation of bills of exchange.

merchant shipper

a person who buys directly from manufacturers with a view to selling overseas. These merchants are also known as ex-port merchants and most belong to the Export House Association.

merge

to come under common ownership or control. To form a single sequence collection of units of data by combining two or more collections that have each been sequenced already.

merti rating

assessing an employee's performance and personal qualities by which his pay can be determined. Also such an assessment of an employee.

micro accounting

accounting for individual, business, nonprofit, or government organization, or for any department or other subdivision thereof.

middle manager

a manger in an organisation who is not a first-line supervisor and is not in a general-management position. Also a person in an organization with the same status as middle mangers in that organization.

middle rate

the arithmetic mean of the buying and selling rates in a

quotation of exchange rates.

mineral lease
a legal contract that permits the lessee to explore for and extract minerals from the leased property under prescribed conditions as to time, rental, or royalties. Also known as mining lease.

min/max system
an industrial procedure for stock reple-nishmet that establishes point at which the minimum quantity on hand indicates the need to reorder so as to return the quantity to the maximum level.

minor
also, infant. In law, a person under legal age, and therefore not able to vote, enter an enforceable contract, etc. In many parts of the world a minor is anyone under 19 years of age.

minority interest
an amount recorded in consolidated accounts to represent the value of the shares in subsidiaries of the holding company that are not owned by the holding company.

mint
the organization authorized by the state to manufacture and issue, on a monopoly basis, the Bank notes and coins which make up the legal tender of a nation.

mint par
(or mint par of exchange). The ratio of the gold content of two currencies which are regulated by the gold standard.

mint ratio
under, a bimetallic standard, the ratio of the weight of one metal or another, determined by the equivalent value of those quantities of metal in terms of the national unit of currency (such as the dollar) as defined by the government.

misery index
index devised by stockholders de Zoete & Bevan which adds together going rate of inflation to rate of adult employment. Indicates that a government should seek re-election when index is going down but could go up.

misrepresentation
if a person induces another to form a contract by falsifying certain information, he is guilty of misrepresentation. This may be innocent or fraudulent. If the person who made the representation can show that he believed them correct, the misrepresentation is innocent. In this case the injured party cannot always claim damages, though he can rescind the contract if he can show (1) that he has not implicitly accepted the mispresentation, (2) that he has acted promptly, (3) that no innocent third parties have obtained rights in the subject matter for value (i.e. some kind of payment), and (4) that the parties can be restored to their former positions. The injured party could claim damages for innocent misrepresentation if (1) an agent has

misrepresented his authority, (2) mispresentations have been made in a prospectus, (3) mispresentation is in the form of a condition or warranty, or (4) there is a special relationship between the parties (a soplictor or banker, for instance, has a legal duty to take care) though in this case there would have to be negligence. The Law gives additional aid to victims of innocent misrepresentation in certain cases.

Fraudulent misrepresention entitles the injured party to damages and rescission.

mistake

generally speaking, when two persons enter into a contract it is taken for granted that they know what they are doing. The law will therefore not interfere, and if one party fails to perform his part he will be liable for breach of contract. Mistakes nevertheless do happen. They may be mutual or unilateral; they may be mistakes of fact or of law. If there is mutual mistake fundamental to the contract, whether about the existence or the nature of its subjects matter, or about some other matter material to the contract, the contract will be void ab initio, for it does not represent the intention of either party and the court will not enforce it. This will not apply where the mistake is superficial, where the parties are getting substantially what they bargained for—though there may be ground for an action for damages.

where the mistake is unilateral the position is rather difficult. Where there has been on the part of one party, whether fraudulent or innocent, particular rules apply. Where there has been no misrepresentation the doctrine of Caveat Emptor will probably apply. However, even where no representations have been made, there are situations where unilateral mistakes can invalidate contracts. For instance, if one party is mistaken on something material to the contract, whether the person with whom he is contracting, or a term in the contract, or the nature of the document, and if the fact that he is mistaken is known to the other party (who need not have contributed to the mistake himself) the contract will not be enforced.

Mistake of law are usually irrelevant as everybody is expected to know the law: However, money paid where there is a mistake of law can sometimes be recovered if it would be inequitable for the other party to retain it e.g. if the payee knew of the mistake.

mixed economy

an economy with both public and private ownership of the means of production, thus combining element of socialism and capitalism.

monetary policy
measures taken by the central bank and the national treasury to manipulate the money supply with the intent to influence the output of goods and services, employment, the price level, the rate of economic growth, or the balance of international payments.

monetary unit
the unit of measure for a country's money, in terms of which all of its coins are paper money and defined.

money at call and at short notice
an item on a balance sheet of a bank. Money at call is money that must be repaid on demand. Money at short notice may be money borrowed for, say, twenty-four hours, at a very low interest rate. There is a great deal of money at short notice circulating in the city. When more money is offered than required, money is said to be 'easy'—when the reverse is true, money is said to be 'tight' in Lombard Street.

monetary policy
it is the policy of a government regarding the money stock in a country.

money
anything that serves as medium of exchange and thus facilitates the economic process of production, distribution, and consumption. Econometricans define money as currency and checking accounts. Superficially, credit cards appear to be money; however credit cards do not immediately demand the movement of currency, and they may be paid for by check from the credit card holder's checking account at the time later than the delivery of the goods or services received by the consumer.

money broker
financial institution that specializes in dealing in the money market in short-term securities and loans and in gold and foreign currencies. Other types of institution dealing in the money market include acceptance houses, commercial bank and discount house.

money had and received
a particular form of action where money paid by one party to another is claimed, not so much because the second party has failed to perform his part of the contract properly, but rather because there has been total failure of consideration, or because the money was obtained under false pretences or under duress and it would be unconscionable for the second party to retain it.

money issue
it often stand for an excess of government spending over tax collection combined with the issue of new money.

money market

in the filed of finance, a center where short-term credit instruments are bought and sold.

money of account

the unit in which accounts are kept and by which values are recorded, the Money of Account is usually the same as the legal tender money. The rupee in India and the dollar in U.S.A. Are both legal tender money and the money of account. The money of account may, however, differ from the money circulation.

money proper

the different currency notes and metallic coins through which business transactions are discharged.

money stock

the amount of money available to residents of a country. There are several ways of measuring this according to the view taken of what constitutes money.

monometalism

the legal tender money which is linked with a particular metal—gold or silver. The money is either made of the chosen metal or may be convertible into it, the value of money in use depends upon the value of metal.

monopolistic competition

refers to a type of market structure in which a reality large number of the sellers of product that are similar but not identical possess some degree of control over their selling price.

monopoly

a monopoly is said to exist where at least one-third of a local or national market is controlled by one person or a group of persons working together. The relevant Acts are the Monopolies and Mergers Acts.There is a Monopolies Commission, appointed by the Board of Trade, which has from four to twenty-five regular members, and is designed to protect the public interest. The Commission may be ordered by the Board of Trade to investigate and report on apparent monopolies in the production or supply of goods and services, or on prospective Mergers between two or more enterprises. It may also report on unregistered restrictive practices. Agreements which must be registered are listed in the Restrictive Trade Practices Act. Registration of these agreements debars investigation by the Commission. Mergers may be referred to the Commission where a monopoly situation may result, or where the value of assets taken over exceeds Rs.250000000. Reference must be made within six months and the Commission must report within another six months plus any extra time (limit three months) allowed by the Board of Trade. The Board of Trade has power to nullify agreements on the basis of the

Comission's investigations. It may also order the break up of a business and has further powers over the regulation of Prices.

there are special provisions, relating to newspaper mergers, again for the protection of the public. These mergers, if they result in one proprietor's controlling an average daily circulation of 500,000 or more copies, must (with limited exceptions) be investigated and must receive the written consent of the board of trade.

monopoly agreements

when there are more then one firm controlling the total of any specified commodity which could be used as near substitutes, they often enter into agreement with one another in order to safeguard their own interest and to obtain the maximum gain.

monopoly price

the function of the marginal cost of production and the elasticity of demand.

monopsony

a market situation in which a single firm is the only buyer of product , although there may be more than one seller; also known as a buyer's monopoly. Mono-psonies occur most frequently in labour markets, when a sinlge firm is the only important employer in a locality. The early textile-mill towns of New England and the coal-mining towns of Pennsylvania were examples of labour monopsony. The improvements in and the increased availability of transportation have enabled labourers to expand their reach beyond the town in which they live or domicile, thus lessening monopony power.

moonlighting

being employed by two employers simultaneously; especially doing one job during the day and another at night.

mortality chart

a group of data on life expectancy commonly used by life insurance companies in the United States for calculating insurability and premium rates.

mortgage bound

any bond secured by a mortgage on a property whose value may or may not be equal to the value of all the mortgage bonds issue against it.

mortgage debentures

they are debentures in which the payment of interest and principal is secured by some charge on any part of whole of the assets of the company. They may be either fixed or floating.

mortgagor

the person who gives rights over his property by a mortgage.

most-favoured nation-clause

this means that each state binds itself not to impose high duties on import from a third country.

motion study

this area of motion and methods study has many names, is known as methods analysis, methods engineering, methods research, work study, and work analysis. Gilbreth curve that displays the estimated. It may also be used to display the define motion study as the science of eliminating wastefulness resulting from using unnecessary ill-directed, inefficient motions. The aim of motion study is to find and prepetuate the scheme of least-waste methods of labour.

motivating the subordinates

management should provide material and psychological incentives to the subordinates so that they are spontaneously impelled to accept the delegated responsibility and duty and exercise the authority entrusted to them. Higher wages, bonus, promotions to better positions act as stimulants for productive performance of duties. In the absence of incentives, subordinates will be reluctant to undertake responsible tasks.

motor insurers' bureau

a bureau set up by various insurance offices for the protection of the general public, when a motorist involved in an accident is not properly insured against third party risks. The bureau pays out and then attempts to recover from the motorist.

multi-column cash book

this is used by large establishments. Its receipts and payments sides are divided into as many columns as there are regular heads of receipts and payments. Particular receipt item, e.g., cash-sales occurring time and again, is placed in the 'sales' column. Periodically, the total of the sales column is posted to the credit of the sales account. This avoids the sorting out of the similar items and economises labour and expense involved in their individual postings. Receipts for debtors and payments to creditors are, however, individually posted.

multilateral trade

the sale of goods in any country while its proceeds are used for the purchase of goods from another country leading to multilateral trading; it is trade between several countries.

multinational

usually applied to companies conducting major business in a number of countries by means of their own local or indigenous manufacturing and/ or marketing organizations.

multiplier

the ratio of an increase in national income to the amount of investment that caused the increase, as per the Keynes's theory of income determination.

multinational research
an expression used in marketing for investigations of the reasons why consumers may choose one product in favour of another.

municipal bond
a bond issued by a state or by a political subdivision such as a country, city, town, village. The term also designates bonds issued by state agencies and authorities.

mutual insurance company
an insurance firm in which each policy holder becomes a member. The policyholders are entitled to name the firm's directors or trustees who oversee its management, and they share in the company's net profit, which is returned to them in the form of either a dividends or rebates on future premiums.

mutual life assurance company
a mutual company is one where there are no shareholders. These companies developed from friendly societies, and were formed by large numbers joining together for their mutual interest. The capital of the company is made up of premiums paid in.

mutual office
insurance company that does not have shareholders but shares out all profits among policyholders. A company that does have shareholders is a propriety office.

named vote
vote taken at a meeting for recording by name the way in which each voter votes. This procedure is usually reserved only for critically important issues.

national account
customer of major 'national' importance often with several locations through a country. May or may not operate a central purchasing operation.

national bus company
this is being set up by the Law. It is to operate in England and Wales as a public authority (there is a separate authority for Scotland: the Scottish Transport Group). The Company is required to supervise the provision of adequate bus services throughout the country and to cooperate where necessary with the Scottish Transport Group, the London Board, the Railways Board and local authorities.

It is authorized to carry passengers by road in or outside England and Wales and also by ship or hovercraft where ancillary. It is also authorized to hire out vehicles for carrying goods, and to act as a travel agent. It may use existing services and will in fact take over the securities of most of the larger bus companies in the country. The provisions which refer to the National Bus Company are many and complicated. Anyone interested should consult the Act.

national capital

since capital is man-made, it can be easily reproduced and increased by concerted human effort. In capital we include all those goods which are used for further production. For example, plants and machines; roads, bridge and railway track; factories, offices and shops all combine to produce goods and services. Hence while capital is a means, production is an end. That is why capital has been defined as 'the produced means of production". In this sense, National Capital includes all goods which a nation has produced in the past but which have not been either used up or consumed by the people for the satisfaction of their current wants, but serve as an infrastructure for future production.

Thus national capital consists of fixed and circulating capital used in the process of production plus the consumers' durables and other goods lying for the use of consumers or households.

national claim

claim for more pay or improved conditions, etc. lodged by trade unions as the first move in industry-wide bargaining.

national dividend

the sum of all the different kinds of wealth producted by the factors of production in a year in a country.

national freight corporation

this was set to cooperate with the Railways Board in promoting properly integrated services for the carriage of goods by road or rail within Great Britain; and also to see that goods are carried by rail whenever this is efficient and economic. The corporation is intended inter alia (1) to carry goods by road in or outside Great Britain, (2) to cooperate with the Railways Board in carrying goods either as agents for the Board or on its own account, (3) to store goods, (4) to operate harbours, (5) to provide transport services by sea where these are provided by organizations taken over by the corporations, (6) to operate jointly with private individuals if necessary, (7) to provide hovercraft services, (8) to let vehicles out for hire. The Freight Corporation is not a common carrier in respect of any activity.

It takes over the Securities of inter alia British Road Services Ltd., British Roadrailer Services Ltd., Pickfords Ltd., Tartan Arrow Service (Holdings) Ltd., and Transport Holding Company Trustees Ltd..

nationalization

the action of a government in assuming ownership of an industry; usually used in reference to an industry that was formerly privately held or operated within the private sector.

national savings certificates
a government of India Secu-rity obtainable at post offices of the country. Certificates are available in multiple units. They may be bought by anyone in his own name or that of another. Repayment follows from written application by the holder of the certificate.

nationalized industries
electricity, gas, coal and iron and steel industries as also Civil Aviation, and major commercial banks are nationalised bodies of the government. In modern socialist societies, Governments are tending to nationalise a number of natural resources and industries of social importance—particularly heavy and basic industries which produce goods for utilization by smaller industries functioning in the private sector.

National Research Development Corporation
this was established by the board or trade in 1949. Its purpose is to develop and exploit inventions from research by government departments and other [public bodies. It may also help in independent research, where this seems to be in the public interest, and this aspect of its work was emphasized by the Law. Funds are obtained by borrowing from the Board of Trade, and adding incomes from royalties Patent right. Grants up to Rs.50000 may be made. If more is required, Board of Trade sanction is necessary.

national wealth
the value of a nation's total resources, including both reproducible tangible assets (buildings machines, inventory) and nonreproducible assets (land, natural resources).

natural business year
a fiscal year the ends at the annual low point of business activity or at the conclusion of a business season.

natural resources
these comprise both the raw materials and the conditions of nature that are required in production they include mineral wealth, soil, climate, waterways, and topography. By means of foreign trade, domestic natural resources may be exchanged for those of another country or for finished products, so that productive labour therefore becomes part of the trade.

near cash
something that can be converted into a known amount of cash at very short notice—for example, a demand deposit.

near money
it does not refer to cash in the bank or in hand but it is such money as may be available at the beck and call at short

notice by any business house or financial institution/bank.

need

a concept taken from behavioural science, assumed by many industrial psychologists to be the initiating and sustaining force of behaviour. A positive need or desire is defined as a force that impels a person toward the achievement of a goal. A negative need is an anxiety, a force that repels a person away from certain objects or conditions, often through fear of failure. Common synonymous for need are drive and want, when positive; fear and aversion, when negative.

negative income elasticity of demand

it occurs when an increase in money income of the consumer is followed by a fall in the quantity of goods bought as in the case of inferior goods.

negligence

in legal procedures, the failure to do what an ordinary, seasonable, prudent person would, do, or the act of doing what an ordinary, reasonable, prudent person would not do. Ordinary negligence arises from errors in judgement, not from ful deceit. Gross negligence is attributable to recklessness and an extreme disregard for common standards.

negligence of directors

generally speaking, directors are not liable for contracts made on behalf of the company where they are not acting ultra vires. They have, however, a duty to take care, and this could involve them in a charge of negligence. A director may be liable for the acts of his fellow directors if he habitually abstains from attending board meeting. He is not liable, when he acts in good faith, for errors of judgment. Also, provided he acts honestly and reasonably, the court can relieve him from responsibility for ultra vires transactions.

negotiable

a document of title is said to be 'negotiable' if, according to custom, anyone who becomes a holder of it for value and in goods faith will not be affected by prior claims to it.

negotiable instruments

claims or rights to payments that are readily transferable from one person to another, that is, capable of being bought and sold. There are four principal kinds of negotiable instrument; the Bill of Exchange (or draft), Cheque, Promissory Note, and Certificate of Deposit.

negotiation credit

a credit under which the beneficiary's bills will be negotiated.

net annual value

the result of substracting a statutory repairs allowance from the annual value of the land under the system of taxing income from land

(Schedule A) that was abolished in 1963.

net asset value

a term usually used in connection with investment trusts, meaning net asset value per share. It is common practice for an investment trust to compute its assets daily, or even twice daily, by totalling the market value of all securities owned. All liabilities are deducted, and the remainder is divided by tire number of shares outstanding. The resulting figure is the net asset value per share.

net book amount

value of a fixed asset after allowing for the amount written off for depreciation and shown in the account of a company. Net book amount is virtually synonymous with written down value.

net change

the change in the price of a security from the closing price on one day to the closing price on the following day in which the stock is traded. In the case of a stock that is entitled to a dividend one day, but is traded exdivided and next, the dividend is considered in computing the change. For example, if the closing market price of a stock on the day it was entitled to receive a 50 percent dividend was $45: a share, and if it sold for $44.50 at the close at the next day when it was exdividend, the price would be considered unchanged. The same applies to a spliup of shares. A stock selling at $100 the day before a 2-for-1 split and on trading day selling at $50 would be considered unchanged.

net effective distribution

retail audit term for the proportion of shops in a survey that actually have the product being surveyed in stock at the time of an audit. Maximum distribution is the term for the proportion of shops that have stocked the product at some time since the last audit.

net income

the net profit of a firm over a period measured after deducting payments of corporate income tax, interest on debt capital and preference dividends. Note that net income includes receipts from transactions that are not related to the firm's main activities and also include the cost of paying interest on loans and debt capital.

net issue market

it is defined as that part of the capital market which serves as the market for new long-term capital. Those organisations requiring capital (industrial, commercial and financial companies and public authorities) offer shares and securities, generally through financial intermediaries which are then purchased by each other as well as by the general public.

net lease

a lease on real property requiring lessee to assume all operating expenses, such as maintenance, insurance, and taxes, in addition to the payment of rent.

net national debt
the sum of debts outstanding of a national government, but not including those of state or local governments or the money owned to government agencies and trust funds.

net operating assets
fixed assets (including trade investments) of a firm plus its stocks and its monetary working capital as recorded in historical cost accounts.

net present value
a term used with particular reference to investment control. When a project is being considered, various devices are employed to discover whether it is profitable. One method is to take the net present value of expected income, i.e. the net income for the years plant will be productive. This is discounted back at a rate of interest consistent with the risk involved, to the date of investment. There will be a figure for each year. If the total exceeds the capital to be invested, the project may be profitable. Another similar method is to find the rate of interest that would reduce the anticipated income to the amount invested. The project is then assessed according to the adequency of the interest rate. The first method is known as the net present value (N.P.V.) technique, the second as the discounted cash flow (D.C.F.). Both method are in common use. There are also other more sophisticated techniques but they are basically variations of these two, i.e. worked on the theory of compound interest.

net price
the amount a buyer pays after all discounts etc., have been deducted. This is also called 'net cost'.

net proceeds
proceeds from the sale or disposition or property or the marketing of an issue of securities less directly related costs.

net profit
the profit that remains after all related costs from sales revenue have been deducted. Also known as net income.

net profit on sales
the balance that remains after selling and other expenses that vary directly with sales have been deducted gross profit sales. Also known as net trading profit.

net purchases
the cost of purchases of goods and services plus freight charges less returns and allowances and usually less cash discounts taken.

net sales
total invoiced charges for the sale of goods or services over a period less cash discounts

taken by customers, the value of returns by customers and any other allowances.

net statutory income
the amount of an individual's income for a year of assessment that is liable to income tax after deduction of allowable deduction.

net working capital
the difference between the values of a firm's total current assets and its total current liabilities at a particular time. (Also known as 'net current assets').

new issue
a stock or bond sold by a corporation for the first time. Proceeds may be used to retire outstanding securities of the company, to build a new plant, to purchase new equipment or as additional working capital. Also known as primary distribution and primary offering.

New York Stock Exchange (NYSE) Index
this compilation covers the price movements of all common stocks listed on the board. It is based on the close of the market on December 31, 1965 as 50.00 and is weighted according to the number of shares listed for each issue. The index is computed continuously by the exchange's market data system and is printed on the ticker tape each half hour of the working day. Point change in the index are converted to dollars and cents so as to provide a meaningful measure of changes in the average price of listed stocks. The composite index is supplemented by separate index for four industry group; industrials, transportation, utilities, and financials.

no-load mutual fund
a type of mutual fund that does not charge sales commissions. These funds are readily identified in the lists of mutual fund quotations appearing in the press because bid and asked prices are identical.

nominal capital
the amount of capital represented by the par or state value of a corporation's issued stock.

nominal partner
an individual who lends his or her name to a partnership but is not actually a partner.

nominal value
term used in connection with the value of shares given to them at the time of their creation; during the period of its currency the value of share gets changed making the share change at a value different from what it was at the time of creation.

noncumulative dividend
a dividend on preferred stock that does not become cumulative or need not be made up at a later, date, if passed (not distributed to stockholders). This may not

hold in all jurisdications, since some courts have declared that such dividends are cumulative.

nominee shareholders

shares need not be registered in the name of their beneficial owner. They may be registered in the name of a nominee or trustee. In this way the true ownership of perhaps substantial holdings may be concealed. The Companies Act 1956 give the Board of Trade drastic powers to investigate true ownership where necessary. They may appoint inspectors, of their own volition, to investigate the membership of a company and discover who is financially interested in its success or who is able to control it. The Companies Act 1956 makes it necessary for directors to give full details of shares held by themselves, or by other persons for their benefit, or by persons closely related to them, such as wives and children.

non-cost payments

payments which reduce the usable funds of the treasury, but reduce correspondingly the debt obligations.

non-instalment credit

a loan that need not be repaid in instalments but can be repaid in a lump sum.

non-operating revenue

the revenue of an enterprise that is received from source not classified as being within the firm's regular activities.

non-operating expenses

expenses that cannot be associated definitely with the activities of the business are non-operating expenses ; for example, interest paid etc.

non-operating income

incomes that cannot be associated with the principal activities of the business are non-operating incomes, for example, rent received, dividend on past investments in shares, etc.

non-profit corporation

an incorporated organization in which no stockholder or trustee shares in the profits or losses, if any, of the enterprise.

non-recurring charge

in accounting procedure, an expense or involuntary loss not likely to reoccur. It the loss is in material, it may be stated on an income statement as an income deduction.

nontariff barrier

trade restrictive practices other than customs tariffs employed either by governments or by pri-vate firms.

nonvoting share

an ordinary share in a company that carries no entitlement to vote at shareholders' meetings.

no par capital stock

capital stock that does not have a specified par or nominal value.

normal profit

the average rate of reward per unit of output in an industry or sector of the economy over a period of time. Normal profit is the minimum rate of profit necessary to ensure that a sufficient number of people will be prepared to invest, undertake risks and organize production.

normative
establishing, or seeking to establish, norms, attempting to set out the proper course of action ; stating what should be rather than what is, was or will be.

note payable
a promissory note of the maker held by the payer as a liability.

notice account
a type of savings account that requires the depositor to give notice of her intent to withdraw funds. Such accounts usually receive a premium rate if interest.

notice of default
a notice field by the owner of a trust deed with the country recorder informing official that a borrower has defaulted and foreclosure proceedings or repossession may be started.

not negotiable
if the words 'not negotiable' are written across a bill exchange, a person taking the bill cannot get a better title than the person whom he took it. The does not prevent the bill from being negotiated but the bill is no longer a negotiable instrument proper.

nursery finance
loans by institutions or stockjobbers to profitable private companies which expect to become public companies within three years or so.

object program
the result of translation by a computer using a translating routine, of a source program. The object program is in a form more readily usable by the computer than the source program.

objects clause
a clause in the memorandum of association of a registered company which states the objects of the company.

obligee
the person for whose benefit a promise is made in a bond.

obsolescence
when assets loss their value after some time whether they are used or not; new inventions reduce the importance and value of the old assets in terms of better and higher production. On the purchase of the latest models of a machine, the old machinery will have to be discarded even if it is in good shape because its use might become uneconomical.

occasional audit
this is the audit which is conducted only once in a while and that also as and when the client desires. Occasional audit is undertaken only in partnership and sole proprietorship concerns where the conduct of audit is not

compulsory by law. As a matter of fact, auditing in such cases loses its basic character. It no longer serves any purpose and the accounts thus audited cannot be relied upon.

occupancy rate

the ratio of apartment units of offices rented a, compared with the total number contained within the building, the ratio leased to total space, expressed as a percentage.

occupational psychology

the study of psychological problems associated with work and which arise in connection with, for example, vocational guidance, design of aptitude tests, personnel selection, training, work study or economics.

ocean marine insurance

the oldest form of commercial insurance; it may be obtained in either domestic or foreign posts. Lloyd's of London has gained fame as an ocean marine insurer.

odd lot

in the securities market, an amount of stock that is less than the established 100-share or 10-share unit of trading from one top 99 shares for the great majority of issues, from one to 9 for the so-called inactive stocks.

odd-lot-dealer

a member firm of the New York stock exchange that buys and sells odd lots of stocks; I to 9 shares in the case of those traded in 10-share units, and 1 to 99 shares for those traded in 100-share units. The odd-lot dealer's customers are commission brokers acting on behalf of their customers.

odd pricing

practice of pricing goods in odd amounts in order to suggest a bargain.

offer

a term used in the law of contract. The offer is the first step. Other things being equal, acceptance of the offer can bind the offeror. The offer may be conditional or unconditional. The acceptance must be in the same terms as the offer. An offer is not operative until communicated to the other party. Posting a latter, for instance, is not sufficient. An offer should not be confused with an invitation to make an offer. A shopkeeper who marks his goods with a price in the window is not offering to sale at the price, or to sell at all : he is inviting persons to come into the shop and offer to purchase the goods.

An offer does not necessary have to be in writing.

offer and acceptance by post

an offer by post in not final until communicated to the offeror and therefore can be revoked until that time. Acceptance is complete when the letter is posted, and proof of posting is proof of acceptance. (Delivery to a postman is not posting—the letter must be placed in the post box). The offeror may be bound even though the acceptance does not reach him.

offer by tender

a method of making a public offer of securities (1) in which the public is invited to submit tenders, (2) for purchasing the securities.

officer

in business management, any principal executive of a corporation to whom authority has been delegated by the board of directors or by the bylaws of a corporation.

official liquidator

a liquidator who is appointed by the court in the compulsory winding up of a company.

official receiver

a public official appointed by the Board of Trade to supervise the winding-up of a bankrupt's or a company's affairs unless or until trustee or liquid is appointed.

off-price

in retail selling same as discount, that is, reduced from the price suggested by the manufacturer or from some other, sometimes fictional higher price.

offshore company

company registered in a country where there is little government control over its financial delaying and where there are usually low tax rates.

off the books payments

payment for labour, services or goods which are not recorded in the business accounting books. Usually illegal payments since they avoid taxation and other statutory charges etc.

off-the-job training

any training that takes place while the trainee is not performing his responsibilities of the normal job.

oil and gas lease

a dead which a landowner grants another party the right to extract oil and gas from the leased property.

oligopoly

it is a situation in which a few independent organizations or business houses tend to control the market of a commodity.

oligopoly, bilateral

a market situation in which a few sellers confront a few buyers.

on account

partial clearing of a monetary obligation, as in payment on account. Also, in credit terminology, the expectation that payment is to be made at a date later than the delivery data, as in purchased on account.

on-board bill of lading

a bill of lading that expressly states that the goods have been received on board a named ship.

on demand

at such time as request is made. For example, if a bill exchange or promissory note is stated to be 'payable on demand' it must be paid immediately a request for payment is made.

on hand

owned or possessed. For example, with reference to a balance sheet item such as inventory on hand, the value listed is for items owned by and in possession of the entrepreneur.

on-the-job-training

on-the-job training involves assignment of a new employee is a specific job at a machine or workplace in the shop, office or laboratory. The worker is trained while he is engaged in the work by utilising the actual work situation for the purpose. He is instructed by an experienced employee, special instructor or his superior.

open account

an account covering the unsecured amount owed by a debtor to a creditor who has delivered services or goods without requiring payment either in advance or on delivery. Also, any account that has not been closed out.

open balance

the balance of an account at the beginning of a specific accounting period, usually a month or a year.

open cheque

a cheque that is not crossed but may be cashed over the counter.

open credit

prior to the common use of the cheque card or credit card, open facilities were an effective way to obtain cash from a bank other than the branch where their own account was kept. By prior arrangement open credit facilities up to a predetermined a mount could be given at a particular bank in another town by a customer's own bank.

open-end investment company

an investment company that can increase its size through the sale of additional stock.

open general licence

importers must obtain licences. There are usually restrictions on some goods imported from some areas, but where no restrictions apply, open general licenses are available.

open indent

the export order is known as indent. An open indent signifies carte balance; i.e. full discretionary power given to an agent in selecting the manufacture (the question of carte balance arises because an importer often appoints to act on his behalf).

open market

it refers to transactions which are exclusively with banks and includes especially the bond markets of great financial centres.

open market operations

these are referred to as operations by the central bank of a country with a view to stabilize interest rates, or adjust the quantity of money in circulation. The Reserve

Bank of India may increase the quantity of money enormously by buying securities on a large scale in the open market. The money it spends will increase the clearing banks, and enable them to lend even greater amount to the public for development of trade and industry.

opening prices
these are the prices at which transactions begin in a market from the start of a firm. In the stock exchange for instance, at the time of official opening dealers begin by quoting prices before they have a full appreciation of the relative strength of supply and demand. If they have any reason to think that demand will be heavy where favourable trends have been released overnight, then they mark up their opening prices, compared with the closing prices of the earlier day.

open policy
in the insurance of property, a policy in which the amount recoverable, up to the face value of the policy contract, is ascertained after a loss has occurred. Fire insurance is the most common example of an open policy.

open pricing
it is a form of restrictive practice in which firms in an industry circulate details of their prices and price changes among themselves or through a trade association, in the hope that will help keep price conformity.

operating budget
amount of money set aside to achieve a particular objective or to finance a functional departments's activities.

operating cycle
the period of time between the purchase of inventory and its conversion to cash receipts.

operating expenses
the expenses incurred by a firm, over a period in carrying out its normal operations a part from financing expenses-such as payment of interest on debt capital. The term is often taken to exclude cost of sales but there is no standard usage.

operating ratio
any comparison of an item from a financial statement with net sales, in calculations, the dollar value for net sales in the denominator.

operating revenue
the gross sales of goods and services, less returns and allowances and cash discounts, together with gross amounts received from any other regular source of income; net revenue from sales.

operation research
developed during world was II, the application of scientific methods of analysis including mathematical models, to process complex information and arrive at decision that often maximum probability for achieving organizational objectives. The British term for

procedure is operational research.

opportunity cost
also, alternative cost. The most favourable price that a factor of production (land, labour or capital) can command.

optimum
as favourable or as satisfactory as is possible under specified conditions or circumstances.

optimum production
the greatest output that can be reasonably achieved given the general social and organizational structure of society at that time.

option
an agreement whereby one person grants another the right to buy or sell certain goods at an agreed price, or within a stated future time. The term is usually used with reference to dealings on the stock exchange. Options to sell are known as deals for the 'put', options to buy as deals for the 'call'. It is also permissible to have a double option, i.e. to buy or sell.

It is a criminal offence for a director of a company to deal in options to buy sell shares or debentures of his company or associated companies. For this purpose a director includes his wife or children

optional capital
the difference in capital costs between two projects or schemes which are alternatives, for example, the difference in capital cost between two suitable machines one of which is more expensive than the other but offers higher efficiency. A higher rate of return may be required from optional capital than from basic investment.

option dealing
stock exchange practice (practise) under which a person can make an agreement to buy or sell shares at their present price at or within a specified future time.

oral contract
a contract that is not in writing or that is not signed by the parties; within the statute of frauds, an oral contract is a real and existing contract that lacks only the formal requirements of memorandum to render it enforceable in litigation.

oral evidence
evidence given by a word of mouth in court. Generally speaking oral evidence cannot be admitted to change a written agreement, though there are certain exceptions to this rule. These are :(1) where the whole contracts is not in writing, when oral evidence may be allowed to supply additional terms, (2) where it is necessary to show trade usage or customs or that the sub-contract was subject to a condition precedent, or (3) to explain that words are used with a meaning other than their everyday meaning (trade

usage perhaps).

order-call ratio
relationship between the number of orders obtained and the number of calls made to get them over a particular period of operation. Establishes a useful comparative tool for sales efficiency supervision.

orderly marketing agreement
in international trade, a market sharing pact that restricts competition and preserves shares in national markets for local manufacturers who would otherwise lose out to cheaper or better products from abroad.

order point
a level of inventory for a specific item at which it must be recorded. The order point is calculated on the basis of estimated demand, replenishment lead time, and safety stock to cover forecast errors.

ordinary annuity
an annuity that is payable at the end-of each period of specified time.

ordinary budget
a type of budget. The ordinary budget would present the budget for functions which are relatively permanent and therefore, ordinary functions.

ordinary policy
a type of insurance policy or contract that covers property only while the property remains at the place or location mentioned in the contract.

organizational audit
complete and perioduic re-assessment of all of an enterprise's plans, procedures, personnel, allocation of resources, etc. to determine if each of those mechanisms is being utilised most efficiently and effectively in pursuit of enterprise goals.

organization manual
denotes enterprise handbook which indicates the functions, authority, duties and relationships of each major enterprise unit. The manual properly prepared, makes possible the availability of complete information on pertinent matters about each position thus increasing understanding and knowledge of the requirements and the relations of the position's components within the position itself as well as the position's external relations to the entire organization structure.

An organization manual supplements and provides additional details to the information shown by the organization chart.

organised entry
an accounting entry that records a transaction in a book or original entry. It may include full information concerning the transaction or refer to supporting vouchers or memoranda that contain the data on the which the entry is based.

original capital
this amount of capital paid into an enterprise at the time of organization or incorporation.

original entry
an accounting entry that records transaction in a book of original entry.

organisation
it involves separation of a company's operation into appropriate divisions and subdivisions for establishment of clear lines of responsibilities for persons incharge of these divisions and sub-divisions. No one department should be responsible for handling all phases of any transaction from beginning to end. The division of responsibility should keep operations, custodianship and accountancy separate from each other. A cross checking will be a possible in this way which will promote accuracy. For instance, the clerks writing the books of first entry should not be allowed to write cash book and ledger, not should the cashier be allowed to have any control over ledgers.

other assets
on a balance sheet, minor assets not classifiable under other usual headings; generally a small part of the total assets.

other revenue
in accounting, income from minor sources or sources that are not the principal activity of the business. Examples include interest on customers' notes, instalment accounts, and overdue accounts; dividends and interest from minor investment; and incidental profit from the disposal of asses other than inventory.

outlay
an expenditure, particularly a cash expenditure, or the incurring of a liability to pay cash.

out-of pocket cost
an expense incurred by an individual, paid for in cash not charged to the individual's personal account, for which reimbursements may be sought.

output
the product of an activity. The quantity produced by a person, a machine, a factory or some other unit in a period of time. Power or energy that is delivered by a generator or engine.

outstanding
1. in accounting banking and finance, a term meaning "uncollected" or "unpaid," applied principally to accounts and notes receivable or payable, bank cheques that have been sent but not yet cleared, and similar obligations.
2. desribing securities issued to the public and currently in public hands.

over-bought
characterized by prices

considered too high, as in reference to a security that has had a rise sharp or to the securities market as a whole after a period of vigorous buying.

over-capitalized
a business in overcapitalized when it has more capital than it can profitably use.

over-draft
an arrangement with the bank that an account may be in debit at any time up to an amount not exceeding an agreed figure, interest being paid not on the agreed maximum debit but on the actual average debit.

overhead rate
the ratio of firm's indirect costs over a period to some specific characteristic of a cost centre number of man-hours worked, (e.g., number of machine hours worked, cost of direct materials), which is used as a basis for overhead absorption.

overinsurance
the insuring of property for more than its fair or reasonable value.

overinvestment theory
a theory of business cycles holding that economic fluctuations are caused by too much investment in the economy as business firms try to anticipate the rise in demands during an upswing, and by sharp cutbacks in investment during a downswing when business firms realize they expand too much in the preceding prosperity.

overnight loan
a loan made by a bank to a bill broker enabling him to take up bills of exchange, the loan being repayable on the following day. It is usually renewed: if not, the broker must turn to the Bank of England and would then be forced to pay bank rate. As this is higher than that charged by the clearing banks, general discount rates may be affected by the broker's assessment of this possibility.

over-priced
more than most customers would be prepared to pay.

oversubscribed
describing a new issue of securities for which there are more buyers than securities available. Usually the underwriters allocate subscriptions.

over-subscription
it means that where a new issue of shares is made and the demand of the shares exceeds the number offered, the issue is said to be over-subscribed.

overtime multiplier
the ratio of the time rate for overtime to a basic rate. Often expressed as, e.g., 'time a half' (i.e., overtime hours are paid for at $1\frac{1}{2}$ times the rate for normal hours).

overtime request

customs officers are sometimes requested to supervise cargo outside ordinary hours, in which case special charges must be paid.

owner's equity

the value of a firm to its owners as presented in a balance-sheet; it consists of the value of the firm's total assets term loans and provision. (Also called 'shareholders' equity, 'stockholders equity,' net assets' or net worth.')

packaging

a process or operation by which a finished product is made ready for transportation, or delivery, usually by placing the product in a container or providing it with a wrapping and/or attaching an identifying label. Also the body of knowledge concerning such operations.

packing list

a statement prepared by the shipper and generally not required by the carrier to show particulars about the merchandise in the shipment.

paid-in-surplus

also, capital surplus. Capital that is contributed by stockholders over and above the par value of the stock. The chief sources for such capital are the of stock at price above its per value, and surplus resulting from recapitalization.

paper

in accounting procedures, a written or printed piece of evidence of short-term indebtedness.

paper gold

colloquial name for special drawing rights or similar suggested schemes.

paper money

documents with a value stated on them but having no value in themselves e.g., five, ten or hundred rupee notes.

paper profit

an unrealized profit on a security that has not been sold by its owner. Although the market value of a security may have increased over the purchase price, such paper profits become realized profits only when the security is sold.

par

in the case of common stock, the dollar value assinged to a share by the company's charter. Par pay also be used to compute the dollar amount of the common shares on the balance sheet. It has little significance as far as market value of common stock is concerned; many companies issue no-par stock give a stated per share value on the balance sheet. At one time par was intended to represent the value of the original investment behind each share in cash, goods, or services. In the case of preferred shares and bonds, however, par is important. It often signifies the dollar value on which dividends on preferred stock and interest on bonds are calculated.

parachute salesmen

inexperienced businessmen who descend on a foreign market, think they can sell quickly and go home, not realising that it takes time and patience to create credibility and be taken seriously.

parallel pricing
practice of increasing the price of a product that is sold by several manufacturers by the same amount at approximately the same time by all the manufacturers.

parent company
a company that controls the finances and operations of subsidiary companies. If the controlling company does not have a trade or business of its own, it is known as a holding company or controlling company.

parity price
the price that yields an equivalence to some defined standard. For example, in agriculture, a price of an agricultural commodity that provides purchasing power, in terms of the goods farmers buy, equivalent to its purchasing power in a previous base period; in international economics, the price or exchange rate between the currencies of two countries that makes the purchasing power of one currency substantially equivalent to the purchasing power of the other.

parito ratio
in agriculture, the prices farmers currently receive divided by tile prices they pay. It is used to measure the economic status of agriculture.

par list
a list of all member banks of the Federal Reserve plus all those non-member banks that agree to take part in the clearing house operations of their regional.

partial release clause
a part of a mortgage or trust deed that provides for removal of certain property from the effect of the lies on payment of an agreed-on sum.

participating preferred stock
a security in a company, entitled to its stated dividend as well as to additional dividends on a specified basis at the time of dividend payment on common stock.

part load
a term used with reference to transport, normally road transport. Rather than hire a vehicle, someone wishing to send goods may buy space in a vehicle already going to a particular area without a full load. This can be a cheap way of sending goods.

participating preference shares
a preference share that carries the right to an additional dividend, without limit, whenever the directors recommend that one should be paid.

partly paid share
a share, only a part of the nominal value of which has

been received by the company that issued it.

partner general
a partner in the full sense of the word, without restrictions on his profits and liabilities and participation in decision-making.

partnership, dissolution of
a partnership firm is said to have been dissolved when all and every one of the members of the firm cease to carry on its business of partnership and none of them stands to any other in relation of a partner. A firm therefore is not said to be dissolved by the fact of one or more members ceasing to be partners in it while others remain. Dissolution of the firm may take place either by the voluntary acts of the partners or by an order of the court. Voluntary dissolution of the firm shall be without the interference of the court.

partners, rights of
every partner has a right to take part in the conduct and management of the business. A partner has a right to be consulted and may express his opinion on each and every matter concerning the partnership business.
Every partner has a right to have access to and inspect and copy any of the books of the firm. Partners are entitled to share equally in the profits earned. Every partner has a right to be indemnified by the firm in respect of payments made and liabilities incurred by him, (a) in the ordinary and proper conduct of the business, and (b) in doing such as act, in an emergency, for the purpose of protecting the firm from loss, as would be done by a person of ordinary prudence in his own case, under similar circumstances.
A partner is entitled to interest at the rate of six percent per annum on all advances of money made by him to the firm for business purposes beyond the amount of capital that he has agreed to subscribe. If a partner is entitled to receive interest on the capital contributed by him, it shall be payable only out of profits.

part performance
a contract needs to be evidenced in writing before either party is able to enforce it, but this evidence may be waived where one party has by his actions indicated that the contract is actually made. This is known as pat performance. It must be proved by a party claiming redress or specific performance. Damages cannot be awarded as a remedy where there is no written evidence.

parts clause
when written into an insurance contract, its intention is to make clear that, even through the article may not be usable following loss or damage to a part the insurer cannot consider that a total loss has occurred merely

because a part has been lost or damaged.

par value capital stock
capital stock each share of which has been assigned a fixed nominal or face value by the term of a corporate charter.

patent
a patent gives the patentee the sole right to make, use, or sell, his invention during the period the patent remains in force. This period is sixteen years from the date of filing, subject to the payment of fees. These are: an initial fee when the patent is registered: and renewal fees payable annually, at present Rs. 300 per year until the fifth year, then gradually increasing to Rs.1500. British patents only apply to the United Kingdom. Protection in other countries can only be obtained by applying for patent. When a person wishes to apply for patent, he must apply to the patent office. Before an invention will be patented it must be proved to contain an element of novelty. Patents are not given if the invention, or its use, is contrary to law or morality, or if it consists of foodstuffs or medicine with no other properties than the ingredients are already known to contain. No financial assistance or advice is given. Information on whether patents are still in force, and in whose name they are registered may be obtained on application to the Patent Office.
When applying for patent it is often advisable to employ a patent agent—a list of registered patent agents can be obtained for is, from the Charted Institute of Patent agents (C.I.P.A).
An international convention for the protection of industrial Property helps to obtain patent rights aboard by giving the holder of the patent in a member country priority in obtaining similar patents in another country. Most well-known countries belong to this convention, including: the U.K., the U.S.A., the U.S.S.R., and most commonwealth and European countries.

patent monopoly
the monopoly power a firm exercises because the government has conferred upon it the exclusive right, through issuance of a parent: to make, use, or market its own invention or discovery.

patent pool
the assignment of a Patent to a trade association or special corporation, so that a number of participants may use it.

patent rights
the rights that a person acquires when he is granted a patent.

pawnbroker
an individual or firm in the business of lending money for a free, with the borrower putting up some tangible personal property as security.

The property, called the pawn, serves as a pledge that the borrower will repay the loan.

payable

in accounting, an unpaid obligation, a liability, a debt owing to another.

payable to bearer

a bill of exchange is payable to bearer when no particular payee is named, or where it is endorsed in blank. A holder, by adding his name, could make the bill payable to order.

pay as you earn (paye)

system for collection of income tax under which an employer deducts tax from all remuneration he pays to employees and sends the tax to the tax collector.

pay back method

a method of comparing the profitability to alternative project; the object is to determine over what period the net cash generated by an investment will repay the cost of the project. It is generally calculated as follows:

Pay Back Period=cost of the probject/annual increase in income (after taxes).

payback period

a term used in assessing investment projects. It refers to the period over which the net income from the investment equals its original cost.

payee

an individual or organization to whom an obligation is paid, in money or another form. Also, the person or organization to whom a note, bill, check, or other instrument is made payable.

payment of results

a payments system in which a worker's earnings are related to the work he has done and to other factors within the control of the worker or of the team or group to which be belongs.

pay pause

a period during which a government attempts to prevent any increases in wages as part of an incomes policy.

pay roll

the list prepared by a firm each week or month, giving details of wages and salaries. It states the name or number, or both, of the employee, and the amounts paid. It may also give information on how the net pay is calculated. For instance: basic pay, plus overtime; minus lost time, gross pay, insurance and other deductions; tax paid, and net pay. When prepared on a machine, pay slips for inclusion in wage packets may be prepared at the same time-the one being a carbon copy of the other. The term 'pay roll' is normally rerserved for the list of weekly wages, and the salaries of those who have not achieved what might be called an executive status. The salaries of these are normally closely guarded secrets, and the equivalent pay roll is compiled quietly, separately and privately.

pay structure
the fixed arrangements or formulae by which an employer determines the pay of individual employees within a defined group; especially when such arrangements are known to all the employees concerned.

pedlar
someone who sells from door to door for cash. He needs a licence, which he can obtain from the police if he has been resident in the district for one months, and can provide two testimonials. Once he has a licence, the pedlar can sell anywhere. The licence costs 5. and is renewable annually.

peg
an exchange rate for a currency which is regarded as normal usually because central banks will take action to prevent the rates at which the currency is actually bought and sold in the foreign exchange market by deviating from the peg by more than a known amount. Also known as 'parity' or 'par value'.

pegged prices
selling prices which are held at a stable level, with the seller absorbing increased costs and possibly subsidised by government action.

penetration pricing
a pricing policy intended to capture as large a share of the market for a product or service early in the life of the product or service as possible.

penny stocks
in securities trading, a lowpriced issue that is often highly speculative and sells: for less than a dollar a share.

per capita income
total income of a nation averaged over its population, thus giving an arbitrary but comparative measure of income per head of the population.

perfect competition
market condition in which there are large numbers of buyers and sellers but quantity demanded or offered by an individual buyer or seller is so small that the market price will not change because of that tranaction.

perfectly discriminating monopoly
a situation in which different prices is charged for every individual unit of a commodity.

performance share
a long-term stock bonus with visiting and payout terms that depend on certain corporate performance conditions such as earnings per-share growth; a form of long-term incentive, and a capital accumulation vehicle.

period bill
a bill of exchange payable at sight but on a particular date.

periodic income
income that is accounted for in periods of time, such as bond interest, rent paid in advance, and profit from an instalment sale.

perishable goods
goods which are likely to be spoiled soon, e.g., milk, eggs, vegetables, fruits, etc.

perishing of goods
in a contact for the sale of goods, it happens sometimes that the goods perish either before the contract was made, or before delivery. Goods 'perish' when they cease to be substaiially the goods contracted for or described. The perishing of unspecified goods is unimportant because then the seller must provide some from another source. Where the sale is of specific goods, if they have perished before the contract was made, the contract is void; if they perish after the contract was made but before the risk passes to the buyer, the contract may still be avoided. The perishing must be the fault of neither party.

perpetual inventory system
a system of inventory control in which a running record is kept of all materials, parts, subssemblies, and finished goods.

personal insurance
insurance against loss of earning power arising through death, giving protection to the family or other dependents of the insured.

personnel manger
an official designated as manger of the personnel department of an enterprise. He assists the line and other executives in the recruitment, development and effective use of human resource for the accomplishment of departmental objectives. He is a staff officer. He is concerned with the development and maintenance of proper relations between the interest of individuals and groups and the interest of the enterprise of which they are a part.

personal saving
that part of income actually received that is not spent for taxes or consumption.

personel management, institute of
a voluntary association with over 7,000 members, aiming to encourage high standards of qualification and performance, and promote investigation and research. There are five grades of membership, based on experience, examination success, or both. There are two corporate grades (corporate membership can be gained by experience only, though academic qualification may be a help): member, and associate member. Three non-corporate grades are : graduate members affiate member and student member. Graduate members must have passed the Institute's Examinations. The institute publishes a quarterly, Personnel Management and a monthly.

personnel management
this is a branch of management that is primarily

concerned with the management of human relationships within an organisation. Its object is the maintenance of those relationships on a basis which, by consideration of the well being of the individual, enables, all those engaged in an undertaking to market their maximum personnel contribution to the effective working of that undertaking. Personel management maximises the contributions and the satisfaction of employees of a business. Activity, function or study of helping managers in an organization to make the best use of the human resources of the organization.

petrodollars
money received by governments as royalties for petroleum oil extracted their territories. Such royalties are normally payable in US dollars.

petty cash
a fund of cash held by an organization and used to make small payments.

petty cash fund
in business accounting, a small amount of cash kept either on hand or on deposit and made immediately available for minor disbursements.

phantom stock
form of bonus in which participants receive partial or complete financial benefit of stock or share ownership without actually owning any stock.

photographic copier
photographic paper copies are produced at the rate of about one per minute. No dark room is required for developing. The copies are immediately washed and when dried are ready for use as reference.

picking
in manufacturing, the act of pulling or withdrawing materials from a storeroom in order to create a kit of parts that are to be delivered to the production line for processing. Also known as pulling.
in wholesale marketing operations, the withdrawal of merchandise from the sheleves of a stockroom in accordance with the requirements of a purchase order prior to packing and shipping.

pictorial chart
a chart readily understood and enjoying widespread use by all management disciplines in chatting statistics. Graphic symbols represent numerical magnitude; quantities are compared or evaluated by means of lengths, heights, or areas of the symbols. Pictorial charts are riot usually studie critically but are intended to convey an instant impression of relative values.

piece rate
a plan under which employees are paid on the basis of a predetermined monetary amount for each acceptable

unit produced. Also known as piece work.

piece-work

wages are generally paid on piece-work basis in the small scale sector. It means that a person's pay is directly related to the number of units produced in the period converted by that pay. It is an alternative to payment on a time basis, a fixed monthly wage for a defined number of hours. Occasionally the two methods of payments are combined, particularly in connection with a productivity bonus and the employee receives a fixed wage plus an additional amount related to production above a fixed minimum.

pie chart

a diagram showing the relative sizes of the components of some quantity by means of a circle divided into sectors the areas of which are proportional to the sizes of the components.

placement

it means putting the right man in the right job. It is one of the most important functions of the personnel department of any management. Determination of a suitable job for the worker ; of providing right type of workers for the job is called placement. Placement has an experimental element, but for most employees it is a decisive step. It consists in matching what the supervisor has reason to think the new employee can do with what the job demands.

planned economy

an economic system in which the government, according to a preconceived plan, plays a role in directing economic resources for the purpose of deciding what do produce, how much, and possibly for whom. A planned economy may or may not be a command economy, depending on whether the government operates within a substantially authoritarian or a substantially democratic framework.

planning-types of

the process of planning may be classified into different categories on the basis of nature of planning, duration of planning or the use of planning.

plate glass insurance

a specialized form of insurance dealing with the replacement of shop windows, etc. The emphasis is on speed. Although the cost of a shop window is high, insurance premiums may be fairly low as breakages are comparatively rare.

pledge

a pledge is a bailment of goods as security for payment of a debt or performance of a promise. A bailment is the delivery of goods by one person to another for some purpose, upon a contract that they shall, when the purpose is accomplished, be returned or otherwise disposed of according to the directions of the person delivering them. (Indian Contract Act). When a banker advance against pledge, he is the pledgee and the borrower the pledger.

pledged asset

an asset that has been placed in trust or given as security for an obligation, loan, or mortgage. Also known as hypothecated asset.

point

in the securities market, when referring to the price of shares of stock, point means $1. In the case of bonds, it means $10. In the case of market averages, it means a change of one whole integer.

point of sale

(or point of purchase). A place where a product is shown to a customer and where the customer can purchase the product if he wishes. Usually applied by a manufacturer to a strategic position in a retail establishment where his products are offered for sale.

point system

a method of job evaluation in which a number of job factors are defined ; for each factor, a rating sale is defined with numerical values called 'points' ; a rating according tc the rating scale is given to each factor of each job and the total number of points for a particular job then represents its evaluation.

policy holder

a person who is insured under a contract or insurance especially a contract of life assurance.

policy method

in accounting, a method of depreciation determined by financial or social policy; sometimes used in public works projects.

political risk

in the securities market, the uncertainty of future returns from a security because of political developments, such as revolution, currency devaluation nationalization of facilities, and so on.

poor country

underdeveloped country. The term suggests that a country ought to be developed or is capable of being developed.

port

a harbor with piers and docks. Also the left side of a ship or other carrier, as determined while facing forward toward the front of the carrier. The opening in the carrier's side for handling freight. Also known as larboard, as distinguished from starboard.

positive cash flow

where more cash is flowing into a project or enterprise than out of it. Where the larger flow is out of the project/enterprise there is said to be negative cash flow.

positive economics

the part of economics that is concerned with proposition about what is rather than about what ought to be. The essence of a positive proposition is its concern with matters of fact, not with matters of values and ethics.

post-balance-sheet

an important event affecting a company and happening between a balance-sheet date and the date when the balance-sheet was approved by the directors of the company.

postdate

to affix a date on a document later than the date on which the document is written or executed. A postdated cheque cannot be cashed or deposited before the date appearing on its face.

post-dated

to give a document especially a cheque of a date that is later than the actual date of writing the document.

post office

at one time a government department, made into a public corporation on 1 October 1969. It deals with inland and overseas communications, written, printed or spoken — apart from radio broadcasting. It is also responsible for numerous ancillary services such as the issue of licences, government bonds, telephone directories, postal and money orders, distribution of social security benefits, etc., runs the post office savings bank and has recently inaugurated the National Giro.

post office : airway letters

letters carried by air on certain routes. They are handed in at one airport and colleted or posted at the other. The weight limit is 1 ib., and the cost, ordinary postage rate plus, for letters not over 2 oz. 18p, 4 oz. 22p, 1 ib. 26p. This service is only available inland, not to the irish republic. Registration is not possible.

post office: cash-on-delivery (inland)

parcels and registered letters may be sent- cash-on-delivery to any address in Great Britain, Northern Ireland, the Channel island or the Isle of Man. The trade charge (i.e. the value of the goods being paid for on delivery) must not exceed Rs.2500. Special labels are available—the package must be marked with name and address of addressee and of sender, and the amount of the trade charge. Present cash-on-delivery fees (in addition to postage and registration) are in the range of 25p for Rs.2500. A certificate of postage can be obtained. The cash is collected by the postman where less than Rs. 1000; otherwise the addressee is notified and collects from the post office. On no account will the parcel be handed over or opened until the trade charge is paid. There are no special rules, so maximum compensation is Rs.250 if the parcel is not registered.

post office : compensation

compensation is available for loss of, or damage to, registered packets, unregistered parcels, recorded-delviery packets, and express-postal packets conveyed entirely by post office messenger, but only if specified packing requirements have been complied with (for instance, money must be sent in the prescribed manner, and fragile goods must be marked 'fragile—with care' even if registered). The post office must be satisfied that the damage occured in the pst. Damanged articles should be retained for inspection. Companies is always limited to the market value of the articles involved. Otherwise, for registered packets post office registration.

post office : datel services

the post office provides facilities for the transmission of information in a form suitable for computer services. Information is transmitted either by telephonic or by telegraphic means. There are various types of conversion equipment supplied for a rental by the post office, e.g. for translating audio signals. The services are continually being elaborated and improved.

post office : evasion of postage

it is not permissible to evade postage by enclosing one letter inside another, unless they are both addressed to the same person. If this happens and is detected, the post office may take out the second letter and send it separately, charging postage.

post office: express delivery (overseas)

Letters can be sent express for an extra charge of 10p (or more if the addressee is outside the normal delivery area). They must be marked 'express' in red. Some countries do not accept express delivery, but these are very few and rather remote. Express deliveries can be sent from these countries but the fee is payable in Great Britain. Similar rules apply to parcels though in some places the addressee is merely notified, by express; and must collect the parcel himself.

post office guide

a booklet issued by the post office corporation annually, with supplements. It gives information about post office services available at the time of going to press, and costs 20p.

post office : late posted packets

letters (by first class mail) can be posted after normal hours at any railway station where there is a travelling post office. Wherever the mail train stops, the letter can be put straight into it if handed in five minutes or more before its departure. There is an additional charge of $\frac{1}{2}$p, or, in the case of registered or recorded-delivery mail, $7\frac{1}{2}$p.

post office : money orders (inland)
these may be purchased and are payable at any post office in Great Britain, Northern Ireland, Channel Island, or the Isle of Man. They may have any value not over Rs.2500. Poundage (cost per order) 25p. A form must be completed giving the name and address of purchasers and payee. The money order may or may not be crossed. Notice of payment will be given for a fee of $7\frac{1}{2}$p. It is possible to defer payment. An order will not be paid unless the payee signs the order and gives the name of the remitter. It is possible to stop payment of an order. The post office is not liable when an order is lost. Money orders may also be remitted by telegraph. There are special regulations concerning overseas money orders and money orders to H.M. forces abroad. Consult the post office guide.
No poundage is payable for certain orders addressed to commissioners of Customs and Excise, the Inland Revenue, of the Minister of Finance in Ireland.

post office : parcels (overseas)
postage rates for parcels sent abroad vary considerably according to distance and cost of handling. Some countries charge a fee for delivery. Size and weight limits are the same as those for inland parcels. There is also a minimum size limit of 4 by $2\frac{3}{4}$ inches for one area (unless the parcel has an attached label measuring $6\frac{3}{4}$ by $1\frac{1}{2}$ inches). Parcles in the form of a roll must measure at least $6\frac{3}{4}$ inches in length plus doubled diameter. There is a maximum size limit of 3 feet 6 inches for length, and 6 feet for length and girth combined. There is also a weight limit of 22 Ibs.
It is necessary to fill in a customs declaration form for each parcel, and advisable to state the contents on the outside to facilitate inspection. Customs duty is payable on a long list of items, and various items are banned by some countries (they may be confiscated if sent). Some goods may only be exported under licence. There are currency controls to be observed, and forms to be filled in where items exceeds a certain value. Certain privileges are enjoyed by gift parcels containing licensable goods worth less than Rs.125, if sent by and to private individuals. For details of all those restrictions, it is best to consult the post office guide or

a post office official.

post office: postal orders

these may be purchased and are payable at most post office in Great Britain, Northern Ireland, the Channel Islands, and the Isle of Man. They are also paid in the Irish Republic. They may also be sent to H.M. Forces abroad. They are available at values of 5p, increasing by $2\frac{1}{2}$p steps to 25p, and from there by 5p steps to Rs.1, and then at Rs.2, Rs.4, and Rs.5. Stamps worth up to $4\frac{1}{2}$p may be affixed to postal orders. Poundage (i.e. the charge per pound) varies between $2\frac{1}{2}$ and 5p. Postal orders are available in bulk. The name of the payee should be filled in also, where possible the name of the post office for payment. Postal orders are not negotiable instruments. They may be crossed like a cheque and are then only payable into a bank. They may be repaid though poundage is retained. They are valid for six months but may be renewed on payment of a new poundage. Application regarding loss of postal orders should be made to the district postmaster or the local head postmaster; the conterfoil should be submitted. The post office is not normally liable once a postal order has been paid. Postal orders cannot be sent overseas except to H.M. forces and persons in the sterling area.

post office: railway parcels

these may be handed in at any express delivery office to be taken by a post office messenger to a station. If necessary, a messenger will also meet the train and deliver the parcel. The charges are : railway charges plus 20p for each mile the messenger travels, plus 5p for each ten minutes he has to wait. The parcel must not contain a letter.

post office : registration

any first letters, parcels, or packets can be registered, but not airway letters, railway letters or railex. The fee is 20p, covering a loss of not more than —Rs. 7500; higher fees are payable where higher compensation would be necessary (up to 30 p. for 25000). The sender is responsible for seeing that an adequate fee is paid on top of postage. Personal delivery to an addresse is not possible. Registered packets etc., must be handed in at the post office and must be sealed —parcels, where tied with string, must be sealed with wax. Used envelopes can rarely be used for registration. Money sent by registered post should be sent in special envelops provided by the post office, as should uncrossed postal orders, dividend warrants, savings stamps etc.. If these envelopes are opened and found unregistered, they will be registered compulsorily. Perishable articles must not be sent. The envelope should be marked 'registered' and where a higher fee is paid this should be stated on the envelope. Inquiries for loss of registered packets must be made on official forms—a fee of 5p is payable. Advice of delivery can be obtained. Registration applies to letters overseas with one or two exceptions. The liability of the British Post office is limited to Rs.170 for total loss when it is in the hands of the Birtish Post Office. When the letter has been passed into the hands of another country the compensation depends on the other country. With reference to loss of contents, or damage to the contents, compensation is only paid when the packet is posted to certain countries. Registration of overseas parcels is not possible but there are facilities for insurance.

post office savings bank since 1 October 1969, the National Savings Bank. Anyone over seven years of age may open new accounts at any savings-bank post office, by depositing a sum of 25p or moreand signing a simple form. Relatives or friends may open accounts for children under seven. Persons may also open accounts jointly; and accounts may also be opened by clubs (but not by companies or business organizations). There are two types of account: ordinary accounts and investment accounts.

In ordinary accounts amounts up to Rs.500,000 may be deposited. Certain organizations may apply for permission to deposit larger sums. The minimum deposit is 25p. Up to Rs.1000 may be withdrawn on demand at a saving-bank post office, but the book will be retained by the post office if more than one demand for over Rs.250 is made in any period of seven days. Only one demand may be made on any one day. Larger amounts can be withdrawn by filling in a notice of withdrawal, obtainable at the post office. Urgent withdrawals may be made by telegraph (for a fee). Transactions are recorded in a bank book which must be sent to Savings Bank Headquarters (1) for interest to be entered, (2) when a warrant is required, (3) when two pages, or the whole book, have been filled with entries, or (4) when two demand for more the Rs.250 have been made in seven days. Interest is at Rs.175 perRs.5000 per annum. Interest begins to accrue on the first day of the month following deposit. Interest must be stated in tax returns: the first Rs. 750 is free of income tax (but not of surtax); husband or wife are entitled to Rs.750 each. Certain firms operate savings group schemes which may be affiliated to the national savings movement. Investment accounts are available to persons with at least Rs.2500 is an ordinary account. The minimum deposit is Rs.50, the maximum Rs.500000. One month's notice of withdrawal is required. Interest rates vary.

post office telephone : directories

these are supplied free to subscribers. Classified directories are free to businessmen. Additional copies obtainable from local telephone managers.

post office telephone : morning and alarm calls

one may arrange to be called by the post office at any time of the day or night. The charge is 10p. Certain country districts do not offer this facility.

post office telephone : prolonged calls under contract

when lines are available it is possible to make prolonged calls of over two hours. Where the contract allows for calls each of more than fifteen minutes duration and totalling more than five hours, the charges are at present: three-quarters of ordinary rates for the first half-hour (or part), and half of ordinary rates for subsequent periods.

post office telephone : transferred charges calls

charges may be reversed if the other party agrees to accept the call. The charge is $2\frac{1}{2}$p. There are no transfer calls to the Irish Republic.

pound-cost averaging

purchasing more share, in a company whose shares one already owns, when the price of the shares falls, so as to reduce the average cost of one's holding.

predetermined cost

an estimate of the amount of a cost to be incurred in the future.

pre-emption

it stands for a business announcement of price. Before an-offer is made to the general public, a prior right to purchase is given to special customers or organizations. That is called pre-emption.

For example, a right of existing members of a company to be offered new shares of the company before they are made available to outsiders. A right of members of a company to purchase any shares that one of them wishes to sell.

preemptive right

the privilege to subscribe for a pro rata share of any new capital stock a corporation is about to issue, given to a stockholder in the corporation's charter or tinder the common law.

preferential debt

a debt that must be paid, when a person is declared bankrupt, before any other debts apart from pre-preferential debts. Preferential debts include taxes incurred in the 12 months preceding the date of the receiving order and wages of the bankrupt's employees for a period of 4 months preceding the date of the receiving order. A debt that must be paid, in the winding up of a company, before any debts aparts from the costs of the winding up.

preference share capital

the part of actual or potential share capital of a company received in exchange for preference shares.

preferential creditor

one who is owed money by a company or individual and takes preference over unsecured creditors in recovering the money. A preferential creditor may be assured of the return of his loan by having a debenture on assets of the debtor company

preferred-stock dividend

a dividend paid to the registered holders of preferred stock, usually at a fixed rate per quarter and expressed as a percentage or in dollars per share.

preferred stockholder

someon who owns one or more shares of the preferred stock of a corporation.

premises of an office

an ideal office should be housed in spacious premises with cheerful surroundings. The office building must be large enough to meet the requirements of the business and there should be also sufficient scope for possible extensions as and when necessary.

premium

in securities trading, the amount by which the price of security exceeds its nominal, face, par, quoted, or market value. In the case of a new issue of bonds or stocks, the premium is the amount the market price rises over the original selling price. The term also refers to a charge sometimes made when a stock is borrowed to make a delivery on short sale.

premium bonus system

a type of bonus system. This is a payment by results. Under which the reward for increased work starts high, but afterwards does not increase proportionately with the work done. This automatically scales down the rate as output of individual worker increases. This system is based on a "standard time" for a given job with a bonus for time saved.

premium on a lease

very often when property is leased, the lesse in addition to paying a rent for an agreed period, pays, a lump sum. This is known as premium, or sometimes as 'key money, was once intended to avoid taxation and disguise the true rent. Premiums for leases granted for fifty years or less are now taxable. For tax purposes the premium is reduced by 2 per cent for every complete twelve months of the lease's length after the first twelve months.

prepaid interest
the excess of the face value of a loan over the amount of money actually received by the borrower, or the difference between the two amounts; often classified as a prepaid expense.

prepay
to pay for a service or the use of a facility before the benefit or enjoyment is actually received.

present value
the value today of future cash flows. For example Rs. 100 to be received to year from now is worth less than it would be if it were in hand today. Also known as present worth.

prestige need
in business management, the desire to be highly regarded by one's associates; the need for recognition. The need may motivate an individual to strive for higher status, inasmuch as prestige or recognition is implicit in a class-stratified society (or organizational structure) and may be made visible in the form of special privileges, perquisites, or office location and furnishing. The need may be associated with the acquisitive need and may or may not be related to the individual's need for achievement.

prestige pricing
practice of setting high selling prices for goods regardless of manufacturing cost because customers would not believe that quality was satisfactory if they were asked to pay a lower price. Also called 'premium pricing'.

pretax income
income reported for accounting purposes before income taxes have been deducted. Also known as pretax earnings.

price
the amount of money payable in exchange for an article or service purchased.

price fixing
the setting of prices by the government or by private individuals of firms.

price index
a statistical device for comparing the amount of which price have changed during a given period of time. A specific year is chosen as the base year and prices in all other years are measured as a percentage of the price in this base year.

price leader
a firm that is one of the suppliers in an obligopoly and usually is the first of the suppliers to change its price—

the other suppliers making similar changes after the price leader.

price maker
a firm that produces goods and sells them at prices which it can determine itself.

price plateau
price level or band which is accepted by customers as being reasonable for a particular product which is part of a range of products sold at different qualities and prices.

price ring
a lose associations of firms for the control of prices by mutual agreement.

price system
adherence by firms in an oligopolistic industry, often tacitly and without formal agreement, to the pricing policies of one of the members of the same industry. Frequently, but not always, the price leader will be the largest firm in the industry, and other firms will simply follow the leader, charging the same price as it charges.

price war
a situation in which competing suppliers of a good reduce their prices drastically in the hope that one competitor will find it impossible to continue supplying that good and will then leave the market.

primage
part of the cost of loading or unloading a ship. This varies from port to port, and is included in the freight charge.

primary account
any account to which external transactions are first carried. At some point in the accounting period, some or all of the primary accounts may be transferred to a secondary accounts.

primary industry
agriculture and extracting industries are considered as primary industries.

primary product
an economic good that is a result of agriculture, forestry, fishing, mining or quarrying and has been subjected to little or no processing or transformation by humans apart from the activity involved in extracting it from its natural source.

prime rate
the rate of interest charged by commercial banks on short-term loans to preferred customers.

principle of differential charging
also known as principle of charging what the traffic will bear, it is one of the different principles of determinations of railway rates and fares.

prior charge
loan which is a first claim on the assets of a company in the event of liquidation or winding up.

private bank
an unincorporated bank, which in the United States is regulated by the state is which it operates. Some states,

however, prohibit private banks entirely.

private corporation
the common corporation created by and for private individuals for non-governmental purposes.

private enterprise
economic activities carried on with the expectation of profit by private individual acting either as individual entrepreneurs or through partnerships, associations, joint stock, companies, or corporations.

private offering
the sale of securities by the issuer to a selected group of subscriber, usually without the intermediation of an investment banker.

private sector
that part of the economy not under direct government control. Included are private enterprises firms and the economic activities of nonprofit organizations and private individuals.

private sector of the economy
part of a nation's economy that is not controlled either by the Government or by nationalized or publicly owned undertakings.

privatization
de-nationalization by selling public utilities and state corporations to private shareholders.

process audit
social audit approach developed by Bauer and Fenn of the Harvard Business School.

process costing
practice or activity of determining the cost per unit of output of a product by a manufacturing firm through dividing total costs to total ouput. Also known as 'unit costing'.

product brokers
syndicators who find an exclusive product such as a foreign product which they ship to home market and other countries, offering exclusive mail order rights in each country.

product invention and improvement
the competition among sellers in their selling activities exerts strong, even irresistible, pressure on those sellers to compete on their basis than that of product. Manufacturers must constantly ask if they should bring out any new products, if there are product improvments that can and should be made, or if there are any new uses for their represent product. In every proposal for product change, there is one basic and all-important question : Can the new product, or the improved products, or the new use of product be sold profitably ? Unless the answer is in the affirmative, the proposal has no practical value.

No new product or service can

be placed on the market and kept there unless it can be sold successfully. Inbventions and improvements mean nothing to the inventor, the worker, the businessman, the consumer, or to our national wealth until they are accepted which means bought by the public. In the case of new products, both the product and its market must be created from scratch. New and better products do not of themselves create buyer-desire or buyer-demand. The histories of electric light, typewriters, cash registers, sewing machines, rail road transportation, and insurance prove this point.

production debt

productive debt. Debt created in the acquisition of money, goods and services to aid in the process of productions to meet payrolls, to purchase inventory, to cover costs of storage and transportion or to purchase land, buildings and equipment used in production.

productive capacity

the potential of the economy and of companies and industries for producing useful goods and services: limited by the stock of capitals goods, the available labour force, and the level technology.

product layout

the arrangement of machines and equipment in a production or processing facility according to the sequence of operations required to fabricate and assemble the items. Machines and workers are specialized in the performance of specific operations part; approach continuous movement.

product mix

range of products which, when viewed as a whole, provides a more than proportionate return than the sum of the individual items if marketed in isolation.

professional salesman—profile of

he possesses a satisfactory amount of basic ability to sell. He consciously chooses the selling field and is proud of it. He is loyal to high ethical standards. He is skilled in his work. His knowledge is thorough. He is true to his obligations. He has had selling experience. He stays up to date because he never stops learning. His integrity is above reproach. He knowns that there is no substitute for hard work. He maintains his self-respect and independence. He knows that to sell is to serve.

professional valuation

a term sometimes used in balance sheets or prospectuses. Assets are said to be at professional valuation, which means that they have been valued by a person who professes to have the expertise necessary to value them, or whose profession or job suggests that he is competent to do so. The valuation is usually written and signed, and valuer could be guilty of negligence if it is not made properly.

professions

professions are careers that invoice the acquiring of a specialised formal education before rendering any service. They need long and intensive preparation and learning. Professional services are rendered in strict confidence for a certain amount of predetermined fee. Unlike hobbies which are practised by a man for one's own satisfaction during leisure time, profession is taken as full time occupation for payment. Members of the propfessional services usually have their own organisations or associations, wherein they are required to be compulsorily enrolled. They are required to observe the rules of conduct laid down by such associations or bodies.

profit

an excess or revenues over associated expenses for an activity over a period or for a particular transaction. Terms with similar meanings include 'earnings', 'income', 'margin' and 'profit'; all these (and profit) may be qualified by two adjectives—gross and net.

profitability index

if the discounted cash flow or present value) method is used, the present value of the earnings of a project can be compared directly with the present value of the earnings of another, even if the investment are of different magnitudes.

profitability ratios

a set of ratios of financial data to focusing on the profit realized by an enterprise and its relationship to the revenue generated or the resources employed. Such ratios include the profit margin on sales defined as net profit divided by sales and the return on total assets defined as net profit divided by total assets; sometimes analysts and investors use the ratio for return on equity, defined as earnings after taxes (EAT) dividend by equity.

profit capitalisation of

conversion of surplus accumulated profits of a company into capital, eg., bonus shares.

profit earnings ratio

often styled the P/E ratio, this refers to the number of year's earnings by which a company is valued according to its quoted share prices.

profit, natural rate of

the term was used by Physiocrats for the necessary rate of profit in an industry to induce the entrepreneur to take up the venture; now the term is more or less equivalent to "normal profit".

profit ploughed-back

the part of profit of a business concern for the year not distributed but retained in the business with a view to utilising it for developmental purpose.

profit-push inflation
a situation in which prices and business profits begin to rise before any increase in wages or other production costs takes places. The process stimulates labour unions to seek wages increases, thereby prompting sellers to make further price increases.

profit; sharing
a method by which some of the profit of a business firm are distributed among employees in the form of money or shares of stock, the distribution usually being made at the end of the fiscal year. The amounts distributed may be in accordance with a pre-determined formula related to years of service of the individual employee or they may be entirely at the discretion of a designated committee or management.

profit, windfall
unexpected profit due to sudden rise in prices of goods and articles which sometimes occurs as a result of changes in taste, fashion, war, inflation, etc. Such profits are temporary in nature.

profit tax
a tax levies in addition to income tax on companies but not on individuals.

pro forma invoice
where a selling firm requires payments before delivery of goods, he issues to the prospective purchaser a pro forma invoices, giving item-wise details of the selling price of the goods plus charges for postage and packing, if chargeable or, in some industries, surcharges applicable to small orders. The pro forma invoice may also show the trade discount applicable to the sale.

pro formal invoice
document stating the value of a transaction used to notify the proposed despatch of a consignment of goods. It is frequently used as means of obtaining prepayment or of permitting the buyer to obtain exchange control sanction for the necessary remittance from another country.

programmed instruction (PI)
method of self-instruction in which the material to be taught is split up into small items called frames and recorded in permanent form e.g., printed or tape recorded.

progress billing
an accounting procedure based on work performed under contract and allowing for, the billing of work at progressive levels of completion.

progress payments
payments made at stages of a construction or manufacturing program as it moves towards completion.

promissory note
as an 'unconditional promise in writing made by one person to another, signed by the

maker, agreeing to pay on demand or at a fixed or determinable future time, a certain sum of money to, or to the order of a specified person, or bearer. The note must be delivered to the payer or to bearer. The person making the note must pay it to a holder in due course ; he has no right to deny the existence of the payee or the capacity of the payee to endorse.

promotion-basis of

ability should be stressed as the basis for the promotion although seniority may be considered if there is a tie between two persons of the same ability. According to Pigou and Myers, "seniority should be considered but only when the qualifications of two candidates for a better job are, for all practical purposes, substantially equal. Sometimes, a senior person able to meet the minimum requirements of the next job may be selected. However, senior positions should generally be filled within and not by direct recruitment.

proof of loss

generally used in the event of loss for which insurance payment is requested, a form that identifies the claimant and the relevant policy number and describes the incident and the extent of the loss. A statement may also be required as to how, in the opinion of the insured, the loss occurred. Fraud in making the proof-of loss statement automatically cancels the policy and removes any obligations on the part of the insurer.

property risk

the possibility of damage to or destruction of property through theft, fire, or other peril.

proportional tax

a tax whose percentage rate remains constant as the tax base increases; so that the amount of tax paid is a fixed proportion of the tax base. Property tax is an example.

prosecution : agreements to stifle

generally, speaking, agreements to stifle prosecution are illegal, being against public policy. There are one or two exceptions: for instance a man may not disclose a fraud if he hopes that by doing so he will enable other frauds to be detracted; or where there are both civil and criminal remedies, an innocent party may sometimes go for the civil action where this is to his benefit. The threat to bring legal proceedings, or give evidence leading to prosecution, could constitute duress in equality, where the purpose of the threat is not to serve the purposes of the law but rather than of the threaterner.

protective duty

a customs duty that is imposed by a government in order to make particular imported goods expensive and thus protect domestic producers of those goods.

protocol

the minutes or records of a diplomatic conference; especially a note of agreement on subsidiary matters which supplements a treaty. A code of diplomatic etiquette and precedence.

provision for renewals

an accounting term for the replacement of minor items of the assets variety. Instead of charging each year's replacement costs a they fall due, a company may include in its accounts an average year's expenses.

proxy

a person acting in place of another. A member of a company can nominate another person (who need not be a member) to attend a meeting and if necessary vote. The proxy can only vote if the member has power to vote, and only on a poll, not on a show of hands unless the articles provide otherwise. Notice calling meetings must state that a member appoint a proxy. The appointment is usually made in writing on a form provide by the company. It must be deposited with the company before the meeting, but the company cannot insist that it be deposited more than forty-eight hours before.

There are various forms of proxy : a general proxy with power to vote at any meeting, and a special proxy (for a particular meeting). Special proxy forms may be: (1) at the discretion of the proxy holder; he may vote as he thinks fit, (2) two-way proxies: these are printed so that the member can state whether he wants the proxy to vote for or against the resolution, and (3) three-way proxies, basically a combination of the first two. The stock exchange insists that companies wanting quotations must provide for the issue of two way proxies. If the member attends the meeting as well as the proxy, the proxy might just as well not be there. It is common practice for directors to issue proxy forms naming themselves as proxies for the members.

prudence in accounting

inclusion of revenue and profits in accounts only when they are realized and inclusion in profits of all known liabilities whether their size and timing are known or can only be estimated.

public accountant

an accountant who offers professional services to the public and who may be wholly competent, but who has not been certified by a state examining body.

public corporation

a corporation is a corporate body created by public authority with defined powers and functions and financially independence. It is administered by a Board. Its capital structure and financial operation are similar to those of a public company, but the shareholders if any have no equality interests and no voting right or powers to appoint the Board Members.

public expenditure

it refers to the expenses of the public authorities—central, state and local governments-either in protecting the citizens or in promiting their economic and social welfare.

public investment

any autonomous increase in net government outlays.

public offer

(or 'public offering'.) A general invitation to the public to buy securities. (Often called a 'prospectus issue'.)

public relations

every modern business house maintains a Public Relationship Department to obtain the goodwill of the public. The ultimate idea of any business is serving the public. Therefore, the goodwill and cooperation of the public is absolutely necessary for any business house to succeed and prosper. The public relations officer is appointed to keep the company's liaision with the public at large and with strategic clients.

punt

stock exchanger term for an investment in shares that have only an outside chance of proving to be profitable.

purchase book

is variously called bought book, bought day book, invoice book and purchase journal. All; the credit trade purchase are recorded in it. The expression 'trade purchases' refers to purchases of merchandise for resale, or/and raw materials for manufacture and sale. Furniture, machinery, building etc., to be retained and used in the business are called non-trade items and their credit purchases are separately recorded in the general journal. But where one trades in any of these items, the same is a trade item to him and recorded the purchase book if bought on credit. All cash purchase go to the cash book.

purchase journal

a book-keeping term for the book in which details of all purchases are first entered. Under the double-entry book-keeping system, the information is afterwards transferred to the personal and general ledgers. The journal gives the name of the purchaser, a description of the goods, the date of purchase, the price charged, trade discounts, etc. Nowadays it is common for these journals to be kept mechanically : they may perhaps be no more than a copy of invoices issued, the journal being the backing sheet where invoices are typed.

purchase money obligation

a mortgage or other type of debt secured by a lien that has priority over any lien subsequently created.

purchase order

a document instructing a supplier to deliver goods, materials, or services per specifications and at a specified price and time. On acceptance by the supplier, the purchase order becomes a legal contract.

purchase tax

a tax which was payable in various countries when certain goods sold by'registered traders' (roughly the equivalent of wholesalers) or people who were not registered traders. The tax was a percentage of the wholesale price of the goods.

purser

a person on board ship who keeps the cash account, and is responsible for cash payments.

puts and calls

options the give the holder the right to sell (put) or buy (call) a fixed amount of a specific stock at a specified price within a specified time period. Puts are purchased by those who think a stock price may go down, and they obligate the seller of the right to take delivery of the stock at the specified price. The purchaser of the put may then buy stock on the open market at the lower price, delivering it at the higher price, thereby realizing a profit.

pyramid sellings

a system of selling in which purchasers buy the right to sell a product. This right usually includes a requirement to purchase a minimum quantity of the product. Titles are often part of the purchase, among them are distributor, dealer, agent sales, supervisor, representative and area manager.

qualified stock option

a stock option plan that qualified for capital gains tax treatment. Under such a plan a stock must be awarded at market value, exercised over no longer than a five-year period, and then held for three years before it is sold; capital gains tax rates then apply.

quality control

activity, process of study of ensuring that the output of production processes conforms to a prescribed standard in respect of raw materials used finishing done.

quantity survey

a technical process for estimating the cost of a new construction, it involves detailed estimates of the quantities of raw materials to be used, the current price of the materials, and the labour costs.

quantity surveyor

among various definitions are 'the economist of the construction industry' and 'one who advises on all cost and contractual arrangements and acts as the accountant of the project'. A quantity surveyor is concerned with construction and provides a link between the architect and the contractor. He is consulted by the architect or engineer responsible for the design and advises on probable costs, perhaps considering alternative possibilities of structure, lay-out or materials. When the design is complete, he prepares a bill of quantities concerning labour and material required. This is concerned with quantity and not price. A copy is sent to each contractor tendering for the work, who then quotes a price. The quantity surveyor may also be required to assess progress payments made to contractors and final settlements. Quantity surveying can be specialized, particularly in the case of civil engineering, or work done for government departments and local authorities. The quantity surveyor may work in a private capacity or for a contractor. Specialization may concern both type and condition of work. A quantity surveyor will belong to one of the recognized institutes, either the Royal Institution of Chartered Surveyors or the Institute of Quantity Surveyors.

quantity discounts

it implies additional discount sometimes offered by supplying companies on bulk sales. It is partly the ability to obtain these discounts that enable supermarkets and hypermarkets to offer goods at prices comparable to those of the smaller shops, despite their larger overheads.

A reduction in the price that a seller offers to anyone who buys than a minimum quantity.

quantum meruit

this applies when someone does not complete work he is contracted to do and may perhaps claim payment quantum meruit, that is, 'as much as he has earned'. For instance, someone supplying the wrong quantity of goods can claim payment in proportion , if the purchaser does not decide to refuse delivery altogether.

quasi contracts

there are contracts in which no proper contract exists. In such cases the court may establish an obligation from one to another. The court can review even illegal contracts and may allow one party to recover money from the other even though the contract was void.

queen's award to industry

an annual announced on 21 April of each year. The closing date for applications is about six months earlier. Winners of the award may display the emblem on the goods they produce. The award is given in recognition of outstanding achievements in industry, either in increasing exports or in making technological innovations. They are generally given to firms, but government agencies, research associations, and educational institutions are also eligible.

quick asset

a current asset normally convertible into cash within a relatively short time period, in the order of one month. Examples are cash call loans, marketable securities, and a commodity or goods that can be sold immediately on the open market at quoted prices.

quorum

the number of persons who must be present at a meeting in order that the meeting can officially be declared in order. In case of companies the quorum for members' meetings is fixed by the articles of association. The Companies Act specifies that, three members should be present in person in the meetings ; however even one member could be a quorum if the articles so allow.

quota

in trade relations, a physical limit, mandatory or voluntary, set on the import of a product. In marketing-sales operations, the definition of a budget for orders in terms of a physical limit the becomes mandatory; a numerical quantity for performance stated in units or dollars, sometimes in both, and generally designated for a geographical region, a sales district, and an individual salesperson or sales account. The fulfilment of cumulative quotas ensures the attainment of the budget. Progress toward achievement of quotas is one tool of management for quantitatively measuring the progress of a specific effort, program, or individual in the sales activity.

quoted investment

it is an accounting term for investments in shares or debentures which are quoted on a recognized stock exchange. The amount at which the quoted investments are shown in accounts is normally their cost at the time of their acquisition. However company law requires that the market value, as also the stock exchange value, be given in the list.

racketerring

in business, carry on a dishonest or illegal scheme in order to make money. (Such an enterprise is called a racket.) It ranges from transporting liquor across state lines to 'avoid excise taxes to bribing a jockey in a horse race.

racking

a customs term for the drawing off of wines and spirits from casks.

rack rent

property is said to be let at a rack rent, when the rent is equal to the total income from the property.

racks

storing equipment used in

warehouses and storerooms. Some of the most common types are pallet, bin, tier, cantilevaer, flow through, drivethrough, A-frame, stationary, rollaway, adjustable arms, fixedarms, single-deck and doubl-deck.

rake-off

slang term for a share of the profit from a deal or enterprise particularly one paid corruptly.

rally

a brisk rise following a decline in the general price level of stock market, or in an individual stock.

rank

to list or arrange things in order of importance (according to some concept of what makes them important) or in order of the degree to which they possess some specified attribute.

rate

a charge or payment e.g., of discount, interest on wages expressed as an amount per unit of what is aid for. A tax levied by a local authority on the occupation (or sometimes ownership) of land within its area. The tax is related to the amount of rent for which it is believed the property could be let for a year.

rate base

in a public utility, the total investment which on the company seeks a return. The amount of this investment depends on the method of calculation used, that is, what values are assigned to tangible property, which items are included and which left out, whether value is based on original cost or reproduction cost, how much is allowed for land, how one assesses intangible assets, etc. The total value is sometimes called fair value, and the return in investment is termed fair return.

rate card

a list prepared by the proprietor of a communication medium to show his standard charges for carrying advertisements.

rate group

in transportation, the group in which a given place is identified for the determination of rates in a tariff.

rate of growth

the percentage increase in the national income per annum.

rate of investment

the net increment during a period of time of the capital of the community.

rate of return over cost

the rate which, employed in computing the present worth of all the costs and the present worth of all the returns will make two equal.

The phrase was introduced by professor Iriving Fisher.

rate of turnover

an accounting term for the speed with which stock is turned over. In a retail business, for instance, if stock averaged Rs.500000 and sales Rs.3750000, the stock would be turned over seven and a half times per annum.

rating

the financial or credit position of a person or a business enterprise as determined by another enterprise or by a credit-checking agency. In the security market, the relative worth of a security as determined by any of several investment advisory services. In the televiswion industry, rating is the result of a survey that indicates percentage of those televisikon sets in use which are tuned to a specific channel or show at a specified time.

In insurance, rating is the measure of insurability, or risk taken by the insurer, and is used in the determination of the premium rate for coverage for specified perils.

ratios

financial ratios are derived from balance-sheet data. Operating ratios are derived from items of income and expense. Ratios serve as a measure of merit of several aspects of an enterprise when data for one accounting period are compared with similar data from another period.

row materials

basic items that come from farms, mines and forests, and include such commodities as grain, wool, are, tobacco, petroleum and wood. Also, semifinished goods purchased for use as an ingredient or component of a finished product.

raw materials stock

stock of materials purchased by a manufacture as the ingredients to be used in making his own products. Other form of stocks include bought-out goods, working-progress and finished goods.

real burden of a tax

it relates to the sacrifice which the imposition of a tax entails on the tax payer.

real cost

in accounting, cost expressed in terms of physical units, such as bushels, pounds , tons, miles, and workers hours. In economic, the cost of goods and services adjusted for factors such as inflation.

real income

income measured in terms of the real goods and services it can buy. It can be calculated by dividing money income by a suitable index of prices.

real income per head per annum

average real income of each member of nation or community in one year. May be better than money income as a guide to standard of living of a nation.

real value

the term real' value is used to describe value of price excluding fluctuations brought about by inflation or deflation. It is mostly used in making comparisons over a period when prices have reacted to arbitrary and artificial pressures not of genuine nature. Determination of real value is important to estimate profits, dividends, wages, etc. Current figures are sated in terms of prices ruling at the time when the figures with which they are compared were compiled, with reference to an appropriate index number.

receipt

a document issued by a creditor to acknowledge payment of a debt. At one time it was demanded as proof of payment. Now, if payment is by cheque made out to the creditor and paid into his account, no receipt is legally necessary.

receiver

a person appointed by a court, or some other competent authority, to take over the property of another person, usually a debtor, for the purpose of receiving the income and paying off the debt. He does not usually manage the business, but is there in a supervisory capacity. Debentures holders are often given power to appoint a receiver.

receiving report

a document prepared by the receiver of a shipment as a formal record of goods received; generally used as a source document for warehouse and inventory accounting and to support shippers' and carrier's invoices. The report usually includes the name and address of the shipper, date the goods were received, name of the carrier, bill of lading number, description, and quantity of goods, and signature of the person actually receiving the property on behalf of the consignee.

receptionist

he or she represents the company to callers or various types. Callers may include customers, prospective customers, sales, representatives, solictiors and promoters, creditors, applicants for positions, and friends of the employer. It is the receptionist's job to handle each visitor in a manner that will build goodwill for the firm and conserve the time and energy of the person or person for whom he or she works.

recession

a downtown in economic activity, one phase of the business cycle. Decreased investment, falling incomes, falling consumption, and increased unemployment are characteristic of this phase.

reconsignment

changing the bill of lading provision with respect to the consignee or destination while the goods are still in transit.

recourse agreement

this is an agreement made in hire purchase transactions. The seller can retake the goods retake the goods if the hirer defaults, according to the agreement.

recovery value

in accounting, estimated revenue from a resale or scrapping of a fixed asset.

rectification of register

where a person convinces a court that his name should be on the register of members of a company but is not, the court may order the register to be rectified at the cost of the person responsible for the error. Similarly, when the court thinks a person's name should be removed from the register it may order that to be done.

redeem

to end an obligation to someone else by making a suitable payment specifically to buy back a security, to end a mortgage by paying off the relevant loan.

redeemable preference shares

preference shares which the company reserves the right to redeem. The fact that the shares are redeemable must be stated in the balance sheet, together with the earliest and latest dates for redemption and premium payable. The shares may only be redeemed out of distributable profits or the proceeds of a further issue of shares. Where redemption is made out of profits, a sum equal to the amount redeemed must be put into a capital reserve, and this cannot be distributed.

redemption date

the date at which a certain category of security becomes due for repayment by the borrower. Also referred to as the 'maturity date'. Where the borrower may have reserved an option to convert them into another security ; and even where no such right has been reserved an attempt may be made, where the borrower is short of cash, to persuade the holders to accept a substitute security in place of cash.

red herring

in finance, a colloquialism for a preliminary prospectus prepared in conjuction with a proposed security offering filed with the Securities and Exchange Commission.

rediscount

a negotiable instrument, previously acquired by a bank, a discount, sold to a Federal Reserve Bank. The act or process of rediscounting such an instrument.

redundancy

a person is redundant when his work is no longer necessary. Many firms make private arrangements to compensate those suffering financial loss though redundancy. Attention seems to be directed more to senior personnel but the Redundancy Payments Act has provided for payments by employers to employees for the benefit of those employed for from than three weeks and then made redundant.

Redudancy, and the appropriate scale of payment, are defined in the Act. Both employers and the State make contributions into a central redundancy fund. In certain circumstances the employer can then claim from the fund when he makes redundancy payments.

refinance credit

an arrangement under which goods are paid for by payment predict but the issuing bank is reimbursed out of the proceeds of discounting an accommodation bill drawn on the advising bank.

refinance credits

credits obtainable by an overseas buyer, where the exporter cannot provide credit and the buyer does not wish to pay cash. A credit is opened at the branch of an overseas bank in favour of the exporters. The exporter is paid on a sight draft drawn on the buyer's credit ; the advising bank accepts a bill of exchange on the buyer ; the bill is discounted and the proceeds credited to the account of the foreign bank that issued the credit, thus off-setting the amount paid to the exporter. The buyer pays nothing until the bill drawn on the local bank matures.

Also refinance credit that goods are paid for by payment credit but the issuing bank is reimburshed out of the proceeds of discounting an accommodation bill drawn on the advising bank. When the accommodation bill becomes due for payment be applicant for the credit is required to reimburse the advising bank. Also called reimbursement credit'.

refinancing

in the securities market, new securities may be sold by a company and the money used to retire other debts. For example, the receipts from a new issue for common stock may be used to redeem, outstanding bonds in order to save interest costs.

reflate

to take action to increase purchases of goods and services in the economy e.g. by making consumer credit more readily available.

refund

to return the money someone has paid for goods because he is dissatisfied with purchase. To repay a loan by means of a further borrowing.

register

the book maintained by an enterprise to record matters of importance. Each enterprise has to maintain a number of registers for that purpose.

registered bond

a bond registered on the books of the issuing company in the name of the owner. It can be transferred only when endorsed by the registered owner.

registered of charges

every company is required to keep a Register of Charges and enter therein all charges and mortgages specifically affecting property of the company and all floating charges on the undertaking or on any property of the company, giving in each case the following particulars: (1) a short description of the property charged (2) the amount of mortgages and charges (3) the names and addresses of mortgagees ore creditors entitled to the property charged.

registered transfer

a transfer where the particulars of the name and address of the shareholder, date of execution and consideration for transfer appear not only on the share or scrip itself but also in the books of the company.

register of companies

a register kept at Bush House. All companies must file certain documents with the Register of Companies before they can obtain a certificate of incorporation. Companies may be struck off the register if the Registrar has reasonable cause for believing that they are not in business. He ascertains this by sending a letter. If he receives nor reply within a month, he sends a registered letter. After another month, if there is still no reply, or if the company replies that it is not in business, he may notify it that it is to be struck off the Register, unless good reason can be given why this should not be done. That company will then be dissolved after three months. Notice that the company has been struck off must be published in the London gazette, or the Edinburgh or Belfast Gazette where applicable.

register of directors

every company must keep a register of directors giving names, former names, addresses, nationalities, business occupations, dates of birth and other director ships held. A copy of this register is sent to the Registrar of companies, who must also be notified of any alternations.

registered office

the official house of a company. Any document which the law requires to be delivered to the company must be delivered to the registered office. The Registrar of Companies must be notified or any change of address.

registrar

usually a trust company or a bank or a person employed by such an institution-charged with the responsibility of preventing a company from issuing more stock than it is authorized to issue.

regulated companies

an obsolete type of company originally formed to regulate particular trades, as professional associations do today.

regulating system
a control system the purpose of which is to hold constant the controlled conditions or to vary these under a predetermined programme.

reinsurance
the insuring of a risk by an insurer. Arrangement by which an insurer finds a second insurer (the 'reinsurer') who will indemnify him against all or part of any claims he has to pay.

reinvestment rate
earnings reinvested in a business expressed as a percentage of equity capital.

relief, age
persons over 65 with an income not exceeding Rs.45000 may obtain a deduction from tax of two-ninths of unearned income. This applies to married couples where one is sixty-five and total income does not exceed Rs.50000. Marginal relief is also available. Age relief is an alternative to age allowance.

relief : earned income
for purposes of income tax, earned incomes are subject to a reduction of two-ninth up to an earned income of Rs.200250 and a further reduction of one-ninth on the following Rs.324000. Earned income is income arising from work done, rather than money invested, but it also includes, family allowances, and some insurance benefits. Any allowable expenses must be deducted before tax.

relief , wife's earned income
a married with a working wife is entitled to an additional allowance in respect of his wife's earned income. This allowance is Rs.16250 or one-ninth of those earnings, whenever is the lowest. The wife is also entitled to reduced rate relief on income after deducting earned income relief. Family allowances do not count as wife's earned income.

rendu price
the delivered price for an imposed goods, that is, including all freight, tariff, insurance and other shipping charges.

renewal fund
a reserve fund established for the replacement or renewal of an asset.

rent
a payment made by one person usually at fixed intervals for the use of someone else's property. The difference between the amount actually paid for using a factor of production and a minimum payment which would bring it into use.

replacement theory
in accounting, a means of determining the optimum balance between the costs of breakdowns or failure versus the cost of replacement under conditions of uncertainty.

replevin
the restoration of goods to an owner after the goods have

been distrained, and while the court is deciding whether the distraint was right and proper.

reporting pay

a guaranteed minimum payment to any employee who reports for work whether there is work for him to do or not.

reputed owner

the person who appears to be the owner of property even though it may in fact belong to some other party. The phrase has a particular meaning in a bankruptcy : if A has allowed B possession of goods knowing that third parties might assume B to be true owner of them, then A may be estopped from denying this if B were to go bankrupt.

requirements contract

a contract wherein one party, to the contract agrees to purchase all his or her requirements of a particular product from another party to the contract.

reserve capital

a company may pass a special resolution stating that a portion of its capital not already called up shall not be capable of being called up except in the event of the company being wound up. This capital is called the reserve capital and sometimes reserve liability. It cannot be turned into ordinary capital without the permission of a court and it cannot be withdrawn by the directors.

reserve currency

a currency that commonly forms a major part of countries's official reserves.

reserved material

in manufacturing, material on hand or an order that is assigned to specific future production orders.

reserve fund

the accumulation of the undistributed profits of the bank, which are kept earmarked for meeting any emergency. This fund is built out of the profits from year to year.

reserve price

a term used with reference to auctions. A lot which is subject to a reserve price, is one which the owner does not wish sold below this price. If the auctioneer sells below this figure, the sale is void provided the catalogue does indeed state that there is a reserve price (it need not of course say what the price is). If there is no indication in the catalogue then, if the auctioneer has signed the memorandum (which he does if the contract must be evidenced in writing), the title will pass to the purchaser. The owner's remedies are to stop the sale before the memorandum is signed or to sue for breach of warranty of authority.

reserves, movements on

the Companies, Act 1956 makes it necessary for companies to show details of movements on all reserve accounts which are not depreciation reserves, showing reasons for increases and decreases.

resolution, extraordinary

this is usually a resolution concerned with the winding-up of a company. To be passed it requires a majority of three-quarters of the votes cast. Notice of the resolution must be included in the notice of the meeting.

resource

a material or an abstract quality that a person or organization uses to perform work, e.g., tools stocks, time, employees. Sometimes one can turn to in case of need. Especially financial backing.

responsibility costing

an accounting method that identifies costs with persons assigned to their control rather than with products or functions.

restraint of trade, contracts in

these, unless there are special circumstance, are contrary to public policy and so void. Restraints are only reasonable if they are in the interest of the contracting parties and sale of the public.

restricted cash

cash deposit that can be withdrawn only under special conditions or for special purposes. Usual practice is to maintain such cash in a separate bank account.

restricter

a workers who performs or produces at a level considered to be the norm for the group of which he or she is part.

restrictive covenants

terms in a contract which restrict the right of one party to contract freely after determination of the contract or during its continuance. They occur in contracts of employment where the employee agrees not to complete with the employer or practuise his trade within a given area or time after leaving his employment. They may also appear in the contract for the sale of a business where the vendor agress not to compete with the purchaser, perhaps within a given area, or in any way diminish the value of the goodwill. Another instance would be a contract for the sale of goods which restricts the rights of the buyer to purchase elsewhere. Such covenants are disliked by the law and are generally only enforceable when they are thought necessary for the protection of the party concerned, and are not against the public interest.

retail banking

aspect of a banking business that is concerned with providing current accounts for individuals.

retained earnings

the profits of a firm that are not distributed to the firm's owners or paid out as interest on debt capital, or paid out as tax, or set aside as a provision for specific future liabilities. Also known as 'earned surplus,' 'retained income' 'retained profits' or 'retentions'.

retailer

a person selling goods directly to the public. These goods have normally been purchased from a wholesaler or from a manufacturer by means of an order placed with his representative.

return on capital

a rather nebulous phrase. In the terminology of investment analysis and accounting it means the profit earned by capital if the profit were Rs.10 and the capital Rs.150, the return would be $\frac{10}{150}$, i.e. $6\frac{2}{3}$ per cent. However, there are so many ways of defining both capital and profits, and so many difficulties involved in each definition, that it is doubtful if the phrase has any valuable meaning. It is often stated as return on capital employed.

return on investment

ratio of net income after taxes have been paid of a firm or a division of a firm over a period to the average value during that period of the operating assets of the firm. Synonym for rate of return.

reveluation of assets

the fixed assets of a business are frequently subject to change in value, both real and nominal. Real value can change where the asset is of a durable type, e.g., land, the demand for which may force up the market prices. Nominal values rise continually in times of inflation where the fall in the value of money is reflected in higher replacement costs. In a business where the asset's current value is calculated in terms of current prices.

revenue account

a profit and loss account, especially of an investment trust or a company specializing in buying and selling real property.

revenue bond

a bond issued by a government for the purpose of financing the construction or purchase of or addition to income-producing facilities repayment of such bonds and the periodic payment of interest their dependent on earnings.

revenue duty

a customs duty or an excise duty that is imposed by a government mainly in order to raise revenue for itself. Revenue duties are always imposed by a Finance Act and are invariably charged according to the quantity of goods involved rather than their value.

revenue tariff

an import tax usually applied to products that are not produced in the importing country, for example, tin, coffee, and bananas in the case of the United States. Typically, rates on revenue tariff are modest.

revolving credit

a facility granted to a specific person whereby he may borrow money, or buy goods on credit, up to a known initial limit ; when money is borrowed or goods are bought, the credit limit is reduced by the value of the borrowing, etc. ; it can be increased again by the amount of any money paid to the granter of the facility, but never to more than the initial limit.

rights of resale

in certain circumstance a seller of goods may resale, for instance after stoppage in transit, or because of a lien. Neither stoppage nor lien rescinds the contracts but the seller can, if the goods are likely to perish, resell the goods and give a good title. He may also resell if the buyer does not pay within a reasonable time after the seller has announced his intention to resell. As the title remains with the buyer the surplus on resale belong to him, after the selelr has reclaimed any expenses.

This does not apply where in the contract the seller reserves the right of resale: then the contract is rescinded.

ring trading

it is a term used with reference to dealings in futures. Dealers come together around what is known as a ring, and bids and offers are called, and prices marked up.

risk

the probability of failure or loss associated with a particular course of action. A hazard covered by a contract of insurance.

risk manager

an insurance specialist who diagnoses risks to which a project or enterprise may be subjected and prescribes appropriate action with respect to insurance coverage.

road haulage contract hire

facilities offered by, e.g. the National Freight Corporation for hiring a fleet of vehicles or even just one vehicle. Each vehicle can be dressed in the customer's livery and is to all intents and purposes the customer's own property. Drives can be supplied, the vehicle can be housed by the customer or the true owner. The contract is normally based on a monthly rental.

rolling forecast

a counting series of periods of marketing activity in the form of a budget.

rotating shift system

a three-shift system in which one group of workers works one type of shift for the 6-8 hours, then a second type of shift for the same period and then a third type of shift for the same period.

route card

a document which accompanies a batch of work

during a manufacturing process and shows the operations that have to be performed and the work centres involved.

route sheets

at each stage of a manufacturing process a part is analysed to determine the operations required and to select and specify the functions required to complete the processing. The routing of the pat is summarized on route sheets.

runout list

a list of items to be scheduled into production in sequence by the dates on which the present available stock is expected to be exhausted.

royalties

the sum paid for the right to use another person's property for productive purposes. For instance , royalties may be paid for working mines to the owner of the land, or by a publisher to an author. There are special taxation rules for dealing with royalties where they apply to books, the object being to spread the income over the period of expenditure. Thus the income may be spread back over the time the book was written.

royalty

money paid to someone in return for being allowed to exercise, but to take over entirely, specified rights of his— especially the right to work a mine, or the right to publish a copyright work. The amount of a royalty is almost invariably related to the benefit from exercising the specified right.

rule in foss v. Harbottle

this is a rule observed by the court limited companies. It will not interfere with the running of a company at the instance of any particular shareholder, if it considers that the shareholder has his own redress within the rules of the company itself. Generally speaking, majority decisions within a company are upheld, assuming there is no fraud on the minority.

rupee

the basic unit of currency in India, Mauritius, Nepal, Pakistan and Sri Lanka.

rural industries bareau

now taken over by the Council for Small Industries in Rural Areas. A bureau offering technical and advisory services to industries employing up to skilled workers either in the countryside twenty or in towns in with a population of less than 10,000. Priority is given to exporting firms. It is financed by government funds.

sale of goods

at one time the doctrine of caveat emptor applied to the sale of goods, but this has now been modified by various statutes, the most important of these being the Sale of Goods Act. This gives various implied warranties and conditions concerning the sale of goods. These will apply unless specifically excluded.

The implied conditions are : (1) that the seler has a good title and will be able to pass a good title; (2) where the sale is by description that the goods actually comply with the description; (3) where the sale is by sample, that the goods comply with the sample, and that the customer will have a reasonable time to make a comparison; (4) where the customer relies on the skill and judgment of the vendor and the goods are of a kind that the vendor usually supplies, that the goods will be fit for the purpose for which they are required. (This is modified by the fact that where the buyer relies on a trade name there is no implied condition.) It is no necessary that the buyer should state that he is relying on the seller's judgment: this may be inferred. If a man buys chips in a chip shop, it may be taken for granted the seller known the purpose for which they are required ; (5) that the goods should be of merchantable quality. Where the customer has had opportunity to examine the goods this does not apply to defects that an examination should have revealed.

The implied warranties are : (1) that the buyer should have and enjoy quiet possession of the goods; (2) that the goods are free from any charge in favour of a third party. A condition can be reduced to a warranty in certain circumstances, e.g. where the customer delays in making a claim.

The tendency for the law today is to afford the customer further advantages: there have been two Consumer Protection Acts and probably more to come based on the Monoley Report. There are also of course independent consumer's Association and a state subsidized consumer council Misrepresentation.

safety margin

sales of a product in excess of its break-even point.

salary administration

activities concerned with fixing and sometimes paying a salaries in an organization.

sale of goods : title

it is often important to known when the title to goods passes. When the sale is of ascertained goods, title will normally pass according to the intention of the parties. Sale of Goods Act states that where the contrary is not defined in the contract, if specific goods are named and are in a deliverable state, then the property passes immediately the contract is made. When the contract is for specific goods, and something remains to be done and to them before they can be delivered, then title passes when that something is done the buyer is notified of it. Goods are in a deliverable state when they are in such a state that the buyer would be bound to accept them.

Where goods are unascertained, e.g. where an order is made for a quantity of goods, and the specific goods are not named, the intention of the parties is still relevant but generally speaking title passes when goods are appropriated to the contract with the assent of the buyer and the buyer has been notified. The assent may be implied, and may even be given before goods are appropriated.

Where goods are on sale or return, title passes when the buyer either signifies his assent to the contract, or retains the goods for an unreasonable length of time.

So far as the title of the seller is concerned, there is an implied condition in the Sale of Goods Act that the seller is entitled to the goods and is able to sell them, or will be when the time of sale comes.

sale or return basis

an arrangement by which goods are supplied by a manufacturer or wholesaler to a retailer on condition that he may return any that he does not sell within a specified period and no charge will be made for the returned goods.

sales journal

in accounting, the book of original entry that is used for recording individual sales or classes of sales by product, department, or other aspect of the enterprise.

sales ledger

this ledger consists of individual debtor's accounts to whom the goods and services are sold on credit. Opening balances are checked up with the last years audited balance sheet. The positings are checked from sale books, sales return book, cash book, bills receivable book and journal. One can confirm the balances directly from the debtors in case there is any basis for doubt.

The bad debts are written off only after proper sanction has been obtained from a person authorized to do so, after the bad debts to be written off have been carefully checked.

sales promotion

any device or arrangement, except advertising using media of mass communication, used by a firm at some cost to itself and intended to draw the attention of potential buyers to one or more of firm's products. Probably the most common form of sales promotion is a reduction in selling price for a limited period. Other forms include consumer contests, premiums, and for retailers trading stamps.

sales representative

a person employed to solicit orders for goods or services.

sales revenue
the total amount of money or a measurement, in monetary terms, of the total value of property, of services receivable by a firm in exchange for goods or services of specified kinds supplied by the firm during a specified period.

sales tax
a tax levied on the sale of goods and services at one or more stages in the process of distribution.

salvage
the reward given to persons who save, in part or whole, a ship or its cargo from shipwreck. The person rendering assistance must show that he did so voluntarily, that there was danger involved and that he showed enterprises, that the ship was in need of help and that some benefit did arise from what he did. Salvage money cannot be claimed by those responsible for the care of the ship. The reward is given by the owners of the ship and cargo.

sample
the sample of a good sent to a prospective customer so that he may decide to make a bulk purchase. It he purchases on the basis of the sample, the bulk that he receives must correspond to it.

sampling distribution
the probability distribution of a random variable that is defined as some characteristic (a statistic) of a sample of a particular size drawn from a given population. Thus the sampling distribution of a statistic shows the pattern of occurrence of that static in all possible samples of a given size.

sampling frame
a means of identifying all the items of a population to be surveyed e.g., a list of households or a map of an area—so that a sample can be chosen.

sanction
literally, enforcement. A sanction is the penalty for the breach of a law. Redress for civil injuries is called civil sanction. Punishment for violation of a criminal law is called pena sanction.

savings bond
a debt security sold by the Treasury to individual investors. These are fully registered securities usually to sold in small amounts to make them affordable to the majority of the population.

scalar chain
chain of superior from top to bottom is called the scalar chain. To facilitate quick communication between one link of the chain and the other, either the chain should not be very long or gang planks may be provided in-between to correspond directly.

scheduling
activity or process of planning when particular actions are to

be carried out. In particular , planning when particular items are to be manufactured to meet the orders in hand.

scrip

a fractional or temporary share of stock or other security. It may be issued in connection with a recapitalization or reorganization and is ultimately converted into regular certificates, Also' scrip is paper "money" issued by corporations to pay wages and is accepted in exchange for merchandise by the corporations' stores.

scrip issue

an issue of shares to existing shareholders made possible by the capitalization of reserves. No payment is necessary, so it is often called a bonus issue. In a case where one new share was issued for every two previously held, the shareholder would be receiving an acknowledgement that his capital has increased by 50 per cent. However if the old rate of dividend were not maintained the share prices would be depressed and the shareholder might not find himself financially better off. If the divided were maintained he would have received something that he could sell. The proceeds, being capital, would not be subject to dividend tax. It may be a good policy to capitalize profits rather than distribute them in the form of dividends, but unless profits are increasing, it will not be possible to maintain dividend rates on an expanding capital. The issue of bonus shares used to be looked on as an alternative to a cash dividend, giving the recipient a saleable assets, the profits not being taxable. This gap was closed by the introduction of capital gains taxes and also by the Finance Act, which provided that where a shareholder could opt for cash or additional shares, the additional shares were to be treated as a distribution is cash, and therefore would be subject to dividend tax. This did apply to redeemable preferences shares.

seasonal index

an index number that shows the relative sizes of the figures in a monthly time series which is used to produce seasonally adjusted data.

secondary market

that part of the money market which deals in the exchange or marketing of securities already in issue, and where dealings can be arranged in such property as unquoted stocks and shares, second mortgages, etc. which are not generally handled by the primary market. A market for a good in which the producers of the good do not participate as sellers. A market for securities in which the issuers of the securities do not participate as sellers.

secondary offering

the redistribution-of a block of stock some time after that stock has been sold by the issuing company. The sale is handled by a securities firm or group of firms, and the shares are usually offered at a fixed price that is related to the current market price of the stock usually the block is a large one, such as might be involved in the settlement of an estate.. The security may be listed or unlisted.

secret profits

profits made by a person who is a fiduciary relationship with another, and makes the profits by reason of the relationship, or, arising out of it, without disclosing them to the other person. When they are discovered, they must be shared and in certain circumstances the guilty party may also be sued by the innocent party. Examples of secret profits are profits made by an agent while working for his principal, profits made by one agent while working for his principal, profits made by one partner while about partnership business, profits made by directors of companies from contracts with other organizations in which they have an interest.

secretary, personal

a person employed as an assistant to deal with correspondence and other not needing the employer's personal attention.

secular price

a price resulting from the interaction of economic forces over a period of years.

secured creditor

a creditor whose debt is secured, e.g. by a charge on the property of the debtor: this may take the form of debentures where a company is concerned. The charge may be a fixed or a floating charge. A fixed charge is one where the actual property is specified; a floating charge is one which attaches to the property of the debtor generally-the actual property only becomes known when the debt is payable, when it is said to crystallize.

security

a document given by a corporation or government called the "issuer" and acknowledging that the issuer has received money, or some other valuable consideration, for issuing the security that some specified person is, in return, entitled to certain rights against the issuer.

self employed

there are entrepreneurs running their own business. They may hire if at all, a few employees, to help them.

self insurance

often confused with non-insurance, which means not taking out an insurance policy; self-insurance as practised by large companies means the actual setting aside of a reserve fund that may be used in the event of loss.

sell and-leaseback agreement

an arrangement whereby a business that owns and occupies improved real estate sells it to an investor and takes a long-term lease (in the property, which it continues to occupy. The agreement may include an option to repurchase the property at the termination of the lease.

seller's market

a situation where market conditions are favourable to sellers, usually because demand is running ahead of supply.

selling

the process or activity of persuading and/or assisting individuals to make purchases.

selling as a productive activity

it is a miconception that selling adds no value to the goods and services it markets or that it is a parasitic form of promotion. The other side of this spuerious coin is that individuals engaged in production and agriculture alone are productive that they do create utility.

The answer to this is that economic exchange is the heart or ore of our economy. There cannot be vast consumption without heavy buying, and heavy buying will not be done without extensive selling. Time, place, possession, and information-utility can result directly from the activities of salesmen.

Selling is productive in that, to be successful, it must benefit the buyer as well as the seller. Practically all vendors must receive repeat orders and purchases from their customers if the vendors are to survive profitably. Most vendors must hold a customer's patronage through many successive purchases and over many years. Clearly, no sensible buyer makes repeated purchases from a seller if those purchases fail to benefit him.

selling out

a stock exchange term covering the situation arising from a buyer not being able to take up the shares tendered for and the owner, or broker, sells for the best price he can get. The original buyer is liable for both the difference between the prevailing price and the price originally contracted plus the expenses incurred in the selling out.

semitrailer

a freight-carrying vehicle that has no power of its own. It is attached to a tractor to obtain motive capabilities.

semi-variable costs

costs partly fixed but partly variable, e.g. costs which are fixed until level of output is reached, and then fixed again, at a higher level until another level is reached. Two part tariffs are another example of semi-variable costs (for instance, there is a fixed charge for the installation of, say, a telephone, and then a variable charge for its use).

service life

the period of usefulness of an asset to the owner of the asset. Service life may be used as the basis for calculating depreciation.

set

a collection of objects of some sort is defined by a rule which unambiguously determines whether or not something is included in the collection. A state of psychological preparedness, of limited duration, which is characteristically taken up in anticipation of a particular type of stimulus or situation.

set off

a set-off is said to take place when two parties are indebted one to the other and one debt can be set off against another by mutual agreement.

severable contracts

this phrase often occurs in contracts for the sale of goods, particularly where the goods are to be delivered in instalments. It is possible to treat separate instalments as separate contracts, but not necessary-in a breach of contact case the court would look to the intention of the parties. Failure to deliver, or pay for, one instalment, might be a breach of the whole contract. On of the other hand, the contract might be treated as severable, and an action brought for only the one particular failure to deliver or pay.

share

a unit for reckoning investor's interests in the contributed capital of a company. Each share is assigned a nominal value, which is the minimum value of capital that must be contributed for the share.

share capital account

account of a company recording receipts, repayments and losses of share capital; other than share premium, which is recorded in a separate 'share premium account'.

shares, deferred ordinary

a special category of share, often issued to the founders of a company. These shares normally give the owner special dividend rights, and often entitle him to all profits after a certain percentage has been paid on the other classes of shares. This type of share is not very common in public companies as it tends to arouse suspicion.

shareholder

someone who owns one or more of a company's shares.

share hawking

at one time it was possible to hawk shares from door to door, but nowadays noboday may deal in securities or shares unless they are licensed dealers like stock brokers.

shares : lien

the Articles of Associations of a Company normally give a first lien on the shares of each member, for debts and liabilities, to the company. The lien usually applies to dividends due: the company cannot enforce it by forfeiting the shares.

share, placing of

a method of issuing shares. The shares, rather than be offered to the public by the company or through an issuing house, are 'placed' by a reliable broker, i.e. sold in perhaps substantial blocks to selected customers: probably financial institutions. These clients will then sell to the public when dealings in the shares begin, i.e. when a quotation has been granted by the stock exchange. If the quotation is not obtained of course no dealings well be possible.

share premium

a sum may be charged on an issue of shares, over and above the nominal value, if their profitability indicates that their real value is in excess of their nominal value. Share premiums are put to a special account (the share premium account), which is a capital preserve, and cannot be distributed to members. It can however be capitalized and form the basis of a scrip issue.

share register

the register kept by a limited company giving the names and addresses of major shareholders. The register records the dates of beginnings and endings of shareholders, and the amounts paid up on shares.

share warrant

a share certificate that does not contain the name of the member, so that title is transferable by delivery. It is not a negotiable instrument. Wattants can only be issued when shares are fully paid. The shareholder's name is struck off the register when the warrant is issued. The articles of association usually allow the warrant holder to vote at meetings on presentation of the warrant. Coupons are usually attached.

A document issued by a company which states that the bearer is the owner of a specified member of shares in the company. Share warrants may be sold without registering the change of ownership with the company and the company has no record of who owns share warrants. An owner of a share warrant usually has the right to surrender it to the company in exchange for a share certificate and his name is then entered on the register of member; this would be necessary if he wanted to vote at a shareholders' meeting.

shares of a company

'share' is a share in the share capital of a company. It is an interest of a person in the share capital of a company which is measured by the sum of money. Shares can be purchased and held like other goods. Huge amount of capital for a new industry may be raised by public subscription of shares by large number of people. The joint stock form of business organisation has made it possible to raise funds not only from a large number of people but also from persons of different temperaments. In order to satisfy needs of all types of investors and to raise sufficient amount of capital, various classes of share are issued by the companies. Funds can now easily be raised from people of speculative tastes to the most cautious investors by issuing securities bearing different degrees of risks. The amount of capital which a company can raise and the various classes of shares which may be issued by a company in order to raise its capital together with their rights are mentioned and fixed by the Memorandum and Articles of Association.

shares, forfeiture of
when a shareholder does not pay the calls due on his shares, they may be declared forfeited by the directors provided the articles of association of the company allow. Forfeited shares may be reissued for fresh sale.

shares, ordinary
these have no particular right to dividend but are entitled to all the profits after prior demands, such as loan interest, or preference dividends. However, whether and when they receive the profits is at the discretion of the directors, who may if they wish put all profits into reserve. The ordinary shareholders are the true owners of a company. The directors are, strictly speaking, stewards. The shareholders meet at least once a year and may put forward any resolution that they wish.

shares, preference
these share have a preferential right to dividend, i.e., they are entitled to a fixed sum beforre anything is paid to holders of ordinary shares. The dividends may or may not be cumulative. In any event, dividends are paid at the final discretion of the directors.

shopping goods
consumer goods whose price, fashion, quality, and service are relatively important to the buyer. Greenly bought infrequently , they are of high unit value, and the buyer may spend considerable time in shopping for price and quality, often at outlets located some distance from the consumer's residence. Items in this class include furniture, automobiles, jewellery, china and furs.

ship chandler
an individual or a company that sells ship's equipment and supplies.

ship-owner's lien
the lien that a ship-owner has for freight and other charges attaching to the goods that he carries. This lien may even exist when the goods have been warehoused if notice has been given to this effect. The lien for freight or general average contributions is a possessory lien. The lien for other expenses in protecting the goods is a martime lien.

shipper
a manufacturer or merchant who sends goods abroad on a ship.

shipping agent
a general agent specializing in the export or import of goods by sea. He deals with shipping documents, insurance, and customs, and sees that cargo-space is available as needed. Some of the shipping agents are connected with particular steamship companies and these circulate information about available space to their agents.

shipping bill
a document used for claiming drawack or other facilities from the customs authorities or the Ministry or Commerce.

shipping claims tribunal
established in 1939 to deal with compensation for requisitioned ships, the Tribunal was never really active. It exists now only theoretically. Each year the Registrar checks that entries in reference books are correct.

shoplifting
taking goods from shop counters without any intention of paying for them. This is a criminal offence and should be distinguished from obtaining goods on credit knowing that one will be unable to pay for them.

shop order
an instruction to a manufacturing department to make or assemble specified items.

short bill
a bill of exchange that is due to be paid in a short time (usually less than 10 days).

shorthand
one of various recognized forms of abbreviated writing. Shorthand is used in business, to take notes in court, to take records of parliamentary proceedings, and so on.

short rate
the disproportionate amount of an insurance premium returned when an insured cancels the policy. The insurance company retains a portion of the unused premium as a cancellation penalty.

short-term debt
any current liability, including the maturing portion of a long liability, short-term debts are usually payable within the next 12-months period.

short-term deposits
monies deposited with banks, finance houses, etc. on terms which allow them to be

withdrawn at short notice. Generally speaking, the shorter the loan, the lower the interest rate, and the greater the liquidity.

short-term interest rates

whereas short term interest rates tend be close to base rates and minimum lending rates, they are generally higher in banking institutions. Banks offer high rates for large sums loaned for a period. These rates are higher than normal deposit account rates as they are determined not by the prevalent minimum lending rate but by the fact that the monies are deposited as a loan for a fixed period, in which withdrawals are not permitted or in the form of loans to banks or similar finance companies only.

silence

a seller does not have to make any respresentations with reference to his goods. Silence does not constitute misrepresentation unless the circumstances are exceptional. When a person makes an offer, he cannot state that silence will be taken as acceptance. However, in contracts which are uberrimae fidei there is a duty to make all relevant facts known.

silent partner

a members of a partnership who takes no active part in the management of the enterprise. This type of partnership enables persons to invest in the business without taking an active part in operations but allows others to handle the day-to-day management situations. A silent partner is a limited partner, one whose financial liability in the business is limited to the extent of his actual investment; however if the silent partner takes an active part in management the personal liability is the same as that of a full partner.

simple arbitrage

taking advantage of the existence of two different market prices for something by arbitrage.

simple interest

the charges made by a lender for the loan of money or for a deferment of the collection of an account. It is calculated by applying an interest rate against the principal of the loan only.

simple trust

a trust that must distribute its income currently but does not distribute capital before its termination.

sinking fund

an accounting term for cash set aside for a particular purpose, and invested so that the correct amount of money will be available when it is needed.

sinking fund bond

any issue of a bond that requires the issuer to set aside periodically a sum that, with interest, will meet the redemption price of the bond or will be equal to a specified fraction of the total.

site audit

an audit conducted on the premises of the organization being examined, especially in financial examinations performed by government agencies such as the IRS.

situational sensitivity

in organizational behaviour, the skill in appraising situational elements in terms of task and relationships demands; Slander Liability Insurance available to radio and television broadcasting stations, credit bureaus, and other organizations that may face accusations of oral defamation of character. Usually written with a high dollar-value deductible clause. The insured company is required to conduct its own legal defense.

slab scale

income tax term for a scale where progressive rates apply to the whole of the taxable income.

small business

a general term related to the quantification or size of an enterprise. Definitions of small business are varied. For example, the Bareau of the Census references the number of employees within the enterprise; the Internal Revenue Service reference sales volume; Dun & Bradstreet reference net worth, the Small Business Administration exercise considerable latitude in defining the difference between "small" and "big"-according to type of business (manufacturing, wholesaling, relating, service) and the dominance of the enterprise within its -specific field of endeavor.

small business investment company

a privately and publicly owned but government regulated company whose sole purpose is to provide long-term financial assistance and management services to small business firms. SBICs are licensed and regulated by the small business administration, from which they may also obtain favourable financing.

social balance

the relative distribution of resources between the public and private sectors.

social benefits

a gain that accrues to individuals and society as a whole, but for which the individual does not, have to pay directly. Highway construction and police: protection are examples.

social costs

a disadvantage to society that may result from private production but that is riot necessarily reflected in the money costs to the individual producer of acquiring the resources needed for production. Pollution is a social cost of production that the market system does no measure.

socialism

an economic system whose basic feature is the ownership of all or most production activity by the government rather than by individuals: factors of production (other than human services), thus eliminating property as source, of individual income-it controls the economy through centralized planning. In democratic socialism, the private sector retains control of agriculture, services, and nonvital industries; the government attempts to redistribute wealth through taxation and social welfare programs.

social security

arrangements made by a government to provide money for people who are unable to provide for themselves.

social security integration

the technique whereby a pension or profit-sharing retirement plan is discounted for social security benefits. This is done by applying a formula, by excluding certain earnings from the benefits, calculation, or by substracting social security under the so-called offset approach.

soft currency

the opposite of a hard or scarce currency. Soft currency are those which are falling in value, usually due to continual balance of payments problems in the countries they represent. They are, by nature, not welcome within an nation's gold and foreign exchange reserves.

sole proprietorship

a form of business enterprise which is established financed, owned , managed and controlled by an individual entrepreneur, who enjoys complete freedom of operation, bears all risks and takes all the profits earned.

sole trader

a person who trades on his own account, rather than in partnership or as a member of a company.

solftening price

a price that has a continuing tendency to decrease.

sole proprietorship-features of

ownership and management of a business by a single entrepreneur is the oldest and still the most common form of business organisation. Sole trader is a person who carries on business exclusively by and for himself. He carries on business on his own account and is alone responsible for the profits and losses of his business. He acts both as the owner and the risk bearer of his business. He brings in his own capital, uses his own skill and labour and is entitled to all the profits of the business. His liability being unlimited, he personally responsible to all the creditors of the business. He alone bear the complete risk of success or failure of the business. In a large business a sole trader may, however, employ large number of persons to help him in the management of business or may borrow funds to finance his expanding business, yet the supreme control vests in his hands and he continues to be solely responsible for all that takes place in business.

single man business is established, financed, owned and managed with almost unlimited freedom by a single individual who not only bears all the risks but also receives the entire gains therefrom.

In a single man business, ownership and control remain vested in the hands of the same person. Direct relationship between effort and reward provide him with the necessary incentive to work hard and to look personally in the affairs of the business. All rou ıd personal touch of the proprietor ensures efficiency in business and lessens wastage of resources.

sole trander

sole trader is a person who runs a sole proprietorship in the field of commerce-local national or international. He brings in his own capital and uses his own skill and labour and is entitled to all the profits of the business. He acts both as the owner and the risk bearer of his business. His liability being unlimited, he is personally responsible to all the creditors of the business. He alone bears the complete risk of success or failure of the business.

A person who carries a business for his own profit, not in partnership with others and not by incorporating a company to carry on the business is called a sole trader.

solicitor

a person working within the precincts of the law. Basically, he is the intermediary between the public and the dispensers of justice. His work consists for the greater part in advising clients on their legal rights, dealing himself with smaller matters from conveyancing to proceedings in magistrate's courts, and putting the client in touch with a barrister where legal action is to be taken at a higher level. The charges made by a solicitor, e.g. for conveyancing, are dictated by the Law Society, which keeps a watchful eye over the profession. A solicitor who engages in nefarious activities, offends against accepted modes of conduct, or misuses his client's monies, may be subjected to servers penalties. A solicitor must be articled to a firm of solicitors for a defined period (two years for graduates, up to six years for others) and pass certain examinations set by the law society.

space advertising
printed advertisements appearing in newspapers, magazines, books, timetables or other publications not published by the advertiser himself.

span of control
a theory and practice of management holding that a supervisor, manager or executive cannot operate efficiently if he has more than a limited number of subdordinates reporting directly to him. Generally, the higher the level of work, the smaller the number of directly reporting subordinates. For example, the: span of control for a general manager might be limited to six to nine subordinates while that of a shop floor supervisor might, include; several hundred.

special audit
an audit or inspection of financial records and accounts that has limited and specified scope. Also known as limited audit.

special deposits
these are deposits made with the Bank of England by Joint Stock Banks, at the direction of the government. This is a means of restricting credit in a period of inflation. The joints stock banks lend in proportion to the money deposited with them, that is, credit given is directly in proportion to total cash held, e.g. 1-20. The special deposits are a means of reducing this cash and therefore reducing the amount of credit accordingly. Special deposits are distinct from current balances which the joint stock banks have with the Bank of England.

special endorsement
a Bill of Exchange are sometimes endorsed to a named person.

special fund
in municipal accounting practice, a fund that must be used in accordance with specified legal or administrative restrictions; also any fund other than a general fund.

specialisation
rationalisation results in specialisation and mechanisation of production. Only those concerns can compete to produce, which are more efficient in their work. Inefficient and wasteful concerns get closed down. Production is pooled and regulated. The constituent concerns, instead of manufacturing the identical variety of goods and competing with each other, concentrate upon the production of some special quality of goods. This sort of specialisation bring an improvement in the methods of production.

specialist block purchase
the purchase by a specialist for his own account of a large block of stock outside the regular

exchange market. Such purchase may be made only when the sale of the block could not be made only when the sale of the block could not be made in the regular market within a reasonable time and at reasonable prices, and when the purchase would aid the specialist in maintaining a fair and orderly market.

specialization in management

specialization involves allocation of functions between different workers according to their qualifications, talents and aptitude. A good organisation always provides for optimum use of technological improvements. It increases the all round efficiency of the workers both quantitatively and qualitatively.

speculate

to purchase goods or securities or futures contracts in the hope of reselling them at a profit because their market price will increase as opposed to buying goods for use in manufacturing or for resale as an intermediary or buying securities because they give an entitlement to interest payments.

speculation

although effectively a sophisticated form of a gambling, speculation is recognized in business as a necessary constituent of a healthy free enterprise economy. In the commodity market particularly, the willingness of dealers to speculate on future price can serve to maintain a fairly stable price level. The speculator sells forward at a price acceptable to the purchaser, with no certain knowledge of the price he will have to pay for the commodity when the time comes to fulfill the contract. If supplies are plentiful and pries low he stands to make a more than adequate profit, but if supplies are scarce, due perhaps to a poor harvest, he may be forced to buy at prices far above those at which he had contracted to sell and may thereby incur considerable losses. Clever speculators, therefore, deal in more than one commodity so as to provide a safeguard. Gains in one may be able to compensate for losses in another.

speculator

one who invests money in a risky venture in the hope of earning a high profit or capital gain: a sophisticated kind of gambler. The attractions of speculation at one time lay in the fact that capital profits were not taxable. This of course no longer applies.

spot cash

cash that is readily available, usually in hand, for an immediate purchase.

spot tranactions

this in the name given to

tranactions carried out in cash rather than in credit or for futures on the stock exchnage in the open market.

spread sheet

the price of a commodity available of immediate sale and delivery. The commodity is referred to as a spot commodity.

staffing

it is one of the very important functions of management. It includes recruitment, selections, placement, training and promotion of the employees. Staffing is important not only for the industry for it may determine its productivity and profitability but it is equally important for the workers, for it greatly influences not only the physical and mental conditions of the worker but also those of the members of his family.

Staffing includes the recruitment and development of the members of the organisation at all levels. It includes proper selection and suitable training of personnel, reasonably defining their participation in the organisation, providing for communication and adequate opportunities for promotion to higher posts etc.

stag

a stock exchange term for an individual who buys heavily on a new issue of stocks or shares in the expectation that the price will raise very quickly, and earn him a large profit. He normally holds shares only for a very short time.

standard coin

coin which is the principal or ultimate means of payment within and without the country.

standard cost

a predetermined cost of using some resource such as labour or materials in the production of something by a manufacturer, which, according to the person who estimated it, is the cost that would be incurred if production were carried out under specified conditions. Such an estimate is used as standard with which to compare actual costs in order to discover inefficiencies.

standard deviaiton

a statistical term for the average deviation of numbers in a series, from the mean. It is normally funds by squaring and summing the difference between the numbers and the mean, dividing this total by the number of numbers the square root.

standard machine time

the time allocated or forecast to be required for the use of a machine in a specific operation. In production process, it may be referred to a specific quantity of output units produced against a time base. Setup and teardown time may be included in the total machine time allocation.

standard rating

the rating in numerical terms of the pace of working at a particular job which is the average at which 'qualified workers' would naturally perform the job, provided they adhere to a specified method and are motivated to apply themselves to their work.

standing order
an instruction to a bank to pay a certain sum at certain intervals, for instance subsriptions or hire purchase instalments.

standing profit
the net amount that should be earned per unit of production when a job or a service is performed tinder an accounting method of standard costs.

stated value
the minimum amount that a company will accept as payment for issuing a no-par shape. Stated values may be set by law, by the constitution of the company or by a resolution of the company's directors.

statement
a list, sent periodically to a firm's customer, of his financial transactions with the firm and the balance owed by or to him.

statement of identity
a questionnaire by which real estate tile companies are helped in identifying a person; such a statement is essential, for example, when records show more than one person with the same name.

statute-barred debt
a debt that cannot be recovered at law because its time limit has elasped. The time limit within which action must be taken is set out in the Limitation Act: it is six years for an ordinary debt, or twelve years for a debt under seal. The time runs from the end of the credit period.

statutory meeting
it is the first meeting of the shareholder of a company held only once in the life-time of the company. Companies limited by shareholders or by guarantee and having a share capital are required to hold a statutory meeting but not the private companies.

stepped cost
a cost that increases in steps with increased volumes of activity.

sterling area
the group of countries with Great Britain at the head agreeing to permit fairly free transfer of funds ámongst themselves and to operate joint control over exchanges of sterling area currencies for external currencies. The currencies of the sterling area countries are officially linked to the pound. For the purpose of the Exchange Control Act, the countries are known as the Scheduled Territories.

stock
as opposed to stock-in-trade, stock is similar to shares. The difference is that whereas shares are issued in specified

amounts. Rs. 10, Rs.100, etc., stock is sold in variable quantities. Share cannot be converted into stock unless they are fully paid. The word stock' is also used to describe government loans.

stock appreciation rights
an executive compensation plan intended to reduce the risk of market declines that may be experienced with conventional stock options. Such a plan also eliminates the need for cash investment.

stock company
a company organized of the purpose of writing insurance coverage and registered as a corporation owned by stockholders who need not necessarily be policyholders. The initial capital subscribed by the stockholders constitutes the company's working capital. Income must be earned from premiums paid by policyholders. In most respects, the financial operations are like those of a general corporation.

stock control
the system operated by a business whereby stock-in-trade or goods and materials is kept at necessary levels. This may involve the use of bin cards which are marked in such a way that the storekeeper is automatically warned to re-order the stocks or it may involve use of mathematical forms of stock analysis, which indicate not only the figures of minimum and maximum stock levels that may be profitably maintained but also quantities which need to be ordered cover projected production levels. The efficiency of the system of stock control within a buisness can determine its resilience to changes in trading patterns and, ultimately, its chances of progress at the desired speed.

stock holder
a person who owns an amount of stock. A firm that has a stock of specified goods.

stock-in-trade
in accounting term which appears in many balance sheets, sometimes abbreviated to 'stock'. It applies to the quantities of raw materials or finished goods in hand, and is often coupled with work in progress.

stockist
a marketing term for a person who agrees to hold certain minimum stock of a specified manufactured product in return for special buying terms, entitling him perhaps to a particularly favourable discount.

stock market
an organized market for securities. Also called a 'stock exchange'.

stocktaking
physical or manual counting of trading stock. May sometimes be used to described an inventory, which includes the counting of all assets within

the firm and not just stock.

stop for freight

orders given to a dock authority by a shipowner or broker, not to allow delivery of goods until freight has been paid.

stop payment

a depositors order to his or her bank that the bank refuse to honour a particular cheque written by the depositor. It is used to invalidate a check that has been lost or stolen or when that goods or services being paid for by the check are unsatisfactory.

store

something that is kept for future use; a stock. A place where stocks are kept. An establishment where retail business is carried on; especially where a diverse selection of goods is offered for sale. A part of a computer or of peripheral equipment that records data or programmes for use when required by the control unit.

stranding

a marine insurance term once defined as : 'a taking of the ground by the vessel, which does not happen solely from those natural causes which are necessarily incident to the ordinary course of the navigation in which the ship is engaged either wholly or in part, but from some accidental or extraneous causes'.

strategy

a general method or policy for achieving specified objectives. In games theory a rule by which one player selects his choice. The rule may be a 'pure strategy'—i.e., a rule that he will definitely select a specified choice—or a 'maxied strategy' a rule that gives the probabilities of his making each of a number of choices.

street trader

a person who sells out of a suitcase in a street, usually with a delightful line of sweet talk. His main object is to dispose of his goods (whose quality he rarely guarantees) before being asked to move on. He is also called door-to-door salesman.

structure of organisation in management

it involves clear definition of authority, responsibility, relationship which facilitates better understanding of the objectives and the policies of the enterprise; Organisation structure lays down both channels and the pattern of communication; workers participation in organisation increases their cooperation and improves their will to work; the implementation of policies and achievement of the targets becomes easier.

subrogation

if a person suffers a loss because of the action of a second person but is entitled to be recompensed for his loss by an insurer then, after the insurer has paid the claim of the assured, the insurer is entitled to take over all risks the assured had to pursue a claim for damages against the person who caused the loss. Pursuit of a claim by an insurer in the circumstances is called 'subsorgation'.

subscribe

to signify one's assent or approval. To state that one is a party to some course of action. Specifically, to sign the memoradum of association of a proposed new registered company and thereby become one of the first members of that company. To promise to purchase and pay for something and not yet in existence-especially securities that are about to be issued, or books or periodicals about to be published. To make a regular, advance payment in return for service.

subscription warrant

a security which entitles its holder in buy another security from the same issuer (usually an ordinary share or share of common stock) for a price. Something, there are time-limits for experiencing the entitlements.

subsidiary

a company most shares of which are owned by one company called its 'holding company' or patent company'.

subsidize

to reduce the price of something by paying a subsidy. To asset a firm or an industry by paying subsidies.

substitution effect

phenomenon of a consumer ceasing to buy something that goes up in price and buying a cheaper substitute instead.

supercargo

a person travelling with a merchant ship to look after the cargo and perhaps obtain additional cargo en vovage.

supermarket

in general usage this term now denotes any large self-service retail outlet. The emphasis is on ease of selection, persuasive advertising, high turnover and equally high profits. Costs are kept at a minimum by economizing on staff, customers serving themselves with little or no supervision, bulk-buying to match the high turnover and often, due to the location of the premises away from town can save by way of low rents and buying rates.

super tax

income tax levied at specially high rates in addition to ordinary rates on incomes above a certain large amount.

surtax

a tax which used to be charged in addition to income tax on personal incomes in excess of Rs. 40,000 a year. Surtax has since been abolished.

surveyor of customs

the superintending officer of a customs house station of warehouse.

systems approach

in systems approach, an organisation is viewed as a network of system. A system is "an organised or complex whole, an assemblage or combination of things or parts forming a complex or unitary whole". In a system approach, the organisation is taken to be system that takes certain inputs and transforms into certain outputs. Every information and process is dealt with as related parts of a single system. Some of the system may be divided into sub-systems. In a systematic approach, management brings integration of different systems.

The system approach looks at the organization as a total system comprising a number of intersecting variables. It studies the organization as an integrated whole encompassing many subsystems, formal organisations, individuals, social systems, environment, etc. It does not view organisation as a static arrangement of jobs but calls for identifying the functions required in terms of the decision areas in achieving goals. All the variable in the system start functioning in an orderly way and preserve organisational integrity.

tabular standard

a monetary standard in which the standard is not the price of a single commodity, but it is based upon the price of a representative list of commodities.

tacking

mortgages acquire priority in order of time when they are executed. If there are three mortgages on the same property, the third mortgagee can, by paying off the first mortgagee, acquire first place. This is called tacking. This is detrimental to the interests of the second mortgagee. Tacking is prohibited in India under Sec 93 of the Transfer of Property Act and hence is illegal.

takeover

the acquisition of a business by another through purchase, exchange of capital stock, or any other device.

takers-in

persons prepared to carry over commitments for bulls by taking up the stock that the bull not wish, to, or cannot, pay for at that particular time.

tally man

this word is used for many purposes. A tallyman may be credit to be paid back in instalments; the word is also used for an accountant who tallies account sheets of business or he may be a person who tallies a ship's cargo against its list.

tally

a piece of wood once used for recording a debt or payment, and once also a formal receipt given for a loan to the Exchequer or sovereign. It is also a distinguishing mark on an item or bale of merchandise.

talon

part of a share warrant or similar bearer security which is torn off by the owner when he has used all the coupons from the security and is exchange by the issuer of the security for new coupons.

tap

a large quantity of securities held by someone who is therefore able to sell to anyone who wants to buy (so that buying is like turning on a tap). Treasury bills issued 'through the tap' are those sold direct to government department instead of by tender.

tap stock

readily available securities, particularly gilt-edged government stock, which can always be obtained on demand like water from a tap. Tap stocks should be distinguished from tap issue.

tare

the weight of the wrapping or container of goods.

target price

a term used in common market trading for the price that has been set as the norm for the sale of farm products under a common agricultural policy. The target price is fixed annually on the basis of estimates of fair return for economic and efficient farmers in the member countries.

tariff

a list of the import duties imposed by a government on the goods that are imported into its country. Also one of the rates of duties in such a list. A list of charges, especially for a public utility.

tariff offices

insurance companies or offices which charge rates set by an organization to which they belong, for instance the Accident Offices Association. Non-tariff offices are free to quote their on rates of insurance premium.

taxation : marriage

there is no tax on marriage-at one time the State made its own contribution to the festivities by affording certain tax advantages in the year of marriage. Until 1968, the husband (ignoring the possibility of separate assessment) could claim a full year's marriage allowance, even though the wedding took place only a few days before the end of the tax year. In addition, the wife could claim a full year's allowance on her income before marriage. What is more, the husband could obtain additional personal relief if his wife continued to work after marriage. Consequently, in choosing a wedding date, it was advisable where possible to allow the wife to earn more than her total allowance as a spinster before marriage and also allow her to earn more than the additional personal relief after marriage.

There benefits have been considerably reduced by the Finance Act 1968. The marriage relief over the single relief) is reduced by one-twelfth for every month between the beginning of tax year and the date of the marriage. The husband can elect to be treated as a single person for that year, if it proves more advantageous.

tax base

in economics, the object on which a tax is levied, such as sales, property, income, and so on.

tax credit

an amount that a taxpayer can offset against any income tax or corporation taxe that he has to pay or can have paid to him in cash by the Central Board of Revenue.

In particular, a credit equal to the amount of advance corporation tax paid on a dividend or other distribution of a company's profits. This credit is allowed to the recipient of the dividend.

taxi

a vehicle licensed to ply for hire, that is, to roam the streets looking for passengers wishing to be conveyed privately to destinations previously unspecified. A taxi normally has a meter showing the cost of the journey.

Taxis should be distinguished from vehicles operated by car hire firms. Certain firms have vehicles licensed to carry passenger which can be ordered (e.g. by telephone) for a specific journey, but these are not allowed to ply for hire. They may often be called taxis but it is illegal for them to stop in the street at the request of a passer-by.

tax loophone

a legal provision that can be used to reduce one's tax liability.

tax return

a document containing details of an individuals's income and expenses and his claims for personal reliefs that is used to asess his income tax.

taxylor's differential piece rate system

under this system, a standard output for the day is fixed after careful time and motion study. Those workers who achieve this standard of produce or more are paid at a higher rate than those who fail to reach the standard.

technical analysis

in the security market, the technique of analysing factors of supply and demand to determine the direction-of security prices.

telegraphic transfer

a swift method of transferring monies abroad, operated by a bank at the customer's request and risk. The bank cables the relevant instructions to its overseas agent, usually another bank or the qverseas branch of the nationalised bank. The agent then effects the necessary credits or debits usually in the currency of the transferee.

telex

the telex service operated by the Overseas Communication Services provides a swift and efficient means of sending and receiving printed information. The process is fully automated and printouts of the message are made by both outgoing and receiving telex machines. Telex message can be sent when the receiving machine is not attended by any individual. This has considerable commercial importance both nationally and internationally as hours of business do not coincide owing to differences of time in different parts of the world.

temporary exports

certain goods to be used as samples or exhibits and to be reimported may be initially exported free of duty if certain customs procedure are observed.

tender

a formal, unconditional offer, specifically of something that will discharge a debt or obligation. A formal offer to perform work which has been specified by the person or organization to which the offer is put at a fixed price. Also the price so stated. Also known as a bid. An unconditional offer to buy something previously described by the person to whom the offer is a made at a particular price.

tender capital issues

shares may sometimes be issued by public or private sector companies by tender. The company issuing the shares asks for tenders at prices above a certain minimum. Tenders will be made at various prices. If an offer is made for all the shares at the highest price, this will be accepted. Otherwise the shares will be issued at the highest practicable price, so that all shares could be disposed of. This means that persons offering the highest prices may receive the shares for less.

tenor

a bill of exchange may be payable sometime in the future. The length of this time is known as the tenor of the bill.

tentative balance sheet

a balance sheet in work form, intended for decussion, review , or any other managerial purpose prior to its publication in final form.

term loan

abbreviation of 'intermediate-term loan'. A loan by a bank to a firm for a period 1 and 15 years which is to be repaid according to an agreed schedule of instalments.

terms of trade

a term used in international trade to describe the current trading pattern of a country.

Terms of trade are said to be good when import prices are generally low compared with the prices commanded by exports. When terms of trade are bad export prices have to be kept low, perhaps artificially, in order to finance the import requirements of the country.
Ratio of an index of export prices of a range of goods exported by a particular country to a comparable index of the country's import prices.

territorial waters
those waters next to the coast of a country over which sovereignty is claimed. This is intended to prevent ships of other countries, from, for instances, fishing in these waters. There is some doubt as to the limit of these waters; some countries claim three miles, some six, some twelve; something different areas are claimed for different purpose, for instance twelve miles for fishing, six miles for other purposes.

test check
the verification of selected items in an account as an indication of the probability of, or the development of an opinion concerning, the accuracy of the entire account or record.

theory of factor prices
a study of the way in which factors of production are priced and not a study of their respective shares in the income of the community.

third class paper
these are bills of exchange, particularly commercial bills. Their grades very with the reputation of the acceptors, so that there are first class, second class, and third class bills. Bills which are not certain to be honoured are placed among third class bills.

third-party rights
an insurance contract is generally between two parties, the insured party and the insurance company. Under certain conditions, such as where an insurance company offers a life insurance contract that specifies a beneficiary who would eventually receive the payment, theat specifies a beneficiary, are recognized.

third world
the entirety of the poor nations that are burdened by problems of underdevelopment, poverty, illiteracy, and technological backwardness.

ticket
a ticket should be distinguished from a receipt. Tickets are issued (for cash) particularly for transport of entertainment. They are usually an essential part of the contract, and contain conditions of the offer or else refer to the existence of these conditions and state where they are to be found. The contract is not closed until the customer accepts the ticket and hands over the money..

A receipt on the other hand is an acknowledgement of payment of a debt already due, and cannot contain further conditions applicable to the contract.

tied loan

in the filed of international trade one country often lends money to another on the condition that the loan is spent in buying goods or services of the lending country. Such a loan is known as tied loan.

tie-in sale

a practice whereby a seller requires the buyer to purchase one or more additional or tied products as a conditions for purchasing the desired or tying product.

tight money

money is said to be tight when credit only be obtained at high interest rates. This may be the result of governmental interference e.g., increasing the minimum lending rate, calling for substantial special deposits by the banks or imposing controls, on the granting of credit-particularly in the hirepurchase field. By acting thus the government may hope to restrict spending and check the rate of inflation without pushing the economy into a slum.

tight money- dear money

money is said to be tight when there is more money being called than lent out.

time bargain

a stock exchange term for dealings in futures.

time bill

a bill of exchange that is due to be paid after a fixed interval of time—generally a few months after it is drawn or a few months after it is presented to the drawee for acceptance. Also known as a 'period bill' or term bill.

time charter

the hiring of a ship, or a space in it, for a particular time. The ship might make any number of voyages within that time.

time deposit

a sum of money deposited with someone at a bank or similar institution such as a savings bank or building society on condition that it can be withdrawn at any time if a set period of notice is given. Interest is paid for time deposits.

time draft

a draft payable within a specified time-usually 30 days-after acceptance by the drawee.

time-scale

a graduated line drawn on a chart or graph to indicate how time intervals are represented. The length of time involved in a project.

time sharing

a term in computer management referring to the practice of two or more businesses using a computer at the same time. This type of sharing is a technique of maximizing the use of expensive computer equipments and reducing their working cost of the organisation who wish to buy time on them.

title company

a company that insures titles and issues title insurance policies to property owners.

token coins

coins, the actual value of whose metal is less than their token value.

tolls

charges made for using certain road, bridges, canal locks, etc. The monies collected are intended to pay for their building and upkeep.

tonnage

the cubic capacity of a ship, not necessarily related to its carrying capacity. A ton is 100 cubic feet. Tonnage dues are payable when a ship enters or leaves port.

top management

loosely, the chief executive of an organization and managers close to him in an organization's structure.

tort

a branch of law dealing with civil actions arising from breach of customs duty imposed by state law or statute. It should be distinguished from the law of contract which deals with breaches of duties arising out of transactions entered into by mutual consent. Examples of offences in tort can arise from trespass, deceit, libel, etc.

traceable cost

a cost element whose origin be can identified even though it may have been transferred from the one account to another.

trade accommodation bill

a trade bill is one that arises out of a trading transaction. If A sells goods to B for Rs. 10,000 on credit and draws on him a bill for the amount, such bill is a genuine trade bill. A trade bill is a self-liquidating asset as it is backed by goods which form the basis for the transaction. In the above case after selling the goods B will be in a position to meet the bill on its due date.

An accommodation bill, on other hand, does not arise out of the trading transaction but is drawn to tide over the financial difficulty, may be in collusion with another person. For example, C who is in need of money may draw a 90 days bill on D for Rs. 10,000. D accepts the bill which C discounts with the banker. D likewise draws a bill for similar amount and tenure which is accepted by C and discounted by D with his banks. On due date both meet their obligations. If there is only one bill the drawer of the bill provides the acceptor with sufficient funds on its due date to meet the bill. An accommodation bill is net self-liquidating as it is not supported by any goods, the sale proceeds of which can be utilised to meet the bill.

tradee acceptance

a bill of exchange drawn on the buyer by the seller of merchandise and unconditionally accepted by the buyer made out in accordance with the terms of the contract between the seller and the buyer.

trade development authority

a 'services institution' set up by the government of India for providing assistance to enterprises at the micro level after the potential of their products and their requirements of assistance.

It undertakes selective export development of industrial products with both short-term and long term prospects term prospects of growth to selected markets. In the discharge of this function, the TDA identifies technically competent and commercially viable units, particularly in the small and medium sector, assists in the expansion of exportoriented production facilities in the selected product and areas, undertakes product development/ adaptation and helps in raising the technological levels of selected industrial exports. The units, products and markets are chosen by the TDA after collecting and processing all relevant information and after a careful study of the factors relevant to a sustained build-up of exports with minimal deployment of scarce resource. It arranges for commercial contracts between selected Indian units and potential foreign buyers of standing and repute, and facilitates conclusion of contracts. A special function of the TDA is to attract international subcontracting of engineering and other components from India and promotion of export-oriented joint ventures in the country in conjunction with the Indian investment centre,

TDA provides a comprehensive range of services to the overseas buyers. It informs and advises them of product availability, price structure, sources of supply, delivery schedules, quality control status, etc. free of cost. To discharge these functions, the TDA has the following division—(1) Information Division, (2) Research and Analysis, Division, and (3) Merchandising division.

trade discount

a discount allowed by their suppliers to a class of customers, such as electrical appliance or business machine dealers. It is based on a published list or suggested end-user price, is usually offered on the basis of volume purchase by the dealers, and is not related to date of payment.

trade investment

in the United Kingdom, an investment by one business

firm in another for the purpose of protecting or expanding the investor's activities.

trade payable

an amount of money owed to a creditors for goods or services received. Also known as account payable.

trader

one who buys and sells goods commodities or securities for his or her own account for short-term profit.

trading certificate

the certificate issued to Public Company by the Registrar of Companies enabling it to commence business. A public company can only commence business if it has satisfied certain conditions. These are : (1) shares must have been allotted up to the minimum subscription and paid for in cash; (2) Directors must have taken up and paid or their shares; they need not have paid for them in full if the total amount on that type of shares has not been called; (3) no monies may be due for repayment to applicants for shares or debentures; (4) a certificate must be filed stating that these conditions have been fulfilled.

trading market

a securities market that does not exhibit a definite price trend and with few traders who are other than professionally engaged in the trading of securities.

transire

a shipping document used by coasting vessels, listing the goods carried, and signed by the master of the ship. There are two copies: one is given up to the customs authorities as a clearance certificate on leaving port; the other is used as a certificate of entry at the next port.

traveller's check

a draft issued by a bank or express company that is payable on presentation by a correspondent of the issuer.

travelling auditor

a staff auditor, whose function is to examine branches and division of a corporation at outlying locations as an aid to corporate control.

treasure trove

gold and silver found in some hiding place. The word 'trove' derives from the french trouve', Treasure Trove must be reported to the police, the Director of the British museum or the nearest corner; failure to do so is a criminal offence. The finder is awarded the saleable value of the find, but the treasure itself goes to the legal owner, if traceable.

A jury meets to decide whether the find is really treasure trove, who found it, and to whom it legally belongs. If the owner cannot be traced it belongs to the crown. In Scotland, all treasure trove belongs to the crown.

trinity house

an organization superintending navigation in British waters. It is responsible for beacons and lighthouses and for appointing pilots. It also conducts the examinations of mariners and is responsible generally for supervising the marine interest of the country.

trust
the merger of interest by a number of companies in the same field, with the object of creating monopoly,. The term is more common in the United States and such groupings are now subject to what are known as the anti-trust laws.

trust and agency fund
in municipal accounting, a fund consisting of money and property received and held by a municipality or an institution as trustee or custodian, or in the capacity of an agent for certain individuals or government units.

trust deed
a conveyance of a title to a trustee to be held until a loan or a performance secured by a note is paid or completed, at which time the title is reconveyed.

trustee
a person who handles monies or property on behalf of another in a trust. He usually has the title to the property but in fact acts merely as a steward and all the benefits belong to persons known as the beneficiaries. Because he has the legal title he can try to dispose of the property to a third party without the consent of the true owner ; that would however be a breach of trust. It is therefore essential that a trustee is one whose integrity is undisputed.

trustee in bankruptcy
when a debtor is adjusted bankrupt, his property shall become divisible amongst his creditors, and shall vest in a trustee.

trust mortgage
a mortgage to a person or a corporation as trustee, who holds the security for the benefit of others in accordance with the terms and conditions set forth in the instrument.

trusts, notice of
on the question of shares, a company is not bound to take notice of trusts. The shares are registered in the names of trustees. Trustees may deal with the shares and the company need not ask whether they are dealing properly with them. The beneficiary can protect his interest by issuing a notice in lieu of distringas.

turnkey contract
a contract, usually on a large scale where the person paying leaves the contractor, usually a specialist organization, to see to details and settle all problems that may occur during the period of the contract. Payment is made on completion of the whole or parts of it as stipulated in the contract. On completion the

contractee has merely to turn the key and launch the unit into action.

turnover tax
a form of sales tax levied at each stage in the distribution process.

two-tier board
a group of people who are responsible for the conduct of a company and are divided into two committees : a 'management board' consisting of full-time employees of the company who are responsible for the company's day-to day operations ; a 'supervisory board' responsible for protecting the interests of the company's shareholders and possibly, of its employees. Usually, the management board is appointed by, and may be dismissed by the supervisoty board.

tycoon
slang expression for a person who has accumulated a large sum of money in industry or commerce.

typewriter-office .
typewriter is an important mechanical appliance which is widely used in the modern offices. It is meant for expediting the writing of letters and other correspondence and securing a neat appearance for letters. It is a mechanical device replacing the work of the pen and thus saving time and labour involved in writing letters and documents by hand. Handwritten letters are often unreadable. Typewritten letters are attractive and distinctly legible. They underline the efficiency of the office staff of the firm and create a better impression on the customers and other addressees.

ullage
this word is used in two senses. Originally it meant the difference between the capacity of a cask and its actual contents; in customs terminology it is now used for the actual contents (the difference is called the vacuity). In marine insurance the difference is still known as 'ullage,' is not usually considered a loss, and is not covered by the insurance policy.

unadmitted asset
an asset determined the have little or no liquidation value. In reporting the financial position of an insurance company, such assets are segregated and deducted as a group.

unamortized debt discount
the portion of debt discount that remains and is to be spread over future fiscal periods. Usually appears as a prepaid expense, if related to a bank loan, or as deferred charge, if related to a long term bond issue.

unapplied cash
in municipal accounting, cash not reserved for a specific purpose and available for use

within the fund of which it is part.

unappropriated earned surplus

the part of earned surplus that has not been transferred to a subordinate account or earmarked for a specific propose. Such surplus therefore remains available for distributing in the form of dividends.

unappropriated profit

the part of the profit of a business not paid out in dividend or allocated to any particular use. It implies authorized acts by directors.

unabilled cost

a recoverable cost that may be identified with specific and uncompleted contracts for goods and services. Such uncompleted contracts are classified as assets or receivables.

uncollacted goods, disposal of

where goods left for repair are not collected, the repairer has certain rights either by customs or law. In U.K. for example an important law is the Disposal of Uncollectd Goods Act 1962, which states that if the goods are not collected or paid for within a reasonable time, the bailee may give notice that the goods are read for collection. If he receives no reply to his notice within twelve months, he may give another notice stating his intention to sell. If no reply is received within two weeks, he may sell the goods, but only by public auction. The proceeds of the sale must be retained and after deduction of costs, including storage, etc., the monies must be handed over to the bailor. A notice that the provisions of the Act apply must be prominently displayed on the bailee's premises.

undated stocks

government stock with no stated date for redemption. They may be permanent funds the government has no intention of ever redeeming, such as consolidated stock. Because they are undated they are often the best indication of the movement of interest rates, as their prices is influenced only by the prevailing rate of interest or risk-free investments.

underemployment

a situation where is riot enough work for workers in a company to do. A situation where there is note enough work is a country to occupy all the workforce.

underwrite

the act as an insurer. To guarantee to purchase any of a public offer of securities that are bought by anyone else.

underwriter

in the securities market, an agent acting between a corporation issuing new securities and the public. The usual practice is for one or more underwriters to make an outright purchase of a corporation's new issue of stocks or bonds and to from a syndicate to sell the securities to individuals and institutions. Underwriters also distribute very large blocks of securities, perhaps held by an estate.

undivided interest

the interest of coowners in a property in which their individual interests are indistinguishable from one another.

undue influence

a form of moral pressure. A contact will not a enforced by a court if it can be shown that the defendant was in a position that prevented him forming a free and unfettered judgment. Undue influence will not be presumed unless certain relation, e.g. parental or confidential, exist between the parties.

unearned increment

in accounting any increase in the value of property due to circumstances beyond the control of the property owner and not attributable to direct expenditures or efforts. An example would be the increased market value of a piece of real property caused by improvements made to neighbouring properties.

uniform accounting system

a system of accounts common to similar organizations. Trade associations, for example, propose accounting system that are uniform in application to all members of their particular associations. Federal and state regulatory agencies, such as public utility commissions may develop and strongly recommend uniform accounting system for organization and institutions that come under their purview.

unilateral contracts

strictly speaking these are not contracts at all, but promises. If someone promises to do something provided something else is done, no other person being named or put under obligation, he is only bound if the condition is fulfilled. For instance, if someone promises to pay an amount 12,000 to anyone who will build a new ward for a hospital, he is only bound if the ward is built.

unissued capital

the difference between authorized capital and issued share capital.

unit

a security which is sold by the management of unit trust and which entitles its owners to demand redemption at any time at a price which is related to the value of the securities held by the unit trust ; and to share in the income derived from the securities held by the trust.

unitary demand

a state existing when quantity bought varies with price charge so that the total revenue remains the same.

unit cost

the cost of a single unit of a product or service. It is equivalent average cost.

United States rule
a method of identifying the amounts of interest and principal included in a partial payment of an interest-bearing debt.

unit trust
a collective investment instition in which the fund of money for investment comes from the sale of units and in which decisions about buying and selling securities, and about the sale of units, are made by a 'management company' which makes out a trust deed nominating a second company to act as trustee.

unit trust of India
an autonomous enterprise, set up by a special statute on December 5, 1963 which stated its activities from July 1, 1964. The initial capital Rs. 5 crores contributed by the reserve bank of India, scheduled commercial banks and other financial institutions. It is managed by a board of directors comprised 9 members. The main functions of the trust are : (1) To set units to small and medium savers of the country and to invest the money thus collected, in selected industrial and business enterprise. Keeping in view the financial conditions of the small and medium savers, the face value of the units have been kept in between Rs. 10 and Rs. 100; (2) To invest money in such a manner that, on an average, not less than 6% income accrues to the enterprise; (3) To arrange selling of units through the branches of the state bank of India and 36 other commercial blanks; (4) At the end of each financial year, to distribute among the unit holders. 90% of the net profits as divided income from unit trust to the extent of Rs. 2,000 is exempted from income tax; (5) to publish regularly in the newspaper the daily buying and selling price of Rs. 10 Face value of unit; (6) To give loans keeping units as security; (7) to keep note of the fact than in no circumstances more than 5% of the investable fund is being invested in any particular enterprise; (8) To distribute the investment in many enterprises; (9) to mobilise and turn small savings through the units into productive investment.
Thus, in the Indian capital, market, contribution of the U.T.I. is significant. It is endeavouring to develop the capital market, which ultimately facilitates achieving faster industrial development.

unity of direction
there should be one head and one plan for activities having similar objectives. No organisation can succeed unless it has a unit of direction. Unit of command relates to the personnel but

the unity of direction relates to the whole body corporate. Unity of direction alone can produce a sense of loyalty and devotion amongst the subordinates.

unlimited company

less common than limited companies. All members are liable for debts while they are members. These companies need not have shares capital but must have articles of associations and these must state the number of original members and share capital if any. An unlimited company can purchase its own shares but cannot borrow money on the security of these shares. It can reduce capital or pay shares capital back to the members without having to apply to the court. It must make an annual return. No ad volerm stamp duty is payable on the capital. It does not have to file annual accounts. With the 1956 Companies Act and the abolition of the status of the Exempt Private Company, these companies could become more popular as also could limited partnership. The Companies Act 1956, provides a straightforward process for converting a limited company into an unlimited one. The conversion does affect the status of the company but apart from this it continues in being, i.e. there is no question of the winding-up of the old company and the formation of a new, thus contracts of employment continue.

unlisted securities

shares are not listed on the official Stock Exchange list, but which are traded on the Unlisted Securities Market.

unload

a slang term in commerce for dumping a large quantity of goods on the market at a low price, to make a quick sale. The supplier is prepared to accept a low profit margin—the gives him competitive advantage.

unpaid dividend

a declared dividend that has not yet been paid; an unclaimed divided. Also, a passed dividend on cumulative preferred stock.

unredeemed pledge

an item give as security for a loan which has not been redeemed by repaving the loan.

unsecured creditors

individuals or companies who have loaned money without obtaining a charge against the borrower's assets. Such creditors rank equally with each and, upon bankruptcy of the borrower, are paid parri passu according to the size of debt after the secured creditors have been fully paid.

unissued capital

the difference between authorized capital and issued (paid up) share capital.

usance

bills of exchange may be drawn as unsance; these will be bills between two foreign countries with separate currencies. They are short-term bills and 'usance' means the time allowed by custom for payment. For instance usance for bills drawn in New York Europe is sixty days.

upset price
in the case of equity proceeding in a bankruptcy, the amount established by the court as the lowest acceptable price for a firm's assets when offered at public auction,.

useful life
in accounting, the normal operating life of a fixed asset or its utility to the owner.

use tax
a tax levied on the use of particular goods or services rather than on their sale.

usuary
lending money in return for payment of interest. At one time this was considered a rather nefarious occupation and was much frowned upon by the church; interest was considered something received for nothing. The occupation was pushed into the shadows and consequent abused for, being outside the law, the lender would charge unfair rates of interest and treat the debtor rather unkindly. For this reason the term 'usuary', now that the lending of money is acceptable, is reserved as a term of abuse and used mainly in adjectival form, e.g. usurious rates of interest.

usufruct
the right to use property owned by another while refraining from actions which might diminish the value of the property or later.

valorize
to attempt to determine the price of a commodity by setting an arbitrary market value, usually by government intervention as in buying up surplus or making loans to producers to enable them to store their products for release to the market at more appropriate times. Valorization is also price fixing by cartels or by agreements.

valuation
act of process of estimating the value of something. Also the estimate of value arrived at by this process.

valuation reserves
an amount deducted by a creditor from the book value of debts due to him, in the expectation that some of them are likely to be defaulted.

value
the price which an item would fetch in an open market. Distinction should be made between value in present use and value in alternative use. Value is also determined by various others factors ranging from sentiment to long-term speculation.

value added
a term for the increment added by each person or organization involved in the manufacture of a particular item, becoming

part of its price. As an example, A provides raw materials at 25p, B works on the material and press them on to C at $37\frac{1}{2}$ p, so B has added $12\frac{1}{2}$ to the value. There have been various suggestion for a tax on value added as an alternative to a sales tax.

value added statement
a financial statement prepared by a business relating to its value added during the accounting period. The statement identifies the value added and shows how this value has been appropriated to various claimants, for example the government, employee wages and salaries, and providers of finance.

value added tax (V.A.T)
the underlying principle of V.A.T. is that tax is levied at each stage of the production of goods or services and on the value added at each stage ; e.g. tax is paid by manufacturers on the cost of making an item, by wholesalers on the price they charge the retailer and by retailers on the price they charge the consumer. Each party in this process must account to the Customs and Excise for the tax on their output. It may deduct from this figure the amount of tax already paid by the party supplying them. A tax charged on the value added by an enterprise over a period.

value analysis
usually performed by the purchasing department, the study of materials, parts or components, purchased or manufactured. The purpose is to determine the value received for the dollars spent and to start specific action intended to improve that value.

valued policy
insurance usually issued for property whose precise value may be difficult to establish, such as a work of art, a coin collection, or a rare book. An example is a life insurance contract under which the dollar amount is fixed and becomes payable on the death of the insured.

variable annuity
a pension benefit plan that fluctuates in value with the changes in the worth of the assets, typically common stocks, in which the pension fund is invested.

variable cost
an operating expense that varies in relating to sales or production volume, facility use, or other indicator of activity.

variety store
a store carrying a wide range of relatively inexpensive goods for the household. Small appliance, dry goods, stationery, and nations are typical of the items offered.

vendors shares
in a company which are issued to the seller of a business

which is converted into a limited company. The shares are issued as consideration for the sale of the business.

verba chartarum fortius accipiuntur contra proferentem

a legal maxim which points out that where any doubt arises as to the precise meaning of a written contract it will be constructed more strongly against the person who drew up the contract. This can be quite important where exemption clauses are concerned.

vertical distintegration

the switching from own production purchase of certain components, induced by the circumstances in which optimum production requires large resources than can be provided by the company.

vertical market

a business environment in which the ownership of natural resources, their manufacture and the ultimate use of the finished products are vested in a single organization.

vested interest

interest now in being, as opposed to interest anticipated. It is a term frequently used in law with regard to the title to goods or land. Property is said to vest when the absolute owner is finally established, and his interest is in no way capable of being terminated by anyone but himself.

vestibule training

vestibule training may be used as a preliminary to on-the-job training. New workers are trained for specific jobs and special machines or equipment in a separate location near the actual place of work under practical work situation. In some cases, an attempt may be made to duplicate as closely as possible the actual work room conditions, but one of the advantages of vestibule training is that it permits more emphasis on teaching the best method than on getting out production.

visible exports

of physical visible goods appearing as receipts in the current of a country's balance of payments statements.

visible imports and exports

goods actually shipped or otherwise sold, as opposed to invisible exports or imports which are services earning, or costing foreign exchange, e.g. shipping, insurance, etc. The united kingdom has thrived for many years on invisible earnings and very rarely has a favourable balance on visible trade.

visible index

it is a system under which all the headings on the cards can be seen without fingering them. Visible indexing is made both with cards and loose leaves set in trays, drawers and binders. In it cards or sheets are fastened to a holder in such a way that the edge of each card or sheet projects the width of one line beyond the edge of the next one. This makes it possible to read the indexed line on every card or sheet without removing it from the folder.

vital statistics

statistics having to do with births, deaths, marriages, health, diseases and related matters.

vocation

vocation is different from business or profession. It refers to those activities pursued by a person more with a view to give expression of his personality and artistic sense than for the production of wealth. The primary object of vocational persons is not to earn profit but to earn a livelihood for oneself. It is very much like an occupation.

vocational training

training is the act of increasing the knowledge and skills of an employee for doing a particular job, according to Fayol. It is an organised activity designed to create a change in the thinking and behaviour of people. It involves application of knowledge with a specific end in view. Vocational training enables the workers adopt more scientific methods of production. It eliminates wastages arising from the adoption of traditional methods. Workers are kept informed about the latest developments so that they may not lag behind others. This ensures greater efficiency, removes wastage and increases the output.

volume rate

in motor carrier tariffs, any rate to which a volume minimum weight applies.

voting rights

the stockholders right to vote in the affairs of the issuing corporation.

voucher

a written documentary proof of payment or receipt of money. It is a document signed to evidence any business transaction. It may be a receipt, bank pay-in-slip, counterfoil of a cheque, an agreement deed and other correspondence etc. With the help of these vouchers, the accuracy of a transaction can be ascertained. Voucher alone can tell us about the nature and source of the transaction, its value and authority. It subtantiates the book entries and confirms their reality. All vouchers relating to the business transaction should be carefully preserved and properly field.

voucher

a document serving as evidence of the disbursement of cash. A document authorizing the disbursement of cash. Written evidence of a business or accounting transaction.

vouching

the process of tracing a

transaction to its source and ensuring that all documentation, recording and posting are correct and appropriate to that transaction.

vowel index

in this index, each page in the book is divided into 6 subdivision according to vowels. When the names are to indexed on one page, they are not entered as in the book indexed, but divided according to the first vowel in name after the first alphabet. Then they are entered in the column reserved for that vowel. This saves time and labour in searching for a name.

wage

any regular payment to an employee of a business for his or her labour by the hour, week, month, or some other period, or by units of output.

wage administration

activities concerned with fixing and system of paying wages in an organization.

wage audit

a regular review, conducted by consultants, of all forms of payment to employees within a company.

wage differentials

a difference between the price of one form of labour and another arising through a particular demand and supply situation for each type of labour. Reasons for differentials vary, but include experience, skill and geographical location.

wage freeze

an attempt by government to hold wages and salaries at a certain level, usually as part of a general policy aimed at stemming inflation.

wager

a contract between two parties involving the staking of value upon the outcome of an event, past or future, on: which the parties differ. Night party must have any interest in the event except in the stake. In Britain wagering contracts are void, although in terms of hours units produced, etc.

wage rate

the rate of remuneration earned by an employee. The rate may be expressed in terms of hours, units produced, etc.,

wagering policy

a marine insurance policy where the insurer has no acceptable insurance interest. These contracts and gambling contracts and are illegal.

wages and salaries

a term for remuneration paid to employees of a business or other organization. Both are fixed by contract and are usually determined by a trade union or national agreement. The distinction between a wage and salary is fairly nebulous, but generally speaking , wages paid are daily or weekly and salaries monthly. When reference are made to a wage freeze or to wage restraint the term wage includes both wages and salaries.

wage theory

any of the varying approaches to or theories for determining the wages paid to employees.

waiters

attendants at the stock exchange who takes messages, run errands, and generally take care of the details of the day to-day running of the Exchange. The word is a relic of the days when dealings took place in coffee houses, and the waiters took messages.

waiting time

in business parlance, time which an employee spends idle, though not through his own fault, e.g. time spent waiting for a machine to be repaired or set up ready for use. It is obviously worth-while to minimize this time.

In some services, for example taxi driving, a charge may be made for waiting time.

waiver

where one person waives his rights in a contract, this is known as a waiver. Though an alternation contract, it is in effect a new agreement.

waiver clause

the abuse in marine insurance policies allowing either party to take steps to minimize a loss without prejudicing rights.

wall street

the street where the New York Stock Exchange is situated. Used as a synonym for the New York Stock Exchange and also for US financial interest generally.

water capital

the excess of capital stock issued, as its par value, over the value of the assets contributed in exchange.

warehouse

a place where goods are stored prior to their being distributed, sold or used. The word is also used in shipping terminology, where it means a public warehouse where goods are stored on being landed from a ship. These warehouses are often responsible for sorting, examining, and delivering goods as well as storing them. The goods may be for home consumption or re-export . Some warehouses are bonded warehouses, where duty need not be paid on the goods until they are actually removed from the warehouse.

warehouse receipt

a warehouse receipt is a document of title to goods. It is the receipt issued by a licensed warehouse keeper that the goods specified in the receipt have been held by him for store-keeping. The warefhous receipt gives full description of the goods stored, but the warehouse-keeper is not liable for the quantity or the quality. The warehouse receipt may be marked either "negotiable" or "non-negotiable". A negotiable warehouse receipt can be transferred by endorsement and delivery but the title of the endorsee is subject to the title of the endorser. A non-negotiable receipt cannot be transferred by endorsement for delivery. A separate letter of transfer should accompany the receipt and warehouse-keeper should have notice of transfer to make the transfer effective. Advances against non-negotiable receipts are generally not made.

A document, issued by someone who regularly stores goods for others for a fee, which states that he is storing specified goods, how much he will charge for storing them and the conditions under which he will release them from his store.

warehousing

the business of running an establishment for the storage or accumulation of goods.

warrant

a receipt for goods deposited in a public warehouse. The receipt identifies the goods and may be transferred by endorsement.

warranty

express or implied undertaking or declarations made by an insured party to an insurance contact which, if not followed or if incorrect, invalidate the contract. 2. An element or statement of fact contained in a contract which, if broken, does not invalidate the contract, the aggrieved party may, however, claim damages.

warranty floating

a warranty which may be enforceable by a third party, i.e., by a person not a party to the contract when the warranty is given.

wash

in accounting, a transaction that is reversed or offset by another transaction in short period of time.

wash sale

the sale and purchase of substantially identical securities within a 30-day period. Losses from such transactions are not legal deductions from income subject to federal income taxes.

wasting assets

assets which are used up in producing goods. It is sometimes applied to fixed assets generally. But is perhaps better applied to assets which are exhausted after a certain period of time, such as quarries, mines, etc.

waste book

a book in which the entries of transactions are made as they occur. From this book the entries are transferred to other books.

waybill

a receipt showing list of the goods accepted for shipment/ despatch issued to a shipper/ consignor by a common land carrier.

watered capital

the excess of capital stock, issued, at its par or stated

value, over the fair value of the assets contributed in exchange.

ways and means advances
short-term loans made to the government by the central bank of a country to government by the central bank of a country to supplement money raised on treasury bills.

wear and tear
another term for depreciation.

welfare state
a country which provides through the central government and its agencies minimum standards of living for the population in terms of income, health, education, housing, etc.

where-used report
in manufacturing, a report that display, for each part, all assemblies that contain the part in their single-level bill of material.

white-collar
of relating to, or performing clerical or supervisory work.

white paper
a publication of the British government with a white cover—a usually statement of policy.

wholesale life insurance
life insurance for individual members or a group that is smaller than the minimum required for a group life insurance policy.

wholesaler
the middle man between manufacturer and earlier. He is able to buy in large quantities and then break these into smaller parcels for the benefit of the retailers. The wholesaler takes a profit either by adding to the manufacturer's price or by charging a commission to the retailer. Where selling prices are fixed by the manufacturer, the manufacturer in effect gives a share of his profit by way of discount to the wholesaler who passes on a share to the retailer. This is often referred to as a trade discount.

wholesaler—function of
(i) assembling (ii) warehousing or storing ; (iii) dispersing ; (iv) transporting ; (v) grading (vi) financing ; (vii) risk bearing ; (viii) pricing.

windfall profit
a profit not anticipated. It might arise perhaps from changes in legislation. An increase in tax, or duty, might result in the manufacturer's making additional profit on stock where on the lower rate of duty has already been paid. Windfall profits being exceptional, they are normally shown separately in company accounts.

winding-up, commencement of
in voluntary liquidation the winding up dates from the resolution. In a compulsory liquidation it dates from the presentation of the petition. For the purpose of preferential payments, it dates from the

appointment of a provisional liquidator.

winding-up, compulsory : procedure

winding-up begis with a petition to a court, supported by an affidavit. The proper court is the County Court if the capital of the company is not more than Rs.500000; the High Court if it is. The court may dismiss the petition, order it to stand over, make an order for winding-up with or without court supervision, or make any other order it thinks fit. If a compulsory winding-up order is made the court appoints a liquidator. Winding-up commences either with the presentation of the petition, or, where the company was previously winding up voluntarily, from the date of the resolution to wind up. From the point of view of preferential debts, it dates either the resolution to wind up voluntarily, or date of the order, or the date a provisional liquidator was appointed.

winding-up : supervision by a court

after a resolution to wind up voluntarily has been passed, a creditor (or any other interested person) may petition the court that the winding-up should proceed under the supervision of the court. The winding up is conducted as a normal voluntary winding-up, except for an restrictions the court may order. One advantage in favour of court supervision is that proceeding against the company cannot be commenced or continued without the leave of the court.

window dressing

a part from its literal meaning of displaying goods in a shop window in a manner that maximizes the chances of passers-by being tempted to buy them or at least to enter the shop, this term has certain specialized meaning in the world of commerce.

window shopping

parading up and down a shopping street, to see new products, items, more is envy rather than purchase.

wind up

to arrange the affairs of a company so that its dislocation can take place. The process starts either with an application by the company itself or by its creditors to a court for a winding-up order, or with a decision by member that their company be wound up known as a 'voluntary winding up'. The assets of the company are sold and proceeds distribnuted to its creditors and members, and the company is finally dissolved. Wind up, dissolve and liquidate all refer to ending the existence of a corporation. Sometimes liquidate is used to refer only to the process of selling the corporation's property and winding up is used for the legal formalities including dissolution.

workers' morale

the moral of workers plays an important role in determining their efficiency. Morale and productivity have a direct relationship with each other. Morale is a state of human of the individuals to achieve the objectives of the business. Vitles describes morale as 'an attitude of satisfaction with desire to continue in, and willingness to strive for the goals of a particular group or organisation.

workers' participation in management

workers' participation in management is a concept shrouded with so much vagueness that for different people it has different meaning. The term has been used in a variety of senses has come to be associated with varying practices in different countries. The practices in different countries differ in respect of range of subjects handled by participation machinery; in the degree of authority exercised with regard to these subjects ; and in the methods of selection of workers' representatives. Notwithstanding these differences, worker's participation in management is a crystalisation of the notion industrial democracy.It is an expression of the employer's desire to bind his employee into a team working together towards a common purpose. This is through fullest cooperation between labour and management.

In general terms, the objective of workers' participation implies the mental and emotional involvement of a worker in a group situation which encourages him to contribute to group goals and share responsibility in them. Labour participation in management has become increasingly important during the recent past. Businessmen have realised the importance of an old saying "a fellow in the boat with you will never bore a hole in it". For better business results, proper understanding and cooperation between the labour and managenment and participation of labour in the management of industry is conducive to increased productivity.

Labour participation in the management of the business provides some 'status' and a felling of self-importance to the employees of the organisation. Such a participation leads to better industrial relations. Workers are encouraged to give their best to the organisation. Productivity increases and a sense of belonging to the industry grows. Hence, for peaceful evolution of the economy on democratic basis, it is essential that the workers participation in the management should be recognised as a fundamental principal.

working capital

an accounting term usually defined as the difference between current assets and current liabilities. It is also sometimes referred to as circulating capital, because assets and liabilities are continually circulated or turned over in the normal course of business. This distinguishes it from fixed capital which comprises fixed assets.

The difference between the values of a firm's current assets and its current liabilities is sometimes called net working capital, whereas gross working capital means the total value of current assets.

working control

theoretically, control of a corporation requires ownership of 51 per cent of the corporations voting stock. In practice, effective (working) control may be exercised through ownership, individually or by a group acting as one, of less than 50 per cent.

wcrk study

a study concerned with improving working methods and deciding how long particular jobs should take. Its aim is to reduce effort involved in various operations, to organize labour in the most economical manner and to provide date for planning, estimating, and financial incentive-schemes.

work-sharing—theory of

as applied to labour relations, it is an attempt to prevent dismissal of some employees by management.

writ

a legal document summoning a person to attend a certain court place or to perform a certain act. These are penalties for failure to comply. A written document containing a command from the Executive of the country to a person to take some specified action.

write-down

the transfer of portion of an asset account to an expense account; the deliberate reduction of the book value of an asset.

write-off

the transfer of the remainder of the value of an asset to an. expense account; the act of reducing book value.

written down value

an accounting term for the cost or valuation of an asset, less the written-off depreciation. It is no indication of the present selling price of that asset.

xenophon

Plato's contemporary, xenophon, gives in his Cyclopaedia an account of the division of labour. He seems to appreciate the nature of private exchange : he distinguishes between the big cities in which division of labour is developed and the small cities in which it hardly exists.

x-fficiency

the efficiency of a firm in buying and using inputs. Most firms do not operate a maximum X-efficiency.

xerography

making copies of documents. The original document to be copied is exposed to a bright light. The name is derived from the Greek Xeros=dry and graphein = to write. Process involved is as follows ; white areas of the original reflect the light while dark areas (i.e., the printing or writing on the document) absorb it. The reflected light therefore outlines an image of the printing or writing on the original. This image is received on a metal plate that is coated with selenium powder. The plate has been electrically charged and has been kept in the dark before the projection of the document. Selenium becomes a good conductor of electricity when exposed to light and therefore during projection the electric charge is conducted away by the metal plate everywhere except the lines that were black on the original document. The uncharged selenium powder is no longer attracted to the metal plate and is brushed away. Copy paper is laid on the plate and electrically charged so that the remaining selenium powder, in the form of an image of the document, is transferred to the paper. The paper is then heated so that the image fuses to it.

year-end dividend

an extra dividend paid at the end of the fiscal year. Some companies pay such dividend only rarely, after exceptionally profitable year; other do so regularly, paying deliberately small regular dividends in order to allow for a year-end dividend.

yearss' purchase

the value of property is frequently indicated as being equal to the rent for a certain number of year.

yield

the return earned on an investment, taking into account the annual income and its present capital value. It also has other, more particular, meaning- perhaps as may as there are financial editors.

yield rate

synonym for internal rate of return.

yield variance

in standard costing, and particularly in process industries, the calculating of the actual amounts produced compared with norms or standards and expressing this variance as a percentage.

Young Allyn

Allyn Young propounded a theory which involves breaking down in practice what is an essential part of the assumption of perfect competition : namely, the indifference on the part of buyers to the sellers from whom they purchase. Or, in other words again, it involves the creation of heterogeneity among the products offered for sale by competing producers. If this can be established, the single market of competition becomes subdivided into a number of special markets for the products of each firm, separated from one another by more or less strong or stable insulating walls of special buyer's preferences. In that situation, cash firm has to consider the demand of two kinds of marginal buyers : those who are marginal in its own special market, and those who are marginal to all.

z chart

a graph displaying a number of successive observations of a time series. If observations are to be shown then for each of the times at which the observations were taken, three points are plotted : (a) the observed value at that time ; (b) the cumulative total of observations since the start of the period shown.

zero balance

refers to the result of a technique of balance if details and totals are both correct.

zero-base budgeting

the practice of justifying budgeted expenditure in relation to the performance to be achieved, without reference to pre-existing plans or achievements.

zero coupon bonds

issued by companies bonds which pay no interest but are priced at a discount of their redemption price; they offer the promise of reward through capital gains, which are normally taxed at a lower rate than income received as interest.

zero defects

a programme for persuading employees to produce faultless products. It a wakens workers against complacent attitude induced by statistical quality control in which a certain proportion of defects is set as an acceptable quality level. Programmes usually attempt to motivate employees by emphasizing pride in performance and craftsmanship and by providing reward for defect-free performance.

zero-price advertising

distributing of advertising at price which does not cover its costs, i.e., a zero money price, while the advertised goods are marked up to finance the advertising.

zero-rated

value added tax at a rate of 0%. Supplies in this category include the supply of most kinds of food (except in the course of catering), books newspapers and power. The effect is that a taxable person who makes zero-rated supplies can have his input tax refunded to him, whereas one who makes exempt supplies cannot have input tax refunded in the related 'monopolistically competitive' markets. Theoretically, its policy may be either one of price reduction to attract buyers away from the competitors, or one of buttressing its monopolaid position by maintaining the thickness of the insulating wall between it and the others through the continued expenditure of sales costs.

zollverein

it is a system of economic unity introduced by Wurtemberg List in Germany in order to extend free trade to a larger market in the country. Due to efforts of the List a study was made of a single economic unit, inside which free trade helped German industry to grow.

zone

trading area, or area to which product launch is temporarily limited a zoned campaign or one that is zonal.

zoning ordinance

an ordiance passed by a city council by virture of its police power and used to regulate and prescribe the kind of buildings, residences, or business that shall be constructed and put into service and use within the city's geographical limits.

z-score

a measure of the solvency of a company calculated from a linear equation, incorporating more than one finance ratio.

zweigniederlassung

in Germany, branch office of foreign company or partnership over which parent company has full legal control.

PART 4
GEOLOGY

aa
a Hawaiian term for black Iava flow, which has solidified into a blocky mass; e.g., Mt. Etna in Italy.

aalenian
a stratigraphic stage name which is used for the lowermost middle or uppermost lower Jurassic geologic time.

abandon
to stop efforts to obtain oil/gas from a well.

abandonment
the voluntary surrender of legal rights or title to a mining claim.

ablation
refers to the wearing away of rocks due to erosion, weathering, or wind action.

ablation moraine
1. a layer of rock particles overlying ice in the ablation of a glacier.
2. drift deposited from a superficial position through the melting of underlying stagnant ice.

abnormal synclinorium
a synclinorium with axial planes of subsidiary folds converging downward.

abrade
refers to wear away by the act of abrasion or friction.

abrasion
mechanical *erosion* by debrischarged wind, water or ice, which also removes the eroded material.

abrasion platform
an uplifted marine peneplain or plain, according to the smoothness of the surface produced by wave erosion, which is of large area.

abrasive
a small, hard, sharp-cornered rock fragment, used by natural agents in abrading rock material or land surfaces. Also known as abrasive ground.

absarokite
a porphyritic basalt having a small amount of orthoclase in the groundmass.

absolute temperature
temperature measured on the Kelvin scale, with respect to absolute zero (-273.15°C).

absolute time
geologic time measured in years, as determined by radioactive decay of elements.

abstraction
refers to the complete absorption of one river by another. In abstraction, a series of smaller valleys are progressively incorporated into a larger one. It is commonly seen in streams which are radiating from a cone, e.g. a volcano.

abutment load
the weight transferred to adjacent solid rock in a deep excavation.

abyss
an abyss is a deep cave or valley. A deep valley on the ocean floor is also often called an abyss.

abyssal deposits
the deposits of the deep sea,

accumulating in depths of more than 2000 metres of water; they comprise organic oozes, various muds, and the red clay of the deepest regions.

abyssal hill

a common low-relief feature of the ocean floor, usually found seaweed of abyssal plains and in basins isolated by ridges, rises, or trenches.

abyssal theory

a theory of the origin of ores in which there occurs the separation of ore silicates from the liquid stage during cooling of the earth.

abyssolith

a molten mass of eruptive material which is passing up without any break, from the zone of permanently molten rock within the earth.

abyssopelagic

referring to open waters of the abyssal zone.

acadian

a series name applied to the Middle Cambrian strata of the Atlantic Province in N. America

acanthodiformes

an order of subclass *Acanthodii,* class *Osteichthyes,* superclass *Pisces;* small, shark-like bony *fish.* Range Upper Silurian-Lower Permian.

acaustobiolith

a noncombustible rock which got formed by the organic accumulation of minerals.

accessory Ejecta

pyroclastic substances which are formed from solidified volcanic rocks that are from the same volcano as the ejecta.

accessory lithic

a *clast* in a pyroclastic rock formed of material torn from a volcanic vent's walls during a volcanic eruption.

accidental block

a solid chip of rock which is broken down from the subvolcanic basement and ejected from a volcano.

accommodation structure

a small structure which allows a bed to fill all available space created during deformation.

accretion

1. refers to a number of processes as a result of which stones or other inorganic substances add to their bulk by adding particles to their surface. It is also known as aggradation.

2. Also, refers to buildup of land on a shore due to wave-action tides, currents, airborne material, or alluvial deposits.

accretion Vein

a type of vein which is formed by the repeated filling of channels followed by their opening due to the development of fractures in the zone undergoing mineralization.

accumulation area

the part of a glacier of snowfield in which during a year's time, the mass balance is positive i.e., accumulating exceeds ablation.

ACF diagram

a triangular diagram used to represent the chemical composition of metamorphic rocks. The three corners of the diagram are AL_2O_3, CaO, and FeO+MgO.

achondrite

a type of stony meteorite which compares closely with some basic igneous rocks such as eucrite.

achroite

a white, potassium-rich variety of tourmaline.

acicular

refers to a tendency due to which crystals are shaped needle-like.

acid

an acid is a kind of chemical which dissolves in water to make an acidic solution. Many acids can dissolve metals. An acid is the opposite of an alkali.

acid clay

a type of clay that gives off hydrogen ions when it dissolves in water.

acidic lava

extruded felsic igneous magma which is rich in silica.

acid rocks

those igneous rocks which contain more than 66% of silica, and which, therefore, when crystalline, carry free quartz as an essential constituent.

acid soil

acid soil contains minerals rich in hydrogen and aluminium. Water leaches minerals, such as calcium, magnesium, potassium and sodium, out of the soil. Most plants need these minerals to grow.

aclinal

without dip; horizontal.

acme-zone

a biozone consisting for a body of strata in which a particular species of genus of an organism occurs with maximum frequency.

acoustic basement

the boundary between overlying sediments and underlying igneous or metamorphic rocks, characterized by strong seismic reflections on a seismogram.

acrobatholitic

a stage in batholitic erosion where summits of cupolas and stocks are exposed without any exposure of the surface separating the barren interior of the batholith from the mineralized upper part.

active fault

any type of fault in which there is recurrent movement in the form of continuous creep, small, abrupt displacements, or seismic activity.

active layer

that part of the soil which is within the suprapermafrost layer and which usually freezes in winter and thaws in summer. Also known as frost zone.

active permafrost

permanently frozen ground which, after thawing by artificial or unusual natural means, reverts to permafrost under normal climatic conditions.

active volcano

a volcano capable of venting lava, pyroclastic material, or gases.

adamantine lustre

a brilliant, sparkling lustre arising from a mineral's being transparent and having a high refractive index, e.g. diamond, cerussite.

adamellite

a variety of granite having a calcium-bearing plagioclase, usually oligoclase, and a potassium feldspar, in roughly equal amounts. For microadamellite, Microgranite.

adaptive radiation (adaptive divergence)

an evolutionary trend by which organisms increase in diversity as they adapt to occupy a large number of ecological environments.

adhesion

a process in which dry sand blown onto a damp surface is held by the surface tension of water rising between the grains by capillary action.

adinole

an argillaceous sediment that has undergone albitization at the margin of a basic intrusion.

adsorption

adhesion to the surface of a material.

adularia

a low temperature form of monoclinic feldspar $KAlSi_3O_2$ found in veins etc.

advance

1. a continuing movement of a shoreline toward the sea.

2. a net movement over a specified period of time of a shoreline toward the sea.

adventive cone

a volcanic cone that is on the flank of and subsidiary to a larger volcano. Also known as lateral cone; parasitic cone.

adventive crater

a crater opened on the flank of a large volcanic cone.

aeolian bounding surface

an erosion surface truncating strata within wind deposited sediments.

aeolian deposit

sediments deposited as a result of transport by wind.

aeolian sand sheet

an extensive area of wind-deposited sand, with only rare slip-faced bed-forms, commonly found around dune field.

aeon

this term is used for an indefinite but lengthy period of time. It is being replaced by a precise usage for 10^9 years. On this basis the age of the Earth is about 4.7 aeons, and the Phanerozoic represents just over half an aeon.

aerial

aerial describes an object which is found in the air. Birds and other animals which feed on flying insects are known as aerial predators.

aerogeology
refers to the geologic study of the earth features by using aerial observations including aerial photography.

aerolites
a general name for stony as distinct from iron meteorites.

aerosiderite
a meteorite composed principally of iron.

affine deformation
a type of deformation in which very thin layers slip against each other so that each moves equally with respect to its neighbours; generally does not result in folding.

aftershock
a smaller earthquake which is felt after a large earthquake. It originates at or near the larger earthquake's epicentre.

agalmatolite
a soft and waxy mineral (or stone) of various colours; used for carving images. Also known as lardite; pagodite.

agate
banded chalcedonic silica.

age
a fourth order geological time unit.

age determination
estimation of the geologic age of samples of biological and geological importance using radiometric methods.

agglomerate
pyroclastic rocks which consist mainly of fragments larger than 2 cm in diameter.

agglutinate
a welded pyroclastic deposit in which the pyroclasts are held together by glassy material.

aggradation
the process of building up a surface with sediment deposited by wind or water.

aggregate
an aggregate is a type of soil. It is made up of tiny rock particles that stick together. Aggregate also describes the sand and gravel that is mixed with cement to make concrete.

agmatite
refers to a migmatite in which the introduced material tends to form a network of veins throughout the host rock.

agnatha
a class of the vertebrate, jawless fish, the fossil forms of which are found in rocks of Devonian age.

agpaite
a group of igneous rocks having feldspathoids. It includes naujaite, lujavrite, and kekortokite.

agricere
a waxy or resinous organic coating on soil particles.

agiuille
refers to the needle-top of the summit of certain glaciated mountains.

air
air is the mixture of gases that surrounds the Earth. Air is mostly made up of nitrogen and oxygen. It also contains carbon dioxide, argon and water vapour.

airgun
a mechanical marine seismic source in which a burst of high-pressure air is suddenly released into the water, forming a bubble which oscillates in a similar fashion to an explosion.

alaskite
a bimineralic, leucocratic, granitic rock composed of quartz and alkali feldspar.

albertan
a stratigraphic stage name which is used for the North American Middle Cambrian.

albian
uppermost Lower Cretaceous geologic time.

albian stage
a division of the Cretaceous System, comprising the rocks between the Aptian stage below and the Cenomanian stage above; approximately equivalent to the English Gault and Upper Greensand.

albion
a stratigraphic stage name which is used for the North American Lower Silurian. It is a synonym of Medinian.

albionian
lower Silurian geologic time.

albitite
a rare type of soda-syenite consisting almost entirely of albite, with a small content of coloured silicates.

albitization
in igneous rocks, the process by which a soda-lime feldspar is replaced by albite.

alcove lands
terrain where the mud rocks or sandy clays and shales that compose the hills are interstratified by occasional harder beds; the slopes are terraced.

alee basin
a basin formed in the deep sea by turbidity currents aggrading courses where the currents were deflected around a submarine ridge.

aleishtite
a bluish or greenish mixture of dickite and other clay minerals.

alexandrian
lower Silurian geologic time.

alexandrite
transparent variety of chrysoberyl used as a gemstone. Its colour is green in daylight and deep red in artificial light.

alfisol
an order of soils with gray to brown surface horizons, a medium-to-high base supply, and horizons of clay accumulation.

algal biscuit
a disk-shaped or spherical mass, up to 20 centimetres in diameter, made up of carbonate that is probably the result of precipitation by algae.

algal pit
an ablation depression that is small and contains algae.

algal reef
an organic reef which has been formed largely of algal remains

and in which algae are or were the main lime-secreting organisms.

algal ridge

elevated margin of a windward coral reef built by actively growing calcareous algae.

algal rim

low rim built by actively growing calcareous algae on the lagoonal side of a patch reef in a lagoon.

algal structure

a deposit, most frequently calcareous, with banding, irregular concentric structures, crusts, and pseudopisolites or pseudoconcretionary forms resulting from organic, colonial secretion and precipitation.

alginite (bituminite)

a coal maceral or the exinite group made up of coalified algal remains, characteristic of boghead coal.

algoman

refers to a stratigraphic division of the Canadian Precambrian, Pre-Algonkian.

aliquot

a small sample of a material assayed to estimate the properties of the whole.

alkali feldspar

a feldspar which consists of potassium feldspar and sodium feldspar, such as orthoclase, microcline albite and anorthoclase; all are regarded as rich in alkali.

alkali flat

a level lakelike plain formed by the evaporation of water in a depression and deposition of its fine sediment and dissolved minerals.

alkali-granite

an acid, coarse-grained rock carrying free quartz and characterized by a large excess of alkali-feldspar over plagioclase. In general, the prefix used with a rock name implies a preponderance of soda—or potash-feldspar or feldspathoid over plagioclase, e.g., alkalidolerite.

alkali lake

a lake in an arid region rich in dissolved sodium and potassium carbonate, sodium chloride and other alkaline salts.

alkinite

$PbCuBiS_3$ a mineral occurring in grey coloured needle shaped crystals; crystallizes in the orthorhombic system.

allalinite

an altered gabbro which has original texture and euhedral pseudomorphs.

alleghenian

lower Middle Pennsylvania geologic time.

alleghenian orogeny

Pennsylvanian and Early Permian orogenic episode which deformed the rocks of the Appalachian Valley and the Ridge and Plateau provinces.

aller

a Permian succession in NW Europe covering the lower part of the Capitanian.

allivalite

a form of gabbro which is composed of anorthite and olivine; accessories include auginite, apatite, and opaque oxides of iron.

allochem

sediment formed by chemical or biochemical precipitation within a depsotional basin; includes intraclasts, fossils, peltets, oolites.

allochetite

a porphyritic igneous rock which is composed of phenocrysts of labradorite, orthoclase, titanaugite, nepheline, magnetite, and apatite in a ground mass of augite, biotite, magnetite, hornblende, nepheline, and orthoclase.

allodapic

descriptive of sediment deposited by mass flow, particularly limestone.

allogene

allogenic mineral or rock constituent such as a pebble in a conglomerate or xenolith in an igneous rock.

allogenic

the term applicable to the derived portion of a sediment, whether minerals or other constituents (e.g., the pebbles in a conglomerate, the grains of quartz making up a sand), which got originated away from the area of sedimentation and gets transported to it for final deposition. It is also known as allothigenous.

allothimorph

a metamorphic rock constituent which retains its original crystal outlines in the new rock.

allothogenic

formed from preexisting rocks which have been transported from another location. Also known as allogenic.

allotriomorphic

a textural term used for igneous rocks describing crystals which show a form related to surrounding previously crystallized minerals rather than to their own internal structure.

alloy

an alloy is a kind of solid substance. An alloy is made by melting a metal and mixing in smaller amounts of other metals or nonmetals. The mixture is then cooled until it becomes solid.

alluvial

(1) composed of or pertaining to alluvium, or deposited by running water. (2) applied to a placer formed by running water, or to the mineral associated with it.

alluvial architecture

the three-dimensional distribution of sedimentary faces in an alluvial deposit, governed by autocyclic and allocyclic controls.

alluvial clay

sediment of the clay grade which has been transported by rivers from the place of its origin, as distinct from that which has originated in situ.

alluvial cone
an alluvial fan with steep slopes formed of lose material washed down the slopes of mountains by ephemeral streams and deposited as a conical mass of low slope at the mouth of a gorge. Also known as cone delta; cone of dejection; cone of detritus; debris cone; dry delta; hemicone; wash.

alluvial dam
a sedimentary deposit which is built by an overloaded stream and dams its channel; especially characteristic of distributaries on alluvial fans.

alluvial deposits
detrital material transported by a river and deposited normally temporarily, at points along the flood plain of a river. They are commonly composed of sands and gravels. Many important ore minerals, such as gold, platinum, diamonds, cassiterite, occur locally concentrated in alluvial deposits. It is also known as alluvium.

alluvial fan
a fan-shaped deposit formed by a stream either where it issues from a narrow mountain valley onto a plain or broad valley, or where a tributary stream joins a main stream.

alluvial flat
a small alluvial plain having a slope of about 5 to 20 feet per mile and built of fine sandy clay or adobe deposited during flood.

alluvial ore deposit
a deposit in which the valuable mineral particles have been transported and left by a stream.

alluvial plain
a plain formed from the deposition of alluvium usually adjacent to a river that periodically overflows. Also known as aggraded valley plain; river plain; wash plain; waste plain.

alluvial slope
a surface of alluvium which slopes down from mountain sides and merges with the plain or broad valley floor.

alluvial soil
a soil deposit developed on flood plain and delta deposits.

alluvial terrace
a terraced embankment of loose material adjacent to the sides of a river valley. Also known as built terrace; drift terrace; fill terrace; stream-built terrace.

alluvial valley
a valley filled with a stream deposit.

alluviation
deposition of sediment by a river.

alluvium
the detrital materials eroded, transported, and deposited by streams; and important constituent of shelf deposits. Also known as alluvial deposit; alluvion.

alnoite
a variety of biotite lamprophyres which are characterized by lepidomelane phenocrysts. It is free from feldspar but has meletite pervoskite, olivine, and carbonate in the matrix.

alpine
alpine describes land above the tree-line on mountains. The name comes from the Alp mountains of Europe, but is used for all such areas in the world. Alpine areas are very rocky. The soil is usually shallow, and the climate is cold.

alportian
the highest stage of the Carboniferous, 325.6-322.8 Ma.

alsbachite
refers to an uncommon porphyritic variety of aplite. A plutonic rock having sodic plagicalse, quartz, and subordinate orthoclase.

alteration
any chemical or mineralogical change in a rock caused by chemical or physical action.

altiplano
a tableland plateau at high elevation; specifically, the altiplano of western Bolivia and southwestern Peru, which is a series of intermontane basins.

altitude
(1) vertical distance measured between a point and some reference surface, usually mean sea level.
(2) vertical angle measured between the plane of the horizontal and a reference line at some higher point such as a summit peak.

altocumulus
altocumulus describes a kind of cloud. Altocumulus clouds are white, fluffy and rounded and appear during fine weather.

alum
a series of double sulphate isomorphs with potash alum, approximating the formula $(KAl(SO_4)_2 . 12 H_2O)$.

alum coal
argillaceous brown coal rich in pyrite in which alum is formed due to weathering.

alumina
the native form of the oxide of aluminium. It is found as corundum or in the hydrated forms, as a crystalline or powdery substance.

alum shale
shale containing potassium alum, formerly worked at Whitby in Yorkshire as a source of the latter.

alunite $KAl_3(SO_4)_2(OH)_6$
a rombohedral white or pink fibrous mineral containing basic potassium aluminium sulphate.

alyphite
bitumen that yields a high percentage of open-chain aliphatic hydrocarbons upon distillation.

ambatoarinite
a mineral which is a mixture of the carbonates of cerium

metals and strontium.

amber

amber is a mineral which can be used as a gem. It can be clear orange or cloudy yellow. Amber comes from the liquid sap, or resin, which oozed from trees many millions of years ago. Some pieces of amber have insects trapped in them. Amber is found in sedimentary rocks and washed up on sea-shores.

amesite

a variety of septechlorite rich in magnesium and aluminium.

amethyst

the term applied to a violet/ purple variety of quartz. It is used as jeweller's stone.

amherstite

a syenodiorite containing andesine and antiperihite.

ammanian

a stratigraphic stage name which is used for the British Lower Westphalian.

ammonite

an extinct fossil cephalopod found in rocks of Mesozoic age, particularly characteristic of the Lias. Frequently coiled in a plane, or nearly plane, spiral.

amorphous

descriptive of a mineral with no regular arrangement of atoms, i.e. non-crystalline.

amphibia

a class of vertebrates living on land and in water. Fossil amphibia have been found in rocks of Upper Devonian to Recent age.

amphibolite

a metamorphic rock which is composed mainly of amphibole, generally with an orientated fabric. The term is not applicable to igneous rocks which consist of entirely of amphibole.

amphidromic point

a nodal point in the sea where no vertical tidal movement occurs, and tidal currents are most rapid.

ampholyte

a substance that can act as either an acid, in the presence of a strong base, or a base, when in the presence of a strong acid.

amphoterite

a stony meteorite containing bronzite and olivine with some oligoclase and nickel-rich iron.

amygdaloid

lava rock containing amygdules. Also known as amygdaloidal lava.

amygdule

1. a mineral filling formed in vesicles of lava flows; it may be chalcedony, opal, calcite, chlorite, or prehnite.

2. an agate pebble.

anabranch

a river channel pattern in which the width of islands is more than three times the river width at average discharge.

anaerobic

organisms that are anaerobic *i.e.,* do not require free atmospheric or dissolved oxygen.

analcimite

an extrusive or hypabyssal rock which consists of pyroxene and analcine.

analcimization

the replacement in igneous rock of feldspar or feldspathoids by analcime.

analcitite

an igneous rock in which abundant plagioclase crystals have been replaced by analcite during the late stage deuteric alteration in which magmatic fluids penetrated cleavages and fractures in the plagioclase.

anamigmatism

a process of high-temperature, high-pressure remelting of sediment to yield magma.

anamorphic zone

the zone of rock flow, as indicated by reactions that may involve decrabonation, dehydration, and deoxidation; silicates are built up, and the formation of denser minerals and of compact crystalline structure takes place.

anamorphism

a deep-seated constructive metamorphic process by which new complex minerals of greater density are formed from pre-existing simpler minerals of low density through silication, decarbonization, deoxidation and dehydration.

anastomosing

of streams, branching and rejoining irregularly to form a net-like pattern.

anatase TIO_2

a mineral, trimorphous with rutile and brooklite.

anatexis

a high-temperature process of metamorphosis by which plutonic rock in the lowest levels of the crust is melted and regenerated as a magma.

anathermal

a period of time between the age of other strata or units of reference in which the temperature is increasing.

andalusite Al_2SiO_5

a brown, red, yellow, or green neosilicate mineral. It crystallises in orthorhombic system. It generally occurs in metamorphic rocks.

anderken

an Ordovician succession in Kazakhstan covering part of the Soudleyan, Longvillian and Marshbrookian.

andradite

the calcium-iron end member of the garnet group.

andrite

a meteorite composed principally of augite with some olivine and troilite.

anemoclast

a clastic rock that was fragmented and rounded by wind.

anemoclastic

referring to rock that was broken by wind erosion and rounded by wind action.

anemometer

an anemometer is an instrument which measures the speed of the wind. In the commonest type of anemometer, the wind turns small cups which are attached to a rod. The harder the wind is blowing, the faster the cups turn.

angaraland

a large continent in the northern hemisphere which existed of Carboniferous and Permian times, comprising the former USSR east of the Urals.

angle of draw

the angle between the end of a subsurface working and the point on the surface to which its associated subsidence extends.

angoumian

a stratigraphic stage name which is used for the European Upper Turonian.

angular unconformity

an unconformity in which the older strata dip at a different angle than the younger strata.

angularity (roudness)

the ratio between the average radius of circles drawn within the corners and edges of a clast and the radius of the largest circle which could be drawn within the clast; thus a measure of the sharpness of the corners of a clast.

anhydrous

denoting a chemical compound lacking water: applied particularly to salts lacking their water of cryctolization.

animikie Series

an important member of the Pre-Cambrian of the Canadian Shield, extending northwards into the Arctic regions. Perhaps 4250 m in thickness, it includes important iron ores, carbonaceous slate, jaspers, and boulder conglomerates. These succeed the Huronian.

anisian

a stratigraphic stage name which is used for the European and Russian Middle Triassic.

ankaramite

an augite-rich olivine mela-basalt.

annelida

this phylum, the worms, does not have much geological importance. The only fossil remains have chititinous jaw structures which are comparable to those found in the modern polychaete worms (the Bristle Worms), which are usually termed as scolecodonts, and are of no stratigraphic importance. The only other fossil traces of this phylum include worm tubes and trails.

annealing

the movement of grain boundaries and grain growth in a polycrystalline rock by which the rock undergoes recovery from deformation. Driven by elevated temperature or occurring slowly over a long period.

annual layer

any sedimentary or precipitated layer of material of variable composition and thickness, presumed to have been deposited during the course of one year. Annual layers are most frequently utilized in the study of varved deposits laid down in glacially fed lakes.

anomalous lead

lead with an isotope ratio which gives an incorrect radiometric age. cf. common lead.

anorthosite

an instrusive igneous rock composed almost entirely of plagioclase feldspar. Although less abundant than basalt or granite, anorthosite often occurs in massive complexes, usually lopolithic or laccolithic.

antaractica

antarctica is the Earth's most southerly continent. Antarctica is the land around the South Pole. Most of the land is covered by ice. Antarctica is the coldest continent on Earth.

antecendent drainage

a drainage system maintaining its general directions by cutting through a localized uplifted area at a rate greater than the uplift.

anthracite

a high grade metamorphic coal which has semimetallic lusture, high fixed carbon content, and high density. It burns with a short blue flame and very little smoke or odour.

anthraxylon

composite term for a coal component (maceral) that has a vitreous lustre. In banded coal it forms bands interlayered with opaque or dull attritus.

anti-

anti- is prefix meaning against or preventing.

anti-alias filter

a filter applied to a signal so as to avoid aliasing.

anticline

a fold, closing in any direction in which the older rocks occupy the core.

anticyclone

an anticyclone is an area of high atmospheric pressure. Anticyclones nearly always bring clear skies and settled weather. The opposite of an anticyclone is a depression, which is sometimes known as a cyclone.

antidune

a transient accumulation of sediment on a stream bed, comparable to a sand dune, that moves upstream. Also, any marking or bed feature, whether moving or stationary, produced by unidirectional flow, and in phase with surface water waves.

antiferromagnetism

rock magnetism in which the magnetic lattices posses magnetizations which are equal and in opposite directions so that the rock has a zero external magnetic field.

antiform

an anticlinelike structure whose stratigraphic sequence is not known.

antiperthite

natural intergrowth of feldspars formed by separation of sodium feldspar and potassium feldspar during slow cooling of molten mixtures; the potassium-rich phase is exolved in a plagioclase host, exactly the inverse of perthite.

antithetic
a term used for fault planes which dip in the opposite direction to the bedding.

apex
an American mining law term denoting the outcrop of a vein reaching the surface or the shallowest point of a subsurface vein.

aphanitic
textural term used for describing igneous rocks having such a fine grain that individual constituents do not become visible to the naked eye, but become visible under suitable magnification.

aphyric
said of the texture of fine-grained igneous rocks, showing two generations of the same mineral but without phenocrysts.

aplacophora
a subclass of class Amphineura, phylum Mollusca; molluscs whose dorsal surface is covered by seven or eight non-calcareous plates, and thus with no fossil record.

apoda
an order of subclass Lissamphibia, class Amphibia; legless, snake-like amphibians. Range Lower Jurassic-Recent.

apophysis
in geology a tongue or other direct offshoot of a larger intrusive body, such as a vein or dike.

apparent velocity
the velocity of seismic waves measured from a segment of the graph of arrival time against range. If the refractor is dipping or undulating, this does not represent a true velocity.

appinite
the term used for a group of coarsegrained igneous rocks which are similar in character to syenites, monzonites, or diorites but rich in ferro-magnesian minerals, e.g., hornblende, biotite, and sometimes pyroxene.

apple coal
easily mined soft coal that breaks into small pieces the size of apples.

apposition beach
one of a series of parallel beaches formed on the seaward side of an older beach.

aquamarine
a transparent, pale blue-green gem variety of beryl. It occurs in pegmatite, in which it may form very large crystals.

aqueous lava
mud lava produced by the mixing of volcanic ash with condensing volcanic vapour or other water.

aquiclude

a porus formation that absorbs water slowly but will not transmit it fast enough to furnish an appreciable supply for a well or spring.

aquifer

a permeable body of rock capable of yielding quantities of ground work to wells and springs. A subsurface zone that yields economically important amounts of water to wells.

aquifer loss

the water lost by flow from the aquifer to the well when drawdown occurs.

aquifuge

an impermeable body of rock which contains no interconnected openings or interstices and therefore neither absorbs nor transmits water.

aquitanian

lower Miocene or uppermost Oligocene geologic time.

arachnida

a class of subphylum Chelicerated, phylum Arthropoda; the spiders and scorpions. Range Silurian-Recent.

aragonite $CaCO_3$

an orthorhombic carbonate mineral, which occurs in sedimentary rocks.

arbuckle orogeny

mid-Pennsylvanian episode of di-astrophism in the Wichita and Arbouckle Mountains of Oklahoma.

archaeomagnetism

palaeomagnetism applied to archaeological phenomena.

archean

it is regarded as synonymous with Precambrain, but sometimes it is used to refer to older Precambrian rock.

archetype

the hypothetical ancestral form of an organism in which all basic characteristics are established without specialization.

archipelago

an archipelago is a group of islands. The islands in an archipelago are usually small, and they often form a line or a curved pattern.

arctic circle

the Arctic Circle is an imaginary line around the Earth, to the north of which lies the Arctic region. The position of the Arctic Circle is at 66 degrees 17 minutes north of the Equator.

arcuate delta

a bowed or curved delta with the convex margin facing the body of water. Also known as fanshaped delta.

arcuation

production of an arc, as in rock flowage where movement proceeded in a fanlike manner.

ardealite $Ca_2(HPO)_4(SO_4).4H_2O$.

a white or light-yellow mineral composed of hydrated calcium hydrogen phosphate-sulphate.

ardennian orogeny

a short-lived orogeny during the Ludlovian stage of the Silurian period of geologic time.

areal eruption

volcanic eruption occurring due to the collapse of the roof of batholith; the volcanic rocks grade into parent plutonic rocks.

areal geology

Distribution and form of rocks or geologic units of any relatively large area of the earth's surface.

arenaceous

of sediment or sedimentary rocks that have been derived from sand or that contain sand. Also known as psammitic; sabulous.

arenicolite

a hole, groove, or other mark in a sedimentary rock, generally sandstone, interpreted as a burrow made by an arenicolous marine worm or a trail of a mollusk or crustacean.

arenigian

a European stage including Lower Ordovician geologic time. Also known as Skiddavian.

arenite

arenaceious rock of any composition.

arete

narrow, jagged ridge produced by the merging of glacial cirques. Also known as arris; crib; serrate ridge.

argentite (silver glance) (Ag_2S)

a high temperature form of the ore mineral acanthite.

argillation

development of clay minerals by weathering of aluminium silicates.

argillic alteration

a rock alteration in which certain minerals are converted to minerals of the clay group.

argilliferous

abounding in or producing clay.

argovian

upper Jurassic a substage of geologic time in Great Britain.

argyrodite (canfieldite) (Ag_8GeS_6)

a grey germanium-silver double sulphide found in vein deposits associated with argentite and other silver minerals.

aridisol

a soil suborder and a major soil of deserts characterized by an ochric epipedon and other pedogenic horizons.

arikareen

a stratigraphic stage name which is used for the North American equivalent of the European Aquitanian. It is approximately synonymous with the Burdigalian (Tertiary System).

arkose

a sandstone in which an appreciable proportion of the grains are made of feldspars, as opposed to the commoner varieties in which most of the grains are made of quartz. Arkoses are thought to be derived from the erosion products of granites and gneisses.

armorican
in the time sense, the term implies an event dating from the interval between the Carboniferous and the Permian Periods. The Armorican mountain ranges were formed at this time, and the Armorican granites were intruded in a belt of country extending from S.W. England into Brittany and Normandy (Armorica).

armoured surface
amouring found in an equilibrium river channel, periodically distrupted during floods. cf. paved bed.

arrested decay
a stage in coal formation where biochemical action ceases.

arrival time (onset time)
the travel time of a seismic wave from source to detector.

arroyo
an arroyo is a rocky ravine. Arroyos occur in dry areas and in deserts. They are a kind of dry river valley. They have steep sides and flat, sandy bottoms. Arroyos are found in the south-west of the United States of America in parts of India and in South Africa.

arterite
a migmatite formed as a result of regional - contact metamorphism during which residual magmas were injected into the host rock.

artesian head
the hydrostatic head of an artesian aquifer.

arthodiran
one of an extinct order of armored, jawed fishes, found in fresh water and marine deposits of the Devonian. They reached their peak during the Late Devonian, when some genera attained lengths of 9m.

arthropoda
the term used for a phylum of segmented animals which have an external shell (exoskeleton or carapace) consisting of chitin, strengthened in some cases by $CaCO_3$, and which have jointed limbs. The phylum Arthropoda includes the largest number of known species, which have colonised every conceivable ecological environment, ranging from abyssal through terrestrial to pools of crude oil (petroleum).

artificial recharge
the replenishment of an aquifer by pumping water into it from surface supplies or other aquifers.

arzrunite
a bluish-green mineral having basic copper sulphate along with chlorides of copper and lead.

asbestiform
with an extremely fibrous form.

asbestine
a material with the properties of asbestos.

asbestos
asbestos is a mineral with a rough, threadlike texture. It is a silicate. Asbestos does not

burn and can be used to protect objects from damage by flames. Asbestos is also resistant to attack by most chemicals. Breathing asbestos dust is very harmful.

asbolite

refers to a black mineral aggregate of hydrated oxides of manganese and cobalt.

aseismic ridge

a submarine ridge that is a fragment of continental crust. It is non-seismic and is thus distinguished from the semically active mid-oceanic ridge.

ash

the unconsolidated fine-grained material which is formed due to volcanic explosions.

ashgill Series

the highest series of the Ordovician System, comprising only one graptolite zone, and, together with the Caradocian, equivalent to the Bala Series of N. Wales.

aso lava

a type of indurated pyroclastic deposit produced during the explosive eruptions that formed the Aso Caldera of Hyushu, Japan.

aspect ratio

the ratio of width to height of an object, shape, etc.

asphalt

a naturally occurring hydrocarbon having highly viscous character. Some asphalts are more or less pourable under normal conditions, while others are virtually solid. They may exist as the high boiling-point residuum of an oil pool after the lighter fraction gets evaporated.

asphaltene

an aggregate of high molecular weight hydrocarbons occurring in asphalt.

asphatite

any of the dark-coloured, solid, naturally occurring bitumens that are insoluble in water, but more or less completely soluble in carbon disulfide, benzol, and so on, with melting points between 250 and 600°F examples are gilsonite and grahamite.

asphalt rock

natural rock asphalt or asphalt-containing rock, such as porous sandstones and dolomites. Also known as asphalt stone; bituminous rock; asphalt.

associated gas

gas produced during the formation of petroleum and accompanying oil in an oilfield. cf. non-associated gas.

assyntite

a plutonic rock which is largely composed of orthoclase and pyroxene, but having lesser amounts of sodalite and nepheline, and accessory biotite, sphene, apatite, and opaque oxides.

asthenolith

a body of magma locally melted

anywhere at any time within any solid portion of the earth.

asthenosphere

that portion of the upper mantle beneath the rigid lithosphere which is plastic enough for rock flowage to occur; extends from a depth of 50-100 kilometres to about 400 kilometres and is seismically equivalent to the low velocity zone.

astian

a European stage of geologic time: upper Pliocene, above Plaisancian, below the Pleistocene stage known as villafranchian. Calabrian, or Günz.

astrobleme

a circular-shaped depression on the earth's surface produced by the impact of a cosmic body.

asymmetric valley

a valley with sides of unequal slope. Possibly the result of the geological structure as in uniclinal shifting. They are common in periglacial regions where they form as a result of differences in slope aspect and thus solar radiation received.

ataxite

an iron meteorite lacking the structure of either hexahedrite or octahedrite and has more than 10% nickel.

atadabanian

a stage of the Cambrian, 560-554 million years.

atlas

an atlas is a collection of maps. Some atlases include maps of the whole world, others may show details of just one or a few countries. Maps of the stars and planets can also be found in atlases.

atoll

a ring-shaped coral reef composed of closely spaced coral islets that enclose a shallow lagoon; may be circular to elliptical in plan view.

atoll texture

the surrounding of a ring of one mineral with another mineral, or minerals, within and without the ring. Also known as core texture.

atomic orbital

a descriptor of the spatial distribution of an electron in an atom.

atterberg scale

a geometric and decimal grade scale for classification of particles in sediments based on the unit value of 2mm and involving a fixed ratio of 10 for each successive grade; subdivisions are geometric means of the limits of each grade.

attican orogeny

late Miocene diastrophism.

attrital coal

a bright coal composed of anthraxylon and of attritus in which the translucent cell-wall degradation matter or translucent humid matter predominates, with the ratio of anthraxylon to attritus being less than 1:3.

attrition
the act of wearing and smoothing of rock surfaces by the flow of water charged with sand and gravel, by the passage of sand drifts, or by the movement of glaciers.

attritus
1. visible-to-ultramicroscopic particles of vegetable matter produced by microscopic and other organisms in vegetable deposits, particularly in swamps and bogs.
2. the dull gray to nearly black, frequently striped portion of material that makes up the bulk of some coals and alternate bands of bright anthraxylon in well-banded coals.

aubrite
an enstatite achondrite consisting almost wholly of crystalline-granular enstatite poor in lime and practically free from ferrous oxide, with accessory oligoclase.

augen
clots of very coarse crystals developing locally in the quartzo-feldspathic bands of some genesis. Rocks having them are called augen-gneisses.

augen structure (rib structure)
an eye-like marking on the surface of a joint.

augite $(Ca,Na)(Mg,Fe(II)_2Al)_2O_6$
dark-coloured pyroxene mineral commonly occurs as dark crystals in many basic ingeous rocks.

aureole
a ring-shaped contact zone which surrounds an igneous intrusion. It is also known as contact aureole; contact zone; metamorphic zone.

auriferous deposit
a natural repository of gold, in the general sense, including gold bearing lodes and sediments such as sands and gravels, or their indurated equivalents, which contain gold in detrital grains or nuggets.

aurora
an aurora is a coloured light which can sometimes be seen in the sky at night, especially in the polar regions. An aurora is caused by electrical particles from the Sun hitting nitrogen and oxygen atoms in the Earth's atmosphere.

austral
of southern hemisphere origin. cf. boreal.

authigenic
pertaining to minerals which have crystallized in a sediment during or soon after its deposition.

autobrecciation
refers to the process whereby portions of the first consolidated crust of a lava flow get incorporated into the still-fluid portion.

autochthon
a large structural unit, e.g. a nappe, which originated close

to its present position. cf. allochthon, parautochthon.

autoclasic

a term applied to rock that have been fragmented in situ by mechanical processes such as faulting, or by shrinkage following desiccation.

autointrusion

the injection of the residual liquid fraction of a magma that is differentiating into fissures formed in the crystallized fraction at a late stage by some deformation.

autometamorphism

changes in the mineral composition of an igneous rock consequent upon the action of solutions and vapours which are derived from the same source as the rock itself.

automorphic

a term describing the texture of rock in which the mineral grains display fully developed crystal form.

autophytograph

an imprint on a rock surface made by chemical activity of a plant or plant part.

autopneumatolysis

the occurrence of metamorphic changes at the pneumatolytic stage of a cooling magma when temperatures are approximately 400-600ºC.

autumn

autumn is the period in the year between summer and winter in temperate regions. Autumn is a time when daylight becomes shorter and the weather may be cool and misty. In some countries it is called the fall.

auxiliary fault

a branch fault; a minor fault ending against a major one.

auxiliary minerals

as defined in the Johannsen classification of igneous rocks, those light-coloured, relatively rare minerals such as apatite, corundum, flourite, muscovite, and topaz.

auxiliary plane

a plane at right angles to the net slip on a fault plane as determined from analysis of seismic data for an earthquake.

avalanche

a sudden, rapid movement of disaggregated ice, snow, earth or rock down a slope.

aventurine

a mineral which consists of sparkling gold-coloured particles, usually cupric or/and chromic oxide.

average velocity

for groundwater, the volume of water passing through a given area of rock in unit time divided by its porosity.

aviolite

a type of hornfels containing mica-cordierite.

avonian

a division of Lower Carboniferous time equivalent to the Dinantian, or to the Tournaisian and Visean. Named after the type-section in the Avon Gorge, Bristol district.

awaruite
native nickel-iron alloy having about 57.7% nickel.

axial angle
refers to the acute angle between the two optic axes of a biaxial crystal.

axial culmination
refers to the distortion of the fold axes upward in a form which is similar to an anticline.

axial element
the lengths, length ratios, and angles which define the unit cell of a crystal.

axial modulus
the ratio of longitudinal stress to longitudinal strain when there is no lateral strain.

axinite
$Ca_2(Mn,Fe(II))\ Al_2BO_3(Si_4O_{12})(OH)$. A mineral of the cyclosilicate group. It is formed by the contact metamorphism of limestone or by pneumatolysis.

axis
an axis is an imaginary line around which an object rotates. The Earth's rotates once around its axis approximately every 24 hours. The Earth's axis runs from the South pole. It crosses the Equator which is an imaginary line circling the Earth.

axis of rotation
the axis passing through the centre of the Earth about which the motion of a plate can be described by a single angle of rotation.

azimuth
the horizontal angle of a direction measured clockwise from north.

azoic
refers to a name given to Precambrian strata which was presumed to have been formed before life appeared on the earth. The name is having doubtful validity and is obsolescent.

azulite
a translucent pale-blue variety of smithsonite which occurs in large masses in Arizona.

azurmalachite
a mixture of azurite and malachite. It is usually occurring massive with concentric banding. It finds use as an ornamental stone.

back
the roof of an underground working.

back-arc spreading
the process whereby an island arc is rifted longitudinally and the two sections moved laterally apart to form a back-arc basin between them.

back bay
a small, shallow body into which coastal stream drain and which is connected to the sea through the pass between barrier islands.

backdeep
an epieugeosynclinal basin; a nonvolcanic postorogenic geosynclinal basin whose sediments are derived from an uplifted eugeosyncline.

backfolding
process in mountain forming in which the folds are overturned toward the interior of an orogenic belt. Also known as backward folding.

background radiation
background radiation is the name given to radiation that is always present on the Earth. Background radiation comes from the natural decay of minerals such as radium and uranium in the rocks and soil. Some radiation comes from rays reaching the Earth from space.

backlands
a section of a river floodplain lying behind a natural levee.

backlimb
of the two limbs of an asymmetrical anticline, the one that is more gently dipping.

back-set bed
cross bedding that dips in a direction against the flow of a depositing current.

backset eddy
a small current swirling in the direction opposite to those of the major oceanic eddies; often observed between the main current and the coastline.

backshore
the upper shore zone that is beyond the advance of the usual waves and tides. Also known as back beach; backshore beach.

backwash
the gravity-fed returns flow of water after a wave breaks on a beach. An important factor in determining beach gradient. cf. swash.

backwash mark
a crisscross ridge pattern in beach sand, caused by backwash.

backwash ripple mark
ripple marks that are broad and flat and parallel to the shoreline, with narrow, shallow troughs and crests about 30 centimetres apart; formed backwash above the maximum wave retreat level.

bafflestone
an autochthonous carbonate rock whose original components were bound organically during deposition, the organism forming baffles to trap finer matrix material. cf. bindstone.

bahamite
a variety of limestone which was formed of sediment similar to a type currently found accumulating in the Bahamas.

bajocian
a stratigraphic stage name which is used for the West European Middle Jurassic.

ballas
an aggregate of spherical masses consisting of small diamond crystals.

ballast
crushed rock used for road beds or on railway tracks.

ball clay
fine-textured and highly plastic detrital clay which, on firing, yields pale-coloured or white

pottery. Mixed with kaolin, it imparts plasticity to the latter. Also called potters' clay.

ballstone

the name applied to masses of fine ustratified limestone, occurring chiefly in the Wenlock Limestone of Shropshire, and representing colonies of corals in position of growth.

banakite

refers to one of a variety of saturated or oversturated trachybasalts. It is composed of plagioclase, sanidine, and biotite, with small quantities of analcime, augite, and olivine.

banded peat

peat formed of alternate layers of vegetables debris.

band theory

an approach to the calculation of the electronic structure of solids in which atoms arranged in a lattice have many neighbours so that the atomic orbitals interact to form a band of molecular orbitals whose energies lie in certain energy ranges. The proximity of these bands governs the facility with which electrons could be excited into an empty orbital, where its high mobility would allow a high thermal and electrical conductivity.

bank erosion

the erosion of a river bank by the dethchment of particles or rotational failure following undercutting.

banket

the name assigned to a conglomerate which consists mainly of quartz pebbles with pyrite. It is found in the Precambrian of South Africa and Ghana.

banquereau

a Cretaceous/Palaeocene succession on the Scotian shelf of Canada covering parts of the Maastrichtian and Danian.

bar

bar is the unit used for measuring the weight of air or atmospheric pressure. Normal atmospheric pressure at sea-level is about one bar, or 1,000 millibars. Bar can also be used to describe a sandbar in a river or an estuary.

barchan

the term used for dune shaped in plane like a crescent. The ends of the dune point in the direction in which the wind generally blows. Barchans may be upto 400 metres wide and 30 metres high.

barite rose

a flower-like group of tabular, sand-filled crystals of barite, arranged in radically symmetrical form. Barite roses usually form in sandstone and are generally reddish brown in colour.

barometer

a barometer is an instrument which is used for measuring atmospheric pressure. An aneroid barometer has a dial marked in units of pressure. A needle moves over this dial as the atmospheric pressure changes. Another kind of barometer measures atmospheric pressure with a column of mercury.

barremian

a stratigraphic stage name which is used for the European mid Lower Cretaceous.

barrier beach (bay bar)

a coastal bar permanently exposed above sea level.

barrier reef

a coral-reef developed parallel with the shore-line and enclosing a lagoon between itself and the land. It marks a stage between a fringing-reef and an atoll.

bartonian Series

the topmost division of the Eocene rocks in Britain; comprising in the type locality the Barton Clay, with its rich molluscan fauna, and the overlying Barton Sands.

basal arkose

partially revoked feldspathic residuum in the lower section of a sandstone that overlies granitic rock.

basal conglomerate

a conglomerate which is formed at the beginning, i.e., the earliest portion of a stratigraphical unit.

basal sapping

the process of undercutting the base of a slope by erosion along a spring-line, salt weathering or glacial action.

basalt

basalt is a kind of igneous rock or stone. Basalt is of dark colour and looks as though it is made up of very tiny pieces of rock. Basalt develops from lava and is one of the main kinds of rock that make up the Earth's crust.

basaltic layer

an outmoded term for the lower continental crust. cf. granite layer.

basanite

an olivine-bearing alkali basalt which consists of feldspar and feldspathoid. It is also known as lydite.

base level

refers to the surface to which long-profiles of rivers have been related. The base level of a stream is generally taken as the sea, but if there are irregularities in the long-profiles local base levels are temporarily created, there by defining a series of sub-profiles, each one cutting down to its particular base level. Examples of these local base levels are surfaces of lakes, tributary streams, waterfalls, or knack points.

base line

any line established with precision instruments for the purpose of making additional azimuthal measurements.

baseflow

the subsurface runoff made up of throughflow and/or groundwater.

bashkirian
a stratigraphic stage name which is used for the Upper Namurian to the Lower Westphalian in Russia (Carboniferous System).

basic rocks
igneous rocks with a low silica content. The limits are usually placed at 45% silica, below which rocks are described as ultrabasic, and 52% silica, above which they are described as intermediate. Basic igneous rocks include basalt, the commonest type of lava, and gabbro, its plutonic equivalent.

basification
development of a more basic rock, usually with more hornblende, biotite, and oligoclase, by contamination of a granitic magma in the assimilation of country rock.

basimesostasis
a process of the partial or entire enclosure of plagioclase crystals in a diabase by augite.

basin-and-range structure
regional structure dominated by fault-block mountains separated by basins filled with sediment.

basin Facies
the sediments and their associated fauna which occur in the deeper parts of a basin.

basining
a settlement of earth in the form of basins due to the solution and transportation underground deposits of salt and gypsum.

basin length
length in a straight line from the mouth of a stream to the farthest point on the drainage divide of its basin.

basin order
a classification of basins according to stream drainage; for example, a first-order basin contains all of the drainage area of a first-order stream.

basin range
a mountain range characteristic of the Great Basin in the western United States and formed by a faulted and tilted block of strata.

basin valley
the filled-in depression of large intermountain areas; an example is Salt Valley in Utah.

basset
the outcropping edge of a layer of rock exposed to the surface.

bastard coal (batt)
1. thin layers of coal found in shales immediately above a coal seam. 2. Any coal with a high ash content.

batch melting model
a partial melting model in which the melt remains at the melting site, in equilibrium with the solid, before migrating as a single batch of magma.

batholite
an older massive protrusion of magma that solidifies as coarse crystalline rock in the deep horizons of the earth's crust.

batholith
a body of igneous rock, 40

square miles or more in area, emplaced at great or intermediate depth in the earth's crust.

bathonian

a European stage of geologic time: Middle Jurassic, below Callovian, above Bajocian. Also known as Bathian.

bathonian Series

the upper part of the Lower Oölite below, followed by the Forest Marble, Bradford Clay, and Cornbrash, in ascending stratigraphical order. Also known as Bradfordian.

bathyal

a term used for describing the environment of the continental slope between 180 and 4,000 m. Conditions have been found to be much more variable than in the abyssal region, due to fluctuations in sedimentation, oxygen content, current action, and changes brought about by slumping on the continental slope. The region between 2,000 and 4,000 m is often one where there occurs the formation of oozes (abyssal deposits).

bathymetric biofacies

the lateral distribution and character of underwater sedimentary strata.

battery ore

a manganese ore of grade suitable for the production of MnO_2 for use in dry cell batteries.

batture

an elevation of the bed of a river under the surface of the water; sometimes used to signify the same elevation when it has risen above the surface.

bauxite

a residual clay, consisting essentially of aluminium hydroxides, formed in triopical regions by the chemical weathering of basic igneous rocks. It is the most important ore of aluminium.

bauxitization

bauxite development from either primary aluminum silicates or secondary clay minerals.

baventian

a stratigraphic stage name which is used for the top of the British Lower Pleistocene (Tertiary System).

bay barrier

a narrow shoal or small point of land projecting from the shore across the mouth of a bay and severing the bay's connection with the main body of water.

bay delta

a usually triangular alluvial deposit formed at the point where the mouth of a stream enters the head of a drowned valley.

bay head

a swampy region at the head of a bay.

bay head bar

a bar formed a short distance from the shore at the head of a bay.

bay head beach
a beach formed around a bay head by storm waves; layers of sediment cover the bay floor and bare rock benches front the headland clefts.

bay head delta
a delta at the head of an estuary or a bay into which a river discharges because of the margin of the land's late partial submergence.

baymouth bar
a bar extending entirely or partially across the mouth of a bay. Also known as bay bar.

bayou
(1) a name given (chiefly in the southern states of North America) to marshy offshoots and overflows of rivers and lakes.
(2) general term for a stagnant inlet or outlet of a bay or lake.

bayside beach
a beach formed at the side of a bay by materials eroded from nearby headlands and deposited by long shore currents.

b-c fracture
a tension fracture parallel with the fabric plane and normal to the *a* axis.

b-c plane
a plane that is perpendicular to the plane of movement and parallel to the *b* direction in that plane.

beach
the zone of unconsolidated material that extends landward from the low-water line to where there is marked change in material or physiographic form or to the line of permanent vegetation.

beach cycle
periodic retreat and outbuilding of beaches resulting from waves and tides.

beach drift
the material transported by drifting of beach.

beach gravel
Gravels in which most of the particles cluster about one size.

beach plain
embankments of wave-deposited material added to a prograding shoreline.

beach profile
intersection of a beach's ground surface with a vertical plane perpendicular to the shoreline.

beach ridge
a continuous mound of beach material behind the beach that was heaped up by waves or other action.

beach rock
a friable to well cemented rock made of calcareous skeletal debris that is cemented together by calcium carbonate.

beach scarp
a nearly vertical slope along the beach caused by wave erosion.

beacon
a beacon is a light or other signal which can be easily seen. Beacons are used to guide ships and aeroplanes on a safe course. A beacon is also

a hill where signal fires used to be lit.

bearing capacity

the maximum load per unit area that a surface can support in safety without shear failure.

beaufort

a stratigraphic stage name which is used for the top of the South African Middle Karroo.

bed

1. A layer of sedimentary rock which has been marked off above and below by surfaces that can be seen. It is made up of material that is the same in all parts.

2. Also, refers to the smallest lithostratigraphical division marked by a well-defined divisional plane from its neighbours above and below.

bedding-cleavage intersection

the intersection of bedding and cleavage which produces a lineation often parallel, or nearly parallel, to a related fold axis.

bedding plane cleavage

a cleavage parallel to the bledding.

bedding Void

refers to a void which is formed between two successive batches of lava that get discharged in a single short activity of a volcano, as well as between flows made a long time apart.

bedrock

a mining term which is used for the unweathered rock below the soil and drift cover.

beef

fibrous calcite occurring in veins in sedimentary rocks. Rarely, other minerals with the same structure and occurrence.

beerbachite

a hornfels produced by contact metamorphism of basic igneous rocks, containing olivine.

beetle-stones

coprolitic nodules akin to septaria which, when broken open, give a fancied resemblance to a fossil beetle.

belemnoidea

the term used for an extinct group of the cephalopoda. Geologically, most important members are belemnites. Their fossil shells have been found to be in the shape of a long cone having a conical hole at the broad end.

bell

a conical nodule or concentration in the roof of a coal mine which may fall without warning.

bell pit

an obsolete, shallow mining method in which material extraction led to a bell-shaped excavation.

benthic

benthic describes the area at the bottom of the sea. It also describes the animals and plants living there. On the continental shelf and near the sea-shore, the benthic zone is

1,000 metres in depth. The opposite of benthic is pelagic.

benthos

the animals living on the sediments of the sea floor including both mobile and non-mobile forms.

bering land bridge

the land connection of Beringia during the Cenozoic, which was the only route available into North America for mammals.

bertrand lens

an auxiliary lens of the petrological microscope between the eyepiece and objective used to view interference figure.

bertrandite

$Be_4Si_2O_7(OH)_2$. A colourless or pale-yellow mineral of beryllium silicate. It occurs in prismatic crystals.

beryl

beryl is a mineral. It is found mostly in granite rocks. Beryl contains the elements beryllium, aluminium, silicon and oxygen. The metal beryllium is made from beryl crystals.

biaxial Crystal

the term used for a crystal of low symmetry in which the index ellipsoid is having three unequal axes.

biaxial stress (plane stress)

a stress system in which the maximum principal stress is greater than the intermediate and the minimum principal stress is zero.

bight

1. a long, gradual bend or recess in the coastline which forms a large, open receding bay.

2. a bend in a river or mountain range.

bimodal

descriptive of a frequency distribution which contains two modes, i.e. two values significantly more common than the rest.

bingham plastic

a fluid which requires an initial yield stress to be overcome before it moves, e.g. some lava flows.

bio-

bio- is a prefix used to refer to living things.

bioclastic

term applicable to sediments made up of broken fragments of organic skeletal material. The commonest type is bioclastic limestones.

bioerosion trace

a trace fossil consisting of drilling or raspings on a hard substrate.

biofacies

1. a rock unit differing in biologic aspect from laterally equivalent biotic groups.

2. lateral variation in the biologic aspect of a stratigraphic unit.

biogenic reef

a mass consisting of the hard parts of organisms, or of a biogenically constructed frame enclosing detrital particles, in a body of water; most biogenic reefs are made of corals or associated organisms.

biogenic sediment

a deposit resulting from the physiological activities of organisms.

bioherm

a circumscribed mass of rock exclusively or mainly constructed by marine sedimentary organisms such as corals, algae, and stromatoporoids. Also known as organic mound.

biohermite

a term used for limestone composed of debris broken from a biochem and forming pocket fillings or talus slopes associated with reefs.

biolite

a concretion formed of concentric layers through the action of living organisms.

biolith

a rock which got formed by organic processes, usually of material, and including bedded structures.

biological

biological describes anything to do with living organisms. For example, biological science is the study of living things.

biomass

the amount of living material in a particular area stated in terms of the weight or volume of organisms per unit area or the volume of the environment.

biopelmicrite

a limestone intermediate in content between biomicrite and pelmicrite.

biophile

the elements which are concentrated in living organisms, e.g., carbon, hydrogen, nitrogen.

biosphere

the biosphere is the name given to the parts of the Earth where living things are found. The biosphere is also called the global ecosystem.

biostary

maximum development of organisms at the time of tectonic repose when residual soils form extensively on land and deposition of calcium carbonate is widespread in the sea.

biostratigraphic classification

the organization of strata into units based on their fossil content.

biostratinomy

the study of the postmortems history of an organism before burial.

biostrome

a bedded structure or layer composed of calcite and dolomitized calcarenitic fossil fragments distributed over the sea bottom as fine lentils, independent of or in association with bioherms or other areas of organic growth.

biotic province

a geographic area that supports one or more ecologic associations which are distinct from those of adjacent provinces.

biotope

a palaeoecological term which means a distinct environmental a unit.

bioturbation

the disruption of sediments mainly by the burrowing activities of organisms, e.g. by feeding.

bird-foot delta

a delta formed by the outgrowth of fingers or pairs of natural levees at the mouth of river distributaries; an example is the Mississippi delta.

bisectrix

a line which is the bisector of the angle between the optic axes of a biaxial crystal.

bismuth

bismuth is an element and a metal. Alloys of bismuth melt at low temperatures. They are used as a safety device in many machines because they melt first, before the machines get too hot. When the alloys melt, the machines stop working. Bismuth is also used to make some medicines.

bitter lake

a lake rich in sulphates and carbonates.

bitumen

the term used for naturally occurring tar-like hydrocarbon mineral of indefinite composition: It ranges in consistency from a thick liquid to a brittle solid.

bituminous coal

a dark brown to black variety of coal which has a high proportion of carbonaceous matter. Also known as soft coal.

bivalvia

a name for the class of Mollusca which is better known as Lamellibranchiata.

bizon

a Silurian succession in the Mirnyy Creek area of NE Siberia equivalent to the Ludlow.

black Band

iron stone, a sedimentary rock having mainly iron carbonate (siderite) and coaly material, which is effectively self-smelting. It can be burnt tu yield iron. It is also known as black-band ironstone.

black ice

dark glacier ice formed by freezing of silt laden water.

black sand

an alluvial or beach placer with a preponderance of dark minerals, usually magnetite or ilmenite.

blairmorite

a rare type of phonolite containing phenocrysts of analcime.

blancan

a stratigraphic stage name which is used the North American equivalent of the European Villafranchin (Tertiary System).

blanket sand

a blanket deposit of sand or sandstone covering as

unusually great area; typically deposited by a transgressive sea. Also known as sheet sand; sand sheet.

blastic

means the growth in situ of crystals in metamorphic rock, e.g., poikiloblastic—a poikilitic-type texture which is developed during metamorphic recrystalization.

blind valley

a steep-sided, river-cut valley which terminates in a steep cliff, common in limestone areas with subterranean flow.

blizzard

a blizzard is a fierce storm of snow. Blizzards are common in open, icy regions such as the Arctic and Antarctica.

block caving

a large-scale method of underground mining in which the ore is undermined and thus collapses into the excavation where it is sufficiently broken up for handling. Surface subsidence is inevitable.

block lava

lava flows which occur as a tumultuous assemblage of angular blocks.

blowhole

a vertical fissure in a sea cliff through which waves and tides cause water to fountain to the surface.

blowing cave

a cave that has a movement of air through its entrance.

blue amber

a variety of osseous amber with a bluish tingle that is probably due to the presence of calcium carbonate.

blue ground

refers to a thoroughly brecciated and altered ultrabasic rock. A mica (phlogopite) peridotite having bronzire and chrome-diopside, formerly used for diamonds.

blue mud

a combination of terrigenous and deep-sea sediments having a bluish gray colour due to the presence of organic matter and finely divided iron sulfides.

bluff

a bluff is a steep cliff. Bluffs may be found at the edge of a valley, or at the sea-shore.

bodden

an irregularly-shaped coastal inlet found in the S Baltic, formed by a rise in sea level over uneven topography.

bog burst

the bursting of a bog under the pressure of its swelling, due to water retention by a marginal dam of growing vegetation. The escaping water produces muddy peat flows over the surrounding area.

bogaz

an elongate, deep ravine in a karst area formed by the widening of large joints by solution.

bohemian ruby

a red variety of crystalline quartz; specifically rose quartz cut as gem.

bohm lamellae

microscopic fluid inclusions in planar arrays, possibly formed by the annealing of deformation lamellae.

boiler plate

1. a fairly smooth surface on a cliff, consisting of flush or overlapping slabs of rock, having little or no foothold.
2. crusty, frozen surface of snow. Flat-rolled steel, usually ¼ to ½ inch thick; used mainly for covering ships and making boilers and tanks. Also known as boiler steel.

bojite

a gabbro having primary amphibole—as opposed to many hornblende gabbros in which the amphibole has been secondary.

bole

a fossil laterite interbedded with lava flows, usually basalts.

bolson

in the southwestern United States, a basin or valley having no outlet.

bomb

any large pyroclast ejected while viscous.

bomb sag

depressed and deranged laminae mainly found in beds of fine-grained ash or tuff around an included volcanic bomb or block which fell on and became buried in the deposit.

bone beds

strata, often sands, gravels, or their indurated equivalents, characterized by an extremely high content of fossil remains. Examples are the Ludlow Bone Bed and the Rhaetic Bone Bed, the former consisting largely of the fragmental remains of primitive fossil fishes, and the latter of reptilian bone-fragments. Such abnormal concentration of fossils is due to some sudden change in conditions adversely affecting the fauna, or to the washing together, by wave or current-action, of scattered bones, shells, etc., into a back-water or sheltered region.

bone cave

a cave that has served as a trap for fossil vertebrates.

bone coal

argillaceous coal or carbonaceous shale that is found in coal seams.

bononian

upper Jurassic geologic time.

book structure

in ore deposits, a formation showing an alternation or interleaving with gangue.

boomerangian

a Cambrian succession in Australia covering the upper part of the Menevian.

borax

borax is a mineral. It contains the elements boron, sodium, hydrogen and oxygen. Borax is used for softening water and for cleaning.

bore

bore is the word used to

describe drilling through rocks. Special drills have to be used to bore through hard rocks and the process takes a long time.

borehole

a hole drilled for exploration or exploitation purposes.

bornhardt

a large inselberg. Bornhardts are dome-shaped monoliths, examples of which are found on every continent except Antarctica. They are best developed in the tropics.

borolanite

a hypabyssal rock which is essentially orthoclase and melanite having subordinate nepheline, biotite, and pyroxene.

boron

boron is an element. The element is rare and is only found as compounds with other substances. Boron is usually found in the form of boric acid or as borax.

bostonite

a fine-grained intrusive igneous rock allied in composition to syenite; essentially feldspathic, and deficient in coloured silicates; type-locality, Boston, Mass.

bostonitic

said of the texture of bostonite in which microlites of rough irregular feldspar tend to form clusters of divergent laths within a trachytoid groundmass.

bothnian

refers to a stratigraphic division of the Baltic Precambrian Post Svionian, Pre-Karelian.

botroyolite

a radiated, columnar variety of datalite with a botryoidal surface.

bottom

the bed of a body of running or still water.

bottomland

a lowland formed by alluvial deposit about a lake basin or a stream.

bottom load

an obsolete term for the material rolled and pushed along the bottom of a stream.

bottomset bed

one of the horizontal or gently inclined layers of sediment deposited in front of the advancing forest beds of delta.

boudin

one of a series of sausage-shaped segments found in a boudinage.

boudinage

a structure in which beds set in a softer matrix are divided by cross fractures into segments resembling pillows.

bouguer anomaly

a gravity value calculated, after corrections for latitude, elevation, and terrain.

bouguer reduction

a correction made in gravity work to take account of the station's altitude and the rock between the station and sea level. Also known as Bouguer correction.

boulder
the unit of largest size occurring in sediments and sedimentary rocks, the limit between pebble and boulder being placed at 100 mm, though some authorities recognize 'cobbles' between pebbles and boulders. Boulders may consist of any kind of rock, may be subangular or well rounded, may have originated in place or have been transported by running water or ice. Accumulations of boulders are boulder beds.

boulder belt
a long, narrow accumulation of boulders elongately transverse to the direction of glacier movement.

boulder clay
the characteristic product of glaciation, consisting of stones to the size of boulders, sometimes faceted and striated, embedded in a clay matrix which is essentially rock powder produced by abrasion of the floor over which the glacier moved.

boulder gravel
an unconsolidated deposit consisting mainly of boulders.

boulder tracing
a method of mineral exploration, usually in a glaciated terrain, involving the tracing of mineralized boulders back to their source.

boulder pavement
a surface of, till with boulders; the till has been abraded to flatness by glacier movement.

boulder stone
a consolidated sedimentary rock consisting of boulders-size particles.

boulder train
glacial boulders derived from one locality and arranged in a right-angled line or lines leading off in the direction in which the drift agency operated.

bounce cast
a short ridge underneath a stratum fading out gradually in both directions.

bounce marks
tool marks produced by an object ('tool') like a pebble, shell or bone which is being bounced along the sea floor. They have been especially associated with turbidites.

boundary layer
the marginal region of a flow where frictional resistance causes the velocity to decrease near the boundary and shear stresses are developed in the fluid.

boundary monument
a pile of stones or other objects placed at or near a boundary line to identify the location of the line.

boundstone
a limestone in which the grains were bound by an organism or organisms.

box fold
a fold in which the broad, flat top of an anticline or the broad, flat bottom of a syncline is

bordered by steeply dipping limbs.

box hole

a meteorite crater in central Australia, 575 feet in diameter.

box stones

hollow concretions. Nodules of sandstone containing molluscan casts found in the Pleistocene deposits of East Anglia.

boxwork

limonite and other minerals which formed at one time as blades or plates along cleavage or fracture planes, after which the intervening material dissolved, leaving the intersecting blades or plates as a network.

brachiopoda

a group of bivalved marine animals. They vary in size from 5 mm to 20 cm and have either a calcareous or a chitinous shell. The shells are arranged dorsally and ventrally, and are generally not equal in size and usually symmetrical. The Brachiopods have been divided into two classes, the Inarticulata and the Articulata. The former are primitive forms, that do not have hinge structure, the shell being commonly chitinous. They range from Lower Cambrian to Recent. Articulate forms are having a hinge structure and commonly have a calcareous shell; they also range from Lower Cambrian to Recent.

brachyanticline

an elongate periclinal dome with varying axial plunge.

brachypinacoid

a pinacoid parallel to the vertical and the shorter lateral axis.

bradfordian

a stratigraphic stage name which is used for the top of the North American Devonian.

braggite $(Pt,Pd,Ni)S_x$

a steel-grey coloured mineral of variable composition.

braid bar

any exposed sand or gravel bar that divides flow and causes a braided pattern in a stream.

braid

a multithread channel formed, for example, by the meltwater flow from a glacier in a sandur.

brait

a term, sometimes used for rough diamond.

branch line

the location in an imbricate fault system where a fault forks and displacement is transferred to another fault.

brannerite $(Ca,Ce,U)(Ti,Fe)_2O_6$

a mineral containing rare element uranium.

bravais Lattice

refers to one of the 14 possible arrangements of lattice points in space like the arrangement of points about any chosen point has been found to be identical with that about any other point.

brea

a rarely used term for viscous

asphalt formed by evaporation of volatile components from oil in seepage.

breach

a breach is a crack or hole in a hard surface. During a violent storm, breakers may make a breach in a sea-wall. The action of weathering may cause a breach in a rock face.

bread-crust bomb

a volcanic bomb with a cracked outer crust and vesicular interior.

breaker terrace

a type of shore found in lakes in glacial drift; the terrace is formed from stones deposited by waves.

break-point bar

an elongated sand bar parallel to beach, deposited as a result of breaking waves.

break thrust

a thrust fault cutting across one limb of a fold.

breccia, reef

angular fragments of coral and limy algae broken from reefs and deposited on their slopes.

breccio-Conglomerate

a rudaceous rock having both angular and rounded pebbles. It is intermediate between breccia and conglomerate in character.

breeze

a breeze is a wind of medium strength. Breezes can vary from light to strong. A light breeze makes leaves rustle and blows at about 6 kilometres an hour. A strong breeze makes large branches, sways and blows at about 45 kilometres an hour. Breezes measure between 2 and 6 on the Beaufort Scale.

breunnerite

a variety of magnesite containing about 9% FeO.

bright coal

the brightest type of coal on scale bright coal, banded bright coal, banded coal, banded dull coal, dull coal.

bringewoodian

a stratigraphic stage name which is used for the British Middle Ludlovian (Silurian System).

brittle mineral

a tenacity descriptor of a mineral that breaks and powders easily.

brockram

a sedimentary rock occurring in the Permian strata in N.W. England; consists of angular blocks which probably accumulated as scree material.

bronsil shales

grey shales occurring in the Malvern Hills, England; equivalent to the Tremadoc Shales of N. Wales; of Upper Cambrian age.

bronzitite

a rock composed of bronzite with smaller amounts of angite and calcic plagioclase. A common constituent of layered basic igneous intrusions, such as those of the Bushveld, South Africa and Stillwater, Montana.

brookite TiO_2
a titanium mineral which occurs as brownish, black, or reddish orthorhombic crystals. It occurs in hydrothermal veins in schists and gneisses.
brown clay ironstone
limonite in the form of concrete masses, often in concretionary nodules.
brown coal
a variety of coal containing upto 50% carbon; intermdiate in rank between peat and lignite. It burns with much smoke and leaves a lot of ash.
brown lignite
a type of lignite with a fixed carbon content ranging from 30 to 55% and total carbon from 65 to 73.6%; contains 6300 Btu per pound. Also known as lignite B.
brown soil
any of a zonal group of soils, with a brown surface horizon which grades into a lighter-coloured soil and then into a layer of carbonate accumulation.
brown stone
ferruginuous sandstone where grains are coated with iron oxide.
brunhes
a magnetostratigraphic epoch of normal polarity in the Pleistocene, 0.71 Ma-present.
bruxellian
a stratigraphic stage name which is used for the European Lower Lutetian (Tertiary System).
bubble pulse
the unwanted seismic signal generated by the oscillation of the bubble formed by an underwater explosion.
bubble wall fragment
a glassy volcanic shard revealing part of vesicle surface which may be curved or flat.
buchite
refers to a partially vitrified inclusion of sandstone in basalt.
buckle fold
a double flexure of rock beds formed by compression acting in the plane of the folded beds.
bulk finite strain
the total finite strain of a volume of rock calculated assuming that the strain is homogeneous.
buoyancy
a term describing the gravitational-powered ascent of relatively low density materials, such as hydrocarbons and evaporites.
buried hill
a hill of resistant older rock over which later sediments are deposited.
buried placer
old deposit of a placer which has been buried beneath lava flows or other strata.
buried river
a river bed which has become buried beneath streams of alluvial drifts or basalt.
burnt alum
a porous, friable material produced by dehydrating alum

at dull red heat, used industrially for dyeing, water purification etc.

bush

bush is a word that describes a habitat with many scattered trees and shrubs. Large areas of southern Africa and Australia are covered by bush.

bustite

an achondrite meteorite which is essentially of enstatite, having small quantities of oligoclase and diopside and some nickel-iron.

butane (C_4H_{10})

a colourless paraffin series gas present in natural gas.

butte

a flat-tapped, steep-walled hill, usually a remnant of horizontal beds, smaller and narrower than a mesa; characteristic of arid or semi-arid regions.

buttress sands

sandstone bodies which are deposited above an unconformity; the upper portion rests upon the surface of the unconformity.

byerite

bituminous coal that does not crack in fire and melts and enlarges upon heating.

bysmalith

a body of igneous rock that is more or less vertical and cylindrical; it crosscuts adjacent sediments.

bytownitite

an igneous rock of the gabbro clan; an anorthosite, a leucocratic, coarse grained plutonic rock.

cabochon

a gem cut in convex form; highly polished but not faceted.

cactolith

an irregular intrusive igneous body of obscurely cactus like form, more or less confined to a horizontal zone and appearing to consist of irregularly related and possibly distorted bracling of and anaestomosing dikes that fed a lacolith.

cadmium

cadmium is an element. It is a bluish-white metal. Cadmium is often found in the same rocks as copper and zinc. Cadmium is used for making alloys. Compounds of cadmium are used in making television sets and batteries. Most cadmium comes from Japan.

caen stone

a light creamy yellow limestone of Jurassic age used as a building stone in N. France and England.

cahnite

$Ca_2B(OH)_4(AsO_4)$. A mineral having borate and arsenate of calcium, occurring in white spheroidal crystals.

calabrian

a stratigraphic stage name which is used for the European Lower Pleistocene (Tertiary System).

calaverite ($AuTe_2$)

an ore mineral of gold.

calc-Alkali

the term used for igneous rocks in which the dominant feldspar is calcium-rich. The converse of calcalkali is alkali. Calc-alkaline rocks have calcium-bearing ferromagnesian minerals—hornblende, augite, etc. This term is also applicable to calcium-bearing minerals, e.g., calc-alkali feldspar.

calcareous

said of a substance containing calcium carbonate. When used with a rock name it generally implies that as much as 50% of the rock is calcium carbonate.

calcareous aggregate

an irregular mass of carbonate grains which have been stuck together, often by microbial processes.

calcareous ooze

a fine-grained pelagic sediment containing undissolved sand- or silt-sized calcareous skeletal remains of small marine organisms mixed with amorphous clay-sized material.

calcareous rocks

the sedimentary rocks containing appreciable quantities of calcium carbonate, or in many cases composed almost entirely of this substance. These include all limestones, magnesian limestones, and dolomites, as well as chalk, and chemically precipitated material such as calc-tufa.

calcareous sandtone

a sandstone cemented with calcite.

calcareous soil

a soil containing accumulations of calcium and magnesium carbonate.

calciclasite

an igneous rock of the gabbro clan; a leucocratic granular plutonic rock; contains largely anorthite.

calcification

1. a pedgenetic process involving the accumulation of calcite or dolomite in soils low in moisture. 2. The process whereby organic tissue is converted to calcite.

calcification

refers to any process of soil formation in which the soil colloids become saturated to a high degree with exchangeable calcium, thereby rendering them relatively immobile and almost neutral in reaction.

calcite compensation depth

the depth in the ocean below which solution of calcium carbonate occurs at a faster rate than its deposition. Abbreviated CCD.

calcite dolomite

a carbonate rock with a composition of 10-50% calcite and 90-50% dolomite.

calcium

calcium is a common element. It is a metal which forms many compounds with other elements and is not found naturally in a pure form. Limestone is made of calcium, carbon and oxygen. Plants and animals need calcium to grow properly.

calclithite

limestone having 50% or more fragments of older limestone that got redeposited after being eroded from the land.

calcisphere

a small (<500 μm) sphere of calcite, commonly found in Palaeozoic limestone, comprising a micrite coating around a hollow or sparitic interior, believed to be of algal origin.

calcrete

a conglomerate of surfical gravel and sand cemented by calcium carbonate.

calc-schist

a metamorphosed, argillaceous limestone showing a schistose structure.

caldera

a large volvanic crater produced by the collapse of underground lava reservoirs or by ring fracture, possibly as a surface expression of cauldron subsidence.

calderite

(1) a variety of antradite.

(2) a manganese iron end member of the garnet group.

caledonian

appertaining to the great mountain-building episode of late Silurian-early Devonian time.

caledonides

a mountain system formed in Late Silurian to Early Devonian time in Scotland, Ireland, and Scandinavia.

caliche

the term used for conglomerate of gravel, rock, soil, or alluvium cemented with sodium salts in Chilean and Peruvian nitrate deposits. It is mainly composed of sodium nitrate, potassium nitrate, and iodate, borate, sulphate, and chloride of sodium.

calmite

giant scouring rush (sphenopsid) with a jointed, ribbed trunk and leaf whorls at the joints.

callovian

a stage in uppermost Middle or lowermost Upper Jurassic which marks a return to clayey sedimentation.

calluna peat

peat that is mainly derived from the common heather Calluna vulgaris.

calm

calm describes gentle weather or sea conditions. In calm weather, there is little or no wind or rain. The opposite of calm is stormy. A calm sea has a flat surface of only very small waves.

calving

the breaking off of a mass of ice from its parent glacier, iceberg, or ice shelf. Also known as ice calving.

camber

1. Refers to a terminal, convex shoulder of the continental shelf. 2. Also, refers to a

structural feature caused by the plastic clay beneath a bed flowing toward a valley so that the bed sags downward and appears to be draped over the sides of the valley.

cambering

the warping and sagging of relatively competent strata which overlies less competent strata, such as of clay, which tend to flow towards adjacent valleys so that a convex top is produced.

cambrian

the earliest period of the paleozoic era, thought to have covered the time span 570 to 500 million years ago; also the corresponding system of rocks.

camerata

a subclass of class Crinoidea, subphylum Pelmatozoa; crinoids with a calyx of variable form in which all plates are united by rigid sutures. Range Ordovician-Permian.

camouflage

describes the relationship between a trace element and a major element whose ionic charge and ionic radius are similar, as a result of which the trace element always occurs in the minerals of the major element but does not form spearate minerals of its own. Thus gallium can be considered to be camouflaged by aluminium.

campanian

a stratigraphic stage name which is used for part of the European Upper Cretaceous.

camptonite

an igneous rock occurring in minor intrusions, and belonging to the family of the lamprophyres. It consists essentially of plagioclase feldspar and brown hornblende.

canada balsam

a mountain medium for thin sections, with a refractive index of 1.54.

canadian

the Lower Ordovician of North America.

Canadian Series

the lowest of the 3 main divisions of the American Ordovician rocks, comprising the Beekmantown and Chazy formations.

Canadian Shield

the name applied to the vast area of Pre-Cambrian rocks which cover 5 million square kilometres in E. Canada.

canal

a canal is a straight waterway, built to carry ships or boats. Some canals link rivers together. Others connect two different seas or oceans. The Panama Canal, in Central America, allows ships to pass from the Atlantic Ocean to the Pacific Ocean and back. The Suez Canal links the Mediterranean Sea with the Red Sea.

cannel coal

a fine-textured, highly volatile bituminous coal distinguished by a greasy luster and blocky, conchoidal fracture; burns with a steady luminous flame. Also known as cannelite.

canneloid

1. coal that resembles cannel coal.
2. coal intermediate between bituminous and cannel.
3. durain laminae in added coal.
4. cannel coal of anthracite or semianthracite rank.

cannel shale

a black shale formed by the accumulation of an aquatic ooze rich in bituminous organic matter in association with inorganic materials such as silt and clay.

cantalite

an igneous rock of the granite clan; An extrusive rock; transparent variety of pitchstone or rhylite-pithstone; sometimes referred to as yellow quartz.

canyon

a deep valley whose vertical sides are excavated by a river and generally associated with rejuvenation. An essential condition is that the rocks should be near horizontal and fairly hard if a canyon is to be formed. Dipping rocks will form the valley asymmetrical, while soft rocks will rapidly collapse into the common V-shaped valley, although ephemeral canyons may be produced by very rapid downcutting. The classic example of a canyon is the Grand Canyon, Arizona.

cape

a relatively large section of land jutting into the sea or some other large body of water from a larger land mass.

caprock model

a theory that waterfalls occur where soft rock is eroded from under a harder rock, but which does not apply in all cases.

caradocian

a stage or series of the Ordovician System in Britain, well represented in the Caradoc region of Salop, Wales, the Lake District, etc.

carapace

the upper normal limb of a fold having an almost horizontal axial plane.

carat

a unit of weight for gemstones. The metric carat equals 200 mg.

carbon

carbon is a non-metallic element. Carbon is one of the commonest elements. It is found in all living things as well as in rocks, coal, oil and other minerals. There are two forms of pure carbon. These are graphite and diamond.

carbonado

the term used for a dark coloured, finegrained diamond aggregate with absence of cleavage planes. It is also known as black, diamond; carbon diamond.

carbonate cycle

the biogeochemical carbonate pathways which involve the conversion of carbonates to carbon dioxide and bicarbonates, and the metabolism and regeneration of it in biological systems.

carbonatite

a rock of apparently magmatic origin consisting chiefly of the carbonates of Ca, Mg and Na, with subordinate feldspar, pyroxene, olivine, and other materials.

carbon cycle

the progression of carbon through the surface, interior and atmosphere of the Earth.

carbon dioxide

carbon dioxide is a colourless gas. It has no smell. The gas is formed when compounds containing carbon are burned and when animals and plants breathe. Carbon dioxide makes up a tiny fraction of the air.

carbonate buildup

a reef complex in the geological record or any large stratigraphic accumulation of limestones and dolomites.

carbonation

1. the process of introducing carbon dioxide into water. 2. The process of chemical weathering in which minerals are replaced by carbonates, commonly by reaction with carbonated water.

carbonatization

a type of wall rock alteration in which dolomite, ankerite and other carbonate minerals form in the wall rocks of epigenetic mineral deposits.

carboniferous

carboniferous describes a period in geological time. The Carboniferous Period lasted from about 360 million years ago to about 286 million years ago.

carbonisation

decomposition of animal or (more often) plant remains to pure carbon as a form of fossil.

carbonization

refers to the reduction of organic tissue to a carbon residue. It refers to an unusual kind of fossilization in which the tissue gets preserved as a carbon film. Plants are commonly preserved in this manner, soft-bodied animals more rarely.

carlsbad twin

a twin, commonly found in the feldspars, in which the twin axis is the c crystallographic axis.

carmeloite

an igneous rock of the gabbro clan; a porphyrite extrusive rock; a type of olivine basalt with olivine phenocrysts altered to iddingsite.

carnalite $KMgCl_3.6H_2O$

a white or red mineral. It is crystallized in orthorhombic fashion and composed of hydrous chloride of potassium and magnesium.

carnelian

carnelian, or cornelian, is a semi-precious stone. It is a red or reddish-brown form of chalcedony. Carnelian is found mostly in India, South America and Japan. It has been used as a gem for thousands of years.

carnosaur
a carnivorous, bipedal, saurischian dinosaur.

carrara marble
a general name for marbles quarried in the vicinity of Carrara, Italy. Several pure varieties are found there, including fine-grade statuary marble. Its colours are mostly white to bluish or blue-veined.

carstone
a variety of sandstone having an exceptional amount of limonitic cement. It is commonly seen as thin bands but not necessarily coincident with bedding.

cascadian orogeny
post-Tertairy deformation of the crust of the earth in western North America.

cascajo
reef derived material composed of coral detritas and other sediment, occurring in old deposits.

case hardening
formation of a mineral coating on the surface of porous rock by evaporation of a mineral bearing solution.

cassiar orogeny
orogenic episode in the Canadian Cordillera during late Paleozoic time.

cassiterite
cassiterite is a mineral. It is brown or black and contains tin and oxygen. Cassiterite is found mostly in igneous rocks.

cast
refers to the impression which is obtained from a mould, i.e., a replica of the original form. Casts and moulds are most commonly considered to be connected with the preservation of fossils, but any three-dimensional feature may undergo replication. e.g., rain prints, triple marks, footprints, etc.

castile
a Permian succession in the Delaware Basin, USA equivalent to the lower part of the Longtanian.

cata
a prefix denoting deepest, at greatest depth.

cataclasis
refers to the process of mechanical fracture of breakup of rocks which is usually associated with dynamic metamorphism or faulting. The term is also applicable to both small-scale, i.e., microscopic, structures, and also large scale phenomena.

cataclasite
a cohesive fault rock with a random fabric containing 10-50% fragments in a finer-grained matrix, probably formed as a result of cataclasis. cf. protocataclasite, ultracataclasite.

catacline
said of the inclination of the cardinal area in either value of a brachiopod lying at right

angles to the orthocline position.

cataract

a cataract is a kind of waterfall. In a cataract, the water flows very fast over a series of rocky falls. Cataracts are found in mountain areas where streams and rivers flow quickly.

catastorpism

the hypothesis, which has now more or less completely discarded. According to this hypothesis changes in the earth take place as a result of isolated giant catastrophes of relatively short duration, as opposed to the idea, implicit in Uniformitarianism, that small changes are occurring continuously.

catena (toposequence)

a sequence of soils found successively along a hillslope which are related by similar parential material.

cat face

(1) a miner's term for glistening balls or nodules of pyrite in the mining face of the coal.

(2) Lenticular deposits of pyrite associated with coal.

cauldron

the structure underlying a caldera, comprising the subsided block and any ring dykes.

caustobiolith

combustible organic rock which is formed by direct accumulation of plant materials. It includes coal peat.

caustic metamorphism

the indurating baking burning and frothing effects of lava flows and small dikes on the rocks with which they come in contact.

cavalorite

an igneous rock of the diorite clan. A granular plutonic rock; contains orthoclase in excess of oligoclase, abundant hornblende and accessory quartz, apatite, magnetite and ilmenite.

cave breccias

breccias formed of fragments falling from the sides and roofs of caves.

cave drapery

a speleothem in the form of a sheet, formed by fluid trickling along a dipping ceiling.

cave earth

a deposit formed of the finer-grained debris of cave walls and roofs, mixed in some cases with a certain amount of water-borne sediment.

cave onyx

a compact, banded cave deposit of calcite or aragonite. It resembles true onyx and can take a high polish.

cavern

a chamber in a rock Caverns are of varying size, and are due to several causes, the chief being solution of calcareous rocks by underground waters, and marine action.

c-axis

1. a vertically oriented crystal axis which is usually the

principal axis; the unique symmetry axis in tetragonal and hexagonal crystals. 2. The reference axis which is perpendicular to the plane of movement of rock or mineral strata.

cay

a flat mound of sand which is built up on a reef slightly above the tide.

cayugan

a Silurian succession in North America covering part of the Gorstian, the Ludfordian and the Pridoli.

cazenovian

a stratigraphic stage name which is used for the base of the North American Middle Devonian.

ceclite

an igneous rock of the gabbro, clan; dark grey, dense texture extrusive rock; it contains nearly 50 per cent leucite with augite, melilite, nepheline, olivine, anorthite, magnetite and apatite.

cell texture

in mineral deposits, a network pattern formed by solution or replacement of organic structure, *e.g.*, cell walls.

cement

any chemically precipitated material, such as carbonates, gypsum, and barite, occurring in the interstices of clastic rocks.

cement bond log

a geophysical borehole log which tests the quality of the cement bond between a borehold casing and its surrounding rock by measuring the attenuation of a seismic signal.

cement clay

a clay rock containing a varying quantity of calcium carbonate, hence used for the manufacture of cement.

cementstone

an argillaceous limestone suitable for cement manufacture.

cement rock

argillaceous limestone containing over 18% of clay.

cenology

an old term for the geology of surficial deposits.

cenomanian

the lowest stage of the upper Cretaceous rocks in western Europe.

cenozoic

refers to the youngest of the eras, or major subdivisions of geologic time, which extends from the end of Mesozoic Eera to the present.

centroclinal

referring to geologic strata dipping towards a common centre, as in a structural basin.

cerite (Ca Fe)$Ce_3Si_3O_{12}$

a brown rare-earth silicate of cerium and other metals found in gneiss.

cerolite

a mixture of serpentine and stevensite found in yellow or green waxy masses.

cesarolite $PbMn_3.H_2O$

a steel-grey mineral consisting of hydrous lead manganate; occurring in spongy masses.

ceylonite
a mineral of the spaniel group which occurs as dark-green, black, or brown matter.

cgs
the centimetre-gram-second system of units.

chaetognatha
a phylum comprising the arrow worms, first appearing in the Carboniferous.

chain structure group
a group of sulphide minerals characterized by a structure comprising rings, the only member being realgar.

chalcedony
a cryptocrystalline variety of quartz. It is found as crusts having rounded or botryoidal surface and as a major constituent of nodular and bedded cherts; varieties are blood-stone, and carnelian.

chalchihuitl
green jadeite of the ancient; also synonym of chalchuite.

chalcophile
descriptive of elements which have a strong affinity for sulphur and are therefore more abundant in sulphide ore deposits than in other types of rock. Lead is an example.

chalcophyllite
$Cu_{18}Al_2(ASO_4)_3(OH)_{27}33H_2O$
a green mineral consisting of arsenate and sulphate of basic copper and aluminium occurring in tabular crystals of foliated masses. Also **known as** copper mica.

chalcopyrite
$CuFeS_2$. The main copper ore. It is a widely occurring mineral which is found mainly in hydrothermal and metasomatic veins.

chalcotrichite
a variety of cuprite occurring in long, straight, needle-like red crystals.

chalk
a white, fine-grained and soft limestone, consisting of finely divided calcium carbonate and minute organic remains. In North-West Europe, it forms, the upper half of the Cretaceous system.

chalk marl
the lowest lithological division of the English Chalk, in which the calcareous matter is mixed with up to 30% of muddy sediment.

champlainian
a stratigraphic stage name which is used for the North American Middle Ordovician.

changshan
a Cambrian succession in Chian covering parts of the Maentwrogian and Dolgellian.

channel-belt deposit
a sediment deposited between successive avulsions in a river channel.

channel capacity
the maximum flow volume that a given channel can sustain without overflowing its banks.

channel sample

a rock sample, usually selected across the face of a rock body or vein to provide an average value.

channel width
the distance across a stream or channel as measured from bank to bank near bankful stage.

char
coke in the form of a granular mass of porous powder which can be briquetted.

charnian
the term used for a stratigraphic division of the volcanic Precambrian in Leicestershire (England).

charnockite
a coarse-grained, dark granitic rock, consisting of feldspars, blue quartz, and orthopyroxene; it occurs typically in Madras and is named after the founder of Calcutta, Job Charnock.

charophyta
large, bushy, green calcarcous algae, mainly found in freshwater ponds and useful biostratigraphically from the Cretaceous to Oligocene, when they underwent great diversification.

chart
a chart is a kind of map. Weather forecasters use charts showing the wind, temperature and atmospheric pressure. Sailors also use charts to map their position at sea.

chassignite
an achondritic stony meteorite composed chiefly of olivine; resembles dunite.

chatoyancy
ability to shine like a cat's eye; having a changeable lustre or colour with an undulating narrow band or white light.

chattermark
a scar on the surface of bedrock made by the abrasive action of drift carried at the base of a glacier.

chattian
upper Oligocene geologic time. Also known as Casselian.

chautauquan
a Devonian/Carboniferous succession in E North America equivalent to the Fameennian and Hastarian.

chazyan
middle ordovician geologic time.

chelonia
an order of subclass Anapsida, class Reptilia; the turtles and totoises. Range Triassic-Recent.

chemical
a chemical is any one of the individual, pure substances from which all materials are made. The simplest chemicals are the elements. Elements join together to make more complicated chemicals called compounds.

chemical precipitates
a sediment formed from precipitated materials as distinguished from detrital particles that have been

transported and deposited.

chemocline
the transition in a meromictic lake between the mixolimnion layer and the monimolimnion layer.

chemostratigraphy
the use of chemical signatures (e.g. carbon, oxygen and strontium isotopes, amino acid residues) in stratal sequences for the purpose of correlation.

chemungian
a stratigraphic stage name which is assigned for the North American mid Upper Devonian.

chenier plain
a coastal plain consisting of progradational, alternate coast - parallel bands of coarse clastic and muddy sediment, occurring in environments undergoing periodic erosion.

chernozem (black Earth)
humus-rich soils developed due to low rainfall. The upper layers are relatively leached.

chert
a siliceous rock consisting of cryptocrystalline silica, and sometimes including the remains of siliceous organisms such as sponges or radiolaria. It occurs as bedded masses, as well as concretions in limestone.

chertification
a kind of silification, especially by a fine-grained or cryptocrystalline quartz.

chesterian
a stratigraphic stage name which is used for the North American Upper Mississippian (Carboniferous System).

cheserite $((Mg,Fe)_{17}Si_{20}O_{54}(OH)_6)$
a biopyribole formed by the alteration of anthophyllite.

chiastolite
a variety of andalusite which is having dark cruciform shaped inclusions.

chibinite
an igneous rock of the syenite clan; a coarse grained, hypautomorphic-granular plutonic rock; contains mainly microcline microperthite, sodaclase, nepheline, pyroxene and eudialyte.

chilled margin
the fine-grained, outer layer of an igneous body formed by rapid cooling.

china clay
a clay consisting mainly of kaolinite, one of the most important raw materials of the ceramic industry. China clay is obtained from kaolinized granite, for example in S.W. England, and is separated from the other constituents of the granite by washing out with high pressure jets of water. Also called kaolin, porcelain clay. Kaolin is used as an internal absorbent for poultices, dusting powers, etc.

chinastone
a kaolinitized granitic rock containing unaltered plagioclase. Also applied to certain limestones of exceptionally fine grain and

smooth texture.

chine

a narrow ravine or canyon running to the sea.

chinook

the chinook is a kind of wind. The chinook is warm and dry and blows down the eastern side of the Rocky Mountains in the United States of America.

chixia

a Permian succession in China equivalent to the Sakmarian and Artinskian.

chkalovite $Na_2Be(SiO_3)_2$

sodium beryllium silicate, existing as orthorhombic, large grains, white semitransparent. It shows vitreous lustre and cleavage in one direction.

chlorite schist

a metamorphic rock whose composition is dominated by members of the chlorite group.

chloritoid

a group of minerals having the formula $(Fe(II)Mg_2(AlFe(III)(Al_3O_2(SiO_4)_2(OH)_4$. Their many features are in common with the chlorites, such as perfect basal cleavage, green colour, monoclinic pseudohexagonal crystallography, and certain optical properties. They are not, however, true layer-lattice minerals, because they have isolated SiO_4 tetrahedra and a brucite-type layer, $Mg_6(OH)_{12}$. Chloritoid is most commonly present in low-grade regionally metamorphosed rocks.

chlorophane

a variety of fluorite; emits bright green fluorescent light on heating.

chokrakian

a Miocene succession on the Russian Platform covering the upper part of the Serravallian.

chondrodite $Mg_5(SiO_4)_2F,OH)_2$

a monoclinic mineral of humite group of yellow-red colour. It occurs in contactmetamorphosed dolomites.

chondrules

small, globular masses of pyroxene, divine and sometimes glass which occur in certain stony meteorites.

chonolith

an igneous intrusion which cannot be classified because of its irregular form.

chorizon

the portion of the parent material in soils which has been penetrated with roots.

chrology

deals with the study of the geographical distribution of organisms.

chrome-spinel

a synonym of picotite; sometimes synonym of magnesiochromite.

chromitite

a rock in which chromite is the dominant mineral.

chromium

chromium is an element. It is a hard, shiny metal. Chromium is used as a coating on steel to protect it from rust. Chromium is also used in alloys.

chron

the time unit equivalent to the stratigraphic unit, subseries, and geologic name of a division of geologic time.

chronosequence

the development of a soil with time.

chrysolite

a variety of olivine which has a magnesium to magnesium-iron ration of 0.9-0.7.

chrysophyric

said of a basalt having olivine phenocrysts.

chrosoprase

an apple green variety of chalcedony.

chrysotile

$Mg_3Si_2O_5(OH)_4$. A common variety of asbestos.

ciders

volcanic lapilli composed mainly of dark glass and containing numerous vesicles.

cinder

fine-grained pyroclastic material ranging in diameter from 4 to 32 millimetres.

cinder cone

a conical elevation formed by the accumulation of volcanic debris around a vent.

cienaga

a term, commonly used in arid regions such as the southwestern U.S., for a marshy area whose wetness is due to springs or seepage.

cincinnatian

strata in N. America equivalent in age to the Upper Ordovician of N.W. Europe.

C.I.P.W.

a quantitative scheme of rock classification based on the comparison of norms; devised by four American petrologists, Cross, Iddings, Pirsson, and Washington.

circumgranular fracture (grain boundary fracture)

a fracture in a granular material which goes round the grains. cf. intergranular fracture, intragranular fracture.

cirrocumulus

cirrocumulus describes a kind of cloud. Cirrocumulus clouds are made of ice crystals. They can be found in the sky above a height of 5,000 metres. The clouds look like strips with rounded edges.

cirrus

cirrus describes a kind of cloud. Cirrus cluds form in the sky at a height of about 5,000 metres. The clouds have a wispy shape.

citrine

a variety of quartz which is transparent and has yellow to brown in colour.

cladistics

a taxoniomic system applied to the study of evolutionary relationships which proposes that a common origin can be demonstrated by shared characteristics. It assumes that each new taxon develops by the splitting of an ancestral lineage into two daughter taxa.

cladogenesis
phyletic branching or splitting, or progressive specialization through evolution.

claim
an area of land staked out by a person who has certain rights to explore for and exploit minerals therein.

clarerdonian
a stratigraphic stage name which is used for the North American equivalent of the European Sarmatian (Tertiary System).

clarite
a microthotype of coal, consisting of vitrinite and exinite group macerals, which makes up to 20% of bituminous coals.

clarkeforkian
a stratigraphic stage name for the North American Upper Thanetian (Tertiary System).

clast
a particle of rock or single crystal which has been derived by weathering and erosion. The basic building rock of a clastic sediment.

clastic ratio
the ratio, in a stratigraphic section, of the amount of clastic material (sandstone, conglomerate) to that of nonclastic material (limestone, dolomite).

clastic rocks
rocks formed of fragments of pre-existing rocks.

clay
an argillaceous rock having particles less than 1/256 mm in diameter. Clays are plastic when wet and do not exhibit bedding. Clays mainly consist of silica, alumina and often with iron, alkalies, and alkaline earths.

clay band
a highly coloured, argillaceous layer in clay ironstone.

clay dune
an aeolian dune composed predominantly of clay aggregates rather than quartz sand grains.

clay loam
soil containing 27-40% clay, 20-45% sand and rest as silt.

clay pan (soil crust)
a compact illuvial layer of clayey material found in the soil zone formed by leaching and eluviation of the upper soil zone.

clay slate
a hard fissile metamorphic rock, derived from argillaceous material.

claystone
clay material cemented by calcite; generally spheroidal and flattened, and sometimes forming large boulders.

clay vein
a clay-body which is similar to an ore vein in form and fills a crevice in a coral scan.

clear water erosion
the erosion of a channel by a river whose sediment load has been removed, e.g. by the construction of a dam.

cleat

vertical breakage planes in coal. It is also spelled cleet.

cleavage fracture

the manner of breaking a crystalline substance along the cleavage plane.

cleavage plane

refers to the plane of mechanical fracture in a rock. Cleavage planes are normally sufficiently closely spaced to break the rock into parallel-sided slices. The term is also applicable to mineral cleavage.

cliachite

a group name for colloidal mixture of aluminium hydroxides containing bauxite also.

clifdenian

a Miocene succession in New Zealand. Equivalent to the Langhian.

cliff

a cliff is a steep rock face rising up from flat ground or the side of a mountain. Many rocky islands have high cliffs. Cliffs are very common at the coast, where waves have eroded the rocks.

climbing adhesion ripple structure

an adhesion structure forming when net deposition occurs by adhesion to a surface kept damp by the capillary rise of water.

climbing dune

a dune that develops on the windward side of mountains or hills.

clinochlore

a mineral of the chlorite group which has green appearance. It occurs as monoclinic crystals.

clinoferrosilite ($FeSiO_3$)

a clinopyroxene.

clinoform

a subaqueous landform, such as the continental slope of the ocean or the forest bed of a delta.

clinometer

a field instrument used to measure the magnitude of dip.

clitter

a type of blockfield made up of a scatter of granite boulders.

clog snow

a sking term for wet, sticky, new snow.

clone

the term used for a colony of animals or plants, all being descendants of the same individual, formed by vegetative reproduction (asexual reproduction), e.g., a coral colony.

cluse

a narrow, gorge, trench or watergap with steep sides that cuts transversely through an otherwise continuous ridge.

coal

a general name for firm brittle carbonaceous rocks; derived from vegetable debris, but altered, particularly in respect of volatile constituents, by pressure, temperature, and a variety of chemical processes. The various types are classified on basis of volatile content, calorific value, caking, and coking properties.

coal ball

a subspherical mass containing mineral matter embedded with plant material, found in coal seams and overlying beds of the late Paleozoic.

coal barrier

a protective pillar composed of coal.

coal basin

a sedimentary basin containing important coal seams.

coal bed

a seam or stratum of coal parallel to the rock stratification. Also known as coal rake; coal seam.

coal breccie

angular fragments of coal within a coal bed.

coalification

formation of coal from plant material by the processes of diagenesis and metamorphism. Also known as bituminization; carbonification; incarbonization; incoalation.

coal measures

the uppermost division of the Carboniferous System, consisting of beds of coal interstratified with shales, sandstones, limestones and conglomerates.

coal petrology

the science that deals with the origin, history, occurrence, structure, chemical composition, and classification of coal.

coal tar

tar produced by the distillation of bituminous coal.

coarse aggregate

said of an aggregate composed of particles greater than 4.76 mm in diameter.

coarse sand

a geologic term for sand composed of grains between 0.5 and 1 mm in diameter.

coast

the coast is the edge of the land where if meets the sea. Some coasts are gently sloping, with sandy beaches. Other coasts are wild and rocky.

coastal bar

a linear accumulation of mainly sand grade sediment lying submerged in the nearshore zone subparallel to the coastline.

cobaltite

CoAsS. A cobalt ore mineral occurring in hydrothermal veins with other cobalt and nickel minerals.

cobalt bloom

an old name for erythrite, a secondary mineral of cobalt.

cobble

a fragment of rock with a particle size between 65mm and 250mm.

coblencien

a Devonian succession in France and Belgium covering the Pragian and part of the Emsian.

coblentzian

upper Lower Devonian geologic time.

coccolith ooze
a fine-grained pelagic sediment containing undissolved sand- or silt-sized particles of coccoliths mixed with amorphous clay-sized material.

cockpit karst (cone karst, kegelkarst)
a karst landscape of humid tropical areas comprising star-shaped, closed depression separated by deep residual hills.

coesite
a high pressure polymorph of SiO_2. It got formed in nature only under unique physical condition usually found in meteor inpect craters.

cognate
pertaining to contemporaneous fractures in a system with regard to time of origin and deformational type.

cognate lithic
a non-vesicular clast found in a pyroclastic rock consisting of juvenile material derived from the same, or closely related, magma as the vesicular clasts in the rock.

coke
a dense, porous product of the carbonization of caking coal in an oven.

col
a col is a gap in a mountain or in a line of hills. A col is often the point where roads and railways cross the mountains or hills because it is lower than the rest of the area. A col can also be known as a pass or saddle.

coleoidea
a subclass of class Cephalpoda, phylum Mollusca; molluscs with an internal shell or lacking a shell, including many squids and the octopoids. Range Upper Mississippian-Recent.

collapse structure
a structure resulting from rock slides under the influence of gravity.

collision zone
a linear belt where two continents or microcontinents have collidated as the result of their intervening ocean having been consumed by subduction.

colloform
referring to rounded, globular texture of mineral which are formed by colloidal precipitation.

colophonite
a variety of andradite; a calcium-iron garnet occurring as coarse, granular crystals of dark reddish or brownish colour with iridescent hues.

colorado topaz
a brown-yellow variety of topaz.

colour index (colour ratio)
the total percentage of mafic (Mg-and Fe-rich, minerals in the modal analysis of an igneous rock, used as an aid to classification.

columnar structure
a form of regular joining, produced by contraction

following crystallization and cooling in igneous rocks, especially those of basic composition. The columns are generally roughly perpendicular to the cooling surface.

comagmatic
descriptive of igneous rocks derived from the same magma.

comanchean
the general name for the Cretaceous strata up to the top of the Albian, as developed in N. America.

comanchian
lower Cretaceous geologic time, of North America.

combe (coombe, comb, coomb)
a small, steep-sided valley which may contain an ephemeral stream.

comleyan
lower Cambrian geologic time.

commissure
a line or plane of junction, such as between the valves of a shell.

common granet
a brownish-red translucent of opaque variety of almandine.

comparator electomagnetic method
an electromagnetic induction exploration method using an artificial, time-varying electromagentic field.

compass
a compass is used for working out a direction. Most compasses contain a needle which has been made into a magnet. This always points to the Earth's magnetic poles.

competent beds
beds or strata capable of withstanding the pressures of folding without flowing or changing in original thickness.

complementary rocks
rocks that have been differentiated from the same magma, and whose average composition remains the same as the parent magma.

composite cone
a large volcanic cone constructed of lava and pyroclastic material in alternating layers.

composite dike
a dike consisting of several intrusions differing in chemical and mineralogical composition.

composite fold
a fold having smaller fold on its limbs.

composite grain
a sedimentary clast formed of two or more original particles.

composite intrusion
a type of multiple intrusion composed of magmas of contrasting composition.

composition plane
a planer composition surface in a crystal which is uniting two individuals of a contact twin.

compound fault
a series of closely spaced parallel or subparallel faults.

compound volcano
1. a volcano consisting of a complex of two or more cones.

2. a volcano with an associated volcanic dome.

compressibility
the inverse of the bulk modulus.

concentration factor
the degree of enrichment of an element or elements above their normal crustal abundance in the formation of an orebody.

concentric fold
a fold in which the original thickness of the strata is unchanged during deformation. Also known as parallel fold.

conchoidal
having a smooth and curved surface. The term is used to describe the fracture surface of a mineral or rock.

concretion
refers to a hard and compact of mineral matter in the pores of sedimentary or fragmental volcanic rock It denotes the concentration of a minor constituent of the enclosing rock or of the cementing material.

concurrent range zone
a zone based on the co-occurrence of two or more species.

condensation
condensation describes how a gas changes into a liquid. The most usual kind of condensation is the change from water vapour to water. Clouds are formed by condensation of water vapour in the atmosphere. The word condensation is also used for the liquid itself.

cone
a cone is a solid shape which is circular at the bottom and pointed at the top. A volcano is often described as cone-shaped. During an eruption, the top of the volcano's cone may be blown away.

cone-in-cone structure
a mineral structure in the form of a series of nested, concentric cones.

confining bed
an impermeable bed adjacent to an aquifer.

confining pressure
the radial stress applied to a cylindrical unit deformed by axially symmetric loading.

conformable
1. Pertaining to the contact of an intrusive body when it is aligned with the internal structures of the intrusion.
2. referring to strata in which layers are formed above one another in an unbroken, parallel order.

congelifraction
the splitting or disintegration of rocks as the result of the freezing of the water contained. Also known as frost bursting; frost riving; frost shattering; frost splitting; frost weathering; frost wedging; gelifraction; gelivation.

congeliturbate
soil or unconsolidated earth which has been moved or disturbed by frost action.

congeliturbation
the churning and stirring of soil as a result of repeated cycles of freezing and thawing; includes frost heaving and surface subsidence during thaws. Also known as cryotourbation; frost stirring; geliturbation.

conglomerate
cemented, rounded fragments of water-worn rock or pebbles, bound by a siliceous or argillaceous substance.

conglomerate test
a palaeomagnetic test for determining the age of a remanent magnetization. If the natural remanent magnetization of the clasts of a conglomerate are randomly oriented, the magnetization predates its formation and vice versa.

congrssite
an igneous rock of the syenite clan; a pale pink, coarsegrained, usually foliated, plutonic rock. It contains much nepheline with mainly orthoclase, albite, sodalite, muscovite, biotite and magnetite.

coniacian
lower Senonian geologic time.

conrad discontinuity
a seismic discontinuity seen in certain regions of the continental crust at a depth of 10-12 km marking the boundary between the upper and lower continental crusts.

conservation deposit
an exterptional fossil deposit in which soft tissues or the impression of soft tissues are preserved.

consolidation
refers to the process by which loose, soft, or liquid earth get coherent and firm.

constructive plate margin (accretive plate margin)
a plate margin at which lithosphere is created, i.e. an ocean ridge, cf. conservative plate margin, destructive plate margin.

contact twin
a twin whose members are separated by a composition plane. cf. interpenetrant twin.

contaminate
to contaminate is to make something less pure by adding another substance. Dangerous chemicals may contaminate drinking water.

contamination
a term nearing the incorporation of country rock into magma.

contemporaneous
1. formed, existing, or originating at the same time.
2. of a rock, developing during formation of the enclosing rock.

continental
formed or generated on land, as opposed to in the ocean or sea. Deposits originating in lakes, swamps, or streams, or moved by land winds, are all continental.

continental accretion

the theory that continents have grown by the addition of new continental material around an original nucleus, mainly through the processes of geosynclinal sedimentation and orogeny.

continental borderland
the area of the continental margin between the shoreline and the continental slope.

continental crust
the basement complex of rock, that is, metamorphosed sedimentary and volcanic rock with associated igneous rocks mainly granitic, that underlies the continents and the continental shelves.

continental deposits
sedimentary deposits laid down within a general land area.

continental divide
a continental divide is a chain of high mountains which separates one part of a continent from another.

continental drift
the concept of continent formation by the fragmentation and movement of land masses on the surface of the earth.

continental geosyncline
a geosyncline filled with nonmarine sediments.

continental growth
the process contributing to the growth of continents at the expense of ocean basins.

continental margin
those provinces between the shoreline and the deep-sea bottom; generally consists of the continental broderland, shelf, slope, and rise.

continental nucleus
a large area of basement rock consisting of basaltic and more mafic oceanic crust and periodotitic mantle from which it is postulated that continents have grown. Also known as continental shield; cratogene; shield.

continental plate
thick continental crust.

continental rise
a transitional part of the continental margin; a gentle slope with a generally smooth surface, built up by the shedding of sediments from the continental block, and located between the continental slope and the abyssal plain.

continental shelf
the zone around a continent, that part of the continental margin extending from the shoreline and the continental slope; composes with the continental slope; composes with the continental terrace. Also known as continental platform; shelf.

continental shield
large areas of Precambrian rocks exposed within the cratons of continents.

continental slope
the part of the continental margin consisting of the declivity from the edge of the continental shelf extending down to the continental rise.

continental splitting
the inititaion of a new ocean by rifting of a continent and subsequent seafloor spreading.

continental terrace
the continental shelf and slope together.

continent formation
a series of six or seven major episodes, resulting from the buildup of radioactive heat and then the melting or partial melting of the earth's interior; the molten rock melt rises to the surface, differentiating into less primitive lavas; the continent then nucleates, differentiates, and grows from oceanic crust and mantle.

continuous deformation
deformation by process of flow rather than by fracture.

contour
a contour is a line drawn on a map, or chart. All the points joined by a contour line on a map are at the same height above sea-level. Maps of the land have contours to show high and low ground. Maps of the sea have contours showing the depth of the water.

contourite
a muddy or sandy sediment reworked and deposited by a contour current.

contraction
the decrease in length of a line during deformation. cf. elongation, stretch.

convection cells
pattern of mass movement of mantle material in which the outer area is downflowing and the central area is uprising due to heat differences. These cells may be of various sizes and shapes.

convection current
a convection current is the movement of a gas such as air caused by convection. During convection, the air or gas moves up or down. The movement is called a current.

convergence
1. metamorphic convergence is said to take place when two rocks of differing original character become closely similar after metamorphism, e.g., a basic igneous rock and an argillaceous limestone may produce similar amphibolerich rocks on metamorphism.
2. Stratigraphic convergence means the reduction of the vertical interval between two beds by the thining of the intervening strata, due to the area of deposition.
3. in palaeontology, evolutinary convergence is considered to have taken place if two groups of organisms develop similar features, even though not genetically related.

convergent evolution
the tendency of unrelated species to evolve similar structures, physiology or appearance due to the same external factors.

convolute
descriptive of a coiled shell in

which the outer whorls embrace the inner ones so that they are nearly invisible. cf. evolute.

cooling joint

a joint in an igneous body forming perpendicular to the cooling surface by thermal contraction.

coombe rock

a sedimentary rock; a mass of unrolled flints and fragments of chalk with some earth interstital matter; considered as result of movement by solifluction during the glacial period.

coordination polyhedron

the shape adopted by the anions around a particualr cation. Used with coordination number in the description of crystal structure.

coorongite

a boghead coal in the peat stage.

copper ore

rock containing copper minerals.

coprolite

petrified excrement.

coquimbite **($Fe_{2-x}Al_x(SO_4)_3 9H_2O$)**

a hydrated copper sulphate found in some ore deposits and fumaroles.

coquina

a coarse-grained, porous, easily crumbled variety of clastic limestone of cemented coarse shell debris, e.g., some of the shelly 'grits' of the English MidJurassic.

coral

a coral is a kind of marine animal which has a hard skeleton. Corals belong to the same family as sea anemones. When the corals die, the skeletons build up to form a coral reef.

coral head

a small reef patch of coralline material. Also known as coral knoll.

coral sand

a sand-grade sediment of carbonate grains derived from the erosion of a coral-algal reef.

corallian

a stratigraphic stage name which is used for the European mid-Upper Jurassic, a synonym of Lusitanian.

corallum

the skeleton of a colonial coral.

coral mud

detrital deposits which are composed of clay-grade and sand-grade sized particles of calcareous material derived from reefs and generally get deposited in the vicinity of such features.

coral pinnacle

a sharply upward-projecting growth of coral rising from the floor of an atoll lagoon.

coral reef

a ridge or mass of limestone built up of detrital material deposited around a framework of skeletal remains of mollusks, colonial coral, and massive calcareous algae.

coral-reef shorelline

a shoreline formed by reefs composed of coral polyps. Also known as coral shoreline.

coral sand

coarse-grade deposits of coral fragments formed around coral islands and coasts bordered by coral reefs.

cordillera

refers to a string of islands in a geosyncline which is a surface expression of a geanticline. They may divide the gensyncline into a number of separate basins.

cordylite ([$Ba_2(Ce,La)_3(CO_3)_5F_3$]

barium and cerium group of rare earths fluorcarbonate. It occurs in pegmatite veins in nepheline syenite with acgirine, ancylite and neptunite.

core analysis

the use of core samples taken from the borehole during to give information on strata age, composition, and porosity, and the presence of hydrocarbons or water along the length of the borehole.

core logging

the analysis of the strata through which a borehole passes by the taking of core samples at predetermined depth intervals as the well is drilled.

core sample

a sample of rock, soil, snow, or ice obtained by driving a hollow tube into the undisturbed medium and withdrawing it with its contained sample or core.

corestone

a large cabble or boulder of relatively pristine rock found within a deep weathering profile.

corneite

a biotite-hornfels formed during deformation of shale by folding.

cornîsh stone

a crushed, partially weathered granite with appreciable feldspar and kaolinite, used in the manufacture of bone china.

cornstones

the term used for concretionary limestones which are generally formed under arid conditions. They are typical of the Devonian and Permo-Trias of the Great Britain.

corona

a zone of mineralization, often showing radial arrangement, surrounding another mineral. The term has been applied to corrosion rims and reaction rims.

corona structure

means the development of a concentric zone or zones of one or more minerals, commonly made-up of radically arranged crystals, surrounding another mineral.

correlation

1. the determination of the equivalence or contemporaneity of geologic events in separated areas.

2. as a step in seismic study,

the selecting of corresponding phases, taken from two or more separated seismometer spreads, of seismic events seemingly developing at the same geologic formation boundary.

cortlandite

a peridotite having large crystals of hornblende with pockitically included crystals of olivine. Also termed as hudsonite.

corundophilite

a ferroan variety of clinochlore.

corundum

corundum is a very hard mineral. It is made up of luminium and oxygen. Red ruby and a blue sapphire are forms of corundum. They are precious stones and are used to make jewellery. A very dark-coloured form of corundum is used in industry as an abrasive.

coset

a term used for a sedimentary unit composed of two or more sets.

cosmogeny

the term deals with the study of the age and origin of the Universe, and more especially the age and origin of the solar system including the earth.

cotectic

allowing the crystallization of two or more solid phases from a single liquid over a finite temperature decrease.

cottonballs

a colloquial term for fine, fibrous crystals of ulexite.

couloir

a steep valley or gorge on a mountainside especially the Alps. The term is also used in mountain-climbing parlance for a passage in cave.

counter point bar

a river bar deposited on the concave side of a channel bend because of a change in flow conditions or meander pattern migration.

country rock

1 rock that surrounds and is penetrated by mineral veins.

2. rock, that surrounds and is invaded by an igneous intrusion.

couvinian

lower Middle Devonian geologic time.

covellite

CuS. A copper ore mineral. It occurs in the zones of secondary enrichment of copper veins.

crack-seal mechanism

a mechanism of vein filling by repeated cycles of extensional fracture followed by cementation.

crag

a steep, rugged point or eminence of rock, as one projecting from the side of a mountain.

crag-and-tail

a streamlined ridge comprising a hill of resistant rock and a tail of less competent material, formed by glacier action.

crater

1. a large, bowl-shaped topographic depression with steep sides.

2. a rimmed structure at the summit of a volcanic cone; the floor is equal to the vent diameter.

crater cone

a cone built around a volcanic vent by lava extruded from the vent.

craton

the large and immobile portion of continents consisting of both shield and platform areas.

creek

a creek is a narrow, winding channel with a stream at the bottom. Creeks are often found in muddy areas, such as salt-marshes. Many creeks are flooded by the sea at high tide.

creep

refers to a slow or gradual movement; applicable to (a) soil and superficial accumulations moving under gravity (gravity transport); (b) progressive deformation of a rock by long-applied stress just below the elastic limit. As soon as the stress is removed, part of the deformation remains and part is lost by elastic recovery.

creep limit

the maximum stress that a material can withstand without observable creep.

creep strength

the long-term strength of a material, i.e. its strength at low strain rate. cf. instantaneous strength.

crenitic

relating to or resulting from the raising of subterranean minerals by the action of spring water.

crescent beach

a crescent-shaped beach at the head of a bay or the mouth of a stream entering the bay, with the concave side facing the sea.

crest

1. the top of a working face of an openpit mine or quarry.

2. the highest part of an anticline.

crest line

the line connecting the highest points on the same bed of an anticline in an infinite number of cross sections.

crest plane

the plane which connects the crest lines of successive beds in an anticlinal fold.

cretaceous

the latest system of rocks or period of the Mesozoic Era, between 136 and 65 million years ago.

crevasse

an open, nearly vertical fissure in a glacier or other mass of land ice or the earth, especially after earthquakes.

crevasse deposit

kame deposited in a crevasse.

crianite

a basic igneous rock comprising intergrown feldspar, titanaugite, olivine and analcite.

crinoidal limestone
a rock which is composed of mainly crystalline joints of crinoids, with foraminiferns, corals, and molluscs.

critical crack extension force (fracture toughness)
a measure of rock strength which is independent of experimental procedure.

critical reflection
a seismic reflection at the critical angle, at which high amplitude waves are generated.

critical velocity
the minimum velocity of a fluid required to entrain a particle.

crocidolite
a common variety of asbestos which looks like lavenderblue, indigo-blue, or leek-green. It is found in fibrous, massive and earthy forms. It is also known as blue asbestos; krokidolite.

cromaltite
an igneous rock of the ultrabasic clan; a black to dark green, coarse to medium grained hypabyssal rock; contains aegirine, augite, melanite, biotite, ilmenite, apatite and pyrite.

cromerian
a stratigraphic stage name which is used for the British and European basal Middle Pleistocene (interglacial between the Weybourne and the Lowestoft Till).

cross fold
a secondary fold whose axis is perpendicular or oblique to the axis of another fold.

cross fracture
a surface marking of a joint surface.

cross vein
a vein intersecting a larger one.

crucible swelling number
a parameter indicating the suitability of coal for coke manufacture, involving the measurement of the profile of the coke residue after heating a small sample of coal to 800^0C under standard conditions.

crude oil
crude oil is the name used for petroleum when it first comes out of the ground. Oil wells pumps crude oil from oilfields deep under the ground or from under the sea. Crude oil is a heavy, brown liquid. It is refined to make many petroleum products.

crudline
a Devonian succession in E Australia equivalent to the Lochkovian.

crush belt
refers to a narrow region of the earth's crust in which the rock is broken and pulverised owing to movement. Sometimes, but not always it coincides with a fault zone. It is also known as crush zone.

crush fold
a fold of large dimensions that may involve considerable minor folding and faulting such as would produce a mountain chain or an occanic deep.

crust

the outermost solid layer of the Earth, distinguished chemically from the underlying mantle beneath the Mohorovicic discontinuity. Oceaninc and continental crust are markedly dissimilar.

cryconite

refers to a dark dust which is transported by wind and deposited on the surface of snow or ice.

cryogenic period

a time period in geologic history during which large bodies of ice appeared at or near the poles and climate favoured the formation of continental glaciers.

cryolite (greenland spar) (Na_3AlF_6)

a fluoride mineral found in pegmatite veins and exploited as a flux.

cryopedology

a branch of geology dealing with the study of intensive frost action and permanently frozen surfaces.

cryoplanation

land erosion at high latitudes or elevations due to processes of intensive frost action.

cryosphere

the part of earth's surface that is frozen throughout the year.

cryptic layering

the gradual change in composition of cumulate minerals of a solid solution through layers in a cumulate igneous rock.

cryptoclastic

composed of extremely fine, almost submicroscopic, broken or fragmental particles.

cryptoperthite

a sub-optical perthite formed by the very rapid cooling of alkali feldspar.

cryptozoic

term meaning "hidden life". It is that part of geologic time represented by rocks in which evidence of life is slight and only of primitive forms.

crystal

refers to a three-dimensional body, the bounding surfaces of which have been arranged symmetrically. For a given substance, with constant angular relationships, it arises from the inherent regular atomic structure of the substance.

crystal class

refers to one of 32 categories of crystals in accordance to inversions, rotations about an axis, reflections, and combinations of these which leaves the crystal invarient. It is also termed as symmetry class.

crystal growth

the process of precipitation following nucleation by which a crystal grows spontaneously and is removed from solution.

crystal habit

the general shape of crystals, *e.g.,* cubic, fibrous.

crystal lattice

means a lattice from which the structure of a crystal could be obtained by associating with every lattice point an assembly of atoms which are identical in composition, orientation, and arrangement. It is also known as space lattice; lattice.

crystal settling

a mechanism for the formation of a cumulate igneous rock by concentration as minerals settle out of a magma.

crystalline massif

a portion of continental crust made up of metamorphic or igneous rocks that is stable relative to its surroundings.

crystallite

a small, rudimentary form of crystal which is of unknown mineralogic composition and which does not polarize light.

crystalloblastic series

a series of metamorphic minerals ordered according to decreasing formation energy, so crystals of a listed mineral have a tendency to form idioblastic outlines at surfaces of contact with simultaneously developed crystals of all minerals in lower positions.

crystalloblastic texture

a crystalline texture resulting from metamorphic recrystallization under conditions of high viscosity and directed pressure.

crystallographic preferred orietation

an alignment or preferred orientation of the axes of symmetry of crystal lattices in a deformed rock.

crystallography

crystallography is the study of crystals. It looks at the outer shape of crystals and also at their inner structure.

crystal symmetry

means the existence of nontrivial operations such as inversions, rotations around an axis, reflections and combination of these, which are able to bring a crystal into a position indistinguishable from its original position.

cubanite [$CuFe_2S_3$]

copper iron sulphide composed of orthorhombic, striated, elongated or thick tabular crystals.

cubic packing

one end member of the different ways perfectly sorted spheres can be arranged, in which orthogonal lines join the sphere centres. A sediment with such packing would have 48% intergranular porosity. cf. rhombohedral packing.

cubic plane

a plane that is at right angles to any one of the three crystalographic axes of the cubic system.

cuesta

a geomorphological unit which consists of a gently inclined surface parallel to the dip of the bedding planes, and an escarpment or scarp face that is steeply inclined in the opposite direction to the dip slope and cutting across the bedding planes.

cuirass
a well-cemented duricrust covering the land surface, protecting underlying unconsolidated material from erosion.

culm
a miner' term which is used for carbonaceous shale and fissile varieties of anthracite (coal). The term is applicable stratigraphically to Carboniferous rocks in Devon and Cornwall.

cummingonite $[(Mg,Fe)_7Si_8O_{22}(OH)_2$
a ferrosilicate mineral with ratio of magnesium to iron greater than 1:1. It contains hydrated magnesium ferrous iron silicate and occurs as a cline-amphibole, identical with anthophllite in composition and therefore an amphibole asbestos. It forms series with grunerite.

cumulate
a layerred igneous mass commonly having rocks which are considered to have formed by 'accumulation' of 'primary precipitate crystals'.

cumulate igneous rock
an igneous rock characterized by a framework of touching or interlocking crystals and grains interpreted to have been concentrated by gravitational settling during magmatic diversification processes.

cumulus
cumulus describes a kind of cloud. Cumulus clouds look rounded and fluffy and can be very tall. They often develop in convection currents of warm air, particularly in hot weather.

cupola
an isolated, upward-projecting body of plutonic rock that lies near a larger body: both bodies are presumed to unite at depth.

current lineation
a lineation caused by the movement of sediment or fluid.

current ripple
a type of ripple mark having a long, gentle slope toward the direction from which the current flows, and a shorter, steeper slope on the lee side.

cursorial
a term applicable to animals having one pair of limbs adapted for running, e.g., ostriches some dinosaurs, man.

cusp
one of the series of low crescent shaped mounds of beach material separated by smoothly curved, shallow troughs spaced at almost regular intervels along and generally perpendicular to the beach face.

cuspate bar
a crescentic bar joining with the shore at each end.

cuspate fold profile
a fold shape with the fold closure in one direction having a broad, arcute shape and in the other direction a cuspoid shape, arising across an

interface separating layers of different competence.

cutbank

the concave bank of a winding stream that is maintained as a steep or even overhanging cliff by the action of water at its base.

cutout

mass of siltstone, sandstone, or shale occupying the space of an erosional channel cut into a coal seam.

cycle of erosion

a concept according to which the various stages in the erosion of a region are considered as parts of a 'cyclic' process. Ideally the cycle start with uplift of a land surface followed by initiation and development of relief, and finally degeneration of relief and ultimate plantation. Further uplifts makes the cycle to recommence. It is very probable that complete plantation is never achieved, uplift taking place at almost any stage in the cycle.

cycle of sedimentation

also known as sedimentary cycle.

1. a series of related processes and conditions appearing repeatedly in the same sequence in a sedimentary deposit.

2. The sediments deposited from the beginning of one cycle to the beginning of a second cycle of the spread of the sea over a land area, consisting of the original land sediments, followed by those deposited by shallow water, then deep water, and then the reverse process of the receding water.

cyclic evolution

the concept that evolution was initially rapid and then followed by a longer phase of more gradual change.

cyclone

a cyclone is a very strong wind. Cyclones sometimes blow around an area of low atmospheric pressure, particularly in the tropics. Cyclone is sometimes used as another name for a depression.

cyclostomata

an order of subclass Monorhina, class Agnatha, superclass Pisces; the lampreys, hagfishers and slime eels. Range? Ordovician-Recent.

cyclothem

a rock stratigraphic unit which has been applied indiscriminately to the 'repeat unit of either cyclic sedimentation or rhythmic sedimentation.

cymatolite

a mixture of albite and muscovite possessing fibrous to wavy structure.

cymophane (Oriental cat's eye)

a variety of chrysoberyl exhibiting chatoyancy.

cymrite

$Ba_2Al_5Si_5O_{19}(OH).3H_2O$. A mineral of zeolite group having a basic aluminosilicate of barium.

cyprine
a variety of idacrase containing traces of copper. It acquires pale to sky-blue or greenish-blue colour due to presence of copper.

cyrtoconic
descriptive of a coiled gastropod shell in the form of a curved, tapering cone.

dachsteinkalk
a triassic succession in the Alps equivalent to the Norian and Rhaetian.

dacian
a stratigraphic stage name which is used for the European Upper Pliocene (Tertiary System).

dacite glass
a natural glass formed by rapid cooling of dacite lava.

dahamite
an anigneous rock of the granite clan; a porphyritic hypabyssal rock; variety of paisanite characterised by abundant albite.

dala
a Carboniferous succession in China covering part of the Bashkirian and the Moscovian.

dalradian
refers to the youngest stratigraphic division of the Precambrian in Scotland and Ireland. The upper part is having a Cambrian fauna.

dam
a dam is a structure which controls the flow of water. Dams are built to hold water in reservoirs, or to stop flooding.

dambo
a linear depression without a well-defined stream channel found on old, gently-sloping, land surfaces, especially in the tropics.

daphnite
a variety of chlorite rich in iron and aluminium.

darriwilian
an Ordovician succession in Australia equivalent to the Llanvirn.

datang
a Carboniferous succession in China equivalent to the Visèan.

datum
the top or bottom of a bed of rock on which structure contours are drawn.

daughter Element
an element which is produced by the radioactive decay of a pre-existing element.

daya
a small, silt-filled, solutional depression on a limestone surface in arid areas of the Middle East and N. Africa.

dead sea
a body of water in which there are no normal aquatic organisms, and from which evaporites are being or have been precipitated.

debris
large fragments arising from disintegration of rocks and strata.

debris avalanche
the sudden and rapid downward movement of incoherent mixtures of rock and soil on deep slopes.

debris cone
1. a mound of fine-grained debris piled atop certain boulders moved by a landslide.
2. a mound of ice or snow on a glacier covered with a thin layer of debris.

debris fall
the near free fall of weathered material from a vertical or overhanging face.

debris flow
a variety of rapid mass movement involving the downslope movement of high-density coarse clast-bearing mudflows, usually on alluvial fans.

debris slide
a type of landslide involving a rapid downward sliding and forward of comparatively dry, unconsolidated earth and rocky debris.

decarboxylation
the thermocatalytic decomposition of oxygen-containing kerogen to release carbon dioxide during burial diagenesis, causing an increase in carbon content and a loss of water.

decay series
the sequence of daughter elements produced by the radioactive decay of a parent element.

deccan basalt
fine-grained, nonporphyritic, tholeiitic basaltic lava consisting essentially of labradorite, clinopyroxene, and iron ore; found in the Deccan region of southeastern India. Also known as Deccan trap.

declination
the horizontal angle between true north and magnetic north.

declivity
1. a slope descending downward from a point of reference.
2. a downward deviation from the horizontal.

decomposition
chemical reaction in which a compound breaks down into simpler compounds or into elements.

decussate Texture
a random arrangement of lath-like or columnar crystals that make up a rock.

decompose
decompose describes the breakingup of a chemical into simpler material. When animals and plants die, the complicated organic substances of their bodies decompose into simpler substances in the ground.

deep coal
coal that is far enough below the surface to require underground mining.

deep-focus earthquake
an earthquake with a depth of focus greater than 300 km. cf. shallow-focus earthquake, intermediate-focus

earthquake.

deerparkian

a stratigraphic stage name which is used for the North American mid Lower Devonian.

deflation

refers to the transport of loose surface debris by wind action.

deflation lag

large particles remaining after the removal of finer material by deflation.

deformation band

a tabular zone of a crystal lattice differing in crystallographic orientation from the rest of the mineral grain.

deformation fabric

the space orientation of rock elements produced by external stress on the rock.

deformation lamella

a type of slipband in the crystalline grains of a material produced by intracrystalline slip during tectonic deformation.

deformation mechanism

the means by which deformation is accomplished at a microscopic scale. The three basic mechanisms are cataclasis, intracrystalline plasticity and diffusive mass transfer.

deformationplane

twinning produced by formation and gliding. A portion of the crystal structure is sheared in such a way as to produce a mirror image of the original crystal.

deglaciation

1. refers to the stage of retreat of a widespread glaciation. 2. Also, refers to the exposure of an area from beneath a glacier or ice sheet due to shrinkage of the ice by melting.

delamination

the process of crust detachment from the mantle during continental collision, or when an upper crustal layer detaches from a lower layer by flake tectonics.

dellenite

an igneous rock of the granite clan; a fine grained extrusive rock; contains basic plagioclase with orthoclase, occasional quartz and some hornblende; its type is intermediate between rhylite and dacite.

delmontian

a Neogene succession on the west coast of the USA covering part of the Messian, the Zanclian and part of the Piacenzian.

delta

a deposit, of sediments usually triangular in shape, which is formed at the mouth of a river, stream, or tidal inlet. It is normally built up only where there exists no tidal or current action which is capable of removing the sediment as fast as it gets deposited, and hence the delta builds forward from the coastline. This process of building-up is complex, and results in the formation of a number of separate channels isolated lagoons, levees, marshy ground, and a network of small creeks.

demagnetization
the removal of natural remanent magnetization by incremental increase in temperature or the strength of an applied magnetic field.

demultiplexing
the recovery of information from a multiplexed signal.

dendritic
this term is used for describing any form that is branching, ramifying or dichotomising, thereby giving the appearance of a tree in silhouette.

density
the mass of a substance per unit of volume. In SI unit it is expressed in kg m^{-3}.

density current
a current driven by the density of the fluid, e.g. turbidity current.

denudation
refers to the sum total of the processes which cause general lowering of the land surface. It involves the processes of weathering, transportation, and erosion.

denudation chronology
the reconstruction of the erosional history of the Earth's surface using erosional remnants where the stratigraphy is incomplete.

depletion drive (dissolved-gas drive, solution gas drive)
the mechanism whereby oil in a reservoir is driven towards a well by the action of dissolved gas in the oil.

depocenter
a site of maximum deposition.

deposit
a deposit is any material which is laid down. The water in a river leaves a deposit, or sediment, of gravel and mud on the river bed.

depositional mark
an irregularity formed on the bedding plane of a sediment during deposition.

depositional sequence
a major but informal assemblage of formations or groups and supergroups, bounded by regionally extensive unconformities at both their base and top and extending over broad areas of continental cratons.

depositional strike
sedimentary deposits that are continuous laterally on a gently sloping surface.

depth ice
small ice particles formed below the surface of sea agitated by wave activity.

depth of compensation
the depth at which isostatic effects cause the pressure due to the overlying rocks to be everywhere equal.

dereliction
a recession of water from the sea or other body of water so that the land is left dry.

deroofing
the uncovering of a pluton by

denudation.

desert

a desert is a dry, open area of land. Deserts usually have less than 25 centimentres of rain a year. A heavier rainfall that evaporates quickly may also occur in a desert. Some deserts, like the Sahara in North Africa, are hot. Other deserts are cold, like the Gobi in eastern Asia. A much smaller range of plants and animals is found in deserts than in other areas. But many kinds of plant and animal are able to live in deserts.

desert armor

a desert pavement surfaced with stony fragments that protect underlying fine-grained material from wind erosion.

desert pavement

a mosaic of pebbles and large stones which accumulate as the finer dust and sand particles are blown away by the wind. Also known as desert crust.

desert polish

a smooth, shining surface imparted to rocks and other hard substances by the action of windblown sand and dust of desert regions.

desert roses

concretions of barytes or sometimes gypsum in sandstone, or clusters of platy crystals containing sand. Barytes acts as cement for sand.

desert soil

in early United States classification systems, a group of zonal soils that have a light-coloured surface soil underlain by calcareous material and a hardpan.

desert varnish

a brown or black stain or crust of manganese or iron oxide characterizing many exposed rock surfaces in the desert.

desiccation breccia

fragments of a mud-cracked layer of sediment deposited with other sediments.

desiccation crack

a crack formed by shrinkage of clay or clayey beds under the influence of heat from the sun.

desmoinesian

a stratigraphic stage name which is used for the North American Middle Pennsylvanian (Carboniferous System).

desmostyla

an order of infraclass Eutheria, subclass Theria, class Mammalia; aquatic, hippopotamus-sized mammals. Range Miocene.

detached core

the inner part of a fold that has been detached or pinched from the parent structure by some process, usually severe compression and folding. The term core is used even though a fold may be composed entirely of one kind of rock.

detachment fault

a fault which marks the displacement along a

detachment horizon or dècollement plane.

detritus

detritus is loose, rocky material produced by the weathering of exposed rock. Detritus is washed away by rivers and rain and gathers at the bottom of seas, rivers and lakes, as well as on land.

deuteric

the term used for describing the alterations in a body of igneous-rock formed by the action of vapours and volatiles, which are obtained from the magma itself during the later stages of consolidation.

deuteric reaction

the permeation of non-water bearing minerals through crystal fractures in a newly crystallized magma and their reactions with primary minerals.

development

the progression of changes in fossil groups which have succeeded one another during deposition of the strata of the earth.

deviatoric stress

the stress remaining in a triaxial stress system when the mean stress is subtracted.

devitrification

means the development of crystals, initially on a very small scale, in a glassy igneous rock like obsidian or pitchstone. Devitrification may ultimately spread throughout a glassy rock leaving it completely crystalline. These completely devitrified rocks are sometimes known as variolites.

devonian

the fourth period of the Paleozoic Era.

dew

dew is a collection of water droplets. The droplets condense from the water vapour in the air on to the ground, or on to plants. Dew forms at night, when the air cools to below the dew point.

dewu

a Carboniferous succession in China equivalent to the Serpukhalian.

dextral

a term which is applicable to tear faults for describing apparent direction of relative movement of each side, in this case to the right.

diachronism

a time-transgressive unit, e.g. lithostratigraphic unit that varies in age.

diadochy

refers to the replacement of one ion in a lattice by another.

diagonal joint

a joint whose strike is in a direction that lies between the strike and direction of dip on the associated rocks.

diallage

an obsolete name for a clinopyroxene.

diamond

a colourless cubic mineral variety of crystalline carbon. It crystallizes in isometric system and may be of gem quality. It occurs in ultrabasic and alluvial deposits. It is used for cutting and abrasive.

diaphthorite

schistose rocks in which minerals have been formed by retrograde metamorphism.

diapir

a dome or anticlinal fold in which a mobile plastic core has ruptured the more brittle overlying rock. Also known as diapiric fold; piercement dome; piercing fold.

diastem

a temporal break between adjacent geologic strata that represents nondeposition or local erosion but not a change in the general regimen of deposition.

diastrophism

1. the general process or combination of processes by which the earth's crust is deformed. 2. The results of this deforming action.

diatom

a microscopic, unicellular, planktonic alga growing in water. Possesses a siliceous cell wall which may contribute to sediment.

diatomaceous earth

a yellow, white, or light-gray, siliceous, porous deposit made of the opaline shells of diatoms; used as a filter aid, paint filler, adsorbent, abrasive, and thermal insulator. Also known as kieselguhr; tripolite.

diatomaceous ooze

a pelagic, siliceous sediment composed of more than 30% diatom tests, up to 40% calcium carbonate, and up to 25% mineral grains.

diatomite

dense, chert-like, consolidated diatomaceous earth.

diatreme

a volcanic vent which is piercing sedimentary strata. It is usually the result of an explosive eruption.

dichroiscope

an instrument for the determination of pleochroism.

dichroism

refers to a variety of plecochroism, in which two colours or shades get displayed due to different absorption coefficients for light which is polarized in different directions.

didymite

a variety of muscovite; contains calcium carbonate as impurity and forms greenish or greyish-white fine scales.

differential stress

the two-dimensional stress difference between the maximum and minimum stresses.

diffluence

a mechanism by which a glacier overflows an obstacle at its lowest point.

diffusivity

a measure of the rate of heat diffusion through a material,

defined as the ratio of thermal conductivity to the product of specific heat and density.

digenite Cu_2S

copper sulphide, occurring usually with some copper deficiency, as octahedral crystal of the blue to black colour, it shows conchoidal fracture and occurs with chalcocite challcopyrite and other copper ores as replacement of bornite.

dikaka

a sand dune covered by scrub or grass.

dike ridge

any small wall-like ridge created by differential erosion.

dike set

a small group of dikes arranged linearly or parallel to each other.

dike swarm

a large group of parallel, linear, or radically oriented dikes.

dike wall

a topographic feature formed when a dike is more erosion resistant than the rock on either side.

dilatant zone

the open space formed in the more steeply-dipping part of a pinch-and-swell structure arising from normal faulting.

dilation vein

a vein formed by the infilling of an existing void caused by fault or fissure.

diluvial

pertaining to, produce by, or resembling a flood.

dimorphism

1. refers to a type of polymorphism in which a substance (or body) exists in two different forms; e.g., calcium carbonate exists as calcite and aragonite.

2. Also, refers to the occurrence of certain species of fossil in two distinct forms, e.g., the megaspheric and microspheric forms of some Foranlinifera.

dinosaur

a general term for the orders saurischia and Ornithschia, subclass Archosauria, class Reptilia which dominated the terrestrial ecology of the Mesozoic, many of which achieved great size.

dinosaur

a dinosaur is any one of a group of reptiles which lived during the Mesozoic Era. Dinosaurs died out at the end of the Cretaceous Period.

diorite

refers to a coarse-grained plutonic rock having intermediate composition including essentially intermediate plagioclase (oligoclase andesine) hornblende, and biotite or pyrexene as ferromagnesian minerals. A diorite may have upto 10% quartz and some alkali feldspar.

Diorites containing more than 7% ferromagnesian minerals are known as meladiorites (this term is taken to include the appinites in part).

diorite model

a type of porphyry copper deposit characterized by the presence of zones of potassic alteration, sericitization, intermediate argillic alteration and propylitic alteration with increasing distance from the mineralization.

dip

the inclination of a planar surface, measured in the vertical plane perpendicular to its strike. cf. apparent dip.

dip fault

a type of fault striking parallel with the dip of the strata involved.

dip joint

a joint that strikes approximately at right angles to the cleavage or bedding of the constituent rock.

dip log

a log of the dips of formations traversed by boreholes.

dip moveout

the moveout generated by a dipping reflector, cf. normal moveout.

diploid

a crystal form in the isometric system which has 24 similar quadilateral faces arranged in pairs.

dip shift

the relative displacement of rock units parallel to the fault dip, but beyond the fault zone itself.

dip slope

a topographic surface dipping in the same direction as the underlying beds. It is often more or less parallel to them.

directional fabric

the fabric in an igneous, sedimentary or metamorphic rock comprising the alignment of minerals caused by motion during the formation of the rock.

directional structure

any sedimentary structure having directional significance; example are cross-bedding and ripple marks. Also known as vectorial structure.

dirt band

a dark layer in a glacier representing a former surface, usually a summer surface, where silt and debris accumulated.

dirt bed

a buried soil containing partially decayed organic material; sometimes occurs in glacial drift.

discharge

the amount of water flowing down a stream channel; it is measured in cubic metres per second, and data for such measurement is always taken at specified location along a given stream.

discoaster

a coccolith with the form of a stellate shield, usually built of six radiating rays.

disconformity

unconformity between parallel beds or strata.

discordant

a term used for describing an igneous rock which shows a cross-cutting relationship to bedding or foliation.

discordant coast

a coast where the structural grain runs transverse to the coastline. cf. concordant coast.

dislocation

a line defect in a crystal, the result of slip along a surface of one or more lattice constants.

dismicrite

fine-grained limestone of obscure origin, resembling micrite but containing sparry calcite bodies.

dispersal pattern

means the distribution pattern of metals in soil, water, rock, or vegetetion.

dispersion

the dependence of propagation velocity on wave frequency, characteristic of surface seismic waves. The general increase in velocity with depth means that lower frequencies travel faster than higher frequencies.

displacement plane

the plane at right angles to the walls of a shear zone, containing the shear direction.

dissection

destruction of the continuity of the land surface by erosive cutting of valleys or ravines into a relatively even surface.

disseminated deposit

a generally low grade deposit in which ore minerals are dispersed throughout a host rock, e.g. diamonds in kimberlite, prorphyry copper deposit.

dissemination

the term used for an ore deposit consisting of fine particles of the ore mineral which are dispersed through the enclosing rock.

distal

descriptive of a feature far from its sources. cf. proximal.

disturbance

a term used in geology for a lesser or minor orogeny such as the Palisades disturbance at the close of the Triassic.

diving seismic wave

a seismic wave that follows a curved path between the seismic source and detector, caused by a progressive increase in seismic velocity with depth.

dog-tooth spar

a form of calcite in the shape of a canine tooth.

dogger

refers to a large spherical or oblately spherical calcareous concretion. This is usually applicable to large masses, as opposed to the smaller nodules.

dolerine

metamorphic rock; a variety of talc-schist; contains feldspar and chlorite as chief minerals.

dolerite

the term used for a medium-grained basic nypabyssal igneous rock which is mineralogically and chemically the same as gabbro and basalt. Porphyritic dolerites are uncommon, but ophitic textures are of frequent occurrence. Dolerites are found mainly as dykes (often in swarms), sills, and small plugs which are often old volcanic necks.

dololithite

a dolostone comprising detrital fragments of dolomite derived by weathering from an existing rock.

dolomite

dolomite is a mineral. It is a compound called calcium magnesium carbonate. Dolomite is one of the chief sources of magnesium. One kind of sedimentary rock, which contains calcium magnesium carbonate, is also called dolomite. Many mountain ranges, especially in Europe, have huge amounts of dolomite rock.

dolomitization

refers to the process by which an original calcium carbonate rock gets converted into the double calcium magnesium carbonate, either wholly or in part. Dolomitization often destroys contained fossils, original sedimentary structure etc.

domain

a subdivision of a larger area of volume that is more homogeneous than the whole.

dome

1. the term used for a circular or elliptical almost symmetrical upfold of anticlinal type of structural deformation.
2. A large igneous intrusion whose surface gets curved upward.

donau glaciation

a Pleistocene glacial time unit in the Alps region in Europe.

doodlebug

also known as douser.

1. any unscientific device or apparatus, such as a divining rod, used to locate subsurface water, minerals, gas, or oil.
2. a scientific instrument used for locating minerals.

dopplerite

a naturally occurring gel of humic acids found in peat bags or where an aqueos extract from a low-rank coal can collect.

dormant

dormant describes a volcano which has not erupted recently, but which might erupt in the future.

dormant volcano

a volcano which is currently inactive but which has erupted within historical time. cf. extinct volcano.

downthrow

the side of a fault whose relative movement appears to have been downward.

downthrown

descriptive of the side of a fault with relative downwards movement. cf. upthrown.

downwash

a process involved in the formation of grèza litèe in which a halffluid mixture of fine sediment is spread over a stony layer.

dowtonlan

uppermost Silurian or lowermost Devonian geologic time.

draa (complex dune, 'uruq)

a large dune formed by a regional wind pattern.

drag fold

a minor fold which is formed in an incompetent bed by movement of a competent bed so as to subject it to couple; the axis is lying at right angles to the direction in which the beds slip.

dgragonian

a stratigraphic stage name for the North American equivalent of the mid Montain (Teritary System).

dreikanter

a pebble shaped with three facets by sandblasting.

dresbachian

lower Croixan geologic time.

dreuss

a Jurassic succession in Utah/ Idaho, USA, covering part of the Callovian.

drewite

calcareous ooze composed of impalpable calcareous material.

driblet cones

small cones which are formed by lavas which are very viscous and usually acidic.

drift

a general term for all rock materials that has been carried by glaciers and deposited directly from the ice or through the agency of meltwater.

drill hole

a metalliferous mining term for borehole.

drilling mud (drilling fluid)

an oil or water-based fluid containing clay, lime or barite forced down a drill hole during drilling to cool and lubricate the bit, seal the sides of the borehole and prevent blowouts.

dripstone

general term for calcite or other mineral deposits formed in caves by dripping water. This includes stalactities, stalagmites, and similar deposits formed by flowing water.

dripstone cave

any cave of calcium carbonate or other mineral which gets formed by the action of dripping water.

dropstone

a clast dropped through the water column into soft sediment, typically released from ice.

drought

a drought is a long period without rain. Wild plants and animals can often survive short droughts, but crops may suffer badly.

druse (Drusy)

refers to a cavity in a rock or mineral vein into which euhedral crystals of the minerals form the rock or vein project.

drystone

a stalagmite or stalactite formed by dropping water.

dry wash

a wash, arroyo, or coulee whose bed lacks water.

duchesnian

a stratigraphic stage name, which is used for the North American equivalent of the European Ludian (Tertiary System).

dull coal

a component of banded coal of grey colour with dull appearance; consisting of small anthraxylon constituents in addition to cuticles and bark like constituents embedded in the attritus.

dumortierite $(Al_7O_3(BO_3)(SiO_4)_3$

a nesosilicate, found in aluminium-rich metamorphic rocks.

dune-bedding

the large-scale crosstatification developed in dunes.

dune-complex

referring to the totality of topographic forms, especially dunes, which are comprising the moving landscape.

dune stabilization

the artificial prevention of erosion or immobilization of a dune for engineering purposes.

dunite

refers to an ultrabasic, monomineralic rock having more or less pure olivine with some chromite and picolite.

duplex

an imbricate structure in which faults branch from an underlying floor thrust and join a common, higher-level roof thrust.

durain

a hard, granular ingredient of banded coal which occurs in lenticels and shows a close, firm texture. Also known as durite.

durargid

a great soil group constituting a subdivision of the Argids, indicating those soils with a hardpan cemented by silica and called a duripan.

duricrust

a general term for the hard crust on the surface or within the upper horizons of a soil in a semi-arid climate.

durinite

the principal maceral of durain; a heterogeneous material, semiopaque in section, micrinite, exinite, cutinite, resinite, collinite, xylinite, subserinite, and fusinite may be present.

duripan

a horizon in mineral soil characterized by cementation by silica.

dust

dust is a collection of powdery particles of earth. In dry weather, dust covers the surface of the soil and finds its way into every hole and corner.

dust avalanche

an avalanche of dry, loose snow.

dust devil

a dust devil is a small, circular column of wind which has picked up dust and soil. It is a kind of small tornado which occurs in dry areas. A dust devil can move quite quickly, at a speed of up to 30 kilometres per hour.

dust storm

a dust storm is a strong wind which picks up and carries dust. Dust storms take place mostly in areas with a hot climate, especially where the soil is fine and dry. Sometimes, small tornados pick up dust and become dust storms.

dyke, Neptunean

a sheet of sediment which fills a crack in another rock.

dyke swarm

a set of dykes, generally subparallel, with a common origin.

dynamic allotropy

a kind of allotropy in which the allotropes are in dynamic equilibrium with each other, *e.g.,* liquid sulphur.

dynamic metamorphism

metamorphism resulting exclusively or largely from rock deformation, principally faulting and folding. Also known as dynamometamorphism.

dyanamic recrystallization

the formation of new crystal species as a result of deformation or tectonism.

dyscrystalline

a term applicable to igneous rocks which are poorly crystalline and poorly crystallized.

dystrophic lake

a lake poor in nutrients and oxygen and rich in undecomposed plant matter. cf. eutrophic lake, oligotrophic lake.

dzhalindite In (OH)

a yellowish brown mineral of indium; an alteration product of indite.

eagle ford

a Cretaceous succession on the Gulf Coasrt of the USA covering part of the Cenomanian and the Turonian.

earth

earth is another name for soil. Earth is the loose material lying above rocks. It is made of tiny pieces of rock, dust and sand.

earth current

static or alternating electric current flowing through the ground and arising either in natural or artificial electric or magnetic fields.

earth flow

refers to the rapid movement of water-laden soil material down a slope.

earth hummock

a type of patterned ground in which rounded hummocks form an irregular net-like pattern as the result of frost heaving.

earth pillars

refers to columns of clay which are capped by large boulders, and develop from spurs arising from valley slopes. As rain erodes the surface, the boulder protects the earth beneath it and remains as perched on a pillar of clay. Where the slope gets sheltered from oblique rain, particularly tall pillars may be occurring. The heights of about 60 meters are recorded in the Tyrol. The material in which the formation of earth pillars is most commonly observed is boulder clay.

earthquake

a sudden release of accumulated stress along a subsurface planer discontinuity according to the elastic rebound theory.

earthquake intensity (intensity)

a subjective measure of the strength of the effects of an earthquake at and around the epicentre, expressed on a scale of I to X or XII. cf. earthquake magnitude.

earthquake swarm

a prolonged series of earthquakes of small to moderate magnitude without a single 'main' event.

earthquake zone

an area of the earth's crust in which movements, sometimes with associated volcanism, occur. Also known as seismic area.

earth science

the branch of science dealing with the study of the earth or any part thereof. It includes geology, geography, geophysics and geochemistry (in their widest senses), geodetics, climatology, and meterology, oceanography, and the astronomical aspects of the earth-moon system.

eastonian

an Ordovician succession in Australia covering the Harnagian, Soudleyan, Longvillian, Marshbrookian, Actonian and part of the Onnian.

eastonite

magnesium sodium potasium aluminosilicate; a silver-white mica similar in composition to a vermiculite.

ecca

a stratigraphic stage name which is used for the base of the Middle Karroo in South Africa.

echo sounder

an echo sounder measures the distance of something under water. It sends out sound waves, which bounce back off the sea-bed, the river bed or an object under water. The echo sounder calculates depth or distance by measuring the time between sending the sound waves and receiving the echo.

eclogite

a metamorphic rock whose chemical composition is similar

to that of a basic igneous rock, but which has crystallized under conditions of high temperature and high pressure. The normal constituents of an clogite include a garnet (usually pyrope), pyroxene, characteristically omphacite, and sometimes a corresponding amphibole, sphene, zoisite, and magnetite are common accessories.

eclogite facies

a set of metamorphic mineral assemblages of basalt composition represented by omphacitic pyroxene and almandine pyrope garnet.

economic geology

geological studies for the explanation and exploration of materials which can be profitable utilized by man.

economic yield

the maximum rate at which water can be extracted from an aquifer without damaging water quality or creating a deficiency.

ecosystem

the interdependence of species with themselves and their environment.

ectexis

magmatization with in site formation of the mobile part.

ectinite

a metamorphic rock which is developed isochemically, i.e., without introduction or loss of material.

ectohumus

an accumulation of organic matter on the soil surface with little or no mixing with mineral material. Also known as mor; raw humus.

eddy viscosity

the component of resistance to deformation in a fluid arising from the generation of eddies in a turbulent flow.

edenite $NaCa_2Mg_5(Si)$

basic sodium calcium magnesium and aluminium flurosilcate; an iron free variety of hornblende.

edge coal

a coal seam of high inclination.

edge dislocation

a dislocation in a crystal occurring as the result of inserting an extra plane of atoms, terminating along the line of dislocation.

efficiency of a water well

the ratio of aquifer loss to total drawdown of a well.

effective porosity

a property of the earth having interconnecting interstices. It is expressed as a percentage of bulk volume which is occupied by the interstices.

effusion

the passage of gases through small apertures under pressure. The relative rates of effusion of different gases under the same conditions are inversely proportional to the square roots of their densities.

Eh

oxidation potential, a measure of the electron concentration of a system in internal equilibrium.

eifelian

a stratigraphic stage name which is used for the European Middle Devonian.

einkanter

a stone shaped by windblown sand only upon one facet.

ejecta

the solid material thrown from a volcano or impact crater.

ekman transport

the net displacement from an Ekman spiral.

elastic rebound theory

a model for the mechanism of an earthquake whereby forces progressively distort a body of rock until its strength is exceeded and energy is suddenly released in a catastrophic event.

elaterite

a variety of bitumen; it is quite amorphous; shows brown streak, soft and elastic with consistency like India rubber when fresh hard and brittle with conchoidal fracture on exposure.

elbaite

a lithium-rich variety of tourmaline, which may be green, pink or blue.

electrical conductivity

the reciprocal of electrical resistivity, unit S m^{-1}.

electrode configuration

the arrangement of electrodes in electrical surveying.

element

an element is a simple substance. An element cannot be changed by chemical reaction into any simpler substance. Carbon, hydrogen and oxygen are all examples of elements. Elements join together to form compounds. Scientists known of just over 100 different elements so far.

eleolite

a dark coloured variety of nepheline with a greasy lustre.

elevation correction

the correction applied to gravity and magnetic survey data to compensate for the varying elevations of observations.

elongation lineation

a lineation formed by a set of parallel, elongate objects in a deformed rock.

elster glaciation

the first of the four glacial periods of northern Europe in the Quatermary.

elutriation

refers to the process by which a granular material can be sorted into its constituent particles sizes by using a moving stream of fluid (usually air or water). Elutriators find extensive use in studies of sediments for determining particle size distribution.

eluviation

refers to the process of leaching in a soil, which mainly removes iron and calcium.

eluvium

disintegrated rock material formed and accumulated in stiu or moved by the wind alone.

elvan
a miner's term from south-west England which is applicable to any dyke of granite, microgranite, or quartz porphyry.

embouchure
1. the mouth of a river.
2. a river valley widened into a plain.

embry and clovan classification
an expanded form of the Dunham classification of limestones.

emerald
emerald is a green, transparent crystal. It is a kind of beryl, which contains traces of chromium. It is a precious stone.

emery
a rock having finely granular corundum and magnetite. It is formed from the thermal metamorphism of a ferruginous.

emplacement
the intrusion of an igneous rock body into an envelope of country rock.

emulsification
the process of dispersing one liquid in another immiscible liquid.

enantiomorphic
a crystallographic term applicable to forms which are similar but not congruent, i.e., they cannot be superimposed even by rotation and/or inversion.

encrinal limestone
a variety of limestone consisting of more than 10% and less than 50% of fossil crinodal fragments.

enderbite
a charnockitic rock comprising quartz, antiperthite, hypersthene and magnetite.

endobatholithic
pertaining to ore deposits along projecting portions of a batholith.

endogenic
of or pertaining to a geologic process, or its resulting feature such as a rock, that originated within the earth. Also known as endogenetic; endogenous.

endometamorphic
refers to a term which describes the changes undergone by an igneous rock due to its assimilating the country rock being invaded.

endoskarn
a skarn deposit formed by the replacement of an intrusion. cf. exoskarm.

en echelon
referring to an overlapped or staggered arrangement of geologic features.

en echelon fault blocks
a belt in which the individual fault blocks trend approximately 45° to the trend of the entire fault belt.

engineering geological map
a map showing units defined by their engineering properties.

englacial
said of something that is

contained embedded, or carried within a glacier or ice sheet, *e.g.,* till or drift.

enrichment
refers to the processes by which the relative amount of one constituent mineral or element contained in a rock gets increased.

entablature
a volcanic layer with fan - like joints, commonly alteration with colonnades.

enveloping surface
the surface which would join the crest or trough lines of a set of folds.

environment
environment is a word which describes our surroundings, or the surroundings of an animal or plant. The environment includes the other animals and plants nearby, as well as the soil, rocks, water and climate.

eocene
the epoch of the Tertiary period between the Palaeocene and Oligocene epochs.

eolation
any action of wind on the land.

eolianite
a sedimentary rock having clastic material which is deposited by wind action.

eon
an eon is one of the divisions of geological time. There are four eons, each covering a very long period of time. The Phanerozoic Eon is the most recent. It is divided into eras, periods and epochs.

eosite
a variety of a quartzite; it is bluish with veins or splotches of brownishred; contains small crystals of pyrites. It is used for ornamental carvings.

eozoon
a pseudo-fossil which consists of rather finely banded calcite and serpentine.

ephermeral stream
a stream or river which does not flow at all times of the year. cf. perennial stream.

epicentral angle
the angle subtended at the centre of the Earth by the epicentre of an earthquake and the location of its detection.

epicentre
a point on the surface of the earth which is directly above the seismic focus of an earthquake and where the earthquake vibrations reach first.

epiclastic
pertaining to the texture of mechanically deposited sediments consisting of detrital material from preexistent rocks.

epicontinental
located upon a continental plateau or platform.

epidosite
a rock having epidote and quartz which may be metamporphic or hydrothermal in origin.

epidotization
an alteration process whereby the feldspar of, commonly, a

basic igneous rock is albitized with the separation of epidote and zoisite.

epifauna

organisms live attached to another. The larger organism is termed as an eplfauna. For example, the growth of corals and bryozoa on brachiopod shells, a growth which may develop during the life of brachiopod or after its death. The attachment is quite haphazard, and no special relationship such as parasitism or symbiosis is necessarily meant.

epimagma

a gas-free, vesicular to semisolid magmatic residue of pasty consistency formed by cooling and loss of gas from liquid lava in a lava lake.

episode

a distinctive event or series of events in the geologic history of a region or feature.

epitaxy

the term used for the growth of one crystal on the surface of another crystal in which the growth of the deposited crystal gets oriented by the lattice structure of the substrate.

epithermal

pertaining to mineral veins and ore deposits formed from warm waters at shallow depth, at temperatures ranging form 50-200°C, and generally at some distance from the magnetic source.

epithermal deposit

one deposit formed in and along openings in rocks by deposition at shallow depths from ascending hot solutions.

epizone

1. the zone of metamorphism characterized by moderate temperature, low hydrostatic pressure, and powerful stress.
2. the outer depth zone of metamorphic rocks.

epoch

a third order geological time unit.

equator

the equator is an imaginary line which is drawn around the globe. Latitudes are measured to the north and south of the Equator, which has latitude 0 degrees. The Equator divides the Earth into two halves, the northern and southern hemispheres.

equigranular

a textural term applicable to a rock in which the constituent grains are all of about the same size.

equilibrium

a state of balance between opposing forces or effects.

era

an era is one of the main divisions of geological time. Each era is divided into periods. The order of eras from oldest to youngest is Paleozoic, Mesozoic and Cenozoic.

erian

middle Devonian geologic time; a North American provincial series.

erian orogeny
one of the orogenies during Phanerozoic geologic time, at the end of the Silurian; the last part of the Caledonian orogenic era. Also known as Hibernian orogeny.

erode
to erode is to wear away the surface of something. The wind, water and ice are constantly eroding the rocks and soils of the Earth.

eroding velocity
the minimum average velocity required for eroding homogeneous material of a given particle size.

erosion
means that part of the process of denudation in which there occurs the wearing away of the land surface by the mechanical action of transported debris.

erosional unconformity
the surface that separates older, eroded rocks from younger, overlying sediments.

erosion cycle
a postulated sequence of conditions through which a new landmass proceeds as it wears down, classically the concept of youth, maturity, and old age, as stated by W.M. Davis; an original landmass is uplifted above base level, cut by canyons, gradually converted into steep hills and wide valleys, and is finally reduced to a flat lowland at or near base level.

erosion pavement
a layer of pebbles and small rocks that prevents the soil underneath from eroding.

erosion surface
a flat plain resulting from erosion and representing the final phase of a cycle of erosion.

erosivity
a measure of the potential ability of an eroding agent, such as rainfall or wind, to cause erosion, based on its kinetic energy.

erratic
refers to a large-pebble, cobble, or boulder which gets transported to some distance from its source. The term is commonly applicable to glacially transported blocks.

erupt
erupt describes how a volcano explodes. Some volcanoes do not erupt for many years, or even centuries. Other volcanoes erupt more frequently.

eruption
the ejection of solid, liquid, or gaseous material from a volcano.

esbiotic crystallization
the process in which the orbicules of an esboite attain oligoclastic composition.

escarpment
a cliff or steep slope of some extent, generally separating two level or gently sloping areas, and produced by erosion or faulting. Also known as scarp.

esker
a term applicable to long, winding ridges of sand and gravel which are unrelated to the surrounding topography and found in previously glaciated regions. They originated within or beneath the ice.

espichellite
an igneous rock of the gabbro clan; a porphyritic hypabyssal rock. It contains phenocrysis of hornblende augite olivine, magnetite and pyrite in black compact groundmass of magnetite hornblende, augite, mica, and labadorite with orthoclase rims.

essential mineral
a mineral whose presence or absence determines the name of a rock. cf. accessory mineral.

essexite
the term used for a rock of igneous origin which is composed chiefly of plagiodase, hornblende, biotite and titanaugite.

estuary
an estuary is the part of a river where fresh water flows into the sea. The fresh river water mixes with the salty sea water. An estuary is affected by the tides. The water in the parts of the river nearest the sea rises and falls as the tide ebbs and flows.

esturarine deposit
a sediment deposited at the heads and floors of estuaries.

esturian deposit
a sediment deposited at the heads and floors of estuaries.

ethmolith
a downward tapering, funnel-shaped, discordant intrusion of igneous rocks.

eucolite
a variety of eudialyte possessing prismatic crystals with large or small basal plane. It shows cleavage in one direction and imperfect in two others.

eucrite
an olivine-bearing gabbro, generally having calcic plagioclase; a meteorite component.

eukaryote
an organism with cells possessing a distinct nucleus. cf. prokaryote.

eulysite
a metamorphic rock which is rich in iron and manganese. Typical minerals are hedenbergite and iron hypersthene, fayalite and manganese fayalite, iron-manganese garnet, etc.

euphotic zone
an ocean zone in which light penetration is sufficient for photosynthesis. It commonly extends from 60-70 m but may be even greater.

euryapsida
a subclass of class Reptilia, characterized by only one temporal opening; possibly not a natural grouping. Range Permian-Upper Cretacceous.

eustatic

refers to absolute changes in sea level, i.e., to world-wide changes and not local changes which are occurring due to local movements of the land or the sea floor.

eutaxitic texture
a texture of flattened glassy discs (fiamme) in an ashy matrix seen in welded tuffs.

eutectic
a solution or an alloy that has the lowest possible constant melting point.

eutectic system
the composition and temperature of substances at the eutectic point.

eutrophic lake
a lake containing much dissolved plant nutrient and a seasonal lack of oxygen in the lowest layer due to significant amounts of decaying organic matter. cf. dystrophic lake, oligotrophic lake.

euxinic
a term used for describing an environment which is characterized by the presence of large volumes of stagnant water which is de-oxygenated, yielding reducing conditions. The characteristic sediments are black carbonaceous pyritic muds. Such conditions are found at present in the deeper parts of the Black Sea.

evaporate
evaporate is a word which describes how a liquid changes into a gas or vapour. When water evaporates, it turns from a liquid into water vapour in the air. Water evaporates when it is heated.

evaporite deposit
a deposit from which various salts can be recovered, principally anhydrite, borax, carnallite, celestine, colemanite, gypsum, halite, kernite, nitrates, sylvite and trona.

evaporite dust
deposits of mineral salts from sea water or salt lakes due to evaporation of the water.

evolute
descriptive of a coiled shell in which all whorls are exposed. cf. convolute.

eversion
the process of pothole formation in riverbeds; plays an important role in denudation.

excavate
to excavate is to dig carefully into the ground in order to find something. Geologists excavate quarries and cliffs when looking for fossils or different rocks.

excelsior
a Triassic succession in Nevada, USA equivalent to the Anisian and Ladinian.

exchangeable sodium percentage
a property of certain clays referring to the percentage of sodium that is readily lost by dissolution. If this is high the clay is very susceptible to erosion.

exfoliation
refers to a process of weathering in which thin sheets of rock split off due to differential expansion and contraction during heating and cooling over the diurnal temperature range.

exinite
a hydrogen-rich maceral group consisting of spore exines, cuticulae matter, resins, and waxes; includes sporinite, cutinite, alginite, and resinite. Also known as liptinite.

exocline
an inverted anticline or syncline.

exogen effect
the effect of an igneous mass on the rock that it invades.

exogeosyncline
a parageosyncline that lies along the cratonal border and obtains its clastic sediments from erosion of the adjacent orthogeosynclinal belt outside the craton. Also known as deltageosyncline; foredeep; transverse basin.

exothermic process
a process in which energy in the form of heat is released.

exotic
used for an organism that has been introduced into a new area from where it grew naturally.

expansive soil
a soil which shrinks and swells with changing moisture content, such as one containing montmorillonite.

explosion crater
a volcanic crater formed by explosion and commonly developed along rift zones on the flanks of large volcanoes.

explosion tuff
a tuff whose constituent ash particles are in the place they fell after being ejected from a volcanic vent.

exploitation well
a well sunk in a proven deposit.

explosive index
the percentage of pyroclastic material in the products of a volcanic eruption.

exsolution
a phenomenon during which molten rock solutions separate when cooled.

exsolution lamellae
layers of sedimentary rock that solidify from solution by either precipitation or secretion.

extension
an increase in the length of a line during deformation.

extension joints
fractures that form parallel to a compressive force.

extinction
if the vibration directions of the ordinary and extraordinary rays of an anisotropic mineral have been found to be parallel to the vibration directions of the polars in a petrological microscope, no light reaches the eye and the mineral is said to be in extinction. This happens because light which can pass the polariser (vibrating E-W) also passes the

mineral (following one of its vibration directions), but gets stopped by the analyser, which has a N-S vibration direction. This phenomenon takes place every 90° of rotation of the mineral.

extract

to extract something is to take it out. Matals are extracted from their ores by melting or by the use of chemicals.

extraction

extraction describes how one substance is taken out of a mixture. Extraction can be done by heating and melting the mixture, or by dissolving the mixture in chemicals.

extrusive

applicable to igneous rock which has flowed out at the surface of the earth, as opposed to intrusive, synonymous with volcanic and effusive.

exudatinite

a coal maceral of the exinite group of secondary origin, found in cavities in other macerals, which was soft and mobile at some stage during coalification.

eye

eye is sometimes used to describe the central part of a storm of circular winds or hurricane. The air in the area of the eye is calm.

eye coal

coal characterized by small circular or elliptic structural discs that reflect light and are arranged in parallel planes either in or normal to the bedding. Also known as circular coal.

eye ridge

a raised line or narrow band extending from the forward and inner part of a trilobite eye to the anterior part of the glabella.

eyebrow scrap

a fault scrap that crosses a piedmont alluvial fan near its apex and that seldom maintains the dip of the fault surface in the unconsolidated gravels of the fan.

fa

a method of indicating olivine composition as a percentage of fayalite, e.g. Fa_{10} indicates a composition of 10% fayalite, 90% forsterite.

fabric

1. refers to the spatial orientation of the elements of a sedimentary rock.

2. Also, refers to the sum of all the structural and textural features of a rock.

fabric cross

orthogonal fabric axes of menoclinic symmetry.

fabric diagram

a graphic representation of the data of fabric elements.

fabric skelton

lines linking the highly populated parts of sterogram showing fabric elements, which define preferred orientations.

face

refers to a single flat surface of a naturally developed crystal, which exists in fixed angular relation to adjoining faces. It may be considered to be one element of a form.

facet

a facet is part of a precious stone or gem. A gem used for jewellery is cut into several flat surfaces. Each of these flat surfaces is called a facet.

facies

refers to the sum total of features like sedimentary rock type, mineral content, sedimentary structures, bedding characteristics, fossil content, etc. which have been found to characterize a sediment as having been deposited in a given environment.

facies fossil

a fossil that represents a particular paleo-environment and therefore, a correspondingly restricted distribution.

faecal pellets

the term used for small masses of the excreta of invertebrates, which are usually not larger than 2-3 mm in diameter. Generally they are ovoid, but occasionally they may be rod-shaped.

facing

the direction in which beds become younger.

fahlband

a stratum containing metal sulfides; occurs in crystalline rock.

fahrenheit

fahrenheit is a scale used for measuring temperature. On the Fahrenheit scale, the freezing point of water is 32 degrees and the boiling point is 212 degrees.

falling dune

a steep-sided stationary dune forming on the lee slope of an obstacle such as a hill where sand collects.

fall line

1. the zone or boundary between resistant rocks of older land and weaker strata of plains. 2. The line indicated by the edge over which a waterway suddenly descends, as in waterfalls.

false-bedding

an inclined bedding produced by currents.

famennien

a Devonian succession in France and Belgium covering parts of the Frasnian and Famennian.

fan, alluvial

refers to a low heap of material, which has a roughly triangular plan, in the form of a cone. Alluvial fans are said to be formed where rivers or streams with a high velocity have their speeds suddenly checked by reaching a flatter region.

fan fold

a fold of strata in which both limbs are overturned, forming a syncline or anticline.

fanglomerate

coarse material in an alluvial fan, with the rock fragments being only slightly worn.

fan shooting

a method of seismic refraction surveying in which the detectors are sited at similar distances from the seismic source from which they radiate out in an arc. Provides information on the three-dimensional form of a refractor.

farlovian

a stratigraphic stage name which is used for the European Upper Devonian (Old Red Sandstons facies).

fasinite

a feldspathoid igneous rock; a coarse grained to porphyritic under saturated plutonic rock. It contains augite, nepheline and subsidiary olivine and biotite.

fault basin

a region depressed in relation to surrounding regions and separated from them by faults.

fault block

a rock mass that is bounded by faults; the faults may be elevated or depressed and not necessarily the same on all sides.

fault breccia

the assembly of angular fragments found frequently along faults. Also known as dislocation breccia.

fault drag

the bending of a marker across a fault.

fault gouge

a fine-grained, clay-like substance formed by the grinding of rock material as a fault develops; it may also be formed by decomposition caused by circulating solutions.

fault inlier

an inlier created by a fault crossing a valley.

fault line

intersection of the fault surface with the surface of the earth or any other horizontal surface of reference. Also known as fault trace.

fault-line scarp

a cliff produced when a soft rock erodes against hard rock at a fault.

fault plane

a planar fault surface.

fault rock

a rock often found along a fault plane and made up of fragments formed by the crushing and grinding which accompany a dislocation.

fault scarp

a steep cliff formed by movement along one side of a fault. Also known as displacement; fault clift; fault escarpment; fault ledge.

fault strike

the angular direction, with respect to north, of the intersection of the fault surface with a horizontal plane.

fault system

two or more fault sets which interconnect.

fault terrace
a step on a slope, produced by displacement of two parallel faults.
fault throw
the amount of vertical displacement of rocks due to faulting.
fault trap
oil or gas reservoir formed by a structural trap limited in one or more directions by subterranean geological faulting.
fault vein
a mineral vein deposited in a fault fissure.
fault wall
the mass of rock on a particular side of a fault.
fault zone
a fault expressed as an area of numerous small fractures. Also known as distributed fault.
faunal province
a region which is characterized by an assemblage of organisms which is distinct from those of neighbouring regions. The term is generally applicable to fairly large areas, e.g., the Australasian Faunal Province, characterized by marsupials.
faunizone
a bed characterized by fossils of a particular assemblage of fauna.
fayalite
Fe_2SiO_4. A brown to black silicate mineral of olivine group, which occurs either massive or in crystalline from. Its hardness on Mohs scale is 6.5.
feather edge
the intersection line on a map of a stratigraphic boundary with a higher boundary such as an unconfomity, which marks the zero isopachyte of the strata between the boundaries.
feather ore
a plumose or acicular form of jamesonite.
fecal pellets
mainly the excreta of invertebrates occurring in marine deposits and as fossils in sedimentary rocks. Also known as castings.
feixianguan
a Triassic succession in China covering the Griesbachian and part of the Nammalian.
feldspar
feldspar is a kind of mineral. Feldspar is made up of crystals. It contains aluminium and silica, with mixtures of sodium, potassium and calcium.
feldspathic
a term used for mineral aggregate containing feldspar. The percentage of feldspar present must usually be within certain limits.
feldspathic graywacke
sandstone containing less than 75% quartz and chert and 15-75% detrital clay matrix, and having feldspar grains in greater abundance than rock fragments. Also known as high-rank graywacke.
feldspathic sandstone

sandstone rich in feldspar; intermediate in composition between arkosic sandstone and quartz sandstone, made up of 10-25% feldspar and less than 20% matrix material.

feldspathization

formation of feldspar in a rock usually as a result of metamorphism leading toward granitization.

feldspathoid

aluminosilicates of sodium, potassium, or calcium that are similar in composition to feldspars but contain less silica than the corresponding feldspar.

felsenmeer

a flat or gently sloping veneer of angular rock fragments occurring on moderate mountain slopes above the timber line.

felsic

an acronymic word which is derived from feldspar and silica, and used to describe light-coloured silicate minerals like quartz, feldspar, and feldspathoids.

felsitic

a texture term applicable to granular cryptocrystalline aggregates which are formed by the devitrification of glassy material; also often used for the groundmass of porphyritic types.

felty

a textural term used for dense holocrystalline igneous rocks, or the dense holocrystalline groundmass of porphyritic igneous rocks consisting of tightly and flatly pressed microlites. These are generally feldspar, interwoven in an irregular manner.

fen

a mire resulting from groundwater rather than precipitation.

fenester (fenster)

a tectonic 'window' through which rocks below a thrust sheet have been exposed by erosion.

fengshan

a Cambrian succession in China covering the upper part of the Dolgellian.

fenite

the rocks surrounding a carbonatite plug commonly show metasomatic alternation, especially the development of nepheline. Fenites commonly have nepheline perthite, and aegirine, and often exhibit a gneissose texture.

feral relief

a landscape in which valley sides are deeply dissected by insequent streams, related to rapid runoff.

ferric

containing trivalent iron. Ferric salts are usually yellow or brown in colour.

ferricrete (laterite)

an iron-rich duricrust often formed in deep weathering profiles in humid tropical and subtropical conditions.

ferroaluminium

an alloy of aluminium (up to 80%) and iron.

ferroboron

an alloy of iron and boron that is added to steel to make it hard.

ferrogabbro

a gabbro rock in which the pyroxene and olivine constituents have a high iron content.

ferromagnesian

containing iron and magnesium.

ferromagnesian mineral

rock-forming silicate mineral having essential iron and/or magnesium. It is a convenient group-name which is used for the common minerals olivine, hypersthene, augite, hornblende, and biotite.

ferroselite

rock forming silicate minerals which contain magnesium and/or iron.

ferrous

ferrous describes something that is made of the metal iron, or that contains iron. A ferrous metal is a metal which contains a large amount of iron.

fertilizer

fertilizer is a chemical or mixture of chemicals added to soil to make it more fertile. Compost and manure are forms of natural fertilizer.

festoon bedding

refers to a type of cross-bedding in which deposition occurs in small troughs and gulleys, the bedding surfaces of the sediments being approximately parallel to the walls of the trough.

fetch

the extent of open water across which a wave-generating wind blows, determining the height and energy, and hence the erosional and depositional potential, of the waves.

fibre growth

a slickenside formation mechanism in which elongate crystals grow on a fault surface in the movement direction.

fibrous fracture

the fracture seen in minerals giving a fibrous appearance.

field geology

that part of geology that is practised by direct observation in the field.

fines

very small particles in a mixture of particles of various sizes. The term is also used for finely crushed ore, mineral, or coal.

fingerlakian

a stratigraphic stage name which is used for the base of the North American Upper Devonian.

finite strain (total strain)

the total change in shape of a deformed body relatively to its shape before deformation.

fireclay

a fossil soil of aragillaceous type in association with coal seams. It finds use as a refractive material.

fire damp

a combustible gas contained in coal comprising a mixture of methane and other hydrocarbons.

fire opal

a variety of opal with a brilliant orange colour.

firn line

the line dividing the ablation area of a glacier from the accumulation area. It is also known as firm limit.

firnification

the process of transformation of snow into firn and then into ice in a glacier.

first arrival (first break)

the earliest seismic signal to be recorded from a particular seismic source.

fissure eruption

the eruption of magma at several points along an elognate volcanic conduct. cf. central eruption.

fissure vein

a mineral deposit of vein like shape, characterized by clearly defined walls as opposed to extensive country-rock replacement.

fjord

a fjord is a deep inlet of the sea with steep mountain slopes on each side. Fjords are found on hilly or mountainous coasts. They were formed when the sea flooded river valleys caused by glaciers.

flaggy

1. of bedding, consisting of strata 10-100 centimetres in thickness. 2. Of rock, tending to split into layers of suitable thickness (1-5 centimetres) for use as flagstones.

flagstone

1. a hard, thin-bedded sandstone, firm shale, or other rock that splits easily along bedding planes or joints into flat slabs.

2. a piece of flagstone used for making pavement or covering the side of a house.

flamboyant structure

the optical continuity of crystals or grains as disturbed by a structure that is divergent.

flandrian

a stratigraphic stage name which is used for the British and European postglacial Pleistocene.

flandrian transgression

the rise in sea level during Holocene and late Pleistocene times caused by the melting of ice sheets of the last glacial.

flasconite

an igneous rock of gabbro clan; a dark grey, compact porhyritic extrusive rock; contains phenocrysts of augite, leucite, anorthite, olivine, biotite, magnetite and apatite.

flaser

streaky layer of parallel, scaly aggregates that surrounds the lenticular bodies of granular material in flasher structure; caused by pressure and shearing during metamorphism.

flaser gabbro

a cataclastic gabbro that contains augen of feldspar or quartz surrounded by flakes of mica or chlorite.

flaser structure

1. a metamorphic structure in which small lenses and layers of granular material are surrounded by a matrix of sheared, crushed material, resembling a crude flow structure. Also known as pachoidal structure.

2. a primary sedimentary structure consisting of fine-sand or silt lenticles that are aligned and cross-bedded.

flash

a water-filled depression caused by surface subsidence.

flat

a more or less horizontal ore bedy which is characteristically replacing a bedded sediment, generally limestone. A crosscutting vein which acted as a feeder may sometimes be seen. Flats commonly take place at the junction between layers of differing lithology.

flaxeed ore

iron ore composed of disk-shaped oölites that have been partially flattened parallel to the bedding plane.

flexural flow

a fold mechanism in which there is layer-parallel shear in the fold limbs without distortion in the hinge zone.

flinn diagram

a graph used to illustrate and analyse the shapes of strain ellipsoids. cf. Hsu diagram.

flint

variety of chalcedony; contains mainly granular chalcedony with small proportion of opal silica and sometimes organic remains. Also known as firestone.

flint clay

a hard, smooth, flintlike fireclay; when it is ground, it develops no platicity, and it breaks with conchoidal gracture.

flocculation

the change taking place when the disposed phase of a colloid forms a series of discrete particles which could settle out from the dispersion medium in geological processes, flocculation is almost inevitably occurring as a result of a colloidal solution mixing with a solution containing electrolytes, e.g., sea water.

floe

a sheet of floating ice, smaller than an ice field; found especially on the surface of the Arctic sea.

floe till

1. a glacial till resulting from the intact deposition of a grounded iceberg in a lake bordering an ice sheet.

2. a lacustrine clay with boulders, stones, and other glacial matter dropped into it by melting icebergs. Also known as berg till.

flood

a flood is a sudden rise in

water level. It covers land that is usually dry. Floods may happen on low-lying land near the coast when there are high tides and strong winds.

flood lava

a lava flow contributing to a plateau lava.

floodplain

the relatively smooth valley floors adjacent to and formed by alluviating rivers which are subject to overflow.

flora

flora is the word used for all of the plants of a particular region or a particular time. The tropical rain forests have the richest flora on Earth.

flour gold

the very finest-grained placer gold.

flowage

refers to the deformation which is formed by the stressing of material beyond its elastic limit, i.e., irreversible deformation. For example the thinning of incompetent beds over crests of anticlines.

flowage line

a contour line at the edge of a body of water, such as a reservoir, representing a given water level.

flow banding

an igneous rock structure resulting from flowing of magmas or lavas and characterized by alternation of mineralogically unlike layers.

flow breccia

a breccia formed with the movement of lava flow while the flow is still in motion.

flow cast

one of the group of bedding plane structures formed in graywacke.

flow cleavage

rock cleavage in which solid flow of rock accompanies recrystallization. Also known as slaty cleavage.

flow fold

folding in beds, composed of relatively plastic rock, that assume any shape impressed upon them by the more rigid surrounding rocks or by the general stress pattern of the deformed zone; there are no apparent surfaces of slip.

flow regime

a classification of flows based on the frictional resistance experienced.

flow structure

the structure which arises when directional movement of a liquid (e.g., a lava) having crystals causes these crystals to take up a parallel orientation. If the result is mineralogical or textural banding, the structure is known as flow banding, as is seen in many rhyolites.

flume

1. a deep, narrow gorge containing a turbulent stream.
2. an apparatus used to reconstruct and study fluid flow and sediment transport.

flourescene

the property of emitting light

when light of a certain wavelength is absorbed.

fluorine

fluorine is an element. It is a yellow gas which is found naturally in the mineral fluorite. Sodium fluoride is a fluorine compound which is sometimes added to drinking water. It helps teeth to grow strong.

fluorspar

material with sufficient fluorite to be exploited commercially.

flute cast

a raised, oblong, or subconical welt on the bottom surface of a siltstone or sandstone bed formed by the filling of a flute.

fluted

having a channelled or grooved structure or texture.

fluvial (fluviatile)

pertaining to a river or stream.

fluvial sand

sand laid down by a river or stream.

fluvial soil

soil laid down by a river or stream.

fluviatile

resulting from river action.

fluxgate magnetometer

a continuous-reading magnetometer for measuring the strength of the geomagnetic field, now largely replaced by more modern instruments.

fluxing

making of a liquid phase in a ceramic body under heat treatment by melting low fusion components.

flysch

a term originated in Switzerland and applicable only to sediments associated with the Alpin orogeny. It is used to describe sediments which are produced by the erosion of uprising and developing fold structures, and are subsequently deformed by later stages in the development of these same fold structures.

focal sphere

a hypothetical sphere centred on an earthquake focus which facilitates representation of focal mechanism solution data on a sterogram.

focus

refers to the point of origin of an earthquake in the earth's crust.

fog

fog is the word used when thick clouds form at ground level. Fog develops when water vapour in the air cools below the dew point.

foid

a collective term used to denote the feldspathoid group of minerals.

fold

a curved or angular shape of an originally planar geological surface.

fold axial trace

the line of intersection of a fold axial surface with the topographic or some other defined surface.

fold culmination
an elevated zone on a fold hinge or crest which is of variable height, or a high point on a folded surface with dome-and-basin structure.
fold hinge line
the line in a folded surface linking the points of maximum curvature.
fold mountain
a fold mountain is a mountain which was formed from a fold in the rocks. The mountains of Scotland, Wales and Norway are fold mountains, and so are the Himalayas in Asia and the Pyrenees in Europe.
fold style
various geometric features of a fold profile considered useful in classification and indicating fold mechanism.
fold tightness
the definition of a fold in terms of the interlimb angle.
foliation
refers to parallel orientation of platy minerals or mineral banding in rocks.
folk classification
a scheme for the classification of limestone.
fondo
a term applied to the environment of sedimentation that lies on the deep floor of a water body.
footwall ramp
a ramp in which truncation of bedding or other datum surface is seen in the footwall.
foraminifera
protozoa having shells, which are commonly divided into parts. The shell may be made of calcite or arenaceous material. Most of the foraminifera are marine. They are valuable in stratigraphical correlation especially in the Tertiary.
forecast
a forecast tells people about what might happen in the future. The weather forecast gives information about future weather. The shipping forecast gives the weather at sea.
foredeep
a long, narrow depression that borders an orogenic belt, such as an island arc, on the convex side.
foredune
a coastal dune or ridge that is parallel to the shoreline of a large lake or ocean and is stabilized by vegetation.
foreland
an area marginal to an orogenic belt, towards which folds have been overfolded and thrusts have moved. The side from which the surface rocks have moved in the hinterland.
foreland basin (foredeep basin)
a tectonic basin on the foreland of an orogenic belt and genetically related to it, ascribed to flexure caused by the load of the belt.
forelimb
the limb of an asymmetric fold with the greater dip. cf.

backlimb.

forest

a forest is a large area of woodland. Many forests grow naturally and may be hundreds years old. Some forests are carefully planted and the wood is cut at intervals.

foreset bed

oen of a series of inclined symmetrically arranged layers of a cross-bedding unit formed by deposition of sediments that rolled down a steep frontal slope of a delta or dune.

foreshore

the zone that lies between the ordinary high-and low-watermarks and is daily traversed by the rise and fall of the tide. Also known as beach face.

form

refers to the group of faces which are generated from an initial face by the operation of the symmetry elements of a particular crystal class. All the faces comprising a form are always present together, except where the crystal is mal-developed. An open form is referred to an assemblage of faces which cannot enclose a volume of space, and hence cannot exist in the absence of a second form. A closed form is referred to as an assemblage of faces which can enclose a volume of space.

formation

a grouping of beds used in lithostratigraphy; the smallest unit mappable on a reasonable scale.

forsterite marble (ophicalcite)

a marble-like rock produced by the contact metamorphism of silica-bearing, dolomitic limestone.

fortunite

an igneous rock of the diorite clan; a brownish-grey, finegrained porphyritic extrusive rock; it contains phenocrysts of enstatite and bronzite with orthopyroxene and clinopyroxene, mica, feldspar and some glass.

fosse

a long and narrow depression between a glacier and the sides of its valley.

fossil

the term used for the organic remains, traces, or imprint of any organism preserved in the crust of the earth since sometime in the geological past.

fossil fuel

fossil fuel is fuel formed from the fossilized remains of plants. Peat, coal and natural gas are all fossil fuels. Fossil fuels contain carbon and are a good source of energy when burned.

fossil man

ancient man which got identified from prehistoric skeletal remains which are archeologically earlier than the Neolithic.

fossil record

all the remains of past animal and plant life found in rocks.

fourchite

an intrusive igneous rock comprising essential titanium-bearing augite and kaersutite in a matrix of analcite or glass.

foyaite

a nepheline syenite; mainly composed of potassium feldspar; it contains orthoclase, nepheline and hornblende with accessory pyroxene mica, iron ore and sodalite nosean, and zircon.

fractography

the study of fracture surfaces, which provides information on fracture propagation.

fracture

a crack, joint, or fault in a rock due to mechanical failure by stress. Also known as rapture.

fracture cleavage

cleavage that occurs in deformed but only slightly metamorphosed rocks along closely spaced, parallel joints and fractures.

fracture plane inclination

gradient or inclination of the plane of fracture formed in a reservoir formation.

fracture system

a stress-related group of contemporaneous fractures.

fracture toughness

a measure of the resistance of a material to brittle failure by the spreading of cracks.

fracture zone

an elongate zone on the deep-sea floor that is of irregular topography and often separates regions of different depths; frequently crosses and displaces the midoceanic ridge by faulting.

framestone

an authochtonous, organically-bound limestone in which the organisms formed a framework during deposition.

franconian

a North American stage of geologic time; the middle Upper Cambrian.

frasch process

a method of extracting subsurface native sulphur by melting it with hot water and blowing the melt to the surface.

frasnian

a stratigraphical stage name for the base of the European Upper Devonian.

free air correction

the correction applied to a gravity measurement to account for the decrease in gravity with height in free air. cf. Bouguer correction.

freestone

a fine-grained stone that can be cut and worked without fracturing.

freeze-thaw

freeze-thaw describes a kind of weathering. In freeze-thaw weathering, the water in rocks or soils freezes and then thaws repeatedly. Water exapnds when it freezes, so it enlarges any cracks in the rocks. Freeze-thaw action is most common

during cold weather in high mountains, and in the polar regions.

french chalk

a variety of talc with a compact form used to mark cloth or remove greases stains.

friable

capable of readily crumbled to a powdered form.

fringing reef

a coral reef attached directly to or bordering the shore of an island or continental landmass.

fritting

refers to the process by which a granular material gets coherent because of partial melting at grain contacts, or diffusion of material across grain contacts, causing adhesion. The process can take place either because of metamorphism or in the hotter parts of volcanic ash deposits.

frondelite

a mineral having basic manganese iron phosphate with proportion of manganese greater than ferric iron. Its crystals are orthorhombic botryoidal masses and crystals with a radial elongated fibrous or fine-columnar structure occurs. It colour has been found to vary from dark green or olivegreen to greenish-black in fresh material becoming brownishgreen or dark reddishbrown on oxidation. Its hardness on Mohs scale is 4.5.

front

a front describes **a** sharp change in the temperature of air. A warm front occurs at the edge of a mass of warm air and a cold front is found at the edge of a mass of cold air masses of different temperatures in the ocean.

frost

grangular or flaky deposit of ice crystals caused by sublimation of water vapour on a surface whose temperature is, below the freezing point of water.

frost action

refers to the weathering process which is caused by cycles of freezing and thawing of water in surface pores, cracks, and other openings.

frozen ground

soil having a temperature below freezing generally containing water in the form of ice. Also known as gelisol; merzlota; taele; tjaele.

fuchsite

a chrome-rich variety of muscovite.

fucoid

a tunnellike marking on a sedimentary structure identified as a trace fossil but not referred to a described genus.

fuel

fuel is any substance which is used to produce energy. Coal, gas and oil are fuels which are burned to obtain heat. Petroleum is another fuel, which is made from crude oil. Nuclear power stations use radioactive chemicals as fuel, usually a form of uranium.

fulgurite
a ramifying or branching tube having fused silica or silicates which is formed by the action of lightning striking sandy soil, e.g., dunes, beaches, etc.

fumarole
a volcanic vent, distinct from those erupting magma, from which volcanic gases escape.

fundamental strength
the maximum stress a material can sustain indefinitely at a given temperature and confining pressure.

funnel
a funnel is an opening in rocks, which is wide at the top and narrow at the bottom.

fusain
the local lithotype strands or patches which are characterized by silky lustre, fibrous structure, and black colour. It is constituent of bituminous coal; charcoal like substance consisting of fusinite. It is formed from alteration of wood in oxidising environment.

fusibility
the property of being capable of conversion from solid to liquid by heating.

fusiform
spindle-shaped; tapering toward the ends.

fusinization
refers to the process of formation of fusain in coal.

fusoclarain
a lithotype of banded coal intermediate between fusain and clarain.

fussain
the local lithotype strands or patches, characterized by silky lustre, fibrous structure, and black colour. It is a constituent of bituminous coal; charcoal like substance consisting of fusinite. It is extremely friable and easily reduced to fine powder. It is formed from alteration of wood in oxidising environment.

fasulinid limestone
a forminiferal limestone composed mainly of fusulinid tests.

gabbro
refers to a group of dark-coloured, intrusive igneous rocks having granular texture. It is composed largely of basic plagioclase (labradorite to anorthite, a pyroxene (augite and/ or hypersthene) and, very commonly divine in substantial amounts. Hornblende, biotite, and quartz may be present in accessory amounts, and magnetite and ilmenite are common accessories.

gabbrophyrite
an igneous rock of the gabbro clan; a prophy ritic plutonic rock, containing phenocrysts of basic plagioclase and sometimes pyroxene and/or olivine in fine-grained equigrangular holocrystalline groundmass of basic plagioclase, pyroxene and

magnetite with accessory biotite, hornblende and iron ores. It is also known as gabbro porphyry.

gahnite (zinc spinel) ($ZnAl_2O_4$)
a zinc-aluminium spinel found in crystaline schist, contact metamorphosed limestones, high temperature replacement ore deposits, granite pegmatites and placer deposits.

galaxite ($MnAl_2O_4$)
a rare, black manganese-aluminium spinel.

gale
a gale is a very strong wind. A gale breaks twigs from trees. A strong gale can damage buildings. A gale measures between forces 7 and 9 on the Beaufort Scale.

galena
it is a bluish-grey to lead-grey mineral having brilliant metallic lustre. It occurs in hydrothermal veins and as a replacement mineral.

gallery
a term used for a horizontal passage way in a cave, it is also used for a horizontal conduit or channel constructed to intercept water.

gamma ray spectometer
an instrument which measures gamma rays in a similar way to a scintillation counter, but which can discriminate between rays produced by uranium, thorium and potassium-40.

gangue
the valueless rock or aggregates of minerals in an ore.

ganister
sedimentary rock with high siliceous sandstone, and consists of medium to fine quartz grains cemented together with silica. It is found in compact form with fine and even grangular texture.

gannister
the term applied to arenaceous seat earth which is found below coal seams. It is a pure silica sand, which is low in alkalies, iron, and aluminium, and is having frequent carbonized traces of plant roots.

gard notation
a method of describing the unit cell relationship in polytypism.

garewaite
igneous rock of ultrabasic clan. A dark-coloured porphyritic hypabyssal rock, contains phenocrysts of corroded diopside in fine-grained hollo crystalline groundmass of olivine. pyroxene, chromite, and magnetite with accessory spinel and labradorite.

gargasian
a stratigraphic stage name which is used for the European Upper Aptian.

garnet
garnet is the name used for a group of minerals found mostly in metamorphic rocks. Garnet crystals are made of silicates of magnesium, aluminium, iron

and calcium. Dark red garnets are used as gems.

garronite $Na_2Ca_5Al_{12}.Si_{20}O_{64}.27H_2O$.
a zeolite mineral which belongs to phillipsite group. It crystallizes in the tetragonal system.

gas cap
free gas accumulated above an oil reservoir. It forms whenever the available gas exceeds the amount that will dissolve in the oil under the existing conditions of temperature and pressure.

gas cap drive
the pressure exerted by a gas cap as oil is removed from a reservoir which drives it towards the well.

gas-condensate reservoir
hydrocarbon reservoir in which conditions of temperature and pressure have resulted in the condensation of the heavier hydrocarbon constituents from the reservoir gas.

gaseous
gaseous is the word used to describe a substance when it is a gas. All substances change to a gaseous form when they reach a high enough temperature.

gaspeite Na_2CO_3
an anhydrous mineral having sodium carbonate with calcite structure.

gas pool
an accumulation of natural gas in a single reservoir and gas trap.

gas reservoir
an accumulation of natural gas found with or near accumulations of crude oil in the earth's crust.

gas spurt
an accumulation of organic matter on certain strata caused by escaping gas.

gas zone
a gas formation containing gas under a pressure large enough to force the gas out if tapped from the surface.

gault
a Cretaceous succession in England covering the upper part of the Albian.

geanticline
1. the term used for the broad uplifted area bordering a geosyncline which is supplying sediments for its infilling. 2. refers to a broad anticlinal uplift which develops within a geosyncline at an early stage of the orogenic phase. It is commonly associated with vulcanaism.

gehlenite $4[Ca_2Al_2SiO_7]$
a mineral which is composed of calcium aluminium silicate in which ferric iron is replacing aluminium and magnesium replacing calcium. It is brittle and exhibits imperfect cleavage in one direction. It hardness on Mohs scale is 5.5-6.5.

gel
the term used for a coagulated colloid of a jelly-like nature, i.e., a two-phase colloidal

system having a solid and a liquid in more solid form than a sol.

gelifuction

a type of solifluction taking place in periglacial environments underlain by permafrost.

gemology

refers to the scientific study which deals with the identification, evaluation, fashioning, and other aspects of gemstones.

general form

a crystal form which has no particular relationship with the symmetry operators present in the special form.

geniculate twin (knee twin)

a twin in which the twin plane changes the crystal shape so that it has the appearance of a knee joint.

genus

a category in plant and animal classification between family and species.

geo

1. a narrow coastal inlet which is bordered by steep cliffs.
2. a prefix which denotes earth.

geochemical anomaly

an abnormal concentration of elements with respect to the background level.

geochemical facies

the region characterized by particular physiocochemical conditions that effect the production and accumulation of sediments.

geochemistry

the study of the chemical composition of the various phases of the earth and the physical and chemical processes which have produced the observed distribution of the elements and nuclides in these phases.

geochesnical cycle

refers to a circle which results from a consideration of the way in which an element, commencing in a primary magma, may circulate through a sequence of geocriemical environments. As shown, the cycle for an individual element may he much more complicated.

geochemistry

deals with the study of chemical composition of the various phases of the earth and the physical and chemical processes which have produced the observed distribution of the elements and nuclides it these phases.

geochronology

1. the dating of the events in the earth's history. 2. a system of dating developed for the purposes of study of the earth's history.

geochronometry

the study of the absolute age of the rocks of the earth based on the radioactive decay of isotopes, such as U^{238}, U^{235}, Th^{232}, Rb^{87}, K^{40}, and C^{14}, present in minerals and rocks.

geocosmogony

the study of the origin of the earth.

geode

a roughly spheroidal, hollow body lined inside with inward-projecting, small crystals; found frequently in limestone beds but may occur in shale.

geodesy

the branch of science which deals with determination of size and shape of the earth and precise location of points on its surface.

geodynamics

the branch of science that deals with the forces, and processes of the earth's interior.

geographer

a geographer is someone who studies or practises geography.

geography

geography is the study of the Earth's surface. Physical geography includes the Earth's climate, vegetation and oceans. Human geography looks at the peoples of the world and their environments. Mathematical geography studies the size, shape and movements of the Earth.

geoid

the equipotential surface of the gravitational field of the Earth represented by the sea level surface, usually taken as the datum plane in gravity reduction.

geological survey

means an examination of the geology of an area. A survey is generally depicted in the form of a geological map and sections, and a report.

geological transportation

the term used for the shifting of material by the action of moving air, ice, or water.

geologic column

refers to the vertical sequence of the strata of various ages found in an area or region. Also, refers to geologic time scale as represented by rocks.

geologic high

an oil-fiel term for a structure on which rocks occur at a higher positions than in the surrounding area.

geologic province

an area in which geologic history has been the same.

geologic section

any succession of rock units found at the surface or below ground in an area. Also known as section.

geologic structure

the total structure features in an area.

geologic time

the period of time covered by historical geology, from the end of the formation of the earth as a separate planet to the beginning of written history.

geologic time scale

the relative age of various geologic periods and the absolute time intervals.

geologist

an individual who specializes in the geological sciences.

geology

geology is the study of the Earth. Different branches of geology deal with the Earth's history, the movements that take place within it, the materials it is made from and the shapes of these materials. Geology also studies the plants and animals that have lived on Earth throughout the different ages.

geomagnetic dipole field
the 80% of the geomagnetic field that can be ascribed to the field of a single, fictitius, magnetic dipole. cf. geomagnetic nondipole field.

geomagnetic event (geomagnetic excursion)
a short period of constant geomagnetic polarity, usually < 10,000 years.

geomagnetic reversal
a change of the earth's magnetic field between normal polarity and reversed polarity.

geomagnetism
geomagnetism is the magnetism of the Earth. It is caused by the metals at the core of the Earth, which act like a huge magnet. These metals, which are mainly iron and nickel, set up a magnetic field around the Earth.

geomorphic
concerning the form of the Earth or its surface features.

geomorphic cycle
refers to the cycle of the change in the surface configuration of the earth. It is also known as cycle of erosion; geographical cycle.

geomorphology
1. deals with the study of the origin of secondary topographic features which are carved by erosion in the primary elements and built up of the erosional debris.
2. Refers to the description and interpretation of land forms.

geopetal
pertaining to top-to-bottom relations in rocks at the time of formation.

geophysical anomaly
a perturbation from the norms in a measured field, usually resulting from a change in the physical properties of the subsurface, e.g. gravity anomaly, magnetic anomaly. In order to be able to recognize such anomalies, all non-geological sources of variation in the field are removed by a reduction process.

geophysics
the physics of the earth and its environment, that is, earth, air, and space.

geopressurized geothermal system
a geothermal system dominated by the presence of hot fluids under high pressure and having higher-than-normal temperatures because of their low thermal conductivity, the presence of interbedded shale layers, or the existence of local, exothermic chemical reactions.

georges banks
an elevation beneath the sea east of Cape Cod, Mass.

georgiaite
any of a group of North American tektites, 134 million years of age, found in Georgia.

georgian
obsolete stratigraphic stage name which is used for the North American Lower Cambrian.

georgiev
a Jurassic succession in W Siberia equivalent to the Kimmeridgian.

geosere
a series of ecological climax communities following each other in geologic time and changing in response to changing climate and physical conditions.

geosphere
1. the solid mass of earth, as distinct from the atmosphere and hydrosphere. 2. the lithosphere, hydrosphere, and atmosphere combined.

geostatic pressure
refers to the vertical pressure at a point in the earth's crust which is caused by the weight of the overlying rock.

geosynclines
refers to the major structural and sedimentational units of the crust of the earth. They comprise of elongated basins which get filled with very great thicknesses of sediment, and because of this fact, progressive subsidence of the basin floor must have taken place. Volcanic rocks occur intercalated with sediments.

geotectonic
relating to major Earth structures, such as orogenic belts, cratons, basins, and the processes forming them.

geothermal
refers to the heat of the interior of the earth.

geothermal energy
the energy that can be recovered from the earth's internal heat.

geothermal field
an area of high heat flow that can produce geothermal energy.

geothermal gradient
refers to the rate of increase of temperature in the earth with depth. It varies from place to place depending on the heat flow in the region and the thermal conductivity of the rocks.

geyser
the term used for a natural spring or fountain that is discharging a column of superheated water or steam into the air at almost regular intervals. Some of the examples of geyser regions are Iceland, New Zealand, and the Yellowstone National Park, Wyoming, U.S.A.

geyser basin
a valley that contains numerous springs, geysers and steaming fissures fed by the same groundwater flow.

ghost reflection
a seismic multiple generated by a seismic reflection at the base of the weathered layer.

ghost stratigraphy
in certain granite masses there are large numbers of xenoliths which, when mapped exhibit a continuation of the stratigraphy and structure of the country rocks to a remarkable degree. In some cases the xenoliths are able to even maintain their correct orientation. This phenomenon is termed as ghost stratiraphy, and is often considered as an evidence in favour of the formation of granite by the replacement of country rock.

gilbertite
a flourine-rich variety of muscovite.

gipping
a stratigraphic stage name which is used for the base of the British upper Pleistocene.

girdle distribution
a pattern of points around a great circle on a sterogram.

givetien
a Devonian succession in France and Belgium covering the lower part of the Givetian.

glabella
refers to the bony prominence on the frontal bone which joins the supraorbital ridges.

glacial
refers to an interval of geologic time which got marked by an equatorward advance of ice during an ice age.

glacial advance
increase in the thickness and area of a glacier.

glacial breaching
glacial breaching is said to take place when the volume of ice in a glacier increases to a point where the original valley system can no longer have it and the pre-glacial watersheds get breached by the escaping ice.

glacial deposit
a sedimentary feature deposited by a glacier, composed mainly of till. Includes braids, drumlins, eskers, kames, moraine and sandurs.

glacial lobe
a large tongue-like protrusion from the margin of an ice sheet.

glacial retreat
a condition in which backward melting at the front of a glacier takes place at a rate exceeding forward motion.

glaciation
glaciation is the way in which land is shaped by ice. Thick layers of ice move slowly over hills and mountains. The ice gouges out the soil and rocks. Glaciantion is also the name for the times in geological history when ice covered the Earth.

glacier
a mass of land ice, which is formed by the further recrystallization of firm and is flowing slowly from an accumulation area to an area

of ablation.
The main types of glaciers are:
(i) Mountain or valley glaciers, are those glaciers whose source is the snow which is lying in that part of the mountain range above the snowline.
(ii) piedmont glaciers, are those which develop when valley glaciers emerge from their confining channels and spread out over a lowland area.

glacier flood
refers to a sudden release of meltwater from a glacier or glacier-dammed lake which is formed by the melting of a drainage channel or by subglacial volcanic activity. It may produce catastrophic flood.

glacier milk
a stream of turbid, whitish melt-water containing rock flour in suspension.

glaciofluvial
pertaining to streams fed by melting glaciers, or to the deposits and landforms produced by such streams.

glaclolacustrine
pertaining to lakes fed by melting glaciers, or to the deposits forming therein.

glaclology
the study of existing or modern glaciers in their entirety.

gladkaite
igneous rock of the diorite clan. A fine-grained hypabyssal rock; contains plagioclase (oligoclase to andesine) abundant quartz, hornblende and a little biotite with accessory magnetite and apatite and secondary muscovite and epidote.

glance pitch
a variety of asphaltite having brilliant conchoidal fracture, and resembling gilsonite but having higher specific gravity and percentage of fixed carbon.

glass
refers to igneous rock constituent, the cryptocryst alline or amorphous material which represents the final phase of magma consolidation takes place as part of the groundmass; may also form extrusive igneous rocks when rapid chilling takes place.

glassy
glassy or vitreous, substances are solids with absolutely no crystalline structure. Rare geologically but can be formed by a variety of processes.

glassy rock
a rock consisting partly or wholly of glass, usually formed when magma is quenched too rapidly for crystallization to occur, but also forming in a fault rock by dynamic metamorphism (pseudotachylite) or by thermal metamorphism (buchite).

glauchroite ($CaMnSiO_4$)
a rare manganese-bearing olivine.

glauconitic sandstone
a quartz sandstone or an arkosic sandstone that has many glacuonite grains.

gley
a sticky subsurface layer of clay in some waterlogged soils.

glide twinning
twinning that occurs when a stress forces part of a crystal to move into a twin-related orientation.

glimmerite
an ultrabasic rock which consists almost entirely of the micas phlogopite and/or biotite.

global
global describes something which affects the whole Earth. An animal or plant that is found throughout the world has a global distribution. Global warming heats up the climate of the whole Earth.

global tectonics
tectonics on a global scale, such as tectonic processes associated with the very large-scale movement of material.

globlgerina ooze
a pelagic sediment consisting of more than 30% calcium carbonate in the form of foraminiferal tests of which Globigerina is the dominant genus.

globulite
a small, isotropic, globular of spherulelike crystallite; usually dark in colour and found in glassy extrusive rocks.

glomeroporphyritic
refers to porphyritic texture in which groups of crystals (either all of the same mineral or of different minerals) get scattered through a finergrained ground mass. It is also known as cumulophyric.

glomeroporphyritic texture
the texture of a rock containing glomerocrysts.

gloss coal
the highest rank lignite; black and compact with a conchoidal fracture and glossy lustre.

gloup
an opening in the roof of a sea cave.

gnamma
a basin on a rock surface, especially ingeous rock and sandstone, produced by weathering.

gneiss
the term used for a variety of rocks having a banded or coarsely foliated structure which is formed by regional metamorphism; included under this heading are a number of rock types which have different origins.

gneissic granodiorite
any of the grandiorite rock with gneissic characteristics.

gobl
sedimentary deposits in a synclinal basin.

gold
gold is an element. It is a soft, bright yellow metal. Gold is rare and valuable and does not react easily with other chemicals.

gold dust
fine specks of gold found in placer deposits.

gondite

high grade regional metamorphic rock. A fine-grained granular rock; contains spessartite, quartz and apatite.

gondwanalad (gondwana)

the southern supercontinent, comprising Africa, Malagasy, India, Sri Lanka, Australasia, Antarctica and South America, which probably formed over 2000 million years ago and began to split some 180 million years ago.

gondwana series

refers to the stratigraphic name for the Indian equivalent of the Karroo Series.

goniometer

a device which is a used for measuring the angles between crystal faces. Two main types in use are as follows;

(i) the contact goniometer, is used with large crystals. It consists of a protractor with a pivoted arm which is kept in contact with crystal faces. Results are, in general, of a low order of accuracy.

(ii) the optical goniometer is suitable for small crystals having brilliant reflecting faces.

gordumite

igneous rock of the ultrabasic clan. A coarse-grained porphytric plutonic rock, massive with indistinct schistosity contains pseudo-phenocrysts of accessory picotite magnetite and rutilè needles.

gorge

refers to a narrow passage between mountains or the walls of canyon, especially one having steep and rocky walls.

gossan

a rusty, ferruginous deposit filling the upper regions of mineral veins and overlying a sulphide deposit. It is formed by the oxidation of pyrites. This process occasionally concentrates highly insoluble elements, such as gold in the gossan.

gothlandian

a stratigraphic name (from the Island of Gothland, Sweden). It is a synonym of Silurian, and was formerly used by Continental authors. It is now obsolete.

grab sample

a random, possibly hurried, sample of mineralized ground with no statistical validity, taken simply to check the type of mineralization.

grade

refers to the slope of the bed of a stream, or of a surface over which water is flowing, upon which the current can just transport its load without either eroding or depositing.

gradient

a gradient is a measure of slope. High up a hill or mountain, the gradient usually becomes steeper.

gradiometer

an instrument measuring the horizontal or vertical gradient

of a potential field, most commonly applied to magnetic survey.

grain

the discrete crystals or particles making up a rock or sediment.

grain fall lamination

a lamination produced in an aeolian system by the fall of sand from suspension in zones of flow separation, i.e. as forest and toeset stratification.

grampian event

a major episode of deformation in Scotland in the Cambrian.

granite aplite

type of aplite with a granitic composition.

granite clan

Igneous rocks having at least 66 per cent silica and an average of 30 per cent quartz. Also have alkalifeldspar and plagioclase with numerous ferromagnesian minerals.

granite-greenstone terrain

a type of Archean crust composed of associated granite batholiths and greenstone belts, typically in the greenschist facies.

granite porphyry

a hypabyssal rock characterised by sparse phenocrysts of mica, amphibole or pyroxene in a medium-to-fine-grained groundmass.

granite series

a scheme pospelated by Read to present the relationships in time and space of the various types of granite.

granitic layer

an outmoded term for the upper continental crust, cf. basaltic layer.

granitization

1. refers to a process whereby various types of rock get converted to granite or closely related material.

2. the name assigned to a group of theories which have a common basis that pre-existing rock can be transformed to granite or granite magma by the action of energetic fluids of appropriate composition arising from the depths.

granoblastic

a term originally applicable to metamorphic rocks which are equigranular. The term is also applicable to diagenetic processes which give rise to an equigranular texture by recrystallization.

granophyre

a fine- to medium- grained, commonly porphyritic, acidic felsic rock characterized by a groundmass containing intergrown quartz and alkali feldspar.

granophyric texture

small-scale graphic texture.

granular texture

refers to the texture of a rock which consists of mineral grains of approximately equal size.

granule

a somewhat rounded rock

fragment ranging in diameter from 2 to 4 millimetres; larger than a coarse sand grain and smaller than a pebble.

granulite

1. granite having musconite. 2. a metamorphic rock of regional metamorphic origin, which has a granular texture. It usually consists of fieldspars, pyroxenes, and garnets. Streaked or banded varieties are known as laptites.

granulite-gneiss belt

a very highgrade metamorphic rock association of the Archaen made up of quartzite, limestone, pelite, bedded iron formation, amphibolite and layered anorthosite complexes.

grapestone

a cluster of sand-size grains, such as calcareous pellets, held together by incipient cementation shortly after deposition; the outer surface is lumpy, resembling a bunch of grapes.

graphic texture

in certain pegmatites, granites and micrograpnites and more rarely in other rocks, there occurs an intergrowth of quartz an alkali feldspar which present on flat surfaces the appearance of Hebrew, cuneiform, runic or hieroglyphic writing. This results from the simultaneous crystallization of the two minerals, in many cases (but not always) from a eutectic mixture. Small scale graphic texture is called micrographic or granophric texture.

graphite

refers to a soft black allotropic form of native carbon, C (hexagonal), which is found in metamorphic rocks, crystalline limestone, igneous rocks, veins and pegmatities. Its hardness on Mohs scale is 1-2, and is sectile and light in weight. It can be recognized by its softness, feel and weight and is distinguished from molybdnite by its black streak.

graphitization

the conversion of amorphous carbon to graphite by heat.

graptolite shale

shale having an abundance of extinct colonial marine organisms called graptolites.

grassland

a grassland is a region where grass is the main kind of plant. Large grasslands are found in East Africa and in parts of central Asia. Grasslands occur where there is not enough rainfall for trees to grow well.

gratonite Pb_9 AS_4 S_{15}

a grey mineral composed of lead arsenic sulphide; occurs as prismatic crystals as well as massive; brittle fracture and shows no cleavage. Its hardness on Mohs scale is 2.5.

gravel

a loose or unconsolidated deposit of rounded pebbles, cobbles, or boulders.

gravel bank

a natural mound or exposed face of gravel, particularly such a place from which gravel is dug.

gravimeter (gravity meter)
a small, portable instrument for measuring changes in gravity.

gravitational force
the force on a body due to its gravitational attraction on other bodies.

gravity (acceleration due to gravity, g)
the acceleration experienced by an object under the influence of the Earth's mass according to Newton's law of gravitation. The measurement of small variations in gravity forms the basis of a geophysical exploration method.

gravity log
a geophysical borehole log in which a specialized gravimeter is read remotely down a borehole in order to provide density information on the formations it penetrates.

gravity separation
refers to the separation of immiscible phases by allowing the denser phase to settle out under the influence of gravity.

gravity survey
a survey in which variation in gravity is measured in order to locate and define subsurface bodies of anomalous density.

gravity tectonies
refers to the operation of gravitational forces to produce faulting, thrusting, and folding by the movement of the cover down the slope of an uplifted region.

graywacke
an argillaceous sandstone which is characterized by an abundance of unstable mineral and rock fragments and a fine-grained clay matrix binding the larger, sandsize detrital fragments. Graywackes, often have irregularities on the bedding planes.

great circle
a circle corresponding to a circumference of a sphere. cf. small circle.

greenhouse effect
the greenhouse effect is a theory which describes the gradual warming of the atmosphere of the Earth. The greenhouse effect is thought to be caused by the build-up of carbon dioxide and methane in the atmosphere. These gases prevent heat escaping from the Earth's surface and the lower part of the atmosphere.

green mud
oceanic argillaceous deposit containing decrial material enriched with glauconite and choleite.

greensand
1. sandstone which is composed of greensand with little or no cement.
2. A lithostratigraphic unit of the Cretaceous in Britain and north-west Europe.

greenschist
a green, schistose,

metamorphic rock coloured green due to the presence of chlorite, epidote or actinolite.

greenstone

a field term which is used for any slightly altered basic igneous rock, e.g., diabase epidiorite, etc.

greenwich meridian

the greenwich meridian is an imaginary line around the Earth's surface. It joins the North Pole and South Pole and crosses the Equator at a right angle. Meridians are a measure of longitude. The Greenwich meridian is 0 degrees longitude. All the other meridians are measured in degrees from the greenwich meridian. The meridian takes its name from greenwich in the British Isles, through which it passes.

greisen

a rock formed granite by the action of flurine rich gases. The feldspar gets altered to muscovite and fluorine rich minerals are formed forming a crumbly white or grey rock having essentially of muscovite and quartz with topaz and fluorite.

greisenization

1. the process of greisen formation.

2. flourine metasomatism.

grenville

refers to a stratigraphic division of the Canadian Precambrian Lower Ontarian.

greywacke (graywacke)

old term for an immature sandstone with > 15% clay minerals.

grike (gryke, klufarren)

a trough separating clients in a limestone pavement, developing in response to solutional widening.

griquaite

a hypabyssal rock having garnet and diopside, and sometimes olivine or phlogopite. It occurs in kimberlite pipes and dikes.

grit

1. a hard, sharp granule, as of sand. 2. a coarse sand.

groove casts

refer to the rounded or sharp, crested, rectilinear ridges that are a few millimetres high and a few centimetres long. They are found on the undersurfaces of sandstone layers which are lying on mudstone.

grossular ($Ca_3Al_2Si_3O_{12}$)

a garnet, frequently found in metamorphosed impure calcareous rocks.

ground frost

ground frost describes a frost which only freezes the surface of the ground. A ground rost is a light frost which usually does little damage to growing plants.

groundmass

refers to the fine-grained material which constitutes the main body of a rock, in which is set larger units. In porphyritic texture, for example, the larger phenocrysts have been set in a fine-grained groundmass.

ground moraine

rock material carried and deposited in the base of a glacier. Also known as bottom moraine; subglacial moraine.

ground morine

rock material carried and deposited in the base of a galcier.

ground roll

the large amplitude oscillation of the ground in the vicinity of an explosion, caused by Rayleigh waves.

ground water

water which is occupying openings, cavities, and spaces in rocks. There are two main sources of such water: juvenile water, which is rising from a deep, magmatic source, and meteoric water, which is due to rainfall having soaked into the under-laying rock.

group velocity

the velocity of the energy in a signal suffering dispersion.

growth fault (synsedimentary fault)

a fault along which movement is contemporaneous with sedimentation.

grus

an accumulation of poorly, sorted, angular rock fragments formed during the weathering of crystalline rocks, particularly granite.

gruss

a loose accumulation of fragmental products formed from the weathering of granite. Also spelled grus.

guadalupian

a stratigraphic stage name which is used for the North American Middle Permian.

guano

phosphatic deposit. Greyish brown. Contains calcium phosphate and various nitrates and carbonates. Compact or friable.

gully

a gully is a narrow channel in rock or in the soil. Gullies are usually formed by erosion. Water may make a gully by wearing away soft earth or rock.

gumbo

a special type of soil which is able to yield a characteristic sticky mud when wet.

gumboti

deoxidized, leached clay that contains siliceous stones.

gumbotil

a clay-rich glacial deposit or leached glacial deposit which is having gumbo properties.

günz-Mindel

the first interglacial stage of the Pleistocene in the Alps, between Günz and Mindel glacial stages.

gushan

a Cambrian succession in China covering parts of the Menevian and Maentwrogian.

gutter

a linear depression in a sediment surface caused by the erosion associated with vortices in the flow.

guyot
a seamount, usually deeper than 100 fathoms, having a smooth platform top. Also known as tablemount.

gymnocodiaceae
a group of calcareous algae with vegetative structure similar to green algae, but with sporangia resembling red algae. Range Permian-Cretaceous.

gypsite
a variety of gypsum consisting of dirt and sand; found as an efflorescent deposit in arid regions, overlying gypsum. Also known as gypsum earth.

gypsum $CaSO_4.2H_2O$
a monoclinic mineral having hydrated sulphate of calcium. It is found in clays and limestones, sometimes associated with sulphur.

gyroconic
descriptive of a gastropod shell which coils loosely.

gyttja
a fresh-water anaerobic mud containing an abundance of organic matter; capable of supporting aerobic life.

gzelian
the youngest epoch of the Carboniferous, 295.1-290.0 million years.

habit
1. the relative development of individual crystal forms and faces.
2. the typical appearance of an organism.

habitat
refers to the environment in which a plant or animal lives.

habit plane
refers to the crystallographic plane or system of planes along which phenomena like twinning take place.

hachure
a short line at some angle to contours, used to denote slopes of the ground in geologic maps.

hackly fracture
a fracture with jagged, sharp-edged surfaces.

hacksaw structure
the irregular, saw-toothed termination of a crystal or mineral particle due to intrastratal situation.

hade
the angle which a fault plane is making with the vertical plane.

haematization (hematization)
the replacement of the hard parts of an organism by haematite. cf. pyritization.

hail
hail is frozen raindrops. The ice pieces in hail are called hailstones. Hailstones may be as large as 5 centimetres in diameter.

hairpin
an abrupt change in the direction of an apparent polar wandering path, usually indicative of a continent-continent collision.

hairstone
quartz embedded with hairlike

crystals of rutile, actinolite, or other mineral.

half-width

the horizontal distance over which a spatial function decays to half its maximum value. Particularly used for magnetic and gravity anomalies, as it can be used to estimate the limiting depth of the causative body.

halite NaCl

it is native salt, which occurs in massive granular compact or cubic-crystalline forms. Its crystal are grown by slowly evaporating a concentrated salt solution.

halmyrolysis

the geochemical reaction of sea-water and sediments in an area of little or no sedimentation.

halocline

the interface between dense seawater and lighter freshwater in an estuary or between waters of different salinity within a water column.

hamagian

a stage of the Ordovician, 462.3-457.5 million years.

hammada

a plateau in a desert region having a rocky surface which is denuded by wind erosion.

hamra

a red, sandy soil with a high clay content found in desert regions.

hamrongite

an igneous rock of the granite clan; a fine grained porphyritic hypabyssal rock. It contains phenocrysts of biotite in a groundmass of quartz, biotite and andesine.

hanging wall

refers to the rock mass above a fault plane, vein, load, ore body, or other structure. It is also known as hanging side

hangingwall ramp

a ramp in which bedding or datum surfaces are seen in the hangingwall.

hardpan

a hard, impervious layer of soil clay cemented by insoluble materials. Also known as caliche.

hard water

hard water is water which contains large amounts of dissolved calcium and magnesium salts. Hard water is often found in limestone areas.

harker diagram

a variation diagram which shows the chemical relationships of a suite of rocks by plotting constituents against silica content.

harmonic folding

refers to folding in the surface of the earth having no sharp changes with depth in the form of the folds.

harringtonite

amorphous chalky white mixture of mesolite and thomosolite from Country Antrim in Northern Ireland.

harzburgite

an ultrabasic rock which is

composed of olivine and orthopyroxene.

hastings beds

a Cretaceous succession in England covering part of the Berriasian and the Valanginian.

haumurian

a Cretaceous succession in New Zealand covering the upper part of the Campanian and the Maastrichtian.

hausmannite Mn_3O_4

a brownish-black, opaque mineral which belongs to spinel group of minerals.

hauterivian

a European stage of geologic time; in the Lower Cretaceous, above Valanginian and below Barremian.

hauyne $(Na,Ca)_{4-8}(Al_6Si_6O_{24})(SO_4,S)_{1-2}$

an isometric silicate mineral of the sodalite group occurring as grains embedded in various igneous rocks. Its hardness on Mohs scale is 5.5-6.0. Also known as hauynite.

hawaiite

name assigned to andesine basalts due to the wide occurrence of these rocks on the Hawaii Islands.

hawleyite (CdS)

a sulphide mineral of the sphalerite group.

haydenite

yellow crystalline variety of chabazite.

hazel sandstone

an arkosic, iron-bearing redbed sandstone from the Precambrian found in western Texas.

head loss

a lowering of the water level, e.g. in an aquifer.

headwall erosion

erosion of the headwall of a ravine after gullying has been initiated, which can occur at very rapid rates.

heat flow

refers to the rate at which heat has been lost from the inner zones of the earth to the atmosphere. The average value has been found to be 1.25×10^{-6} calories per cm^2 per second, but higher values have been found in some areas of the ocean basins which it may be due to uprising convection currents in the mantle.

heave

refers to the measure of the horizontal displacement between the upthrown sides of a fault.

heavy mineral

a mineral with a specific gravity greater than 2.85, i.e. which sinks in bromoform.

heazlewoodite (Ni_3S_2)

a sulphide mineral of the metal excess group.

hectare

a hectare is a metric unit of measurement. It measures area. One hectare is equal to 10,000 square metres.

hedreocraton

a craton that influenced later continental development.

hedrumite

an igneous rock of the syenite clan, a fine to medium-grained porphyritic hypabyssal rock; contains phenocrysts of microperthite and lepidomelane in a groundmass of microperthite, nepheline, analcine, algirine, lepidomelane and hornblende.

helderbergian

a North American stage of geologic time, in the lower Lower Devonian.

held water

the water retained above the water table by capillary action.

helicitic

a textural term originally applicable to S-shaped or reversed-S (S)- shaped trails of inclusions in poikiloblastic crystals, especially garnets and staurolite which are found in regionally metamorphosed rocks. The term has been extended to include any arrangement of inclusions which are representing a relict texture preserved from an earlier metamorphism. Similar S-shaped trails found by rotation during metamorphism should not be referred to as helicitic.

helictite

a small calcium carbonate speleothem growing in curved or spiral shapes in limestone caves.

helvetian

a stratigraphic stage name which is used for the European Middle Miocene.

hemichordata

a phylum which includes the acorn worms, related to the Chordata, and originating in the M.Cambrian.

hemihedral

the term applicable to the class of a crystal system having reduced symmetry, so that the general form is having one half of the number of faces of the corresponding form in the holohedral class, e.g., in the cubic system the hemihedral general form is having 24 faces, in comparison with 48 in the holohedral class.

hemingfordian

a stratigraphic stage name which is used for the North American equivalents of the Lower Vindobonian + Upper Burdigalian.

hemipelagite (hemipelagic deposit)

a generally fine-grained structureless sediment of decimetric thickness formed by the settling of grains from suspension and from low density, low viscosity turbidity currents, nepheloid layers and other ocean currents.

hemisphere

hemisphere describes one half of the globe. The northern and southern hemispheres are separated by the Equator.

hemitropic

referring to a twinned structure in which, if one part is rotated 180° the two parts become parallel.

herangi
a Jurassic succession in New Zealand comprising the Aratauran and Uniroan.

heretaungan
an Eocene succession in New Zealand covering parts of the Ypresian and Lutetian.

hermatypic coral
a coral with symbiatic algae, living in water < 50 m deep. cf. ahermatypic coral.

heronite
an igneous rock of the syenite clan; a fine-grained hypabyssal rock; contains analcite, orthoclase, labradorite and aegirine.

hessonite (cinnamon stone)
a yellow-brown variety of grosular containing iron.

heterogeneous strain
strain in which the relationship between displacement and distance changes abruptly. cf. homogeneous strain.

heteropygous
a term applicable to trilobites which have a cephalon larger than the pygidium.

hettangian
a stage of Lower Jurassic geologic time.

heumite
an igneous rock of the syenite clan; a fine-grained grangular hypabyssal rock; contains soda-orthoclase, soda-microcline, barkevikite, biotite, nepheline and sodalite.

hexagonal pyrrhotite ($Fe_9S_{10}Fe_{11}S_{12}$)
a sulphite mineral of the nickel arsenide group.

hexagonal system
a crystal system having three equal axis which are intersecting at 120° and lying in one plane; a fourth unequal axis is perpendicular to the other three.

hexahedrite
an iron meteorite composed of single crystals or aggregates of kamacite, usually containing 4-6% nickel in the metal phase.

high-angle fauit
fault with a dip greater than 45°.

high energy window
a period during the mid-Holocene when wave energy was higher than at present.

high-rank coal
coal consisting of less than 4% moisture when air-dried, or more 84% carbon.

highwoodite
refers to an igneous rock of the syenite clan. A coarse-grained granular plutonic rock; has soda orthoclase, labradorite, diopside, biotite, and apatite.

hill creep
slow gravity movement of rock and soil waste down a steep hillside. Also known as hillside creep.

hilt's law
the law that in a small area the deeper coals are of higher rank than those above them.

Himalyan mountain belt
a broad mountain chain formed by continental collision, either

a single collision or a series involving several suspect terranes, possibly followed by indentation tectonics. cf. Andean mountain belt.

hinge fault

a fault whose movement is an angular or rotational one on a side of an axis that is normal to the fault plane.

hinge line

1. the line separating the region in which a beach has been thrust upward from that in which it is horizontal.

2. a line in the plane of a hinge fault separating the part of a fault along which thrust or reverse movement occurred from that having normal movement.

hinterland

1. the region from which the surface rocks have been translated in an orogenic belt. cf. foreland.

2. an area of land drained by a river system.

3. the area supplying sediment to a depositional system.

hirantite

an igneous rock of thee diorite clan; a fine grained grangular plutonic rock. It contains albite, chlorite and augite.

historical geology

a branch of concerned with the systematic study of bedded rocks and their relations in time and the study of fossils and their locations in a sequence of bedded rocks.

histosol

an order of wet soils consisting mostly of organic matter, popularly called peats and mucks.

hitch

1. a fault of strata common in coal measures, accompanied by displacement.

2. a minor dislocation of a vein or stratum not exceeding in extent the thickness of the vein or stratum.

hjulström curve

an empirical curve showing the critical condition for erosion of river channel bed deposits in terms of mean flow velocity.

hoar frost

hoar frost is a kind of frost which is produced when the air near the ground cools down very fast at night. Hoar frost coats the grass and trees with crystals of ice.

hogback

refers to alternate ridges and ravines in certain regions of mountains which are caused by the erosive action. of mountain torrents.

holmquistite

lithium rich variety of glaucophane.

holoblast

a mineral formed entirely during metamorphism.

holocene

holocene describes the most recent epoch in geological time. It began about 10,00 years ago and continues today. The word Holocene means recent.

holocrystalline
descriptive of a rock which is completely crystalline.

holohedral
refers to the class of a crystal system in which the maximum symmetry has been displayed, and the general form is having the maximum number of faces possible, e.g., 48 in the cubic system.

holokarst
any limestone landscape with a fully developed range of karst features.

holomictic lake
a lake whose waters undergo complete mixing during periods of circulation overturn.

holothuroidea
a class of subphylum Eleutherozoa, phylum Echinodermata; worms-like invertebrates with a non-rigid calcite skeleton, poorly preserved as fossils. Range Silurian-Recent.

homeomorphism
crystalline substances that have a dissimilar composition but similar habit.

homoblastic
the term used for a metamorphic crystalloblastic texture which is having constituent minerals of approximately the same size.

homogenous simple shear
simple shear in which the relationship between displacement and distance is linear or continuously changing. cf. heterogeneous simple shear.

homomorphy
the term used for the superficial similarities in the morphology of members of different phyla, e.g., the Rudistid lamellibranchs and corals.

homoplasy
the similarity between parts of different organisms as a result of convergent evolution rather than a common ancestor. cf. homology.

hoodoo
a pillar of rock or weakly consolidated sediment formed by differential erosion, found in arid to semi-arid regions.

hopper crystal
a crystal with recessed faces caused by more rapid growth at its edges.

horizon
a time plane which can be recognised in rocks by some characteristic feature such as flora, fauna, or lithology.

horn
a glacial erosion featur formed when a mountain is eroded from all sides to leave a pyramidal peak.

hornblende schist
a rock having essentially orientated crystals of hornblende which gives rise to a linear schistosity. Other minerals which may occur are plagioclase, quartz, epidote, calcium garnet, biotite, calcite, and sphene.

hornfels

refers to a medium or fine-grained granulose rock which is produced by thermal metamorphism. It does not show cleavage, schistosity, or parallel alignment or minerals due to metamorphism, although relict fabrics (either depositional or compressional) may persist.

horse
a large rock caught along a fault.

horseback
a low and sharp ridge of sand, gravel, or rock.

horse-tailing
a feature made up of a number of mineralized fractures with the general appearance of a horse's tail, which is sometimes found at, or near, the end of a vein.

horst
1. A block of the earth's crust uplifted along faults relative to the rocks on either side.
2. a mass of the earth's crust limited by faults and standing in relief.
3. one of the older mountain masses limiting the Alps on the west and north. 4. A knobby ledge of limestone beneath a thin soil mantle.

host grain-controlled replacement
replacement that is selective or specific to sites of high surface free energy in the host mineral or grain, typical of solutions of low chemical reactivity. cf. precipitate controlled replacement.

hotspot
a heat source of limited areal extent arising from a mantle plume persisting for tens of millions of years and remaining nearly stationary with respect to the mantle.

howardite
an achondritic stony meteorite composed chiefly of calcic plagioclase and orthopyroxene.

howlite $Ca_2BsSiO_9(OH)_5$
a mineral consisting of basic calcium borosilicate. It does not show cleavage. Its hardness on Mohs scale is 3.5.

hoxnian
a stratigraphic stage name which is used for the British Middle Pleistocene (the interglacial between Lowest oft and Gipping Tills).

huashiban
a Carboniferous succession in China covering the lower part of the Bashkirian.

hullite
a mineral composed of iron, magnesium, calcium and alkaline aluminosilcate of uncertain crystal system. Its hardness on Mohs scale is 2.0.

humic coal
a coal whose attritus is composed mainly of transparent humic degradation material.

humid
humid describes the atmosphere when it contains a large amount of water vapour. Warm air holds more water

vapour than cold air so it can be more humid.

humification
formation of humus.

humite
refers to series of magnesium neosilicate minerals which are closely related in crystal structure and chemical composition.

hummocky cross-stratification
a bedding structure consisting of gently curved, low-angle cross-stratification, possibly forming under storm conditions or by a flow regime with a unidirectional component.

humus
refers to the amorphous, colloidal matter which is present in the soil.

hungarite
an igneous rock of the diorite clan; a fine grained porphyritic extrusive rock. It contains phenocrysts of hornblende and plagioclase in groundmass of plagioclase.

hurbachong
a Triassic succession in China equivalent to the Norian.

huronian
refers to a stratigraphic division of the Canadian Precambrian Pre-Algonkian.

huygen's principle
' a point on an advancing wavefront can be regarded as the centre of a fresh disturbance.' Used to predict the path of a wavefront of e.g. a seismic wave.

hyalobasalt
volcanic glass with the composition of basalt.

hyaloclastite
a tuffilike deposit formed by the flowing of basalt under water and ice and its consequent fragmentation. Also known as aquagene tuff.

hyalophane **($(K,Ba)(Al,Si)_2Si_2O_8$)**
a rare barium feldspar.

hyalopilitic
a variety of pilotaxitic texture in which the felt of crystals or crystallites gets embedded in a glassy base.

hybrid
a term applicable to rocks which are formed by the mixing of two magmas or the assimilation of one igneous rock by another.

hybrid joint
a type of joint intermediate between a shear joint and an extension joint.

hydration layer dating
a dating method for obsidian artefacts based on the phenomenon of obsidian's absorbing water at a rate dependent on its chemical composition and the ambient temperature.

hydraulic fill
earth or waste materials that have been excavated, transported, and flushed into place by flowing water.

hydraulic gecmetry
the study of channel form in

relation to the external controls of discharge and sediment.

hydraulic radius
the ratio of a stream's wetted perimeter length to the cross-sectional flow in a channel, a measure of the efficiency of a section in conveying flow.

hydroaulically smooth
a term indicating that sediment particles or other irregularities on a bed have a diameter less than the thickness of the viscous sublayer of a flow, and turbulence is probably not generated. cf. hydraulically rough.

hydrocarbon
a hydrocarbon is a compound made of hydrogen and carbon. Hydrocarbons are the most important chemicals found in oil and they are used to make fuels.

hydrocarbon saturation
the condition of a reservoir in which the pore fluid has been reduced to the minimum possible level by hydrocarbons. This can be determined using resistivity logging.

hydrograph
the graph of the discharge of a river or stream plotted against time for a particular point.

hydrography
hydrography is the making of maps or charts of the waters of the world. It includes describing and surveying rivers, lakes, oceans and the coast.

hydroisostasy
an isostanic reaction to the removal or loading of a mass of water.

hydrolith
(1) a rock that is free from organic substance.
(2) a chemically precipitated aqueous rock, such as rock salt.

hydrology
refers to the study of all waters in and upon the earth. Waters include underground water, surface water, and rainfall, and embraces the concept of the hydrological cycle.

hydrolysis
hydrolysis is the chemical weathering of rocks. Water combines with minerals in the rocks to make salts which cannot dissolve. Hydrolysis often takes place in igneous rocks which contain silica. Hydrolysis usually leads to clay being formed.

hydromagnesite ($Mg_5(CO_3)(OH)_2 4\text{-}H_2O$
hydrated magnesium hydroxide and carbonate found in amorphous masses and rarely as crystals in serpentinite.

hydrophane
white variety of opal which has a low reractive index and is virtually transparent when placed in water.

hydrosphere
the term used for the total body of water of the earth, i.e., the oceans, rivers, lakes,

underground and atmospheric water.

hydrostatic
the condition in which the pressures or stresses on a body are the same in all three dimensions.

hydrothermal
of or pertaining to heated water, to its action or to the products of such action.

hydrothermal alteration
refers to rock or mineral phase changes which are caused by the interaction of hydrothermal liquids and wall rock. These are including sepentinization of olivine and rhombic pyroxenes, chloritization of ferromagnesian minerals, saussuritization, uralitization, and propylitization.

hydrothermal deposit
a mineral deposit precipitated from a hot, aqueous solution.

hydrothermal processes
the name assigned to the various processes associated with igneous activity which involves heated or superheated water.

hydrothermal solution
hot, residual watery fluids derived from magmas during the later stages of their crystallization and commonly containing large amounts of dissolved metals which are deposited as ore veins in fissures along which the solutions often move.

hydrothermal synthesis
mineral synthesis in the presence of heated water.

hydrothermal vent
the location of the exhalation of hydrothermal solutions; such as are found along ocean ridge systems, including black smokers and white smokers. Probably the source of many massive sulphide deposits.

hydrozincite (zinc bloom) ($Zn_3(CO_3)_2(OH)_6$)
a secondary mineral produced by the alteration of zinc ore.

hygrometer
a hygrometer is an instrument used for measuring the humidity of the atmosphere. One kind of hygrometer has two thermometers, one dry and one wet. The difference in temperature between the two gives a measure of humidity.

hypabyssal
descriptive of an igneous rock crystallizing nearer the surface than a plutonic rock and further from the surface than a volcanic rock.

hypabyssal rock
a term applicable to intrusive igneous rocks which get crystallized under conditions intermediate between plutonic and volcanic. In general, hypabyssal rocks are medium-grained, and have been formed nearer the surface than plutonic rocks. Dykes and sills are typical examples.

hypautomorphic
having some trace of crystal form.

hypermelanic

a term applicable to igneous rocks which have almost exclusively dark minerals with a colour index greater than 90° on Shand' scale.

hypersaline
geologic material with high salinity.

hypersolvus granite
a granite which crystallized above the solvus temperature and thus contains only one type of alkali feldspar. cf. subsolvus granite.

hypersthene MgFe (II) S:O$_3$
a member of a continuous series of minerals in the pyroxene group which occurs in basic and ultrabasic rocks having low calcium, content, and in some metamorphosed rocks.

hypersthenite
an igneous rock of the ultrabasic clan; coarse-grained grangular plutonic rock composed of hypersthene.

hypidiomorphic
a term used for describing the texture of a rock in which the mineral grains exhibit some trace of crystal form. Also known as hypantomorphic; subidiomorphic.

hypidiotopic fabric
a fabric characterized by the presence of some minerals which exhibit their crystal form.

hypogene
a team used for describing processes which are originating within the earth, especially the formation of mineral deposits by ascending fluids.

hypothermal
a term used to represent high temperature environment (300-500°C) high temperatures.

hypothermal deposit
mineral deposit formed at great depths and (300-500°) high temperatures.

hypsographic curve
a graph of the distribution of elevation and depth with reference to sea level. cf. hypsometric curve.

hypsometry
refers to the measuring of elevation with reference to sealevel.

hysteresis
the difference between the paths followed with time during loading and unloading, e.g. of elastic loading, magnetization.

ibexian (Canadian)
a Cambrian/Ordovician succession in the E USA covering part of the Dolgellian, the Tremadoc and the early Arenig.

ice
ice is frozen water. Pure water freezes at 0° Celsius. Salt water freezes at a lower temperature, so the sea freezes only when it is very cold. When water becomes ice, it swells and takes up more space. Ice is lighter than water, so it floats on the surface of water.

ice age

refers to a major interval of geologic time during which glacial ice spreads over regions which are not normally ice-covered.

iceberg

an iceberg is a large piece of ice floating in the sea. icebergs break off from ice-sheets or from glaciers and drift on ocean currents. Only about one ninth of an iceberg can be seen above the water.

ice cap

refers to a perennial cover of ice and snow having the shape of a dome or plate on the summit area of a mountain through which the mountain peaks get emerged. An ice cap is considerably smaller than an ice sheet.

ice cliff

any vertical wall of ice, e.g., a glacier or mass or shelt ice.

ice erosion

erosion due to freezing of water in rock fractures.

ice-field

an ice-field is an area of ice which is floating in the sea. It usually measures more than 10 kilometres across.

iceland spar

a pure and transparent variety of calcite which gets easily cleaved to form rhombohedral crystals that are doubly refracting. It is also known as iceland crystal.

ice period

the period of time from freeze up to break-up of ice.

ice wedge

wedge-shaped, foliated ground ice formed in permafrost. It occurs as a vertical or inclined sheet, dike or vein and originates by the growth of hoar frost or by freezing of water in a narrow crevice.

ichnite

a trace fossil comprising a footprint.

ichnology

the study of trace fossils or their recent counterparts.

ichors

one of the names assigned to the fluids by which, it has been postulated, rocks may get transformed to granite or granite magma during granitization.

idamean

a Cambrian succession in Australia covering parts of the Maentwrogian and Dologellian.

idioblastic

a term describing the texture of a metamorphic rock in which the grains display fully developed crystal form.

ibioblastic texture

a texture of a metamorphic rock in which grains show fully-developed crystal forms.

igneous body

a volume of igneous rock with discrete boundaries with the surrounding country rock into which it was emplaced.

igneous facies

a part of an igneous rock differing in structure, texture or composition from the main mass.

igneous foliation
a foliation in an igneous rock defined by compositional variation or changes in crystal size or shape, possibly produced by differentiation or flow in a magma.

igneons rocks
refers to one of the three main groups of rocks which are generally considered as the primary source of the material comprising the earth's surface. They characteristically appear crystalline. Most igneous rocks appear to have crystallized from a silicate melt, the magma.

ignimbrite
a poorly-sorted, pyroclastic rock, comprising mainly pumice and ash, possibly with broken phenocrysts and dismembered vent wall material, of large volume (1 km^3-2000 km^3).

ijolite
a plutonic rock of nepheline and 30-60% mafic materials, generally sodic pyroxene, with accessory apatite, sphene, calcite and titaniferous garnet.

ikakiy
a Permian succession on the eastern Russian Platform equivalent to the Artinskian.

illite
the term used for a group of grey, green, or brown micalike clay minerals which are found in argillaceous sediments.

illuviation
the accumulation of material in the lowest soil zone by the leaching and eluviation of fine-grained material and water-soluble minerals from the upper soil zone and their downward transport.

illuvium
material leached by chemical or physical processes from one soil horizon and deposited in another.

imaginary component (out-of-phase component, quadrature)
the part of the secondary electromagnetic field that is 90° out of phase with the primary field in electromagnetic induction methods. It is larger in the presence of a good conductor and at low EM frequencies.

imbibition
the term is defined as the tendency of granular rock or any porous medium to absorb a fluid usually water under the force of capillary action and in the absence of any pressure.

imbricate fault
one of a number of closely-spaced faults in an imbricate structure.

imbricate structure
1. a sedimentary structure characterized by shingling of pebbles all inclined in the same direction with the upper edge of each leaning downstream or toward the sea. Also known as shingle structure.
2. Tabular masses that overlap

one another and are inclined in the same direction. Also known as schuppen structure; shingle-block structure.

imbrication

formation of an imbricate structure. Also known as shingling.

immature oil

heavy, low API gravity, naphthalene-or asphalt-rich oil, which has not undergone sufficient cracking to convert it into a light oil.

immature soil

a soil in which erosion has exceeded the rate at which the soil develops downward.

immiscible

descriptive of two or more liquids that are incapable of mixing to form a single liquid and separate into two phases. cf. miscible.

impact crater

a depression formed by the impact of an unspecified projectile especially a crater formed on the earth or moon surface where the nature of impacting body is unknown.

impact grater

a depression which is formed by the impact of an unspecified projectile especially- a crater formed on the earth or moon surface where the nature of impacting body is not known with certainty.

impactite

glassy fused rock or meteor fragments resulting from heat of impact of a meteor on the earth.

impactogen

a continental rift valley system in the distal region of continent-continent collision oregon resulting from tensional stresses associated with indentation tectonics.

impersistent

geologists usually use 'impersistent' as the converse of 'persistent', instead of 'non-persistent'. It carries the connotation of discontinuity (especially in an areal sense) and spasmodicity.

impervious

impervious describes materials through which water cannot pass. Rocks which do not have gaps or cracks may be impervious. The opposite of impervious is pervious.

impoundment

the process of forming a lake or pond by some sort of barrier such as a dam or dike. The body of water formed in this manner is also called an impoundment.

impression

a form left on a soft soil surface by plant parts; the soil hardens and usually the imprint is a concave feature.

impsonite

a black, asphaltic pyrobitument with a high fixed-carbon content derived from the metamorphosis of petroleum.

inarticulata

a class of phylum Brachiopoda, characterized by the absence

of hinging between the valves. Range Tommotian-Recent.

inclined bedding

a type of bedding in which the strata dip in the direction of current flow.

inclined contact

a contact plane of gas or oil with water underlying, in which the plane slopes or is inclined.

inclusion

a portion of one substance which' is enclosed within another. For example, a piece of older rock included in a younger rock.

inclineds trail

a linear array of microscopic inclusion within a crystal, commonly fluids, iron oxides and iron hydroxides.

incompetent bed

a bed not combining sufficient firmness and flexibility to transmit and to lift a load by bending.

incongruent solution

dissolution yielding a solution with different proportions from those in the solid.

incongruous

or a drag fold, having an axis and axial surface not parallel to the axis and axial surface of the main fold to which it is related.

index fossil

the ancient remains and traces of an organism that lived during a particular time period, and that characterises a specific horizon by its abundance, although not restricted to it in time.

index mineral

a mineral which is occurring in a series of metamorphic rocks whose first occurrence marks the outer limit of metamorphic zone, as one is moving in the direction of increasing metamorphic grade.

index plane

a surface used as a reference point in determining geological structure.

indicatrix

a three-dimensional geometrical figure that represents geometrically the different vibration directions in a mineral in terms of an ellipsoid whose axis are proportional to the refractive index of a ray travelling parallel to it.

indigskiy

a Permian succession in the Timan area of the former USSR equivalent to the L. Asselian.

induan

a stratigraphic stage name which is used for the base of the European Lower Triassic.

induced fission

fission taking place only as a result of bombardment of nucleus with neutrons, gamma rays or other carriers of energy.

induced polarization

a geophysical exploration method based on the phenomenon that metallic minerals can store electric charge, which is gradually released when the energizing current is removed. The only method capable of detecting disseminated deposits.

industrial diamond

a diamond of less than gem quality, used for drilling, cutting, lapping etc.

inertinite

a carbon-rich maceral group, which is including micrinite, sclerotinite, fusinite, and semifusinite.

inertodetrinite

a coal maceral consisting of broken fragments of inertite and sclerotine.

infiltration

the entry of water into the soil, usually by downward flow through the surface.

infrastructure

a name assigned to a magmatite zone which shows complex tectonics, and lay below a more simply folded, non-magmatitic zone.

inground meander

a continually growing or expanding incised menander formed during a single cycle of erosion by the enlargement or accensuation of an initial minor curve while the stream was actively down cutting; a meander that grows in place.

injection complex

refers to an association of igneous rocks and, very commonly, regionally metamorphosed rocks, in which the relationships between the various rock bodies become intricately intermixed. It is usually found that more than one period of igneous activity gets involved, and several stages of metamorphism may also be detected.

injection structure

a structure in a sediment formed when one layer forces into another.

inlet

(1) a small, narrow groove in a shoreline, through which water penetrates into the land.

(2) an inflowing stream, as into a lake.

inlier

a circular or elliptical area of older rocks surrounded by strata that are younger.

inner core

refers to the central part of the earth' core which extends from a depth of about 5100 km to the centre (6371 km) of the earth. Its radius is about one-third of the whole core. It is equivalent to G layer.

inorganic

inorganic is the word used to describe substances which do not contain any of the organic chemicals that make up living things. The rocks of the Earth's crust are inorganic. The opposite of inorganic is organic.

inosilicate (band silicate, chain silicate)

a crystal structure classification in which the coordination polyhedra are Si tetrahedra and these form chains when each tetrahedron shares two corners with adjacent tetrahedra.

insects

members of superclass Hexapoda, phylum Uniramia. Range Devonian-Recent.

inselberg

a large, steep-sided residual hill, knob, or mountain, generally rocky and bare, rising abruptly from an extensive, nearly level lowland erosion surface in arid or semiarid regions. Also known as island mountain.

insequent

the term used for a stream or drainage system controlled by the associated rock structure or surface features. It wanders irregularly across the region of low relief.

insequent stream

a stream developed as a result of indeterminate features. cf. anteconsequent, inconsequent, obsequent, resequent and subsequent streams.

inshore zone

the zone of variable width extending from the shoreline at low tide through the breaker zone.

insolicate

a class of structural type of silicate in which the SiO_4 teahedrons are linked together by the sharing of oxygen to form linear chains of indefinite length.

insolation

refers to the effect of the solar heat on rocks at the surface of the earth; especially refers to the effect of changes in temperature on the mechanical weathering of rocks.

insoluble residue

material remaining after a geological specimen is dissolved in hydrochloric or acetic acid.

inspissation

the process of drying of oil that has reached the surface.

insular slope

an area of the ocean floor analogous to the continental shelf but surrounding an island.

interbedded

means between two layers with different characteristics; e.g., a lava flow may take place interbedded between two layers of sediments.

intercalation

a layer located between layers of different character.

intercepts

distances which are cut off a crystal's reference axis by planes.

interconnectedness

an index of the proportion of individual sediment bodies of specific type that are in touch with each other in a given succession.

interface

(1) the boundary separating the top of the uppermost layer of the sediment from the water in which the sedimentation process is taking place.

(2) the contact between fluids in a reservoir.

interference figure
refers to a pattern of light and dark areas which are observed with a conoscope when a birefringent crystal is kept in a convergent beam of linearly polarized light.

interference ripple
a bedding surface sedimentary structure comprising ripples in at least two orientations at a high angle forming a polygonal pattern, produced by simultaneous or sequential currents in different directions.

interfluve
the term used for the high land between two streams belonging to the same drainage system.

interglacial
pertaining to or formed during a period of geologic time between two successive glacial epochs or between two glacial stages.

intergrade
a soil that is transitional between two other soils.

intergrowth
a textural term applicable to interlocking arrangements of two minerals, usually occurring due to simultaneous crystallization of the phases or the exsolution of one phase from another.

interior basin
a depression surrounded by higher land from which no stream flows outward to ocean.

interlayer slip
deformation accomplished by displacement along bedding or foliation surfaces.

intermediate moraine
a type of lateral moraine which is formed at the junction of two adjacent glacial lobes. It is also known as interlobat moraine.

intermediate sulphur crude oil
crude oil with 0.6-1.7% sulphur.

intermontane
located between or surrounded by mountains.

intermonatane glacier
a glacier that is formed by the confluence of several valley glaciers and occupies a trough between separate ranges of mountains.

intermontane trough
1. a subsiding area in an island arc of the ocean, lying between the stable elements of a region. 2. a basinlike area between mountains.

international geomagnetic reference field (IGRF)
a complex formula used to compute the geomagnetic correction in the reduction of magnetic survey measurements.

international program for ocean drilling (IPOD)
a phase of the Deep Sea Drilling Program.

interpenetrant twin
a twinning phenomena in which two individuals appear to have grown through each

other.

interpluvial
pertaining to an episode or period of geologic time that was dryer than the pluvial period occurring before or after it.

intersection lineation
a lineation produced by the intersection of two planes, e.g. cleavage and bedding.

intersertal
a term referring to the texture of a porphyritiric; igneous rock in which the groundmass is forming a small proportion of the rock and filling the interstices between unoriented feldspar laths.

interstadial
a phase of relative warmth during a major glacial, or insufficient magnitude and/or duration to be classed as an interglacial.

intertidal zone
the intertidal zone is an area of the sea-shore. It is covered by water at high tide and is dry at low tide. It is part of the littoral zone. Some animals and plants are found only in the intertidal zone.

interstitial crystal defect
a crystal defect in which an alien atom occupies a small gap between atoms in the regular arrangement.

intra
a prefix denoting within or inside.

intraclast
a fragment of limestone which is formed by erosion within a basin of deposition and redeposition there to form a new sediment.

intragranular displacement
displacement taking place within a grain during deformation. cf. intergranular displacement, transgranular displacement.

intrenched meander
a meander in a river channel that is incised into the landscape as a result of erosion.

intrusion
refers to a body of igneous rock which is forced itself into pre-existing rocks, either along some definite structural features e.g., bedding planes, joints, cleavages, etc., or by deformation and cross-cutting of the invaded rocks.

inverse problem
a problem common to the interpretation of potential fields relating to the fact that the anomaly of any given body can be computed, but the derivation of the body responsible for any particular anomaly has no unique solution.

inversion twinning
a twinning phenomenon resulting from a phase transition during which crystal symmetry is lowered and the twin orientations are in the highest symmetry.

inverted relief
a topographic surface that is out of phase with the geologic

structure as where valleys are underlain by anticlines and mountains by syncline.

iodine
iodine is an element. It is composed of greyish-black crystals. All living things need iodine to grow. Some iodine compounds can be used to prevent infection.

ion milling
a preparation method for transmission electron microscopy in which beams of agron ions or atoms are fired at a demounted, polished thin-section eroding its surface to provide small, electron-transparent holes.

iowan glaciation
the fourth of the glaciations experienced by North America in the Quaternary.

ipswichian
a stratigraphic stage name which is used for British Upper Pleistocene Interglacial between Gipping Till and Newer Drift.

iridescence
a shimmering effect exhibited by some minerals caused by the diffraction of light by fine-grained lamellar intergrowths.

iridescent
many coloured, often the result of interference effects in the light reflected by the surface.

iron
iron is an element. It is a dark grey metal. Iron reacts with damp air to form rust, which is a reddish-brown colour. Iron is a very common element in the Earth's crust.

iron meteorite (siderite)
a meteorite comprising iron plus $< 20\%$ nickel.

ironstone
name applicable to agrillaceous, arenaceous, or calcarecous sedimentary rocks which have a high percent age of iron minerals. The minerals may occur as a result of primary deposition or later alteration.

irregular mullion
a mullion structure comprising cylinders with irregular cross-sections.

isentropic
of equal or constant entropy.

island
an island is an area of land entirely surrounded by water. An island can be only a few metres across or many thousands of kilometres wide. The largest island on Earth is the continent of Australia.

isoanomaly
a line joining points of equal geophysical anomaly; *e.g.*, magnetic anomaly, gravity anomaly.

isoash map
a coal quality map showing trends in the ash content of a coal.

isobar
an isobar is a line drawn on a weather map to join points of equal pressure. If the isobars on a weather map are close together, the winds are strong.

isobath
a line which joins the points of equal depth of horizon below the surface or a datum plane.

isochore
a line which joins points of equal vertical interval between two datum planes.

isocline
a fold of strata so tightly compressed that parts on each side dip in the same direction.

isoclinic
a line joining points of similar principal stress orientations.

isoclinic line
a line which connects points on the earth's surface and has the same magnetic inclination. It is also known as isoclinial.

isofacies map
a stratigraphic map showing the distribution of one or more facies within a particular stratigraphic unit.

isoflor
a line which connects points of similar flora. A concept which was used by palaceoclimatologists in an attempt to ascertain climatic zones.

isogonic line
a line connecting points of equal magnetic declination.

isogor map
oil reservoir contour-line map showing constant gas-oil ratios.

isograd
a line on a map joining those rocks comprising the same metamorphic grade.

isogyre
the name assigned to the black areas of an interference figure.

isohaline
a line on a chart connecting all points of equal salinity.

isohume
a line of a map or chart connecting points of equal moisture content in a coal bed.

isolith map
a contour-line map depicting the thickness of an exclusive lithology.

isomegathic solution
solutions formed of solute molecules of almost same size.

isomorphism
the phenomenon of two or more minerals of similar chemistry crystallizing with the same crystal symmetry.

isomorphous
a term originally applicable to two substances crystallizing in the same form but now this term is restricted to cases where the two substances are forming a series of solid solutions, e.g., rock salt and fluorite, both crystallize in cubes but are not said to be isomorphous because they are not forming a solid solution.

isopach line
a line which joins point of equal bed thickness. It is also known as isopachyte.

isopach map
map of the areal extent and thickness variation of a stratigraphic unit; used in geological exploration for oil

and for underground structural analysis.

isopachous line
one of the lines drawn on a map to indicate equal thickness.

isopachyte (isopach)
a line joining points of equal stratigraphic thickness. cf. isochore.

isopleth
any line which is joining points of equal value, abundance, frequency, etc., on a map, e.g., contour lines, isobars, isotherms, (isoline is a synonym).

isopycnal
a line joining points of equal pressure in water.

isoseismal
referring to points which are having equal intensity of earthquake shock, or referring to a line on a map of the earth's surface which is connecting such points.

isostatic anomaly
the Bouguer anomaly minus the effect of the compensation predicted by the Airy or Pratt hypotheses. Non-zero values indicate isolatic equilibrium is not extant.

isostatic compensation
the process in which lateral transport at the surface of the earth by erosion or deposition is compensated by lateral movements in a subcrustal layer. Also known as isostatic adjustment; isostatic correction.

isostructural
a term used for describing two or more minerals which are having similar physical, chemical, and crystallographic features, but which show little or no tendency to form a solid solution, e.g., grossular and almandine varieties of garnet.

isotherm
an isotherm is a line on a weather map which joins places where the temperature is the same.

isotherm line
a line connecting points at an equal temperature in graphs or thermodynamic relation.

isotones
atoms whose nuclei contain the same number of neutrons but have a different atomic number.

isotopic abundance
the ratio of the quantity of an isotope to the total amount of the element.

isotopic number
the difference between the number of neutrons in an isotope and the number of protons.

isotropic
having no order or preferred orientation. Does not affect doubly polarized light.

isotropic point
the point where the principal stresses are equal.

isotype
the term used for crystalline substance whose chemical formula is analogous to, and

whose structure is like, that of another specified (reference) compound.

isovol

a line joining points of equal volatile content in coal.

itabirite

regional metamorphic rock. A shistose rock containing quartz, hematite, oligoclase and muscovite.

itacolumnite

a micaceous sandstone with interlocking clasts so that the rock bends when in the form of a thin slab.

itsindrite

an igneous rock of the syenile clan a fine to a coarse-grained granular hypabyssl rock; contains microcline, nepheline, biotite, and aegirine.

ivorian

a stage of the Carboniferous, 353.8-349.5 million years.

ixiolite $(Ta,Nb,Sn,Mn,Fe)_4O_8$

a mineral previously considered to be a mixture of cassiterite with columbite or tapiolite.

j

in earthquake seismology, an S wave generated by conversion from a P wave at the boundary between the inner and outer core and reconverted on exit.

jackson

an Eocene succession on the Gulf Coast of the USA equivalent to the Priabonian.

jacupirangite

an igneous rock of the ultrabasic clan; a fine-grained grangular plutonic rock consisting mainly of titan-augite and aegirine-augite with accessory nepheline.

jade

the name assigned to two distinct minerals which are hard, compact, dark-green or greenish-white gemstone composed of either jadeite—a pyroxene, or nephrite—an amphibole, when they occur in the form of a tough compact aggregate. This material, especially the green and white varieties, finds use extensively as a gem material. It is also known as jadestone.

jamesonite $(Pb_4FeSb_6S_{14})$

a minor ore mineral of lead.

jargoon

colourless or smoky variety of zircon from Sri Lanka.

jasper

refers to a dence, opaque to slightly translucent, red, crystalling quartz having iron oxide as impurity. Also known as jasperite; jaspis.

jasperiod

the term used for dense, chertlike siliceous rock in which chalcedony or cryptocrystalline quartz replaces the carbonate materials of limestone or dolomite; a silicified limestone.

jaspoid

the term used for a black, green, or brown volcanic glass which is formed from basaltic magma. It is also known as basalt glass; sordawalite, tachylite.

jefferisite

a mineral having magnesium aluminium silicate of uncertain crystal system and formula. It snows perfect basal cleavage. Its hardness on Mohs scale is 1.5.

jeffreys-bullen model

a model for the seismic velocity structure of the Earth, in which velocity varies only radically.

jet

jet is a hard form of coal. When it is cut and polished, it is very shiny and looks like black glass. It is used to make jewellery and ornaments.

jet coal

a hard, iustrous, pure black variety of lignite, occurring in isolated masses in bituminous shale; thought to be derived from waterlogged driftwood. Also known as black amber.

jiangtangjiang (chientangkiang)

an Ordovicin succession in China covering part of the Harnagian, the Soudleyan, Longivillian, Marshbrookian, Actonian, Onnian and Ashgill.

joint

fefers to a fracture in a rock between the sides of which there occurs no observable relative movement. A series of parallel joints is known as a 'joint set'; two or more sets intersecting are said to produce a 'joint system'; two sets of joints nearly at right angles to one another, produced by the same stress system, are said to be conjugate. A master joint (a quarryman's terms) is defined as a persistent joint or set which may be horizontal or vertical.

joint block

a body of rocks that is bounded by joints; the rock that occurs between the adjacent joint.

joint set

a group of joints with a common orientation.

joseite $Bi_3Te(Se,S)$

a mineral having telluride of bismuth, along; with small amounts of sulphur and selenium.

jotnian

the youngest division of the Baltic Precambrian.

jotnian orogeny

an orogeny affecting the Baltic shield in the Proterozoic.

juanite $Ca_{10}Mg_4Al_2Si_{12}O_{39}\cdot 4H_2O$

a white orthorhombic mineral. Its hardness on Mohs scale is 5.5.

jumillite

igneous rock of the syenite clan.

junction

(1) the meeting of two or more streams, also the place of such a meeting; a confluence.

(2) a point common to two or more survey lines.

jurassic

also known as jura.

1. The second period of the Mesozoic era of geologic time. 2. The corresponding system of rocks.

juvenile

a term applicable to gases and water arising from an underground magmatic source.

juvenile gas

gas originating in the interior of the Earth, not previously having been at the surface.

juvenile water

water derived from magma.

juvite

igneous rock of the syenite clan.

juxtaposed ice stream

ice from a tributary glacier that is set into the surface of a glacier and extends to the bed.

k-cycle

a concept of land evolution involving the cyclic erosion of soils on upper slopes during unstable climatic phases and soil development during stable phases.

kaersutite

black titanium rich variety of hornblende.

kaiatan

an eocene succession in New Zealand covering the upper part of the Bartonian.

kainite $MgSO_4.KCl.3H_2O$; or, $KMgSO_4Cl.3H_2O$.

a colourless to yellowish, reddish, grey or blue, monoclinic mineral. It is, found in bedded salt deposits of oceanic origin associated with halite, rylvite, polyhalite, carnallite, and other salt minerals. It finds use as a fertilizer and as a source of magnesium and potassium compounds.

kaiwekite

a volcanic rock containing phenocrysts of olivine, titanaugite, barkevikite and anorthoclase.

kakirite

dynamic metamorphic rock; contains augens of residual material surrounded by zones of granulation and recrystallization.

kalevian

refers to a stratigraphic division of the Baltic Precambrian, the younger Karelian.

kakirite

dynamic metamorphic rock which contains augens of residual material surrounded by zones of granulation and recrystallization.

kalisilite

high temperature polymorph of kaliophilite.

kalisyenite

a medium to coarsegrained granular plutonic rock which contains orthoclase, microperthite, biotite, anorthoclase, hornblende, diopside and minor quartz.

kalitordrillite

a fine-grained porhyritic extrusive or hypabyssal rock which contains phenocrysts of quartz, orthoclase, anorthoclase, and albite in a groundmass of intergrown quartz and orthoclase.

kame
an irregular, undultaing mound of bedded sands, and gravels deposited unevenly along the front of a stationary or decaying ice sheet.

kame terrace
terrace-like body of startified drift, left by a glacier against an adjacent valley wall after the ice has melted.

kandite
a group of clay minerals including kaolinite, dickite, nacrite, halloysite and meta-halloysite.

kaolin (China clay)
an important mineral product composed principally of kaolinite.

kaolinization
the formation of kaolin by weathering of aluminium silicate minerals or other clay minerals.

kapitean
a neogene succession in New Zealand covering parts of the Messian and Zanclian.

karakan
an Ordovician succession in Kazakhstan covering the upper part of the Llanvirn.

karelian
refers to a stratigraphic division of the Baltic Precambrian Post-Sveccofennian.

karroo system
glaciated strata formed in Permian times in southern Africa.

karst
a topography formed over limestone, dolomite, or gypsum and characterized by sinkholes, caves, and under ground drainage.

karst plain
a plain on which karst features are developed.

kashirskian
a stage of the Carboniferous, 309.2-307.1 million years.

kata-
a prefix which denotes deepest, greatest or maximum depth.

katazone
a depth zone of high temperature and very high hydrostatic pressure.

kawhia
a Jurrasic succession in New Zealand comprising the Temaikan, Heterian and Ohauan.

kazanian
a stratigraphic stage name which is used for the base of the East European Upper Permian.

kazankite
an igneous rock of the gabbro clan; a black fine grained granular hypabyssal rock; contains olivine plagioclase, magnetite and spinel.

kelyphitic rim
a rim of one mineral around another in an igneous rock resulting from reaction of the enclosed mineral with other constituents of the rock.

kelyphytic rime
a peripheral zone of pyroxene or amphibole developed around olivine in some igneous rocks. Also known as kelyphytic border.

kentallenite
1 refers to igneous rocks of diorite clan. A medium-grained granular plutonic rock; has olivine, augite, biotite, orthoclase, and plagioclase. 2. A special variety of olivine monzonite.

keralite
type of hornfels containing quartz and biotite as essential minerals.

keratophyre
a rock of the spilite suite made up of albite, chlorite, epidote and iron-titanium oxides, formed by the alteration of intermediate volcanic rocks.

kerogen
the term used for the complex fossilized organic material which produces petroleum-type hydrocarbons on heating and distillation. Also known as petroloyen.

kersantite
refers to the igneous rock of the diorite clan. A fine-grained porphyritic hypabyssal rock; having phenocrysts of oligocalse, biotite, and hornblende in a groundmass of plagioclase and diopside.

kesterite Cu_2ZnSnS_4
a sulphide mineral derived from the sphalerite structure by ordered substitution.

kettle
a bowl-shaped depression with steep sides in glacial drift deposits that is formed by the melting of glacier ice left behind by the retreating glacier and buried in the drift. Also known as kettle basin; kettle hole.

keuper
a European stage of geologic time, especially in Germany; Upper Triassic.

keupur
a stratigraphic stage name which is used for the West European Upper Triassic.

keweenawan
the younger of two Precambrian time systems that constitute the Proterozoic period in Michigan and Wisconsin.

key bed
also known as index bed; key horizon; marker bed.
1. A stratum or body of strata that has distinctive characteristics so that it can be easily identified.
2. A bed whose top or bottom is employed as a datum in the drawing of structure contour maps.

khamsin
the khamsin is a wind. It is very hot, dry and dusty and blows from the south, across the Sahra in north Africa. The khamsin usually blows from April to June.

kharakovian
an Oligocene succession in the former USSR equivalent to the

Rupelian.

kick

a surge or thrust against the normal fluid circulation in an oil well, as a result of a well pressure that exceeds the pressure exerted by the drilling mud Arriva.

kidney ore

a form of haematite with a fibrous, radiating, internal structure and a reniform, red, external surface.

kieserite $MgSO_4H_2O$

a white mineral which crystallizes in monoclinic system and occurs chiefly in sedimentary deposits of oceanic origin associated with halite and other salts and rarely as a product of volcanic activity.

kimberlite

refers to a thoroughly breciated peridotite which contains essential mica (phlogopite), bronzite and chromediopside

kimmeridglan

a European stage of geologic time; middle Upper Jurassic, above Oxfordian, below Portlandian.

kinderhookian

lower Mississippian geologic time, above the Chautauquan of Devonian, below Osagian.

kinematic

referring to motion; used to describe phenomena related to the relative motion of an object.

kinematic symmetry axes

the direction of flow, the plane of flow and the plane normal to these, assuming plane strain.

kink

a type of fold with an angular profile.

kink band

a deformation band in a single crystal or in foliated rocks in which the orientation is changed due to slipping on several parallel slip planes. Also known as knick zone.

kinking

the fold process forming a kink.

kjelsasite

calcium-rich and alkalipoor type of larvikite.

klabava

an Ordovician succession in Bohemia equivalent to the Arenig.

klint

an exhumed coral reef or biohern which is more resistant to the processes such as erosion than the rocks that enclose it so that the core remains in relief as hills and ridges.

knick point

refers to the intersection between the old and new long profiles of a river arising because of the process of rejuvenation.

knoll

a knoll is a small, rounded hill.

knott's equations

equations which define now seismic wave energy is partitioned between reflected P and S waves when it impinges on a discontinuity; similar to Zoepptitz' equations.

kokhanskiy

a Permian succession on the eastern Russian Platform equivalent to the Upper Asselian.

komatiite

an igneous suite of Archean rocks that were among the first documented perioditic magmas.

komichanskiy

a Permian succession in the Timan area of the former USSR equivalent of the Upper Artinskian.

kopaly

an Ordovician succession in Kazakhstan covering the lower part of the Llanvirn.

korangian

a Cretaceous succession in New Zealand covering parts of the Aptian and Albian.

kraton

refers to a major structural unit of the earth's crust which consists of a large stable mass of rock generally igneous and/ or metamorphic sometimes with a thin veneer of sediment. A typical kraton is the Canadian (Precambrian) Shield.

krotovina (crotovina)

an animal burrow filled by later material.

krypton

krypton is an element. It is a gas which is found in small amounts in the atmosphere. Krypton forms very few compounds with other elements. It is called an inert gas.

kungurian

a European stage of geologic time; Middle Permian, above Artinskian, below Kazanian.

kunzite

the term used for the lilac coloured, gem quality variety of spodumene from California, U.S.A.

kurtosis

a measure of the 'peakedness' of a frequency distribution.

kuyalnitskian (cimmeridian)

a Pliocene succession on the Russia Platform covering parts of the Zanclian and Piacenzian.

kvellite

an igneous rock of the ultrabasic clan. A medium grained porpoyritic hypabyssal rock; contains phenocrysts of lepidomelane, . olivine, barkevikite, apatite, ilmenite, and magnetite in a groundmass of anorthoclase.

kyanite Al_2SiO_5

refers to a blue or light green coloured neosilicate mineral which crystallizes in triclinic system.

kyanite group

an industrial name for the sillimanite minerals.

kylity

refers to the igneous rock of the gabbro clan. A fine-grained granular hypabyssal rock; has augite labradorite, olivine, ilmenite, and nepheline.

kymoclastic rock
a hydroclastic rock containing marine and other wave formed fragments.

l
letter used to indicate a phase of lineation formation subscripted to denote each separate phase.

laagte
a broad, almost level drainage course in the veld of south western Africa, dry for most of the year, less well defined them a valley.

labradite
igneous rock of the gabbro clan. An anorthosite, a grey plutonic rock; composed mainly of labradorite and clinopyroxenes.

labradorescence
the brilliant play of colours shown by labradorite.

laccolith
a body of igneous rock intruding into sedimentary rocks so that the overlying strata have been notably lifted by the force of intrusion.

lacustrine
belonging to or produced by lakes.

lacustrine sediments
sediments that are deposited in lakes

lacustrine soil
soil that is uniform in texture but variable in chemical composition and that has been formed by deposits in lakes which have become extinct.

ladder ripples (ladder-back ripples)
interference ripples comprising a set of long wavelength wave ripples and a second set of shorter wavelength orthogonal to them, observed to form during a fall in water level.

ladinian
a European stage of geologic time; upper Middle Triassic.

ladogian
refers to a stratigraphic division of the Baltic Precambrian the older Karelian.

lag deposit
residual accumulation of coarse, unconsolidated rock and mineral debris left behind by the winnowing of finer material.

lag fault
a minor low-angle thrust fault occurring within an overthrust; it develops when one part of the mass is thrust farther than an adjacent higher or lower part.

lagomorpha
an order of infraclass Eutheria, subclass Theria, class Mammalia; the rabbits and hares. Range Upper Eocene-Recent.

lagoon
a lagoon is a shallow pool of salt water near the coast. A lagoon is usually cut off from the sea by a ridge of sand or shingle. In an atoll, the central lagoon is surrounded by a coral reef.

lagoon beach

the sandy fringe on the innerprotected side of a reef island facing toward the lagoon.

lahar

mud-flows and deposits which are resulted from torrential downpours of rain mass, melting of snow and ice or the breaching of a crater lake which acts upon loose finegrained pyroclastic material (ash) on the flanks of a volcanic cone.

lahn-dill iron deposit

a synegentic, conformable, iron-rich layer or lens, dominantly siliceous at the base and calcareous at the top. The principal minerals are hematite, magnetite, siderite and limonite. Probably of volcanic-exhalative origin.

lakarpite

igneous rock of the syenite clan. A course-grained plutonic rock similar in appearance to dirite; contains orthoclase or microcline with albite, amphiboles and minor aegirine, apatite, and altered nepheline.

lamellar flow

a movement of a liquid in which individual particles move in parallel sheets slide over one another. Magma beneath the surface of the earth shows lamellar flow.

lamina

the term used for a thin, clearly differentiated layer of sedimentary rock or sediment, which is usually less than 1 centimetre thick.

laminar flow

a non-turbulent flow in which the mean flow a velocity and instantaneous velocities at any point are exactly the same characterized by the dominance of viscous forces over inertial forces, and Reynolds numbers < 500. cf.turbulent flow.

lamination

means the development of thin, discrete layers of rock. The individual layers may be different from one another or may be homogeneous, the layers being separated by a physical discontinuity, e.g., bedding planes.

lampadite

a variety of wad containing copper; composed of hydrous mangenese oxides with about 18% copper oxides and often associated with cobalt oxide.

lamprobolite

a product which is formed by heating common hornblende to about 800°C.

lamp shells

a popular name which is used for the Branchiopoda, especially the Terebratulid group.

lamproite

a potassium- and magnesium-rich to ultramafic alkaline lamprophyre-type rock of volcanic or hypabyssal origin composed of Tirich phalogopite, clinopyroxene, alkali amphibole, olivine, leucite and sanidine with accessory chrome spinel, priderite, wadeite, nepheline, ilmenite, sherbakovite, jeppeite, apatite, perovskite, sphene and amphibole.

lancefieldian

an Ordovician succession in Australia covering parts of the Tremadoc and early Arenig.

land Bridge

refers to a strip of land linking two land masses which is often subject to temporary submergence, but permitting migration of organisms.

landenian

a European stage of geologic time: upper Paleocene

landerite

a pink to rose-pink variety of grassular garnet.

land mass

a land mass is a large piece of land. A continent is a land mass.

landsat satellites

a series of satellites used in remote sensing to provide images particularly useful for geological studies. Previously known as the ERTS satellites.

landscape

refers to the distinct association of landforms which can be seen in a single view.

land slide

refers to the movement of a mass of rock or soil, or both down a slope under the influence of gravity. A landslide is different from an earth flow in that the mass of rock remains more or less in one piece. Also known as landship.

landslide breccia

a breccia that is largely fragmented and whooly assembled by the force gravity, as by rockfall or a rockclide.

landslide terrace

a short, rough-surfaced terrace resulting from a landslide.

lang topographic method

an X-ray diffraction method for the direct imaging of microstructural crystal defects.

lapies

a limestone pavement.

lapilli

Pyroclasts that range from 1 to 64 millimeters in diameter.

lapilli-tuff

a pyroclastic deposit that is indurated and consists of lapilli in a fine tuff matrix.

lapis lazuli

refers to an azure-blue, violet blue, or greenishblue, translucent to opaque crystalline rock. It is chiefly composed of lazurite and calcite with some haiiyne, sodalite, and other minerals. It finds use as a semi-precious stone. It is also known as lazuli.

laramide orogeny

an orogeny responsible for the formation of the Rocky Mountains of America in late Cretaceous and Palaecocene times.

large-scale

large-scale is a term used when something is shown in great detail. A large- scale map covers all the features of a small area. A large-scale diagram is drawn large enough to show a very detailed view of the subject.

larvikite

refers to a coarse-grained syenite which consists largely of anorthoclase feldspar showing blue schillerization. It is mainly used as an ornamental stone when cut and polished. Also known as laurvigite.

lassenite

unaltered form of volcanic glass.

lateral accretion

the digging away of material at the outer bank of a meandering stream and the simultaneous building up to the water level by deposition of material brought there by pushing and rolling along the stream bottom.

lateral erosion

the action of a stream in undermining a bank on one side of its channel so that, material falls into the stream and disintegrates; simultaneously, the stream shifts toward the bank that is being undercut.

lateral moraine

drift material, usually thin, that was deposited by a glacier in a valley after the glacier melted.

lateral planation

reduction in land in interstream areas in a plane parallel to the stream profile; the reduction is caused by lateral movement of the stream against its banks.

lateral resistivity log

an electric geophysical borehole log which measures the resistivity of the formations to a considerable distance from the borehole.

lateral secretion

a supposed phenomenon whereby a lode's or vein's mineral content is derived from the adjacent wall rock.

laterite

weathered material composed principally of the oxides of iron, aluminum, titanium, and manganese; laterite ranges from soft, earthy, porous soil to hard, dense rock.

lateritic soil

1. soil containing laterite.
2. any reddish soil developed from weathering. Also known as latosol.

laterization

those conditions of weathering that lead to removal of silica and alkalies, resulting in a soil or rock with high concentrations of iron and aluminum oxides (laterite).

lateroid

the metasomatic replacement product. It contains hydrated iron or magnesium oxides.

laterolog

an electric geophysical borehole log which measures the resistivity of the formations within a thin circular disc around the borehole.

latite

the term used for a propyritic extrusive rock which has phenocrysts of plagioclase and potassium feldspar in almost equal amounts, with little or no quartz, and a finely crystalline to glassy groundmass.

latosol

a great group of zonal soils which are characterized by deep weathering and abundant hydrous-oxide material.

lattice constant

a parameter defining the unit cell of a crystal lattice i.e., the length of the edge of the cell or an angle between edges. Also known as lattice parameter.

lattorfian

a stratigraphic stage name which is used for the European Lower Oligocene.

laue back-reflection method

an X-ray diffraction method in which the incident beam is directed at the sample through the centre of a flat piece of film. Back-diffracted radiation causes a pattern of spots on the film which can be interpreted with the aid of a net.

laurasia

laurasia is the name of a large continent. Some scientists think that it formed when the super-continent of Pangaea split about 215 million years ago, during the Mesozoic Era. Laurasia may have gradually split further, to create North America, Greenland, Europe and Asia.

laurdalite

an alkalic syenite having more than 10 per cent modal feldspathoids and characterized by porphyritic texture. Igneous rock of the syenite clan. A very coarse-grained pseudorphyritic plutonic rock; contains nepheline, anorthclase, soda-or-thoclase, diallage and diopside.

laurentia

a supercontinent present during and subsequent tc the Variscan orogeny comprising the Canadian shield, Greenland, parts of NW Europe and some other parts of North America.

lava

the material which is extruded by a volcano. It consists of molten or partially molten silicate material and reaches the earth's surface through volcanic vents and fissures. Their composition ranges from acidic to ultrabasic, although basic lavas account for more than 90% of the whole. Acid lavas have been highly viscous and rarely cover very large areas, while basic lavas have a much lower viscosity and flow readily.

lava blister

a small hollow steepsided swelling raised on the surface

of a lava flow by gas bubbles puffing up the viscous crust of the flow.

lava cave

a cave formed as molten rock solidified, possibly termed a pseudokarst feature.

lava cone

a volcanic cone that was formed of lava flows.

lava done

the term used for a done-shaped mountain of solidified a lava in the form of many individual flows which is formed by the extrustion of highly fluid lava.

lava field

a wide area of lava flow; it is commonly several square kilometres in area and forms along the base of a large compound volcano or on the flanks of shield volcanoes.

lava flow

1. a lateral, surficial stream of molten lava issuing from a volcanic cone or from a fissure.
2. the solidified mass of rock formed when a lava stream congeals.

lava fountain

a jetlike eruption of lava that issues vertically from a volcanic vent or fissure. Also known as fire fountain.

lava lake

a lake of lava that is molten and fluid; usually contained within a summit volcanic crater or in a pit crater on the flanks of a shield volcano.

lava plain

a broad stretch of level or nearly level land usually many hundreds of squares kilometres in extent underlain by a relatively thin succession of lava flows most of which are basaltic and the product of fissure eruptions.

lava plateau

an elevated tableland or flat-topped highland that is several hundreds to several thousands of square kilometres in area; underlain by a thick succession of lava flows.

lava tube

the term used for a hollow space beneath the surface of a solidified lava flow which is formed by the withdrawl of molten lava after the surficial crust. It is also known as lava cave, lava tunnel.

law

a regularity which applies to all members of a broad class of phenomena.

law of accordant junctions (play fair's law)

'Tributary rivers enter a main river at the same level as that river without any sudden drop.' Not always correct, as channel sizes may affect the form of the junction.

law of divides

'the nearer the divide, the steeper the slope, with all points on a single being interdependent.' A law explaining the smooth slopes in badland areas.

law of equal declivities

the law stating that where homogeneous rocks have been maturely dissected by consequent streams all hillside slopes of valleys cut by the streams tend to develop at the same slope angle thereby forming symmetrical profiles of ridges spars, and valleys.

law of Faunal Succession
a general law of geology stating that fossil organisms are succeeding one another in a definite and recognizable order each geologic formation having a different total aspect of life from that in the formation above it and below it. The law also states that the relative ages of the rocks can be determined from their fossil content.

law of includedfFragments
the law states that if recognizable fragments of one rock have been found enclosed in another rock, then the enclosing rock must have been produced later than the rock material of the included fragments.

law of mineral stability
'minerals are in thermodyanmic equilibrium only in the environment in which they form.' An expansion for many eogenetic reactions.

law of nature
a generalization of science representing an intrinsic orderliness of natural phenomena or their necessary conformity to reason.

law of rational indices
the term used for the statement in cryptography that crystal faces are making simple rational intercepts on suitable-crystal axes, i.e., the axes of reference or the three axes that form the edges of the unit cell of each crystal lattice.

law of superposition
a law upon which all geologic chronology is based which states that in any sequence of sedimentary strata which is not overturned the youngest stratum is at the top and the oldest at the base. It means that each bed is younger than the bed beneath, but older than the bed above it.

laxfordian
a stratigraphic division of the Scottish Precambrian the younger Lweisian.

laxfordian orogeny
an orogeny affecting NW Scotland in the Precambrian from 1800-1600 million years.

layer
a tabular body of rock, ice, sediment, or soil lying parallel to the supporting surface and distinctly limited above and below.

layeredpernafrost
ground consisting of perennially frozen layers alternating with unfrozen layers or taliks.

layer sulphides group
a group of sulphide minerals characterized by a structure derived from the nickel

arsenide group by the omission of a complete cation layer, with metal atoms in octahedral coordination and octahedra in the same layer sharing edges.

layered igneous rock
an igneous rock which displays mineralogical and/or chemical layering.

lazuli
a synonym of lapis lazuli. Also spelled lazule.

leaching
1. refers to the dissolution of soluble constituents of a mixture by a liquid solvent.
2. refers to the extraction of soluble metals or salts from an ore by using slowly percolating solutions.

lead
lead is an element. It is a very heavy, dark grey metal. There are several lead ores. The most common is galena. Lead can be used as a building material, in alloys with other metals and in many other ways.

leader
a thin mineralized vein relate to the main ore-carrying vein and which aids its discovery.

leaf mold
a soil layer or compost consisting principally of decayed vegetable matter.

leancannel coal
cannel coal that is low in hydrogen and transitional to bituminous coal in rank.

lechatelierite
naturally occurring fused silica glass which occurs in quartzose enclosures in volcanic rocks.

ledian
lower upper Eocene geologic time. Also known as Auversian.

lee
the side of a hill, dune or other object that is sheltered or turned away from the wind.

lee side
the downstreams side of a body sheltered from the dominant flow direction. cf. stoss side.

left lateral fault
a fault in which movement is such that an observer walking toward the fault along an index plane would turn to the left to find the other part of the displaced index plane. Also known as sinisterly fault.

legend
explanation of the symbols and patterns shown on a diagram of map.

leintwardinian
a stratigraphic stage which is used for the name for the base of the British Upper Ludlovian (Silurian System).

lenan
a Cambrian succession in Siberia covering part of the Atdabanian, the Lenian and part of the Solvan.

lenticle
a bed or rock stratum or body that is lensshaped.

leonardian
a North American provincial series: Lower Permian

lepiodoblastic
a texture term applicable to

foliations or schistosity which are produced by planar minerals, e.g., mica.

lepidoblastic texture

a metamorphic texture comprising foliation or schistosity.

lepodocystoidea

a class of phylum Echinodermia close to the common ancestry of the Crinoidea and Cystoidea. Range Lower Cambrian.

leptite

a quartz-feldspathic metamorphic rock which is finegrained having little or no foliation. It is formed as a result of regional metamorphism of the highest grade.

leptogeosyncline

a deep oceanic trough that has not been filled with sedimentation and is associated with volcanism.

leptynite

medium grade regional metamorphic rock. A light coloured coares grained granular rock; contains quartz, feldspar, mica and chlorite.

letna

an Ordovician succession in Boheam covering part of the Costonian and the Harnagian.

leucitite

refers to a fine-grained or porphyritic extrusive rock or hypabyssal igneous rock. It is mostly composed of pyroxene and Lucite.

leucosome

a centimetric- to metricscale, coarse-grained, quartzofeld-spathic vein found in peltic and psammitic metamorphic rocks, which may represent a migmaitic product of a low melting point liquid segregated from the sediment during high-grade metamorphism.

leucotephrite

a geological term used to denote leucite rich, nepheline free, tephrites.

levantian

a stratigraphic stage name which is used for the top of the European Pliocene (Tertiary System).

levy-mises equations

a fundamental law of plasticity in which strain rates are proportional to deviatoric stress.

lewisian

a stratigraphic division of the Scottish Precambrian, the oldest in Britain, covered, uncomfortably by Torridonian.

lherzolite

an ultrabasic rock having olivine and ortho-and clinopyroxenes.

liassic

the Lower Jurassic period of geologic time. Also known as Lias.

liangshan

a Permian succession in China equivalent to the Asselian.

lichenometry

a relative or absolute dating method for the exposure of a surface using the concentric growths of long-lived lichen, often used in the dating of glacial deposits.

lift force

the force experienced by a sediment grain, in a direction at right angles to the flow direction, generated by pressure differences over its surface.

lignite

a brown-black coal. It is intermediate in coalification between peat and sub-bituminous coal. It is consolidated coal having a calorific value less than 8300 BTU/lb.

limb

the area of fold between adjacent fold hinges; it may be planar or slightly curved.

limburgite

a dark basalt glass having olivine and augite phenocysts with little or no feldspar. Analysis reveals that it is commonly undersaturated.

lime

lime is a solid, white compound. It is also the name used for salts of calcium. The two forms of lime are quicklime and slaked lime. Quicklime is an oxide of calcium and is used as a fertilizer. When water is added, quicklime becomes calcium hydroxide. This is slaked lime which is used in cements.

lime mud

the unconsolidated micritric component of a limestone.

limestone

a rock comprising > 50% calcium carbonate, since the Cambrian partly or wholly of biogenic origin.

limiting depth

the maximum depth at which the top of an anomalous body could lie and still give rise to an observed geophysical anomaly.

limnic

a descriptive term which is applicable to the environment of freshwater lakes. It is employed especially of coal basins, as the opposite of paralic.

limnology

deals with the scientific study of fresh waters, especially of ponds and lakes.

limurite

high grade contact metamorphic rock. A coarse granular rock; contaisaxinite, diopside, actionlite, zoisite, albite, and quartz; produced at granite, calcareous rock contacts.

lindoite

refers to a igneous rock of the granite clan. It is a medium to coarse-grained hypabyssal rock having microcline-microperthite, arfvedsonite, quartz, and zircon.

linear circuit

the property of metamorphic rocks of breaking into long planar fragments.

line mapping

detailed geological mapping at

scales of 1:2500 or more, used for complex areas, in which offsets are taken to an exposures from a surveyed base line.

lineation

a repeated or penetrative linear structure in a rock mass. Commonly used for a metamorphic fabric of non-specific genesis, but also applied to features of fault planes, folds, elongate crystal alignment in igneous rocks and current lineation, etc. in sedimentary rocks.

link

an unbroken section of a stream channel between two notes in a drainage network.

linsen

a sand lens of lenticular bedding in mud.

liplodatrinite

a maceral of coal within the exinite group, having no recognizable structure and low reflectance and florescence.

liptobiolith

a fossil gum or resin, e.g. amber.

liquation deposit

an oxide-sulphide deposit forming as the result of liquid immiscibility in a mixed sulphide-silicate magma. The dense sulphides form globules that sink and accumulate at the base of the magma.

liquefied petroleum gas (LPG)

liquefied propane and butane extracted from wet gas.

liquid-crystal display

a digital display in an electronic device like calculator, etc., based on liquid crystal cells that change their reflectivity in an applied electric field.

liquid limit

may be defined as the minimum amount of water which is to be mixed with a sediment or soil so that, under standard conditions of test, the mineral is capable of flowing like a liquid.

lissamphibia

a subclass of class Amphibia; the frogs, toads and Apoda. Range Triassic-Recent.

listric

a term applicable to fracture planes which are curving either to near horizontal ones which are steepening, or to near-vertical ones which are becoming less steep. Those which are concave upwards conform to the definition most strictly, and the term 'negatively listric' is applicable to those which are concave downwards. The term 'shoulderthrust' is also used for the latter type.

litenschichten

a Silurian succession in Bohem covering the Rhuddanian, Aeronian, Telychian, Sheinwoodian and part of the Homerian.

lithic

a descriptive term which is applied to rock fragments occurring in a later formed rock, e.g., lithic tuff.

lithic block

a pyroclastic fragment of initially solid rock over 64mm in size.

lithic tuff

type of volcanic tuff. Dominant constituent of later formed rock fragments.

lithification

1. Conversion of a newly deposited sediment into an indurated rock. Also known as lithifaction.

2. Compositional change of coal to bituminous shale or other rock.

lithiophorite

lithium rich variety of wad. It has metallic lustre and shows blackish-grey streak. Its hardness on Mohas scale is 3.0.

lithium

lithium is an element. It is a soft, silvery metal. Pure lithium cannot be found because it joins with other elements so easily. Lithium is used in batteries, for alloys and in medicine.

litho

a prefix which means rock or stone.

lithoclast

a class of an origin not associated with the main depositional system. cf. intraclast.

lithofacies

a subdivision of a specified stratigraphic unit distinguished on the basis of lithologic features.

lithofacies map

the facies map of an area based on lithologic characters; shows areal variation in all aspects of the lithology of a stratigraphic unit.

lithofraction

refers to the breaking of rock fragments during transportation in streams or by wave action on breaches.

lithographic limestone

a dense, compact, fine-grained crystalline limestone having a pale creamy-yellow or grayish colour. Also known as lithographic stone; litho stone.

lithology

a term which is usually applicable to sediments, referring to their general characteristics. It has been used in several rather loose senses, e.g., 'lithological variation', which refers to variation in composition and texture; 'lithology of a formation', which means the rock types present in a stratigraphic sub-division. Lithology is generally related to descriptions which are based upon hand-specimens and outcrops rather than microscopic or chemical features.

lithophile

elements having a strong affinity for oxygen, concentrated in the silicate minerals.

lithophysa

a cenitmetric-scale, rounded mass found in glassy and partly crystalline, felsic volcanic rocks comprising concentric shells separated by voids. Possibly formed during rapid crystallization alternating with gas expansion or by the chemical alteration of spherulites, with which they are found.

lithophysae
hollow bubble like structures which consist of concentric shells of finely crystalline alkali feldspar, quartz and other minerals. It is found in certain silicic volcanic rocks.

lithosome
a sediment body deposited under uniform physical and chemical conditions.

lithosol
a group of shallow soils lacking well-defined horizons and composed of imperfectly weathered fragments of rock.

lithosphere
1. The rigid outer crust of rock on the earth about 50 miles thick, above the asthenosphere. Also known as oxysphere.
2. since the development of plate tectonics theory, a term referring to the rigid, upper 100 kilometres of the crust and upper mantle, above the asthenosphere.

lithotope
1. the environment under which a sediment is deposited.
2. an area of uniform sedimentation.

lithotype
a macroscopic band in humic coals, analysed on the basis of physical characteristics rather than botanical origin.

lithotypes of banded coal
the four basic constituents of banded coal that can be used for identification in hand specimen and classification; clarain, durain, fusain and vitrain.

lit-par-lit
pertaining to the penetration of bedded, schistose, or the foliate rocks by innumerable narrow sheets and tongues of granitic rock.

little Ice Age
a period of expansion of mountain glaciers, marked by climatic deterioration, that began about 5500 years ago and extended to as late as A.D. 1550-1850 in some regions, as the Alps, Norway, Iceland, and Alaska.

littoral
refers to the benthic environment of depth zone which is present between high water and low water. It also refers to the organisms of that environment.

littoral drift
materials moved by waves and currents of the littoral zone. Also known as longshore drift.

littoral sediments
deposits of littoral drift.

littoral transport
the movement of littoral drift.

liver opal (menilite)
opal with a colour resembling liver.

lizzie
a Carboniferous/Permian succession in Queensland. Australia, covering parts of the Upper Carboniferous and Asselian.

llandellian
a stratigraphic stage name which is used for the European Lower Ordovocian.

llano
a term for extensive plane, with or without vegetation.

llanvirnian
a stratigraphic stage name which is used for the European Lower Ordovician.

load cast
an irregularity at the base of an overlying stratum, usually sandstone, that projects into an underlying stratum, usually shale or clay.

loam
soil mixture of sand, silt, clay, and humus.

local magnitude
an earthquake magnitude scale for the crustal events, within 600 km of the seismograph, based on wave amplitudes and a simple correction for distance.

local peat
peat formed by groundwater. Also known as basin peat.

lochkovium
a Devonian succession in Bohemia equivalent to the Lochkovian.

lode
a fissure in consolidated rock filled with mineral; usually applied to metalliferous deposits.

lodestone
common name for magnetite, Fe_3O_4. It shows well defined polarity when it is freely suspended.

lodranite
a stony iron meteorite composed of bronzite and olivine within a fine network of nickel-iron.

loess
an essentially unconsolidated, unstratified calcareous silt; commonly it is homogeneous, permeable, and buff to gray in colour, and contains calcareous concretions and fossils.

loess kindchen
an irregular or spheroidal nodule of calcium carbonate that is found in loess.

log
a record of the rocks which are passed through by a borehole or a well.

logan canyon
a Cretaceous succession on the Scotian shelf of Canada covering the Aptian, Albian and part of the Cenomanian.

lomonosovite $Na_5Ti_2Si_2PO_{13}$
a dark brown mineral of uncertain crystal system; composed of sodium titanium-phosphorosilicate; show suneven fracture and poorcleavage. Its hardnesson

Mohs scale is 3.0-4.0.

longitude

refers to the angular distance between the meridian of a given place and the prime meridian of Greenwitch, England. It is measured east or west to a maximum value of 180°.

longitudinal dune

a type of linear dune ridge that extends parallel to the direction of the dominant dunebuilding winds.

longitudinal fault

a fault parallel to the trend of the surrounding structure.

longmyndian

the term used for a stratigraphic division of the English Precambrian, the Shrophsire Post-Uriconian sediments.

long river profile

the elevation of a river channel plotted against distance downstream.

longshore bar

a ridge of sand, gravel, or mud built on the seashore by waves and currents, generally parallel to the shore and submerged by high tides. Also known as offshore bar.

longshore drift

the shore-parallel transport of sediment in one direction as the result of oblique wave action.

longshore trough

a long, wide, shallow depression of the sea floor parallel to the shore.

lonsdaleite (c)

a hexagonal polymorph of diamond found in iron meteorites.

loparite

alkali bearing variety of perovskite from the Kola Peninsular, USSR.

lopolith

the term used for a saucer-shaped igneous intrusion which is concave upwards. Small lopoliths are intruded into folded strata and their shape has been controlled by the folding. However, the name is also used for very large basin-shaped masses of igneous rock.

losing stream

a stream which loses water when flowing across permeable rocks. cf. gaining stream.

lostriver

(1) a dried up steam in an arid region.

(2) a stream that disappears underground in a darkest region.

love wave

a seismic surface wave in which particle motion is horizontal and perpendicular to the direction of propagation. The wave travels by multiple reflection in the surface low velocity layer.

low-angle fault

a fault that dips at an angle less than 45°

lower cambrian

the earliest epoch of the Cambrian period of geologic

time, ending about 540,000,000 years ago.

lower continental crust
the continental crust between 10-12 km depth or the Conrad discontinuity and the Mohorovicic discontinuity, formed of granodioritic rocks in the granulite facies with a density approximately of 3.0 Mg m^{-3}. cf. upper continental crust.

lower devonian
the earliest epoch of the Devonian period of geologic time, extending from about 400 to 385,000,000 years ago.

lower greensand
a Cretaceous succession in England covering the Aptian and parts of the Albian.

lower Jurassic
the earliest epoch of the Jurassic period of geologic time, extending from about 185 to 170,000,000 years ago.

lower mantle
the portion of the mantle below a depth of about 1000 kilometre. Also known as inner mantle; mesosphere; pallasite shell.

lower Mississippian
the earliest epoch of the Mississippian period of geologic time, beginning about 350,000,000 years ago.

lower Ordovician
the earliest epoch of the Ordovician period of geologic time, extending from about 490- to 460,000,000 years ago.

lower Permian
the earliest epoch of the Permian period of geologic time, extending from about 275- to 260,000,000 years ago.

lower silurian
the earliest epoch of the Silurian period of geologic time, beginning about 420,000,000 years ago.

lower-stage plane bed
a flat sediment bed forming at low shear stresses from sand coarser than 0.6 mm diameter and replacing the ripples of finer sediment.

lower triassic
the earliest epoch of the Triassic period of gologic time, extending from about 230- to 215,000,000 years ago.

lowestoftian
a stratigraphic stage name which is used for the British mid Middle Pleistocene.

low-moor bog
a bog that is at or slightly below the ground water table.

low-moor peat
peat found in low-moor bogs or swamps and containing little or no sphagnum. Also known as fen peat.

low pressure
low pressure is an area of the atmosphere where atmospheric pressure is low. During a period of low pressure, or depression, the weather is often wet.

low-rank metamorphism
a metamorphic process that occurs under conditions of low to moderate pressure and temperature.

low-tide terrace
a flat area of a beach adjacent to the low-water line.

low-volatile coal
a coal that is nonagglomerating, has 78% to less than 86% fixed carbon, and 14% to less than 22% volatile matter.

ludhamian
a stratigraphic stage name which is used for the British Lower Pleistocene.

ludlovian
a European stage of geologic time; Upper Silurian, below Gedinnian of Devonian, above Wenlockian.

lugarite
Igneous rock which has intermediate composition between syenite and gabbro clans. It contains barkevikite, titanaugite, labradorite, and nepheline.

luisian
a North American stage of geologic time: Miocene

lujavrite
igneous rock of the syenite clan; contains microline-micropesrthite, oligoclase, nepheline, aegirine and arfvedsinite.

luminescence
the emission of light by a material when irradiated by electromagnetic radiation of different wavelength.

lunarite
a general term for lighttoned, highly reflecting surface rocks of the lunar highlands or errace.

lunette
a broad, low crescentic mound of windblown fine silt and clay.

lusclalite
igneous rock which is having intermediate composition between syenite and gabbro clans. It is coarse-grained plutonic rock and has plagioclase, orthoclase, olivine, biotite, and nepheline.

lusitanian
lower Jurassic geologic time.

lustre
lustre is the shine on the surface of a mineral. Different kinds of stones and minerals have different lustres.

lutaceous
used for a sedimentary rock which is formed from mud; pertaining to lutite.

lutecite
a fibrous, chalcedonylike quartz with optical anomalies that have led to its being considered a distinct species.

lutite
a fine-grained sedimentary rock in which silt makes up one third to two thirds of the total.

luxullianite
refers to an igneous rock of the granite clan. A porphyritic plutonic rock; having phenocrysts of orthoclase in a groundmass of quartz; tourmaline, orthoclase, mica and cassiterite.

lycopsida
a class of division Trachaeopyta, kingdom

Plantae; the club mosses and related plants. Range Devonian Recent.

lyddite

the term used for a dense black variety of chert formerly used as a touchstone.

lynchert

a bank of earth that accumulates on the downhill side of an ancient plongeo hed field as the disturbed soil moves downslope under gravity.

lysocline

refers to the level of ocean depth at which the rate of solution of calcium carbonate just exceeds its combined rate of deposition and precipitation.

ma okou

a Pernian succession in China equivalent to the Kungurian and Zechstein.

maar

a volcanic crater.that is created by violent explosion but is not accompanied by igneous extrusion;sometimes, it is filled by a small circular lake.

macedonite $PbTiO_3$

1. a mineral having oxides of lead and titanium.
2. a basaltic rock having orthoclase, biotite olivine, sodic plagioclase, and rare pyriboles.

maceral

the microscopic organic constituents found in coal.

maceration

refers to the process of disintegrating sedimentary rock like coal and shale to extract and concentrate acid insoluble microfossils. This process is widely used in palynology.

mackensite $Fe_6Si_3AlO_{15}(OH)_3$

a greenish-black, monoclnic mineral composed of basic iron aluminosilicate.

macrinite

a coal maceral of the inertinite group resembling fusininte but without cell structure.

macro-axis

the term used for the larger lateral axis of an orthorhombic or triclinic crystal, it is usually the b-axis.

macrofauna

1. widely distributed fauna.
2. fauna of a macrohabitat.

macrofossil

a fossil large enough to be studied without the aid of a microscope.

macrophyric

descriptive of the texture of a medium-to fine-grained igneous rock with phencrysts >2 mm long. cf. microphyric.

macropore

a pore in soil of a large enough size so that water is not held in it by capillary attraction.

maculose

of a group of contact-metamorphosed rocks or their structures, having spotted or knotted character.

made ground

an area of land that has been constructed by man, often using a landfill of natural materials.

maestrichtian
a European stage of geologic time; Upper Cretaceous.

mafic
a general term; used for describing ferromagnesian minerals. It is not applied to rocks which consist mainly of ferromagnesian minerals for which melanocratic has been the correct term.

mafite
an alternate name for aphanite.

maghemite.y-Fe_2O_3
a member of the magnetite series of minerals; occurs in the form of iron oxide that is strongly magnetic.

magma
a melt, generally containing suspended crystals and dissolved gases or volatiles, formed by total or partial melting of solid crust or mantle rocks. Comprises polymers of interconnected, disordered Si-O tetrahedra with cations such as magnesium, iron, calcium, sodium and potassium in loose coordination with the oxygens and may range in composition from ultramafic through basalitic, andesitic, dacitic and rhyolitic. Magma diversification can take place through the process of magmatic differentiation (including fractional crystallization, liquid immiscibility and vapour transport), assimilation or magma mixing.

magma blister
a pocket of magma whose formation has raised the overlying land surface.

magma chamber
a larger reservoir in the crust of the earth that is occupied by a body of magma.

magma geothermal system
a geothermal system in which the dominant source of heat is a large reservoir of igneous magma within an intrusive chamber or lava pool; an example is the Yellowstone Park area of Wyoming.

magmatic differentiation
the separation of an initially homogenous magma into two or more magmas of contrasting composition by the processes of fractional crystallization, liquid immiscibility or vapour transport.

magmatic emanations
refers to fluids of magmatic origin; the term has been found to be more or less synonymous with volatiles.

magmatic stoping
a process of igneous intrusion in which magma gradually works its way upward by breaking off and engulfing blocks of the country rock.

magmatic water
water which arises from an underground magmatic source.

magnafacies
a major, continuous belt of deposits that is homogeneous in lithologic and paleontologic

characteristics and that extends obliquely across time planes or through several time-stratigraphic units.

magnesian limestone

1. the name used for a stratigraphic formation in the permain of Great Britain.

2. A limestone having less than 15% of magnesium carbonate in which the mineral dolomite could not be detected by the older staining tests. Newer techniques are able to detect this mineral and modern usage of the term means,a limestone having a low percentage of dolomite.

magnesiokatophorite

a magnesium rich member of the catophorite series.

magnesite ($MgCO_3$)

a carbonate mineral, the source of magnesia.

magnesium

magnesium is an element. It is a silvery-grey metal. Magnesium is found in many minerals and also in sea water. It burns with a very bright flame.

magnetic anomaly

the variation in the geomagnetic field arising from variation in the magnetic properties of underlying rocks.

magnetic dating

a relative or absolute dating method making use of the secular variation of the geomagnetic field, polarity reversals or apparent polar wander, which cause remanent magnetization directions to vary with time. Comparison of directions for different regions at the same time will demonstrate if they have moved relative to each other since the magnetization was acquired.

magnetic epoch

a time interval of constant geomagnetic field polarity, normally longer than 10,000 years.

magnetic equator

a line of zero magnetic dip lying fairly near the geographical equator. Also known as aclinic line; geomagnetic equator.

magnetic log

a geophysical borehole log in which the geomagnetic field is measured down a borehole to provide information on the presence of magnetic rocks.

magnetic moment

(1) the torque experience by a magnetic dipole in a field of unit magnetic field strength. It is measured in webre metres. This is also called magnetic dipole moment.

(2) the product IA, where I is the current flowing through a small loop of wire of area A. It is measured in ampere metres square (Am^2). This is also called the electromagnetic moment.

magnetic north

magnetic north is the position of the magnetic pole at the northern point of the Earth. It is in Canada, near the geographic North Pole.

magnetic observatory
a fixed installation which continuously monitors all the magnetic elements and thus records diurnal and secular variation of the geomagnetic field.

magnetic pole
the points at which the lines of magnetic force surrounding a dipole converge (single poles very rarely exist in isolation). The Earth's magnetic poles are displaced from the geographic poles and are not exactly antipodal.

magnetic potential
the work which must be done against a magnetic field to bring a magnetic pole of unit strength from a reference point to point under consideration. Also known as magnetic scalar potential.

magnetic quiet zone
a region with few or no magnetic anomalies, particularly an area of oceanic crust with no magnetic lineations due to an absence of geomagnetic polarity reversals or the loss of original magnetizations.

magnetic spectrometer
an instrument that can be attached to a transmission electron microscope which allows the energy lost by in-elastically-scattered electrons to be measured. This is characteristics of the elements present and allows microanalyses to be made.

magnetic storm
a magnetic storm is a disturbance in the Earth's magnetic field. It is caused by changes in the activity of the Sun. Magnetic storms can interfere with radio waves and satellites.

magnetic variometer (variometer)
an early form of magnetometer based on a small dipole suspended in the geomagnetic field.

magnetometer
an instrument for measuring a magnetic field. Fluxgate, proton and cesium vapour magnetometers are used in magnetic surveys to measure the geomagentic field. Spinner and cryogenic magnetometers measure the fields associated with rock sample in palaeomagnetic studies.

magnitude
magnitude describes the force of an earthquake. The magnitude of an earthquake is measured on he Richter scale.

major element
an element present in a rock in high concentration, so that it controls the presence of minerals such as feldspar and pyroxene. cf. trace element.

major fold
a large-scale fold with which minor folds are usually associated.

malachite
a fine-grained lamprophyre

with small, rare phenocrysts or hornblende, labradorite and sometimes biotite embedded in a matrix of hornblende, andesine, and some quartz.

malakovian

a Triassic succession in New Zealand equivalent to the Nammalian.

malignite

igneous rock of the syenite clan and contains orthoclase, nepheline, apatite, biotite, and aegirine-augite.

mallardite $MnSo_4.7H_2O$

a light palerose coloured monoclinic mineral composed of hydrous mangaese sulphate.

malleable

a tenacity descriptor indicating a mineral that can be hammered into a thin sheet.

malm

the Upper Jurassic geologic series, above Dogger and below Cretaceous.

malvernian

refers to the stratigraphic division of the English Precambrian, the Herefordshire Pre-Uriconian.

mammalia/mammals

a class of vertebrate animals that suckle their young, the fossils of which are classified by their teeth. Range late Triassic-Recent.

manganese nodule

small, irregular black to brown concretions consisting chiefly of manganese salts and manganese oxide minerals; formed in oceans as a result of pelagic sedimentation or precipitation.

mangaotanian

a Cretaceous succession in New Zealand covering parts of the Cenomanian and Turonian.

mangrove swamp

an intertidal region of mudflats and mangrove vegetation found along sheltered, low-energy shorelines in tropical areas.

manjak

a variety of bitumen possessing brilliant lustre.

mantle

the term used for that portion of the earth' interior which is lying between the Mohorovicic and Gutenburg Discontinuities, i.e., from a depth of 35 km. to 2,900 km. The density has been found to range from 3.3 at the Mohorovicic Discontinuity to 5.7 at the Gutegburg Discontinuity.

mantle bedding

a uniform thickness of pyroclastic material over all but the steepest topography.

mantle transition zone

a layer in the mantle between 400 and 700 km across which there is an increase in seismic velocity due to phase changes of the minerals present to more closely-packed, denser forms.

manto

a sedimentary or igneous ore body occurring in flat-lying depositional layers.

maozhung

a Cambrian succession in China covering parts of the Lenian and Solvan.

marble

1. a metamorphic limestone rock, which is produced by recrystallization under conditions of thermal metamorphism, although marbles of regional metamorphic origin are not uncommon.
2. Commercially, any crystallized carbonate rock, including true marble and certain types of limestone, that can take polish and can be used as architectural or ornamental stone.

march analysis

the analysis of the behaviour of passive markers in homogeneous body that is deforming by viscous flow. Elongate markers originally parallel to the axis of shortening rotate symmetrically from this direction by an amount dependent on the strain to form a bimodal preferred orientation.

marekanite

rounded to subangular obsidian bodies that occur in masses or perlite.

mare material

dark and relatively smooth, heavily created igneous rock, chiefly of mafic, ultramafic composition, underlying the lunar maria.

margarite

(1)a string of beadlike globulites; commonly found in glassy igneous rocks.

(2) $CaAl_2(Al_2Si_2)O_{10}(OH)_2$ A pink, reddish, or yellow, brittle mica mineral.

margarosanite $PbCa_2(SiO_3)_3$

a colourless or show-white triclinic mineral which occurs in lamellar masses.

marginal escarpment

a seaward slope of a marginal plateau with a gradient of 1:10 or more.

marginal fissure

a magma-filled fracture bordering an igneous intrusion.

marginal ore

ore which just repays the cost of exploitation.

marginal plateau

a relatively flat sheft adjacent to a continent and similar toporagaphically to, but deeper than, a continental shelf.

marginal sea

a semi-closed sea adjacent to a continent, floored by submerged continental mass.

marine band

refers to a layer of sediment which is characterized by the presence of marine fossils and interbedded with non-marine sediments. The term is especially applicable to such bands in coal-bearing strata, where they constitute a major means of correlation between basin of deposition.

marine-cut terrace

a terrace or platform cut by

wave erosion of marine origin. Also known as wave-cut terrace.

marine erosion

refers to the processes which are responsible for the wearing back and destruction of coastilines. Erosion is carried out by the sea itself which acts as a 'hammer' on the rocks and thereby shatters them, but the process gets reinforced if the waves are armed with rock fragments, and if the air contained in crevices and cavities of the rocks is suddenly compressed by the waves. In some areas (limestone), erosion may also get augmented by seawater taking material into solution.

marine swamp

an area of low, salty or blackish water found along the shores and characterized by abundant grasses, trees and similar vegeation. Also known as paralic swamp.

maritime

maritime describes something which is near the sea or which is affected by the sea. A maritime climate is temperate, and has mild weather all year. The temperature do not change much from winter to summer and there is no dry season.

mariupolite

refers to the igneous rock of the diorite clan. A coarse-grained porphyritic plutonic rock. It consists of phenocrysts of nepheline in a groundmass of sodaclase, nepheline, aegirite, and lapidomelane.

markfieldite

the term used for igneous rock of the granite clan. It is a fine-grained porphyritic hypabyssal rock and has phenocrysts of plagioclase in a groundmass of quarts, orthoclase, and muscovite.

marl

a deposit of crumbling earthy material composed principally of clay with magnesium and calcium carbonate; used as a fertilizer for lime-deficient soils.

marlstone

an indurated rock of about the same composition as marl; i.e., anearthy limestone; it is less fissile than shale.

marly

pertaining to, containing, or resembling marl.

marmorize

refers to the process of recrystallization of limestone by heat (with or without pressure effects) to form marble. The term is now obsolete, but is occasionally applicable to slight thermal effects which are produced by a dyke or sill intruded into limestone.

marmolite

a pale-green serpentine mineral which occurs in thin laminations. It is a variety of chrysotile.

marosite

an igneous rock of the diorite

clan, a medium to coarse-grained plutonic rock; contains biotite, augite, apatite, sandine, plagioclase, nepheline and sodalite.

marsh

a marsh is an area of low, wet ground. In a marsh, the drainage is poor and the water often floods over the surface. Marshes can form at estuaries when the land becomes flooded with salt water.

mascon

a large, high-density lunar mass concentration below a ringed mare on the surface of the moon.

massif

a massif is a large mountain or group of mountains. A massif stands out clearly from the surrounding lowlands.

massive

of a mineral deposit, having a large concentration of ore in one place.

mass movement

unit downslope movement of aportion of the land surface, as in creep, landslide or slip.

matrix

the natural material in which a rock of mineral is embedded.

matrix porosity

core-sample porosity determined from a small sample of the core, in contrast to total porosity, where the whole core is used.

maturity

1. the second stage of the erosion cycle in the topographic development of a landscape or region characterized by numerous and closely spaced mature streams, reduction of level surfaces to slopes, large well-defined drainage systems, and the absence of swamps or lakes on the uplands. Also known as topographic maturity.

2. a stage in the development of a shore or coast that begins with the attainment of a profile of equilibrium.

3. the extent to which the texture and composition of a clastic sediment approach the ultimate end product.

4. the stage of stream development at which maximum vigour and efficiency has been reached.

maturity index

a measure of the progress of a clastic sediment the direction of chemical or mineralogic stability; for example, a high ratio of quartz + cherts/ feldspar + rock fragments indicates a highly mature sediment.

maucherite 16[$Ni_{11}As_8$]

a tetragonal mineral which is composed of nickel arsenide. It consists of tabular crystals and shows blackish-grey streak, uneven fracture, and no cleavage. Its hardness on Mohs scale has been 5.0.

maximum subsidence

the maximum amount of subsidence in a basin.

maze cave

a consisting of repeatedly rejoined passages.

meander

the term used for any naturally occurring bend which a river or stream may develop along its course, often forming a series of re-entrant curves. The precise cause of meandering is that meanders are formed as a result of the river taking a preferred route which is decided by gradient, cross-sectional area of channel, and ratio of rate of discharge to load. Only in few circumstances is a meander formed by casual obstructions.

meander belt

the zone along the floor of a valley across which a meandering stream periodically shifts its channel.

meander core

a hill encircled by a stream meander. Also known as rock island.

meandering stream

a mature stream having a pattern of successive meanders. Also known as snaking stream.

meander niche

a conical or crescentic opening in the wall of a cave formed by downward and lateral stream erosion.

meander plain

a plain built by the meandering process, or a palin of lateral accretion.

meander scar

a crescentic, concave mark on the face of a bluff or valley wall formed by a meandering stream.

meander spur

an undercut projection of high land that extends into the concave part of, and is enclosed by, a meander.

measures

a mining term which is formerly applicable to sequences of sedimentary rocks which could be measured in bore-holes or mine shafts. In this sense the term is almost obsolete, although preserved in some 'Coal Measures', in Western Europe. Occasionally the term is employed as a synonym for 'beds' or 'division' of strata.

mechanical weathering

breakdown or weathering of the earth's surface by mechanical means as frost wedging and root wedging.

medial moraine

1. an elongate moraine carried in or upon the middle or a glacier and parallel to its sides. 2. A moraine formed by glacial abrasion of a rocky protuberance near the middle of a glacier.

median particle diameter

the middlemost particle diameter of a rock or sediment, larger than 50% of the diameter in the distribution and smaller than the other 50%.

medinian

refers to a stratigraphic stage name which is used for the North American Lower

Silurian. It is a synonym of Albion.

megabreccia

a rock consisting of randomly oriented clests with sharp edges and of very large size.

megacyclothem

a cycle of or combination of related cyclothems.

megaripple

a large sand wave.

megatectonics

the tectonics of the very large structural features of the earth.

melanocratic

dark-coloured, referring to igneous rock containing at least 50-60% mafic minerals. Also known as chromocratic; melanic.

meltegite

refers to feldspathoid igneous rock. It is a medium-grained granular plutonic rock which contains biotite, nepheline, pyroxene, and garnet.

meltegite

feldspathoid igneous rock; a medium-grained granular plutonic rock which contains biotite, nepheline, pyroxen and garnet.

menapian

a stratigraphic stage name which is being used for the top of the European Lower Pleistocene.

mendip

1. a buried hill that is exposed as an inlier. 2. A coastal-plain hill that was originally an offshore island.

meramecian

a stratigraphic stage name which is being used for the North American Middle Mississippian.

meridian

a meridian is an imaginary line around the Earth. The meridians run from the North Pole to the South Pole and cross the Equator at a right angle. Meridians are measurements of longitude. They are numbered from 0 to 180° to the east and to the west of the Greenwich meridian. The Greenwich meridian is 0° longitude.

meridional

pertaining to longitudinal movements or directions, that is, northerly or southerly.

mesa

Spanish term which is used for an isolated table-land area having steep sides, the result of a horizontal capping of hard strata having resisted denudation. In the course of time with continual erosion of the sides a mesa gets reduced to a smaller flat-topped hill—a butte. Mesas and buttes are found often in groups and may be considered, as a late stage in the dissection of a region of horizontally layered rocks.

mesocratic

term originally used for the group of rocks which are now described as mesotype. Mesotype is preferred, as the suffix 'cratic' means dominance and for the 'mean' to be dominant in this connotation has been obviously absurd.

mesocratic

a term used for rocks especially igneous ones that contain between 30 and 60% of dark mineral; *i.e.,* whose colour index lies between leucocratice and melanocratic.

mesogene

said of a mineral deposit or enrichment of mingled hypogene supergene solutions; also said of such solution and environment.

mesosiderite

a stony-iron meteorite containing about equal amounts of silicates and nickel-iron, with considerable troilite. Also known as grahamite.

mesostasis

in igneous rocks, it refers to the last fraction of the melt to consolidate in the spaces between the earlier-formed crystals. It may be taking the from of a glass or a eutectic, or may be appearing as a reaction rim around an earlier crystal.

mesotil

a semiplastic or semifriable derivative of chemically weathered hill; form beneath a partially drained area.

mesotype

a group of zeolite minerals, including natrolite, mesolite and scolecite.

mesotype

a term applicable to igneous rocks which have approximately equal quantities of light and dark minerals with a colour index of between 30 and 60 on Shand's scale.

mesozoic

mesozoic describes one of the three major eras in geological time. The Mesozoic Era lasted from about 248 million years ago until about 65 million years ago. Some scientists think that during this time the continents which we know today separated from Laurasia and Gondwanaland. The Mesozoic Era contains the Triassic, the Jurassic and the Cretaceos periods.

meta

a prefix which denotes metamorphism of the rock so qualified.

metaanthracite

anthracite coal containing at least 98% fixed carbon.

metabassite

any metamorphosed basic igneous rock.

metabentonite

altered bentonite, formed by compaction or metamorphism; it swells very little and lacks the usually high colloidal properties of bentonite.

metahalloysite

a term used in Europe for the less hydrous form of halloysite. Also known as halloysite in the United States.

metafentonite

altered bentonite, formed by

compaction or metamorphism; it swells very little and lacks the usual high colloidal properties of bentonite.

metalimnion

the term used for the horizontal layer of a thermal stratified lake in which the temperature decreases rapidly.

metalliferous

metal-bearing; pertaining to mineral deposit from which metals can be extracted by metallurgical operations.

metallogenic province

a region characterized by a particular mineral assemblage, or by one or more specific types of mineralization. Also known as metallographic province.

metamict

a term used for describing a mineral having radioactive elements which, although having external crystal form, fails to produce a normal X-ray diffraction pattern. It can be due-to an imperfect developments of the atomic lattice which destroys the basic pattern upon which the X-ray diffraction is based. The development of metamict structures is now assumed to be brought about by radioactive bombardment by atoms of uranium and /or thorium contained within the minerals in contact with it.

metamorphic facies

a set of metamorphic rocks characterized particular mineral associations indicating origin under restricted temperature and pressure conditions.

metamorphic rock reservoir

uncommon type of formation for oil reservoir; developed when secondary porosity results from fracturing or weathering.

metamorphisms auto

refers to changes which take place during the cooling of auigneous mass because of the activity of residual fluids within the mass.

metamorphism, thermal

metamorphic process involving heat alone, without significant pressure effects. It is normally associated with igneous, when the term contact metamorphism may be used.

metaquartzite

a quartzite which is formed by metamorphic recrystallization, as distinguished from an orthoquartzite, whose crystalline nature forms diagenetic origin.

metaripple

an asymmetrical sand ripple.

metasediment

a sediment or sedimentary rock which shows evidence of metamorphism.

meteor

any relatively small fragment of solid material which gets associated with a meteor and made luminous because of friction during passage throw the earth's atmosphere.

meteoric water

a term applied to water which enters the rocks from the atmosphere i.e., rain, dew, hail, snow and also the water of rivers and streams.

meteorite

any meteoroid that has fallen to the earth's surface.

meteorite crater

an impact crater on the surface of the earth or of a celestial body caused by a meteorite; a characteristic feature on the earth is the upturened rim, which formed as the rocks rebounded following the impact.

meteorograph

a meteorograph is an instrument. It is used by meteorologists to record information about the Earth's atmosphere. It is attached to a balloon and floats in the stratosphere.

metharmosis

changes that occur in a buried sediment after uplift or consolidation but before the onset of weathering. Also spelled metaharmosis.

meyerhofferite $Ca_2B_6o_{11}.6H_2O$

a colourless hydrated borate mineral which crystallizes in triclinic system.

miarolithic

a chorismite type of igneous rock having miarolitic cavities or vestiges thereof.

mica

mica is a kind of mineral. Mica has a smooth texture and breaks easily into sheets. Mica contains potassium, aluminium and silicon.

micaceous

consisting of; containing, or pertaining to mica.

micrite

1. a descriptive term used for the semiopaque crystalline matrix of limestones. It consists of chemically precipitated carbonate mud crystals less than 4 microns in diameter, and interpreted as lithified ooze.

2. a limestone having less than 1% allochems and consisting dominantly of micrite matrix.

microgranite

refers to a medium-grained acid igneous rock which has very similar mineralogical and chemical properties of granites (or adamellites in the case of microadamellites, and granodiorite in the case microgranodiorite). Microgranodites and their associates are found in dykes, sills, and small plug but much larger bodies of granophyre occasionally occur.

microgranular

1. said of the texture of a microcrystalline xenomorphic igneous rock, also said of a rock with such texture.

2. said of the texture of a carbonate sedimentary rock wherein the particles have been mostly 10 to 60 microns in diameter and are well sorted whereas the finer clay sized

matrix is absent, also said of a rock with such texture.
3. said of a forminiferal wall which is made of minute calcite crystals.

microhill
a very rough, small sand columns raised by the formation of piprakes, ranging from a few millimeters to several centimeters high.

microlite
1. refers to a very small crystal, but not so small as to be completely indeterminate. It is usually found embedded in glassy material.
2. an isometric mineral of the pyrochlore group which is found in pegmatites and constitutes an ore of tantalum.

micrologo

microlog
a drill-hole resistivity log recorded with electrodes mounted at short distance from each other in the face of a rubber-padded microresitivity sonde.

microsomite
chlorine rich variety of cancrinite.

microvitrain
a coal lithotype; fine vitrainlike lenses of laminae in clarain.

mid-Atlantic ridge
the mid-oceanic ridge in the Atlantic.

middle Cambrian
the geologic epoch between Upper and Lower Cambrian, beginning approximately 540,000,000 years ago.

middle Cretaceous
the geologic epoch between the Upper and Lower Cretaceous, beginning approximately 120,000,000 years ago.

middle Devonian
the geologic epoch between the Upper and Lower Devonian, beginning approximately 385,000,000 years ago.

middle Jurassic
the geologic epoch between the Upper and Lower Jurassic, beginning approximately 170,000,000 years ago.

middle ordovician
the geologic epoch between the Upper and Lower Ordovician, beginning approximately 460,000,00 years ago.

middle Pennsylvania
the geologic epoch between the Upper and Lower Pennsylvanian.

middle Permian
the geologic epoch between the Upper and Lower Permian, beginning approximately 260,000,000 years ago.

middle Silurian
the geologic epoch between the Upper and Lower Silurian.

middle Triassic
the geologic epoch between the Upper and Lower Triassic, beginning approximately 215,000,000 years ago.

midfan
the portion of an alluvial fan between the fanhead and the outer, lower margins.

mid-oceanic ridge
a continuous, median, seismic mountain range on the floor of

the ocean, extending through the North and South Atlantic oceans, the Indian Ocean, and the South Pacific Ocean; the topography is rugged, elevation is 1-3 kilometres, width is about 1500 km, and length is over 84, 000 km. Also known as mid-ocean ridge; mid-ocean rise; oceanic ridge.

miharaite

an igneous rock of the gabbro clan; a fine-grained poryphyrite extrusive rock; contains phenocrysts of bytwownite and hypershthene in a groundmass of a augite, plagioclase, and megnetite.

milky quartz

refers to an opaque milky white variety of crystalline quartz often having a greasy lustre; milkness has been due to the presence of air-filled cavities.

mill rock

a variety of coarse, braccia found in or close to the volcanic units.

mimetic

means imitative; e.g., mimetic crystallization—the fabric of a recrystallized metamorphic rock which has initiated a pre-existing fabric.

mindel glaciation

the second glacial stage of the Pleistocene in the Alps.

mindel-Riss interglacial

the second interglacial stage of the Pleistocene in the Alps; follows the Mindel glaciation.

mineral facies

rocks of any region whose constituents have been formed within the limits of pressure-temperature range characterized by the stability of certain index minerals.

mineralization

means the introduction of ore minerals and gangue minerals into pre-existing rock, whether by veins replacement, or in a disseminated fashion. Mineralization can be taken into account on any scale, from a hand specimen to a region of several thousand square kilometres. The term is also used in a stratigraphic sense; e.g., one can refer to a 'post Carboniferous mineralization', i.e., it means the formation of the mineral deposits associated with the Hercynian (Armorican) granites.

mineralize

to convert to, or impregnate with, mineral material; applied to processes of ore vein deposition and of fossiolization.

mineralizer

a gas or fluid dissolved in a magma that aids in the concentration and crystallization of ore minerals.

mineralogenetic province

geographic region where conditions were favourable for the concentration of useful minerals.

mineralogy

means the study of minerals which involves their formation, occurrence, properties, composition, and classification.

mineraloid

a naturally occurring, usually inorganic substance that is not considered to be a mineral because it is amorphous and thus lacks characteristic crystal form e.g. opal.

mineral resources

valuable mineral deposits of an area that are presently recoverable and may be so in the future; includes known ore bodies and potential ore.

mineral soil

soil composed of mineral or rock derivatives with little organic matter.

mineral water

mineral water is water which comes from springs in the Earth. Different kinds of mineral water contain different mineral salts. A few types of mineral water are fizzy because they contain carbon dioxide. Mineral waters are sometimes used for treating illnesses such as rheumatism and arthrits.

minette

1. refers to a syenitic variety of lamprophyre which is composed principally of biotite phenocrysts in a matrix of orthoclase and biotite.

2. also refers to sedimentary ironstones of Jurassic Age in the Lorrine area of France. Sometimes applicable to any sedimentary iron ore, especially if it consists mainly of limonite.

mining

mining is the process of taking metals, valuable stones and minerals from the Earth. Most mining is done with large machines, such as drills and diggers.

mining geology

the gelogical aspects of mineral deposits, with special regard to problems related to mining.

miocene

a geologic epoch of the Tertiary period, extending from the end of the Oligocene to the beginning of the Pliocene.

miogeosyncline

the nonvolcanic portion of an orthogeosyncline, located adjacent to the craton.

miotian

a stratigraphic stage name which is being used for the base of the North American Upper Miocene.

mire

wet spongy earth, as of a marsh, swamp, or bog.

misfit stream

under normal, uninterrupted conditions, a stream is cutting a valley into which it fits precisely. A misfit stream or river is defined as one which flows in a valley which is too large for it, i.e., a meandering stream which flows in a meandering valley. Such streams are formed by a reduction in the total amount of water available. It has been postulated that one possible cause has been a reduction in the average annual rainfall.

mispickel FeAsS

old name for the mineral arsenopyrite.

mississappian

refers to the older of the two sub-systems into which the Carboniferous period in North America has been divided.

missourite

refers to feldspathoid igneous rock. A mottled grey, coarsegrained granular plutonic rock; having augite, biotite, leucite, and olivine.

mist

mist is tiny drops of water suspended in the air. When clouds form at ground level, it is called mist. Mist is difficult to see through. It is thicker than haze, but it is not thick as fog.

mixed ore

any ore with both oxidized and unoxidized minerals.

moat

1. a ringlike depression around a the base of a seamount. 2. A valleylike depression around the inner side of a volcanic cone, between the rim and the lava dome.

mobile belt

a long, relatively narrow crustal region of tectonic activity.

mobilization

the term used for any process by which solid rock gets sufficiently soft and plastic to allow it to flow or to allow geochemical migration of mobile components.

mode

1. refers to the mineral composition of a rock which is usually expressed as percentages of total weight by volume.

2. the value or group of values that are formed with the greatest frequency in a set of data; the most typical observation.

modulus

a constant factor or multiplier for the conversion of units from one system to another.

mofette

a small opening emitting carbon dioxide in an area of late-stage volcanic activity.

moffette

a small opening in an area of late-stage volcanic activity that allows carbon dioxide to move out. It is a type of fumarole.

moho

an abbreviation for the Mohorovicic discontinuity.

mohole drilling

drilling aimed at penetration of the earth's crust, through the Mohorovicic discontinuity, to sample the mantle.

moine

refers to a stratigraphic division of the Scottish Precambrian which is the metamorphic equivalent of the Torridonian in Scotland, which passes into the Lower Dalradian.

molasse

a paralic sedimentary facies

consisting mainly of shale, subgraywacke sandstone, and conglomerate; it is more clastic and less rhythmic than the preceding flysch and is generally postorogenic.

moldavite

a translucent, olive-to brownish-green or pale-green tektite from western Czechoslovakia, characterized by surface sculpturing due to solution etching. Also known as moldauite; pseudochrysolite; vitavite. A variety of ozocerite from Moldavia.

mollisol

an order of soils having dark or very dark, friable, thick A horizons high in humus and bases such as calcium and magnesium; most have lighter -coloured or browner B horizons that are less friable and about as thick as the A horizons; all but a few have paler C horizons, many of which are calcareous.

mollusca

the term used for a group of invertebrate animals which may be terrestrial, freshwater, or marine in habitat. They are commonly having a shell secreted by the mantle. The shell may be either external univalve, external bivalve, internal or missing. The molluscs have a muscular 'foot' which gets modified in the various groups.

molysite $FeCl_3$

a brownish-red or yellow mineral composed of native ferric chloride.

monadnock

a remanant hill of resistant rock rising abruptly from the level of a peneplain; commonly represents an outcrop of rock that has withstood erosion. Also known as torso mountain.

monazite

refers to a yellow to brown, monoclinic rare-earth mineral. It occurs as an accessory mineral in acid igneous rocks, in pegmatite dykes, and in detrital sand. It forms a principal ore of rare-earths and of thorium. It is also known as cryptolite.

monmouthite

the term used for igneous rock of the syenite clan. It is coarsegrained granular plutonic rock and has apatite, calcite, hastingsite, nepheline, and sodaclase.

monochiquite

a lamprophyre composed of olivine, pyroxene, and usually mica or amphibole phenocrysts embedding glassoranalcine groundmass.

monocline

a stratigraphic unit that dips from the horizontal in one direction only, not as part of an anticline or syncline.

monogenetic

resulting from the process of formation or derived from one source, or originating or developing at one place and time; *e.g.*, said of a volcano built up by a single eruption.

monogeosyncline

a primary geosyncline that is long, narrow, and deeply subsided; composed of the sediments of shallow water and situated along the inner margin of the borderlands.

monomictic

the term used for a lake having only one yearly overturn. Tropical lakes overturn in the winter while polar lakes in the summer.

monomorphic

a term used for a bryzoan colony in which all zooids in zones of astogenetic repetition are feeding zooids of similar morphology.

monsoon

a monsoon is a kind of wind which brings heavy rain. Monsoons occur in tropical regions and mark the change from the dry to the wet season.

montian

a European stage of geologic time: Paleocene (above Danian, below Thanetian).

montmerillonite

the term used for the group name for all clay minerals having an expanding structure, except vermiculite.

moor

a moor is an area of high, open land where shrubs, such as heather, grow. Moors are found mainly in regions with a damp, temperate climate, such as north-west Europe. The soil contains much peat.

moor coal

a friable lignite or brown coal.

moraine

an accumulation of glacial drift deposited chiefly by direct glacial action and possessing initial constructional form independent of the floor beneath it.

moraine bar

a terminal moraine serving as a bar, rising out of deep water at some distance from the shore.

moraine kame

one of a group of kames characterized by the same topography, constitution, and position as a terminal moraine.

morgannian

a stratigraphic stage name which is being used for the European Upper Westphalian (Carboniferous System).

morphogenesis

refers to the origin and early development of landforms or a landscape.

morphology

1. the term dealing with the study of form and structure of animals and plants or their fossil remains especially of the relations and development of organs apart from their functions. In this form also features included are form and structure of an organism or any of its parts.

2. refers to the study of the distribution patterns of horizons in a soil profile and

of the soil's properties.

mortar structure

the term used for early stage in the development of a mylonite in which the larger crystals in a rock get surrounded by finely granular material which has been formed by the crushing of interstitials crystals. It most often occurs in quartzo-feldspathic rocks.

mosaic

1. in aerial photography, it refers to an overall picture of an area which is built up by fitting together (and overlapping wherever necessary) a series of individual air photographs.

2. refers to granobalstic texture in a rock which is formed by dynamic metamorphism in which the boundaries between individual grains are straight or slightly curved.

3. referring to a texture in a crystalline sedimentary rock in which contacts at grain boundaries have been more or less regular.

mottled

the term used for a soil or sedimentary rock which is irregularly marked with spots of various colours.

mound

1. a low, isolated, rounded natural hill, usually of earth. Also known as tuft.

2. a structure built by fossil colonial organisms.

mountain pediment

a plain of combined erosion and transportation at the base of and surrounding a desert mountain range; at a distance it has the appearance of a broad triangular mass.

mouth

the mouth is the part of a river where the water flows out into the sea or a lake. The mouth of a cave is the entrance.

mud

the term used for a wet mass of clayey material in a liquid or semi-liquid state. The term is also applicable to the artificial slurries used when drilling bore holes.

mud cone

a cone of sulfurous mud built around the opening of a mud volcano or mud geyser, with slopes as steep as 40° and diameters ranging upward to several hundred yards. Also known as puff cone.

mud crack

an irregular fracture formed by shrinkage of clay, silt, or mud under the drying effects of atmospheric conditions at the surface. Also known as desiccation crack; sun crack.

mud flat

a relatively level, sandy or muddy coastal strip along a shore or around an island; may be covered by shallow water. Also known as flat.

mudflow

a flowing mass of fine-grained earth material having a high degree of fluidity during movement.

mudlump
a diapric sedimentary structure consisting of clay or silt and forming an island in deltaic areas, produced by the loading action of rapidly deposited dalta front sands upon lighter-weight prodelta clays.

mud polygon
a nonsorted polygon whose centre lacks vegetation but whose peripheral fissures contain pat and plants. Also known as mud crack polygon.

mudstone
an indurated equivalent of mud in the form of a blocky or massive, fine-grained sedimentary rock containing approximately equal proportions of silt and clay; lacks the fine lamination or fissility of shale.

mud volcano
a conical accumulation of variable admixtures of sand and rock fragments, the whole resulting from eruption of wet mud and impelled upward by fluid or gas pressure. Also known as hervidero; macaluba.

mugearite
the term used for a dark coloured finegrained igneous rock in which the main feldspar is oligoclase, plus orthoclase and olivine with some apatite and opaque oxides. It gets originated by differentiation and volcanic crystallization of primary magma.

multicycle
referring to landscape or landform which is produced during more than one cycle of erosion, and bearing the traces of former condition (s).

multiple
a term applicable to igneous intrusions where several emplacements of more or less identical material have occurred to make up the whole mass.

multiplex
a stereoscopic plotting instrument. It is mainly used for preparing topographic maps from aerial photographs.

muschelkalk
a European stage of geologic time equivalent to the Middle Triassic, above Bunter and below Keuper.

mylonite
the term used for a hard, compact, coherent, chertlike often glassy-looking rock which has suffered extreme mechanical deformation and granulation but has remained chemically unchanged; it may be having steaky, finity, or banded structure, but the nature of parent rock could be easily recognised.

mylonitic structure
refers to a structure characteristic of mylonites, which was produced by extreme microbrecciation and shearing that gives the appearance of a flow structure.

mylonitization

rock deformation produced by intense microbrecciation without appreciable chemical alteration of granulated materials.

myrmekite

means an intergrowth of plagioclase feldspar (usually oligoclase) and quartz which is generally replacing potassium feldspar and formed during the later stages of consolidation in an igneous rock or during a subsequent period of plutonic activity. The quartz is found as blobs, or wormlike shapes within the feldspar.

myrmekitic

1. referring to texture of an igneous rock which is marked by intergrowths of feldspar and vermicular quartz.

2. Possessing characteristic properties of myrmekite.

nacreous

possessing an iridescent lustre resembling that of mother-of-pearl. It is also known as pearly.

nagatelite

a black, monoclinic mineral composed of phosphosilicate of aluminium, rare-earth elements, calcium, and iron. It occurs in tabular masses. Its hardness on Mohs scale is 5.5.

naked karst

karst that is developed in a region without soil cover, so that its topographic features are well exposed.

nakhlite

an achondritic stony meteorite composed of an aggregate of diopside and olivine.

namurian

a European stage of geologic time; divided into a lower stage and an upper stage.

nanofossil

a collective term used for fossil discoasters and coccoliths, both primarily calcareous microfossils, near the limit of resolution of the light microscope and hence are best studied with electron microscope.

nanoplankton

the name used for the fossil material of ultramicroscopic size in the range 5-60 micrometres; in general it has been so small that it can only be seen by employing the highest power of a phase-contrast microscope or an electron microscope. As the organisms are planktonic they occur over enormous geographical ranges and have been practically independent of facies excluding continental and freshwater ones).

These fossils are proved useful in correlating both short range and long range, and a particular point supporting them is that they are found in rocks which are barren of other fossils. They are also recorded from unmetamorphosed Precambrian sediments and the possibility exists that they will give a means of correlation for these beds.

nappe
the term used for a sheetlike, allochthonous rock unit that has moved in a predominantly horizontal surface. The mechanism had been thrust faulting, recumbent folding, or gravity sliding.

nassauian
a stratigraphic stage name which is being used for the European Middle Dinantian (Carboniferous System).

native asphalt
exudations or seepages of asphalt occurring in nature in a liquid or semiliquid state. Also known as natural asphalt.

native element
any of 20 elements, such as copper, gold, and silver, which occur naturally uncombined in a nongaseous state; there are three groups—metals, semimetals, and nonmetals.

natrocalcite $NaCu_2(SO_4)(OH)\text{-}H_2O$
an emrald-green mineral composed of hydrous basic sulphate of copper and sodium.

natrolunite
a mineral having basic sulphate of sodium and aluminium; shows conchoidal fracture and good cleavage in one direction. Its hardness on Mohs scale has been 3.5-4.0.

natrojarosite $NaFe_3(SO_4)_2(OH)_6$
a yellow to brown hexagonal mineral which shows conchoidal fracture and perfect cleavage in one direction. Its hardness on Mohs scale has been 3.0.

natural
natural describes something which has not been made or altered by the activities of people. Natural vegetation describes plants which have not been disturbed by people or by farmed animals.

natural bitumen
native mineral pitch, tar, or asphalt.

natural bridge
an archlike rock formation spanning a ravine or valley and formed by erosion. Also known as natural arch.

natural gas
this term generally refers to gaseous hydrocarbons, which may be found in association with oil accumulations.

naturalist
a naturalist is someone who studies the wild plants and animals of a region.

navajo sandstone
a fossil dune formation of Jurassic age found in the Colorado Plateau of the United States.

navigation
navigation is a word which describes how a ship or boat is guided across the sea, a plane through the skies, or a vehicle along roads.

navite
refers to an igneous rock of the gabbro clan. It is a medium-grained porphyritic hypabyssal rock which contains

phenocrysts of augite, labradorite, and olivine in a groundmass of augite and feldspar.

neap tide

a tidal pattern in which the difference in level between high low tide is a minimum. Neap tides occurs when the earth and sun are at right angles with respect to the moon; *i.e.,* during the first and third quarter moon.

nebrasken drift

rock material transported during the Nebraskan glaciation; it is buried below the Kansan drift in Iowa.

nebraskan glaciation

the first glacial stage of the Pleistocene epoch in North America, beginning about 1,000,000 years ago, and preceding the Aftonian interglacial stage.

neck

1. refers to a volcanic plug.
2. A narrow strip of land which connects two larger areas.
3. the narrow bank or rip of water which forms the part of a rip current where feeder currents converge and flow swiftly through the incoming breakers or surf and out to the head.

negative crystal

1. a pseudomorph which consists of a hollow mould of a crystal shape, the original crystal having been removed from it by solution. Also applicable to cavities which have the form of crystals enclosed within a crystal.
2. also refers to a uniaxial crystal in which the extraordinary wave is travelling faster than the ordinary wave, e.g., calcite.

negative element

a large structural feature or part of the earth's crust, characterized through a long geologic time period by frequent and conspicuous downward movement (subsidence) or by extensive erosion, or by an uplift that is considerably less rapid or less frequent than that of adjacent positive elements. Also known as negative area.

negative movement

subsidence of a part of the earth's crust, actual in relation to sea level or relative in relation to adjacent parts of the crust.

nekton

nekton describes all those animals which can swim freely in the open sea. Animals of the nekton do not drift with the tides and currents, unlike the plankton. They can move in any direction. They range in size from a few millimetres long to many metres long. The nekton does not include the animals of the benthos.

nematoblastic

a texture term applicable to a foliation which is formed by prismatic minerals, e.g., hornblende and augite.

neocomian

a European stage of Lower Cretaceous geologic time; includes Berriasian, Valanginian, Hauterivian, and Barremian.

neogene

the name assigned to the Miocene and Pliocene periods of the Tertiary, when grouped together. The use of this term has been almost obsolete.

neoglaciation

the removal of glacier ice growth in certain mountain areas during the Little Ice Age, following its shrinkage or disappearance during the Altithermal interval.

neotype

a specimen selected as type subsequent to the original description when the primary types are known to be destroyed, a nomenclatural type.

nepheline phonolite

the fine grained equivalent of nepheline syenite.

nephelinite

refers to a dark-coloured, aphanitic rock of volcanic origin which is composed essentially of nepheline and pyroxene; texture has been usually posphyritic with large crystals of augite and nepheline in a fine-grained matrix.

nephrite

refers to an exceptionally tough, compact, fine-grained, bluish or greenish premalite or actionalite, constituting the less rare kind of jade and formerly worn as a remedy of kidney diseases.

neptunism

the obsolete theory that all rocks of the earth's crust were deposited from or crystallized out of water. Also known as neptunianism; neptunian theory.

neritic

of or referring to the ocean environment or depth zone between low tide level and 100 fathoms, or approximately the edge of the continental shelf; also referring to the organisms living in that environment.

nesosilicates

a mineral like olivine which is composed of independent silicon-oxygen tetrahedra bonded by ionic bonds, without sharing of oxygen atoms.

net slip

on a fault, the distance between two formerly adjacent points on either side of the fault; defines direction and relative amount of displacement. Also known as total slip.

nevadan orogeny

orogenic episode during Jurassic and Early Cretaceous geologic time in the western part of the North American Cordillera. Also known as Nevadian orogeny; Nevadic orogeny.

nevadite

an igneous rock of the granite clan; a fine-grained porphyritic extrusive rock; it contains phenocrysts of biotite, hornblende, quartz, and sanidine in a very fine groundmass.

newbournian
obsolete stratigraphic stage name which was used for the (post Ludhamian) base of the British Pleistocene.

new global tectonics
comprehensive theory relating the formation of mountain belts, island arcs, and ocean trenches to the relative movement of regionally extensive lithospheric plates which are delineated by the major seismic belts of the earth.

niagaran
a stratigraphic stage name which is being used for the North American middle Silurian.

nick point
American spelling of knick point.

niggli classification
a classification of cocks which was done on the basis of their chemical composition. It is similar in some respects to the CIPW classification.

nival surface
the hypothetical planar surface containing all of the different snowlines of the same geologic time period.

nivation
rock or soil erosion beneath snowbank or snow patch, due mainly to frost action but also involving chemical weathering, solifluction, and meltwater transport of weathering products. Also known as snow patch erosion.

nivation hollow
a small, shallow depression formed, and occupied during part of the year, by a snow patch or snowbank that, through nivation, is thought to initiate glaciation. Also known as nivation cirque; snow niche.

node
(1) the point on a fault at which the apparent displacement changes.
(2) that point on a standing wave at which there is no vibration.

nodular chert
chart occurring as nodular or concretionary segregations.

nodule
means a spherical, oval, or similarly rounded concretion (of either type), which is not exceeding 256 mm in diameter. The terms nodule and concretion have been often used synonymously, nodule being preferred for more rounded types. Nodular rhyolites have rather large spherulites which have weathered out from the rest of the rock.

nominal conservanda
the term used for the names of organisms which although technically invalid have to be retained, as it is thought that their replacement by other names would create confusion.

nominal diameter
the diameter computed for a hypothetical sphere which would have the same volume as the calculated volume for a specific sedimentary particle. Also known as equivalent diameter.

non
non- is a prefix that changes the meaning of the original word to the opposite meaning.

nonbanded coal
coal without lustrous bands, composed mainly of clarain or durain without nitrain.

noncaking coal
hard or dull coal that does not cake when heated. Also known as free-burning coal.

noncalcic Brown soil
a great soil group having a slightly acidic, light-pink or reddish-brown A horizon and a light-brown or dull-red B horizon, and developed under a mixture of grass and forest vegetation in a subhumid climate. Also known as Shantung soil.

nonclastic
of the texture of a sediment or sedimentary rock, formed chemically or organically and showing no evidence of a derivation from preexisting rock or mechanical deposition. Also known as nonmechanical.

nonconformity
a type of unconformity in which rocks below the surface of unconformity are either igneous or metamorphic.

non-plunging fold
a fold whose hinge line is horizontal.

non-porous
non-porous describes substances which do not let water through. Hard rocks which do not have cracks or gaps in them are non-porous. Solid clay is also non-porous. The opposite of non-porous is porous.

non sequence
refers to a synonym of non-depositional unconformity, where the break in sedimentation has been short and often localized.

nonsorted polygon
a form of patterned ground which has a dominantly polygonal mesh and an unsorted appearance due to the absence of border stones, and whose borders are generally marked by wedge-shaped fissures narrowing downward.

nordmarkite
refers to igneous rock of the syenite clan. A reddish, medium-grained granular plutonic rock which has biotite, hornblende, microperthite, oligoclase, and quartz.

norite
refers to a coarse-grained plutonic rock having labradorite as the chief constituent and differing from gabbro by presence of hypersthene as the dominant mafic mineral.

normal cycle
a cycle of erosion whereby a

region is reduced to base level by running water, especially by the action of rivers. Also known as fluvial cycle of erosion.

normal dispersion

the dispersion of sesmic surface waves in which the recorded wave period increases with time.

normal soil

a soil having a profile that is more or less in equilibrium with the environment.

normal zoning

zoning in a crystal of plagioclase in which the zones become progressively more sodic outward.

northfieldite

an igneous rock of the granite clan, a white, coarsegrained granular plutonic rock; contains muscovite and quartz.

north pole

the north pole is the most northern point on the Earth. There are two north poles. These are the geographical North pole and the magnetic pole.

novaculite

a siliceous sedimentary rock that is dense, hard, even-textured, light-coloured, and characterized by dominance of microcrystalline quartz over chalcedony. Also known as razor stone.

novaculitic chert

a gray chert that fragments into slightly rough, splintery pieces.

nugget

1. the term used for small mass of metal which occurs free in nature.
2. a water worn lump of placer gold or other metal.

nummulitic limestone

a sedimentary rock composed chiefly of nummulite shells.

nunatak

an isolated hill, knob, ridge, or peak of bedrock projecting prominently above the surface of a glacier and completely surrounded by glacial ice.

oasis

a fertile, vegetated area in the midst of a desert, where the water table have come close enough to the surface for whells and springs of seepages to exist, thus making it suitable for human habitation.

obsequent fault-line scarp

a fault-line scarp which faces in the direction opposite to that of the original fault scarp or in which the structurally upthrown block is typographically lower than the downthrown block.

obsidian

a jet-black volcanic glass, usually of rhyolitic composition, formed by rapid cooling of viscous lava; generally forms the upper parts of lava flows. Also known as hyalopsite; Iceland agate; mountain mahogany.

obstruction

a morine formed where the movement of the ice is obstructed, as by a ridge of bedrock.

occult mineral
the term used for a mineral component of rock which cannot be seen through microscope, but whose presence can be known by chemical analysis.

ocean
an ocean is a very large sea. There are five oceans. These are the Pacific, Atlantic, Indian, Arctic and Southern oceans. Together, the oceans cover 71 per cent of the Earth's surface.

ocean basin
refers to the great depression which is occupied by the ocean on the surface of the lithosphere.

ocean floor
the near-horizontal surface of the ocean basin.

oceanic crust
a thick mass of igneous rock which lies under the ocean floor.

oceanic island
any island which rises from the deep sea floor rather than from shallow continental shelves.

oceanic rise
a long, broad elevation of the bottom of the ocean.

oceanite
a picritic basalt in which olivine has been more abundant than plagioclase.

oceanization
process by which continental crust is converted into oceanic crust.

oceanographer
an oceanographer studies the oceans of the world. Some oceanographers study the physical and chemical properties of the oceans. Others study the biological life of the oceans.

ocher
an earthy, powdery, red, brown, or yellow oxide of iron which finds use as pigment. Also spelled ochre.

ochoan
a North American provincial series: uppermost Permian.

octahedral plane
the plane in a cubic lattice having three numerically equal Miller indices.

octant
defined as a sector of space which is defined by three intersecting planes, no two of which are parallel, and all of which are passing through a common point, the origin.

odonotolite
fossil bone or tooth coloured by vivianite and partly replaced by apatite or calcite. Its hardness on Mohs scale is 5.0.

offiap
the successive lateral contraction extent of strata due to their deposition in a shrinking sea or on the margin of a rising landmass. Also known as regressive overlap.

offset ridge
a ridge consisting of resistant sedimentary rock that has been made discontinous as a

result of faulting.

offset well

an oil well drilled near the boundary of a property and opposite to producing or completed well on an adjoining property, for the purpose of preventing the drainage of oil or gas by the earlier well. An obligation to drill such offset wells contained in oil and gas leases.

offshore

refers to the comparatively flat zone of variable width which is extending from the outer margin of the shoreface to the edge of the continental shelf.

offshore drilling

means the drilling of oil or gas wells into water covered locations which are usually on submerged continental shelves.

oil base mud

a drilling mud with clay particles suspended in oil rather than in water.

oil pool

an accumulation of petroleum locally confined by subsurface geologic features. Also known as oil accumulation; oil reservoir.

oil sand

an unconsolidated, porous sand formation or sandstone containing or impregnated with petroleum or hudrocarbons.

oil shale

a finely layered brown or black shale that contains kerosene and from which liquid or gaseous hydrocarbons can be distilled. Also known as kerogen shale.

oil trap

an accumulation of petroleum which, by a combination of physical conditions, is prevented from escaping laterally or vertically. Also known as trap.

oil water contact

the boundary layer or surface between an oil accumulation and the underlying bottom water.

old age

the last stage of the erosion cycle in the development of the topography of a region in which erosion has reduced the surface almost to base level and the land forms are marked by simplicity of form and subdued relief. Also known as topographic old age.

old mountain

a mountain that has formed prior to the tertiary period, especially a fold mountain formed before the Alpine crogeny.

old red sandstone

a devonian formation in Great Bratain and northwestern Europe, of nonmarin, predominantly red sedimentaey rocks, consisting principally of sandstone. Conglomerates. and shales.

olenokian

a stratigraphical stage name which is being used for the base of the East European

Lower Triassic.

oligocene
refers to the epoch of the Tertiary period between the Eocene and Miocene epochs.

oligomict
a term used for detrital rock having fragments of only one kind of material (or with one kind in great predominance). It is applicable especially to rudaceous rocks.

oligosiderite
a neberoite containing a small amount of metallic iron.

olistolith
an exotic block or other rock mass that has been transported by submarine gravity sliding or slumping and is included in the binder of an olistostrome.

olistostrome
a sedimentary deposit composed of a chaotic mass of heterogeneous material that is intimately mixed; accumulated in the form of a semifluid body by submarine gravity sliding or slumping of unconsolidated sediments.

olivine basalt
any of a group of olivine bearing basalts.

ombrotiphic
pertaining to a short lived pond which gets its water mainly from rain.

omphacite
refers to a dark-green to palegreen, granular or foliated, high temperature aluminious clinopyroxene mineral which has a viterous lustre. It commonly occurs in the rock eclogite. It is a variety of augite.

onesquenthawan
north American stage; Lower and Middle Devonian.

onlap
a type of overlap characterized by regular and progressive pinching out of the strata toward the margins of a depositional basin; each unit transgresses and extends beyond the point of reference of the underlying unit. Also known as transgressive overlap.

onshore
onshore describes something which is at the sea-shore or which moves towards the sea-shore. An onshore breeze is a breeze blowing towards the sea-shore from the sea. The opposite of onshore is offshore.

ontorian
a stratigraphic stage name which is being used for the oldest Canadian Precambraian.

onyax marble
refers to a compact, usually banded, generally translucent variety of calcite which resencers true onyax in appearance.

oolite
a sedimentary rock, usually a limestone, made up chiefly of ooliths cemented together.

oomold
a spheroidal opening in a

sedimentary rock, or insoluble residue, produced by the dissolutiong of an oolith.

ooze

1. a pelagic sediment which consists of at least 30% skeletal remains of calcareous or siliceous pelagic organisms, the rest being clay minerals.
2. refers to a soft and muddy piece of ground, such as a bog which is usually resulting from the flow of a spring or brook.
3. Soft mud or slime, which is typically covering the bottom of a lake or river.

opal

opal is a mineral. An opal is a form of silica and a semi-precious stone. Opals can be white or they may have rainbow colours. Some of the finest opals come from Australia.

open fold

a fold having only moderately compressed limbs

open form

a crystal whose faces do not enclose space *e.g.,* trigonal prism.

ophiolite

refers to basic and ultrabasic lavas and minor intrusions which are associated with the infilling of a geosyncline. The term is also applicable to their metamorphic equivalents, which are usually rich in albite and amphiboles.

optical activity

the property of a substance *e.g.,* quartz, to rotate the plane of polarization of light. Such a substance is said to be optically active.

optical axis

the term used for a line which is passing through a radically symmetrical optical system such that rotation of the system about this line does not change it in any detectable way.

optical calcite

crystalline calcite so clear that it finds use in making Nicol prism. It is usually iceland spar.

optic orientation

refer to the spatial relationships between the optical elements and the crystallographic elements of a mineral.

orbicule

a nearly spherical body. up to 2 or more centimetres in diameter. In which the components are arranged in concentric layers.

orbit

an orbit is the path followed by an object as it circles another object in space. The Earth follows an orbit around the Sun. Satellites and space stations circle the Earth in orbits.

ordinary ray

1. the term used for the ray which-vibrates at right angles to the optic axis in uniaxial crystals. Also known as O ray.
2. refers to one of the two rays in which a ray incident on an anisotropic uniaxial crystal

gets splitted.

ordosite

a dark-coloured syenite containing about 60% sodic clinopyroxene.

ordoviclan

The second period of the Paleozoic era, above the Cambrian and below the Silurian, form approximately 500 million to 440 million years ago.

ore

1.the naturally occurring material from which economically valuable minerals can be extracted.

2. specifically, a natural mineral compound of the elements, of which one element at least is a metal.

3. more loosely, all metalliferous rock, though it contains the metal in a free state.

4. occasionally, a compound of nonmetallic substances, as sulphur ore.

ore bed

an economic aggregation of minerals occurring between or in rocks of sedimentary origin.

orebody

generally, a solid and fairly continuous mass of ore, which may include low-grade ore and waste as well as pay ore, but is individualized by form or character from adjoining country rock.

ore control

any tectonic, geochemical or lithologic feature thought to have influenced the formation and placement of ore.

ore cluster

a group of interconnected ore bodies.

ore control

a geologic feature that has influenced the ore deposition.

ore deposit

rocks containing minerals of economic value in such amount that they can be profitably exploited.

ore district

a combination of several ore deposits into one common whole or system.

ore-lead age

measurement of the age of the earth by comparing the relative progress of the two redioactive decay schemes U^{235}- pb^{206}

ore magma

a magma that may be able to crystallize into an ore; the sulphide, oxide, or other metallic facies of a solidified magma.

ore mineral

the term used for a mineral from which a useful metal could be extracted, which may act as a source of this metal if it could be profitably worked.

organic reef

a sedimentary rock which is composed almost exclusively of the remains of cords, algae, bryozoans, sponges, and other sedimentary of colonial organisms.

organic soil

the term used for any soil or

soil horizon which consists chiefly of or, contains at least 30% of organic matter, e.g., peat soils and muck soils.

organic texture

a sedimentary texture resulting from the activity of organisms.

oriented

pertaining to a specimen that is so marked as to show its exact, original position in space.

orocline

an orogenic belt with an imposed curvature or shors bend.

orogenesis

the term used for the process of mountain building, which has lead to the formation of the intensely deformed belts which constitute mountain ranges. Most orogenic belts have been arising on the sites of geosynclines and the resulting mountains therefore have sediments and volcanic rock deformed and metamorphosed to a greater or lesser extent in accordance to their position and depth in the orogenic belt. Regional metamorphism and granite emplacement always occurs in the deeper levels of an orogenic belt.

orogenic belt

a linear region that has undergone folding or other deformation during the orogenic cycle. Also known as fold belt; orogen; orogene.

orogenic cycle

a time interval during which a mobile belt evolved into an orogenic belt, passing through preorogenic, orogenic, and postorogenic stages. Also known as geotectonic cycle.

orogeny

the process or processes of mountain formation especially the intense deformation of rocks by folding and faulting which, in many mountainous regions, has been accompanied by metamorphism, invasion of molten rock, and volcanic eruption; in modern usage, orogeny produces the internal structure of mountains, and epeirogeny produces the mountainous topography. Also known as orogenesis; tectogenesis.

orology

the scientific study of mountain building and mountain formation.

orthoclasite

an igneous rock of the syenite clan. A medium to find grained granular hypabyssal rock; contains orthoclase and minerals.

orthoconglomerate

a conglomerate with an intact gravel framework held together by mineral cement and deposited by ordinary water currents.

orthogeosyncline

a linear geosynclinal belt lying between continental and oceanic cratons, and having internal volcanic belts (eugeosynclinal) and external nonvolcanic belts (miogeosynclinal). Also known as geosynclinal couple; primary geosyncline.

orthognelss

gneiss originating from igneous rock.

orthograde

pertaining to uniform distribution of dissolved oxygen in hypolimnion of alake, dependent only on conditions at circulation and on subsequent physical events.

orthomagmatic

the name assigned to the stage in the crystallization of an igneous mass during which the main mass of silicates get crystallised. It gets followed by the postmagmatic phase, during which processes such as pneumatolysis, hydrothermy, and pegmatite formation take place.

orthomagmatic stage

the principal stage in the crystallization of silicates from a typical magma; up to 90% of the magma may crystallize during this stage. Also known as orthotectic stage.

orthopyroxene

a series of pyroxene minerals which crystallise in orthorhombic system. Its members include enstatite, bronzite, hypersthene, ferrohypersthene, eulite, and orthoferrosilica.

orthorhombic system

a crystal system which could be divided into three symmetry classes. This system has been including all crystals which are referred to three axes mutually at right angles and employing different parameters on each axis.

orthotill

a till formed by immediate release from transporting ice, as by ablation and melting.

osagean

a provincial series of geologic time in North America; Lower Mississippian (above kinderhookian, below Meramecian).

oscillation ripple mark

a symmetric ripple mark having a sharp, narrow, and relatively straight crest between broadly rounded troughs, formed by the motion of water agitated by oscillatory waves on a sandy base at a depth shallower than wave base. Also known as oscillation ripple; oscillatory ripple mark; wave ripple mark.

ossicle

refers to a single echinoderm plate. They have been often so abundant that they may comprise the greater part of a limestone.

ouenite

an igneous rock of the gabbro clan. A fine grained granular hypabyssal rock; contains anothite, bronizite, diopside and olivine.

outcrop

refers to the total area over which a particular rock unit

exists at the surface—whether visibly exposed or not. The term has been especially used for the delineation of such an area on a geological map.

outer core

the outer core is part of the interior of the Earth. It lies inside the mantle, about 2,300 kilometres below the surface of the Earth. The outer core is very hot. It is thought to be made of molten rocks, with large amounts of nickel and iron. Inside the outer core lies the inner core.

outflow cave

a cave from which a stream issues out.

outlier

a group of rocks separated from the main mass and surrounded by outcrops of older rocks.

outwash

soil mineral washed down a hill by rainwater and deposited upon gently sloping region.

outwash cone

a cone-shaped deposit consisting chiefly of sand and gravel found at the edge of shrinking glaciers and ice sheets.

outwash plain

a broad, outspread flat or gently sloping alluvial deposit of outwash in front of or beyond the terminal moraine of a glacier. Also known as apron; frontal apron; frontal plain; marginal plain; morainal apron; morainal plain; morainal apron; morainal plain; outwash apron; overwash plain sandur; wash plain.

overburden

1. Useless material which is overlying a bed of useful material, e.g., shale overlying a coal seam.

2. Any loose unconsolidated material which is resting upon solid rock.

overdeepening

the erosive prosive process by which a glacier deepens and widens an inherited preglacial valley to below the level of the subglacial surface.

overfold

a fold that is overturned.

overlap

a term used for describing the relationship of the beds in an unconformity where progressively younger members of an upper series are resting upon an older series.

overseepened valley

an ice-free valley in which one side is higher and steeper than the other.

overstep

refers to an unconformity which is developed during a marine transagression when the younger series is resting upon progressively older members to the underlying series.

oversteepening

the process by which an eroding alpine glacier speepens the sides of an inherited preglacial valley.

overturned

of a fold or the side of a fold, tilted beyond the perpendicular. Also known as inverted; reversed.

oxfordian

a European stage of geologic time, in the upper Jurassic (above Callovian, below Kimmeridgean). Also known as Divesian.

oxidates

refers to a geochemical division of the sedimentary rocks having the sedimentary iron and manganese ores.

oxidized zone

a region of mineral deposits which has been altered by oxidizing surface waters.

ozocerite

a natural, brown to black paraffin wax which occurs in irregular veins and consists primarily of hydrocarbons. It is soluble in chloroform and has a variable melting point. It is also known as earth wax; fossil wax; ozokerite.

ozone

ozone is a compound and a colourless gas. Ozone is a type of oxygen. It is formed when oxygen is exposed to radiation, especially in the upper atmosphere. Ozone is poisonous to breathe in large quantities.

paar

a depression formed as result of the morning-apart of crustal blocks rather than by subsidence within a block.

pacific-type continental margin

a continental margin typified by that of the western Pacific where oceanic lithosphere descends beneath an adjacent continent and produces an intervening island are system.

packsand

a fine grained sandstore that is so loosely consolidated by calcareous cement so as to be readily cut by knife.

packstone

the term used for a sedimentary carbonate rock whose granular material has been arranged in a self-supporting frame work, yet also has matrix of calcareous mud.

padparadschah

the term used for the orange coloured gem variety of corundum.

pahoehoe

a type of lave flow whose surface is glassy, smooth, and undulating; the lave is basaltic, glassy, and porous. Also known as ropy lava.

paint pot

a mud pot containing multicoloured mud.

paisanite

refers to the igneous rock of the granite clan. It is a fine-grained porphyritic hypabyssal rock and contains phenocyrsts of quartz and riebeckite in a groundmass of microperthite and quartz.

palaeobiology

a branch of palaeontalogy which deals with the study of

fossils as organisms rather than as features of historical geology.

palaeoclimatology

refers to the study of the climatic conditions which were obtained in past geological eras. Detailed study of sedimentary rocks and their enclosed fossils reveals the estimates of climatic factors such as wind direction, rainfall, atmospheric and oceanic temperatures, and the effects of atmospheric changes.

palaeoecology

deals with the study of the relationships which exist between ancient organisms and their environment.

palaegonite

a brown to yellow altered barsaltic glass found as interstitial material or amygduled in pillow laves.

palaeomagnetism

refers to the study of natural remanent magnetization so as to determine the intensity and direction of earth's magnetic field in the geologic past. Some rocks attain a permanent record of the earth's magnetic field due to certain iron-bearing minerals which they contain.

palaeoslope

refers to the inclination of an ancient land surface as it was existing in some period of geological history.

palagonite

a brown to yellow altered basaltic glass found as interstitial material or amygdules in pillow lavas.

palasite

the most abundant of the intermediate types of meteorites, consisting of olivine enclosed in a nickel-iron matrix.

paleo-

paleo- is a prefix meaning old or ancient.

paleontologist

a paleontologist is someone who studies fossils. Some paleontogists collect and describe fossils. Others use the fossil traces left by extinct animals and plants to help them reconstruct the animal or plant.

palette

a broad sheet of calcite which represents a solutional remnnant in a cave. It is also known as shield.

paleocene

a major worldwide division of geologic time of the Tertiary period; extends form the end of the Cretaceous period to the Eocene epoch.

paleoclimate

the climate of a given period of geologic time. Also known as geologic climate.

paleoclimatic sequence

the sequencxe of climatic changes in geologic time; it shows a succession of oscillations between warm periods and ice ages, but superimposed on this are numerous shorter oscillations.

paleoclimatology
the study of climates in the geologic past, involving the interpretation of glacial deposits, fossils, and paleogeographic, isotopic, and sedimentologic data.

paleogene
a geologic time interval comprising the Oligocene, Eocene, and Paleocene of the lower Tertiary period. Also known as Eogene.

paleogeography
the geography of the geologic past; concerns all physical aspects of an area that can be determined from the study of the rocks.

paleogeologic map
An areal map of the geology of an ancient surface immediately below a buried unconformity, showing the geology as it appeared at some time in the geologic past at the time the surface of unconformity was completed and before the overlapping strata were deposited.

paleogeology
the geology of the past, applied particularly to the interpretation of the rocks at a surface of unconformity.

paleolithologic map
a paleogologic map indicating lithologic variations at a buried horizon or within a restricted zone at a specific time in the geologic past.

paleoslope
the direction of initial dip of a former land surface, such as an ancient continental slope.

paleosol
a soil horizon that formed on the surface during the geologic past, that is, an ancient soil. Also known as buried soil; fossil soil.

paleotectonic map
regional map that shows the structural patterns that existed during a particular period of geologic time for example, the Lower Cretaceous in Western Canada.

paleotemperature
1. the temperature at which a geologic process took place in ancient past.
2. the mean climatic temperature at a given time or place in the geologic past.

paleotopography
the topography of a given area in the geologic past.

paleozolc
the era of geologic time from the end of the precambrian (600 million years before present) until the beginning of the mesozoic era (225 million years before present).

palette
a broad sheet of calcite representing a solutional remnant in a cave. Also known as shield.

palimpasset
the fabric or texture of a metamorphic rock in which remains of a pre-existing fabric

or texture are still preserved.

palingenesis

1. refers to the melting or partial melting of preexisting rocks to form new magma.

2. Refers to the recapitulation of morphological and other features of adult ancestors at earlier stages during the life of the descendants.

palinspastic map

a paleogeographic or paleotectonic map showing restoration of the features to their original geographic positions, before thrusting or folding of the crustal rocks.

palygorskite

1. refers to a chain structure type of clay mineral.

2. a group of light tough fibrous clay minerals which shows extrusive substitution of aluminium for magnesium.

pampa

a vast treeless grassy plain of temperate regions.

pandiomorphic

a texture term which is applicable to a rock made up of well-developed crystals.

panfan

a graded bedrock surface consisting of a series of coal escing pediments and representing the penultimate stage of an arid cycle of erosion.

pangea

postulated former supercontinent supposedly composed of all the continental crust of the earth, and later fragmented by drift into laurasia and gondwana.

pannonian

a stratigraphic stage name which is being used for the European Upper Miocene (Tertiary System).

panplain

a broad, level plain formed by coalescence of several adjacent flood plains. Also spelled panplane.

panthalassa

the ocean that surrounded Pangaea before its fragmentation.

paperspar

a crystallized variety of calcite, occurring in thin lamellae.

parabolic dune

a long. scoop-shaped sand dune having a ground plan approximating the form of a parabola, with the horns pointing windward (upwind). Also known as blowout dune.

paraconformity

a type of unconformity in which strata are parallel; there is little apparent erosion and the unconformity surface resembles a simple bedding plane. Also known as nondepositional unconfornity; pseudoconfornity.

paraffin-base crude

crude oil that will yield large quantities of paraffin during distillation.

paragenesis

refers to the relationship of minerals which is expressed in terms of a time sequence, i.e., if conditions have been changing progressively along a time-axis, then a particular mineral will appear as a derivative of an earlier mineral, and may ultimately convert into yet another mineral, the process taking place being recrystallization.

parageosynline

an epeirogenic geosynclinal basin located within a craton or stable area.

paraglomerate

a conglomerate which contains more matrix than gravel-sized fragments and was deposited by subsqueous turbidity flows and glacier ice rather than normal aqueous flow.

paralic

a term applicable to sedimentary basins which get developed in marginal marine environments, e.g., lagoons, littorals basins, etc.

paralic coal basin

coal deposits formed along the margin of the sea.

parallel cleavage

an obsolete term for bedding-plane cleavage.

parallel fold

a fold in which the thickness of the layers is almost constant.

parallel ripple mark

a ripple mark characterized by a relatively straight crest and an asymmetric profile.

parameter

1. refers to any of the axial lengths of interaxial angles which are used to define a unitcell.

2. On a crystal face, it refers to the rational multiple of the rational length intercepted by a plane, which determines the position of the plane relative to the crystal lattice.

paramorph

a pseudomorph having the same composition as the original crystal.

paramorphism

refers to the property of a mineral whose internal structure gets changed without change in composition or external form. It was formerly known as allomorphism.

popararipple

a large, symmetric ripple whose surface slopes gently and which shows no assortment of grains.

parataxitic

a term used for describing the streaky appearance of some pyroclastic rocks.

paratill

a till formed by ice-rafting in a marine or lacustrine environment.

parautochthonous

a term used for describing a feature which gets formed at great distance from the place in which it is found. It has been most commonly used for describing nappe structure in the Alps.

parental magma

the naturally occurring mobile rock material from which a

particular igneous rock solidified or from which another magma was derived.

parkerite
a bright, bronze coloured mineral which is composed of sulphide of nickel bismuth and lead.

partial pluton
that part of a composite intrusion representing a single intrusive episode.

particle diameter
the diameter of a sedimentary particle considered as a sphere.

particle shape
it is possible to define the shape of clastic fragments in terms of the ratio of the dimensions of the fragment. The three measurements necessary for this purpose may be length, breadth and thickness.

particle size
the general dimensions of the particles or mineral grains in a rock or sediment based on the premise that the particles are spheres; commonly measured by sieving, by calculating setting velocities, or by determining areas of microscopic images.

parting
1. refers to a small joint, specially in a coal seam.
2. refers to a thin layer of shale which separates two parts of a coal seam.
3 refers to a plane along which a crystal will divide, which is not a true cleavage plane.

partiversal
pertaining to formations that dip in different directions roughly as far as a semicircle.

parvafacies
a body of rock constituting the part of any magnafacies that occurs between designated time stratigraphic planes or key beds traced across the magnafacies

pass
a pass is a narrow path or channel. It is usually an area of lower ground through hills or mountains. A pass connects one valley with another valley.

passage bed
a stratum marking a transition form rocks of one geological system to those of another.

patch reef
1. a small, irregular organic reef with a flat top forming a part of a reef complex.
2. a small, thick, isolated lens of limestone or dolomite surrounded by rocks of different facies.

patina
a thin, coloured film produced on a rock surface by weathering.

patterned ground
any of several well-defined, generally symmetrical forms, such as circles, polygons, and steps, that are characteristic of surficial material subject to intensive frost action.

pay streak
the portion of a vein which

carries a profitable ore.

peat bog
a bog in which peat has formed under conditions of acidity. Also known as peat bed; peat moor.

peat-sapropel
a product of the degradation of organic matter that is transitional between peat and sapropel. Also known as sapropel-peat.

peat soil
soil containing a large amount of peat; it is rich in humus and gives an acid reaction.

peat tar
tar obtained from the distillation of peat.

pebble
a rock fragment which has a diameter of between 4 and 64 mm i.e., larger than gravel and smaller than cobble.

pebble armor
a desert armour made up of rounded pebbles.

pebble coal
a type of coal that is transitional between peat and brown coal.

pebbly mudstone
a delicately laminated till-like conglomeratic mudstone.

pebbly sand
an unconsolidated sediment containing at least 75% sand and the amount of pebbles not exceeding 25% of the total aggregate.

pedalfer
a soil in which there is an accumulation of sesquioxides; it is characteristic of a humid region.

pedestal boulder
a rock mass supported on a rock pedestal. Also known as pedestal rock.

pediment
refers to a plain of eroded bedrock (which may or may not be covered by a thin veneer of alluvium) in an arid region which is developed between mountain and basin areas.

pedimentation
the actions or processes by which pediments are formed.

pediment pass
a flat, narrow tongue that extends form a pendiment on one side of a mountain to join a pediment on the other side.

pedion
a crystal form consisting of only one face.

pediplain
a rock-cut erosion surface formed in a desert by the coalescence of two or more pediments. Also known as desert peneplain; desert plain; panfan.

pediplaination
the actions or processes by which pediplanes are formed.

pediplane
any planate erosion surface formed in the piedmount area of a desert, either bare or covered with a veneer of alluvium.

pedocal
a soil containing a concentration of carbonates,

usually calcium carbonate; it is characteristic of arid or semiarid regions.

pedology

pedology is the study of soils. It includes studying how different kinds of soil are made, and what the soils are made from. Pedagogy also involves making maps of different soils to show where they are found.

pegmatite

the term used for exceptionally coarse-grained igneous rock which consists of interlocking crystals. It is usually found as irregular dikes, lenses, or veins, especially at the margins of patholiths. Most grains are having more than 1 cm in diameter.

pegmatitization

formation of or replacement by a pegmatite.

pegmatoid

an igneous rock that posses the course-grained texture of a pegmatite but lacks graphic intergrowths and/or typically granitic composition.

peg model

three dimensional model used to illustrate and study stratigraphic and structural conditions of subsurface geology; consists of a flat platform onto which vertical pegs of varying heights are mounted to represent the contours of various strata.

pelagic

pertaining to regions of a lake at depths of 10-20 meters or more, characterized by deposits of mud of ooze and by the absence of vegetation. Also known as eupelagic.

pelagic limestone

a fine textured limestone formed in relatively deep water by the concentration of calcareous tests of pelagic foraminifera.

pelean-type eruption

a type of volcanic eruption characterized by gaseous clouds and the development of volcanic domes.

pelees hair

the term used for a fine mass of hairlike glass which gets formed because of lava being exuded through a small orifice and blown about by the wind.

pelelith

Vesicular or pumiceous lava in the throat of a volcano.

pele's hair

a spun volcanic glass formed naturally by blowing out during quiet fountaining of fluid lava. Also known as capillary ejecta; filiform lapilli; lauoho o pele.

pele's tears

volcanic glass in the form of small, solidified drops which precede pendants of Pele's hair.

pelite

a sediment or sedimentary rock, such as mudstone, composed of fine, clay- or mud-size particles. Also spelled pelyte.

pelitic

partaining to, characteristic of,

or derived from pelite.

pelmicrite

a limestone containing less than 25% each of intraclasts and ooliths, having a volume ratio of pellets to fossils greater than 3 to 1, and with the micrite matrix more abundant than the sparry-calcite cement.

pelogloea

marine detrital slime from settled plankton.

pencil gnelss

a gneiss that splits into thin, rodlike quartz- feldspar crystal aggregates.

pencil ore

hard, fibrous masses of hematite that can be broken up into splinters.

penecontemporaneous

of a geologic process or the structure or mineral that is formed by the process, occurring immediately following deposition but before consolidation of the enclosing rock.

peneplain

refers to the end-product of the cycle of erosion in humid climates, in accordance with the scheme of W.M. Davis.

peninsula

a peninsula is a narrow area of land which stretches out into the sea or into a lake. A peninsula can be small, or very large like the Malay peninsula in South-east Asia.

pennsylvanian

a division of late Paleozoic geolovic time, extending from 320 to 280 million years ago, varying by considered to rank as an independent period or as an epoch of the Carboniferous period; named for ontcrops of coalbearing rock formations in pennsylvania.

pentalith

a cocolith formed by five crystal units.

penutian

a North American stage of geologic time; lower Eocene.

peperino

the term used for a rock of mixed pyroclastic and sedimentary origin such as pyroclastic material, and weathered and eroded volcanic material such as scoriae, cinders, etc. cemented together.

peperite

a breccialike material in marine sedimentary rock, considered to be either a mixture of lava with sediment, or shallow intrusions or magma into wet sediment.

perched block

a large. detached rock fragment presumed to have been transported and deposited by a glacier, and perched in a conspicuous and precarious position on the side of a hill. Also known as balanced rock; perched boulder; perched rock.

percussion mark

a small crescent shaped scar produced on a hard, dense pebble by a blow.

pereletok
a frozen layer of ground, at the base of the active layer, which may persist for one or several years. Also known as intergelisol.

perezone
a zone in which sediments accumulate along coastal lowlands; includes lagoons and brackish water bays.

pergelation
the formation of permafrost in the present or in the past.

pericline
a fold characterized by central orientation of the dip of the beds.

peridot
peridot, or olivine, is a mineral. It is made of silica, iron and magnesium. Peridot is hard and glassy, with an olive-green colour. Good crystals of peridot are used as gems.

peridotite
refers to a class of ultrabasic rocks which consist of predominantly olivine with or without other ferromagnesian minerals.

periglacial
of or pertaining to the outer perimeter of a glacier, particularly to the fringe areas immediately surrounding the great continental glaciers of the geologic ice ages, with respect to environment, topography, areas, processes, and conditions influenced by the low temperature of the ice.

peristerite
a gem variety of albite that resembles moonstone and has a blue or bluish-white lustre; characterized by sharp internal reflections of blue, green, and yellow.

perknite
the term used for igneous rock of the ultrabasic clan. It is fine to coarsegrained granular plutonic rock and consists of monoclinic amphiboles and pyroxenes. It is a class of ultrabasic rocks which consist of predominantly of ferromagnesian minerals other than olivine.

perlite
a rhyolitic glass with abundant spherical or convolute cracks that cause it to break into small pearllike masses or pebbles, usually less than a centimetre across; it is commonly gray or green with a pearly luster and has the composition of rhyolite. Also known as pearlite; pearlstone.

perlitic texture
the term used for describing texture which is found in glassy and devitrified igneous rocks, and consists of curved or spherical to sub-spherical cracks. These are formed by contraction during cooling and occasionally are so strongly developed that the rocks break to form a series of spherical units.

permafrost
perennially frozen ground, occurring wherever the

temperature remains below 0°c for several years, whether the ground is actually consolidated by ice or not and regardless of the nature of the rock and soil particles of which the earth is composed.

permafrost table
the upper limit of permafrost. Also known as pergelisol table.

permeability
the term used for the capacity of a porous rock, soil, or sediment by which a fluid could be transmitted without damage to the structure of the medium. Permeability may be shown by the rock which is being either porous or pervious. Permeability in a rock is measured in darcies.

permeable
permeable describes something through which water can pass. A permeable soil is a soil which allows free drainage of water. The opposite of permeable is impermeable.

permeaition
penetration by passing through the imterstices, as of a rock or soil, without causing physical change.

permian
the last period of geologic time in the Paleozoic era, from 280 to 225 million years ago.

permineralization
the term used for the process of fossilization by which minerals get deposited in the pore spaces of originally hard mineral parts.

permo-triassic
said of strata not differentiated between the Permian and Triassic systems particularly in regions where the boundary occurs within a nonmarine red-beds succession.

perpendicular slip
the component of a fault slip measured at right angles to the trace of the fault on any intersecting surface.

perpendicular throw
the distance between two points which were formerly adjacent in a faulted bed, vein, or other surface, measured at right angles to the surface.

persalic
in the CIPW classification of igneous rocks, the rocks in which the ratio of salic to femic minerals is greater than 7.

perthite
a parallel to subparallel intergrowth of potassium and sodium feldspar; the potassium-rich phase is usually the host form which the sodium rich phase evolves.

perthitic
of a texture produced by perthite, exhibiting sodium feldspar as small strings, blebs, films, or irregular veinlets in a host of potassium feldspar.

perthosite
refers to syenite which consists almost entirely of alkali feldspar but having small amounts of aegirine and other ferromagnesian minerals, and

often nepheline.

perxenic
in the CIPW classification of igneous rocks, the rocks in which the ratio of rock crystal to chadacrysts is less than 1/7.

petrifaction
refers to a fossilization process whereby inorganic matter dissolved in water has been replacing the original organic materials converting them to a stony substance.

petrogenesis
refers to a branch of petrology that is concerned with the origin and formation of rocks especially igneous rocks.

petrographer
an individual who does petrography.

petrographic facies
facies distinguished principally by composition and appearance. Also known as petrofacies.

petrographic period
the time represented by a rock association.

petrographic province
a broad area in which similar igneous rocks are formed during the same period of igneous activity. Also known as comagmatic region; igneous province; magma province.

petrography
refers to the systematic description of rocks in hand specimen and thin section.

petroleum geology
the branch of economic geology dealing with the origin, occurrence, movement, accumulation and exploration of hydrocarbon fuels.

petroleum trap
stable underground formation of such nature as to trap and hold liquid or gaseous hydrocarbons; usually consists of sand or porous rock surrounded by impervious rock or clay formations.

petrologist
an individual who studies petrology.

petrology
the branch of geology concerned with the origin, occurrence, structure, and history of rocks, principally igneous and metamorphic rock.

petromict
of a sediment, composed of metastable rock fragments.

petzite
a grey to black mineral which is composed of silver gold telluride.

phacolith
a minor, concordant, lens-shaped, and usually granitic intrusion into folded sedimentary strata.

phancritic
said of texture of an igneous rock being visibly crystalline.

phanerocrystalline
a textural term which is applicable to igneous rock in which the crystals comprising it could be separately distinguished with the naked eye.

phanerozoic
the part of geologic time for which there is abundant evidence of life, especially higher forms, in the corresponding rock, essentially post-Precambrian.

phantom
a bed or member that is absent from a specific stratigraphic section but is usually present in characteristic position a sequence of similar geologic eye.

phantom horizon
in seismic reflection prospecting, a line constructed so that it is parallel to the nearest actual dip segment at all points along a profile.

phengite
a variety of muscovite possessing high silica content.

phenoclast
a general term which is used for a large fragment (larger than 4 mm) in a sedimentary rock i.e., a pebble, cobble, or boulder.

phenocrysts
refers to the relatively large crystals which have been found set in a finer-grained groundmass constituting the texture which is termed prophyritic, 'inset' is a synonym. Phenocrysts are generally idiomorphic.

phi grade scale
a logarithmic transformation of the Wentworth grade scale in which the diameter value of the particle is replaced by the negative logarithm to the base 2 of the particle diameter.

phlebite
melamorphite or migmatite with roughly banded veined appearance.

phonolite
it is a igneous rock of the syenite clan. It is a fine-grained porphyritic extrusive rock which is a light-coloured aphanitic rock of volcanic origin, and composed largely of alkali feldspar, feldspathoids, and smaller amounts of mafic minerals.

phorogenesis
slipping of earth's crust over the mantle.

phosphatic nodule
a dark, usually black, earthy mass or pebble of variable size and shape, having a hard shiny surface and occurring in marine strata.

phosphorite
a sedimentary rock which is composed of phosphate minerals. It is also known as phosphate rock.

phosphorus
phosphorus is an element. It is found in many different types of rock and mineral, mainly as a compound with calcium. Phosphorus is used to make matches and fertilizers. All living things need phosphorus.

photogeology
the geologic interpretation of landforms by means of aerial photographs.

phreatic Eruption
means a volcanic eruption or explosion, of steam, mud, or other material which is not incandescent. It takes place by the heating and consequent expansion of ground water due to an underlying igneous heat source like lava. Such eruptions are generally not accompanied by the usual products of volcanic eruption.

phretomatic explosion
a volcanic explosion that extrudes both magmatic gases and steam; caused by the contact of magma with groundwater or shallow surface water.

phyllonite
the term used for a metamorphic rock which occupies an intermediate position between phyllite and mylonite in which recrystallization or growth of new minerals has occurred.

physical geology
that branch of geology concerned with understanding the composition of the earth and the physical changes occurring in it, based on the study of rocks, minerals, and sediments, their structures and formations, and their processes of origin and alteration.

physiographic province
a region which possesses a pattern of relief features or landforms and is different significantly from that of adjacent regions.

picotite
a dark-brown variety of hercynite having chronium is commonly found in dunites. Also known as chrome spinel.

piedmont
a piedmont is a gentle slope running down from a mountain to a plain. A piedmont is found at the foot of a mountain.

piedmont benchland
one of several successions or systems of piedmont steps. Also known as piedmont stairway; piedmont treppe.

piedmont scarp
a small, low cliff formed in alluvium on a piedmont slope at the foot of a steep mountain range; due to dislocation of the surface, especially by faulting. Also known as scarplet.

piedmont step
a terracelike or benchlike piedmont feature that slopes outward or downvalley. Also known as piedmont bench; piedmont flat.

pillow lava
refers to lava in the form of distorted globular masses which gets extruded under water.

pillow structure
a primary sedimentary structure that resembles a pillow in size and shape. Also known as mammillary structure.

pilotaxitic
a texture having a felted mass of acicular or lath-like crystals

which are sometimes showing flow structure. Hyalopilitic is a variety of pilotaxitic texture in which the felt of crystals or crystallites gets embedded in a glassy base.

pimple mound

a low, flattened, roughly circular or elliptical dome consisting of sandy loam that is entirely distinct from the surrounding soil; peculiar to the Gulf coast of eastern Taxas and southwestern Louisiana.

pimple plain

a plain distinguished by the presence of numerous, conspicuous pimple mounds.

pindobonian

a European stage of geologic time, middle Miocene.

pipe amygdule

an elongate amygdule occurring toward the base of a lava flow, probably formed by the generation of gases or vapour from the underlying material.

pisolite

1. a sedimentary rock, which is commonly a limestone and made up chiefly of cemented pisoliths; a coarse-grained oolite.

2. a term often used for describing pisolith.

pisolith

small, more or less spherical particles found in limestones and dolomites, having a diameter of 2-10 millimeters and often formed of calcium carbonate.

pisolitic tuff

of a tuff, composed of accretionary lapilli or pisolites.

pitch

1. in a fold, it refers to the angle between the horizontal and the axis measured on the axial plane. It is a synonym of asphalt.

pitchstone

a glassy igneous rock often somewhat devitrified, and is characterized by a dull, 'pitchy' lustre and a rather flat fracture, as opposed to the conchoidal fracture of obsidian. Pitchstones have been found to vary in composition from acidic to near basic.

pit-run gravel

a natural deposit of a mixture of gravel, sand, and foreign materials.

pitted outwash plain

an outwash plain characterized by numerous depressions such as kettles, shallow pits, and potholes.

placer

a mineral deposit at or near the surface of the earth, formed by mechanical concentration of mineral particles from weathered debris. Also known as ore of sedimentation.

plagiaplite

refers to the igneous rock of the syenite clan. It is a medium-grained granular hypabyssal rock and has oligoclase, hornblende, quartz, biotite, and muscovite.

plain

a plain is a flat area of lowlands. Many plains stretch for hundreds of kilometres. The plains of East Africa are covered with trees and grasslands. The great Plains of North America are used for growing grain crops.

plaisancian

a European stage of geologic time; lower Pliocene. Also known as Piacention; Plaisanzian.

planar cross-bedding

cross-bedding characterized by planar surfaces of erosion in the lower bounding surface.

planatlon

erosion resulting in flat surfaces, caused by meandering streams, waves, ocean currents, wind, or glaciers.

planosol

an intrazonal, hydromorphic soil having a clay pan or hardpan covered with a leached surface layer; developed in a humid to subhumid climate.

plastic

capable of being deformed permanently without rupture.

plasticity index

the percent difference between moisture content of soil at the liquid and plastic limits.

plastic limit

the water-content limit of a sediment.

plateau basalt

one or a succession of high temperature basaltic lava flows from fissure eruptions which accumulate to form a plateau. Also known as flood basalt.

plate crustal

an ice crystal exhibiting typical hexagonal [rarely triangular] symmetry and having comparatively little thickness parallel to its axis.

plate tectonics

global tectonic's based on a model of the earth characterized by a small number of semiringid plates which float on some viscous underlayer in the mantle; each plate moves more or less independently and grinds against the others, concentrating most deformation, volcanism, and seismic activity along the periphery. Also known as raft tectonics.

platform

1. any level or almost level surface; a small plateau.

2. a continental area covered by relatively flat or gently tilted, mainly sedimentary strata which overlay a basement of rocks consolidated during earlier deformations; platforms and shields together constitute cratons.

platinum

platinum is an element. It is a silvery metal. Platinum is normally found combined with sulphur. It is rare and valuable, and used to make jewellery.

playa

a low, essentially flat part of a basin or other undrained area in an arid region.

playfair's law

the law that each stream cuts its own valley, the valley being proportional in size to its stream, and the stream junctions in the valley are accordant in level.

plazolite

a cubic mineral which is composed of hydrated calcium aluminium silicate and carbonate.

pleistocene

an epoch of geologic time of the Quaternary period, following the Tertiary and before the Holocene. Also known as Ice Age; Oiluvium.

pliensbachian

a European stage of geologic time; Lower Jurassic .

pliocene

a worldwide epoch of geologic time of the Tertiary period, extending fro m the end of the miocene to the beginning of the Pleistocene.

plug

a plug is a mass of solid lava in the vent of a volcano which is dormant or extinct. Sometimes, a plug is left exposed when the softer rock surrounding it erodes away.

plug dome

a volcanic dome characterized by an upheaved, consolidated mass filling the conduit.

plum

a clast embedded in a matrix of different kind.

plumasite

it is an igneous rock of the diorite clan. It is a medium-grained granular hypabyssal rock. It is an undersaturated oligoclase-corundum diorite.

plumbago

an obsolete name which was used for the mineral.

plunge

the inclination of a geologic structure, especially a fold axis, measured by its departure from the horizontal. Also known as pitch; rake.

plunging fole

a fold in which the hinge line is inclined to the horizontal.

pluton

1. an igneous intrusion.
2. a body of rock formed by metasomatic replacement.

plutonic

pertaining to rocks formed at a great depth. Also known as abyssal; deep-seated; plutonian.

plutonic breccia

breccia consisting of older annular rock fragments enclosed in younger plutonic rock.

plutonic rock

a rock formed at considerable depth by crystallization of magma or by chemical alteration.

plutonism

1. pertaining to the processes associated with pluton formation.
2. the theory that the earth

formed by solidification of a molten mass.

pluvial

of a geologic process or feature. effected by rain action.

pluvial lake

a lake formed during a period of exceptionally heavy rainfall; specifically, a Pleistocene lake formed during a period of glacial advance and now either extinct or only a remnant.

pneumatolysis

refers to those changes which are brought about by the action of hot gaseous substances (other than water) associated with igneous activity. The commonest volatiles involved in Pneumatolysis include fluorine, hydrofluoric acid, and fluorides of boron.

pneumatolytic

formed by gaseous agents.

pod

an ore body of an elongate or lenticular shape.

podzol

a soil group characterized by mats of organic matter in the surface layer and thin horizons of organic minerals overlying gray, leached horizons and dark-brown illuvial horizons; found in coal forests to temperate coniferous or mixed forests.

poikilitic

a textural term which means the occurrence of a number of orientated or unorientated crystals which are totally enclosed within a larger crystal, e.g., small rounded olivine crystals have been enclosed within large crystals of hornblende, thereby giving rise to the phenomenon of lustre mottling. The use of the term is normally limited to igneous rocks.

poikiloblastic

used for a texture of metamorphic rocks in which small grains of one mineral are lying within larger metacrysts of another. It is also spelled as poeciloblastic.

point diagram

a fabric diagram in which poles representing linations, normals to fabric planes, or crystallographic directions have been plotted.

polar-cap

an ice sheet which is centered at on of the poles of the earth.

polar wandering

migration during geologic time of the earth's poles of rotation and magnetic poles. Also known as Chandler motion: polar migration.

pole

the poles of the Earth are the points at its extreme north or south. The North Pole and the South Pole are directly opposite each other. They are known as the geographical poles. The north pole is over the frozen arctic ocean. The South Pole is over the ice-covered ontinent of Antarctica.

polje

refers to a large depression in

a karst region having steep sides and a flat floor.

pollenite

igneous rock of the diorite clan. A greenish-grey, fine-grained porphyritc extrusive rock; contains phenocrysts of sanidine and andesine in agroundmass of olivine, and esineaugite, hornblende, biotite and glass.

polygeosyncline

a geosynclinal geoanticlinal belt along the continental margin, receiving sediments from a boderland on its oceanic side.

polygonal ground

a ground surface consisting of polygonal arrangements of rock, soil and vegetation formed on a level or gently sloping surface by frost action. Also known as cellular soil.

polymict

a term used for describing detrital rock which consists of fragments of many different materials. The term is cable especially to rudaceous rocks.

polymorphism

a substance is said to exhibit polymorphism if it exists in two or more distinct forms having identical chemical compositions. Calcite (hexagonal) and aragonite (orthorhombic) are regarded as polymorphs of calcium carbonate.

polynya

any nonlinear opening enclosed in ice, especially a large expanse of water, surrounded by sea ice, but not large enough to be called open water.

polyzenite

feldspathoid igneously rock. A medium-grained porphyritic hypabyssal rock; contains phenorcrysts of anomite in a groundmass of lazurite melilite, olivine and phalogopite.

porcelaneous

resembling unglazed porcelain.

pore

1. Means a small to minute opening or interstice in a rock or soil.

2. also refers to a small opening in the wall or shell of an invertebrate animal e.g., from the exterior through theeal plates of a crystoid.

pore compressibility

the fractional change in reservoir-rock pore volume with a unit change in pressure upon that rock.

pore-size distribution

variations in pore sizes in reservoir formations; each type of rock has its own typical pore size and related permeability.

pore space

open space or void between individual grains in a rock mass; it varies greatly in size and shape.

porous

porous describes something through which water is able to pass. Gravel is very porous, and so are soils which contain a lot of sand or organic matter.

porphyritic

a texture term used for describing igneous rocks which have relatively large crystals set in a finer-grained groundmass. Porphyritic crystals are usually euhedral.

porphyroblastic

pertaining to the textures of a recrystallized metamorphic rock having large idioblasts of minerals in a finer grained crystalloblastic matrix.

porphyry

rock names which are usually applied to hypabyssal rocks having phenocrysts—in the strictest sense alkali feldspar phenocrysts. In practice the terms are used for any medium-grained rock having phenocrysts of any mineral. 'Porphyrite' is now restricted to a porphyry having andesine phenocrysts, but the term is almost obsolete.

portlandian

a European geologic stage of the Upper Jurassic, above Kimmeridgian, below Berriasian of Cretaceous.

positive area

an area where deposition is not taking place. The opposite of a basin of deposition or negative area.

postglacial

referring to the interval of geologic time since the total disappearance of continental glaciers in middle latitudes or from a particular area.

postmagmatic

pertaining to geologic reactions orevents occurring after the bulk of the magma has crystallized.

postorogenic

of a geologic process or event, occurring after a period of orogeny

potash

potash is a compound of potassium. It is made of potassium carbonate and other potassium salts. Potash is found with other salts, such as common salt, in salt lakes. It is also found in ash, Potash is used as a fertilizer for plants.

potassium-argon dating

dating of archeological, geological, or organic specimens by measuring the amount of argon accumulated in the matrix rock through decay of radioactive potassium.

potassiumbentonite

a clay of the illite group that contains potassium and is formed by alteration of the volcanic ash. Also known as potash benttonite.

pothole

refers to a shaftlike cave which opens upward to the surface.

potstone

a massive greyish-green, dark-green, iron-grey, or brownish black variety of talc.

pozzolan

a finely ground burnt clay or shale resembling volcanic dust, found near Pozzuoli, Italy; used in cement because it hardens underwater.

prairie

the prairie is the treeless, grassy plain in the centre of the North American continent. On the prairie, the rain falls mostly in the summer, when it is also hot. In the winter, it is dry and cold.

prasopal

a green variety of common opal containing chromium.

precambrian

refers to the period of time from the consolidation of the earth's crust to the base of the Cambrian. The terms Proterozoic, Azoic, and Archaean are used either as synonyms or partial synonyms. Most precambrian rocks, have undergone one or more Precabrian orogenies, as well as post - cambrain ones. Precambrian rocks are exposed at the surface in shield areas.

precipitates

refers to a geochemical division of the sedimentary rocks which ate including the chemically formed limestones.

predazzite

a crystallized limestone that resembles pencatite, but contains less brucite than calcite.

preferred orientation

any rock in which the constituent units have been arranged in any but a random way is said to exhibit a preferred orientation fabric. The units constituting the rock may get oriented themselves according to:

(a) some shape characteristic.

(b) some crystallographic characteristic.

(c) their magnetic characteristics, or

(d) some other physical characteristic.

preglacial

1. refers to geologic time which is immediately preceding the Plesitocene epoch. 2. said of materials, which are underlying glacial deposits.

premineral

in economics geology, said of a structure or other feature extant before mineralization.

pressure gradient

a pressure gradient is the difference in pressure between two points. There is a steep pressure gradient between an area of high pressure ad one of low pressure. A steep pressure gradient, with strong winds, is marked on a weather chart by isobars placed close together. Widely-spaced isobars show a weak gradient and light winds.

prevailing current

the ocean current most frequently observed during a given period.

primary

1. an obsolete name which was used for the Precambrian, subsequently the Precambrian + Palaeozoic, later the Palaeozoic only.

2. in its ordinary sense of

'original', it is applicable to those features of a rock which are developed at the time of its formation.

primary porosity

the porosity that developed during the final stage of sedimentation or that was present within sedimentary particles at the time of deposition.

prismatic

said of a crystal with one dimension markedly greater than the other two. May also refer to a metamorphic texture characterized by such crystals.

problematic fossil

a structures making, object or other feature in a rock whose nature presents a problem, such as a doubtful organic nature or origin.

prod cast

the cast of a prod mark. Also known as impact cast.

prodelta

the part of a delta lying beyond the delta front, and sloping gently down to the basin floor of the delta; it is entirely below the water level.

prodelta clay

fine sand, silt, and clay transported by the river and deposited on the floor of a sea or lake beyond the main body of a delta.

prod mark

a short tool mark oriented parallel to the current and gradually deepening downcurrent. Also known as impact mark.

profile

1. the outline formed by the intersection of the plane of a vertical section and the ground surface. Also known as topographic profile. 2. Data recorded by a single line of receivers from one shot point in seismic prospecting.

profile of equilibrium

1. the slope of the floor of a sea, ocean, or lake, taken in a vertical plane, when deposition of sediment is balanced by erosion. 2. the longitudinal profile of a graded stream. Also known as equilibrium profile; graded profile.

progressive metamorphism

systematic change in metamorphic grade from lower to higher in any metamorphic terrian.

progressive sand wave

a sand wave characterized by downcurrent migration.

prong reef

a wall reef that has developed irregular buttresses normal to its axis in leeward and seaward directions.

propylitization

refers to the hydrothermal alteration of a finegrained igneous rock (especially andesite) to a mass of secondary minerals like chlorite, epidote, quartz, carbonates, and sub-micas such as 'sericite'.

proterobase

a disbase in which the mafic

mineral is primary hornblende.

proterozoic

proterozoic describes an eon in geological time. The Proterozoic Eon lasted from about 2,500 million years ago to about 590 million years ago. The Proterozoic Eon is the later part of Precambrian time.

protolith

the unmetamorphosed rock from which a given metamorphic rock was formed by metamorphism.

protore

material having ore minerals in too low a concentration for economic working, but which may become a workable ore where secondary enrichment, especially supergene oxidation, has been carried out.

provenance

refers to the source area or areas of the material which are making up a sediment, more especially the nature of the rocks from which the material is derived.

provitrain

vitrain in which some plant structure can be discerned by microscope. Also known as telain.

proximal

(1) said of an ore deposit formed adjacent to a volcanic feature to which it is genetically related and from which its constituents have been derived.

(2) said of a sedimentary deposit consisting of coarse clastics, formed nearest the source area.

psammitic

pertaining to, characteristic or, or derived from a grenite.

psephite

a sediment or sedimentary rock composed of fragments that are coarser than sand and which are set in a qualitatively and quantitatively varying matrix; equivalent to a rudite or, generally, a conglomerate.

psephitic rocks

a synonym of rudaceous rocks, which is more commonly used for describing the metamorphic equivalents of these rocks.

psephyte

a lake-bottom deposit consisting mainly of coarse, fibrous plant remains.

pseudimorphic

applied to mineral appearing in the crystal form of another, due to alternation for example, where serpertines may retain the crystal shape of the original olivines.

pseudofossil

means a structure, natural object, or mineral of inorganic origin which may resemble or be mistaken for a fossil.

pseudoporphyritic

refers to a rock which is not a true porphyry, but resembles one due to the rapid growth of some of the crystals.

pseudovolcano

a larger circular hollow or crater which is not associated

with volcanic activity.

pteroceriań

a stratigraphic stage name which is being used for the European Lower Kimmeridgian.

pteropod ooze

a pelagic sediment containing at least 45% calcium carbonate in the form of tests of marine animals, particularly pteropods.

ptygma

pegmatitic material with migmatite or gneiss, resembling disharmonic folds. Also known as ptygmatic fold.

ptygmatic folds

granitic material within migmatite or gneiss, having the appearance of disharmonic folds. The genesis of this type of folding is controversial.

pudding stone

in Britain, a conglomerate having rounded pebbles whose colours are in marked contrast with the matrix, yielding a section of a rock the appearance of a raism pudding.

pulaskite

a sysenite which consists almost entirely of alkali feldspar, but having some aegirine and other ferromagnesian minerals, and often nepheline.

pull-apart

a precompaction sedimentary structure having the appearance of bondage and consisting of beds that have been stretched and pulled apart into relatively short slabs.

pumice

a light coloured cellular glassy rock which is commonly having the composition of rhyolite. It is usually sufficiently buoyant to float on water. It is economically useful as light-weight aggregate and as an abrasive.

pumic fall

pumice falling from a volcano eruption cloud.

punky

said of a semi-indurated rock, such as leached limestone; also said of a tuff that is weakly welded.

puy

a volcanic plug, especially as occurring in the Auvergne district of the Central Massif of France, where the volcanic necks stand up as steep-sided pillar-like hills.

pyreneite

a black or greyish-black variety of andradite.

pyriboles

a 'portmanteau' word for pyroxenes and/or amphiboles.

pyrite

pyrite is a mineral. Crystals of pyrite are very shiny and have a gold colour. Pyrite is sometimes called fool's gold. It is made of iron and sulphur and is found in sedimentary and igneous rocks.

pyritization

a common process of hydrothermal alteration involving introduction of or replacement by pyrite.

pyroclast
an individual pyroclastic fragclast.

pyroconductivity
electrical conductivity which is developed in a material only at high temperature, mainly at fusion, in solids which are practically nonconductive at normal temperatures.

pyroelectric crystal
a crystal that exhibits pyroelctricity, such as tourmaline, lithium sulphate monohydrate, cane sugar, and ferroelectric barium titante.

pyroelectricity
the term used for the property of certain crystals to produce a state of electrical polarity by a change of temperature.

pyromagma
a highly mobile lava, oversaturated with gases that exists at shallower depths than hypomagma.

pyrometamorphism
refers to an intense form of thermal metamorphism which gets developed at or near a contact with a high-temperature igneous intrusion.

pyrometasomatic
a term used for describing metasomatic changes taking place in rocks under condition of high temperature and pressure at or near contacts with high temperature igneous intrusions. The effects have been most easily observable in limestones, and high-temperature skarns form under these conditions. The formation of some ore bodies, e.g., magnetite pyrrhotite, is attributed to this process.

pyrophanite
a bloodred, rhombohedral mineral which consists of manganese titanate; and is isomorphous with ilmenite.

pyroschist
a schist or shale that has sufficiently high carbon content, so that it burns with a bright flame.

pyrosphere
the zone of the earth below the lithosphere.

pyrostilpmite Ag_3SbS_3
it is a hyacinth-red mineral which is occurring in monoclinic crystal tufts; it is polymorphous with pyrargerite.

pyrixene monzonite
a quartz-poor member containing approximately equal amounts of microperthite and plagioclase.

pyroxenide
an informal term for any holocrystalline, medium to coarse grained igneous rock composed mainly of pyroxene, *e.g.,* pyroxenite.

pyroxenite
refers to a dark-coloured heavy, phaneritic igneous rock which is composed mainly of pyroxene having smaller amounts of olivine and hornblende; it is formed by crystallization of gabbraic

magma.

pythmic

pertaining to the bottom of a lake.

quagmire bog

a peat bog floating or growing over water-saturated land which shakes or trembles when walked on.

quaking bog

a peat bog which is floating or growing over water-saturated land. It shakes or trembles when walked on.

quaquaversal

of strata and geologic structures, dipping outward in all directions away from a central point.

quarry

a quarry is an open pit made by digging for rocks or minerals. The surface soil is removed to reach the rocks or minerals below. Stone for building and slate, sand and gravel are dug from quarries.

quartzarenite

a sandstone which is composed primarily of quartz.

quartz-flooded limestone

a variety of limestone characterized by abundance of quartz particles that were imported suddenly from a nearby source by wind or water currents.

quartzine

chalcedony characterized by fibres having positive crystallographic elongation.

quartzite

metaquartzite is considered to be a metamorphosed arenaceous rock. The constituent grains recrystallise and develop an interlocked mosaic texture, having little or no trace of cementation. Impurities in the original rock may produce metamporphic minerals e.g., argillaceous impurity will produce chlorite or biotite; calcite may produce wollastonite. Quartzites are usually considered to be as thermally metamorphosed rocks, but regional metamorphism also gives rise to them, usually with the development of an orientated fabric which distinguishes them from the thermally metamorphosed kinds. Also refers to orthoquartzite.

quartzitic sandstone

sandstone having 100% quartz grains cemented with silica.

quartzose

containing quartz as a principle constituent; especially applied to sediments and sedimentary rocks consisting chiefly of quartz.

quartz topaz

a frequently used but incorrect term for citrine.

quarternary

the second period of the cenozoic era, following the Tertiary. It began about two or three million years ago and extends to the present.

queenston shale

a red bed series from the Ordovi cian found in Niagara

Gorge; it is composed of deltaic red shale.

quenselite 4[PbMnO$_2$,OH]
a pitchblack, monoclinic mineral.

quick clay
clay that loses its shear strength after being disturbed.

quicksand
a highly mobile mass of the fine sand consisting of smooth, rounded grains with little tendency to mutual adherence, usually thoroughly saturated with upward-flowing water; tends to yield under pressure and to readily swallow heavy objects on the surface. Also known as running sand.

quilted surface
a land surface characterized by broad, rounded, uniformly convex hills separating valleys which are relatively narrow.

race
the term used for a group of organisms having similar characteristics but not distinctive enough to be classified as a species or sub-species.

radial drainage pattern
a drainage pattern characterized by radiating streams diverging from a high central area. Also known as centrifugal drainage pattern.

radial fault
faults arranged like the spokes of a wheel, radiating from a central point.

radiation
radiation is a kind of energy. It includes the particles given off by elements which are radioactive. Some radiation is harmful in large doses and can destroy living cells.

radioactive clock
a radioactive isotope like potassium-40 which spontaneously decays to yield a stable end product at a constant rate, thereby allowing absolute geological age to be determined.

radioactive emanation
a radioactive gas given off by certain radioactive elements; all of these gases are isotopes of the element radon. Also known as emanation.

radiochronology
an absolute-age dating method based on the existing ratio between radioactive parent elements and their radiogenic daughter isotopes.

radiogenic
said of a product which is obtained from a radioactive process.

radiogenic isotope
an isotope that is produced by radioactive decay, but which itself may or may not be radioactive.

radiolarian chert
a homogeneous cryptocrystalline radiolarite with a well-developed matrix.

radiolarin earth
a porous, unconsolidated silliceous sediment formed from the opaline silica skeletal remains of Radiolaria; formed

from radiolarian ooze.

radiolarian ooze

a deep-sea pelage sediment containing at least 30% opaline silica tests of radiolarians.

radiolarite

the hard fine-grained chert-like homogenous consolidated equivalent of radiolarian earth.

radiometric age

geologic age expressed in years determined by quantitatively measuring radioactive elements and their decay products.

radon

radon is an inert gas. It is found in small quantities in the atmosphere. Radon is given off when the metal radium decays.

rafting

transporting of rock by floating ice or floating organic materials (such as logs) to places not reached by water currents.

rainbow

a rainbow is an arch of colours seen in the sky. There are six main colours in a rainbow. These are red, orange, yellow, green, blue and violet. When sunlight shines through rain, the raindrops split up the sunlight into these colours.

rain prints

small , shallow depressions formed in the soft sediment of mud by the impact of falling raindrops. Also known as raindrop impressions; raindrop imprints.

rain shadow

a dry region on the lee side of a topographical obstacle, generally a mountain range, where rainfall is significantly less than on the windward side.

raised beach

refers to a wave-cut platform, with or without a covering of beach deposits, which has been now raised above the present sealevel.

rammelsbergite $NiAs_2$

a grey mineral which is isomporphous with pararemmelsbergite.

ramp valley

a trough between faults, forced downward by lateral pressure.

rang

a unit of subdivision in C.I.P.W. classification of igneous rocks.

range zone

formal biostratigraphic zone made up of a body of strata comprising the total horizontal and vertical range of occurrence of a specified taxon of a group of taxa.

rank

1. a coal classification based on degree of metrmorphism.

rapakivi

a variety of granite or quartz monozite characterized by orthoclase phenocrysts mantled with plagioclase. Also known as wiborgite.

rapids

rapids are very fast-flowing parts of a river. In the rapids, the water rushes quickly over a series of waterfalls.

rauracian
it is a synonym of Argovian (Jurassic System).

ravine
a ravine is a deep, narrow river valley. Ravines are formed when rivers rush over rocks and wear away a channel. A ravine is similar to a gorge, but the sides are not as steep.

reaction pair
any of the two minerals, one of which is formed at the expense of the other by the reaction with liquid.

reaction rim
a peripheral zone around mineral grains that are typically anhedral corroded grains of the unstable high temperature phase of a mineral. The rim is composed of another minerals species, and represents the reaction of the earlier solidified mineral with the surrounding magma.

realgar
a mineral, which occurs in association with orpiment in hydrothermal sulphide veins and as a deposit from hot springs and vulcanicity.

rebound
the isostatic readjustment upward of a landmass depressed by glacial loading.

recent
an epoch of geologic time (late Quaternary) following the Pleistocene; referred to as Holocenen in several European countries.

recombent fold
an overturned fold in which the axial surface is more or less horizontal.

rectangular cross ripple mark
an oscillation cross ripple mark consisting of two sets of ripples which intersect at right angle, enclosing a rectangular pit.

rectangular drainage pattern
a drainage pattern characterized by many right-angles bends in both the main streams and their tributaries. Also known as lattic drainage pattern.

recumbent fold
an overturned fold with a nearly horizontal axial surface. Also known as reclined fold.

redbed
continetally deposited sediment composed principally of sandstone, siltsitone, and shale; red in colour due to the presence of ferric oxide. Also known as redrock.

red clay
a fine-grained, reddish-brown pelagic deposit consisting of relatively large proportions of windblown particles, meteoric and volcanic dust, pumic, shark teeth, manganese nodules and debris transported by ice. Also known as brown clay.

red mud
a reddish terrigenous mud composed of up to 25% calcium carbonate and deriving its colour from the presence of

ferric oxide; found on the sea floor near deserts and near the mouths of large rivers.

red snow

a snow surface of reddish colour which is caused by the presence within it of certain microscopic algae or/and particles of red dust.

reduzate

a sediment accumulated under reducing conditions and consequently rich in organic carbon and in iron sulfide minerals; examples are coal and black shale.

reedmergnerite

it is a colourless, triclinic borate mineral which represents the boron analog of albite.

reef detrius

fragmented material derived from erosion of an organic reef. Also known as reef debris.

reef flat

a flat expanse of dead reef rock which is partly or entire by dry at low tide; shallow pools, potholes, gullies and patches of coral debris and sand are features of the reef flat.

reef limestone

limestone which is composed of the remains of sedentary organisms like sponges, and of sediment-binding organic constituents such as calcareous algae. It is also known as coral rock.

reef patch

a single large colony of coral formed independently on a shelf at depths less than 70 meters in the lagoon of a barrier reef of an atloo. Also known as patch reef.

reef plnnacle

a small, isolated spire of rock of coral, especially a small reef patch.

reefrock

a hard unstratified rock composed of sand, shale and the calcareous remains of sedentary organisms; cemented by calcium carbonate.

reef talus

massive inclined strata composed of reef detritus deposited along the seaward margin of an organic reef. Also known as reef conglomerate.

refolding

means a process by which folds of one generation get subjected to and stressed by a force of different orientation.

refoliation

a foliation that is subsequent to and oriented differently from an earlier foliation.

reg

a reg is a kind of desert. It has a flat surface covered in gravel. Wind has swept away any small particles of loose sand.

regime

the existence in a stream channel of a balance between erosion and deposition over a period of years.

regional dip

the nearly uniform and generally lowangle inclination

of strata over a wide area. Also known as normal dip.

regional geology

the geology of a large region, treated from the viewpoint of the spatial distribution and position of stratigraphic units, structural features, and surface forms.

regional metamorphism

geological metamorphism affecting an extensive area.

regional slope

the generally uniform dip of rock strata or land surface over a wide area.

regional slope deposit

a sedimentary deposit widely distributed as a thin sheet over a regional slope.

regional uncontormity

a continuous unconformity extending throughout a wide region that may be nearly continentwide, and usually represents a long period of time.

regmagenesis

diastrophic production of regional strike-slip displacements.

regolith

refers to the loose, incoherent mantle of rock fragments, soil, blown sand, alluvium, etc., which is resting upon solid rock, i.e., the bedrock.

regosol

in early United States soil classification systems, one of an azonal group of soils that form from deep, unconsolidated deposits and have no definite genetic horizons.

regressive sediments

sediments deposited during the retreat or withdrawal of water emergence of the land; characterized by an off lap arrangement.

rejuvenate

the act of stimulating a stream to renewed erosive activity either by tectonic uplift or a drop in sea level.

rejuvenated fault scarp

a fault scarp revived by renewed movement along an old fault line after partial dissection or erosion of the initial scarp. Also known as revived fault scarp.

rejuvenation

the restoration of youthful features to fluvial landscapes; the renewal of youthful vigour to low-gradient streams is usually caused by regional upwarping of broad areas formerly at or near base level.

relative geologic time

non-absolute geologic time in which events may be placed relatively to one another.

relative humidity

relative humidity is a measure of the amount of moisture in the atmosphere. If the relative humidity is very high, mist, fog or rain can occur. The relative humidity is usually lower during the day than during the night. It is measured using a hygrometer.

relative permeability

specific permeability of a porous rock formation to a particular phase at a particular saturation and a particular saturation distribution; for example, ratio of effective permeability to a specified phase to the rock's absolute permeability.

relaxation

in experimental structural geology, the diminution of applied stress with time, as the result of any of various creep processes.

release fracture

a fracture formed as a result of a decrease in the maximum principal stress.

relic

1. a landform that remains intact after decay or disintegration or that remains after the disappearance of the major portion of its substance. 2. a vestige of a particle in a sedimentary rock, such as a trace of a fossil fragment.

relict dike

in a granitized mass, a tabular, crystalloblastic body that represents a dike which was emplaced prior to and which was relatively resistant to, the granitization process.

relict permafrost

permafrost formed in the past which persists in areas where it would not form today.

relict sediment

a sediment which was in equilibrium with its environment when first deposited but which is unrelated to its present environment even though it is not buried by later sediments, such as a shallow-marine sediment on the deep ocean floor.

relict soil

a soil formed on a preexisting landscape but not subsequently buried under younger sediments.

relict texture

in mineral deposits, an original texture that persists after partial replacement.

relizean stage

a subdivision of the Miocene in the California-Oregon-Washington area.

remain fossils

refers to organic skeletal material which get accumulated over a considerable period of time, which is rolled and abraded, more or less in situ, before its eventual burial. The high concentration of fossils occurs either due to a paucity of sediment or by current action preventing the deposition of sediment. Many bone beds are produced by these methods.

rendzina

refers to ore of an intrazonal calcimorphic group of soils which are characterized by a brown to black, friable surface horizon and light-grey or yellow, soft underlying horizon. They occur under forests of grasses in humid to semiarid climates.

replacement
a term widely used in geology for describing the process whereby one constituent in a system has been progressively substituted by another.

replacement dike
a dike which is made by gradual transformation of wall rock by solutions along fractures or permeable zones.

replacement texture
the texture which has been exhibited due to the replacement of mineral by the other.

replacement vein
a mineral vein formed by the gradual transformation of an original vein by secondary fluids.

resequent fault-line scarp
a fault-line scarp which faces in the same direction as the original fault scarp or in which the downthrown block is topographical lower than the upthrown block.

reservoir fluid
the subterranean fluid which has been trapped by a reservoir formation; may include natural gas, liquid and vapours of petroleum, and interstitial water.

reservoir rock
friable, porous sandstone containing deposits of oil or gas.

residual
1. of a mineral deposit, formed by either mechanical or chemical concentration.
2. pertaining to a residuae left in a place after weathering of rock.
3. of a topographic feature, representing the remains of a formerly great mass or area and rising above the surrounding surface.

residual anticline
in salt tectonics, a relative structural high resulting from the depression of two adjacent rim synclines. Also known as residual dome.

residual clay
very finely divided clay material formed in place by weathering of rock. Also known as primary clay.

residual ochre
an earthy, red, yellow or brownish iron oxide powder of iron oxide produced during chemical weathering.

residual soil
soil formed in place by the decomposition of rocks like those on which it lies.

resinite
a variety of exinite composed of resinous compounds, often in elliptical or spindle-shaped bodies.

resinous coal
coal in which large proportions of resinous material are contained in the attritus.

resistate
a sediment consisting of minerals that are chemically resistant and are enriched in the residues of weathering

process. Also known as residual sediment.

resorption
refers to the partial refusion or solution of a phenocryst in a porphyritic igneous rock. The process may produce a border of secondary minerals.

resurgence
the emergence of an underground river from a cavern, usually at the base of a scrap face or cliff in limestone (spring or seepage, in which a smaller quantity of water is involved).

revelly ground
rock that breaks into small pieces when drilled and tends to cave or slough into the hole when the drill string is pulled, or binds the drill string by becoming wedged or locked between the drill rod and the borehle wall.

reversal of dip
change in the dip direction of bedding near a fault such that the beds curve towards the fault surface in a direction exactly opposite that of the drag folds. Also known as dip reversal.

reversed arc
a curved belt of islands which is concave toward the open ocean, the opposite of most island arcs.

reverse fault
a fault along which the hanging wall is displaced upward with respect to the footwall.

reverse slope
a hill descending away from a ridge.

revolution
a little-used term to describe a time of profound crustal movements, on a continentwide or worldwide scale, which led to abrupt geographic, climatic and environmental changes that were related to changes in forms of life.

rework
any geologic material that has been removed or displaced by natural agents from its origin and incorporated in a younger formation.

rhaetain
the stratigraphical stage name which is being used for the European Rhaetic.

rhegmagnesis
orogeny characterized by the development of large-scale strike slip faults.

rheid
a substance (below its melting point) which deforms by viscous flow during applied stress at an order of magnitude at least three times that of elastic deformation under similar circumstances.

rheidity
relaxation time of a substance which is divided by 1000.

rheomorphism
a term which is more or less synonymous with viscous flow. It is applicable to rocks which have been deformed when partial melting takes place. The

use of the term is also extended to many types of plastic or plastico-viscous deformation.

rhodocrosite $MnCO_3$

a hexagonal carbonate mineral, which is found in metasomatic deposits.

rhodonite $MnSiO_3$

a manganese mineral, a pyroxenoid. It is sometimes found in hydrothermal venis or metasomatic deposits.

rhodusite

fibrous variety of glaucophane.

rhombohedral close packing

a tight arrangement of uniform solid spheres in a cluster sediment or crystal lattice in which the unit cell has six planes passing through the centres of light sphere located at the corners of a regular rhombohedron; an aggregate so packed has minimum porosity.

rhombiod ripple mark

an aqueous current ripple mark characterized by a reticular arrangement of diamond shaped tongues of sand, with each tongue having two acute angles, one pointing upcurrent and the other pointing downcurrent.

rhylite

a light coloured, aphanitic volcanic rock composed largely of alkali feldspar and free silica with minor amounts of mafic minerals. Mineralogically they are similar to granites and micrograniticas although chemically they appear somewhat richer in SiO_2. Occasionally quartz in rhyolites is replaced by the high temperature beta-form, and very rarely by tridymite or cristobalite. Ferromagnesian minerals are less obvious than in the corresponding plutonic rocks. Rhyolites in the strict sense are divided into sodic and potassic forms, according to the type of feldsper present.

rhyodacite

the term used for a group of extrusive prophyritic igneous rocks that have quartz, plagioclase, and biotite phenocrysts in a fine-grained to glassy groundmass. It is composed of alkali feldspar and silica minerals. It is also known as dellenite.

rhyolitic glass

volcanic glass that is chemically equivalent to rhyolite.

rhyolitic lava

a highly viscous, silica-rich lava.

rhyolitic tuff

a tuff composed of fragments of rhyolitic lava.

rhythmic accumulations

refers to the regular pattern of ripples and cusps in sediment on the beach or the sea floor which is formed by current and waves.

rhythmic sedimentation

a repetitious, regular sequence of rock units formed by sedimentary succession and indicating a frequent, predictable recurrence of the same sequence of conditions.

rhythmic stratification
the occurrence of sediment layers in repetitive patterns, such as a regular alternation of layers of lime and clay.

rhythmite
an independent unit of a rhythmic succession or of beds that were developed by rhythmic sedimentation.

rib- and- furrow
the bedding-plane expression for micro-cross-bedding, consisting of sets of small, transverse arcuate marking confined to long, narrow, parallel grooves oriented parallel to current flow and separated by narrow ridges.

ribbon
refers to one of set of parallel bands in a rock or mineral.

ribbon conveyor
a continuous geological cross section that is drawn in perspective along a curved or sinuous line.

ribbon diagram
a continuous geologic cross-section that is drawn in perspective along a curved or sinous line.

ribbon rock
a succession of thin layers of different mineralogy and texture often contorted and deformed.

richmondian
a stratigraphic stage name which is being used for the North American mid Upper Ordovician.

rideau
a small ridge or mount of earth, or a slightly elevated piece of ground.

ridge
an elongate, narrow, steep-sided elevation of the earth's surface or the ocean floor.

riebungsbreccia
a breccia developed during folding.

riedel fracture
a branching fault which gets developed in the cover because of movement in the basement.

riegel
a low, traverse ridge of bedrock on the floor of a glacial valley. Also known as rock bar; threshold; verrou.

rift
1. a narrow opening in a rock caused by cracking or splitting.
2. a high, narrow passage in a cave.

rift block mountain
a mountain range which is horst block bounded by normal faults.

rift rock valley
a valley which occupies a graben.

rift valley
a deep, central cleft with a mountainous floor in the crest of a midoceanic ridge. Also known as central valley; midocean rift.

rill erosion
the formation of numerous, closely spaced rills due to the uneven removal of surface soil

by streamlets of running water. Also known as rilling; rill wash; rillwork.

rill mark

a small, dendritic channel formed on beach mud or sand by a rill, especially if on the lee side of a partially buried obstruction.

rim cement

a thin layer of calcium carbonate, hematite, or silica developed on the surface of detrital grains during diagenesis.

rime

refers to a white or milky and opaque granular deposit of ice, which is formed by the rapid freezing of supercooled water drops as they impinge upon an exposed object.

rim rock

a top layer of resistant rock on a plateau outcropping with or near by vertical walls.

ring dike

an almost ring circular dike that is vertical or inclined away from the centre of the arc.

ring dike

a roughly circular dike that is vertical or inclined away from the centre of the arc. Also known as ringfracture intrusion.

ring structure

refers to a composite igneous in which the individual members are appearing as circular or partially-circular outcrops. The two main constituents of such structures include ring dykes and cone-sheets. Ring structures have been commonly associated with volcanic episodes. Examples of granitic ring complexes are seen in Glencoe and Ben Nevis, Scotland, and in Nigeria and adjoining territories.

ripple

refers to a small curling or undulating wave which is controlled to a significant degree by both surface tension and gravity.

ripple drift

a pattern of cross-lamination formed by sedimentry deposits on both sides of a migrating ripple.

ripple index

on a rippled surface, the ratio of the crest-to-crest distance to crest-to-trough distance.

ripple load cast

a load cast of a ripple mark showing evidence of penecontemporaneous deformation in the accumulation of its trough and crest and in the overstepping of the components laminae.

ripple mark

1. a surface pattern on incoherent sedimentary material, especially loose sand, consisting of alternating ridges and hollow formed by wind or water action.

2. one of the ridges on a ripple-marked surface.

rise

a long, broad elevation which

rises gently from its surroundings, such as the sea floor. The increase in height or the value of something, such as a rise of tide or a rise of temperature.

riser

a steplike topographic feature, such as a steep slope between terraces.

riss

1. a European stage of geologic time; Pleistocene.

2. the third stage of glaciation of the Pleistocene in the Alps.

riss-würm

the third interglacial stage of the pleistocene in the Alps, following the Riss glaciation and preceding the Würm glaciation.

river basin

the area drained by a river and all of its tributaries.

riverbed

the channel which contains, or formerly contained, a river.

river capture

means the abstraction of the head-waters of one river by a more actively eroding stream. It occurs usually by the breaching of a local watershed Certain cases of capture arise because of glacial breaching Rejuvenation may also produce this phenomenon.

river profile

the longitudinal profile of a river.

river terrace

it marks the position of the former flood plain which had developed if the river flowed at a higher level. It has usually a bench on the side of the valley and is covered with the usual flood plain deposits of clay, sand, and gravel.

river valley

an elongated depression in the earth's surface, carved by river or stream erosion in conjunction with mass wasting or collapse of river banks.

roche moutonnee

a small, elongate hillock of bedrock sculptured by a large glacier so that its long axis is oriented in the direction of ice movement, the upstream side is gently inclined, smoothly rounded, but striated, and the downstream side is steep, rough, and hackly.

rock

rock is the term used for hard mineral deposits. The Earth's crust is made of solid rocks about 70 kilometres deep. Rocks are named according to the way they were formed. The main types of rock are igneous, metamorphic and sedimentary. Small, individual rocks are called stones.

rock avalanche

a very rapidly moving, turbulent mass of broken-up bedrock. Movement in a rock avalanche is a flowage on a grand scale.

rock control

the influences of differences in earth materials on development of landforms.

rock creep
a form of slow flowage in rock materials evident in the downhill bending of layers of bedded or foliated rock and in the slow downslope migration of large blocks of rock away from their parent outcrop.

rock crystal
refers to a clear variety of quartz. It is also known as mountain crystal.

rock cycle
the term used for the interrelated sequence of events by which rocks have been initially formed, altered, destroyed and reformed because of magmatism, erosion, sedimentation, and metamorphism.

rock-defended terrace
1. a river terrace having a ledge or outcrop of resistant rock at its base which serves as protection against undermining. 2. a marine terrace having a mass of resistant rock at the base of the cliff which protects against wave erosion.

rock desert
an upland desert in which bedrock is either exposed or is covered with a thin veneer of coarse rock fragments.

rock failure
fracture of a rock that has been stressed beyond its ultimate strength.

rockfall
1. the fastest-moving landslide; free fall of newly detached bedrock segments from a cliff or other steep slope; usually occurs during spring thaw.
2. the rock material moving in or moved by a rockfall.

rock fan
a fan-shaped rock surface whose apex is where a mountain stream debouches upon a piedmont slope, and which occupies an area where a pediment meets the mountain slope.

rock flour
a fine, chemically unweathered powder of rock-forming minerals produced by pulverization of rock fragments during natural transport or crushing. Also known as glacial flour.

rockforming
referring to any minerals which commonly occur in important proportions in common rocks.

rock glacler
boulders and fine material cemented by ice about a meter below the surface. Also known as talus glacier.

rock mechanics
deals with the study of the mechanical properties of the rocks, especially those properties which may be of interest to the civil engineer. The various properties are as follows: the determination of physical properties such as crushing strength, binding strength, shear strength, moduli of elasticity, internal

angle of friction, porosity, and permeability density, etc. and their interrelationships.

rock pediment
a pediment formed on the surface of bedrock.

rock permeability
the ability of a rock to receive, hold, or pass fluid materials by nature of the interconnections of its internal porosity.

rock pillar
a column of rock formed by differential weathering or erosion, as along a joint plane. Also, a column-like structure that is residual bedrock.

rockslide
the sudden, rapid downward movement of newly detached bedrock segments over a surface of weakness, such as of bedding, joining or faulting. Also known as rock slip.

rock-stratigraphic unit
a lithologically homogeneous body of strata characterized by certain observable physical features, or by dominance of a certain rock type or combination of rock types; rock-stratigraphic units include groups, formations, members and beds. Also known as geolith, lithologic unit; lithostratic unit; lithostratigraphic unit; rock unit.

rock stream
rocks moving in a mass down a slope under the influence of their own weight.

rock terrace
a stream terrace on the side of a valley composed of resistant bedrock which remains during erosion of weaker overlying and underlying beds.

roesslerite $MgH(AsH_4).7H_2O$
a monoclinic mineral which is composed of hydrous acid arsenate of magnesium and is isomorphous with phosphorroesslerite.

roof pendant
the term used for a large mass of the country rock which forms the roof of a major igneous intrusion. They occur most commonly around the margins of batholiths.

rossi-forell scale
refers to an arbitrary scale of earthquake intensity, which has now supplanted by the Modified Mercalli Scale.

rotary fault
a fault in which displacement is downward at one point and upward at another point. Also known as pivotal fault; rotational fault.

rotten stone
a siliceous residue which is produced from the weathering or partial weathering of certain lime-stones which, when suitably crushed and graded, could be used as a mild abrasive.

roundness
the degree of abrasion of sedimentary particles; expressed as the radius of the average radius of curvature of

the edges or corners to the radius of curvature of the maximum inscribed sphere.

rouvillite
an igneous rock of the gabbro clan. A mottled, medium to coarse grained plutonic rock; contains augite hornablende, labradorite, and nepheline.

rubellite
refers to the red to violet coloured tourmaline which is rich in lithium; its hardness on Mohs scale is 7.0-7.5.

rubicelle
yellow or orange-red gem variety of spinel.

ruby
the term used for the red variety of corundum, which is having small amounts of chromium; in its fine quality, it finds use as gemstone.

ruby mica
the first grade of Indian mica; used for electrical capacitors.

rudistids
refers to the aberrant lamellibranchs, reef-builders, which had developed a coral-like form. They lived in the Cretaceous period.

runoff
runoff is that part of the rainfall which reaches the streams and rivers. The rest either evaporates back into the air or seeps into rocks under the ground.

rupelian
a stratigraphic stage name which is being used for the European Middle Oligocene.

ryazanain
a stratigraphic stage name which is being used for the base of the Lower Cretaceous in Eastern Europe.

saalian
a stratigraphic stage name which is being used for the base of the European Upper Pleistocene.

saamite
variety of apatite having strontium and rare earths in place of calcium.

saccharoidal
having a granular texture resembling that of a loaf of sugar. The term is used to describe some marbles and sandstone.

saddle back
a hill or ridge which has concave outline along its crest.

saddle fold
a flexural fold perpendicular to the parent fold and having an additional flexure at its crest.

saematian
a European stage of geological time; the upper Miocene, above Tortonian, below Pontian.

safflorite
a mineral which is composed of cobalt arsenide. It occurs in tin-white masses and is dimorphous with smaltite.

sagenitic
containing acicular minerals.

saint peter sandstone
an artesian aquifer of early Lower Paleozioc age which underlies part of Minnesota, Wisconsin, Iowa, Illinoise and

Indiana.

sakmarian

a European stage of geologic time; the lowermost Permian, above Stephanian of Carboniferous and below Artinskian.

salado formation

a red-bed formation from the Permian found in southest New Mexico; contains rock salt and potash salts.

saleite $Cu(IO_3)(OH)$

a bluish-green mineral composed of hydroxy-iodate of copper(II).

salic

a soil horizon enriched with secondary salts, at least 2 percent, and measuring at least, 15 centimeters in thickness.

salina

an area, such as a salt flat, in which deposits of crystalline salts are formed or found.

salinity

salinity is a measure of the amount of any salt which is dissolved in water. All water even fresh water, contains some salt. Sea water has a high salinity because it contains a large amount of salt. Some lakes have ever higher levels of salinity than sea water.

salopian

obsolete stratigraphic stage name which was used for the Ludlovian plus Wenlockian in Britain (Silurian System).

salt anticline

a structure like a salt dome but with a linear salt core. Also known as salt wall.

salt dome

a diapiric or piercement structure in which there is a central, equidimensional salt plug.

salt lake

a body of water in and or semi-arid region, having no outlier to the sea and containing a high concentration of salt and Louisiana sulphur.

salt pan

a salt pan is a small salt lake. Common salt can be collected from salt pans. The water in a salt pan evaporates in the Sun and wind, and the salt is left behind as crystals.

saltpeter -cave

a cave in which there are deposits of saltpeter earth.

saltpeter earth

a deposit containing calcium nitrate and found in caves.

sand

1. the term used for a detrital particle which is smaller than a granule and larger than a silt grain, having a diameter in the range or 1/16 to 2 mm.

2. refers to a loose aggregate of such particles, most commonly of quartz.

sand-bank

a sand-bank is a mound of sand which is found in the sea, an estuary or a river. A sand-bank forms when a water current which is carrying sand slows.

The sand falls through the water and is deposited as a mound. Sand-banks can be a danger to boats as they can usually be seen only at low tide.

sandbar

a bar or low ridge of sand bordering the shore and built up, or near, to the surface of the water by currents or wave action. Also known as sand reef.

sand crystal

a large crystal loaded up to 60% with detrital sand inclusions formed in a sandstone during or as a result of cementation.

sand drift

1. movement of windblown sand along the surface of a desert or shore. 2. An accumulation of sand against the leeward side of a fixed obstruction.

sand dune

a mound of loose windblown sand commonly found along low-lying seashores above high-tide level.

sandkey

a small sandy island parallel with the shore. Also known as sand cay.

sand plain

a small outwash plain formed by deposition of sand transported by meltwater streams flowing from a glacier.

sand sheet

a thin accumulation of coarse sand or fine gravel having a flat surface.

sandspit

a spit consisting principally of sand.

sandstone

sandstone is a kind of sedimentary rock or stone. It is made of sand grains held tightly together by mud. Sandstone is easy to cut and shape, and is often used for building. Sandstone is often a red colour.

sand wave

a small, ridgelike primary structure which resembles a water wave on the upper surface of a sedimentary bed, which is formed by high-velocity air or water currents. It is also known as sand ridge.

sand wedge

a wedge-shaped accumulation of sand with the apex downward formed by the filling in of winter contraction cracks.

sangamon

the third interglacial stage of the Pleistocene epoch in North America, following the Illinoian glacial and preceding the Wisconsin.

sannoisian

a stratigraphic stage name which is being used for the European Lower Oligocene.

santa catherina

a stratigraphic name for the Brazillian equivalent of the Karroo.

santonian

a stratigraphic stage name which is being used for the European mid Upper

Cretaceous.

saprogenous ooze
ooze formed of putrefying organic matter.

saprolite
a soft, earthy-brown or red decomposed igneous or metamorphic rock that is rich in clay and formed in place by chemical weathering. Also known as saprolith.

sapropel
a mud, slime, or ooze deposited in more or less open water.

sapropel-clay
a sedimentary deposit in which the amount of clay is greater than that of sapropel.

sapropelic coal
coal formed by putrefaction of organic matter under anaerobic conditions in stagnant or standing bodies of water. Also known as sapropelite.

sard
the term used for a reddish or brownish variety of chalcedonic silica. It is also known as sardine; sardius.

sarmatian
a stratigraphic stage name which is being used for the European Upper Miocene.

satin spar
properly, a name assigned to fibrous calcite, but is now commonly applicable also to fibrous gypsum.

savanna
savanna is a kind of dry, lowland plan found in the tropics. In a savanna, there are patches of grassland with scattered bushes and trees.

saxonian
a stratigraphic stage name which is being used for the West European Middle Permian.

scabland
elevated land that is essentially flat-lying and covered with basalt and has only a thin soil cover, sparse vegetation and usually deep, dry channels.

scalenohedron
the term used for closed crystal from whose faces are scalene triangles; the hexagonal scalenohedron is having twelve faces, and the tetragonal scalenohedron is having eight faces.

scapolitization
introduction of or replacement by scapolite.

scar
a steep, rocky eminence, such as a cliff or precipice, where bare rock is well exposed. Also known as scaur; scaw.

scarped plain
a terrain characterized by a succession of faintly inclined or gently folded strata.

scarpline
a relatively straight line of cliffs of considerable extent, produced by faulting or erosion along a fault.

scarp slope
the steep face of a cuesta, or asymmetric ridge, facing in an opposite direction to the dip of the strata. Also known as front slope; inface; scarp face.

schalstein
a slaty rock which is formed by shearing basaltic or andestic tuff or lava.

schist
a large group of coarse-grained metamorphic rocks which readily split into thin plates or slabs as a result of the alignment of lamellar or prismatic minerals.

schistose
pertaining to rocks exhibiting schistosity.

schistosity
a type of cleavage characterstics of metamorphic rocks, notably schist and phyllites, in which the rocks tend to split along parallel planes defined by the distribution and parallel arrangement of platy mineral crystals.

schlieren
the term is generally applicable to elongated 'streakedout', patches in an igneous rock. The patches are somewhat different in composition from the host rock and generally have rather diffuse boundaries.

schmidt projection
a lambert azimuthal equal-area projection of the lower hemisphere of a sphere onto the plane of a meridian; used in structural geology.

schonfelsite
a type of basalt having embedded crystals of olivine and augite in a complex, dense fine-grained groundmass.

schorlite
the black, iron-rick, opaque variety of tourmaline; occurs in the form of radiating clusters of needles. Also known as schorl.

schrund line
the base of the bergschrund or deep crevasse, at a late stage in the excavation of a cirque; the schrund line separates the steep slope of the cirque wall from the gentler slope below.

schungite
amorphous carbon-rich material occurring in Precambrian schists.

scissors fault
a fault on which the offset or separation along the strike increases in one direction from an initial point and decreases in the other direction. Also known as differential fault.

scolite
any of small tubes in rock believed to be the fossilized burrows of forms.

scoria
a vesicular cindery crust on the surface of lava flows, the cellular nature of which has been due to the escape of volcanic gases before solidification. It has been found to be heavier, darker and more crystalline than pumice.

scourian
refers to a stratigraphic division of the Scottish Precambrian older Lewisian. The division between it and the Laxfordian has been done on

the basis of the number of orogenies affecting these groups.

scree

a mound of loose, angular material, less than 10 centimeters .

screw dislocation

a dislocation in which atomic planes form a spiral ramp widing around the line of dislocation.

scyelite

it is an igneous rock of the ultrabasic clan. It is a hornblende biotite periodotite in which the biotite poikilitically is enclosing the olivine.

scyrthian stage

a stage in the lesser Triassic series of the alpine facies. Also known as Werfenian stage.

sea

the sea is the great mass of salt water that covers more than three-quarters of the Earth's surface. Enormous areas of the sea are known as oceans.

sea-bed

the sea-bed is the bottom of the sea. Like dry land, the sea-bed can be flat or can have huge mountain ranges and deep valleys.

sea cave

a split, or hollow opening, usually at sea level, in the base of a sea cliff, formed by waves acting on weaker parts of the weathered rock. Also known as marine cave; sea chasm.

seam

a seam is a band of a mineral trapped between tow layers of rock. Coal is often found in long seams.

seamount chain

several seamounts in a line with bases separated by a relatively flat sea floor.

seamount group

several closely spaced seamounts not in a line.

seamount range

three or more seamounts having connected bases and aligned along a ridge or rise.

sea peak

a peaked elevation of the sea floor, rising 1000meters or more from the floor.

seascarp

a submarine cliff that is relatively long, high, and straight.

seashore

1. the strip of land that borders a sea or ocean. Also known as seaside; shore.

2. the ground between the usual tide levels. Also known as seastrand.

season

a season is a part of the year which has a particular climate. In temperate regions, the four seasons are spring, summer, autumn and winter. These vary in both temperature and rainfall. In the tropics, there are usually two seasons. These are the hot, dry season and the hot, rainy season.

sebstianite

an igneous rock of the diorite clan. A coarse-grained anorthite, apatite, augite, and granular plutonic rock contains biotite.

secondary

1. an obsolete name which was used for the Mesozoic Era. 2. a term which is approximately equivalent to 'late' or 'subsequent', e.g., as in the phrase 'secondary alteration product' especially pertaining to weathering or hydrothermal action. It may also imply a second generation of a mineral, e.g., secondary calcite.

secondary coast

a relatively stable seacoast or shoreline whose features are the results of present day marine processes.

secondary enrichment

the addition to a vein or ore body of material that originated later in time from the oxidation of decomposed ore masses that overlie the vein.

secondary mineral

refers to a mineral which is produced in an enclosing rock after the rock was formed because of weathering or metamorphic or solution activity, and usually at the expense of primary material that came into existence earlier.

secondary structure

a structure that originated after the deposition or emplacement of the rock in which it was found e.g., a fault; especially, an epigentic sedimentary structure, such as concretion or sedimentary dike.

second bottom

the first terrace rising over a floodplain.

sedimentary dike

refers to a tabular mass of sedimentary material which is cutting across the structure or bedding of pre-existing rock in the manner of an igneous dike. It is formed by the filling of a crack or fissure by forcible injection of sediments, under abnormal pressure, or by simple infillings.

sedimentary facies

a stratigraphic facies differing from another part or parts of the same unit in both lithologic and paleontological characters.

sedimentary iron ores

sedimentary iron ores have been of considerable economic importance and form a major proportion of iron ore. They may be classified as follows:

(i) Detrial

(ii) Residual

(iii) Replacement and late diagenetic

(iv) Marine

(v) Freshwater

Sedimentary iron pyrites are not regarded as iron ore. The role of bacteria and possible other organisms in the deposition of iron minerals in sediments is not understood.

sedimentary ore

a sedimentary rock of ore grade;

an ore deposit formed by sedimentary processes; *e.g.* saline residues and phosphatic deposits.

sedimentary structure

a structure in sedimentary rocks, such as cross-bedding, ripple marks, and sandstone dikes, produced either contemporaneously with deposition or shortly after deposition.

sedimentary tectonics

buckling and folding of strata in geosynclinal basins produced by subsidence of the geosyncline.

sedimentary trap

refers to an area between a high energy and low energy environment in which sedimentary materials get accumulated.

sedimentary tuff

a tuff containing a small amount of nonvolcanic detrital material.

sedimentary volcanism

the expelling, extruding or breaking through of overlying formations by a mixture of sediment, water and gas, driven by the gas under pressure.

sedimentation

1. the act or process of accumulating sediment in layers.

2. the process of deposition of sediment.

sedimentation basin

a depression in the ocean floor with a wide, flat bottom in which sediments accumulates.

sedimentation curve

a curve showing cumulatively and in successive units of time, the amount of sediment accumulated or removed from an originally uniform suspension.

sedimentation diameter

the diameter of a sedimentary particle, determined from the measurement of a hypothetical sphere of the same gravity and settling velocity as those of a given sedimentary particle in the same fluid.

sedimentation radius

one-half of the sedimentation diameter.

sedimentation trough

a depression in the ocean floor with a narrow U- or V-shaped bottom in which sediment accumulates.

sedimentation unit

a sedimentation deposit formed during one distinct act of sedimentation.

sedimentology

sedimentology is the study of sedimentary rocks. Sedimentology helps in the exploration for oil, natural gas and coal.

seep

it refers to a spot where water or petroleum oozes from the earth. It often forms the source of small trickling stream.

segrgation banding

a compositional band in geneisses that is the result of segregation of material from an originally homogenous rock.

seismic wave
a general term which is used for all elastic waves produced by earthquakes or generated artificially by explosions. It incorporates both body waves and surface waves.

seismology
seismology is the study of seismic waves. It gives us information about earthquakes, the structure of the Earth and about what happens inside the Earth.

selagite
an igneous rock of the syenite clan; a fine grained porphyritic extrusive rock; contains phenocrysts of biotite in a ground mass of orthoclase, diopside, oligoclase and apatite.

selective fusion
the fusion of only a portion of a mixture, such as rock.

selvage
a marginal zone of a rock form, showing some distinguishing peculiarity, such as in composition or fabric.

semianthracite
coal which is between bituminous coal and anthracite in metamorphic rank, and which has a fixed-carbon of 86-92%.

semifusinite
a coal maceral with a well-defined woody structure and optical properties intermediate between those of nitrinite and those of fusinite.

semitumous coal
coal that is harder and more brittle than bituminous coal, has a high fuel ratio, contains 10-20% volatile matter, and burns without smoke; ranks between bituminous and sendimanthracite coals.

senonian
a stratigraphic stage name which is being used for the European Upper Cretaceous.

seriate
having crystals, that vary gradually in size.

serrate
said of topographic feature that are notched or have a saw-toothed profile, e.g., a serrate divide.

sessile
a term used for describing a non-mobile organism, which may or may not be fixed.

shaft
a shaft is a straight tunnel going into the ground. Many mines are made by digging shafts.

shale
a fine-grained laminated or fissile sedimentary rock which is made up of slit-or clay-size particles or mud; it is well indurated but it is not as hard as argillite or slate. It may be brown, red, grey or black in colour. It has nearly one-third quartz, one-third clay materials, and one-third miscellaneous minerals, including carbonates, iron oxides, feldspar, and organic

matter.

shale clay

a clay made from ground slate.

shale reservoir

underground hydrocarbon reservoir in which the reservoir rock is a brittle, siliceous, fractured shale.

shallow inland seas

epeiric seas which periodically cover cratonic areas as result of continental subsidence or eustatic rises in sea level.

shallow marginal seas

epeiric seas along the cratonic margins.

shallow-pool test

a well located within the known limits of an oil or gas pool and drilled with the object of searching new producing zones above the producing zone of the pool.

shaly bedding

laminated bedding varying between 2 and 10 millimetres in thickness.

sharkskin pahoehoe

a type of pahoehoe displaying numerous tiny spines or spicules on the surface.

sharpsand

an angular-grain sand which is free of clay, loam, and other impurities.

sharpstone

ant rock fragment having angular edges and corners and being more than 2 mileometers in diameter.

shatter cone

a striated conical rock fragment along which fracturing has occurred.

shear fold

a similar fold whose mechanism is shearing or slipping along closely spacd planes that are parallel to the fold's axial surface. Also known as glide fold; slip fold.

shear fracture

a fracture that results from stresses that tends to shear one part of a rock past the adjacent part.

shear joint

a joint that is a shear fracture; it is a potential plane of shear. Also known as slip joint.

shear structure

a local structure in which earth stresses have been relieved by many small, closely spaced fractures.

shear zone

a tabular area of rock that has been crushed and brecciated by many parallel fractures resulting from shear strain; often becomes a channel for underground solutions and the seat of ore deposition.

sheet deposit

a stratiform mineral deposits that is more or less horizontal and extensive relative to its thickness.

sheeted fissure

a closely spaced fissure.

sheeted vein

a vein filling a shear zone.

sheeted zone

an area of mineral deposits consisting of sheeted veins.

sheet erosion

erosion of thin layers of surface materials by continuous sheets of running water. Also known as sheetflood erosion; sheetwash; surface wash; unconcentrated wash.

sheeting

the process by which thin sheets, slabs, scales, plates, or flakes of rock are successively broken loose or stripped from the outer surface of a large rock mass in response to release of load. Also known as exfoliation.

sheet sandstone

a thin, blanket-shaped deposit of sandstone of regional extent.

sheetwash

1. the detritus deposited by a sheetflood.

shelf

1. solid rock beneath alluvial deposits

2. a flat, projecting ledge of rock.

shelf channel

a valley formed in a shelf by erosion.

shelf edge

the demarcation without dramatic change in gradient, between continental shelf and continental slope.

shelf facies

a sedimentary facies characterized by carbonate rocks and fossil shells and produced in the neritic environments of marginal shelf seas. Also known as foreland facies; platform facies.

shield

refers to a major structural unit of the earth's crust, which consisted of a large mass of Precambrian rocks, both metamorphic and igneous, which remain unaffected by later orogenies. Well-known examples include the Canadian and Baltic Shields. The term is partially synonymous with kraton.

shield basalt

means a basaltic lava flow from a group of small, close spaced shield volcano vents which get coalesced to from a single unit.

shield cone

a cone or dome-shaped volcano built · up successive outpourings of lava.

shift

the relative displacement of the units affected by a fault but outside the fault zone itself.

shingle

pebbles, cobbles, and other beach material, coarser than ordinary gravel but roughly the same size and occurring typically on the higher parts of a beach.

shingle rampart

a rampart of shingle built along a reef on the seaward edge.

shoal

a shoal is a bank of sand or mud in a river or in the sea. Shoals form when slow-flowing river water deposits the sediment it has been carrying.

shock wave

refers to a fully developed compressional wave having large amplitude, across which density pressure, and particle velocity change drastically.

shock zone

a volume of rock which is surrounding an explosion or impact crater in which the effects of shock metamorphism have been present.

shonkinte

a melanocratic feldspar-rich syenite, which consists largely of pyroxenes, a little olivine, and potassic feldspars (traces of nepheline may also occur).

shore

the narrow strip of land bordering any water-body; the most seaward part of the coast.

shoreline

the intesection of a specified plan of water, especially mean high water, with the shore; a limit which changes with the tide or water level. Also known as strandline; waterline.

shoreline cycle

the cycle of changes through which sequential forms of coastal features pass during shoreline development, from the establishment of a water level to the time when the water can do no more work.

shoreline of emergence

a straight or gently curving shoreline formed by the dominant relative emergence of the floor of an ocean or a lake. Also known as emerged shoreline; negative shoreline.

shoreline of submergence

a shoreline characterized by bays, promontories and other minor features, formed by the dominant relative submergence of a landmass. Also known as positive shoreline; submerged shoreline.

shore platform

the horizontal or gently slopping surface produced along a shore by wave erosion. Also known as scar.

shore terrace

a terrace produced along the shore by wave and current action.

shungite

a black, hard, coal-like amorphous material, composed of more than 98% carbon.

shutter valley

a valley which gets affected by a tear fault at Tight angles to the axis of the valley so that two halves do not coincide.

sial

a petrologic name for the upper layer of earth's crust, composed of rocks rich in silica and alumina. It is an acronym for silica and alumina.

sialma

a layer of the earth's crust which is intermediate in depth as well as composition between sial and sima.

siderophile

elements which have weak affinities for oxygen and sulphur, but are soluble in molten iron. They are assumed to be concentrated in the core of the earth, and occurs in metal phases of meteorites.

sierozem

a soil found in cool temperate arid regions, characterized by a brownish-gray surface on a lighter layer based on a carbonte or hardpan layer.

sierra

a sierra is a mountain chain containing a number of peaks. A famous example of a sierra is the Sierra Nevada in Spain.

silerete

a conglomerate consisting of surficial sand and gravel cemented into a hard mass by silica.

silexite

chert occurring in calcareous beds.

silica sand

sand having a very high percentage of silicon dioxide; a source of silicon.

silicates

silicates are the most common minerals. Silicates are compounds containing silicon and oxygen, with one or more extra element.

silicated

said of a rock in which the process of silication has taken place.

siliuceous ooze

any pelagic deep-sea sediment containing at least 30% siliceous skeletal remains, such as radiolarians.

siliceous sinter

a white, light-weight, porous, opaline variety of silica deposited by hot springs.

sillar

a pyroclastic igneous rock of the granite clan; white to salmon red unconsolidated rock.

silt

silt is a dust-like substance made up of tiny particles of rock. Rivers and streams carry silt, which settles on the river bed as sediment. Silt can build up in reservoirs.

siltstone

indurated silt having a shalelike texture and composition. Also known as siltite.

silurian

1. a period of geologic time of the Paleozoic era, covering a time span of between 430-440 and 395 million years ago.

2. the rock system of this period.

sima

a petrological name for the lower of the earth's crust, composed of rocks that are rich in silica and magnesia. It is equivalent to oceanic crust and to the lower portion of the continental crust underly the sial. Also known as intermediate layer.

similar fold

a fold in deformed beds in which the successive folds resembles each other.

simple dike

an igneous dike emplaced in a

single episode.

sinemurian

a stratigraphic stage name which is being used for the base of the European Lower Jurassic.

sinistral

a term applicable to tear (strike) faults for describing the apparent direction of apparent movement, in this case to the left.

sink

a circular or ellipsodal depression formed by collapse on the flank of or near to a volcano.

sinter

sinter is a deposit which is made of silicates. It is found around the edges of hot springs or geysers.

sinter

a chemical sedimentary rock which gets deposited by precipitation from minerals waters, especially siliceous sinter and calcareous sinter.

sinus

a groove, silt, or notch, as developed in shells or several invertebrates.

skarn

a lime-bearing silicate derived from nearly pure limestone and dolomite with the introduction of large amounts of silicon, aluminium, iron and magnesium.

skiddavian

a local stratigraphic stage name which is being used for the Arenigina plus part of the Cambrian in Great Britain.

skip cast

the cast of a skip mark.

skip mark

a crescent-shaped mark that is one of a linear pattern of regularly spaced marks made by an object that skipped along the bottom of a stream.

skythian

refers to a synonym of Bunter (Triassic system). Also spelled Scythian.

slaking

1. crumbling and disintegration of earth materials when exposed to air or moisture.

2. the breaking up of dried clay when saturated with water.

slate

slate is a kind of metamorphic rock or stone. It is formed from shale or mudstone. Slate has smooth surface and it splits easily in flat slabs. Slate is used for building and for roofing tiles.

slice

an arbitrary section of some uniform standard, such as thickness of a stratigraphic unit that is otherwise indivisible for purposes of analytic study.

slick

area in which capillary waves are absent or suppressed.

slickens

a layer of fine silt deposited by a flooding stream.

slickenside

a surface that is polished and

smoothly striated and results from slippage along a fault plane.

slickensides

If one surface of a rock is moved over another surface in close contact under pressure, the two surfaces develop a kind of polish, with linear grooves and ridges which are parallel to the direction of movement. This is known as slickensiding and is commonly seen on faulty surfaces.

slickolite

a vertically discontinuous slip-scratch surface made by slippage and shearing and developed on sharply dipping bedding planes of limestone that shapes the wall of a solution cavity.

slide

1. refers to the movement of descent of a landslide or rock-slides, also the mass of material so moved.

2. refers to the track of bare rock or furrowed earth which has been left by a landslide.

slip bedding

convolute bedding formed as the result of subaqueous sliding.

slip cleavage

cleavage that is superposed on slaty cleavage or schistosity, characterized by spaced cleavage with thin tabular bodies of rock between the cleavage planes. Also known as close-joints cleavage; crenulation cleavage; shear cleavage; strain-slip cleavage.

slip-off slope

the long, low, gentle slope on the inside of the downstream face of a stream meander.

slip surface

the displacement surface of a landslide.

slope failure

the downward and outward movement of a mass of soil beneath a natural slope or other inclined surface; four types of slope failure are rockfall, rock flow, plane shear and rotational shear.

slope stability

the resistance of an inclined surface to failure by sliding or collapsing.

slope wash

1. the mass-wasting process, assisted by nonchanneled running water, by which rock and soil is transported down a slope, specifically, sheet erosion.

2. the material that is or has been transported.

sludge

the term used for a soft or muddy bottom deposit as on tideland or in a stream bed.

sludge lump

an irregular mass of sledge formed as a result of strong winds.

slump

a type of landslide characterized by the downward slipping of a mass of rock or unconsolidated debris, moving as a unit or several subsidiary units, characteristically with backward rotation on a horizontal axis parallel to the slope; common on natural cliffs and on the sides of artificial cuts and fills.

slump bedding

also known as slurry bedding

1. any disturbed bedding.
2. convolute bedding produced by subaqueous slumping or lateral movement of newly deposited sediment.

slump block

a coherent mass of material form away during the formation of a slump, the slide mass remains virtually intact and moves outward and downward.

slurry

the term used for a highly fluid mixture of water (or any liquid) and finely divided material, e.g., of pulverized coal and water for movement by pipeline.

small-scale

small-scale is a term which describes a kind of map. A small-scale map covers a large area, but does not show much detail.

smaragdite

a green amphibole mineral that is pseudomorphous after pyroxene in rock such as eclogite.

snow

a type of precipitation consisting of water vapour which has frozen into ice crystals. Several ice crystals join together to form a snowflake, which will gradually fall down to earth. Some snowflakes may melt as they fall, especially if the temperature is only just down to freezing point. Under such condition sleet occurs, and for the same reason it is possible for clouds to give snowfall on mountains, while producing rainfall on adjacent lowland areas. Snowline is the line on a mountainside above which there is perpetual snow. There may be snow below the line during the winter months but it will not persist throughout the year. The altitude of the snowline varies with latitude.

snowfield

a snowfields is a wide expanse of permanent snow. Snowfields are found in high mountains and around the North Pole and South Pole. Some snowfields may turn to ice and form glaciers.

soapstone

refers to the popular name for any very soft rock which has a greasy 'feel'. Most soapstones are talc rocks.

sodalite

refers to a white, grey, or green mineral tectosilicate of feldspathoid group which crystallizes in isometric system.

soffione

a jet of steam and other vapours issuing from the ground in a volcanic area.

soil

1. unconsolidated rock

material over bedrock.
2. Freely divided rock-derived material containing an admixture of organic matter and capable of supporting vegetation.

soil air
the air and other gases in spaces in the soil; specifically, that which is found within the zone of aeration. Also known as soil atmosphere.

soil colloid
colloidal complex of soils composed principally of clay and humus.

soil complex
a mapping unit used in detailed soil surveys; consists of two or more recognized classifications.

soil creep
the slow, steady downhill movement of soil and loose rock on a slope. Also known as surficial creep.

soil erosion
soil erosion is the loss of soil from the surface of the ground. When the wind blows, dry soil may be blown away. Water can also cause soil erosion when heavy rainfall washes the soil away.

soil genesis
the mode by which soil originates, with particular reference to processes of soil-forming factors responsible for the development of true soil from unconsolidated parent material. Also known as pedogenesis; soil formation.

soil profile
a vertical section of a soil, showing horizons and parent material.

soil science
the study of the formation, properties, and classification of soil; includes mapping. Also known as pedology.

soil series
a family of soils having similar profiles, and developing from similar original materials under the influence of similar climate and vegetation.

soil shear strength
the maximum resistance of a soil to shearing stresses.

soil stripes
alternating bands of fine and coarse material in a soil structure.

soil structure
arrangement of soils into various aggregates, each differing in the characteristics of its particles.

soil survey
the systematic examination of soils, their description and classification, mapping of soil types, and the assessment of soils for various agricultural and engineering uses.

solar energy
solar energy is energy which comes directly from the Sun. Solar energy can be used to make electricity and to heat water.

solar faculae
bright steaks or regions on the surface of the sun, especially

near solar sunsport.

solar system

the sun and the celestial bodies moving about it; includes nine planets: Mercury, Venus, Earth, Mars, Jupiter, Saturn, Uranus, Neptune and Pluto: and of the belt of asteroids revolving in elliptical orbits round the sun, along with satellites of the planets, commets, and meteor swarms. Over 99% of the mass of the system is concentrated in the sun. The solar system as a whole moves in an approximately circular orbit about the centre of the Galaxy, taking about 2.2 × 108 years to complete its orbit.

sole

1. the bottom of a sedimentary stratum.

2. the middle and lower portion of the shear surface of a landslide.

3. the underlying fault plane of a thrust nappe. Also known as sole plane.

sole injection

an igneous intrusion that was put in place along a thrust plane.

solfatra

a fumarole from which sulphurous gases are emitted.

solid

a term which is used for describing geological survey or other maps from which the superficial deposits have been omitted, thereby leaving the outcrops of the pre-superficial formation unobscured.

solifluction

a rapid soil creep, especially referring to downslope soil movement in periglacial areas. Also known as sludging; soil flow; soil fluction.

solifluction lobe

an isolated, tongue-shaped feature of the land surface with a steep front and a smooth upper surface formed by more rapid solifluction on certain sections of the slope. Also known as solifluction tongue.

solifluction mantle

the locally derived, unsorted material moved downslope by solifluction. Also known as flow earth.

solifluction sheet

a broad deposit of a solifluction mantle.

solifluction stream

a narrow, streamlike deposit of a solifluction mantle.

solodize

to improve a soil by removing alkalies from it.

solonchak soil

one of an intrazonal, balamorphic group of light-coloured soils rich in soluble salts.

solonetz soil

one of an intrazonal group of black alkali soils having a columnar structure.

soloth soil

one of an intrazonal halomorphic group of soils formed from saline material;

the surface layer is soft and friable, and overlies a light-coloured leached horizon which, in turn, overlies a dark horizon. Also known as Solid soil.

solum

the upper part of a soil profile, composed of A and B horizons in mature soil. Also known as ture soil.

solution pool

a pool in a rock that is formed by the dissolution of the rock in ocean water.

solution potholes

potholes produced in carbonate rocks by the dissolution.

solution transfer

a process whereby pressure solution of detrital mineral grains at contact areas is followed by recrystallization on the less strained parts of the grains surface.

sonar

sonar is a system which uses sound waves to measure the depth of water. An instrument sends out pulses of sound, which bounce back off the sea-bed. The depth of water is measured on a depth scale. Shoals of fish can also be detected using sonar. Some forms of sonar are called echo sounders.

sorotiite

a type of meteorite similar to the pallasites, with troilite substituting for olivine.

sorted polygon

a patterned ground having a sorted appearance due to a border of stones and characterized by a polygonal mesh. Also known as stone polygon.

sorting

the process by which similar in size, shape, or specific gravity sedimentary particles are selected and separated from associated but dissimilar particles by the agent of transportation.

sorting index

a measure of the degree of sorting in a sediment based on the statistical spread of the frequency curve of particle sizes.

sounding sand

a lead used for determining the depth of water.

source bed

the original stratigraphic horizon from which secondary sulfide minerals were derived.

source rock

1. rock from which fragments have been derived which form a later, usually sedimentary rock. Also known as mother rock; parent rock. 2. sedimentary rock, usually shale and limestone, deposited together with organic matter which was subsequently transformed to liquid or gaseous hydrocarbons.

southern hemisphere

the southern hemisphere is the part of the Earth which lies south of the Equator. The continents of Australia and most of South America lie in the southern hemisphere.

spandite

name assigned to garnet which is intermediate in composition between spessartite and andradite.

spar

a term imprecisely applied to any transparent or translucent lightcoloured mineral that is somewhat lustrous and usually shows easy cleavage.

sparagmite

late Precambrian fragmental rocks of Scandinavia, characterized by high proportions of microcline.

sparite

1. a descriptive term which is being used for the crystalline transparent or translucent interstitial component of limestone which is consisting of clean, relatively coarsegrained calcite or aragonite that either accumulated during deposition or got introduced later as a cement. 2. A limestone in which the Sparite cement has been more abundant than the micrite matrix.

sparnacean

a European stage of geologic time; upper Paleocene, above Thanetian, below Ypersain of Eocene.

specularite Fe_2O_3

the popular name which is being used for haematite crystallized in the form of brilliant, black, metallic crystals. Also known as iron hat, grey hamatite.

spelean

of or pertaining to a feature in a cave.

speleology

the study and exploration of caves.

speleothem

a secondary mineral deposited in a cave by the action of water. Also known as cave formation.

spending beach

in a wave basin, the beach on which the entering waves spend themselves, except for the small remainder entering the inner harbour.

spergenite

a biocalcarenite containing ooliths and fossil debris and having a maximum quartz content of 10%. Also known as Bedford limestone; indiana limestone.

sperrylite

a mineral which is composed of platinum arsenide, and crystallizes in cubic system, shows poor cleavage.

sphalerite ZnS

the main zinc ore which occurs in metasomatic deposits along with galena, in hydro-thermal vein deposits, and in replacement deposits. It is also known as jack; mock lead; mock ore; steel jack; pseudogalana; zinc blende.

sphenoid

a term denoting wedgeshaped.

sphenolith

a wedgelike igneous intrusion

that is partly concordant and partly discordant.

spherulilte

a spherical body or coarsely crystalline aggregate having a radial internal structure arranged about one or more centres.

spike

the known amount of an isotope added to a sample to determine the unknown amount present in analysis by isotope dilution.

spilite

a basaltic rock type, having chlorite in lieu of augite and olivine, and albite as the plagioclase. Trachytic and rhyolitic types having sodipotassic feldspars, and sometimes quartz, are called keratophyres. Spilites and their associates generally occur as pillow lavas interbedded with geosynclinal sediments.

s-p interval

in earthquake seismology, it refers to the time interval between the first arrivals of longitudinal and transverse waves, which forms a measure of the distance from the earthquake source.

splash erosion

erosion resulting from the impact of falling raindrops.

spliced

refers to veins which pinch out and get overlapped at that point by another vein.

splint coal

the term used for a type of banded coal which is dull, blocky, and greyish-black in colour, with uneven fracture and granular texture. Quantitatively, it has been defined as having more than 5 per cent anthraxylon and more than 30 per cent opaque attritus. It is also known as splent coal.

split

a coal seam that cannot be mined as a single unit because it is separated by a parting of other sedimentary rock. Also known as coal split; split coal.

spodosol

a soil order characterized by a spodic or placic horizon overlying a fragipan.

spongework

a pattern of small irregular interconnecting cavities on walls of limestone caves.

spongolite

a rock or sediment composed chiefly of the remains of sponges. Also known as spongolith.

sporinite

a variety of exinite composed of spore exines which have been compressed parallel to the stratification.

spread

(1) a marsh or shallow-water resulting from the expansion in width of a stream, as where a natural obstruction impedes flow.

(2) in seismology, the layout of geophone groups from which

the data from a single shot are recorded simultaneously.

spur

an area of high ground which protrudes into an area of lower ground such as river valley. Spurs alongside valleys are gradually eroded by the river but in the upper and middle courses especially, they often form interlocking spurs. In galcia valley many of the spurs will have been truncated.

squall

a squall is a kind of wind. A squall is sudden, short and rather violent. Squalls are common during storms.

stability

1. the resistance of a structure, spoil heap or clay bank to sliding, overturning, or collapsing.
2. chemical durability, resistance to weathering.

stack

erosional remnant in the form of a small bedrock island a short distance off shore. Stacks are pillar-like formations detached from a headland by marine erosion.

stade

a substage of a glacial stage marked by a secondary advance of glaciers.

staffordian

a stratigraphic stage name which is being used the British equivalent of the European Morgannian (Carboiferous system).

stage

1. a development phase of an erosion cycle in which landscape features have distinctive characteristic forms.
2. a phase in the historical developement of a geologic feature.
3. a major subdivision of a glacial epoch.
4. a time-stratigraphic unit ranking below series and above substage.

stalactite

a conical or roughly cylindrical speleothem formed by dripping water and hanging from the roof of a cave; usual composed of calcium carbonate.

stalagmite

a general term applicable to the massive calcium carbonate deposits which are found in limestone caverns, but more specifically for the upward projection corresponding to stalactite.

starved basin

a sedimentary basin in which the rate of subsidence exceeds the rate of sedimentation.

steatite

1. a compact, massive rock consisting mainly of talc but usually containing large quantities of other materials; an impure talc-rich rock.
2. a term originally used as an alternative mineral name for talc, often restricted to grey-green or brown massive talc that can be easily carved.

steatite talc

a high-grade variety of talc which has been suitable for use in electronic insulators. It has been the purest commercial form of talc.

steatization

introduction of or replacement by talc or steatite.

steinkern

1. rock material formed from consolidated mud or sediment that filled a hollow organic structure, such as a fossil shell.

2. the fossil formed after dissolution of the miod. Also known as endocast; internal cast.

stenohaline

said of a marine organism that tolerates only a narrow range of salinities.

step fault

one of a set of closely spaced, parallel faults. Also known as distributive fault; multiple fault.

stephanian

a stratigraphic stage name which is being used for the top of the European Upper Carboniferous.

steppe

a steppe is a dry, grassy plain without trees which is found in central Europe and Siberia. Steppes are found in climates which are deep and fertile. In North America, these grassy plains are called prairies.

steptoe

an isolated hill which is surrounded by a lava flow, i.e., an upstanding part of the original relief which is projecting above the lava flow which has otherwise sub-merged it.

sternberg's law

the wearing away of transported particles is proportional to their weight in water and distance travelled.

stewartite

a steel- gray, iron-containing variety of bort that has magnetic properties.

stillstand

refferring to a land area a continent or an island, or an island, to remain stationary with respect to the interior of the earth or to sea level.

stinkstone

a stone containing decomposing organic matter that gives off an offensive odour when rubbed or struck.

stock

refers to an intrusive mass of plutonic igneous rock which is smaller in size than a batholith and usually having a more or less circular or elliptical cross-section. The contacts with the country rock have been found to vary from steep to low angle.

stockwork

refers to a large-scale ramifying and dichotomising series of fissures which become filled with mineral matter.

stone

in geology the word 'stone' is

allowed only in combination such as limestone, sandstone, etc., or where it has been used as the name for extracted material like building stone, road stone. It is not to be used as a synonym for rock or pebble.

stone line

a line or angular or subangular rock fragment that parallels a sloping topographic surface at a depth of several metres. It crops out in natural and artificial cuts.

stope

an underground excavation formed by the extraction of ore.

stoping

1. in mining this term is used for describing a method of extracting ore from a vertical of steeply dipping vein by driving tunnels along the strike of a vein and getting the ore from above and below the tunnel-overhand and underhand stopping respectively.

storm berm

a low beach ridge marking the upper limit of wave action during storms.

stoss

said of the side of a hill, knob, or prominent rock, which faces the upstream side of a glacier.

strait

1. a narrow waterway which is connecting two layer water-bodies. 2. Also refers to a neck of land.

stratification plane

a demarcation between two layers of sedimentary rock, often signifying that the layers were deposited under different condition.

stratified ocean

an ocean where there is a vertical gradient of density.

stratigraphic throw

the term used for the thickness of strata which had originally separated two beds brought into contact at a fault. It is also known as stratigraphic separation.

stratigraphic unit

a stratum of rocks or a body of strata classified as a unit on the basis of character, property, or attribute.

stratopause

the stratopause is part of the Earth's atmosphere. It is the upper edge of the stratosphere, and lies at a height of about 50 kilometres above the surface of the Earth.

stratum

it is synonymous with bed. Rocks which display layering or bedding may be regarded to be displaying stratification.

stratus

stratus describes a kind of cloud. Stratus clouds form low in the sky. They are light grey with flat bases. They form when warm and cold air mix together. Stratus clouds usually bring a fine, long-lasting rain.

stream

a stream is a small channel of

water which flows continually. Streams start at a spring or lake and join together to form rivers. Stream can also be used to describe a current or a continuous flow of a liquid or a gas, such as molten rock or air.

streamline
a line which is every where parallel to the direction of fluid flow at a given instant.

stretching
in metamorphic rocks, the elongation of mineral grains, or other features; a type of lineation.

stria
the term used for one of a series of parallel straight lines present on the surface of crystal, as in pyrite which is indicative of an oscillation between two crystal forms; also, one of a series of such lines on the cleavage planes of a mineral, as of plagioclase which is indicative of polysynthetic twinning.

strike joint
a joint that strikes parallel to the strike or lineation of the enclosing rock.

striped ground
a pattern of alternating stripes formed by frost action on a sloping surface. Also known as striated ground; striped soil.

stripped plane
the upper, exposed surface of a resistant stratum that forms a stripped structural surface when extended over a considerable area.

stripped structural surface
an erosion surface formed in an area underlain by horizontal or gently sloping strata of unequal resistance where the overlying softer beds have been removed by erosion. Also known as stripped surface.

stromatite
chorismite having flat or folded parallel layers of two or more textural elements. Also known as stromatolith.

stromatolite
a structure in calcareous rocks consisting of concentrically laminated masses of calcium carbonate and calcium magnesium carbonate which are believed to be of calcareous algal origin; these structures are irregular to columnar and hemispheroidal in shape, and range from 1 millimetre to many meters in thickness. Also known as callenia.

stromatolith
1. a complex sill like igneous intrusion interfingered with sedimentary strata.

strombolian
a type of volcanic eruption characterized by fire fountains of lava from a central crater.

structural
of or pertaining to rock deformation or to features that result from it.

structural bench
a bench typifying the resistant edge of a terrace that is being

reduced by erosion. Also known as rock bench.

structural geology

a branch of geology concerned with the form, arrangement and internal structure of the rocks.

structural high

any of various structural features such as a crest, culmination, anticline or dome.

structural low

any of various structural features such as a basin, a syncline, a saddle, or a sag.

structural terrace

a terrace-like landform developed where generally steeply inclined and otherwise uniformly dipping strata locally flatten.

structural trap

containment in a reservoir bed of oil or gas due to flexture or fracture of the bed.

structural valley

a valley whose form and origin is attributable to the underlying geologic structure.

structure

1. refers to the relationship between different parts of a rock. Examples of structures are amygdaloidal, beddings cleavage, flow, jointing.

2. a term used for describing the overall relationship of rock-masses, e.g., faulting, folding, unconformities.

3. implying structural feature; e.g., petroleum geologist says about 'drilling a structure', implying drilling a structural feature which may be an oil trap.

structure contour

a contour that portrays a structural surface, such as a fault. Also known as subsurface contour.

structure-contour map

a map that uses structure contour lines to portray subsurface configuration. Also known as structure map.

structure section

a vertical section showing the observed or inferred geologic structure on a vertical surface or plane.

strunian

a stratigraphical stage name which is being used for the transition beds of the European Devonian Carboniferous Systems.

stylolite

an irregular surface, generally parallel to bedding plane, in which small toothlike projections on one side of the surface fit into cavities of complementary shape on the other surface; interpreted to result diagenetically by pressure solution.

subaerial

pertaining to conditions and processes occurring beneath the atmosphere or in the open air, that is, on or adjacent to the land surface.

subage

a subdivision of a geologic age.

subaqueous dune

a dune resulting from

entrainment of grains by the flow of moving water.

subarkose

sandstone that is intermediate in composition between arkose and pure quartz sandstone; it contains less feldpar than arkose.

subconchoidal

pertaining to a fracture that is partly or vaguely conchoidal in shape.

subcrop

an occurrence of strata beneath the subsurface of an inclusive stratigraphic unit that succeeds an unconformity on which there is marked overstep.

subduction

the process by which one crustal block descends beneath another, such as the descent of the Pacific plate beneath the Andean plate along the Andean Trench.

suberinite

a variety of provitrinite composed of corky tissue.

subgelisol

unfrozen ground beneath permafrost.

subglacial

pertaining to the area in or at the bottom of, or immediately beneath, a glacier.

subhedral

descriptive of a crystal which has partially developed crystal faces.

subjacent

a mass of igneous recks is considered to be subjacent if no evidence of a base can be actually observed or inferred, at depth.

sublacustrine

existing or formed on the bottom of a lake.

sublacustrine channel

a channel eroded in a lake bed either before the lake existed or by a strong current in the lake.

sublimation vien

a vein of mineral that has condensed from a vapour.

submarinee

submarine describes an object or habitat which is found below the surface of the sea.

submarine canyon

steep-sided valleys winding across the continental shelf or continental shelf or continental slope, probably originally produced by Pleistocene stream erosion, but presently the site of turbidity flows.

submarine fan

a shallow marine sediment that is fan- or cone- shaped and lies off the seaward opening of large rivers and submarine canyons. Also known as abyssal cave; abyssal fan; sea fan; submarine cave; submarine delta; subsea apron.

submarine isthmus

a submarine elevation joining two land areas and separating two basins or depression by a depth less than that of the basins.

submarine peninsula
an elevated portion of the submarine relief resembling a peninsula.

submarine pit
a cavity on the bottom of the sea. Also known as submarine well.

submarine relief
relative elevations of the ocean bed, or the representation of them on a chart.

submarine topography
configuration of a surface such as the sea bottom or of a surface of given characteristics within the water mass.

submarine weathering
a slow alteration of the form, texture, and composition of the sea floor from chemical, thermal and biological causes.

submerged coastal plain
the continental shelf as the seaward extension of a coastal plain on the land. Also known as coast shelf.

submerged lands
lands covered by water at any stage of the tide, as distinguished from tidelands which are attached to the mainland or an island and are covered or uncovered with the tide; tidelands presuppose a high-water line as the upper boundary, submerged lands do not.

submergence
a change in the relative levels of water and land either from a sinking of the land or a rise of the water level.

subsequent
referring to a geologic feature that followed in time the development of a consequent feature of which it is a part.

subsequent valley
a valley eroded by a stream developed subsequent to the system of which it is a part.

subsoil
subsoil is the soil below the surface soil, or topsoil. The subsoil is less often disturbed than the topsoil and contains less organic material. The subsoil also has more clay and minerals than the topsoil. The subsoil lies above the bedrock.

subsurface geology
the study of geologic features beneath the land or sea-floor surface. Also known as underground geology.

sudburite
a basic basalt composed of hypersthene, augite, and magnetite, among other minerals.

suevite
a greyish or yellowish fragmental rock associated with meteorite impact craters; resembles tuff breccia or pumiceous tuff but is of non volcanic origin.

sulfur ball
a bubble of hot volcanic gas encashed in a sulfurous mud skin that solidified on contact with air.

sulphur
a non-metallic native element, which occurs in areas of recent

volcanic activity and around hot springs and in sedimentary rocks having gypsum and limestone. It is found as orthorhombic crystals.

summer

summer is the name for the warmest season of the year in temperate climates. In the summer, the Sun is at its highest point in the sky and the days are longest. In the northern hemisphere, summer lasts from May to August. In the southern hemisphere, summer lasts from November to February.

sun

the Sun is a star. Scientists think that it has a liquid centre, surrounded by a large mass of very hot gas. In orbit around the Sun is a solar system of nine planets. Our world, Earth, is the third planet from the Sun. Radiation from the Sun reaches Earth as heat and sunlight. This solar energy allows life to exist on our world.

sunstone

refers to the reddish-grey gem variety of oligoclase. Also known as heliolite.

supercapillary interstice

an interstice that is too large to hold water above the free water surface by surface tension; it is larger than a capillary interstice.

super-continent

a super-continent describes one of the huge continents which may have existed very early in the history of the Earth. Some scientists think that the continents of today were once joined together in a single super-continent, called Pangaea.

superimposed

pertaining to layered or stratified rocks.

superimposed fan

an alluvial fan developed on, and having a steeper gradient than, an older fan.

superimposed glacier

a glacier whose course is maintained despite different preexisting structures and lithologies as the glacier erodes downward.

supermature

pertaining to a texturally mature clastic sediment whose grains have become rounded.

superposition

1. the order in which sedimentary layers are deposited, the highest being the youngest.

2. the process by which the layering occurs.

superstructure

refers to a series of folded sedimentary or metamorphosed sedimentary rocks which are overlying a migmatitic zone. The two zones get folded disharmonically with the migmatite developed in the antiformal folds.

supracrustal rocks

rocks that overlie basement rock.

supratidal sediment
the sediment deposited immediately above the high-tide level.

supratidal zone
pertaining to the shore area immediately marginal to and above the high tide level.

surface creep
a stage of the wind erosion process in which grains of sand move each other along the surface.

surface geology
the scientific study of the features at the surface of the earth.

surface soil
the soil extending 5 to 8 inches below the surface.

surficial deposit
unconsolidated alluvial, residual, or glacial deposits overlying bedrock or occurring on or near the surface of the earth. Also known as superficial deposit; surface deposit.

surficial geology
the scientific study of surficial deposits, including soils.

surf ripple
a ripple mark formed on a sandy beach by wave-generated currents.

suspension
the term used for the process by which material which is light enough has been carried in the zone of turbulent flow and does not settle out of this zone.

svionian
refers to the oldest stratigraphic division of the Baltic Precambrian.

swallow-hole
a large pothole in a limestone area down which a river is flowing. The hole will be an enlarged joint, which has been weathered by solution and also eroded by running water.

swash
1. a narrow channel or ground within a sand bank, or between a sand bank and the shore.
2. a bar over which the sea washes.

swash mark
a fine, wavy or arcuate line or minute ridge consisting of fine sand, seaweed, and other debris on a beach; marks the farthest advance of wave uprush. Also known as debris line; wave line; wavemark.

sweet
said of crude oil or natural gas containing very little or no sulphur compounds.

swell
1. the volumetric increase of soils on being removed from their compact beds due to an increase in void ratio.
2. a local enlargement or thickening in a vein or ore deposit.
3. a low dome or quaquaversal anticline of considerable areal extent; long and generally symmetrical waves contribute to the mixing process in the surface layer and thus to its sound transmission properties

genetally rising ground, or a rounded hill above the surrounding ground or ocean floor.

swelled ground
a soil or rock that extends when wetted.

syenogabbro
refers to type of gabbro in which orthoclase occurs. Plutonic rock is having basic plagioclase orthoclase, and a ferromagnesium mineral.

symmict
referring to a sedimentation unit that is structureless and in which coarse-and fine grained particles are mixed more extensively in the lower part.

symplectic texture
refers to the texture which is produced by the intergrowth of two different minerals, e.g., graphic texture, ophitic texture, poikilitic texture.

symplektite
refers to any secondary intergrowth of two minerals in which one is present as worm-like inclusions within the other. Myrmekite is a special case. The texture has been described as symplektitic.

synantexis
deuteric alteration.

synchronous
geological rock units or features formed at the same time.

sychronous pluton
any pluton whose time of emplacement coincides with a major orogeny.

syncline
the term refers to a fold of which the core is having the stratigraphically younger rocks. It is generally concave upward.

synegabbro
an instrusice rock differing from gabbro by the presence of alkali feldspar.

syngenesis
the term used for the formation of unconsolidated sediments in place; early diageneis.

syngenetic
1. pertaining to a primary sedimentary structure formed contemporaneously with sediment deposition.
2. pertaining to a mineral deposit formed contemporaneously with the enclosing rock. Also known as ideogenous.

synonym
if two distinct names have been assigned to the same organism or group of organisms the names are termed as synonymous. In general the mere recent synonym is considered to be invalid.

synorogenic
referring to a geologic process occurring at the same time as orogenic activity.

syntectonic
refers to a geologic process or event occurring during tectonic activity. Also known as synkinematic.

syntexis

magma made by the melting of two or more rock types and the assimilation of country rock. Also known as syntectic.

syntype

the term used for a series of type specimens of a genus selected for showing the range of variation in the organism.

systematic joints

joints occurring in patterns or sets and oriented perpendicular to the boundaries of the constituent rock unit.

tabbyite

a variety of solid asphalt which occurs in Western United States. It is mainly used as rubber filler with roofing materials.

tableland

a tableland is a landscape with a large area of flat, high land. The surface of the land is flat, like a table.

table reef

a small, isolated organic reef which has a flat top and does not enclose a lagoon.

tabula

a transverse spectum that closes off the lower part of the polyp cavity in certain extinct corals and hydroids.

tabular

referring to a sedimentary particle whose length is two to three times its thickness.

tachygenesis

the extreme crowding and eventual loss of those primitive phylogenetic stages that are represented early in the life of an individual.

tachylite

a black, green, or brown volcanic glass formed from basaltic magma. Also known as basalt glass; basalt obsidian; hyalobalaly; jaspoid; sodawalite; wichtisik.

tachylyte

name assigned to natural glass in extrusive igneous rocks. It is also known as hyalobasalt; jaspoid; sordawalite; wichtisite.

taconite

the siliceous iron formation from which high grade iron ores of the Lake Superior district have been derived; consists chiefly of fine-grained silica mixed with magnetic and hamatic.

tahuian

a local Eocene time subdivision in Australia whose identification is based on foraminiferans.

talasskite

a brown variety of fayalite containing about 12 per cent ferric oxide.

talc

talc is a soft mineral. Its colour is white to pale green. Talc is found in metamorphic rocks, and contains magnesium and silicon. There are large deposits of talc in India and in Austria. When it is ground up, it is called talcum powder. The solid form of talc is also called soapstone.

talcose rock
a rock having a soft and soapy feel, that is, resembling talc.

talus
the term used for rock fragments which are usually coarse and angular and lying at the base of a cliff or steep slope from which they are derived; also the heap or mass of such broken rock which is considered as a unit. It is also known as scree.

talus creep
the slow downslope movement of talus, either in individual rock fragments or the moss as whole.

taphrogeosyncline
a synonym of rift valley.

tarn
a small lake which is formed in a cirpue.

tar pits
the term used for describing relatively small areas where soft asphaltic (or bituminous) 'tar' wells up to the surface and fills a hollow. The material is coming from some underground source of hydrocarbons. Some tar pits have a mass of bones of animals which got trapped in the tar. The most famous of these are at Rancho El Brea, California.

tar sand
a type of oil sand; a sand whose interstices are filled with asphalt that remained after the escape of the lighter fractions of crude oil.

tar seep
natural tar that, because of its close proximity to the ground surface, seeps from cracks in the earth or from between rocks, often forming pits or pools.

tasmanite
an impure coal, transitional between cannel coal and oil shale. Also known as combustible shale; Mersey yellow coal; white coal; yellow coal.

tautonym
the name of species in which the term designating the genus is the same as that for species.

tawite
a feldspathoid igneous rock; a coarse-grained granular plutonic rock; contains sodalite and aegirite.

tear fault
a very steep to vertical fault associated with and perpendicular to the strike of an overthrust fault.

tectogene
the term used for hypothetical deep, tightly-folded downward which is present below an orogenic belt. It is suggested as an explanation of the greater thickness of sialic material beneath mountain ranges.

tectonic breccia
an aggregation of angular rock fragments that have formed as a result of tectonic movement; a crush breccia.

tectonic cycle
the orogenic cycle which

relates larger crustal features, such as mountains belts, to a series of stages of development. Also known as geosynclinal cycle.

tectonic framework

the relationship in space and time of subsiding, stable and rising tectonic elements in a sidemintary source area.

tectonic land

linear fold ridges and volcanic islands which existed for a short time in the interior sections of an orogenic belt during the geosynclinal phase.

tectonic lens

an elongate sausage-shaped body of rock formed by distortion of a continuous incompetent layer enclosed between competent layers, similar to a bounding, but genetically distinct.

tectonic map

a map which shows the architecture of the upper portion of the earth's crust.

tectonic moraine

an aggregation of boulders incorporated in the base of an overthrust mass.

tectonic rotation

internal rotation of a tectonite in the direction of transport.

tectonite

the term used for a rock in which crystallizations has occurred under stress, forming the mineral constituents taking up a preferred orientation or fabric.

tectosilicate

a class of structural type of silicate characterized by the sharing of all four oxygens of the SiO_4 tetrahedra with neighbouring tetrahedra, and with Si:O ratio of 1:2, e.g., quartz, SiO_2.

tectosome

a body of strata representing a tectotope.

teilzone

a time term which was originally introduced for designating the local duration of existence of a species.

tektite

a collective term applied to certain objects of natural glass of debatable origin that are widely strewn over the land and in sediments under the oceans; composition and size vary, and overall shapes resemble splash forms; most tektites are believed to be of extraterrestrial origin. Also known as obsidianite; tectite.

telemagmatic

pertaining to a hydrothermal mineral deposit that is distant from its magmatic source.

telethermal

pertaining to a hydrothermal mineral deposit precipitated at a shallow depth and at a mild temperature.

telinite

a variety of provitrinite composed of plant cell-wall material.

temporary base level

ant base level, other than sea level, below which a land area temporarily cannot be reduced by erosion. Also known as local base level.

tender

a barge anchored alongside an offshore drilling platform.

tenor

means the proportion of ore mineral in an ore.

tenorite CuO

a monoclinic mineral composed of cupric oxide; occurs as elongated lath-like crystals; shows conchoidal to uneven fracture and poor cleavage. Its hardness on Mohs scale is 3.5.

tension joint

a joint that is a tension fracture.

tension fracture

a minor rock fracture developed at right angles to the direction of maximum tension. Also known as subsidiary fracture.

tepee structure

a disharmonic sedimentary structure consisting of a fold that resembles an inverted depressed V in cross section.

tephra

all fragmental material ejected from a volcanic vent and transported through the air, *e.g.,* ash, pumic, bombs, etc; a synonym for pyroclasic material ash, cinders, lapilli, scoriae, pumice, bombs *etc.*

tephrite

refers to the igneous of the gabbro clan. It is a finegrained porphyritic extrusive rock which contains phenocrysts of augite and labradorite in a groundmass of augite, labradorite, leucite, and nepheline.

tephrochronology

the dating of different layers of volcanic ash for the establishment of a sequence of geologic and archeologic occurrences.

terminal moraine

an end moraine that extends as an arcuate or crescentic ridge across a glacial valley; marks the farthest advance of a glacier. Also known as marginal moraine.

terra

an upland or mountains region on the surface of the moon, characterized by a lighter colour than that of a mare, by relatively high albedo and by a rough texture formed by large overlapping craters.

terracette

a small steplike form developed on the surface of a slumped soil mass along a steep grassy incline.

terrain

terrain is the surface of an area of country. In a flat terrain, the surface is level, but in hilly terrain it is very bumpy.

terra rossa

a reddish-brown soil overlying limestone bedrock.

terrestrial sediment

a sedimentary deposit on land above tidal reach.

terrigeneous

derived from the land or a continent.

terrigenous sediment

shallow marine sedimentary deposits composed of eroded terrestrial material.

tertiary

the older major subdivision of the Cenozoic era, extending from the end of Cretaceous to the beginning of the Quaternary, from 70,000,000 to 2,000,000 years ago.

teschenite

refers to the igneous rock of the gabbro clan. It is a fine to coarse-grained hypabyssal rock which consists of hornblende, augite, labradorite, and analcite. Barkevicite is common, whereas olivine-teschenites are of frequent occurrence; the presence of alkali feldspar produces the variety glenmuirite.

test

(1) a drill-stem test or other procedure for sampling the content of an oil or gas reservoir. (2) The shell or supporting skeleton of many invertbrates, *e.g.,* of an echinoid or a formainifer.

test well

the term used for well which is drilled to determine the presence of petroleum oil and its potential commercial value in terms of abundance and accessibility.

tethys

refers to a Mesozoic geosyncline which got developed between Laurasia and Gonwanaland, and covered southern Europe, the Mediterranean, North Africa, Iran, and the Himalayan region, possibly extending into Burma and southeast Asia, it happened to be the site of the Alpine orogeny.

tetrahedron

an isometric crystals form in cubic crystals, in the shape of a fourfaced polyhedron, each face of which is a triangle.

texture

the physical nature of the soil according to composition and particle size.

thalassocratic

1. pertainig to a thalassocration.

2. referring to a period of high sea level in the geologic past.

thalassocraton

a cration that is part of the oceanic crust.

thallasso

a prefix which means pertaining to the sea.

thanatocoenosis

refers to an assemblage of fossils which consists of the remains of organisms that had not been not associated during life. The remains have usually been brought together after death by the action of current.

thanetian

a European stage of geologic time; uppermost Paleocene, above Mountain, below Ypresian of Eocene.

thaw

thaw describes the melting of a substance which has been frozen. Snow or ice thaw when the temperature rises above freezing, or 0° Celsius.

thaw lake

a shallow, rounded depression containing a circular or semi-circular pond in a lowland periglacial region. Thaw lakes are very common feature of thermokarst, and result from the surface thawing of frozen ground (for example, at points where he vegetation cover has been disrupted). This produces localized collapse, and the formation of an irregular depression which becomes occupied by meltwater.

thenardite Na_2SO_4

a colourless or milky-white orthorhombic mineral.

thermal

(1) pertaining to or caused by heat.

(2) a vertically moving current of air that is caused to rise by differential heating of the ground below it.

(3) an interglacial interval.

thermal diffusion

a phenomenon in which a temperature gradient in a mixture of fluids gives rise to flow of one constituent relative to the mixture as a whole. Also known as thermodiffusion.

thermal spring

a spring whose water temperature is higher than the local mean annual temperature of the atmosphere.

thermocline

the thermocline is found in the sea and in large lakes. The thermocline is the layer of water between the warm water at the surface and the cold, deeper water. The water at the top of the thermocline is warmer than the water at the bottom. The thermocline in the sea lies at a depth of about 100 to 200 metres.

thermokarst topography

an irregular land surface formed in a permafrost region by melting ground ice.

thermoluminescent

a term applicable to a substance which emits characteristic light when warmed.

thermonatrite $4[Na_2CO_3H_2O]$.

an orthorhombic mineral composed of hydrous sodium carbonate; shows poor cleavage. Its hardness on Mohs scale is 1.0-1.5.

thick-bedded

pertaining to a sedimentary bed that ranges in thickness from 60 to 120 centimeters

thick-skinned structure

any large-scale structure such as a fold or fault, believed to have originated as a result of basement movement beneath overlying rocks.

thin bands

a field term that, in accordance with a scale established for use in describing banded coal, denotes vitrain bands with a range of thickness from 0.5 to 20 mm.

thin Bedded

a relative term applicable to sedimentary beds having a thickness in the range of 5-60 cm; a bed which is less than 5 cm but more than 1 cm thick being very 'thinbedded'.

thin out

gradual thinning of a stratum, vein or other body of rock until the upper and lower surfaces meet and the rock disappears.

thixotropic

a term applicable to certain types of solid/liquid systems which remain effectively solid when stationary but which become mobile liquids when they are subjected to shearing stresses. Once started, they start flowing down a slope as long as the velocity remains sufficient to maintain the minimum shearing stress required for liquidity. Certain clay-water systems form sediments which are thixotropic, and these produce certain sedimentary structures.

tholeite

the term applicable to important type of basalt which consists of basic plagioclase and pigeonite (a pyroxene), having interstitial glass or quartz-akali feldspar intergrowths.

thorianite ThO_2

it is a radioactive mineral that crystallizes in isometric system and occurs in worn cubic crystals.

thread-lace scoria

scouira whose vesicle walls have collapsed and are represented only by a network of threads.

three-point method

a method used to determine the dip and strike of a structural surface from three points of varying elevation along the surface.

through flow

the sub-surface movement of water in a downslope direction, by contrast with the vertical movement of percolating rainwater towards the water table. Throughflow may be concentrated in the subsoil, especially where it lies above relatively impermeable bedrock, and may follow matural pipes in the soil (percolines). Throughflow is probably a far more important process than overland flow in the disposal of rainwater in hill-slopes in humid temperate regions.

through valley

1. a depression eroded across a divide by glacier ice of meltwater streams.
2. a valley excavated by a through glacier.

throw

refers to the measure of the vertical displacement between the up-thrown and down thrown sides of a fault.

thrust

overriding movement of one crystal unit over another.

thrust fault

the term used for a low-angle (less than 45°) fault along which the hanging wall is moved up relative to the football. It is also known as reverse fault; reverseslip fault; thrust-slip fault.

thrust nappe

the body of rock that makes up the hanging wall of a thrust fault. Also known as thrust block; thrust plate; thrust sheet; thrust slice.

thucolite

concentrations of carbonaceous matter in ancient sedimentary rocks.

thuringian

a stratigraphic name which is being used for the European Upper Permian.

thurnian

a stratigraphic stage name which is being used for the British mid Lower Pleistocene.

tidal current

the alternating horizontal movement of water associated with the rise and fall of the tide caused by the astronomical tide-producing forces.

tidal delta

a sand bar or shoal formed in the entrance of an inlet by the action of reversing tidal currents.

tidalite

any sediment transported and deposited by tidal currents.

tidal wave

a tidal wave is a large wave usually caused by the movement of the tides. Tidal waves called tsunamis can also be caused by the shock waves that follow an earthquake or volcanic eruption. Tidal waves can cause a great deal of damage when they flood the land close to the coast.

tideland

land which is under water at high tide and uncovered at low tide.

tiff

originally a colloquial term for the mineral ($BaSO_4$) barite. The term has also been used in the field of drilling.

tiffanian

refers to a stratigraphic stage name for the North American equivalent of the European Lower Thanetian.

tiger's eye

a yellowish brown crystalline variety of quartz; a translucent, fibrous, broadly chatoyant gemstone that may be dyed.

till

unsorted and unstratified drift consisting of a heterogeneous mixture of clay, sand, gravel and boulders which is deposited by and underneath a glacier. Also known as boulder clay; glacial till; ice-laid drift.

till billow

an undulating mass of glacial drift that is disposed in an irregular pattern with regard to the direction of movement of the ice.

tilloid

a nonglacial till-like deposit.

till plain

an extensive, relatively flat area overlying a till.

till sheet

a sheet, layer, or bed of till.

tilt block

a tilted fault block.

tilted interface

oil-water interface in which water moves in a generally linear direction under an oil accumulation which is, for instant, in an anticline.

timazite

an altered igneous rock of the diorite clan. A fine-grained porphyritic extrusive rock; it contains phenocrysts of hornblende and biotite largely altered to augite and magnetite in a groundmass of plagioclase and quartz.

tombolo

a bar or barrier joining an island with a mainland or another island; occurs along shorelines of submergence, where islands are common.

time line

1. a line that indicates equal geologic age in a correlation diagram.

2. a rock unit represented by a time line.

time-stratigraphic facies

a stratigraphic facies based on the amount of geologic time during which deposition and nondeposition of sediment occurred.

time-stratigraphic unit

a stratigraphic unit based on gelogic age or time of origin. Also known as chronolith; chronolitholoc unit; chronostratic unit; chronostratigraphic unit; time-rock unit.

time transgressive unit

a laterally continous; lithologically homogeneous rock unit whose are differs regionally.

tin

tin is an element. It is a white metal. The most common tin ore is cassiterite. Tin may be used to coat other metals. Cans for food are often made with tin. Tin is also used to make alloy.

tioughniogan

a stratigraphic stage name which is being used for the North American mid Middle Devonian.

tithonian

southern European equivalent of the Portlandian stage (uppermost Jurassic) of geologic time.

toarcian

a stratigraphic stage name which is being used for the top of the European Lower Jurassic.

tobanite

a variety of coal that resembles a carbonaceous shale in outward appearance; it is fine-grained, black to brown, and tough. Also known as bitumenite; kerosine shale.

toe

the leading edge of a thrust nappe.

tombolo

a sand or gravel bar or spit that connects an island with another island or an island with the mainland. Also known as connecting bar; tie bar; tying bar.

tonalite

refers to an igneous rock of the diorite clan. It is a medium to fine-grained granular plutonic rock and contains quartz, oligioclase, biotite, and hornblende.

tongrian

a European stage of geologic time; lower Oligocene (above Ludian of Eocene, below Rupelian). Also known as Lattorfian.

tonsbergite

an igneous rock of the syenite clan. A red coarse-grained granular plutonic rock; contains orthoclase, andesine, pyroxene, and biotote.

tonstein

kaolinitic bands in certain coalfields which have characteristic fossil fauna from short-lived but widespread marine invasions.

tool mark

any of the wide variety of current marks, such as groove marks, prod marks, and skip marks, produced by the continuous contact or intermittent impact of solid, current-borne objects against a muddy bottom.

topaz

topaz is a mineral. It may have yellow, blue or colourless crystals. Topaz contains aluminium and silica. It is found mainly in igneous rocks. Topaz is a semi-precious stone which is used in jewellery.

topoclinc

a clinc related to a geographic zone and usually unrelated to any ecologic condition.

topography

topography describes all the surface features of a landscape. These features include the hills and slopes of the land, the soils and vegetation, and things that have been made by people.

topotype

any specimen which is obtained from the same locality as the holotype.

topset bed

one of the nearly horizontal sedimentary layers deposited on the top of an advancing delta.

tor

a tor is a small area of rock which is exposed at the top of a rounded hill. Tors appear when the surrounding rocks have been worn away by erosion. Some tors at the top of hills have become landmarks.

torbanite

a mineral substance intermediate between oil shale

and coal. Often referred to as a type of boghead coal, or as a synonym for boghead coal.

tordrillite

refers to the igneous rock of the granite clan. It is a fine-grained granular extrusive rock and-contains quartz, soda-class, albite, and minor ferromagnesian minerals.

torose load cast

one of a group of elongate load casts with alternate contractions and swellings, which may terminate down current in bulbous, teardrop, or spiral forms.

torridonian

refers to a stratigraphic division of the Scottish Precambrian. It is the umnetamorphosed equivalent of Moinian.

torrox

a suborder of the order Oxisol that is dry for some part of the year.

toscanite

it is an igneous rock of the granite clan. It is a fine-grained porphyritic extrusive rock and consists of phenocrysts of quartz and labradorite, in a groundmass of biotite, sanidine, hypersthene, labradorite, and quartz.

total porosity

the ratio of total void space in porous oil-reservoir rock to the bulk volume of the rock itself.

tournaisian

a stratigraphic stage name which is being used for base of the European Lower Carboniferous.

T plane

a term used in crystal plasticity to denote the crystal-lographic slip plane; known as translation plane.

trace element

a trace element is an element which plants and animals need for healthy growth. Only small amounts of trace elements are required. Manganese, boron and cobalt are examples of trace elements.

trace fossil

a fossilized track, trail, boring, or burrow formed by the movement of an animal in soft sediments.

trace slip

that component of the net slip in a fault which is parallel to the trace of an index plane on a fault plane.

trace- slip fault

a fault whose net slip is trace slip.

trachyandesite

the term used for a volcanic rock which is intermediate in character between trachyte and andesite; the volcanic equivalent of monzonite.

trachybasalt

an extrusive rock with a composition intermediate between trachyte and bsalt. Both calcic plagioclase and alkali feldspar are present, as well as augite and olivine. Leucite or analcime may be minor constituents.

trachydolerite
a term applicable to rocks which are intermediate in character between dolerites and alkali dolerites.

trachytoid
physically or chemically similar to trachyte group of igneous rocks, *e.g.*, fine-grained with a structure of parallel rods of feldspar.

track
a fossil structure which consists of a mark left in soft material by the foot of an animal.

traction
transport of sedimentary particles along and parallel to a bottom surface of a stream channel by rolling, sliding, dragging, pushing, or saltation.

trail
a line of rock fragments that were picked up by glacial ice at a localized outcropping and left scattered along a fairly well-defined tract during the movement of a glacier.

transcurrent fault
a strike-slip fault characterized by a steeply inclined surface. Also known as transverse thrust.

transfer
a single process occurring continuously in space-time in which erosion is followed by transportation and deposition of sediment.

transformationg twin
a crystal twin developed by a growth transformation form a higher to a lower symmetry.

transform fault
a strike-slip fault with offset ridges characteristic of a midoceanic ridge.

transformism
a theory explaining the origin of granite because of granitization, opposed to magmatism.

transgression
geologic evidence of landward extension of the sea. Also known as invasion; marine transgression.

transgressive deposit
sediment deposited during transgression of the sea or during subsidence of the land.

transition series
refers to a group of beds which link twos series of sediments formed in contrasting environments.

translational movement
movement as of fault blocks, that is uniform, without rotation, so that parallel features maintain their orientation.

transportation
a phase of sedimentation concerned with movement by natural agents of sediment or any loose or weathered material from one place to another.

transversal jade
a mineral that is not a true jade but a green grossularite garnet.

transverse bar
a slightly submerged sand bar extending perpendicular to the

shoreline.

transverse dune

a sand dune with a nearly straight ridge crest formed by the merger of crescenting dunes; elongated at right angles to the direction of prevailing winds, with a gentle windward slope and steep leeward slope.

transverse fault

a fault whose strike is more or less perpendicular to the general structural trends of the region.

transverse gallery

an auxiliary crosscut which had been made in thick deposits across the one body so as to divide it into sections along the strike.

transverse ripple mark

a ripple mark formed nearly perpendicular to the direction of the current.

transverse valley

1. a valley perpendicular to the general strike of the underlying strata.

2. a valley cutting perpendicular by across a ridge, range, or chain of mountains. Also known as cross valley.

trap-door fault

a curved fault bounding a block that is hinged along one edge. It is an intrusion displacement structure in Little Rocky Mountains of Montana.

trapezohedron

1. an isometric crystal having 24 faces, each face of which is ideally a four-sided figure having no two sides parallel.

2. a crystal having six, eight, or twelve faces, half of which above are offset from the other half below.

traverse

a line of survey or sampling across a thin section of geological region.

tread

the flat or gently sloping surface of one of the series of natural steplike landforms, such as those of a glacial stairway or of successive terraces; a bench level.

tree

a tree is a large, woody plant with a tall trunk. Some trees are evergreen and keep their leaves all year round. Others are deciduous and lose their leaves every year. The largest trees live for hundreds of years and may reach heights of over 100 metres.

tremadocian

a stratigraphic stage name which is being used for:

1. The top of the British Upper Cambrian.

2. The basal Ordovician in Europe and elsewhere.

3. For the position of the Tremadocian, Cambrian.

trempealeauan

a stratigraphic stage name which is being used for the top of the North American Upper Cambian.

trench

a trench is a long, deep valley on the ocean floor. The deepest trench is the Mariana Trench in the western Pacific Ocean. This reaches a depth of more than 11,000 metres. Trenches have steep sides and are often found by subduction zones at the edge of tectonic plates.

trend
the direction of an outcrop of a layer, vein, fold, or other geologic feature. Also known as direction.

trentonian
a North American stage of geologic time; Middle ordovician equilent to the upper Mohawkian.

triangular diagram
refers to a graphical method of expressing the composition of a particular material in terms of three 'components' of which it has. These three 'components' may be forming whole of a system or part of a more complex system.

triangular facet
a triangular-shaped steep-sloped hill or cliff formed usually by the erosion of a fault-trucated hill.

triassic
the first period of the Mesozoic era, lying above Permian and below Jurassic, 180-225 million years ago.

tributary
a tributary is a small river or stream which flows into a larger one. Most rivers are joined by many tributaries as they flow from their source down towards the sea.

trichite
a block, straight or curved, hairlike crystallite.

trihedral
any figure obtained from three non-coplaner lines intersecting at a common point.

trilling
refers to a cyclic crystal twin which consists of three individual crystals.

trimorphism
a type of polymorphism in which there are three crystal forms, known as trimorphs.

tripoli
a lightweight, porous, friable, siliceous sedimentary rock that may have a white, gray, pink, red or yellow colour; used for polishing metals and stones.

troctolite
refers to an igneous rock of the gabbro clan. It is a coarse-grained granular plutonic rock and contains labradonte and olivine. It is also known as forellenstein.

trolly
a basin-shaped depression in strata. Also known as lum.

troosite
a manganese-bearing variety of willemite.

tropical
tropical describes something found in the tropics. A tropical climate is one with no cool season. It often has a heavy rainfall as well.

tropopause

the tropopause is part of the Earth's atmosphere. It marks the upper limit of the troposphere. The tropopause lies about 18 kilometres above the Equator, but only about 6 kilometres above the poles.

troposphere

the troposphere is part of the Earth's atmosphere. It can rise to about 18 kilometres above the Earth's surface. The troposphere contains most of the water vapour and clouds in the air.

trought

1. the line which is connecting the lowest points of a fold.
2. refers to any narrow elongate depression in the surface of the earth.
3. refers to a small, straight depression which is formed just offshore on the bottom of a sea or lake or on the landward side of a longshore bar.
4. refers to an elongate depression on the sea floor which is wider and shallower than a trench.

trough surface

a surface or a plain connecting the troughs of the bed of a syncline. Also known as synclinal axis; through plane.

truncation

replacement of one edge or corner of a crystal by a plane.

tufa

refers to a spongy porous limestone which is formed by precipitation from evaporating spring and river waters.

tuffite

a consolidated mixture of pyroclastic and sedimentary detrius usually well-bedded and sorted according to grain size.

tundra

a Laphish term used for soils which were produced under conditions of extreme cold. They are often waterlogged due to a layer of permafrost at shallow depth.

turbidite

refers to any sediment or rock which gets transported and deposited by a turbidity current. It is generally characterized by graded bedding, large amounts of matrix, and commonly showing a Bouma sequence.

turbulent flow

refers to any flow which is not laminar, i.e., the stream lines of the fluid, instead of remaining parallel, become confused and intermingled.

turonian

a European stage of geologic time: Upper or Middle Cretaceous.

turquoise

turquoise is a mineral. It is light blue or blue-green in colour. Turquoise contains copper, aluminium and phosphorus. It is a semi-precious stone which can be used as a gem.

tuxtlite

pyroxene intermediate in composition and properties

between diopside and jadeite.

type locality

1. refers to the locality from which a type specimen comes. 2. A locality which is selected as a standard for comparison of a stratigraphic unit. It is the type section of the unit.

type section

refers to the sequence of strata which are identified as the original sequence for a location or area; the standard against which other stratigraphy of parts of the area could be compared. Also known as section.

type specimen

the term used for the single specimen on which the original description of a particular species has been based.

twin law

a statement relating two or more individuals of a twin to one another in terms of their crystalography.

two-cycle valley

a valley that is the result of two cycles off erosion, as shown by a narrow inner valley bordered by high level terraces.

type specimen

the single specimen on which the original description of a particular species is based, which serves as a permanent point of nomeclature reference for application of the name of that species. The type specimen may be a holotype, a neotype, or a lectotype.

udalf

suborder of the soil order Alfisol; brown soil formed in a udic moisture regime and in a mesic or warmer temperature regime.

ugrandite

group name for uvarovite, grossular, andradite.

uintan

a stratigraphic stage name, which is the North American equivalent of the European Bartonian (Tertiary System).

ukrainian

the term used for a stratigraphic division of the Russian Precambrian Pre-Saamian.

ulrichite

an igneous rock of the syenite clan. A fine-grained porphyritic hypabyssal rock; contains phenocrysts of nepheline, sanidine, barkevikite, and olivine in a groundmass of sanidine hornblende, and aegirine.

ulsterian

a stratigraphic stage name which is being used for the North American Lower Devonian.

ultramafic

the term used for an igneous rock which is composed chiefly of mafic minerals, e.g., monomineralic rocks composed of hypersthene augite, or olivine.

ultrasim

the supposedly ultrabasic layer of the earth below the sima, immediately beneath the

Mohorovicic discontunity.

ultravulcanian
a type of volcanic eruption which is characterized by periodic violent gaseous explosions of lithic dust and solid blocks, with little if any, fiery scoria.

umber
the term used for a naturally occurring pigment which is comprised mainly of hydrated oxides of iron and manganese, and sometime clay. Raw umber is having brownish colour which becomes a characteristic red-brown when heated.

umbrept
a suborder of the Inceptisol soil order; has dark A horizon more than 10 inches thick, brown B horizons, and slightly paler C horizons; soil is strongly acid, and clay minerals are crystalline; occurs in cool or temperate climates.

umptekite
an igneous rock of the syenite clan. A fine to coarse-grained granular plutonic rock; contains orthoclase, microcline microperthite, sodalite, arfvedsonite, aegirine, biotite, and nepheline.

unaka
a large residual mass rising above a peneplain that is less well developed than one having a monodnock.

unconformable
said of strata that do not suceed the underlying rocks in immedaite order of age or in parallel position; especially younger strata that do not have the same dip and strike as the under-lying rocks. Also said of contact between unconformable rocks.

unda
said of the environment of sedimentation that lies in the zone of wave action. It may be used alone or as a combining form.

underclay limestone
a thin, freshwater limestone that is relatively free of fossils and is dense and nodular; found in underlying coal deposits.

undercliff
a subordinate cliff or terrace formed by material that has fallen or slide from above.

underfit stream
a misfit stream which is like to be too small to have eroded the valley in which it flows.

underflow conduit
a permeable deposit underlying a surface stream channel.

underlie
to lie or be situated under: to occupy a lower position, or to pass beneath.

undermelting
the melting from below of any floating ice.

undersaturated
a term used for describing the igneous rocks which are deficient in SiO2, so that unsaturated minerals develop. The term is often applicable to feldspathoidal rocks.

underthrust

a thrust fault in which the lower, active rock mass has been moved under the upper, passive rock mass.

undertow

undertow is the backward movement of water below the surface of the sea. When a wave breaks on the sea-shore, the undertow drags backwards as the crest of the wave moves forwards.

unfreezing

the upward movement of stones to the surface as a result of repeated freezing and thawing of the containing soil.

unguligrade

a term applicable to animals having both pairs of limb adapted for running. The adaptation suits them to life on steppes and plans.

uniclinal seift

a stream which is able to follow the outcrop of soft strata and may cut down until it reaches a harder bed below. Further downcutting gets deflected down dip by the harder bed, and this shift has been described as uniclinal.

uniformitarianism

classiclally, the concept that the present is the key to the past; the principle that contemporary geologic processes have occurred in the same regular manner and with essentially the same intensity throughout geologic time, and that events of the geologic past can be explained by phenomena observable today. Also known as principle of uniformity.

uniserial

having a single row or series, e.g., the plates of a primitive crinoid arm.

unit cell

the unit of which a crystal lattice is constructed, for example, the body-centred and face centred lattices are forms of a cubic unit cell.

unit form

a crystal form in a system other than the cubic, which has intercepts on the chosen crystal axis that define the: axial ratio Unit forms have Miller indices {111}, {110}, {011}, and {101}.

unsaturated

a term used for such minerals which cannot develop in stable equilibrium in the presence of excess silica. Such minerals are olivine, feldspathoids, corundum, spinels, and certain garnets.

unstratified

not formed or deposited in strata; specifically said of massive rocks or sediments with an absence of layering, such as granite or glacial till.

upper

pertaining to rocks or strata that normally overlie those of earlier formations of the same subdivision of rocks.

upper cambrian

the latest epoch of the

Cambrian periods of geologic time, beginning approximately 510 millions years ago.

upper carboniferous
the European epoch of geologic time equivalent to the Pennsylvanian of North America.

upper cretaceous
the late epoch of the Cretaceous period of geologic time, beginnig about 90 million years ago.

upper devonian
the latest epoch of the Devonian period of geological time, beginning about 365 million years ago.

upper jurassic
the latest epoch of the Jurassic period of the geologic time, beginnig approximately 155 million years ago.

upper mantle
the portion of the mantle lying above a depth of about 1000 kilometers. Also known as asthenosphere; outer mantle; peridotite shell.

upper mississippian
the latest epoch of the Mississippian period of geologic time.

upper ordovician
the latest epoch of the Ordovician period of geologic time, beginnig approximately 440 million years ago.

upper pennsylvanian
the latest epoch of the Pennsylvanian period of geologic time.

upper permian
the latest epoch of Permian period of geologic time beginning about 245 million years ago.

upper silurian
the latest epoch of Silurian period of geological time.

upper triassic
the latest epoch of Triassic period of geological time, beginnig about 200 million years ago.

upthrow
1. the fault side thrown upward.
2. the amount of vertical fault displacement.

upwarp
a broad anticline with gently sloping limbs formed as a result of differential uplift.

uralian
a synonym of Stephanian (Carboniferous System).

uralitization
1. a process of replacement whereby pyroxene undergoes alteration resulting in uralite.
2. development of amphibole from pyroxene.

uraninite UO_2
an isometric uranium mineral, that is highly radioactive and is the primary ore of uranium. It usually occurs in granular masses or aggregates. Uranium is found in pegmatites and high-temperature hydrothermal veins in sedimentary clastic deposits with mineral of lead, tin, and copper. Its varieties are broeggerite, cleveite,

pitchblende and nasturan.

uranium- lead dating
a method for calculating the geologic age of a material in years based on the radioactive decay rate of uranium-238 to lead-206 and of uranium-235 to lead-207.

uranothroianite
uranium rich variety of thorite.

ureilite
an achondritic stony meteorite consisting principally of oilvine and clinobronzite, with some nickel-iron, troilite,diamond and graphite.

uriconian
a stratigraphic name which is being used for the volcanic precambrian underlying the Longmyndian in Shropshire, England.

urtite
feldspathoid igneous rock. It is medium-grained granular plutonic rock and has nepheline, aegirine, and apatite.

urstromthal
a large channel cut by a stream of water from melting ice, flowing along the edge of an ice sheet.

utahlite
compact nodular variety of variscite.

urtite
feldspthoid igneous rock. It is a medium-grained granular plutonic rock and has nepheline, aegirine, and apatite.

u-shaped valley
a type of valley with a broad floor and steep walls produced by glacial erosion. Also known as trough valley; U valley.

ustalf
a suborder of the soil order Alfisol; red or brown soil formed in a ustic moisture regime and in a mesic or warmer temperature regime.

ustert
a suborder of the Vertisol soil order; has a faint horizon and is dry for an appreciable period or more than one period of the year.

vadose water
water that is present between the ground surface and the water table, i.e., the unsaturated zone. However it is accepted that vadose water is equivalent to meteoric water, and the term may be ambiguous.

vagrant benthos
bottom-dwelling organism that are capable of movement on, in, or above the substratum.

valanginian
a stratigraphic stage name which is being used for the base of the European Lower Cretaceous.

valencianite
a variety of potassium feldspar from Mexico; a synonym of adularia.

valley fill
unconsolidated sedimentary deposit which fills or partly fills a valley.

valley flat

the small plain at the bottom of a narrow valley with steep sides.

valley floor

the broad, flat bottom of a valley. Also known as valley bottom; valley plain.

valley train

a long, narrow body of outwash, deposited by meltater far beyond the margin of an active glacier and extending along the floor of a valley. Also known as outwash train.

valve

refers to one or more of the major skeletal units which form a complete shell, e.g., a gastropod is having a singlevalved shell, lamellibranchs and branchiopods are having two-valved shells.

vanishing tide

when a high-water and low-water 'meet' together into a period for several hours with a nearly constant water level.

vapour

vapour is the gas into which most liquids change when they are heated. Water turns into water vapour when it evaporates into the air.

vapour

vapour is the gas into which most liquids change when they are heated. Water turns into water vapour when it evaporates into the air.

variation diagram

the term used for a graph or other similar diagram which is obtained by plotting the chemical features of a series of rocks against each other, or occasionally against some other property, e.g., colour index, specific gravity. The commonest type is the Harker diagram which is obtained by plotting percentages of elements (as oxides) against silica percentages. The diagrams reveal genetic and other relationships between rocks of a series.

variole

a spherule the size of a pea, usually consisting of radiating plagioclase or pyroxene crystals.

variolite

the term used for an igneous rock of the diorite clan. It was originally glassy, and has developed variolitic structure throughout and contains varioles of plagioclase, augite and limenite in a groundmass of augite and devitrified glass.

variscan orogeny

the late Paleozzoic orogenic era in Europe, extending through the Carboniferrous and Permian. Also known as Hercynian orogeny.

varve

a sedimentary bed, layer, or sequence of layers deposited in a body of still water within a year's time and usually during a season. Also known as glacial varve.

varved clay

a lacustrine sediment of

distinct layers consisting of varves. Also known as varve clay.

varvite

name given to a graded lamilnated clay which resembles a varve clay but was produced by nonglacial processes.

vaughanite

a pure light-grey, fine-textured limestone, that breaks with a smooth conchoidal fracture; contains relatively few fossils, and has a white chalky appearance on weathered surface.

vein

refers to a tabular or shaet-like body of minerals which gets intruded into a joint or fissure, or system of joints and fissures, in rocks. Most veins are directly or indirectly having igneous origin, although in certain circumstances fissures may become filled because of sedimentary processes, e.g., calcite veins filling fissures in limestone.

vein dike

a pegmatitic intrusion that has the characteristics of both a vein and a dike.

velocity discontinuity

an abrupt change of the rate of propagation of seismic waves within the earth, as at a sesmic discontinuity.

velocity profile

refers to a seismic arrangement which is used to record reflections over a large range of shot-to-geophone distances. It is used for determining seismic velocity from the time-distance relationship.

veneer

a thin layer of sediment convering a rock surface.

vent

the opening of a volcano on the surface of the earth.

ventifact

a stone or pebble whose shape, wear, faceting, cut or polish is the result of sandblasting. Also known as glyptolith; rillstone; wind-cut stone; wind-grooved stone; wind-scoured stone; wind-shared stone.

venus' hair

needle-like crystals of rutile. They are usually of a golden-brown or yellow colour and occurring embedded in quartz crystals.

vermiculite

Vermiculite is a mineral. It contains magnesium, aluminium and silicon. When heated, vermiculite expands to become light and squashy. It is used for heat insulation and for packaging.

vertical intensity

the magnitude of vertical component of any vector, e.g., of earth's magnetic or gravitational field at any point.

vertical slip

the vertical component of the net sliop in a fault. Also known as vertical dip slip.

vesicular structure

the term used for describing small spherical or ellipsoidal cavities which are found in volcanic lavas, and are produced by bubbles of gas trapped during solidification of the rock. If these are filled with a secondary mineral they are known as amygdales. Lavas which have abundant vesicles are pumice (acid lava) and scoriae (basic lava). Such frothlike material often gets ejected from the volcano as pyroclastic material.

vicinal face
a crystal face that modifies a normal crystal face, which it closely approximates in angle.

vindobonian
a stratigraphic stage name which is being used for the European Middle Miocene.

virgation
a fold pattern in which the axial surfaces diverge or fan out from a central bundle.

virgence
refers to the converging or diverging of 'fans' of axial plane cleavage.

virglorian
a stratigraphic stage name which is the Western European equivalent of Anisian (Triassic System).

visean
a stratigraphic stage name which is being used for the top of the European Lower Carboniferous.

vitrain
refers to an ingredient of banded coal which is characterized by brilliant vitreous lustre, black colour, and cubic cleavage having conchoidal fracture. Vitrain bands or lenticles have been amorphous and thick enough to be visible to the unaided eye.

vitreous
having the lustre and appearance of glass.

vitric tuff
tuff composed principally of volcanic glass fragments.

vitrification
formation of a glassy or noncrystalline material.

vitrinite
a maceral group rich in oxygen and is composed of humic material which is associated with peat formation.

vitrinoid
vitrinite occurring in bituminous coking coals; characterized by a reflectance of 0.5-2.0 per cent.

vitroclastic
pertaining to a pyroclastic rock structure characterized by fragmented bits of glass; also said of a rock having such a structure.

vitrophyre
a porphyritic texture in which the groundmass is, glassy.

vogesite
refers to an igneous rock of the syenite clan. It is a fine-grained prophyritic hypabyssal rock and contains phenocrysts of hornblende and diopside in a groundmass of orthoclase,

hornblende, and diopside.

volatile component

a component of magma whose vapour pressures are high enough to allow them to be concentrated in any gaseous phase. Also known as volatile flux.

volcanic

refers to one of the three groups into which rocks have been divided. The volcanic assemblage are including all extrusive rocks and the associated intrusive ones. The group has been dominantly basic strictly magmatic, and usually but necessarily associated with orogeny.

volcanic arc

an arcuare string of volcanic islands associated with and parallel to a subduction zone along convergent plate boundaries, often found closely adjacent to a deep ocean trough.

volcanic ash

fine pyroclastic material; particle diameter is less than 4 millimeters.

volcanic bombs

refers to pyroclastic ejecta; the lava fragments, liquid or plastic at the time of ejection, acquire rounded forms, markings, or internal structure during flight or upon landing.

volcanic breccia

a pyroclastic rock. It is composed of angular volcanic fragments having a diameter larger than 2 mm and that may or may not be having a matrix.

volcanic chain

linear arrangement of a number of volcaneos, apparently associated with a major geologic feature such as a fault or subduction zone.

volcanic dust

very fine particles of lava shot out of volcanoes; carried to great distances by wind and may remain suspended in air for a long time.

volcanic gases

volatile matter composed principally of about 90% water vapour, and carbon dioxide, sulfer dioxide, hydrogen, carbon monoxide, and nitrogen, released during an eruption of a volcano.

volcanic glass

natural glass formed by the cooling of molten lava, or one of its liquid fractions, too rapidly to allow crystallization; constituent of extrusive igneous rocks.

volcanic mud

sediment containing large quantities of ash from a volcanic eruption, mixed with water.

volcanic mudflow

the flow of volcanic mud down the slope of a volcano.

volcanic rift zone

a zone comprising volcanic fissures with underlying dike assemblages; occurs in Hawaii.

volcanic rift zone

a zone comprising volcanic

fissures with underlying dike assemblages.

volcanic rock

finely crystalline or glassy igneous rock resulting from volcanic activity at or near the surface of the earth. Also known as extrusive rock.

volcanic vent

subcircular bodies composed of lava and fragmented volcanic rock; contacts are generally steep, and vents range in diameter from a few tens to thousands of feet.

volcanism

the movement of magma and its associated gases from the interior into the crust and to the surface of the earth. Also known as volcanicity.

volcano

a vent in the surface of the earth through which magma and associated gases and ash enrupt: the structure produced by the ejected material is usually in the form of a cone.

volcanogenic

formed by processes directly connected with volcanism. Said of a mineral deposit considered to have been produced through volcanic agencies and demonstrable associated with volcanic phenomena.

volcanology

the branch of geology dealing with volcanism, its causes and phenomena.

vraconian

a stratigraphic stage name which is being used for the Albian Cenomanian transition beds in Europe (Cretaceous System).

vugh

a cavity in a rock which is usually having a lining of crystalline minerals. A term used especially of cavities ill mineral veins.

vulcanian eruption

a volcanic eruption characterized by periodic explosive events. Also known as paroxysmal eruption; Plinian eruption; Vesuvian eruption.

vulpinite

a grangular variety of anhydrite found at Vulpino in Lombardy, Italy.

vulsinite

an igneous rock of the syenite clan. A mottled-grey, fine-grained porphytitic extrusive rock; contains phenocrysts of sodaclase, anorthite and augite in a groundmass of sodaclase, labradorite, and augite.

waalian

a stratigraphic stage name which is being used for the European Lower Pleisocene.

wacke

the sandstone composed of a mixture of angular unsorted or poorly sorted fragments of minerals and rocks and an abundant mixture of clay and fine silt. The term is properly used only in terms of greywacke and its use in any other sense is undesirable.

wad

the term used for a soft black earthy mass which is composed of hydrated manganese oxides, usually having iron oxides and occasionally having barium or cobalt compounds as well.

wadi

in the desert regions of southwestern Asia and northern Africa, a stream bed or channel, or a steep-sided ravine, gulley, or valley which carries water only during the rainy season. Also spelled wady.

wake dune

a sand dune occurring on the leeward side of a larger dune and moving away in the direction of the wind.

wall rock

refers to the country rock of a vein or lode.

warm front

a warm front is the place where a mass of warm air moves over a mass of cold air. A warm front occurs when a depression arrives and brings warmer air and lower atmospheric pressure. As the warm air rises above the colder air, many cluds form and often produce rain.

warp

1. an upward or downward flexure of the earth's curst.

2. a layer of sediment deposited by water.

wasatchian

a stratigraphic stage name which is being used for the North American equivalents of the Cuisian plus Ypresian.

washover

material deposited by overwash, especially a small delta produced by storm waves and built on the landward side of a bar or a barrier. Also known as strom delta; wave delta.

water drive

energy within an oil or gas pool, resulting from hydrostatic or hydrodynamic pressure transmitted from the surrounding aquifer.

waterfall

refers to a point in the course of a river where the water is descending more or less vertically. Waterfalls are produced by: (i) Differential erosion of a soft rock which lies across the course of river; (ii) The knickpoint of a rejuvenated stream; (iii) the damming of a stream; (iv) the damming of a stream by a landslip. Waterfalls are temporary features.

water gap

a deep and narrow pass that cuts to the base of a mountain ridge and through which a stream flows; the Delaware Water Gap is an example.

water level

water level is the height of water in the sea, rivers or lakes. The water level in a lake or reservoir varies with the amount of rainfall.

water opening
a break in sea-ice, leaving the sea surface.

watershed
the term used for the region of higher ground which is situated between two non-communicating drainage system. It may be considered to be the boundary between two adjacent drainage systems.

water table well
a well that taps into unconfined groundwater. Its water level does not necessarily lie at the water-table level.

waucoban
a stratigraphic stage name which is being used for the North American Lower Cambrian.

wave
a wave describes the regular up-and-down movement of a substance. Waves are the ridges of water which move along on the surface of the sea. As a wave passes, the water rises and then falls again, until the next wave appears. Waves on the sea are caused by the wind and sometimes by the tides.

wave basin
a basin close to the inner entrance of a harbour in which the waves from the outer absorbed, thus reducing the size of the waves.

wave-cut cliff
a cliff formed by the erosion action of waves on rock.

way-Up Criteria
the term used for any geological phenomenon which helps the original orientation of a rock mass to be determined. The most important use of such criteria has been the determining sequences in layered rocks, i.e., sediments and interbedded lavas.

wealden
a stratigraphic name which is being used for the local fresh-water facies of the British Neocomian (Cretaceous System).

weathered layer
in seismology, the zonee of the earth that is immediately below the surface, characterized by low seismic-wave velocities.

weathering
weathering is the gradual breaking down of rocks and minerals on the Earth's surface. Weathering turns rocks into sand and soil. The action of wind, water, ice or chemical reactions can cause weathering.

websterite
refers to the igneous rock of the ultrabasic clan. It is a coarse-grained granular plutonic rock and has hypersthene and diopside.

wedge out
disappearance of a thinning, tensing or truncated layer as its thichness reduces to zero.

wehrlite
refers to a igneous rock of the ultrabasic clan. It is a coarse-

grained granular plutonic rock and is having olivine, dialage, and hornblende.

welding

consolidation of sediments by pressure; water is squeezed out and cohering particles are brought within the limits of mutual molecular attraction.

well

a well is a deep hole dug in the ground. Wells are dug to reach a liquid or gas lying below the surface. Some wells provide water, others are made to reach deposits, such as crude oil and natural gas.

well log

a record of variations with depth in a well of various geological features and parameters; including resistivity, spontaneous potential, radioactivity, acoustic velocity, gravity and lithology.

well ties

wells existing or specially drilled yielding information to oil interperation or test the accuracy of a seismic profile.

wemmelian

a stratigraphic stage name which is being used for the top of the European Upper Eocene (Tertiary System).

wennebergite

an igneous rock of the syeniet clan. A fine-grained porphyritic hypabyssal rock; contains phenocrysts of orthoclase, biotite, and quartz in a groundmass of apatite, sphene, and glass.

westphalian

a stratigraphic stage name which is being used for the European mid Upper Carboniferous.

whitbian

a stratigraphic stage name which is being used for the base of the British Upper Lias (Jurassic System).

whitneytie

variety of native copper containing arsenic.

whitleyite

an achondritic metorite consisting essentially of enstatite with fragments of black chonodrite.

whitneyan

a stratigraphic stage name which is the North American equivalent of the European Chattian (Tertiary).

wildcat

a borehole (or more rarely a mine) which is sunk in the hope of getting oil (or ore) in a region where deposits of oil or metallic ores are recorded. As usually employed, the term implies any highly speculative exploratory operation which is carried out generally in search of oil.

wildflysch

a type of flysch facies that represents a stratigraphic unit with irregularly sorted boulders resulting from fragmentation, and twisted, confused beds resulting from slumping or sliding due to the influence of gravity.

wilsonite

magnesium potassilum alulminosilicate of uncertain formula. Its colour varies from pinkish-white to red; an altered scapolite.

wind gap

a shallow, relatively high level notch in the upper part of a mountain ridge. It is usually an abandoned water gap. Most wind gaps are produced by glacial breching; river capture; climatic changes, accidental diversion.

windrow

refers to any accumulation of material formed by wind or tide action.

winter

winter is the coldest season of the year in a temperate climate. Winter is also the time when the days are shortest. In the northern hemisphere, winter lasts from about November to Frebruary. In the southern hemisphere, winter lasts from about May to August.

winterbourne

a stream which flows in winter but dries up in summer when the water-table is lower. Such streams are found mainly in chalk areas. The name winterbourne is used only in southern England.

wisconsin

pertainig to the fourth, and last, glacial stage of the Pleistocene epoch in the North America; followed the Sangamon interglacial, beginnig about 85,000 ±15,000 years ago and ending 7000 years ago.

witherite $BaCO_3$

a barium mineral. It occurs in hydrothermal veins associated with barytes galena.

wleback dune

a smooth, elongated mound or hill of desert sand shaped generally like a whale's back; formed by passage of a succession of longtitudinal dunes along the same path. Also known as sand levee.

wolfcampian

a North America provincial series of geological time; lowermost Permian.

wolff net

a coordinate system which is used in crystallography to plot a polar stereographic projection with conservation of equal angles.

wollastonite

a mineral of the pyroxenoid group.

wood

wood is the substance from which tree trunks are made. Wood contains a chemical called cellulose which gives it strength. Wood is a valuable natural resource which is used for building and a fuel. Wood is also used to make paper.

woodendite

an igneous rock of the syenite clan. A black, fine-grained granular extrusive rock; contains augite, enstatite, olivine, and magnetite, in a glass of feldspar composition.

wood tin

botryoidal or renilform variety of calltterite with a radiating fibrous habit.

wrench fault

a lateral fault with a more or less vertical fault surface. Also known as basculating fault: torion fault.

wurm

the fourth of the four classical glacial stages of the Pleistocene of Europe, above the Riss.

wurtzilite

a black, massive, sectile, infusible, asphaltic pyrobitumen derived from the metamorphosis of petroleum.

wyomingite

a lava having leucite, phlogopite, and a pyrozene in a glassy groundmass. On the basis of the composition of the glassy groundmass it is quite likely that the rock gets related to the phonolites rather than the alkali basalts.

xanthite

a yellowish-brown variety of idocrase.

xenoblastic

a textural term which is applicable to metamorphic rocks. It is applicable to mineral grains which are developed without exhibiting crystal faces and corresponds to allotriomorphic in the igneous textural terminology.

xenocryst

a crystal resembling a phenocrysts in an igneous rock, but unrelated to the rock body in which it occurs.

xenolith

refers to an inclusion in an igneous rock which is not genetically related, like uumelted fragment of country rock. Xenoliths may undergo extensive reaction with the igneous rock and may have undergrone partial assimilation.

xeralf

a suborder of the soil order Alfisol; brown or red soil formed in a xeric moisture regime.

xeret

a suborder of the soil order Vertsol; formed in a xeric moisture regimle.

xerert

a suborder of the soil order Vertisol, formed in a Mediterranean climate; wide surface cracks open and close once a year.

xeroll

a suborder of the soil order Mollisol, formed in a xeric moisture regime; may have a calcic, petrocalcic, or gypsic horizon or a duripan.

xerothermic period

a postglacial interval of a warmer, drier climate. Also known as xerothermal period.

xeruit

a suborder of the soil order Ultisol, formed in a xeric moisture regime; browhish or reddish soil with a low to moderate organic-carbon content.

xerult

a suborder of the soil order Ultisol, formed in a xeric moisture regime; brownish or reddish soil with a low to moderate organic carbon-content.

xyloid coal

a variety of brown coal which has the fibrous structure of wood. It is also known as broad coal; bituminous wood; xyloid lignite.

yamaskite

an igneous rock of the gabbro clan. A coarse-grained, granular plutonic rock; contains hornblende, titanaugite and anorthite.

yarmouth integlacial

the second integlacial stage of the Pleistocene epoch in North America, following the Kansan glacial stage and before the Illinoian.

yatalite

an igneous rock of the diorite clan. A coarse-grained granular pegmatite; contains uralite, albite, titanite, and quartz.

yeovilian

a stratigraphic stage name which is being used for the top of the British Upper Lias.

young valley

a valley in its early stages, when it is relatively straight and has a high gradient; a V-shaped cross-section, and short tributaries.

ypresian

a stratigraphic stage name which is being used for the European Lower Eocene.

yuksporite

a red mineral composed of calcium strontium barium and alkali silicate and fluoride of uncertain composition and crystal system; occurs as lamellar masses or fibres.

zechstein

a European stratigraphic stage name which is equivalent to Thuringian (Permian System).

zeolite

the term used for a group of colourless or white (sometimes red or yellow) tekto silicates having true water of crystallization; one of the few mineral groups which are displaying reversible dehydration. The cations present typically are sodium, potassium, calcium and barium. Zeolites have powerful base exchange properties and sodium zeolites were originally employed for softening water. Most zeolites occur in amygdales and other cavities in basic volcanic rocks, but they may also occur in other volcanic rocks.

zeolite facies

metamorphic rocks formed in the transitional period from diagensis to metamorphism, at pressures of about 200-3000 bars and temperatures of 475-575K.

zeugen

tabular erosional remnats

formed in desert regions by the erosional effect of sand-laden winds; masses of resistant rock resting on supports of softer rock, becoming separated by erosion from the once continuous horizontal stratum.

zinc

zinc is an element. It is a bluish-white metal and is poisonous. Zinc is used to coat iron and steel. It is also used in medicines.

zinnwaldite

a grey to brown mica similar to lepidolite containing appreciable iron, found in tin veins and granite pegmatites.

zircon $ZnSiO_4$

a brown, green, pale-blue, red, orange, goldenyellow or colourless neosilicate mineral which occurs in granites, syenites, schists and crystalline limestones.

zirconite

a grey or brown variety of zircon.

zone

a zone is a series of layers in rocks. Each zone may be distinguished by a particular collection of fossils.

zone fossil

refers to a fossil species which characterizes a particular horizon, and gets restricted to it in time.

zone of aeration

a subsurface zone containing water below atmospheric pressure and air or gases at atmospheric pressure.

zone of plastic flow

the part of earth's crust that is under sufficient pressure to prevent fracturing. i.e., ductile, so that deformation is by flow.

zone of weathering

the layer of the earth's crust above the water table that is subject to destructive atmospheric processes, and in which soils develop.

z-phenomenon

refers to a possible time lag (a few seconds or less) which occurs between the issuance of P and S waves from an earthquake focus.

zontation

the subdivision of a stratigraphic unit by means of fossils.

zussmanite

a basic aluminosilicate of potassium and iron which occurs in metamorphosed shales, iron-stones; and limestones.

zweikanter

a ventifact which has two faces and are intersecting in two sharp edges.